FRANK WOOD'S

BOOK-KEEPING AND ACCOUNTS

Eighth Edition

Frank Wood BSc(Econ), FCA

and

Sheila Robinson BA(Hons), Cert Ed, FMAAT

PEARSON

Harlow, England • London • New York • Boston • San Francisco • Toronto • Sydney • Auckland • Singapore • Hong Kong
Tokyo • Seoul • Taipei • New Delhi • Cape Town • São Paulo • Mexico City • Madrid • Amsterdam • Munich • Paris • Milan

Pearson Education Limited

Edinburgh Gate
Harlow
Essex CM20 2JE
England

and Associated Companies throughout the world

Visit us on the World Wide Web at:
www.pearsoned.co.uk

First published 1981 (print)
Second edition published 1986 (print)
Third edition published 1992 (print)
Fourth edition published 1997 (print)
Fifth edition published 2001 (print)
Sixth edition published 2004 (print)
Seventh edition published 2009 (print)
Eighth edition published 2013 (print and electronic)

ISBN 978-0-273-77306-1 (print)
978-0-273-77310-8 (eBook)
978-0-273-78072-4 (eText)

British Library Cataloguing-in-Publication Data
A catalogue record for this book is available from the British Library

Library of Congress Cataloging-in-Publication Data
A catalog record for this book is available from the Library of Congress

10 9 8 7 6 5 4 3 2 1
16 15 14 13 12

Typeset in 10.5/12.5pt ITC Garamond by 35
Printed and bound by L.E.G.O. S.p.A., Italy

Contents

Part 4 Adjustments to financial statements

Part 5 Financial statements of other organisations

Part 6 Associated accounting topics

Companion Website

For open-access **student resources** specifically written to complement this textbook and support your learning, please visit **www.pearsoned.co.uk/wood**

Lecturer Resources

For password-protected online resources tailored to support the use of this textbook in teaching, please visit **www.pearsoned.co.uk/wood**

Preface to the eighth edition

This eighth edition of Book-keeping and Accounts has again been revised and updated to take account of changes in the accounting standards and assessment requirements of the accountancy bodies.

It is a valuable text for students studying accounting for the first time and for those wanting to begin the path to professional accountancy qualifications. Where schools are introducing accounting to their curriculum the book is a very appropriate text.

This latest edition sees many new developments due mainly to the UK changing over from domestic accounting rules to international rules. The book covers the development of international accounting standards with the preparation and presentation of financial statements. Throughout, new terminology is introduced initially alongside the UK equivalent; the following lists the main changes:

International	*Traditional UK*
Accounts payable	Creditors
Accounts receivable	Debtors
Allowance for doubtful debts	Provision for doubtful debts
Income statement	Profit and loss account
Inventory	Stock(s)
Loan note	Debenture
Non-current assets	Fixed assets
Non-current liabilities	Long-term liabilities
Retained profits	Profit and loss account figure (usually shown on the statement of financial position)
Statement of financial position	Balance sheet

Value Added Tax (VAT) has been introduced earlier in the book incorporating the latest VAT rates, i.e. 20%, at the time of writing. These changes have been followed through in all subsequent chapters, i.e. purchase and sales invoices, credit notes, the day books and ledgers, cash book, petty cash, etc.

Several chapters have been completely rewritten including Accounting standards, rules and concepts, and Limited company accounts, while others have been revised and refreshed.

Each chapter follows a logical structure from the initial learning objectives, working through the chapter topic, a reminder summary and finally exercises to practise and assess ones competence.

A comprehensive glossary can be found in the Appendices along with multiple-choice questions and answers and model layouts for financial statements and worksheets.

Acknowledgements

The author wishes to thank Malcolm Robinson for his support and contribution in the production of this book and to Stephen Clark, information technology advisor, for his continued help and assistance. The author woold also like to thank Rosemary Evans, a Chief Examiner for the AAT (Association of Accounting Technicians).

The author also wishes to thank all the lecturers and teachers who kindly provided feedback and suggestions for this latest edition which she has endeavoured to incorporate in this new edition.

Sheila Robinson
June 2012

Publisher's acknowledgements

We are grateful to the following for permission to reproduce copyright material:

Figures

Figures on page 80, page 103, page 181 from *Edexcel International GCSE Accounting* 1st ed., Edexcel (Robinson, S. 2010) Pearson Education Ltd.

Text

Exercise 9.7 from Northern Examinations and Assessments, Paper 1, Level H, Paper ref 1407, Question 3, AQA(AEB)/AQA/NEAB/AQA examination materials are reproduced by permission of the Assessment and Qualifications Alliance; Exercise 19.4 from OCR Bk-k, Stage 1, Paper ref NOV 107, Nov 1998, Question 1; Exercises 20.6, 25.4, 26.8, 30.7, 35.7 from Administration and Assessment Manual, AAT (2002); Exercise 20.7 from Administration and Assessment Manual, AAT (2000); Exercises 23.6, 25.6, 28.4, 38.6, 39.4, 39.5 from *Edexcel International GCSE Accounting* 1st ed., Edexcel (Robinson, S. 2010) Pearson Education Ltd; Exercise 24.3 from OCR Bk-k, Stage 1, Paper ref MAR 107, Mar 1999, Question 1; Exercise 27.5 from Southern Examining Group, Paper 3, Level H, Paper ref 3260/3, Question 2, AQA, AQA(AEB)/AQA/NEAB/AQA examination materials are reproduced by permission of the Assessment and Qualifications Alliance; Exercise 27.6 from Northern Examinations and Assessments, Paper 2, Level H, Paper ref 1408, Question 5, AQA, AQA(AEB)/AQA/NEAB/AQA examination materials are reproduced by permission of the Assessment and Qualifications Alliance; Exercise 28.5 from Northern Examinations and Assessments, Paper 1, Level H, Paper ref 1407, Question 4, AQA, AQA(AEB)/AQA/NEAB/AQA examination materials are reproduced by permission of the Assessment and Qualifications Alliance; Exercise 29.8 from Bk-k & A/c, Level 2, Paper ref NU-BKA 12/01058, Question 5, City & Guilds, City & Guilds Qualifications;

Exercise 29.9 from Southern Examining Group, Paper 2 Level F, Paper ref 3260/2, Question 2, AQA, AQA(AEB)/AQA/NEAB/AQA examination materials are reproduced by permission of the Assessment and Qualifications Alliance; Exercise 30.6 from Administration and Assessment Manual, AAT (1999); Exercises 31.6, 31.7, 35.8 from Administration and Assessment Manual, AAT (1998); Exercise 33.2 from Bk-k & A/c, Level 2, Paper ref NU-BKA 12/90093, Question 2, City & Guilds, City & Guilds Qualifications; Exercise 33.3 from Bk-k & A/c, Level 2, Paper ref NU-BKA 12/01054, Question 2, City & Guilds, City & Guilds Qualifications; Exercise 33.8 from Northern Examinations and Assessments, Paper 3, Level H, Paper ref 1408, Question 4, AQA, AQA(AEB)/AQA/NEAB/AQA examination materials are reproduced by permission of the Assessment and Qualifications Alliance; Exercise 34.10 from from Southern Examining Group, Paper 3, Level H, Paper ref 3260/3, Question 5, AQA, AQA(AEB)/AQA/NEAB/AQA examination materials are reproduced by permission of the Assessment and Qualifications Alliance; Exercise 34.11 from Southern Examining Group, Paper 1, Level F, Paper ref 3260/1, Question 8, AQA, AQA(AEB)/AQA/NEAB/AQA examination materials are reproduced by permission of the Assessment and Qualifications Alliance; Exercise 35.5 from Administration and Assessment Manual, AAT (2001); Exercise 35.9 from A/c, Level 3, Paper ref NU-ACC 13/70111, Question 3, City & Guilds, City & Guilds Qualifications; Exercise 36.6 from A/c, Level 3, Paper ref NU-ACC 13/70111, Question 1, City & Guilds, City & Guilds Qualifications; Exercise 36.7 from Assessment and Qualifications Alliance, Paper 2, Level F, Paper ref 3122/F, Question 4, AQA, AQA(AEB)/AQA/NEAB/AQA examination materials are reproduced by permission of the Assessment and Qualifications Alliance; Exercise 38.3 from Southern Examining Group, Paper 3, Level H, Paper ref 3260/3, Question 4, AQA, AQA(AEB)/AQA/NEAB/AQA examination materials are reproduced by permission of the Assessment and Qualifications Alliance; Exercise 38.5 from A/c, Level 3, Paper ref NU-ACC 13/70107, Question 4, City & Guilds, City & Guilds Qualifications; Exercise 39.2 from A/c, Level 3, Paper ref NU-ACC 13/70111, Question 5, City & Guilds, City & Guilds Qualifications; Exercise 39.3 from Northern Examinations and Assessments, Paper 1, Level H, Paper ref 1407, Question 5, AQA, AQA(AEB)/AQA/NEAB/AQA examination materials are reproduced by permission of the Assessment and Qualifications Alliance.

In some instances we have been unable to trace the owners of copyright material, and we would appreciate any information that would enable us to do so.

PART 1

Introduction to principles of accounting

This part of the book is concerned with the basic principles of the double entry system of book-keeping. It also includes capital and revenue expenditure.

CHAPTER 1

Introduction to accounting principles

Learning objectives

After you have studied this chapter you should be able to:

- understand the aims of a business
- distinguish between the different types of business organisations
- appreciate the need and importance of accounting
- identify the main users of accounting information
- know that the two most important financial statements are:
  1 the income statement
  2 the statement of financial position
- understand the concept of financial control
- understand that the accounting sequence is the basis for preparing financial statements
- understand the process of internal control.

1.1 Aims of a business

The aim of any business is to make a profit and to ensure it remains in operation for the long term. To achieve these aims the owners of the business must practise sound management techniques. These can include the ability to sell the product/service, to purchase materials and products wisely, to manage and motivate staff but crucially to manage the finances of the business.

In setting up the business the owners would have invested money in what they felt was a worthwhile venture. This would normally be referred to as 'introducing capital' in accountancy terms. The capital introduced would be used to enable the business to start trading. In the simplest of terms this would involve purchasing goods and then selling them at a higher price. The owners would have worked hard to establish good trading relationships with their customers but there can be difficulties if some customers are late paying for the goods or default altogether.

To ensure that capital is not put at risk and the trading effort has not been wasted good financial control is vital. A good control system would inform the owners of the financial status of the business at all times and enable them to make appropriate decisions.

1.2 Types of business organisations

There are a number of different trading organisations from the smallest, a sole trader, to major public limited companies, plcs. The difference between them is their legal status and the financial reporting required of them, and these are shown below:

- **Sole trader** – an individual trading alone with their own name or a recognised trading name. The main features are:
  - the sole trader is legally responsible for the business
  - when successful they can take all the profits
  - if unsuccessful they are liable for all the business debts
  - their financial information is not available to the public.
- **Partnership** – two or more people, normally up to a maximum of 20, who carry on a business with the aim of making a profit. The main features are:
  - bound by the Partnership Act 1890
  - the partnership agreement may be written or oral
  - partners are liable for debts incurred by the partnership
  - their financial information is not available to the public.

  Note: this topic is covered fully in Chapter 36.
- **Public limited company (plc)** – a company owned by the shareholders. The main features are:
  - regulated by the various Companies Acts, the latest being the Companies Act 2006
  - the issued share capital must be at least £50,000
  - must have at least two shareholders and two directors
  - must have a qualified company secretary
  - registered (incorporated) at Companies House
  - is a separate legal entity
  - the shareholders have limited liability (see below).

  Note: this topic is covered fully in Chapter 37.
- **Private limited company** – defined in the Companies Act 2006 as 'any company that is not a public company'. The main features are:
  - regulated by the various Companies Acts (see above)
  - must have at least one shareholder and one director who may be the sole shareholder
  - registered (incorporated) at Companies House
  - no need to have a company secretary
  - is a separate legal entity
  - the shareholders have limited liability (see below).

  Note: this topic is covered fully in Chapter 37.
- **Non-trading organisations** – include clubs, associations and other non-profit-making organisations which are normally run for the benefit of their members to engage in a particular activity rather than to make a profit. Their financial statements will take the form of an income and expenditure account, see Chapter 35.

1.3 Importance and need for accounting

Both newly formed and existing businesses need to operate profitably and be continuously viable otherwise they will fail and the investment in those businesses will be lost. To sustain profitability businesses must sell their goods or services at a higher price than the cost of providing such goods or services.

The other crucial factor in maintaining viability is that the business must be receiving more money in than it is paying out in any particular period. The cash flow must be positive; no or low cash flow and *down they go!*

Financial control is the recording of transactions and presenting the information to the owners and is carried out by the business's accounts department.

The two most important **financial statements** are:

1 The **income statement** - shows the calculation of gross and net profits.
2 The **statement of financial position** - shows the assets, liabilities and capital of the business.

At the end of the financial period both these statements are prepared for use by the owner(s) of the business and other parties who are interested in the performance of the business. The interested parties are shown in Exhibit 1.1.

Exhibit 1.1

Interested party	Reason
HMRC	Legally required to collect tax such as employees' tax, national insurance contributions, business tax, VAT, etc.
Investors	Could be private individuals, companies, banks, etc. who want to monitor the performance of the business to ensure it is profitable.
Suppliers	They will need to be assured of the viability of the business before accepting orders.
Customers	Before placing orders with a business they will need to know that it is financially stable.
Employees	They need to know of a business's financial status usually via unions or professional bodies.

1.4 Basic concept of financial control

All businesses whether small, i.e. sole traders, through to very large organisations use the same concept of financial control as shown in Exhibit 1.2.

Exhibit 1.2 The basis of financial control

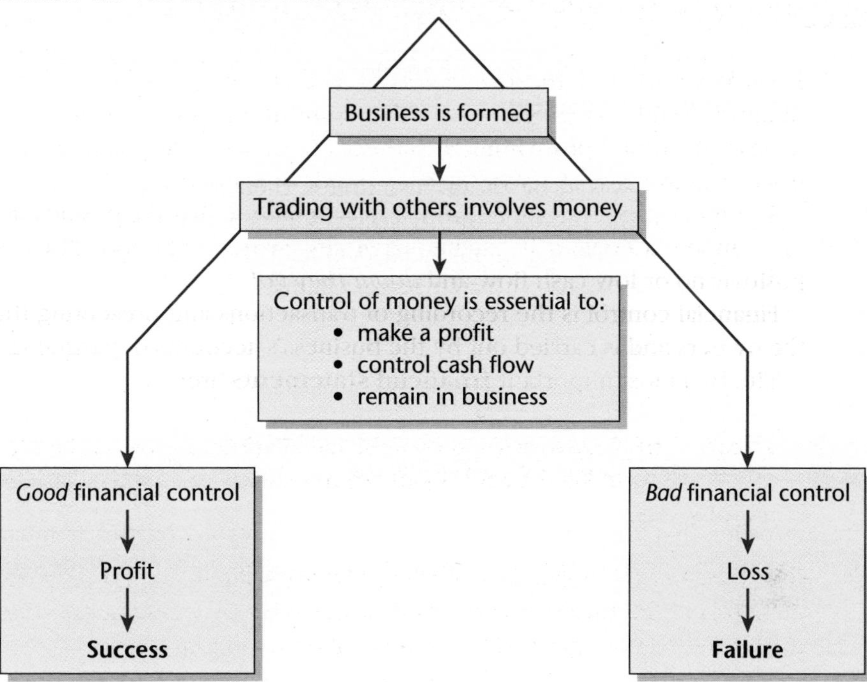

This can be further illustrated using the following example:

Thomas recently won some money on the lottery and decided that he would like to use some of his winnings to start his own business selling leather goods. He rents a shop, purchases leather goods and commences trading on 1 July.

The cost of the initial inventory of leather goods was £14,000 which Thomas sold for £20,000 during the first three months of trading. His expenses for the same period, including the rent for the shop, amounted to £2,800. How successful has Thomas been in his first months of trading?

	£
Thomas sells his goods for	20,000
Less Cost Price	14,000
Profit (before expenses)	6,000
Less Expenses	2,800
Profit (after expenses)	3,200

As can be seen from the above example Thomas has bought his inventory of goods wisely and been able to sell them for more than he paid for them producing a **profit** before expenses of £6,000. After paying his rent and other expenses his profit is £3,200. His venture for his first three months of trading is certainly successful.

Financial control is a major function of a business but there are other aspects that are equally important if a business is to be successful:

- a competitive product and/or service
- a good business strategy
- a competent workforce.

None of these would be of any use unless there is a market (people or businesses willing to buy the product and/or service). It is, however, a fact that businesses that practise good recording of financial data will have the information to make sound management decisions with a far better chance of success.

1.5 The accounting sequence

In order that the business can satisfy all interested parties it must follow certain accounting procedures and practices in a formal sequence. This sequence is shown in Exhibit 1.3.

Exhibit 1.3 The accounting sequence

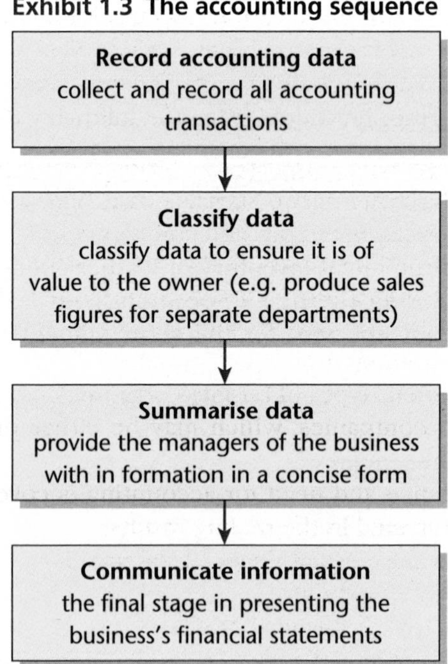

Book-keeping is the process of recording, in the books of account or on computer, the financial effect of business transactions.

Accounting is the skill or practice of maintaining accounts and preparing reports to ensure the financial control and management of a business.

1.6 Internal financial control

The role of the accounts department in providing financial statements to external parties was discussed in section 1.3. However, the department's role is crucial in providing internal financial information to the managers in their day-to-day running of the business.

Normally, the steps taken by a business in a commercial environment are to determine potential sales over a particular period, say, one year. A sales plan is developed in the form of a sales **budget**. This would then need to be monitored throughout the year to ensure that sales targets are being met.

In the case of a manufacturing company the sales budget would impact on the production facilities in terms of the number of employees needed, the materials to be purchased and the overheads that would be incurred.

Assuming a sales budget of £520,000 and a gross profit of 30% means that the total costs must not exceed £400,000. To ensure the costs do not exceed the £400,000 limit, budgets will be drawn up for various aspects of the business, e.g. wages, materials, overheads, and will need to be strictly adhered to (see Chapter 38).

If the sales target looks as if it will be exceeded then the sales budget needs to be amended. Consequently production facilities would need to be increased.

If the sales target has been too optimistic the sales budget will have to be decreased with an adverse affect on production facilities.

The monitoring of these various aspects is known as **cost control** and its function is to identify any overspend in any of the relevant budgets. The activities described above are in effect the basis of management accounting.

Chapter summary

- The basis of any business is trading with others and providing good products and/or services to meet customer requirements, to manage the business well, ensure costs are controlled and cash flow maintained, resulting in a successful and profitable business.
- There are various types of business organisations, including: sole traders, partnerships and limited companies, which may be either public or private, and non-trading organisations.
- The importance and need for accounting is covered including the various parties who are interested in the trading results.
- The two most important financial statements are:
  - the income statement
  - the statement of financial position.
- The basic concept of financial control is where goods purchased are sold for more than they cost and a profit is made after expenses have been paid.
- The accounting sequence for dealing with transactions is as follows:
  - record accounting data
  - classify data
  - summarise data
  - communicate information.

- It is important to use the financial data to assist in the day-to-day running of the business by providing information to enable planning and budgets to be prepared, monitored and controlled.

Reminder: A glossary of accounting terms can be found in Appendix A at the end of the book.

EXERCISES

Note: Questions with the suffix 'X' shown after the question number do ***not*** *have answers shown at the back of the book. Answers to the other questions are shown in Appendix E.*

1.1 Explain briefly why good financial control is important to any business.

1.2 There are a number of bodies or individuals, other than the owners, who will have an interest in the financial performance statements of a business. List these interested parties and explain briefly the reasons for their interest.

1.3 List the main types of business organisation and explain each one's basic structure.

1.4X Profit is the aim of all businesses. Explain in simple terms how this can be attained.

1.5X A sole trader is an individual trading alone. State one drawback and one positive aspect of trading in this way.

CHAPTER 2

The accounting system

Learning objectives

After you have studied this chapter you should be able to:

- describe and explain the accounting system
- understand the source documents used within an organisation
- understand the need for books of original entry and what each one is used for
- appreciate how the books of original entry are used alongside the ledgers employing the double entry system of book-keeping
- distinguish between personal and impersonal ledgers
- distinguish between the different types of ledgers
- appreciate that at the end of the financial year the accounts are balanced off and a trial balance prepared
- understand that from the final trial balance the financial statements are prepared consisting of the income statement (formerly the trading and profit and loss account) and the statement of financial position (formerly the balance sheet).

2.1 Introduction

This chapter gives an overview of the **accounting system** starting with the source documents that are used initially to enter a transaction in the books of account. It explains the books of original entry and provides an introduction to the double entry system of book-keeping and the ledgers. The difference between personal and impersonal accounts is discussed together with the meaning of real and nominal accounts.

Finally, a summary is given of the procedures followed by organisations at the end of the accounting year to 'balance off' the accounts and prepare the trial balance. From the final trial balance the financial statements are prepared which show the results of the year's trading, be it an income statement, together with the statement of financial position that indicates the financial position of the organisation at a specific point in time.

All the topics covered in this overview chapter are dealt with thoroughly in later chapters.

2.2 The accounting system

Traditionally businesses operate on a 12-month cycle, which may be the same as the calendar year January to December or perhaps the same as the tax year which runs from 6 April of one year to 5 April of the following year. Alternatively, some businesses operate from the date the business first began, for example 1 September of one year to 31 August of the following year.

During the 12-month period the business receives many documents of a financial nature that have to be entered in the books of account using either a manual or a computerised system. At the end of each month the books are usually 'balanced off' and a trial balance drawn up from which the financial statements may be prepared. Also, at the end of each month, outstanding accounts are usually settled, wages and salaries paid and monies received during the month are all recorded.

If the organisation uses a computerised system of accounting then, at the end of each month, a great deal of useful information can also be obtained such as the amount of money outstanding each month and the length of time the debt has been owing, and the amount of money that the organisation owes. Other financial information is also available that enables management to carry out an appraisal of the business, to budget and to forward plan. While this information is also available using a manual system of book-keeping it is not as readily available or as easily reformatted and processed as the information from a computerised system.

It is usual for the financial statements of a business to be prepared on an annual basis since they are required for taxation purposes and for the use by the owners of the business.

This chapter shows how source documents are recorded in the accounting records of an organisation and the various stages that are followed in preparing the financial statements (*see* Exhibit 2.1).

2.3 Source documents

Source documents are documents where original information is found, for example, sales and purchase invoices and credit notes. All businesses and organisations which are involved in either trading activities or providing a service use these important documents.

Invoice An invoice is a document prepared by the seller when they sell goods or provide services on credit. The invoice, usually numbered for easy identification and for filing in a suitable storage system, contains the following information:

- seller's name and address
- purchaser's name and address
- purchaser's order number and date
- date of delivery
- description of goods and services supplied including part number and catalogue reference
- quantity and price per item

Exhibit 2.1 The accounting system for a profit-making organisation

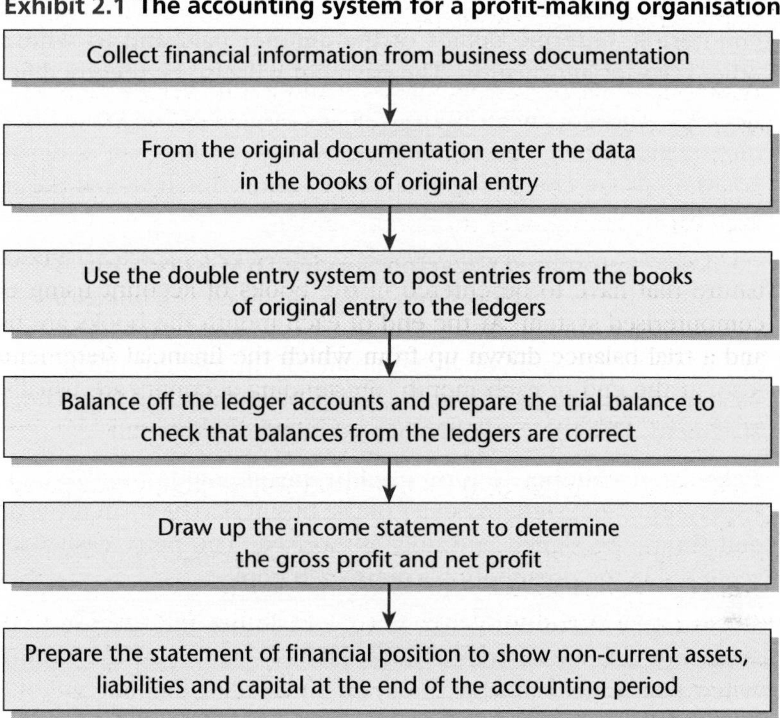

- total amount due
- terms and conditions of sale.

From a book-keeper's point of view the invoice is one of the most important documents since details of the transaction need to be entered in the books of account of both the seller and the buyer. In the seller's records the invoice is a sales invoice and in the purchaser's records it is a purchase invoice.

Credit note. This document is raised by the supplier when goods have been returned by the purchaser due to their being damaged, faulty or supplied to the wrong specification, or when an overcharge has been made on an invoice. The amount owed by the customer will be reduced by the amount of the credit note. Credit notes are sometimes printed in red to distinguish them from invoices. Again, credit notes are important documents that need entering in the books of both the supplier and purchaser.

Debit note. If the supplier agrees, goods bought previously may be returned. When this happens a debit note is raised by the purchaser and sent to the supplier giving details of the goods returned and the reason for their return. The debit note shows that the purchaser expects the seller to bear the charge.

Paying-in slips. These are forms used for paying money into a bank account. The recipient of the money must record on the counterfoil of the bank paying-in slip details of the amount paid and by whom so that these may be recorded in the organisation's cash book.

Cheque counterfoil. When a cheque is made out it is important to complete the counterfoil, entering details of the amount paid and to whom together with any other relevant information. The payment will also be recorded in the cash book.

Receipt. This document acknowledges the receipt of money from a customer and is often issued when a customer purchases goods for cash rather than on credit. Again counterfoils are completed and used to enter the details of the receipt of cash in the cash book.

Bankers' Automated Clearing Service (BACS) receipt. BACS enables the transfer of money between banks and other financial organisations. The supplier's bank can receive payment direct from the customer's bank. The customer usually sends an advice to the supplier giving details of the amount of the payment, which is then used to record the receipt in the books of account and later checked against the bank statement. This topic will be covered fully in Chapter 20.

Petty cash voucher. A form used by anyone requesting payment for a small item of expenditure incurred on behalf of the business. The form gives details of the expense and should be signed and duly authorised. The petty cash voucher expenditure is recorded in the organisation's petty cash book.

Occasionally correspondence from a customer may be used as a source document to record a financial transaction that may be out of the ordinary. This may occur when a customer is unable to pay an outstanding amount and offers to settle the debt by giving the supplier an asset. Such a transaction would be entered in the journal (see Chapter 24). Internal documents such as a memorandum from a senior member of the organisation may be used in the same way.

It is important to note that all information of a financial nature must be supported by a source document and it is from this document that the details are entered in the business's book-keeping system. Source documents may also be referred to as **prime documents**.

2.4 Books of original entry

These are books in which the transaction is first entered. There are separate books for different types of transaction, as follows:

- **Purchases day book** (also called **purchases journal**) – this is similar to the sales day book, but contains lists of purchase invoices received from suppliers of goods or services. The purchases day book may also contain analysis columns depending upon the accounting system.
- **Purchases returns day book** (also called **returns outwards day book** or journal) – this is used to record goods returned to suppliers.
- **Sales day book** (also called **sales journal**) – a book used for listing sales invoices. It gives details of the date of the sale, to whom and the amount of the sale. Sales day books may also contain analysis columns to analyse sales between different goods, departments and so on.
- **Sales returns day book** (also called **returns inwards day book** or journal) – this is used to list any returns made by customers. This will lead to a credit note being issued to them.

- **Cash book** – this is another book of original entry used to enter cash and bank receipts and payments. The cash book provides a record of the business's bank account and also provides details of the amount of cash in hand. It is both a book of original entry and part of the double entry system as it contains the balances of both cash in hand and cash at bank.
- **Petty cash book** – a cash book used for making small (petty) payments, details of which are entered from petty cash vouchers supported if possible by a receipt.
- The **journal** – this is used to record items that are much less common and sometimes complicated and are not recorded in any other book of original entry.

2.5 An introduction to the double entry book-keeping system

The system of **double entry book-keeping** is a method of recording transactions in the books of account of a business. In the section above, source documents, which provide all the relevant information, were discussed followed by the books of original entry. The next important stage is to understand the double entry system of book-keeping.

Business transactions deal with money or money's worth and each transaction always affects two things. For example, if a business buys goods valued at £500 and pays for them by cheque, two things will have occurred:

1 The inventory is increased by £500.
2 The money in the business's bank account will have decreased by £500.

If the business then pays cash for a piece of equipment, then:

1 The money in the cash account will be reduced.
2 The business will have acquired equipment.

The dual aspect of treating each transaction is then recorded in an account. An account shows us the 'history' of a particular business transaction, for example, the bank account or equipment account. If manual accounting records are kept, then each account is usually shown on a separate page. If a computerised system is used, then each account is given a separate code number. The following shows an example of an account.

Reference no.

Name of account

Date	*Details*	*Folio*	*£*	*Date*	*Details*	*Folio*	*£*
	'Debit side'				'Credit side'		

Double entry book-keeping is shown using a step-by-step approach in Chapters 4, 5 and 6.

2.6 The ledgers

In a double entry system the accounts, as mentioned above, are kept in a ledger. If the business is very small then only one ledger may be used, but once the business expands it is better to have more than one ledger to allow different members of staff to be able to record transactions at the same time.

Once details from the source documents are entered in the books of original entry then the next stage of the book-keeping procedure is to show the effect of the transactions by putting them into double entry accounts. The different types of ledgers used are as follows (their alternative names are shown in brackets).

Types of ledger		
Sales ledger	**Purchase ledger**	**General ledger** (Nominal ledger)
Shows records of customer's personal accounts – the accounts receivable	Shows records of suppliers' personal accounts – the accounts payable	Contains the remaining double entry accounts, such as expenses, non-current assets and capital

2.7 Classification of accounts

Accounts are divided into **personal accounts** and **impersonal accounts**. Personal accounts are accounts that deal with people and businesses - in other words, the **accounts receivable** and **accounts payable**. Accounts receivable are people who owe money to the business and accounts payable are people or businesses to whom money is owed. Accounts receivable records are maintained in the sales ledger, while the accounts payable are kept in the purchases ledger.

Impersonal accounts are divided into real and nominal accounts:

- **Real accounts** are those which deal with possessions of the business, for example, buildings, machinery, computer equipment, fixtures and fittings, inventories (stock of goods), etc.
- **Nominal accounts** are those in which expenses and income are recorded, for example, sales, purchases, wages, electricity, commissions received, etc.

Private ledger

In order to ensure privacy for the proprietor(s), the capital, drawings and other similar accounts are sometimes kept in a **private ledger**. This prevents office staff from seeing items of a confidential nature.

Exhibit 2.2 illustrates the classification of accounts.

Exhibit 2.2 Classification of accounts

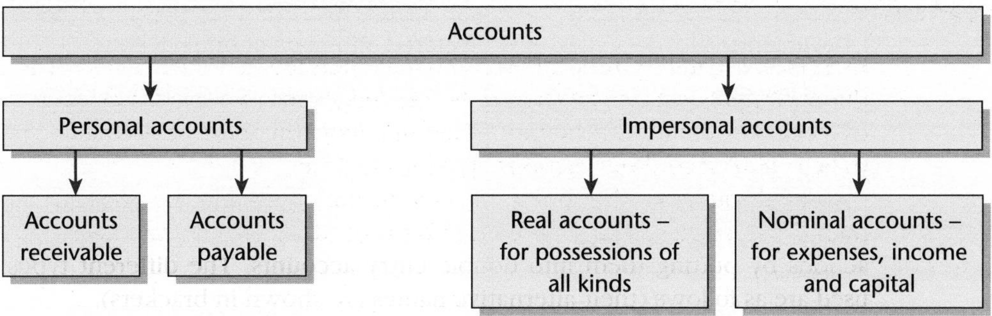

2.8 Balancing off accounts and the trial balance

Businesses usually balance off their accounts at the end of each month and prepare what is called a **trial balance**. The trial balance is prepared for several reasons: first of all it is important to check periodically that the transactions have been entered correctly in the books of account; second it is useful to know how much money is outstanding and how much the business owes. Also, with the use of accounting software, the business can easily prepare draft financial statements showing the profit or loss to date and the financial position of the firm at a specific date. Both the trial balance and the financial statements are dealt with in later chapters of this book.

2.9 Financial statements

At the end of the financial year a trial balance is drawn up and from that and other information and adjustments the financial statements are prepared by an organisation. The financial statements include:

- an **income statement** which shows the gross and net profits or losses made during the period, and
- the **statement of financial position**, which indicates the financial position of the business at a particular point in time.

As the name implies, the final accounts are the end product of the recording of all the business transactions throughout the financial year. Once prepared, they are used by the owner(s) of the business for information, interpretation and planning purposes.

2.10 Summary of the accounting system

This chapter has shown how the accounting procedures of a business are recorded and the information that is derived from those records. It may be useful to list them once again at this point. Source documents are received as follows:

Source documents	
Documents	**Entered into book of original entry**
Sales invoices	Sales day book (also called sales journal)
Credit notes (sent to customers)	Sales returns day book (also called returns inwards day book)
Purchase invoices	Purchases day book (also called purchases journal)
Credit notes (received from suppliers)	Purchases returns day book (also called returns outwards day book)
Cash and cheques received	Cash book (also a ledger account)
Cheques paid out	Cash book (also a ledger account)
Small cash payments	Petty cash book (also a ledger account for cash in hand)
Miscellaneous correspondence	The journal

Once the details of the transaction have been entered into the books of original entry, the information is then entered into the ledgers by means of the double entry system. This procedure is often referred to as **posting**. Sales transactions are posted to the sales ledger, purchases transactions are posted to the purchases ledger and items involving the real and nominal accounts are posted to the general ledger.

At the end of each month the books are balanced off and a trial balance prepared to check the arithmetical accuracy of the book-keeping entries. At the end of the accounting period the final trial balance is used to prepare the year-end accounts, i.e. the income statement and statement of financial position. The accounts are then presented to the owner(s) of the business for their information, interpretation and action in the form of planning and budgeting for the next accounting period, and for forward planning.

Chapter summary

- The accounting system is the sequence in which financial data is recorded and processed prior to the preparation of the financial statements at the end of the trading period.
- All information that is entered into the book-keeping records comes from a source document such as an invoice, credit note, debit note, cheque book counterfoil, paying-in book, petty cash voucher, etc.
- The books of original entry are used as a basis for posting the transactions to the double entry accounts in the various ledgers.
- At the end of the accounting period the accounts are balanced off and a trial balance prepared.
- The final trial balance is used to prepare the year-end accounts. These are the income statement, which shows the profit or loss made for the period, and the statement of financial position, which shows the financial position of the business at a specific date.
- A summary of the accounting system is shown together with a recap of the various stages of the accounting procedures.

Reminder: There is a glossary of accounting terms in Appendix A at the end of the book.

EXERCISES

*Note: Questions with the suffix 'X' shown after the question number do **not** have answers shown at the back of the book. Answers to the other questions are shown in Appendix E.*

2.1 Source documents are very important.

(*a*) Describe the contents of both an invoice and a credit note.
(*b*) State when each of these would be used.

2.2 Describe the service offered by BACS and in what circumstances might a business use this facility.

2.3X The books of original entry are used to record initial accounting information and separate books are used for different types of transactions. List the various books used and give a brief explanation as to how each is used.

2.4 For what purpose would you use the following ledgers:

(*a*) General or nominal ledger
(*b*) Sales ledger
(*c*) Purchases ledger?

2.5X Distinguish between personal and impersonal accounts giving examples of what each might contain.

CHAPTER 3

The accounting equation and statement of financial position

Learning objectives

After you have studied this chapter you should be able to:

- understand the accounting equation
- understand what is meant by assets, liabilities and capital
- draw up statements of financial position (formerly balance sheets) after different transactions have occurred
- explain the meaning of the terms assets, capital, liabilities, accounts receivable (debtors) and accounts payable (creditors).

3.1 Introduction

This chapter looks at one of the financial statements used in businesses called the **statement of financial position**. The statement of financial position is just one of the statements prepared at the end of the financial year, the other statements being **income statements**. Although these are separate accounts they are usually shown as one financial statement, and will be discussed in later chapters.

The statement of financial position is a financial statement that is usually prepared at the end of an organisation's financial year. Quite simply the statement details everything that the organisation *owns* and what it *owes* as at a specific date. The items an organisation owns are known as **non-current assets** and what it owes are called **liabilities**. Also included in the statement of financial position is the **capital**, which is the amount of money supplied by the owner(s) of the business.

3.2 The accounting equation

Accounting is based upon a concept known as the **accounting equation**, which is simply that at any point in time the total amount of resources supplied by the owner equals the resources in the business. Assuming that the owner of the new business supplies all the resources then this can be shown as follows:

Resources supplied by the owner = Resources in the business

In accounting the various terms have special meanings. The amount of resources supplied by the owner is called **capital**. As mentioned above the actual resources that are in the business are called **assets**. If the owner of the business has supplied all of the resources, the accounting equation can be shown as:

Capital = Assets

In many cases other people besides the owner of the business will have supplied some of the assets. The amounts owing to these people for these assets is called **liabilities**, as stated above. When this is the case the accounting equation changes to:

Capital = Assets – Liabilities

This is the most common way in which the accounting equation is presented since the two sides of the equation will have the same totals because we are dealing with the same thing but from two different points of view. First, the value of the owners' investment in the business and secondly the value of what is owned by the business, which is ultimately owned by the owners.

Unfortunately, with this form of the accounting equation, it is no longer possible to see at a glance what value is represented by the resources in the business. This can be seen more clearly if you change assets and capital around to give an alternative form of the accounting equation:

Assets = Capital + Liabilities

This can then be replaced with words describing the resources of the business:

Resources: what they are = Resources: who supplied them
(Assets) (Capital + Liabilities)

It is a fact that no matter how you present the accounting equation, the totals of both sides will *always* equal each other, and this will *always* be true irrespective of the number of transactions. The actual assets, capital and liabilities may change, but the total of the assets will always equal the total of capital + liabilities. Or, reverting to the more common form of the accounting equation, the capital will always equal the assets of the business minus the liabilities.

Assets consist of property of all kinds, such as buildings, machinery, equipment, inventories (stocks of goods) and motor vehicles. Other assets include debts owed by customers and the amount of money in the bank account.

Liabilities include amounts owed by the business for goods and services supplied to the business, and expenses incurred by the business but still outstanding. Funds borrowed by the business are also included.

Capital is often called the owner's **equity** or **net worth**. This is comprised of the funds invested in the business by the owner plus any **profits** retained for use in the business less any share of the profits paid out to the owner by the business.

3.3 The statement of financial position and the effects of business transactions

As mentioned above the statement of financial position shows the financial position of an organisation at a point in time. In other words, it presents a snapshot of the organisation at the date when the statement was prepared.

The statement of financial position is not the first accounting record to be made, nor the first record that you will learn to enter, but it is a convenient place to start considering accounting.

In the following activities you will see how a series of transactions affect the statement of financial position.

1 The introduction of capital

On 1 January 2012, K Astley started in business and put £50,000 into a bank account for the business. The statement of financial position would appear:

K Astley
Statement of Financial Position as at 1 January 2012

	£
Assets: Cash at bank	50,000
Capital	50,000

Note how the top section of the statement of financial position contains the assets and the bottom section contains the capital. The information is always presented in the statement of financial position in this way.

2 The purchase of an asset by cheque

On 3 January 2012, Astley buys a small shop for £30,000. The effect of this transaction on the statement of financial position is that the money in the bank is decreased and the new asset, shop, is added:

K Astley
Statement of Financial Position as at 3 January 2012

	£
Assets: Shop	30,000
Cash at bank	20,000
	50,000
Capital	50,000

Note how the two parts of the statement of financial position 'balance': the total of the assets equals the total of the liabilities, i.e. the money invested in the business by K Astley, the capital, is owed by the business to him.

3 The purchase of an asset and the incurring of a liability

On 5 January 2012, K Astley buys goods for £5,000 from D Moore and agrees to pay for them some time within the following two weeks. The effect of this is that a new asset, **inventory**, is acquired, and a liability for the goods is created. A person to whom money is owed for goods is known in accounting language as an **accounts payable (creditor)**. The statement of financial position is now shown below:

K Astley
Statement of Financial Position as at 5 January 2012

		£
Assets:	Shop	30,000
	Inventory	5,000
	Cash at bank	20,000
		55,000
Less:	Accounts payable	5,000
		50,000
Capital		50,000

Note how the liability (the account payable) is shown as a deduction from the assets. This is exactly the same calculation that is presented in the most common form of the accounting equation.

4 Sale of an asset on credit

On 10 January 2012, goods which cost £1,000 were sold to P Hall for the same amount, the money to be paid at a later date. The effect is a reduction in inventory (stock of goods) and the creation of a new asset. A person who owes the business money is known in accounting terms as an **accounts receivable (debtor)**. Once this transaction has been recorded the statement of financial position would appear as follows:

K Astley
Statement of Financial Position as at 10 January 2012

		£
Assets:	Shop	30,000
	Inventory	4,000
	Accounts receivable	1,000
	Cash at bank	20,000
		55,000
Less:	Accounts payable	5,000
		50,000
Capital		50,000

5 Sale of an asset for immediate payment

On 16 January 2012, goods which cost £2,000 were sold to M Clark for the same amount. Clark paid for them immediately by cheque. Here one asset, inventory, is reduced, while another asset, bank, is increased. The statement of financial position after these transactions is now shown:

K Astley
Statement of Financial Position as at 16 January 2012

		£
Assets:	Shop	30,000
	Inventory	2,000
	Accounts receivable	1,000
	Cash at bank	22,000
		55,000
Less:	Accounts payable	5,000
		50,000
Capital		50,000

6 The payment of a liability

On 17 January 2012, K Astley pays a cheque for £3,000 to D Moore in part payment of the amount owing. The asset of bank is therefore reduced, and the liability to the creditor is also reduced, as shown below:

K Astley
Statement of Financial Position as at 17 January 2012

		£
Assets:	Shop	30,000
	Inventory	2,000
	Accounts receivable	1,000
	Cash at bank	19,000
		52,000
Less:	Accounts payable	2,000
		50,000
Capital		50,000

Note how the total of each part of the statement of financial position has not changed. The business is still worth £50,000 to the owner K Astley.

7 Collection of an asset

P Hall, who owed K Astley £1,000, makes a part payment of £750 by cheque on 31 January 2012. The effect is to reduce one asset, account receivable, and to increase another asset, bank, as shown below:

K Astley
Statement of Financial Position as at 31 January 2012

		£
Assets:	Shop	30,000
	Inventory	2,000
	Accounts receivable	250
	Cash at bank	19,750
		52,000
Less:	Accounts payable	2,000
		50,000
Capital		50,000

3.4 Equality of the accounting equation

It can be seen that every transaction has affected two items. Sometimes it has changed two assets by reducing one and increasing the other. In other cases, the effect has been different. You will notice, however, that in all cases apart from the very first (when the owner started the business by putting in cash of £50,000) no change has been made to the total of either section of the statement of financial position and the equality between their two totals has remained the same. The accounting equation has held true throughout the example and, in fact, always will.

The effect of each of the seven accounting transactions, shown above, upon the two sections of the statement of financial position is now illustrated in Exhibit 3.1.

Exhibit 3.1

Type of transaction	Effect	
1 Owner pays capital into the bank	⬆ Increase asset (Bank)	⬆ Increase capital
2 Purchase shop premises by cheque	⬇ Decrease asset (Bank)	⬆ Increase asset (Shop premises)
3 Buy inventory on credit	⬆ Increase asset (Inventory)	⬆ Increase liability (Accounts payable)
4 Sale of inventory on credit	⬇ Decrease asset (Inventory)	⬆ Increase asset (Accounts receivable)
5 Sale of inventory for cash or cheque	⬆ Increase asset (Cash or bank)	⬇ Decrease asset (Inventory)
6 Pay creditor (accounts payable)	⬇ Decrease asset (Bank)	⬇ Decrease liability (Accounts payable)
7 Debtor pays money owing by cheque	⬆ Increase asset (Bank)	⬇ Decrease asset (Accounts receivable)

Each transaction has, therefore, maintained the same total for assets as for capital + liabilities. This can be shown:

Number of transactions as above	Assets	Capital and Liabilities	Effect on balance sheet totals
1	+	+	Each side added to equally
2	− +		A minus and a plus both on the assets side thus cancelling out each other
3	+	+	Each side added to equally
4	− +		A minus and a plus on the assets side
5	+ −		A plus and a minus both on the assets side cancelling out each other
6	−	−	Each side reduced equally
7	+ −		A plus and a minus on the assets side

3.5 More detailed presentation of the statement of financial position

The statements of financial position shown in this chapter are presented in what is referred to as the 'vertical presentation'. This method will be used throughout the book since it is the most common method of presentation used today.

A more detailed statement of financial position of K Astley is now shown in line with how you will present the information in later stages of your studies:

K Astley
Statement of Financial Position as at 31 January 2012

		£
Non-current assets		
Shop		30,000
Current assets		
Inventory	2,000	
Accounts receivable	250	
Cash at bank	19,750	
	22,000	
Less: Current Liabilities		
Accounts payable	2,000	20,000
		50,000
Capital		50,000

The terms **non-current assets**, **current assets** and **current liabilities** shown in the above statement of financial position are explained below. The terms are dealt with more fully in Chapter 11.

- **Non-current assets** are assets which have an expected useful life of at least a year and beyond, for example, buildings, machinery, fixtures, motor vehicles. They are used in the business to enable it to carry on the purpose of earning income and are not intended for resale.
- **Current assets** are assets which change from day to day, for example, the value of stock in hand goes up and down as it is bought and sold. Similarly, the amount of money owing to us by debtors will change quickly, as we sell more to them on credit and they pay their debts. The amount of money in the bank will also change as we receive and pay out money.
- **Current liabilities** are those liabilities which have to be paid within the near future, for example, accounts payable for goods purchased.

Chapter summary

- The statement of financial position is a financial statement prepared at a particular point in time. It contains assets, capital and liabilities.
- The whole of accounting is based on the accounting equation namely that resources supplied by the owner (the capital) will always equal the resources in the business (the assets).

- Other people may also supply some of the assets to the business. The name given to any amounts that are owed by the business to other people are called liabilities.
- When assets are supplied by other people as well as the owner of the business the accounting equation becomes Capital = Assets – Liabilities.
- The two sides of the accounting equation are represented by the two sections of the statement of financial position.
- The totals of each part of the statement of financial position should always agree, i.e. balance.
- Every transaction affects two items in the accounting equation. Sometimes that may involve the same item being affected twice, once positively (going up) and once negatively (going down).
- Every transaction affects two items in the statement of financial position.

Reminder: There is a glossary of accounting terms in Appendix A at the end of the book.

EXERCISES

*Note: Questions with the suffix 'X' shown after the question number do **not** have answers shown at the back of the book. Answers to the other questions are shown in Appendix E.*

3.1 Examine the following table and complete the gaps:

	Assets £	*Liabilities* £	*Capital* £
(*a*)	34,282	7,909	?
(*b*)	276,303	?	213,817
(*c*)	?	6,181	70,919
(*d*)	?	109,625	877,138
(*e*)	88,489	?	78,224
(*f*)	456,066	51,163	?

3.2X Examine the following table and complete the gaps:

	Assets £	*Liabilities* £	*Capital* £
(*a*)	?	59,997	604,337
(*b*)	346,512	?	293,555
(*c*)	47,707	?	42,438
(*d*)	108,129	11,151	?
(*e*)	515,164	77,352	?
(*f*)	?	19,928	179,352

3.3 Determine which are assets and which are liabilities from the following list:

(*a*) Computer equipment
(*b*) Inventory of goods held for sale
(*c*) Loan from H Barlow
(*d*) Motor vehicles
(*e*) Accounts payable for inventory
(*f*) Bank balance.

3.4X Which of the following are assets and which are liabilities?

(*a*) Premises
(*b*) Accounts receivable
(*c*) Cash in hand
(*d*) Accounts payable
(*e*) Loan from finance company
(*f*) Owing to bank
(*g*) Machinery
(*h*) Motor vehicles.

3.5 State which of the following are shown under the wrong headings for S Murphy's business:

Assets	*Liabilities*
Cash in hand	Money owing to bank
Accounts payable	Accounts receivable
Premises	Inventory
Motor vehicles	
Loan from C Shaw	
Machinery	

3.6X Which of the following are shown under the wrong headings?:

Assets	*Liabilities*
Cash at bank	Machinery
Computer equipment	Motor vehicles
Account payable	Loan from W Barlow
Capital	
Accounts receivable	
Inventory	

3.7 Ann Wood decides to open a retail shop selling greetings cards and gifts. Her uncle lends her £30,000 to help her with financing the venture. Ann buys shop premises costing £50,000, a motor vehicle for £10,000 and inventory of a stock of goods costing £5,000. Ann did not pay for her stock of goods in full and still owes £2,100 to her suppliers in respect of them. After the events described above and before she starts trading, Ann has £100 cash in hand and £7,000 cash at the bank.

You are required to calculate the amount of capital that Ann invested in her business.

3.8X Suman Patel decides to start his own retail business and his father agrees to lend him £3,000. Before starting trading he decides to buy some shop fittings costing £4,000 and a secondhand motor van costing £6,100.

Suman also buys an inventory of a stock of goods costing £5,720, paying £3,000 when he placed the order, the balance being due in two months. After paying for the above items Suman has £4,200 in the bank and £120 in cash.

You are required to calculate Suman's capital.

3.9 Draw up T Lymer's statement of financial position, using the vertical presentation method, from the following information as at 31 December 2012.

	£
Capital	34,823
Delivery van	12,000
Accounts receivable	10,892
Office furniture	8,640
Inventory	4,220
Cash at bank	11,722
Accounts payable	12,651

3.10X Draw up A Pennington's statement of financial position as at 31 March 2012 from the following information:

	£
Premises	50,000
Plant and machinery	26,500
Accounts receivable	28,790
Accounts payable	32,320
Bank overdraft	3,625
Inventory	21,000
Cash in hand	35
Capital	90,380

3.11 Complete the columns to show the effects of the following transactions:

	Effects upon		
	Assets	*Capital*	*Liabilities*
(*a*) Bought goods on credit £400.			
(*b*) F Drew lends the business £500 by cheque.			
(*c*) We return goods £50 to a supplier whose account was still outstanding.			
(*d*) We pay a supplier £330 by cheque.			
(*e*) The owner of the business introduces £5,000 into the business by cheque.			
(*f*) Bought computer £880 for office use paying by cheque.			
(*g*) Sold goods for cash £45.			
(*h*) A customer pays us in cash £77.			

For each item shown above, you are required to state how it changes assets, capital or liabilities.

For example the answer to (*a*) will be:

	Assets	*Capital*	*Liabilities*
(*a*)	+ £400	–	+ £400

CHAPTER 4

The double entry system for assets, liabilities and capital

Learning objectives

After you have studied this chapter you should be able to:

- understand what is meant by the double entry system
- explain how the double entry system follows the rules of the accounting equation
- understand the rules for double entry book-keeping
- draw up 'T accounts' and understand the terms 'debit' and 'credit'
- record transactions affecting assets, liabilities and capital in the T accounts.

4.1 Introduction and history of the double entry system of book-keeping

Since early times, various forms of record keeping existed to record such things as rents, taxes and fines due, although at this time no formal or standard system of book-keeping was present. It was not until the fifteenth century, when Father Luca Pacioli first invented the 'double entry system of accounting', that the process of formalised book-keeping and accounting began. Since that time the principle of 'double entry' has progressed to the world-wide system we see today.

In the previous chapter we saw how the concept of the 'accounting equation' was introduced whereby the resources supplied by the owner of the business, i.e. the capital, will always equal the resources owned by the business, i.e. the assets. In other words, the **transaction** has affected *two* items, i.e. the capital and the assets. Double entry book-keeping is thus based upon the accounting equation in that every transaction affects two aspects.

4.2 The double entry system

The system of double entry book-keeping is a method of recording transactions in the books of account of a business. In the previous chapter we saw how every transaction affected two items. We now need to show these effects when the transaction is first recorded in the books of account. The information for every item that is entered into the books of account is obtained from a source document, i.e. an invoice, credit note, cheque book stub, paying in book, etc. (see Chapter 15). The next important stage is to understand the double entry system of book-keeping.

Business transactions deal with money or money's worth and each transaction always affects two things. For example, if a business buys goods valued at £500 and pays for them by cheque, two things have occurred:

1 the money in the business's bank account will have decreased by £500
2 the stock of goods is increased.

Here is another example: if a business buys a motor van costing £10,000 and pays for it by cheque then again two things have been affected:

1 the money in the business's bank account will have decreased by £10,000
2 the motor van will have been acquired for the business and that asset account will have increased.

This is the book-keeping stage of accounting and the process used is called **double entry**; sometimes this may also be referred to as **double entry book-keeping**, either term is correct.

In the previous chapter a new statement of financial position was drawn up after each transaction. This can be done quite easily if there are only a few transactions per day. However, if there are hundreds of transactions per day then it will become impossible to draw up numerous statements of financial position. There simply would not be enough time to carry out such a task.

Therefore, instead of constantly drawing up amended statements of financial position after each transaction what we have instead is the double entry system. The basis of this system is that the transactions that have occurred are entered in the books of account, as mentioned above. An **account** shows us the 'history of' a particular business transaction. It is the place in the records where all the information referring to a particular asset, liability or capital is entered, for example, the bank account or motor van account. If manual records are kept, then each account is usually shown on a separate page; if a computerised system is used, then each account is given a separate code number and the information is stored on the accounting package and back-up systems.

4.3 The accounts for double entry

Each account should be shown on a separate page. The double entry system divides each page into two halves. The left-hand side of each page is called the **debit** side, while the right-hand side is called the **credit** side. The title of each account is written across the top of the account at the centre - see Exhibit 4.1.

Exhibit 4.1

Title of account written here					
Date	Details	£	Date	Details	£

Left-hand side of the page. This is the 'debit' side.

Right-hand side of the page. This is the 'credit' side.

The words 'debit' and 'credit' in book-keeping terms do not mean the same as in normal language and should be viewed differently from the start to avoid confusion. Students new to studying double entry may find it useful to think of 'IN' when looking at the entry of a debit item, and to think of 'OUT' when looking at the entry of a credit item. We will consider this later in section 4.5.

4.4 Rules for double entry

Double entry is relatively easy to learn and understand if the following four rules are learnt and understood:

1 Double entry means that every transaction affects two things and should, therefore, be entered twice: once on the *Debit* side and once on the *Credit* side. Later on in your studies you may have more than two accounts to record a transaction, for example, when an item is purchased and part of it is paid for in cash and part paid by cheque.
2 The order in which the items are entered does not matter – although students may find it easier to deal with any cash or bank transaction first using the 'IN' and 'OUT' principle.
3 A **debit** entry is always an asset or an expense. A **credit** entry is a liability, capital or income.
4 To increase or decrease assets, liabilities or capital, as seen in Chapter 3, the double entry rules are as shown in Exhibit 4.2.

Exhibit 4.2

Accounts	To record	Entry in the account
Assets	↑ an increase ↓ a decrease	Debit Credit
Liabilities	↑ an increase ↓ a decrease	Credit Debit
Capital	↑ an increase ↓ a decrease	Credit Debit

Let us look once again at the accounting equation:

	Capital	= Assets	– Liabilities
To increase each item To decrease each item	Credit Debit	Debit Credit	Credit Debit

The double entry rules for liabilities and capital are the same, but they are the opposite of those for assets. Looking at the accounts the rules will appear as:

Capital account		Any asset account		Any liability account	
Decreases –	Increases +	Increases +	Decreases –	Decreases –	Increases +

In a real business, at least one full page would be taken for each account in the accounting books. However, as we have not enough space in this book to put each account on a separate page, we will list the accounts under each other.

4.5 The 'IN' and 'OUT' approach

To help students having difficulty in deciding on which side of each account the items should be entered, a useful hint is for them to think of the debit side being 'IN' to the account, and the credit side being 'OUT' of the account.

To give two examples of this approach, we will use the following:

Example 1: Paid cash £2,000 to buy machinery.

The double entry for this transaction would be as follows:

Effect	Action
(*a*) Machinery comes 'IN' (*b*) Cash goes 'OUT'	A *debit* entry in the Machinery account A *credit* entry in the Cash account

Example 2: Took £500 out of the cash in hand of the business and paid it into the bank account of the business.

The double entry for this transaction would be as follows:

Effect	Action
(*a*) Money comes 'IN' to the bank (*b*) Cash goes 'OUT' of the cash till	A *debit* entry in the Bank account A *credit* entry in the Cash account

4.6 T accounts

The type of accounts that are going to be demonstrated are known as **T accounts**. This is because the accounts are in the shape of a T, as illustrated in Exhibit 4.3.

Exhibit 4.3

Account title here: the top stroke of the T

Debit side	Credit side

The line divides the two sides and is the downstroke of the T.

4.7 Worked examples

The entry of a few transactions can now be attempted:

Example 3: The proprietor starts the business with £30,000 in cash on 1 August 2013.

Effect	Action
(*a*) Increases the *asset* of cash (*b*) Increases the *capital*	Debit the cash account – cash goes 'IN' Credit the capital account – cash comes 'OUT' of the owner's money

These are entered as follows:

Cash Account

'IN'			'OUT'		
2013		£			
Aug 1		30,000			

Capital Account

'IN'			'OUT'		
			2013		£
			Aug 1		30,000

The date of the transaction has already been entered. Now there remains the description which is to be entered alongside the amount. The double entry to the item in the cash account is completed by an entry in the capital account, and therefore the word 'Capital' will appear in the cash account. Similarly, the double entry to the item in the capital account is completed by an entry in the cash account, and therefore the word 'Cash' will appear in the capital account.

The finally completed accounts are therefore:

Cash Account

'IN'			'OUT'		
2013		£			
Aug 1	Capital	30,000			

Capital Account

'IN'			'OUT'		
			2013		£
			Aug 1	Cash	30,000

This method of entering transactions therefore fulfils the requirements of the double entry rules as shown in section 4.4. Now let us look at the entry of some more transactions.

Example 4: A motor van is bought for £17,500 cash on 2 August 2013.

Effect	Action
(*a*) Decreases the *asset* of cash (*b*) Increases the *asset* of motor van	Credit the cash account – Cash goes 'OUT' Debit the motor van account – Motor van comes 'IN'

Cash Account

'IN'		'OUT'	
		2013	£
		Aug 2 Motor van	17,500

Motor Van Account

'IN'		'OUT'	
2013	£		
Aug 2 Cash	17,500		

Example 5: Fixtures bought on credit from Shop Fitters for £1,500 on 3 August 2013.

Effect	Action
(*a*) Increases the *asset* of Fixtures (*b*) Increases the *liability* to Shop Fitters	Debit the Fixtures account – Fixtures go 'IN' Credit the Shop Fitters' account – Fixtures come 'OUT' of the supplier's account

Fixtures Account

'IN'		'OUT'	
2013	£		
Aug 3 Shop Fitters	1,500		

Shop Fitters' Account

'IN'		'OUT'	
		2013	£
		Aug 3 Fixtures	1,500

Example 6: Paid the amount owing in cash to Shop Fitters on 17 August 2013.

Effect	Action
(*a*) Decreases the *asset* of cash (*b*) Decreases the *liability* to Shop Fitters	Credit the cash account – Cash goes 'OUT' Debit the Shop Fitters' account – Cash goes 'IN' to the supplier's account

Cash Account

'IN'		'OUT'	
		2013	£
		Aug 17 Shop Fitters	1,500

Shop Fitters' Account

'IN'		'OUT'	
2013	£		
Aug 17 Cash	1,500		

***Example** 7*: Transactions to date.

Taking the transactions numbered 3 to 6 above, the records will now appear thus:

Cash Account

'IN'		'OUT'	
2013	£	2013	£
Aug 1 Capital	30,000	Aug 2 Motor Van	17,500
		Aug 17 Shop Fitters	1,500

Capital Account

'IN'		'OUT'	
		2013	£
		Aug 1 Cash	30,000

Motor Van Account

'IN'		'OUT'	
2013	£		
Aug 2 Cash	17,500		

Shop Fitter's Account

'IN'		'OUT'	
2013	£	2013	£
Aug 17 Cash	1,500	Aug 3 Fixtures	1,500

Fixtures Account

'IN'		'OUT'	
2013	£		
Aug 3 Shop Fitters	1,500		

Before you read further, you are required to work through Exercises 4.1 and 4.2 at the end of the chapter.

***Example** 8*: Now you have actually made some entries in accounts, you are to go carefully through the example shown in Exhibit 4.4. Make certain you can understand every entry.

Exhibit 4.4

Transactions	Effect	Action	IN/OUT
2013 May 1 Started an engineering business putting £10,000 into a business bank account. (A)	↑ Increases *asset* of bank. ↑ Increases *capital* of owner.	Debit bank account. Credit capital account.	IN OUT
May 3 Bought works machinery on credit from Unique Machines £2,750. (B)	↑ Increases *asset* of machinery. ↑ Increases *liability* to Unique Machines.	Debit machinery account. Credit Unique Machines account.	IN OUT
May 6 Withdrew £2,000 cash from the bank and placed it in the cash box. (C)	↓ Decreases *asset* of bank. ↑ Increases *asset* of cash.	Credit bank account. Debit cash account.	OUT IN
May 7 Bought a secondhand motor van paying in cash £1,800. (D)	↓ Decreases *asset* of cash. ↑ Increases *asset* of motor van.	Credit cash account. Debit motor van account.	OUT IN
May 10 Sold some of the machinery for £150 on credit to B Barnes. (E)	↓ Decreases *asset* of machinery. ↑ Increases *asset* of money owing from B Barnes.	Credit machinery account. Debit B Barnes account.	OUT IN
May 21 Returned some of the machinery, value £270 to Unique Machines. (F)	↓ Decreases *asset* of machinery. ↓ Decreases *liability* to Unique Machines.	Credit machinery account. Debit Unique Machines account.	OUT IN
May 28 B Barnes pays the business the amount owing, £150, by cheque. (G)	↑ Increases *asset* of bank. ↓ Decreases *asset* of money owing by B Barnes.	Debit bank account. Credit B Barnes account.	IN OUT
May 30 Bought another secondhand motor van for £4,200, paying by cheque. (H)	↓ Decreases *asset* of bank. ↑ Increases *asset* of motor vans.	Credit bank account. Debit motor van account.	OUT IN
May 31 Paid the amount of £2,480 to Unique Machines by cheque. (I)	↓ Decreases *asset* of bank. ↓ Decreases *liability* to Unique Machines.	Credit bank account. Debit Unique Machines account.	OUT IN

In account form this is shown thus:

Bank Account

'IN'			'OUT'		
2013		£	2013		£
May 1 Capital	(A)	10,000	May 6 Cash	(C)	2,000
May 28 B Barnes	(G)	150	May 30 Motor van	(H)	4,200
			May 30 Unique Machines	(I)	2,480

Cash Account

'IN'			'OUT'		
2013		£	2013		£
May 6 Bank	(C)	2,000	May 7 Motor van	(D)	1,800

Capital Account

'IN'			'OUT'		
			2013		£
			May 1 Bank	(A)	10,000

Machinery Account

'IN'			'OUT'		
2013		£	2013		£
May 3 Unique Machines	(B)	2,750	May 10 B Barnes	(E)	150
			May 21 Unique Machines	(F)	270

Motor Van Account

'IN'			'OUT'		
2013		£			
May 7 Cash	(D)	1,800			
May 30 Bank	(H)	4,200			

Unique Machines Account

'IN'			'OUT'		
2013		£	2013		£
May 21 Machinery	(F)	270	May 3 Machinery	(B)	2,750
May 31 Bank	(I)	2,480			

B Barnes Account

'IN'			'OUT'		
2013		£	2013		£
May 10 Machinery	(E)	150	May 28 Bank	(G)	150

4.8 Abbreviation of 'Limited'

The abbreviation 'Ltd' will be seen in examples and exercises throughout the book and this refers to limited companies. When you see the name of a business, for example, Skinners Ltd, the suffix indicates a limited company. In our books, the transaction with Skinners Ltd will be entered in the same way as for any other customer or supplier.

4.9 Value Added Tax (VAT)

Students studying accountancy will be aware that in the UK many goods and services are subject to Value Added Tax (VAT). You will have noticed that in this chapter VAT has been ignored. This has been done deliberately to avoid confusion to the student since it was felt by the authors that it is best to concentrate on the principles of double entry book-keeping initially before including VAT. VAT will be introduced later in this book (see Chapter 14).

Chapter summary

- The chapter covers the concept of double entry book-keeping whereby every transaction affects two things. Each item has to be entered twice in the book-keeping records, once on the debit side of an account and once on the credit side of an account.
- Double entry follows the rules of the accounting equation.
- Transactions are entered into the accounts rather than directly into numerous statements of financial position.
- The use of 'T accounts' to record information is discussed.
- The chapter contains a fully worked example illustrating how transactions cause increases and decreases in asset, liability and capital accounts.

EXERCISES

*Note: Questions with the suffix 'x' shown after the question number do **not** have answers shown at the back of the book. Answers to the other questions are shown in Appendix E.*

4.1 Complete the following table showing which accounts are to be credited and which are to be debited:

	Account to be debited	Account to be credited
(*a*) Bought motor van for cash		
(*b*) Bought office machinery on credit from J Grant & Son		
(*c*) Introduced capital in cash		
(*d*) A customer, J Beach, pays us by cheque		
(*e*) Paid a supplier, A Barrett, in cash.		

4.2X Complete the following table showing which accounts are to be debited and which accounts are to be credited:

	Account to be debited	Account to be credited
(*a*) Bought computer equipment for office paying by cheque		
(*b*) A customer, Bush Ltd, pays us by cheque		
(*c*) Owner of the business puts further money into the business by cheque		
(*d*) Paid a supplier, Ash & Co, by cheque		
(*e*) Bought office chair paying by cash		
(*f*) Bought a motor car paying by cheque		
(*g*) Mike Meredith lent the business £5,000 paying by cheque		
(*h*) Sold old motor van, received cash, £600		
(*i*) Paid a supplier, Skinners Ltd, by cash		
(*j*) Bought desk for computer paying by cheque.		

4.3 Write up the asset and liability and capital accounts to record the following transactions in the records of G Powell.

2012
July 1 Started business with £25,000 in the bank
July 2 Bought office furniture by cheque, £1,500
July 3 Bought machinery £7,500 on credit from Planers Ltd
July 5 Bought a secondhand van paying by cheque, £6,000
July 9 Sold some of the office furniture – not suitable for the business – for £600 on credit to J Walker & Sons
July 16 Paid the amount owing to Planers Ltd, £7,500, by cheque
July 23 Received the amount due from J Walker, £600, in cash
July 31 Bought more machinery by cheque, £2,800.

4.4X You are required to open the asset, liability and capital accounts and record the following transactions for May 2012 in the records of John Morgan & Co.

2012
May 1 Started in business with £12,000 in cash
May 2 Paid £11,750 of the opening cash into a bank account for the business
May 4 Bought office furniture on credit from Office Supplies Ltd for £770
May 11 Bought computer equipment £2,000 paying by cheque
May 17 Bought benches for workroom on credit from Baxter's Ltd, £1,500
May 22 Returned one of the work benches, costing £500, which was broken to Baxter's Ltd. They agreed to credit our account.
May 24 Paid amount owing to Office Supplies Ltd by cheque
May 28 Bought secondhand motor van paying by cheque, £3,000
May 30 Bought secondhand work bench paying by cash, £100
May 31 Paid the amount outstanding to Baxter's Ltd by cheque.

4.5 Write up the asset, capital and liability accounts in the books of A Burton to record the following transactions:

2012
July 1 Started in business with £15,000 in the bank
July 3 Bought secondhand motor car and paid by cheque, £6,500
July 9 Bought office furniture from Cheetham & Co £1,150 paid by cheque
July 12 Bought computer on credit from Computext Ltd, £2,400
July 17 Took £200 out of the bank and put it in the cash till
July 19 Bought office chair and paid by cash, £42
July 25 Paid Computext Ltd £1,000 on account
July 27 Bought secondhand motor van, £2,450 paid by cheque
July 29 Bought desk for reception area and paid cash, £100
July 31 Paid the outstanding account to Computext Ltd by cheque.

4.6X Write up the various accounts needed in the books of S Russell to record the following transactions:

2012
April 1 Opened business with £10,000 in the bank
April 3 Bought office equipment for £700 on credit from J Saunders Ltd
April 6 Bought secondhand motor van, paying by cheque, £3,000
April 8 Borrowed £1,000 from H Thompson – he gave us the money by cheque
April 11 Russell put further capital into the business in the form of cash, £500
April 12 Paid £350 of the cash in hand into the bank account
April 15 Returned some of the office equipment costing £200 – it was faulty – to J Saunders Ltd
April 17 Bought more office equipment, paying by cash, £50
April 19 Sold the motor van, as it had proved unsuitable, to R Jones for £3,000. R Jones will settle for this by three payments later this month
April 21 Received a loan in cash from J Hawkins, £400
April 22 R Jones paid us a cheque for £1,000
April 23 Bought a suitable secondhand motor van £3,600 on credit from Phillips Garages Ltd
April 26 R Jones paid us a cheque for £1,800
April 28 Paid £2,000 by cheque to Phillips Garages Ltd
April 30 R Jones paid us cash, £200.

CHAPTER 5

The double entry system for inventory

Learning objectives

After you have studied this chapter you should be able to:

- understand the terms cost price and selling price, the monetary difference between the two being the profit which is one of the main aims of a business
- understand the need to use various accounts in recording the movement of stock, i.e. sales, purchases, sales returns (returns inwards) and purchases returns (returns outwards) accounts
- record the purchase and sale of goods both by credit and cash using the double entry system
- record the return of goods in the sales returns account using the double entry system when customers return goods to the business
- record the return of goods in the purchases returns account using the double entry system when the business returns goods to their supplier
- explain the meanings of the terms 'purchases' and 'sales' as used in accounting
- understand the differences in recording sales for cash compared with sales made on credit.

5.1 Introduction

As stated in Chapter 1 it is the aim of all commercial organisations to make a profit and to remain in business. Section 1.4 demonstrated the need to sell goods for more than was paid for them and it is important to record the cost of goods purchased and the sale of goods at selling price. The accounts needed to record these transactions are now considered.

5.2 Inventory movements

A business, on any particular date, will normally have goods which have been bought previously and have not yet been sold. These unsold goods are known as the business's inventory (stock of goods). The inventory in a business is therefore constantly changing because some of it is bought, some of it is sold, some is returned to the suppliers and some is returned by the business's customers.

To keep a check on the movement of inventory (stock of goods), various accounts are opened as shown in the table below:

Account	Reason
Purchases Account	For the purchase of goods
Sales Account	For the sale of goods
Sales Returns Account	For goods returned to the business by its customers
Purchases Returns Account	For goods returned by the business to its suppliers

As inventory is an asset, and these four accounts are all connected with this asset, the double entry rules are those used for assets.

We shall now look at some specific entries in the following sections.

5.3 Purchase of inventory on credit

On 1 August 2012, goods costing £1,650 are bought on credit from D Henry.

First, the twofold effect of the transaction must be considered so that the book-keeping entries can be worked out. We have the following:

(*a*) *The asset of inventory is increased.* An increase in an asset needs a debit entry in an account. Here, the account is recording the particular movement of inventory; in this case it is the 'purchases' movement, so the account must be the purchases account.

(*b*) *There is an increase in a liability.* This is the liability of the business to D Henry because the goods supplied have not yet been paid for. An increase in a liability needs a credit entry, and so in order to enter this part of the transaction a credit entry is made in D Henry's account.

Here again, we can use the idea of the debit side being 'IN' to the account, and the credit side being 'OUT' of the account. In this example, purchases have come 'IN', thus creating a debit in the Purchase Account; and the goods have come 'OUT' of D Henry, needing a credit in the account of D Henry. Thus:

Purchases Account

'IN'		'OUT'	
2012	£		
Aug 1 D Henry	1,650		

D Henry Account

'IN'		'OUT'	
		2012	£
		Aug 1 Purchases	1,650

5.4 Purchases of inventory for cash

On 2 August 2012, goods costing £2,200 were bought, cash being paid for them immediately. As a result:

(*a*) *The asset of inventory is increased.* Thus, a debit entry will be needed. The movement of inventory is that of a purchase, so it is the Purchases Account which needs debiting. (Purchases have come 'IN' – debit the Purchases Account.)

(*b*) *The asset of cash is decreased.* To reduce an asset a credit entry is called for, and the asset is that of cash so the Cash Account needs crediting. (Cash has gone 'OUT' – credit the Cash Account.)

Purchases Account

'IN'		'OUT'	
2012	£		
Aug 2 Cash	2,200		

Cash Account

'IN'		'OUT'	
		2012	£
		Aug 2 Purchases	2,200

5.5 Sales of inventory on credit

On 3 August 2012, a business sold goods on credit for £2,500 to K Leach. Then:

(*a*) *An asset account is increased.* This is the account showing that K Leach is a debtor for the goods and is classed as 'an account receivable'. The increase in the asset of accounts receivable requires a debit and the debtor is K Leach, so the account concerned is that of K Leach. (Goods have gone 'IN' to K Leach – debit K Leach's account.)

(*b*) *The asset of inventory is decreased.* For this, a credit entry to reduce an asset is needed. The movement of inventory is that of 'Sales' and so the account credited is the Sales Account. (Sales have gone 'OUT' – credit the Sales Account.)

Thus:

K Leach Account

'IN'		'OUT'	
2012	£		
Aug 3 Sales	2,500		

Sales Account

'IN'		'OUT'	
		2012	£
		Aug 3 K Leach	2,500

5.6 Sales of inventory for cash

On 4 August 2012, goods are sold for £55, the cash for them being paid immediately. Then:

(*a*) *The asset of cash is increased.* A debit in the cash account is needed to show this. (Cash has come 'IN' – debit the Cash Account.)

(*b*) *The asset of inventory is reduced.* The reduction of an asset requires a credit and the movement of inventory is represented by 'Sales'. So the entry needed is a credit in the Sales Account. (Sales have gone 'OUT' – credit the Sales Account.)

Cash Account

'IN'			'OUT'		
2012		£			
Aug 4	Sales	55			

Sales Account

'IN'			'OUT'		
			2012		£
			Aug 4	Cash	55

5.7 Sales returns

Sales returns represent goods sold which have subsequently been returned by a customer. This could be for various reasons, such as:

- the goods sent to the customer are of the incorrect size, colour or model
- the goods have been damaged in transit
- the goods are of poor quality.

As the original sale was entered in the double entry system, so the return of those goods must also be entered.

On 5 August 2012, goods which had previously been sold to F Lowe for £290 have been returned by him. As a result:

(*a*) *The asset of inventory was increased by the goods returned.* A debit representing an increase of an asset is needed, and this time the movement of stock is that of 'Sales Returns'. The entry required therefore is a debit in the Sales Returns Account. (The goods have come 'IN' – debit the Sales Returns Account.)

(*b*) *An asset is decreased.* The debt of F Lowe to the business is now reduced, and to record this a credit is required in F Lowe's account. (The goods have come 'OUT' of F Lowe – credit the F Lowe Account.)

The movements are shown thus:

Sales Returns Account

'IN'			'OUT'		
2012		£			
Aug 5	F Lowe	290			

F Lowe Account

'IN'		'OUT'	
		2012	£
		Aug 5 Sales returns	290

An alternative name for a sales returns account is a returns inwards account.

5.8 Purchases returns

Purchases returns represent goods which were purchased, and are now being returned to the supplier. As the original purchase was entered in the double entry system, so also is the return to the supplier of those goods.

On 6 August 2012, goods previously bought for £960 are returned by the business to K Howe. Thus:

(*a*) *The liability of the business to K Howe is decreased by the value of the goods returned to him.* The decrease in a liability needs a debit, this time in the K Howe Account. (The goods have gone 'IN' to K Howe – debit the K Howe Account.)

(*b*) *The asset of inventory is decreased by the goods sent out.* A credit representing a reduction in an asset is needed, and the movement of inventory is that of 'Purchases Returns', so the entry will be a credit in the purchases returns account. (The returns have gone 'OUT' – credit the Purchases Returns Account.)

K Howe Account

'IN'		'OUT'	
2012	£		
Aug 6 Purchase returns	960		

Purchases Returns Account

'IN'		'OUT'	
		2012	£
		Aug 6 K Howe	960

An alternative name for a purchases returns account is a returns outwards account.

5.9 A worked example

Enter the following transactions in suitable double entry accounts:

2013
May 1 Bought goods on credit £680 from D Small
May 2 Bought goods on credit £770 from A Lyon & Son
May 5 Sold goods on credit to D Hughes for £600
May 6 Sold goods on credit to M Spencer for £450

May 10 Returned goods £150 to D Small
May 12 Goods bought for cash, £1,000
May 19 M Spencer returned £160 goods to us
May 21 Goods sold for cash, £1,500
May 22 Paid cash to D Small, £530, on account
May 30 D Hughes paid the amount owing by him £600 in cash
May 31 Bought goods on credit £640 from A Lyon & Son.

The double entry accounts can now be shown as:

Purchases Account

'IN'		'OUT'	
2013	£		
May 1 D Small	680		
May 2 A Lyon & Son	770		
May 12 Cash	1,000		
May 31 A Lyon & Son	640		

Sales Account

'IN'		'OUT'	
		2013	£
		May 5 D Hughes	600
		May 6 M Spencer	450
		May 21 Cash	1,500

Purchases Returns Account

'IN'		'OUT'	
		2013	£
		May 10 D Small	150

Sales Returns Account

'IN'		'OUT'	
2013	£		
May 19 M Spencer	160		

D Small Account

'IN'		'OUT'	
2013	£	2013	£
May 10 Purchases returns	150	May 1 Purchases	680
May 22 Cash	530		

A Lyon & Son Account

'IN'		'OUT'	
		2013	£
		May 2 Purchases	770
		May 31 Purchases	640

D Hughes Account

'IN'		'OUT'	
2013	£	2013	£
May 5 Sales	600	May 30 Cash	600

M Spencer Account

'IN'		'OUT'	
2013	£	2013	£
May 6 Sales	450	May 19 Sales returns	160

Cash Account

'IN'		'OUT'	
2013	£	2013	£
May 21 Sales	1,500	May 12 Purchases	1,000
May 30 D Hughes	600	May 22 D Small	530

5.10 Special meaning of 'sales' and 'purchases'

It must be emphasised that 'sales' and 'purchases' have a special meaning in accounting language.

Purchases in accounting means *the purchase of those goods which the business buys with the prime intention of selling*. Sometimes the goods may be altered, added to or used in the manufacture of something else, but it is the element of *resale* that is important. To a business that trades in computers, for instance, computers are purchases. If something else is bought, such as a motor van, such an item cannot be called purchases, even though in ordinary language it may be said that a motor van has been purchased. The prime intention of buying the motor van is for use by the company and not for resale.

Similarly, **sales** means the *sale of those goods in which the business normally deals and that were bought with the prime intention of resale*. The description 'sales' must never be given to the disposal of other items.

5.11 Comparison of cash and credit transactions for purchases and sales

The difference between the records needed for cash and credit transactions can now be seen.

The complete set of entries for purchases of goods where they are paid for immediately by cash would be:

(*a*) **debit the purchases account**
(*b*) **credit the cash account.**

On the other hand, the complete set of entries for the purchase of goods on credit can be broken down into two stages. First, the purchase of the goods and second, the payment for them. The first part is:

(*a*) **debit the purchases account**
(*b*) **credit the supplier's account**.

The second part is:

(*c*) **debit the supplier's account**
(*d*) **credit the cash account**.

The difference can now be seen. With the cash purchase, no record is kept of the supplier's account. This is because cash passes immediately and therefore there is no need to keep a check of indebtedness (money owing) to a supplier. On the other hand, in the credit purchase the records should show to whom money is owed until payment is made. A study of cash sales and credit sales will reveal a similar difference.

Cash Sales	Credit Sales
Complete entry: ● debit cash account ● credit sales account	First part: ● debit customer's account ● credit sales account Second part: ● debit cash account ● credit customer's account

Chapter summary

- Goods must be sold at a higher price than the cost price to make a profit. If sold at a lower price than the cost price a loss would occur.
- Various accounts are used to record the movement of inventory because it is normally sold at a higher price than its cost.
- The accounts used to record the movement of inventory are:
  - **purchases account** to record the purchases of inventory as debit entries in the account since the goods come 'IN' to the business
  - **sales account** for the sale of the goods as credit entries in the account because the goods go 'OUT' of the business
  - **sales returns account** to record goods that a customer returns to the business as debit entries since the goods are returned 'IN' to the business
  - **purchases returns account** to record goods that the business returns to its suppliers as the goods go 'OUT' of the business.
- The special meaning in accounting terms of 'purchases' and 'sales', namely that purchases refer to goods bought for resale. Purchases of assets such as a motor van to be used in the business, are recorded separately in the asset account, motor van. Sales refers to goods sold in the normal course of business. The disposal of an asset such as equipment should never be recorded in the sales account but recorded separately in a disposal account to be discussed later.

- Purchases for cash are *never* entered in the supplier's account while purchases on credit are *always* entered in the supplier's account.
- Sales for cash are *never* entered in the customer's account while sales on credit are *always* entered in the customer's account.

EXERCISES

*Note: Questions with the suffix 'X' shown after the question number do **not** have answers shown at the back of the book. Answers to the other questions are shown in Appendix E.*

5.1 Complete the following table showing which accounts are to be credited and which are to be debited:

	Account to be debited	Account to be credited
(*a*) Goods bought on credit from P Hart		
(*b*) Goods sold for cash		
(*c*) Bought motor car from Morgan Motors on credit		
(*d*) Bought goods on credit from Cohens Ltd		
(*e*) Returned some of the goods, which were faulty, to P Hart		
(*f*) Sold goods on credit to H Perkins		
(*g*) Goods sold, a cheque being received on the sale		
(*h*) Sold some of the office furniture for cash		
(*i*) H Perkins returned some of the goods to us		
(*j*) Goods brought on credit from P Griffith.		

5.2X Complete the following table:

	Account to be debited	Account to be credited
(*a*) Bought goods on credit from J Needham		
(*b*) Bought goods paying by cheque		
(*c*) Sold goods for cash		
(*d*) We returned goods to J Needham		
(*e*) Bought computer for the office on credit from Smith Computers Ltd		
(*f*) Sold goods on credit to H Broad		
(*g*) Goods returned to us by H Broad		
(*h*) Bought goods for cash		
(*i*) We paid a supplier, W Simms, by cheque		
(*j*) Bought motor car on credit from Smithy Garage.		

5.3 Paul Garner decided to start his own business and asks you to assist him by entering the following transactions in the books of account for March 2013:

2013
March 1 Started business with £4,000 in cash
March 2 Bought goods £1,230 on credit from Flynn Bros
March 4 Bought goods for cash, £345
March 7 Sold goods for cash, £120

March 10 Opened a bank account and took £3,500 out of the cash and put it in the bank
March 14 Bought a computer to use in the office paid by cheque, £1,000
March 16 Sold goods on credit to D Knott, £600
March 20 Bought goods £450 on credit from Flynn Bros
March 23 Sold goods on credit to Bateson's Ltd, £570
March 25 We returned goods to Flynn Bros, £75
March 27 Paid the amount due to Flynn Bros by cheque
March 30 Bateson's Ltd returned some faulty goods to us value, £109.

5.4 The following are the business transactions of Grace Andrews, a retailer of ladies wear, for the month of September 2012:

2012
Sept 1 Started in business with £10,000 in the bank and £100 of cash
Sept 3 Bought shop fittings £1,900 on credit from Duffy & Son
Sept 5 Bought goods on credit from Barrett's Fashions, £2,378
Sept 9 Bought computer for use within the business, £1,020 paid by cheque
Sept 10 Bought desk for office, £65 and paid cash
Sept 12 Sales of goods £800 paid into bank
Sept 15 Returned faulty goods to Barrett's Fashions, £180
Sept 22 Paid Duffy & Son by cheque, £1,900
Sept 25 Sales of goods £600 paid into bank
Sept 28 Bought goods on credit from Barrett's Fashions, £1,434
Sept 30 Sold goods for cash, £280
Sept 30 Bought secondhand motor car, £4,750.

As accounts assistant you have been asked to record the above transactions in the books of account for September 2012.

5.5X Ahmed's Ltd has just started his own business selling computer equipment and software. The following transactions took place during his first month of trading, June 2013. You are required to enter them into the books of account:

2013
June 1 Started in business with £20,000 in the bank
June 3 Bought stock of computers for resale £8,000 on credit from Computers Wholesale Ltd
June 4 Bought shop fittings paying by cheque, £1,690
June 8 Bought stock of software for resale, £1,000 paid by cheque
June 9 Bought motor car paying by cheque, £7,000
June 12 Sold goods, £1,700 by cheque
June 16 Returned faulty goods to Computers Wholesale Ltd, £900
June 20 Sold goods for cash, £340
June 26 Bought desk and chair for office, £300 paying by cheque
June 28 Sold goods on credit to Law & Co, £1,600
June 29 Paid Computers Wholesale Ltd £5,000 on account by cheque
June 30 Bought goods from Computers Wholesale Ltd on credit, £850
June 30 Law & Co return goods to us, £220
June 30 Sold goods, £2,300 by cheque.

5.6X You are to enter the following in the accounts needed:

2013
June 1 Started business with £1,000 cash
June 2 Paid £800 of the opening cash into a bank account for the business
June 3 Bought goods on credit from H Grant, £330
June 4 Bought goods on credit from D Clark, £140
June 6 Sold goods on credit to B Miller, £90
June 8 Bought office furniture on credit from Barrett's Ltd, £400
June 10 Sold goods for cash, £120
June 13 Bought goods on credit from H Grant, £200
June 14 Bought goods for cash, £60
June 15 Sold goods on credit to H Sharples, £180
June 16 We returned goods worth £50 to H Grant
June 17 We returned some of the office furniture, cost £30, to Barrett's Ltd
June 18 Sold goods on credit to B Miller, £400
June 21 Paid H Grant's account by cheque, £480
June 23 B Miller paid us the amount owing in cash, £490
June 24 Sharples returned to us £50 of goods
June 25 Goods sold for cash, £150
June 28 Bought goods for cash, £370
June 30 Bought computer on credit from J Kelly, £600.

CHAPTER 6

The double entry system for expenses and revenues

Learning objectives

After you have studied this chapter you should be able to:

- understand the concept of profit and loss by comparing revenue with expenses
- see the effects of profits and losses on capital and the relationship to the accounting equation
- understand why separate accounts are used for each type of expense and revenue
- record expenses and revenues using the double entry system
- understand the term 'drawings', be able to record them and recognise the effects of drawings on capital.

6.1 The nature of profit or loss

To an accountant, **profit** means the amount by which **revenues** are greater than **expenses** for a set of transactions. The term 'revenues' means the sales value of goods and services that have been supplied to customers. The term 'expenses' means the value of all the assets that have been used up to obtain those revenues.

If, therefore, we had supplied goods and services valued for sale at £100,000 to customers, and the expenses incurred by us to be able to supply those goods and services amounted to £70,000, then the result would be a profit calculated as follows:

		£
Revenues	Goods and services supplied to customers for the sum of	100,000
Less Expenses	Value of all the assets used up to enable us to supply the above goods and services	70,000
Profit		30,000

On the other hand, it is possible for expenses to exceed revenues for a set of transactions. In this case the result is a loss. For example a **loss** would be incurred given the following.

		£
Revenues	What we have charged to our customers in respect of all the goods and services supplied to them	60,000
Less Expenses	Value of all the assets used up to supply these goods and services to our customers	(80,000)
Loss is therefore		(20,000)

6.2 The effect of profit and loss on capital

Businesses exist to make profits and so increase their capital. Let us look at the relationship between profits and capital in an example.

On 1 January the assets and liabilities of a business are:

- Assets: Fixtures £10,000, Inventory £7,000, Cash at the bank £3,000.
- Liabilities: Accounts payable £2,000.

The capital is found from the accounting equation:

Capital = Assets – Liabilities

In this case capital works out at Assets £10,000 + £7,000 + £3,000 – Liabilities £2,000 = £18,000.

During January the whole of the £7,000 inventory is sold for £11,000 cash. On 31 January the assets and liabilities have become:

- Assets: Fixtures £10,000, Stock nil, Cash at the bank £14,000.
- Liabilities: Accounts payable £2,000.

The capital is now £22,000:

Assets £10,000 + £14,000 – Liabilities £2,000 = £22,000

It can be seen that capital has increased from £18,000 to £22,000 = £4,000 increase because the £7,000 inventory was sold for £11,000, a profit of £4,000. Profit, therefore, increases capital.

Old Capital + Profit = New Capital
£18,000 + £4,000 = £22,000

On the other hand, a loss would *reduce* the capital so:

Old Capital – Loss = New Capital

6.3 Profit or loss and sales

Profit will be made when goods are sold at more than cost price, while the opposite will mean a **loss**.

6.4 Profit or loss and expenses

In section 6.1 it was shown that profit was made when the goods were sold for more than the cost price. As well as the cost of the goods, a business incurs other **expenses** such as rent, salaries, wages, telephone costs, motor expenses, and so on. Every £1 of expenses will mean £1 less profit.

All expenses could be charged to one Expense Account, but it would then be difficult to identify specific areas of the business's expenditure, such as the amount spent on motor running costs or rent. To facilitate the need to know different types of expenses, a separate account is opened for each type of expense, for instance:

- Rent Account
- Telephone Account
- Stationery Account
- Salaries Account
- Advertising Account
- Motor Expenses Account
- Wages Account
- Insurance Account
- Postages Account

In the same way that separate accounts are opened for each type of expense, separate accounts are also opened for any additional *revenue* that the business may receive, such as rent received or bank interest received. Again, separate revenue accounts can be opened as follows:

- Rent Receivable Account
- Commission Received Account
- Bank Interest Received Account

It is purely a matter of choice in a business as to the name of each expense or revenue account. For example, an account for postage stamps could be called 'Postage Stamp Account', 'Postage Account' or even 'Communication Expenses Account'. Also some businesses amalgamate expenses, for example, 'Printing, Stationery and Advertising Account'. Infrequent or small items of expense are usually put into a 'Sundry Expenses Account' or 'General Expenses Account'.

6.5 Debit or credit?

We have to decide whether expense accounts are to be debited or credited with the amounts involved. Assets involve expenditure by the business and are shown as debit entries. Expenses also involve expenditure by the business and therefore should also be debit entries. Why? Because assets and expenses must ultimately be paid for. This payment involves a credit to the bank account (or to the cash account) so the original entry in the asset account or in the expense account must be a debit.

An alternative explanation may also be used for expenses. Every expense results in a decrease in an asset or an increase in a liability, and because of the accounting equation this means that the capital is reduced by each expense. The decreases in capital needs a debit entry and therefore expense accounts contain debit entries for expenses.

Revenue is the opposite of expenses and, therefore, appears on the opposite side to expenses – that is, revenue accounts appear on the credit side of the books. Pending the periodic calculation of profit, therefore, revenue is collected together in appropriately named accounts, and until it is transferred to the profit calculations it will need to be shown as a credit.

Consider, too, that expenditure of money pays for expenses, which are used up in the short term, or assets, which are used up in the long term – both for the purpose of gaining revenue. Both of these are shown on the debit side of the accounts, while the revenue which has been gained is shown on the credit side of the accounts.

6.6 Effect of transactions

A few illustrations will demonstrate the double entry required.

Example 1: Rent of £200 is paid in cash. Here the twofold effect is:

(*a*) *The total of the expenses of rent is increased* – a benefit goes 'IN'. As expense entries are shown as debits, and the expense is rent, so the action required is the debiting of the Rent Account.

(*b*) *The asset of cash is decreased* – money goes 'OUT'. This means crediting the Cash Account to show the decrease of the asset.

Summary:
- debit the rent account with £200 – 'IN'
- credit the cash account with £200 – 'OUT'.

Example 2: Motor expenses are paid with a cheque for £230. The twofold effect is:

(*a*) *The total of the motor expenses paid is increased* – a benefit is received 'IN'. To increase an expenses account needs a debit, and so the action required is to debit the Motor Expenses Account.

(*b*) *The asset of money in the bank is decreased* – money goes 'OUT'. This means crediting the Bank Account to show the decrease of the asset.

Summary:
- debit the motor expenses account with £230 – 'IN'
- credit the bank account with £230 – 'OUT'.

Example 3: £60 cash is paid for telephone expenses.

(*a*) *The total of telephone expenses is increased* – a benefit received goes 'IN'. Expenses are shown by a debit entry, and therefore to increase the expense account in question the action required is to debit the Telephone Expenses Account.

(*b*) *The asset of cash is decreased* – money goes 'OUT'. This needs a credit in the Cash Account to decrease the asset.

Summary:
- debit telephone expenses account with £60 – 'IN'
- credit the cash account with £60 – 'OUT'.

It is now possible to study the effects of some more transactions showing the results in the form of a table. See Exhibit 6.1.

Exhibit 6.1

	Increase	Action	Decrease	Action
June 1 Paid for postage stamps by cash £20	Expense of postages	Debit postage account (IN)	Asset of cash	Credit cash account (OUT)
2 Paid for advertising by cheque £290	Expense of advertising	Debit advertising account (IN)	Asset of bank	Credit bank account (OUT)
3 Paid wages by cash £900	Expense of wages	Debit wages account (IN)	Asset of cash	Credit cash account (OUT)
4 Paid insurance by cheque £420	Expense of insurance	Debit insurance account (IN)	Asset of bank	Credit bank account (OUT)

The above four examples can now be shown in account form:

Cash Account

'IN'		'OUT'	£
		June 1 Postages	20
		June 3 Wages	900

Bank Account

'IN'		'OUT'	£
		June 2 Advertising	290
		June 4 Insurance	420

Advertising Account

'IN'	£	'OUT'	
June 2 Bank	290		

Insurance Account

'IN'	£	'OUT'	
June 4 Bank	420		

Postage Account

'IN'	£	'OUT'	
June 1 Cash	20		

Wages Account

'IN'	£	'OUT'	
June 3 Cash	900		

6.7 Drawings

The owner may want to take cash out of the business for his or her private use. This is known as **drawings**. Money taken out as drawings will reduce capital.

Each amount taken as drawings will be debited to a drawings account and at the end of the year this is transferred to the capital account and will be explained later.

Example 4: On 25 August a proprietor takes £200 cash out of her business for her own use.

Effect	Action
1 Capital is decreased by £200 2 Cash is decreased by £200	Debit the drawings account £200 Credit the cash account £200

Cash Account

'IN'		'OUT'	£
		Aug 25 Drawings	200

Drawings Account

'IN'	£	'OUT'	
Aug 25 Cash	200		

Sometimes *goods* (rather than money) are taken for private use. These are also known as drawings. Entries for such transactions will be described later in the book.

6.8 Revenues and double entry

We have just looked at instances of expenses being recorded. There will also be the need to record revenues. We will now look at an example.

Example 5: On 5 June it is decided that part of a business's premises are not needed at the moment. The business agrees to sublet the surplus space to another business and receives rent of £500 by cheque. Here, the twofold effect is:

(*a*) *The asset of the bank is increased* – money comes 'IN'. This means debiting the bank account to show the increase of the asset.

(*b*) *The total of the revenue of rent received is increased* – the benefit comes 'OUT' of rent received, so the action required is the crediting of the rent received account.

Summary:
- debit the bank account with £500 – 'IN'
- credit the rent received account with £500 – 'OUT'.

This will therefore appear as:

Bank Account

'IN'	£	'OUT'	
June 5 Rent received	500		

Rent Received Account

'IN'		'OUT'	£
		June 5 Bank	500

Chapter summary

- The calculation of profit is achieved by comparing revenues with expenses incurred in running the business.
- A loss occurs when the expenses incurred are more than the revenue earned.
- If a business makes a profit, that profit belongs to the owner of the business and consequently their capital is increased by that amount.
- When a loss is incurred then the owner must bear the losses and such a loss will reduce their capital account.
- It is important to record expenses in separate expense accounts to enable the business to identify various areas of expense such as motor expenses, stationery, etc.
- Different types of revenue should also be recorded in separate accounts to provide information of the income received.
- The procedure for recording expenses and revenue in the various accounts uses the double entry system.
- 'Drawings' are recorded in a separate account. They are then deducted from the owner's capital account and are never an expense of the business.

EXERCISES

Note: Questions with the suffix 'X' shown after the question number do ***not*** *have answers shown at the back of the book. Answers to the other questions are shown in Appendix E.*

6.1 Complete the following table:

	Account to be debited	Account to be credited
(*a*) Paid rent by cash		
(*b*) Paid for goods by cash		
(*c*) Received by cheque a refund of rates already paid		
(*d*) Paid general expenses by cheque		
(*e*) Received commissions in cash		
(*f*) Goods returned by us to T Jones		
(*g*) Goods sold for cash		
(*h*) Bought office fixtures by cheque		
(*i*) Paid wages in cash		
(*j*) Took cash out of business for private use.		

6.2X Complete the following table

	Account to be debited	Account to be credited
(*a*) Sold surplus stationery, receiving proceeds in cash		
(*b*) Paid salaries by cheque		
(*c*) Rent received for premises sublet, by cheque		
(*d*) Goods returned to us by Royal Products		
(*e*) Commission received by us previously in error, now refunded by cheque		
(*f*) Bought machinery by cheque		
(*g*) Paid lighting expenses in cash		
(*h*) Insurance rebate received by cheque		
(*i*) Buildings bought by cheque		
(*j*) Building repairs paid in cash.		

6.3 You are required to enter the following transactions in the double entry accounts of B Cartwright:

2012
Jan 1 Started business with £20,000 capital, which was deposited in the bank
Jan 3 Paid rent for premises by cheque, £1,000
Jan 4 Bought goods on credit from M Parkin for £580 and J Kane for £2,400
Jan 4 Purchased motor van for £5,000, paying by cheque
Jan 5 Cash sales of £1,005
Jan 10 Paid motor expenses in cash, £75
Jan 12 Paid wages in cash, £120
Jan 17 Bought goods on credit from M Parkin, £670
Jan 19 Paid insurance by cheque, £220
Jan 25 Sold goods for £800, payment being received as a cheque, which was banked immediately
Jan 31 Paid wages in cash, £135, and electricity by cheque, £78.

6.4X The following are the transactions of G Dunn for the month of May 2012. You are required to enter the transactions in the appropriate accounts using the double entry system.

2012
May 1 Started in business with £12,000 in the bank
May 2 Purchased goods £1,750 on credit from M Mills
May 3 Bought fixtures and fittings for £1,500, paying by cheque
May 5 Sold goods for cash, £1,300
May 6 Bought goods on credit for £1,140 from S Waite
May 10 Paid rent by cash, £250
May 12 Bought stationery, £87, paying by cash
May 18 Goods returned by us to M Mills, £230
May 21 Let part of the premises receiving rent by cheque, £100
May 23 Sold goods on credit to M Street for £770
May 24 Bought a motor van, paying by cheque £3,000
May 30 Paid wages for the month, £648, by cash
May 31 The proprietor, G Dunn, took cash for himself amounting to £200.

6.5 You are required to enter the following transactions, completing the double entry in the records of K Walsh for the month of July 2013.

2013
July 1 Started in business with £8,000 in the bank
July 2 Paid for rent of premises by cheque, £375
July 3 Bought shop fittings for £800 paid by cheque
July 5 Bought goods on credit from A Jackson, £450; D Hill, £675; and E Frudd, £1,490
July 6 Paid insurance by cheque, £130
July 7 Bought motor van for £5,000 on credit from High Lane Motors
July 11 Cash sales of £1,500
July 13 Paid for printing and stationery by cheque, £120
July 15 Paid wages in cash, £200
July 18 Bought goods from A Jackson, £890, on credit
July 21 Cash sales, £780
July 25 Paid motor expenses, £89, by cash
July 30 Paid High Lane Motors, £5,000 by cheque
July 31 Paid wages in cash, £300, and stationery, £45, in cash.

6.6X Write up the following transactions in the books of J Blake for March 2013:

2013
March 1 Started business with £15,000 capital in cash
March 2 Paid £14,000 of the cash into a bank account for the business
March 2 Bought goods on credit from J Paul for £592
March 4 Paid for rent of premises by cash, £250, and bought a secondhand motor van for £3,000, paying by cheque
March 5 Bought goods, paying by cheque for £2,100
March 9 Sold goods to E Ford for £323 and received a cheque
March 11 Paid for printing of stationery, £45, by cash
March 14 Cash sales of £490
March 18 Goods returned by us to J Paul, £67
March 19 Bought goods from J Paul on credit, £720
March 21 Paid for advertising, £60, by cheque
March 24 Sold goods for cash, £500
March 25 Paid the following expenses by cheque: wages, £540; motor expenses, £110; stationery, £82
March 28 Paid J Paul £1,245 by cheque
March 31 Sold goods for cash, £526.

6.7X Enter the following transactions using double entry for S Littleton for the month of April 2013:

2013
April 1 Started in business with capital of £7,500 in the bank account and £1,000 in cash
April 3 Bought a secondhand motor car, £4,000, paying by cheque
April 5 Paid for rent of office, £275 in cash
April 7 Paid for motor expenses, £50 in cash
April 9 Paid for telephone charges, £95 by cheque
April 14 Bought stock of goods on credit from K Woodburn, £2,300, and A Veale, £2,600
April 16 Sold goods, £1,900, receiving the money by cheque
April 19 Paid for motor expenses, £60 in cash
April 20 Returned faulty goods to A Veale, £240
April 25 Cash sales of £875, paid for insurance, £180 in cash
April 28 Paid salaries, £1,210 by cheque
April 29 Paid K Woodburn £1,500 on account by cheque
April 30 Bought further goods from K Woodburn on credit, £770.

CHAPTER 7

Balancing off accounts

Learning objectives

After you have studied this chapter you should be able to:

- understand what is meant by 'balancing off' accounts
- balance off accounts at the end of a period and bring down the opening balance to the next period
- distinguish between a debit balance and a credit balance
- prepare accounts in a three-column format, as used in computerised accounts.

7.1 Introduction

In the previous two chapters entries into the various accounts have been shown. In this chapter we will now look at what is known as 'balancing off' accounts, a procedure which is usually carried out at the end of each month prior to the preparation of the trial balance.

'Balancing off' simply means finding the difference between the two sides of an account, i.e. the difference between the total debit entries and the total credit entries in a particular account. The 'difference' between the two sides is known as the 'balance' and this figure is inserted on the side of the account that shows the least amount of money. If both sides of the account are then totalled up, they should agree, having inserted the 'balance'; if they do not add up correctly, then an error may have been made in the calculation of the balance or perhaps in adding up the account. The calculation will then need to be rechecked.

Sometimes an account simply requires closing off; this is when both the debit and credit sides total up to exactly the same amount and thus there is no balance.

7.2 Balancing the accounts

Balancing off the accounts is a procedure carried out by most businesses on a monthly basis so that they can keep a check on various accounting issues such as knowing;

- how much money they have in their cash account
- the balance in the bank account
- how much money they owe to other people, i.e. accounts payable (creditors)

- how much money other people owe the business, i.e. accounts receivable (debtors)
- the value of the business's assets
- the amount incurred on various expenses
- how much their inventory has cost, i.e. purchases
- what the sales figures are to date
- the capital invested in the business by the owner(s) and any drawings taken.

In the following examples we will consider balancing off accounts at the end of a period and bringing down the balances to the next accounting period.

7.3 Accounts for debtors (accounts receivable)

Where debtors have paid their accounts

So far we have considered how to record transactions in the accounting books by means of debit and credit entries. At the end of each accounting period the figures in each account are examined to see what they reveal. One of the most obvious reasons for this is to find out how much money our customers owe us for goods we have sold to them. As mentioned above, this procedure is usually carried out monthly.

We will now look at the account of one of our customers, K Tandy, for transactions in August 2013.

K Tandy Account

2013	£	2013	£
Aug 1 Sales	144	Aug 22 Bank	144
Aug 19 Sales	300	Aug 28 Bank	300

This shows that during the month of August we sold a total of £444 in goods to Tandy, and have been paid a total of £444 by him. At the close of business at the end of August he therefore owes us nothing; his account can be closed off on 31 August 2013 by inserting the totals on each side, as follows:

K Tandy Account

2013	£	2013	£
Aug 1 Sales	144	Aug 22 Bank	144
Aug 19 Sales	300	Aug 28 Bank	300
	444		444

Notice that totals in accounting are shown with a single line above them, and a double line underneath. Totals on accounts at the end of a period are always shown on a level with one another, as shown in the following completed account for C Lee:

C Lee Account

2013	£	2013	£
Aug 11 Sales	177	Aug 30 Bank	480
Aug 19 Sales	203		
Aug 22 Sales	100		
	480		480

In this account, C Lee also owed us nothing at the end of August 2013, as she had paid us for all sales to her.

If an account contains only one entry on each side and they are equal, you don't need to include totals. For example:

K Wood Account

	£		£
2013	£	2013	£
Aug 6 Sales	214	Aug 12 Bank	214

Where customers (accounts receivable) still owe for goods

Not all customers will have paid their accounts by the end of the month and will have amounts outstanding on their account. In these cases, the totals of each side would not equal each other. Let us look at the account of D Knight for August 2013:

D Knight Account

	£		£
2013	£	2013	£
Aug 1 Sales	158	Aug 28 Bank	158
Aug 15 Sales	206		
Aug 30 Sales	118		

You will see that the debit side adds up to £482 and the credit side adds up to £158. The difference of £324 (i.e. £482 – £158) represents sales of £206 and £118 not paid for and is, therefore, still owing to us on 31 August 2013.

In double entry, we only enter figures as totals if the totals on both sides of the account agree. We do, however, want to close off the account for August, but showing that Knight owes us £324. If he owes £324 at close of business on 31 August 2013, then he will still owe us that same figure when the business opens on 1 September 2013. We show this by **balancing the account**, which is done in five stages:

1. Add up both sides to find out their totals. Do not write anything permanent in the account at this stage, but you could write the figures lightly in pencil.
2. Deduct the smaller total from the larger total to find the balance.
3. Now enter the balance on the side with the smallest total. This now means the totals will be equal.
4. Enter totals on a level with each other.
5. Now enter the balance on the line below the totals. The balance below the totals should be on the opposite side to the balance shown above the totals.

Against the balance above the totals, complete the date column by showing the last day of that period. Below the totals show the first day of the next period against the balance. The balance above the totals is described as balance *carried down*. The balance below the total is described as balance *brought down*.

Knight's account when 'balanced off' will appear as shown in Exhibit 7.1.

Exhibit 7.1

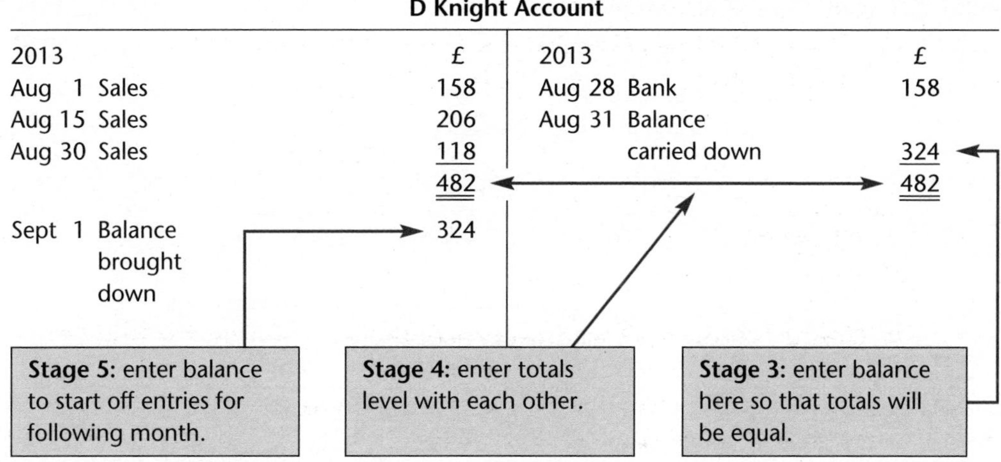

D Knight Account

2013		£	2013		£
Aug 1	Sales	158	Aug 28	Bank	158
Aug 15	Sales	206	Aug 31	Balance	
Aug 30	Sales	118		carried down	324
		482			482
Sept 1	Balance brought down	324			

We can now look at another account prior to balancing:

H Henry Account

2013		£	2013		£
Aug 5	Sales	300	Aug 24	Sales returns	50
Aug 28	Sales	540	Aug 29	Bank	250

We will abbreviate 'carried down' to 'c/d' and 'brought down' to 'b/d' from now on.

H Henry Account

2013		£	2013		£
Aug 5	Sales	300	Aug 24	Sales returns	50
Aug 28	Sales	540	Aug 29	Bank	250
			Aug 31	Balance c/d	540
		840			840
Sept 1	Balance b/d	540			

Notes:

- The date given for the balance c/d is the last day of the period which is finishing and that for the balance b/d is given as the opening date of the next period.
- As the total of the debit side originally exceeded the total of the credit side, *the balance is said to be a debit balance*. This being a personal account (i.e. for a person), the person concerned is said to be a debtor – the accounting term for anyone who owes money to the business.

If accounts contain only one entry, it is unnecessary to enter the total. A double line ruled under the entry will mean that the entry is its own total. For example:

B Walters Account

2013		£	2013		£
Aug 18	Sales	51	Aug 31	Balance c/d	51
Sept 1	Balance b/d	51			

7.4 Accounts for suppliers (accounts payable)

Exactly the same principles apply when the balances are carried down to the credit side. *This balance is known as a 'credit balance'*. We can look at two accounts of our suppliers which are to be balanced off.

E Williams Account

2013	£	2013	£
Aug 21 Bank	100	Aug 2 Purchases	248
		Aug 18 Purchases	116

K Patterson Account

2013	£	2013	£
Aug 14 Purchases returns	20	Aug 8 Purchases	620
Aug 28 Bank	600	Aug 15 Purchases	200

We now add up the totals and find the balance, i.e. stages 1 and 2. When balanced off, these will appear as:

E Williams Account

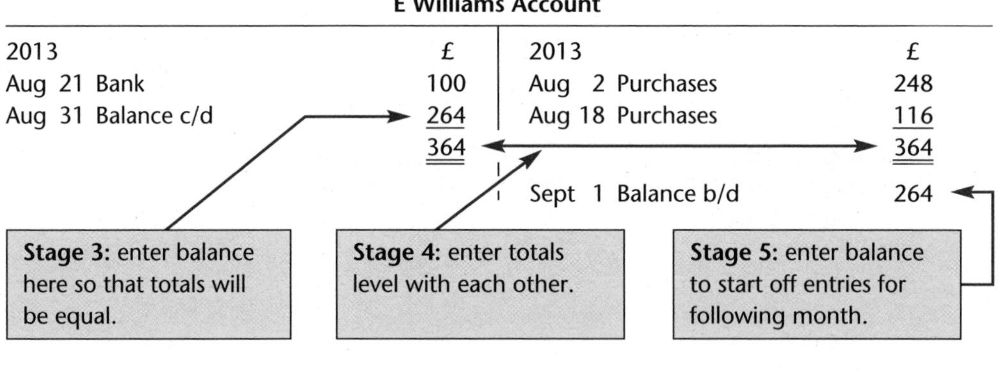

2013	£	2013	£
Aug 21 Bank	100	Aug 2 Purchases	248
Aug 31 Balance c/d	264	Aug 18 Purchases	116
	364		364
		Sept 1 Balance b/d	264

K Patterson Account

2013	£	2013	£
Aug 14 Purchases returns	20	Aug 8 Purchases	620
Aug 28 Bank	600	Aug 15 Purchases	200
Aug 31 Balance c/d	200		
	820		820
		Sept 1 Balance b/d	200

The accounts of E. Williams and K. Patterson have credit balances. They are **accounts payable** – the accounting term for anyone to whom money is owed.

The type of accounts which have been demonstrated so far are often known as 'T accounts' (see section 4.6) since the accounts are in the shape of a letter T. The following accounts show the three-column method, which is used in computerised accounting systems.

Before you read further, attempt Exercises 7.1 and 7.2 at the end of this chapter.

7.5 Three-column accounts

Through the main part of this book, the type of account used shows the left-hand side of the account as the debit side and the right-hand side as the credit side. However, when most computers are used, the style of the ledger account is different. It appears as three columns of figures, there being one column for debit entries, another column for credit entries, and the last column for the balance. If you have a current account at a bank, your bank statements will normally be shown using this method.

The accounts used in this chapter will now be redrafted to show the ledger accounts drawn up in this way.

K Tandy Account

	Debit	Credit	Balance (and whether debit or credit)	
2013	£	£	£	
Aug 1 Sales	144		144	Dr
Aug 19 Sales	300		444	Dr
Aug 22 Bank		144	300	Dr
Aug 28 Bank		300	0	

C Lee Account

	Debit	Credit	Balance	
2013	£	£	£	
Aug 11 Sales	177		177	Dr
Aug 19 Sales	203		380	Dr
Aug 22 Sales	100		480	Dr
Aug 30 Bank		480	0	

K Wood Account

	Debit	Credit	Balance	
2013	£	£	£	
Aug 6 Sales	214		214	Dr
Aug 12 Bank		214	0	

D Knight Account

	Debit	Credit	Balance	
2013	£	£	£	
Aug 1 Sales	158		158	Dr
Aug 15 Sales	206		364	Dr
Aug 28 Cash		158	206	Dr
Aug 31 Sales	118		324	Dr

H Henry Account

	Debit	Credit	Balance	
2013	£	£	£	
Aug 5 Sales	300		300	Dr
Aug 24 Sales returns		50	250	Dr
Aug 28 Sales	540		790	Dr
Aug 29 Bank		250	540	Dr

B Walters Account

	Debit	Credit	Balance	
2013	£	£	£	
Aug 18 Sales	51		51	Dr

E Williams Account

	Debit	Credit	Balance	
2013	£	£	£	
Aug 2 Purchases		248	248	Cr
Aug 18 Purchases		116	364	Cr
Aug 21 Bank	100		264	Cr

K Patterson Account

	Debit	Credit	Balance	
2013	£	£	£	
Aug 8 Purchases		620	620	Cr
Aug 14 Purchases returns	20		600	Cr
Aug 15 Purchases		200	800	Cr
Aug 28 Bank	600		200	Cr

You will notice in the above accounts that the balance is calculated after every entry. This can be done quite simply when using a computer accounting package since the software can automatically calculate the new balance after each entry.

However, when manual methods are being used, it is often too much work to have to calculate a new balance after each entry. Also, the greater the number of calculations, the greater the possibility of errors. For these reasons, it is usual for students to use two-sided accounts. However, it is important to note that there is no difference in principle; the final balances are the same using either method.

Chapter summary

- This chapter describes what is meant by 'balancing off' accounts at the end of a period.
- Balance off appropriate accounts at the end of a period and bring down the opening balance to the beginning of the next period.
- Opening balances brought down on the debit side are referred to as debit balances whereas those brought down on the credit side are known as credit balances.
- 'Debtors' are people or organisations who owe money to the business. On the Statement of Financial Position they are shown as 'Accounts Receivable'.
- 'Creditors' are people or organisations that the business owes money to. On the Statement of Financial Position they are shown as 'Accounts Payable'.
- 'T accounts' are used generally for recording transactions where there is a manual system of accounting.
- Computerised accounting packages use three-column accounts. Illustrations of preparing three-column accounts are shown.
- Both the 'T accounts' and the three-column accounts show the same information and the balances will be identical whichever method is used.

EXERCISES

*Note: Questions with the suffix 'X' shown after the question number do **not** have answers shown at the back of the book. Answers to the other questions are shown in Appendix E.*

7.1 Enter the following items in the appropriate account receivable accounts (i.e. your customers' accounts) only; do *not* write up other accounts. Then balance off each of these personal accounts at the end of the month. (Keep your answer – it will be used as a basis for question 7.3.)

2012
May 1 Sales on credit to D Binns £1,035, C Cade £450, H Teate £630
May 3 Sales on credit to J Watts £627, M Lowe £99
May 9 Sales returns from D Binns £60, H Teate £30
May 12 C Cade paid us by cheque, £450
May 16 H Teate paid us by cheque, £600
May 25 D Binns paid us £450 on account in cash
May 31 Sales on credit to J Watts, £135.

7.2 Enter the following in the appropriate accounts payable accounts (i.e. your suppliers' accounts) only. Do *not* write up the other accounts. Then balance off each of these personal accounts at the end of the month. (Keep your answer – it will be used as the basis for question 7.4X.)

2012
July 2 Purchases on credit from G Birks £687, A Weale £180, T Potts £1,012
July 5 Purchases on credit from K Lee £150, B Dixon £1,320
July 11 We returned goods to T Potts £33, G Birks £87
July 17 Purchases on credit from G Birks, £120
July 21 We paid B Dixon by cheque, £1,320
July 27 We paid G Birks £300 on account by cash
July 31 We returned goods to A Weale, £42.

7.3 Redraft each of the accounts given in your answer to 7.1 as three-column ledger-style accounts.

7.4X Redraft each of the accounts given in your answer to 7.2 as three-column ledger-style accounts.

7.5 Enter the following in the personal accounts (i.e. the accounts payable and accounts receivable) only; do *not* write up the other accounts. Balance off each personal account at the end of the month. After completing this, state which of the balances represent accounts receivable and which represent accounts payable.

2013
Oct 1 Sales on credit to T Tickle £690, S Ames £330,
Oct 3 Purchases on credit D Stott £116, D Owen £347, J Rhodes £98
Oct 9 Sales on credit to S Ames £645, T Johnson £376
Oct 11 Purchases on credit from D Owen £135, J Ahmed £367
Oct 14 Sales returns from S Ames £45, T Tickle £46
Oct 19 We returned goods to D Owen £36, D Stott £19
Oct 23 We paid D Stott by cheque, £97
Oct 25 T Tickle paid us by cheque, £674
Oct 29 We paid J Ahmed by cash, £367
Oct 30 S Ames paid us £500 on account by cheque
Oct 31 T Johnson paid us by cheque, £376.

7.6X Enter the following in the necessary personal accounts; do *not* write up the other accounts. Balance each personal account at the end of the month. (Keep your answer – it will be used as the basis of question 7.8X.)

2012
Aug 1 Sales on credit to L Sterling £445, L Lindo £480, R Spencer £221
Aug 4 Goods returned to us by L Sterling £15, R Spencer £33
Aug 8 Sales on credit to L Lindo £66, R Spencer £129, L Banks £465
Aug 9 We received a cheque for £430 from L Sterling
Aug 12 Sales on credit to R Spencer £235, L Banks £777
Aug 19 Goods returned to us by L Banks £21, R Spencer £25
Aug 22 We received cheques as follows: R Spencer £300, L Lindo £414
Aug 31 Sales on credit to L Lindo £887, L Banks £442.

7.7X Enter the following, which are personal accounts only. Bring down balances at end of the month. After completing this, state which of the outstanding balances represent accounts receivable and which represent accounts payable.

2013
May 1 Credit sales to B Flynn £241, R Kelly £29, J Long £887, T Fryer £124
May 2 Credit purchases from S Wood £148, T DuQuesnay £27, R Johnson £77, G Henriques £108
May 8 Credit sales to R Kelly £74, J Long £132
May 9 Credit purchases from T DuQuesnay £142, G Henriques £44
May 10 Goods returned to us by J Long £17, T Fryer £44
May 12 Cash paid to us by T Fryer, £80
May 15 We returned goods to S Wood £8, G Henriques £18
May 19 We received cheques from J Long £500, B Flynn £241
May 21 We sold goods on credit to B Flynn £44, R Kelly £280
May 28 We paid by cheque the following: S Wood £140; G Henriques £50; R Johnson £60
May 31 We returned goods to G Henriques, £4.

7.8X Redraft each of the accounts given in your answer to 7.6X as three-column accounts.

CHAPTER 8

The trial balance

Learning objectives

After you have studied this chapter you should be able to:

- understand the purpose of a trial balance
- understand why the trial balance totals should equal one another
- draw up a trial balance from a given set of figures
- appreciate that some kinds of errors can be made but the trial balance totals will still equal one another
- understand what steps to take if the trial balance doesn't balance.

8.1 Introduction

A trial balance is an essential stage in ensuring the accuracy of the book-keeping entries prior to the preparation of the financial statements. It is a list of account titles and their balances in the ledger on a specific date. The trial balance lists the name of each account together with the balance shown in either the debit or credit columns. Since every entry in double entry book-keeping should have a corresponding credit entry then, provided no errors have occurred, the two columns should agree when totalled.

It is important to note that the trial balance is not part of the double entry system, it is merely a list of balances drawn up to check the arithmetical accuracy of the book-keeping entries. It does, however, serve two purposes:

1 It checks the accuracy of the double entry transactions.
2 It facilities the preparation of the financial statements of the business (this is a topic covered in Part 2).

8.2 Total debit entries = total credit entries

Using the double entry system of book-keeping it has been shown that:

- for each debit entry there is a credit entry
- for each credit entry there is a debit entry.

All the items recorded in all the accounts on the debit side should equal *in total* all the items recorded on the credit side of the accounts. We need to check that for each debit entry there is also a credit entry. In order to do so, we prepare a trial balance which may be drawn up at the end of a period.

Each account needs to be balanced off, as shown in the previous chapter, and the balances entered in the trial balance. If the outstanding balance is a debit balance it would be entered in the debit column of the trial balance; if a credit balance it would be entered in the credit column. The trial balance would then be totalled and if both sides agree this is proof that certain types of errors have not been made. However, some errors may have occurred which the trial balance does not detect. This is discussed in section 8.5 and later in Chapters 32 and 33.

Using the worked exercise from section 5.9, the trial balance would be as follows:

Trial Balance as at 31 May 2013		
	£	£
Purchases	3,090	
Sales		2,550
Purchases returns		150
Sales returns	160	
A Lyon & Son		1,410
M Spencer	290	
Cash	570	
	4,110	4,110

Here the two sides 'balance', in other words both the debit column and the credit column add up to the same amount: £4,110.

This form of trial balance is the easiest to extract when there are more than a few transactions during the period and it is the one accountants use. As mentioned in the introduction to this chapter, the main purposes of preparing a trial balance is to ensure that no errors have been made and to facilitate the preparation of the financial statements. The financial statements consist of an 'income statement' which shows how much profit the business has earned in a period. The 'statement of financial position' shows what the assets and liabilities of a business are at the end of a period. Both these financial statements are dealt with in Part 2.

8.3 A worked example

The following accounts, for K Potter, have been entered up for May 2013 and balanced off. Note the entries used to 'balance off' the accounts have been highlighted.

K Potter's Books:

Bank Account

2013		£	2013		£
May 1	Capital	9,000	May 21	Machinery	550
May 30	T Monk	300	May 29	T Wood	860
			May 31	Balance c/d	7,890
		9,300			9,300
June 1	Balance b/d	7,890			

Cash Account

2013		£	2013		£
May 5	Sales	180	May 30	K Young	170
May 12	Sales	210	May 31	Balance c/d	220
		390			390
June 1	Balance b/d	220			

T Wood Account

2013		£	2013		£
May 6	Purchases returns	40	May 2	Purchases	900
May 29	Bank	860			
		900			900

K Young Account

2013		£	2013		£
May 28	Purchases returns	80	May 3	Purchases	250
May 30	Cash	170	May 18	Purchases	190
May 31	Balance c/d	190			
		440			440
			June 1	Balance b/d	190

T Monk Account

2013		£	2013		£
May 10	Sales	590	May 23	Sales returns	140
			May 30	Bank	300
			May 31	Balance c/d	150
		590			590
June 1	Balance b/d	150			

C Howe Account

2013		£	2013		£
May 22	Sales	220	May 25	Sales returns	10
			May 31	Balance c/d	210
		220			220
June 1	Balance b/d	210			

AB Ltd Account

		2013	£
		May 31 Machinery	2,700

Capital Account

		2013	£
		May 1 Bank	9,000

Purchases Account

2013	£	2013	£
May 2 T Wood	900	May 31 Balance c/d	1,340
May 3 K Young	250		
May 18 K Young	190		
	1,340		1,340
June 1 Balance b/d	1,340		

Sales Account

2013	£	2013	£
May 31 Balance c/d	1,200	May 5 Cash	180
		May 10 T Monk	590
		May 12 Cash	210
		May 22 C Howe	220
	1,200		1,200
		June 1 Balance b/d	1,200

Sales Returns Account

2013	£	2013	£
May 23 T Monk	140	May 31 Balance c/d	150
May 25 C Howe	10		
	150		150
June 1 Balance b/d	150		

Purchases Returns Account

2013	£	2013	£
May 31 Balance c/d	120	May 6 T Wood	40
		May 28 K Young	80
	120		120
		June 1 Balance b/d	120

Machinery Account

2013	£	2013	£
May 21 Bank	550	May 31 Balance c/d	3,250
May 31 AB Ltd	2,700		
	3,250		3,250
June 1 Balance b/d	3,250		

After each account has been balanced off, a trial balance (see Exhibit 8.1) can then be prepared as follows:

K Potter Trial Balance as at 31 May 2013		
	Dr £	*Cr* £
Bank	7,890	
Cash	220	
K Young		190
T Monk	150	
C Howe	210	
AB Ltd		2,700
Capital		9,000
Purchases	1,340	
Sales		1,200
Sales returns	150	
Purchases returns		120
Machinery	3,250	
	13,210	13,210

Exhibit 8.1 The trial balance

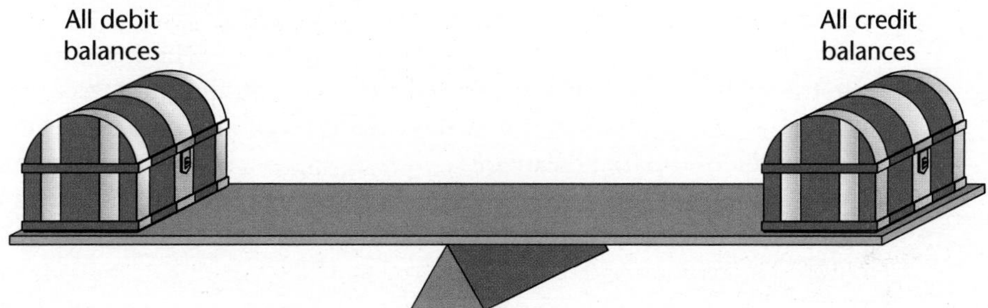

8.4 The uses of the trial balance

Trial balances may be used:

- to check that the books 'balance', i.e. that every debit entry has been accompanied by a credit entry
- to ascertain the net amount of the error(s), should an error(s) have been made
- as a basis from which the financial statements are prepared, i.e. the income statement and the statement of financial position (these will be explained in Part 2).

8.5 Trial balance and errors

Students new to accounting often assume that when a trial balance 'balances', the entries in the accounts must be correct. *This, however, may not be true*. It means that certain types of error have not been made, but there are several types of error that will not affect the balancing of a trial balance, such as omitting a transaction altogether. Another example might be a credit sale of £87 to a customer that is inadvertently debited to the sales account instead of being credited; the customer's account then being credited instead of being debited. Since both the debit and the credit entries are of the same amount then this will not affect the agreement of the trial balance.

Examples of the errors which would be revealed, provided there are no compensating errors which cancel them out, are addition errors, using one figure for the debit entry and another figure for the credit entry, entering only one aspect of a transaction, and so on. These will be considered in greater detail in later chapters.

8.6 Steps to take if the trial balance does not balance

If the trial balance does not balance, i.e. the two totals are different, then this is evidence that one or more errors have been made in either the double entry bookkeeping or in the preparation of the trial balance itself. In this case, the following eight steps should be taken to locate the error(s):

1 If the trial balance is badly written and contains many alterations, then rewrite it.
2 Again add each side of the trial balance. If you added the numbers 'upwards' the first time, then start at the top and work 'downwards' the second time, and vice versa.
3 Find the amount of the discrepancy and then check in the accounts for a transaction of this amount and, if located, ensure that the double entry has been carried out correctly.
4 Halve the amount of the discrepancy. Check to see whether there is a transaction for this amount and, if located, ensure the double entry has been carried out correctly. This type of error may have occurred if an item had been entered on the wrong side of the trial balance.
5 If the amount of the discrepancy is divisible by nine, this indicates that when the figure was originally entered it may have had digits transposed, for example £63 entered in error as £36, or £27 entered as £72.
6 Check that the balance on each account has been correctly calculated and entered onto the trial balance in the right column using the correct amount.
7 Ensure that every outstanding balance from all the ledgers and the cash book have been included in the trial balance and tick each balance after ensuring it is entered correctly.
8 If the error has still not been identified, then the error must be sought in the accounts themselves. It may be necessary to check all the entries from the date of the last trial balance.

8.7 Multiple-choice self-test questions

A growing practice of examining boards is to set multiple-choice questions in Accounting. This type of question certainly gives an examiner the opportunity to cover large parts of the syllabus briefly but in detail. Students who omit to study areas of the syllabus will be caught out by an examiner's use of multiple-choice questions. No longer will it be possible to say that it is highly probable that a certain topic will not be tested – the examiner can easily cover it with a multiple-choice question.

We have deliberately set blocks of multiple-choice questions at given places in this book, rather than a few at the end of each chapter. Such questions are relatively easy to answer a few minutes after reading the chapter, and so by asking the questions later your powers of recall and understanding are far better tested. It also gives you practice at answering a few questions in one block, as in an examination.

Each multiple-choice question has: a 'stem', namely that part which poses the problem; a 'key', which is the one correct answer; and a number of 'distractors', i.e. incorrect answers. The key plus the distractors are known as the 'options'. If you do not know the answer you should guess. You may be right by chance, or you may remember something subconsciously. In any event, unless the examiner warns otherwise, he will expect you to guess if you don't know the answer.

You should now attempt Set 1 in Appendix C, which contains 20 multiple-choice questions.

Chapter summary

- A trial balance is a list of account titles and their balances in the ledger at a specific date which is prepared to check the arithmetical accuracy of the book-keeping entries.
- A trial balance also assists in the preparation of the financial statements.
- A worked example of a trial balance is shown.
- The balancing of a trial balance does not always indicate that no errors have been made since certain errors can be made and the trial balance will still agree.
- What steps to take if a trial balance does not balance.

EXERCISES

Note: Questions with the suffix 'X' shown after the question number do ***not*** *have answers shown at the back of the book. Answers to the other questions are shown in Appendix E.*

8.1 You are required to enter the following transactions for the month of May 2012, for a small electrical retailer. Balance the accounts off and extract a trial balance as at 31 May 2012.

2012
May 1 Started in business with capital of £2,500, which was paid into the bank
May 2 Bought goods on credit from the following: D Ellis £540; C Mendez £87; K Gibson £76
May 4 Sold goods on credit to: C Bailey £430; B Hughes £62; H Spencer £176
May 6 Sold goods for cash, £500
May 8 Paid rent by cash, £120
May 9 C Bailey paid us £250 by cheque on account
May 10 H Spencer paid us £150 on account by cheque
May 12 We paid the following by cheque: K Gibson £76; D Ellis £370 on account
May 15 Bought stationery for cash, £60
May 18 Bought goods on credit from: D Ellis £145; C Mendez £234
May 19 Paid rent by cash, £120
May 25 Sold goods on credit to: C Bailey £90; B Hughes £110; H Spencer £128
May 31 Paid C Mendez £87 by cheque.

8.2 Enter up the books from the following details of a Do-it-yourself Shop for the month of March, and extract a trial balance as at 31 March 2012.

2012
March 1 Started business with £8,000 in the bank
March 2 Bought goods on credit from the following persons: K Henriques £76; M Hyatt £27; T Braham £560
March 5 Cash sales, £870
March 6 Paid wages in cash, £140
March 7 Sold goods on credit to: H Elliott £35; L Lane £42; J Carlton £72
March 9 Bought goods for cash, £46
March 10 Bought goods on credit from: M Hyatt £57; T Braham £98
March 12 Paid wages in cash, £140
March 13 Sold goods on credit to: L Lane £32; J Carlton £23
March 15 Bought shop fixtures on credit from Betta Ltd, £500
March 17 Paid M Hyatt by cheque, £84
March 18 We returned goods to T Braham, £20
March 21 Paid Betta Ltd a cheque for £500
March 24 J Carlton paid us his account by cheque, £95
March 27 We returned goods to K Henriques, £24
March 30 J King lent us £600 by cash
March 31 Bought a motor van paying by cheque, £4,000.

8.3X Record the following transactions in the books of C Hilton. Balance off the accounts and extract a trial balance as at 30 June 2013.

2013
June 1 C Hilton started in business with £9,000 in cash
June 2 Paid £8,000 of the cash into a bank account
June 4 Paid rent for shop £300 by cheque
June 6 Bought goods on credit from Moorlands & Co. £675; J Swain £312; B Merton £225
June 12 Sold goods for cash, £450
June 13 Bought fixtures, paying by cheque, £230
June 15 Sold goods on credit T Green £180; K Wood £367; P Brown £256
June 18 Sold goods for cash, £220
June 20 Paid Moorlands & Co by cheque £675 and B Merton £225
June 21 Returned goods to J Swain £112 and paid the outstanding balance on their account by cheque
June 24 Bought goods on credit from Moorlands & Co £220 and J Swain £92
June 26 Paid wages in cash, £366
June 27 Cash drawings, £200
June 29 Bought motor van, paying by cheque, £4,000
June 30 Sold goods on credit to T Green £300; K Wood £50; P Brown £60
June 30 Received cheques from the following: T Green £180 and K Wood £367

8.4X You are required to enter the following transactions in the necessary accounts for April 2012 of a home furnishing business. At the end of the month balance off the accounts and prepare a trial balance.

2012
April 1 Started in business with £15,000 in the bank
April 3 Bought goods on credit from: Bowman Furnishers £320; Howe Homes £460; W Hunt £1,800; J Bond £620
April 7 Cash sales, £480
April 9 Paid rent by cheque, £500
April 11 Paid rates by cheque, £190
April 12 Sold goods on credit to: L Clark £480; K Allen £96; R Gee £1,170
April 14 Paid wages in cash, £400
April 17 We returned faulty goods to: Bowman Furnishers £28; J Bond £60
April 20 Bought goods on credit from: J Bond £220; W Hunt £270; Bowman Furnishers £240

April 23 Goods were returned to us from: K Allen £20; L Clark £40
April 25 Bought motor car on credit from Bates Motors, £5,000
April 26 Cash sales, £175
April 27 We paid the following by cheque: Bowman Furnishers £532; Howe Homes £460; W Hunt £2,070
April 28 Bought secondhand motor van, £3,000 paid by cheque
April 29 Bought stationery and paid in cash, £56
April 30 Received cheques from: L Clark £440; K Allen £76
April 30 Paid Bates Motors by cheque, £5,000.

8.5 Correct and balance the following trial balance.

Trial balance of P Brown as at 31 May 2013

	Dr £	*Cr* £
Capital		20,000
Drawings	7,000	
General expenses		500
Sales	38,500	
Purchases		29,000
Accounts receivable		6,800
Accounts payable	9,000	
Bank balance (Dr)	15,100	
Cash		200
Plant and equipment		5,000
Heating and lighting		1,500
Rent	2,400	

8.6 Reconstruct the trial balance after making the necessary corrections.

Trial balance of S Higton as at 30 June 2013

	Dr £	*Cr* £
Capital	19,956	
Sales		119,439
Stationery	1,200	
General expenses	2,745	
Motor expenses		4,476
Cash at bank	1,950	
Inventory 1 July 2012	7,668	
Wages and salaries		9,492
Rent and rates	10,500	
Office equipment	6,000	
Purchases	81,753	
Heating and lighting		2,208
Rent received	2,139	
Accounts receivable	10,353	
Drawings		4,200
Accounts payable		10,230
Motor vehicle	7,500	
Interest received	1,725	
Insurance		3,444
	153,489	153,489

8.7X From the following list of balances, prepare a trial balance as at 31 December 2013 for Ms Anita Hall:

	£
Plant and machinery	21,450
Motor vehicles	26,000
Premises	80,000
Wages	42,840
Purchases	119,856
Sales	179,744
Rent received	3,360
Telephone, printing and stationery	3,600
Accounts payable	27,200
Accounts receivable	30,440
Bank overdraft	2,216
Capital	131,250
Drawings	10,680
General expenses	3,584
Lighting and heating	2,960
Motor expenses	2,360

8.8X State whether the following accounts would be either a debit or credit balance.

(*a*) Capital
(*b*) Sales
(*c*) Stationery
(*d*) Cash
(*e*) T Khan (a supplier)
(*f*) Machinery
(*g*) Rent
(*h*) D Allen (customer)
(*i*) Bank loan
(*j*) Purchases

CHAPTER 9

Capital and revenue expenditures

Learning objectives

After you have studied this chapter you should be able to:

- distinguish between capital expenditure and revenue expenditure
- understand that some expenditure is part capital expenditure and part revenue expenditure
- understand that if revenue expenditure is incorrectly treated as capital expenditure, or vice versa, then it will affect the profit and the financial statements.

9.1 Introduction

This chapter will deal with the distinction between capital and revenue expenditure and show the importance of careful classification, which can ultimately affect the recorded profits and valuations in the statement of financial position.

9.2 Capital expenditure

Capital expenditure is incurred when a business spends money to either:

- buy non-current assets, or
- add to the value of an existing non-current asset.

Included in such amounts should be the costs of:

- acquiring non-current assets
- bringing them into the business
- legal costs of buying buildings
- carriage inwards on machinery bought
- any other cost needed to get the non-current asset ready for use.

9.3 Revenue expenditure

Revenue expenditure is expenditure that does not increase the value of non-current assets but is incurred in the day-to-day running expenses of the business.

The difference from capital expenditure can be seen when considering the cost of running a motor vehicle for a business. The expenditure incurred in acquiring the motor vehicle is classed as capital expenditure, while the cost of the petrol used to run the vehicle is revenue expenditure. This is because the revenue expenditure is used up in a few days and does not add to the value of the non-current asset.

9.4 Difference between capital and revenue expenditure

The difference between capital and revenue expenditure can be seen more generally in the following table (Exhibit 9.1). Revenue expenditure is the day-to-day running expense of the business and, as such, is chargeable to the income statement. Capital expenditure, in contrast, results in an increase in the non-current assets shown in the statement of financial position.

Exhibit 9.1

Capital	Revenue
Premises purchased	Rent of premises
Legal charges for conveyancing	Legal charges for debt collection
New machinery	Repairs to machinery
Installations of machinery	Electricity costs of using machinery
Additions to assets	Maintenance of assets
Motor van	Repairs to van
Delivery charges on new assets	Carriage on purchases and sales
Extension costs of new offices	Redecorating existing offices
Cost of adding air-conditioning to room	Interest on loan to purchase air-conditioning

Buying a van is capital expenditure

Repairs to a van is revenue expenditure

Source: *Edexcel International GCSE Accounting* 1st edn, Edexcel (Robinson, S. 2010) Pearson Education Ltd.

9.5 Joint expenditure

In certain cases, an item of expenditure will need dividing between capital and revenue expenditure. Suppose a builder was engaged to carry out some work on your premises, the total bill being £60,000. If one-third of this was for repair work and two-thirds for improvements, then £20,000 should be charged to the income statement as revenue expenditure, and £40,000 should be identified as capital expenditure and added to the value of the business's premises and shown as such in the statement of financial position. See Exhibit 9.2.

Exhibit 9.2 Joint expenditure

Builder's cost for repairs and improvements to premises £60,000

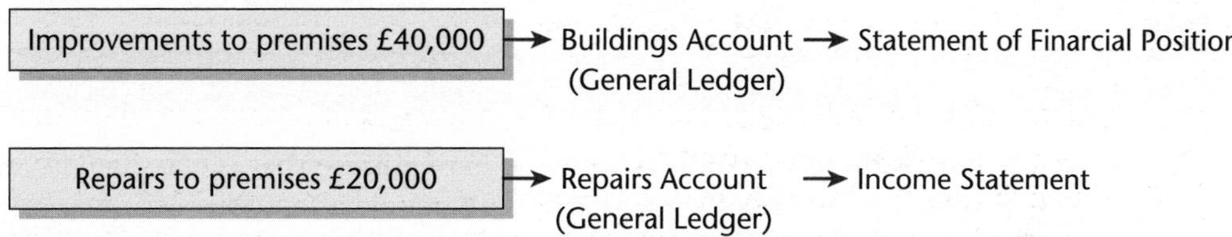

9.6 Incorrect treatment of expenditure

If one of the following occurs:

- capital expenditure is incorrectly treated as revenue expenditure, or
- revenue expenditure is incorrectly treated as capital expenditure,

then both the statement of financial position figures and income statement figures will be incorrect. This means that the net profit figure will also be incorrect.

If capital expenditure is incorrectly posted to revenue expenditure - for example, if the purchase of a photocopier is posted in error to the stationery account instead of the office equipment account - then:

> **Net profit** would be understated, *and* the statement of financial position would not include the value of the asset.

If revenue expenditure is incorrectly posted to capital expenditure - for example if stationery is posted to office equipment instead of the stationery account - then:

> **Net profit** would be overstated, *and* the statement of financial position would show the non-current assets overvalued.

If the expenditure affects items in the trading account, then the **gross profit** figure will also be incorrect.

9.7 Treatment of loan interest

If money is borrowed to finance the purchase of a non-current asset, then interest will have to be paid on the loan. The **loan interest**, however, is *not* a cost of acquiring the asset but is simply a cost of financing its acquisition. This means that loan interest is revenue expenditure and *not* capital expenditure, and should be charged to the income statement.

9.8 Capital and revenue receipts

When an item of capital expenditure is sold, the receipt is called a capital receipt. Suppose a motor van is bought for £10,000, and sold five years later for £2,000. The £10,000 was treated as capital expenditure; the £2,000 received is treated as a capital receipt.

Revenue receipts are sales or other revenue items, such as rent receivable or commissions receivable.

Chapter summary

- It is important to distinguish between expenditure that is classified as 'capital' and that which is 'revenue' since this can ultimately affect the recording of profits and the statement of financial position valuations.
- Expenditure can be either:

Capital expenditure *or*	**Revenue expenditure**
(a) Buying non-current assets	(a) For daily running expenses of the business
(b) Adding value to non-current assets	(b) Not adding value to non-current assets

- Some items are both capital and revenue expenditure and the costs involved need to be apportioned carefully.
- If capital expenditure or revenue expenditure is mistaken one for the other, then either gross or net profit (or both) will be incorrectly stated. The value of the assets in the statement of financial position will also be affected.
- It is also important to classify capital receipts, i.e. the sale of a non-current asset, from revenue receipts which are accounted for from sales or other revenue items.

EXERCISES

*Note: Questions with the suffix 'X' shown after the question number do **not** have answers shown at the back of the book. Answers to the other questions are shown in Appendix E.*

9.1 Newton Data Systems specialises in providing computer services to small commercial businesses.

You are required to state whether the following transactions should be classified as capital or revenue expenditure, giving reasons for your choice:

(*a*) Salaries of the computer operators.
(*b*) Purchase of new computer for use in the office.
(*c*) Purchase of computer printout paper.
(*d*) Insurance of all the company's computer hardware.
(*e*) Cost of adding additional storage capacity to a mainframe computer to be used by the company.
(*f*) Cost of providing additional security to the company's offices.

9.2 Cairns Engineering Company extracted the following information from their financial records:

	£
(*a*) New stationery and brochures	411
(*b*) Purchase of new pickup truck	18,000
(*c*) Purchase of new lathe	5,200
(*d*) Delivery cost of new lathe	200
(*e*) Electricty (including new wiring £1,800, part of premises improvement)	3,900
(*f*) Wages (including wages of two of Cairn's employees for improvement work on Cairns premises, amount involved £20,000)	65,000

You are required to:

- State whether each of the items listed above are capital or revenue expenditure and state how much the company has spent on each category for the year.
- Briefly explain the difference between capital and revenue expenditure.

9.3X (*a*) Star Fashions Ltd, which manufactures children's clothing, is planning to purchase a new cutting machine costing £20,000. Would the following items of expenditure be classed as capital or revenue expenditure?
   (i) The purchase price of the cutting machine.
   (ii) The cost of installing the machine.
   (iii) The significant cost of initial training for the staff to operate the new machine.
   (iv) The cost of future repairs and maintenance of the machine.

(*b*) If capital expenditure is treated as revenue expenditure, then:
   (i) How would the total expenses and the net profit for the period be affected?
   (ii) What effect would the error have on the value of the non-current assets in the statement of financial position?

9.4 T Taylor has drawn up his financial statements for the year ended 31 December 2013. On examining them, you find that:

(*a*) Taylor has debited the cost of office equipment £311 to the purchases account.
(*b*) Taylor has debited the cost of repairing office equipment £290 to the motor repairs account.
(*c*) Sale of a building for £10,000 has been credited to the sales account.
(*d*) Repayment of a loan £500 has been debited to the loan interest account.

From his figures he had calculated gross profit as £95,620 and net profit as £28,910.

Ignoring any adjustments for depreciation, calculate revised figures of gross and net profits after taking (*a*) to (*d*) into account.

9.5X S Simpson has calculated her gross profit for the year to 30 June 2013 as £129,450 and her net profit as £77,270. You find that Simpson's books show:

(*a*) Sale of a motor vehicle for £4,100 has been credited to the sales account.
(*b*) Fixtures, bought for £750, have been debited to the repairs account.
(*c*) Receipt of a loan for £6,000 has been credited to the sales account.
(*d*) Repairs to motor vehicles £379 have been debited to the general expenses account.

Ignoring any adjustments for depreciation, calculate the revised figures of gross and net profits.

9.6X A business has incorrectly charged some of its expenditure in its final accounts. The incorrect figures shown were as follows:

(*a*) Gross profit £216,290
(*b*) Net profit £110,160
(*c*) Non-current assets £190,000
(*d*) Current assets £77,600.

Required:
You are to show, for each of the following, the effects on the calculations of (*a*) gross profit, (*b*) net profit, (*c*) non-current assets in the statement of financial position and (*d*) current assets in the statement of financial position. (Ignore depreciation.)

(i) Motor van costing £5,500 debited to motor expenses account.
(ii) Carriage outwards £77 debited to fixtures account.
(iii) Rent £2,000 debited to buildings account.
(iv) Machinery £6,000 debited to fixtures account.
(v) Office equipment £790 debited to purchases account.
(vi) Discounts allowed £2,380 debited to machinery account.

9.7X (*a*) For each of the following transactions place *one* tick (✓) in the appropriate column to indicate whether the item is an example of capital expenditure, revenue expenditure, revenue receipt or capital receipt.
Transaction (i) is done as an example for you.

Transaction	*Capital expenditure*	*Capital receipt*	*Revenue expenditure*	*Revenue receipt*
(i) Purchase of goods for resale			✓	
(ii) Rent received for office sublet				
(iii) Purchase of stationery for office use				
(iv) Sale of old equipment no longer required				
(v) Cost of building an extension to premises				
(vi) Sale of inventory				
(vii) Repairs to existing premises				

(*b*) How should items of capital expenditure be treated when preparing final accounts?

NEAB (GCSE)

PART 2

The financial statements of sole traders

This part of the book is concerned with preparing the financial statements of sole traders from the double entry records. A chapter on accounting concepts, standards and policies is also included.

CHAPTER 10

Income statements: an introduction

Learning objectives

After you have studied this chapter you should be able to:

- understand the importance of knowing a business's profit for the trading year
- appreciate the importance of preparing the trading and profit and loss account and income statements
- understand the difference between the gross profit and the net profit
- calculate the cost of goods sold
- explain how an adjustment needs to be made for the closing inventory at the end of the trading period
- close off sales, purchases and relevant expense accounts at the end of the trading period using double entry and transfer the balances to the trading account and profit and loss account
- prepare an income statement from the information given in the trial balance
- transfer the net profit and drawings to the capital account at the end of the period
- appreciate that after preparing the trading account and profit and loss account all remaining balances in the books of account are required for the preparation of the statement of financial position.

10.1 Purpose of the income statement

The main reason why people go into business is to make a profit as discussed in Chapter 1. Here the owner of a business bought goods at cost price, £10,000 and later sold them at a selling price of £15,000 thereby making a profit of £5,000 and after expenses of £3,000 his profit became £2,000.

As you will see in this chapter we are now ready to prepare financial statements at the end of a business's trading year. This involves closing off the revenue and expense accounts at the end of the financial year by transferring the balances to either the trading account or the profit and loss account. The information from these two accounts is then used to prepare what is known as an **income statement**.

The information contained in the trading and profit and loss accounts which, as stated above, is used to prepare the income statement, is one of the most important financial statements since it reports to the owner of the business the actual profits made. It must be pointed out, however, that if the business is unsuccessful it could easily make a loss. This will occur when the expenses are greater than the income.

Not only is the owner of the business interested in the results of the year's trading but there are other parties who are interested in the financial results:

- the bank, should the business require a loan
- HM Revenue and Customs, for taxation purposes
- a prospective purchaser of the business or a new partner who is interested in joining the business.

In addition the current year's results are also used for budgeting purposes and planning for the year(s) ahead.

Income statements are usually prepared at least once a year but with the increasing use of computer-based accounting packages they can be made available much more frequently.

10.2 Uses of the trading and profit and loss account

Gross profit

One of the most important uses of the trading and profit and loss account is that of comparing the results obtained with the expected or budgeted results. In a trading organisation, much attention is paid to how much profit is made, *before* deducting expenses. This is known as the **gross profit** and appears in the first section of the trading and profit and loss account.

Net profit

The gross profit is brought down from the trading account section and against this figure the expenses of running the business are deducted to arrive at a figure of **net profit**. This lower section of the financial statement is called the profit and loss account.

Gross profit: calculated in the Trading Account	This is the excess of sales over the **cost of goods sold** in the period.
Net profit: calculated in the Profit and Loss Account	This is what is left of the gross profit after all expenses have been deducted.

Note: Both the trading account and the profit and loss account *are* part of the double entry system as illustrated in section 10.3. The information taken from these two accounts is then used to prepare the Income Statement which is *not* part of the double entry system but merely a financial statement showing details of the business's income and expenditure for the accounting period.

10.3 Preparation of a trading and profit and loss account

In the previous chapters we saw how the various items of revenue and expenditure were recorded in the books of account using the double entry system and at the end of the period the accounts were balanced off and a trial balance drawn up. This contains nearly all the information needed to prepare the trading and profit and loss account. (Later on in this book you will see that certain adjustments have to be made, but we will ignore these at this stage.)

Set out in Exhibit 10.1 is the trial balance of K Wade made up to the end of his first year's trading. This information is needed to prepare his trading and profit and loss account for the year ended 31 December 2013. For the moment we will assume that K Wade has no closing inventory at 31 December 2013.

To calculate gross profit

Remember that:

Sales – Cost of Goods Sold = Gross Profit

Exhibit 10.1

K Wade
Trial Balance as at 31 December 2013

	Dr	*Cr*
	£	£
Sales		39,650
Purchases	27,150	
General expenses	2,550	
Fixtures and fittings	6,840	
Accounts receivable	2,460	
Accounts payable		2,180
Capital		8,800
Drawings	7,750	
Bank	3,820	
Cash	60	
	50,630	50,630

We could in fact calculate this by simply using arithmetic. However, we must remember that we are using double entry methods. The answer will be the same whether normal arithmetic or proper double entry methods are used. To enable you to see fully how the calculations are performed using double entry, we will show the balances for sales and purchases, as in Exhibit 10.1, and how the entries are made to transfer these items into the calculations within the trading account.

The following steps should be carried out:

Step 1 Transfer the credit balance of the sales account to the credit of the trading account portion of the trading and profit and loss account.

Debit: sales account
Credit: trading account.

Step 2 Transfer the debit balance of the purchases account to the debit of the trading account.

Debit: trading account
Credit: purchases account.

Remember that, in this case, there is no inventory of unsold goods. This means that purchases = **cost of goods sold**.

Step 3 If sales are greater than the cost of goods sold, the difference is gross profit. (If not, the answer would be a **gross loss**.) We will carry this gross profit figure from the trading account part down to the profit and loss part.

The double entry for gross profit is:

Debit: trading account
Credit: profit and loss account.

The double entry for the above transfers are shown in Exhibit 10.2.

Exhibit 10.2

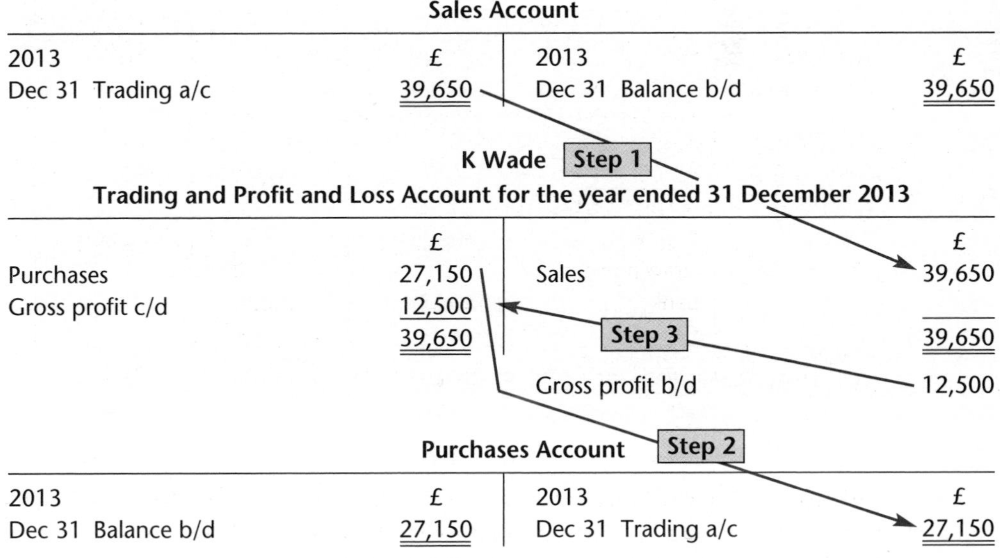

Sales Account

2013		£	2013		£
Dec 31	Trading a/c	39,650	Dec 31	Balance b/d	39,650

K Wade
Trading and Profit and Loss Account for the year ended 31 December 2013

	£		£
Purchases	27,150	Sales	39,650
Gross profit c/d	12,500		
	39,650		39,650
		Gross profit b/d	12,500

Purchases Account

2013		£	2013		£
Dec 31	Balance b/d	27,150	Dec 31	Trading a/c	27,150

Notice that, after the trading account has been completed, there are no balances remaining in the sales and purchases accounts. They are now said to be 'closed'.

To calculate net profit and record it

Remember that:

Gross Profit – Expenses = Net Profit

Remember also (from Chapter 6) that:

Old Capital + Net Profit = New Capital

The double entry needed to carry out these calculations is:

Step 1 Transfer the debit balances on expenses accounts to the debit of the profit and loss account.

Debit: profit and loss account
Credit: expenses accounts.

Step 2 Transfer the net profit, when found, to the capital account to show the increase in capital.

Debit: profit and loss account
Credit: capital account.

The results are shown in Exhibit 10.3.

Exhibit 10.3

K Wade
Trading and Profit and Loss Account for the Year ended 31 December 2013

	£		£
Purchases	27,150	Sales	39,650
Gross profit c/d	12,500		
	39,650		39,650
General expenses	2,550	Gross profit b/d	12,500
Net profit	9,950		
	12,500		12,500

Step 1

General Expenses Account

	£		£
2013		2013	
Dec 31 Balance b/d	2,550	Dec 31 Profit and loss a/c	2,550

Step 2

Capital Account

			£
		2013	
		Dec 31 Balance b/d	8,800
		Dec 31 Net profit	9,950
			18,750

Note: See section 10.4 for completion of this account.

10.4 Completion of capital account

You have seen that we credit the capital account with the amount of net profit. We have, therefore, recorded the increase in capital.

In the trial balance, Exhibit 10.1, we can see that there are drawings of £7,750. **Drawings** are withdrawals of capital.

After entering the net profit in the capital account we can now complete the account. To do this we transfer the drawings to the capital account. Thus:

Debit: capital account
Credit: drawings account.

The completed capital and drawings accounts are as follows:

Drawings Account

		£			£
2013			2013		
Dec 31	Balance b/d	7,750	Dec 31	Capital	7,750

Capital Account

		£			£
2013			2013		
Dec 31	Drawings	7,750	Dec 31	Balance b/d	8,800
Dec 31	Balance c/d	11,000	Dec 31	Net profit	9,950
		18,750			18,750
			2014		
			Jan 1	Balance b/d	11,000

10.5 Inventory of unsold goods at end of period

Usually some of the goods bought (purchases) have not been sold by the end of the accounting period.

We have already seen that gross profit is calculated as follows:

Sales – Cost of Goods Sold = Gross Profit

However, purchases only equals cost of goods sold if there is no inventory at the end of a period. We can calculate cost of goods sold as follows:

What we bought in this period:	Purchases
Less Goods bought but not sold in this period:	Closing Inventory
	= Cost of Goods Sold

Remember, we are concerned here with the trading and profit and loss account of a business where there is no opening inventory. In section 12.4 we will look at the later years of a business.

Now let us look at the preparation of a trading and profit and loss account for B Swift. His trial balance is shown as Exhibit 10.4 and was drawn up after his first year of trading:

Exhibit 10.4

B Swift
Trial Balance as at 31 December 2013

	Dr	*Cr*
	£	£
Sales		38,500
Purchases	29,000	
Rent	2,400	
Electricity	1,500	
General expenses	600	
Fixtures and fittings	5,000	
Accounts receivable	6,800	
Accounts payable		9,100
Bank	15,100	
Cash	200	
Drawings	7,000	
Capital		20,000
	67,600	67,600

Note: On 31 December 2013, at the close of trading, B Swift had goods costing £3,000 that were unsold. This figure is found by B Swift carrying out a check of his unsold inventory. First, the cost of goods sold figure needs to be calculated:

	£
Purchases	29,000
Less Closing inventory	3,000
Cost of goods sold	26,000

The gross profit will be:

	£
Sales	38,500
Less Cost of goods sold	26,000
Gross profit	12,500

The net profit will be:

	£	£
Gross profit		12,500
Less Expenses		
Rent	2,400	
Electricity	1,500	
General expenses	600	
		4,500
Net profit		8,000

The double entry for the above transactions is now shown in Exhibit 10.5.

Exhibit 10.5

Sales Account

2013	£	2013	£
Dec 31 Trading a/c	38,500	Dec 31 Balance b/d	38,500

Purchases Account

2013	£	2013	£
Dec 31 Balance b/d	29,000	Dec 31 Trading a/c	29,000

Rent Account

2013	£	2013	£
Dec 31 Balance b/d	2,400	Dec 31 Profit and loss a/c	2,400

Electricity Account

2013	£	2013	£
Dec 31 Balance b/d	1,500	Dec 31 Profit and loss a/c	1,500

General Expenses Account

2013	£	2013	£
Dec 31 Balance b/d	600	Dec 31 Profit and loss a/c	600

To record the inventory we need to:

Debit: closing inventory account
Credit: trading account

as shown below:

Closing Inventory Account

2013	£		
Dec 31 Trading a/c	3,000		

B Swift
Trading and Profit and Loss Account
for the year ended 31 December 2013

2013	£	2013	£
Purchases	29,000	Sales	38,500
Gross profit c/d	12,500	Closing inventory	3,000
	41,500		41,500
Rent	2,400	Gross profit b/d	12,500
Electricity	1,500		
General expenses	600		
Net profit	8,000		
	12,500		12,500

The figures shown in Exhibit 10.5 show that there is now a balance on the inventory account. We had to record it there because at 31 December 2013 we had an asset, namely £3,000 inventory (of stock), but there was no record of that fact in our books. We have now brought our records up to date by showing the inventory in our accounts. Without the inventory account at 31 December 2013, our records would have been incomplete.

10.6 The capital account

The capital account for B Swift can now be completed, thus:

Capital Account

2013		£	2013		£
Dec 31	Drawings	7,000	Jan 1	Cash	20,000
Dec 31	Balance c/d	21,000	Dec 31	Net profit from profit and loss a/c	8,000
		28,000			28,000
			2014		
			Jan 1	Balance b/d	21,000

Drawings Account

2013		£	2013		£
Dec 31	Balance b/d	7,000	Dec 31	Capital	7,000

10.7 The income statement

Having transferred the balances of the sales and purchases accounts to the trading account and the various expense accounts to the profit and loss account, together with the figure for closing inventory (stock) we now have all the information required to prepare the income statement for B Swift for the year ended 31 December 2013. This is shown below:

B Swift
Income Statement for the year ended 31 December 2013

	£	£
Sales		38,500
Less Cost of goods sold		
Purchases	29,000	
Less Closing inventory	3,000	
		26,000
Gross profit		12,500
Less Expenses		
Rent	2,400	
Electricity	1,500	
General expenses	600	
		4,500
Net profit		8,000

You can see that the figures used are exactly the same as shown in the trading and profit and loss account.

10.8 The balances remaining in the books of account

Taking Exhibit 10.5, including the adjustment of closing inventory valued at £3,000, we can now ascertain the balances still remaining in the books of account after the preparation of the trading and profit and loss accounts. The following accounts have been closed in this process:

Sales Purchases	}	transferred to trading account
Rent Electricity General expenses	}	transferred to profit and loss account
Drawings	}	transferred to capital account

With the remaining balances we can draw up a trial balance which is now shown in Exhibit 10.6.

Exhibit 10.6

B Swift
Trial Balance as at 31 December 2013
(after Trading and Profit and Loss Accounts completed)

	Dr	*Cr*
	£	£
Fixtures and fittings	5,000	
Accounts receivable	6,800	
Accounts payable		9,100
Inventory	3,000	
Bank	15,100	
Cash	200	
Capital		21,000
	30,100	30,100

The one account that was not in the original trial balance was the inventory account. It was not brought into our books until the trading account was prepared. These balances will be used when we look at the statement of financial position in the next chapter. They are also carried forward to the next accounting period.

Chapter summary

- The trading and profit and loss account is prepared to determine the profit/losses made in the period. This information is ultimately used to prepare the income statement.
- One of the main uses of the trading and profit and loss account is to provide information on the profit/losses made in the period and compare these figures with previous year's results.
- How to calculate the cost of goods sold, gross profit and net profit.
- How to close off the sales, purchases and relevant expense accounts at the end of a period and post the entries to the trading and profit and loss account.
- How to transfer the net profit and drawings to the capital account at the end of a period.
- How to treat inventory of unsold goods at the end of a period.
- The preparation of the income statement account from a trial balance.
- Any balances still remaining in the books of account after preparation of the trading and profit and loss account represent non-current assets, liabilities and capital. These balances are entered into the statement of financial position (see the next chapter) and then carried forward to the next accounting period.

EXERCISES

*Note: Questions with the suffix 'X' shown after the question number do **not** have answers shown at the back of the book. Answers to the other questions are shown in Appendix E.*

10.1 From the following details of I Simpson, draw up her income statement for the year ended 31 December 2012, this being her first year of trading:

Year to 31 December 2012	£
Purchases	24,190
Sales	38,220
Rent	4,170
Wages and salaries	5,390
Postage and stationery	840
Electricity expenses	710
General expenses	370

Note: At 31 December 2012, the inventory was valued (at cost) at £4,310.

10.2X From the following details of C Newman, draw up his income statement for his first year of trading for the year ended 31 December 2012.

Year to 31 December 2012	£
Rent	4,990
Motor expenses	2,370
Sundry expenses	410
Travel expenses	600
Office expenses	720
Sales	57,090
Purchases	42,910

Note: Inventory at 31 December 2012 amounted in value to £8,220.

10.3 From the following trial balance of G Singh, extracted after one year's trading, prepare the income statement for the year ended 31 December 2013. A statement of financial position is not required.

G Singh
Trial Balance as at 31 December 2013

	Dr £	*Cr* £
Sales		73,848
Purchases	58,516	
Wages	8,600	
Motor expenses	2,080	
Rates	2,680	
Insurance	444	
General expenses	420	
Premises	20,000	
Motor vehicle	12,000	
Accounts receivable	7,800	
Accounts payable		6,418
Cash at bank	6,616	
Cash in hand	160	
Drawings	8,950	
Capital		48,000
	128,266	128,266

Inventory at 31 December 2013 was valued at £10,192.
(Retain your answer – it will be used later in Exercise 11.1.)

10.4X From the following trial balance of R Cairns after his first year's trading, you are required to draw up a income statement for the year ended 30 June 2013.

R Cairns
Trial Balance as at 30 June 2013

	Dr £	*Cr* £
Sales		99,082
Purchases	71,409	
Rates	2,000	
Printing and stationery	562	
Electricity	1,266	
Wages	9,492	
Insurance	605	
Premises	145,000	
Computer equipment	8,000	
Accounts receivable	9,498	
Sundry expenses	1,518	
Accounts payable		3,618
Cash at bank	6,541	
Drawings	12,200	
Motor vehicle	16,500	
Motor expenses	3,109	
Capital		185,000
	287,700	287,700

Inventory at 30 June 2013 was valued at £11,498.

(Retain your answer – it will be used later in Exercise 11.2X.)

10.5 Mrs P Stewart commenced trading as a card and gift shop with a capital of £6,855 on 1 April 2012. At the end of her first year's trading on 31 March 2013, she was able to identify from her accounting records that she had received £24,765 sales in the year. These sales had cost her £13,545 to purchase, and she had an inventory of £2,345 cards and gifts, at cost on 31 March 2013. In the year she had also spent £2,100 on staff wages, and drawn personal cash of £5,500. Other overhead costs incurred were:

	£
Rent and rates	1,580
Electricity	565
Motor expenses	845
Insurance	345
General expenses	245

On 31 March 2013, Mrs P Stewart had cash in hand of £135, a bank balance of £2,675, and had accounts payable of £3,285. Mrs Stewart's business owned a car, which had a value of £5,875 at 31 March 2013. She had also bought shelving and fixtures and fittings in the year to the value of £1,495.

You are required to draw up her income statement for the first year's trading.

(*Exam hint*: Before you attempt to draw up the income statement, it would be a good idea to extract the trial balance at 31 March 2013 from the information given.) The closing inventory figure should be shown as a note at the foot of the trial balance.
(Keep your answer – it will be used later in Exercise 11.3.)

10.6X Miss R Burgess has just completed her first year of trading for the year ended 30 April 2012, as a manufacturer of model railway accessories. Her initial capital was £9,025. At 30 April 2012, she was owed £5,600 by customers, and owed £4,825 to suppliers. She calculated that she had inventory in hand, at cost, at the year end of £7,670, and her bank account was overdrawn by £2,560. The petty cash float held £25 at 30 April 2012.

From her records, she calculated her income and expenditure for the year ended 30 April 2012 as:

	£
Sales	56,540
Purchases	34,315
Rent of factory	6,000
Drawings	10,000
Motor expenses	1,735
Insurance	345
General expenses	780
Salaries	7,550

Miss R Burgess had plant and equipment to the value of £3,750 and a van worth £2,850 at 30 April 2012.

You are required to draw up the income statement for the first year's trading.
(Keep your answer – it will be used later in Exercise 11.5X.)

10.7X A business has been trading for one year. Extract an income statement for the year ended 30 June 2013 for M Kent. The trial balance as at 30 June 2013 is as follows:

M Kent
Trial Balance as at 30 June 2013

	Dr	*Cr*
	£	£
Rent and rates	1,560	
Insurance	305	
Lighting expenses	516	
Motor expenses	1,960	
Salaries and wages	4,850	
Sales		35,600
Purchases	30,970	
Trade expense	806	
Motor van	3,500	
Accounts payable		3,250
Accounts receivable	6,810	
Shop fixtures	3,960	
Shop buildings	28,000	
Cash at bank	1,134	
Drawings	6,278	
Capital		51,799
	90,649	90,649

Inventory at 30 June 2013 was £9,960.
(Keep your answer – it will be used later in Exercise 11.6X.)

CHAPTER 11

Statements of financial position

Learning objectives

After you have studied this chapter you should be able to:

- define a statement of financial position
- understand that a statement of financial position is prepared from the remaining balances in the trial balance after preparation of the trading and profit and loss accounts
- explain why a statement of financial position is not part of the double entry system
- explain the meaning of the terms non-current assets, current assets, current liability and long-term liability
- prepare a statement of financial position using the vertical method of presentation
- understand the importance of the term net current assets/working capital
- know which items appear in the owner's capital account.

11.1 Definition of a statement of financial position previously known as a 'balance sheet'

A **statement of financial position** is a financial statement setting out the book values of assets, liabilities and capital 'as at' a particular point in time. In simple terms the statement of financial position shows what a business *owns* and what it *owes* at a specific date.

Details of the assets, liabilities and capital have to be found in the records of the business and then written out in the statement of financial position. These details are readily available since they consist of all the balances remaining in the records once the trading and profit and loss account and income statement for the period have been completed. All balances remaining have to be assets, liabilities or capital since the other balances should have been closed off when the trading and profit and loss account was completed.

11.2 Preparing the statement of financial position

Let us look at Exhibit 11.1, the trial balance of B Swift (from Exhibit 10.6) as on 31 December 2013 after the trading and profit and loss account and income statement had been prepared.

Exhibit 11.1

B Swift
Trial Balance as at 31 December 2013
(after Trading and Profit and Loss Accounts completed)

	Dr	Cr
	£	£
Fixtures and fittings	5,000	
Accounts receivable	6,800	
Accounts payable		9,100
Inventory	3,000	
Bank	15,100	
Cash	200	
Capital		21,000
	30,100	30,100

We can now draw up a statement of financial position as at 31 December 2013, and this is shown in Exhibit 11.2. The layout is discussed further in section 11.4.

Exhibit 11.2

B Swift
Statement of Financial Position as at 31 December 2013

	£	£
Non-current assets		
Fixtures and fittings		5,000
Current assets		
Inventory	3,000	
Accounts receivable	6,800	
Cash at bank	15,100	
Cash in hand	200	
	25,100	
Less Current liabilities		
Accounts payable	9,100	
Net current assets/working capital		16,000
Non-current liabilities		
Long-term loan		–
Net assets		21,000
Financed by:		
Capital account		
Cash introduced		20,000
Add net profit for the year		8,000
		28,000
Less Drawings		7,000
		21,000

11.3 No double entry in statements of financial position

It may seem strange to you to learn that statements of financial position are *not* part of the double entry system.

If accounts are drawn such as the cash account, rent account, sales account, trading and profit and loss account, and so on, we are writing up part of the double entry system. We make entries on the debit and credit sides of these accounts.

In preparing a statement of financial position, we do not enter anything in the various accounts. We do not actually transfer the fixtures balance or the motor vehicles balance, or any of the others, to the statement of financial position. All that we do is to list the balances for assets, capital and liabilities to form the statement. This means that none of these accounts have been closed off. *Nothing is entered in the accounts.*

When the next accounting period starts, these accounts are still open containing balances. As a result of business transactions, entries are then made in these accounts to add to, or deduct from, the amounts shown in the accounts using normal double entry.

Hint: If you see the word 'account' you will know that it is part of the double entry system, and it will include debit and credit entries. If the word 'account' cannot be used, it is not part of double entry. For instance:

Trial balance:	A list of debit and credit balances in the accounting records.
Income statement:	A list of revenues received and expenses incurred during a specific period of time. The results of which show the business's gross and net profits for the period.
Statement of financial position:	A list of balances arranged according to whether they are assets, capital or liabilities.

11.4 Layout of the statement of financial position

The statement of financial position is one of the most important financial statements and as such it is important that the reader of this statement finds it easy to follow and understand. Over the years various ways of presenting the financial information have evolved. The present format of the statement is shown in Exhibit 11.2 above.

You will see that the statement of financial position starts by listing all the assets which the business 'owns'. These assets are split into two categories, non-current and current assets, and this is followed by details of the funds acquired to finance the business.

In Appendix B there is a model layout of the financial statements of a sole trader, namely the income statement and statement of financial position. You may find it useful to take a copy of these layouts and use them when undertaking exercises on the preparation of the financial statements.

Assets

Assets are shown under two headings, namely non-current assets and current assets.

Non-current assets

Non-current assets are assets that:

- are to be used in the business
- are expected to be of use to the business for a long time, and
- were not bought only for the purposes of resale.

Examples are buildings, machinery, motor vehicles, fixtures and fittings.

Non-current assets are listed first in the statement of financial position starting with those that the business will keep the longest, down to assets with the shortest life expectancy. For instance:

Non-current assets
1 Land and buildings
2 Fixtures and fittings
3 Machinery
4 Motor vehicles

Examples of non-current assets

Source: *Edexcel International GCSE Accounting* 1st edn, Edexcel (Robinson, S. 2010) Pearson Education Ltd.

Current assets

Current assets are assets that are likely to change in the near future and usually within 12 months of the date of the statement of financial position. They include goods for resale at a profit, accounts receivable, cash at bank and any cash in hand. These are listed starting with the asset that is least likely to be turned into cash, finishing with cash itself. The accepted order is listed as:

Current assets
1 Inventory
2 Accounts receivable
3 Cash at bank
4 Cash in hand

Liabilities

There are two categories of liabilities, **current liabilities** and **non-current liabilities**.

Current liabilities

Current liabilities are liabilities due for repayment in the short term, usually within one year. Examples are bank overdrafts, accounts payable for the supply of goods bought on credit and for resale.

Current liabilities are deducted from the current assets, as shown in Exhibit 11.2, to give the **net current assets** or **working capital**. This figure is very important in accounting since it shows the amount of resources the business has in the form of readily available cash to meet everyday running expenses.

Non-current liabilities

Non-current liabilities are liabilities not due for repayment in the near future. Examples are bank loans, loans from others such as friends or relatives, and mortgages. Non-current liabilities are deducted from the total figure of assets plus the net current assets as illustrated in Exhibit 11.2.

Capital account

This is the proprietor's or partners' account with the business. It will start with the balance brought forward from the previous accounting period, to which is added any personal cash introduced into the business and the net profit made by the business in this accounting period. Deducted from the capital account will be amounts drawn from the business and any loss made by the business. The final balance on the capital account should equal the net assets or net liabilities figure – and hence the statement of financial position balances. Exhibit 11.3 gives the standard format.

Exhibit 11.3

Capital Account

	£	£
Balance b/d		X
Add Cash introduced		X
Net profit for the period		X
		X
Less Drawings	X	
Net loss for the period	X	
		X
		X

It is important to note that the statement of financial position shows the position of the business at one point in time: the statement of financial position date, i.e. 'as at 31 December 2013'. It is like taking a snapshot of the business at one moment in time. On the other hand the income statement shows the profit/loss of that business for a period of time (normally a year), i.e. 'for the year ended 31 December 2013'.

Chapter summary

- The statement of financial position is a financial statement which lists the book values of assets, liabilities and capital 'as at' a specific date. It shows what a business 'owns' and 'owes' at a particular point in time.
- The statement of financial position is prepared from the remaining balances in the trial balance after the trading and profit and loss account and income statement has been completed.
- The statement of financial position is *not* part of the double entry system.
- The term 'non-current assets' means assets of a more permanent nature such as land and building, equipment and cars that are owned by the business. These are listed in the statement of financial position in descending order with the most permanent asset shown first.

- The term 'current assets' refers to assets that are likely to change within one year, for example, inventory, accounts receivable, cash at bank and cash in hand. These are listed in order of liquidity with the least liquid of the assets shown first, i.e. inventory and the most liquid asset shown at the bottom, i.e. cash in hand.
- The term net current assets or working capital is an important figure in accounting since it represents the amount of resources readily available for paying everyday running expenses.
- The capital account contains money invested by the owner of the business plus the net profit for the period less amounts taken out by the owner in the form of 'drawings'. If there is no net profit then a net loss will have been incurred.

EXERCISES

*Note: Questions with the suffix 'X' shown after the question number do **not** have answers shown at the back of the book. Answers to the other questions are shown in Appendix E.*

11.1 Complete exercise 10.3 by drawing up a statement of financial position as at 31 December 2013 for G Singh.

11.2X Complete exercise 10.4X by drawing up a statement of financial position as at 30 June 2013 for R Cairns.

11.3 Complete exercise 10.5 by drawing up a statement of financial position as at 31 March 2013 for Mrs P Stewart.

11.4 Miss V Holland had been trading for a number of years as a cheese retailer, making up accounts each year to 30 June. As at 30 June 2013 she was able to extract the following information from her accounting records and has asked you as her accountant to draw up the statement of financial position at that date:

(*a*) She owed amounts to businesses that had supplied her with cheese, totalling £4,565
(*b*) She was owed £2,375 by a customer who bought goods on credit
(*c*) She had cash in hand of £150
(*d*) Her bank account was overdrawn by £1,785
(*e*) She had stock of cheese unsold totalling £1,465
(*f*) She had a van that was used for deliveries and that was valued at £3,400 on 30 June 2013
(*g*) She had equipment valued at £2,885 at the year end
(*h*) She had introduced £2,000 of her own money in the year, when she was nearing her overdraft limit
(*i*) The business made a net profit of £2,525 in the year to 30 June 2013
(*j*) Miss V Holland drew £50 each week, for the whole year, and had no other drawings from the business
(*k*) The business had a loan from V Holland's mother for £2,000. This was not due to be repaid until the year 2015.

11.5X Complete exercise 10.6X by drawing up a statement of financial position as at 30 April 2012 for Miss R Burgess.

11.6X Complete exercise 10.7X by drawing up a statement of financial position as at 30 June 2013 for M Kent.

CHAPTER 12

Income statements and statements of financial position: further considerations

Learning objectives

After you have studied this chapter you should be able to:

- record sales returns and purchases returns in the trading account section of the income statement
- record carriage inwards on goods purchased as part of the cost of goods sold
- record carriage outwards as an expense in the profit and loss account section of the income statement
- adjust the financial statements to record the opening and closing inventory for the period
- appreciate that the cost of putting goods into a saleable condition is charged to the trading account
- prepare an income statement showing if either a gross profit/net profit is made or, alternatively, if a gross loss/net loss is incurred.

12.1 Dealing with sales and purchases returns in the trading account section of the income statement

When businesses are involved with the purchase and sale of goods it is inevitable that there are occasions when goods have to be returned by the purchaser to the supplier because they are damaged, faulty or perhaps not to the specification ordered. This was discussed fully in Chapter 5 where both sales and purchases returns were entered into the double entry system (see sections 5.7–5.9). In this chapter, we are going to take these returns into consideration when preparing the trading account section of the income statement and determining the gross profit.

In the trading account the sales returns and purchases returns are dealt with as follows:

- **sales returns** should always be deducted from **sales**
- **purchases returns** should always be deducted from **purchases**

Suppose that in Exhibit 10.1, the trial balance of K Wade, shown again below:

Exhibit 10.1

K Wade Trial Balance as at 31 December 2013 (extract)		
	Dr	*Cr*
	£	£
Sales		39,650
Purchases	27,150	

rather than simply containing a sales account balance of £39,650 and a purchases account balance of £27,150, the balance showing the inventory movement had been:

K Wade Trial Balance as at 31 December 2013 (extract)		
	Dr	*Cr*
	£	£
Sales		40,000
Purchases	27,350	
Sales returns	350	
Purchases returns		200

If we compare the two trial balances, i.e. the one shown in Exhibit 10.1 and the one shown above, the gross profit amount will be exactly the same. Sales in the original example were £39,650, while in the above example the sales returns are deducted from the sales as follows:

	£
Sales	40,000
Less Sales returns	350
Net sales	39,650

Purchases were originally shown as £27,150 but in the above example purchases returns will need to be deducted from purchases to ascertain the amount of goods retained by the business as shown below:

	£
Purchases	27,350
Less Purchases returns	200
Net purchases	27,150

The trading account section of the income statement using the figures from the above example will now appear as in Exhibit 12.1.

Exhibit 12.1

K Wade
Trading Account section of the Income Statement for the year ended 31 December 2013

	£	£
Sales		40,000
Less Sales returns		350
		39,650
Less Cost of goods sold		
Purchases	27,350	
Less Purchases returns	200	27,150
Gross profit		12,500

Student hint:
Many students have difficulty deciding whether sales returns should be deducted from sales or purchases figures and vice versa. The same applies to the purchases returns figure. The following illustration shows that the returns are always deducted from the figure on the opposite side so forming an 'X' on the trial balance:

K Wade
Trial Balance as at 31 December 2013 (extract)

	Dr £	*Cr* £
Sales		40,000
Purchases	27,350	
Sales returns	350	
Purchases returns		200

12.2 Carriage

When a business buys goods from a supplier the cost of delivering or transporting the goods also has to be paid. In accountancy terms, this cost of transport is often referred to as 'carriage'. Carriage charges for transporting goods purchased into a business is known as **carriage inwards**, whereas carriage charges for the delivery of goods to a business's customers is known as **carriage outwards**.

Carriage inwards

When goods are purchased one supplier may include carriage within the purchase cost while another may charge separately for carriage. When this happens the carriage inwards charge is always added to the cost of purchases in the trading account section of the income statement.

Carriage outwards

Carriage outwards is the cost of delivering the goods to the business's customers. It is an expense and not part of the selling price of the goods. Carriage outwards is always charged as an expense in the profit and loss account section of the income statement.

12.3 Dealing with carriage in the trading and profit and loss account

Suppose that in the illustration shown earlier of K Wade the goods had been bought for the same total figure of £27,350 but, in fact, £27,200 was the figure for purchases and £150 for carriage inwards. Let us also assume that part of the general expenses figure of £2,550, in Exhibit 10.1 was, in fact, carriage outward amounting to £400.

The trial balance would appear as in Exhibit 12.2.

Exhibit 12.2

K Wade Trial Balance as at 31 December 2013 (extract)		
	Dr £	*Cr* £
Sales		40,000
Purchases	27,200	
Sales returns	350	
Purchases returns		200
Carriage inwards	150	
Carriage outwards	400	
General expenses	2,150	

The trading and profit and loss account sections of the income statement would then be shown in Exhibit 12.3.

Exhibit 12.3

K Wade Income Statement for the year ended 31 December 2013		
	£	£
Sales		40,000
Less Sales returns		350
		39,650
Less Cost of goods sold		
Purchases	27,200	
Less Purchases returns	200	
	27,000	
Add Carriage inwards	150	27,150
Gross profit		12,500
Less Expenses:		
General expenses	2,150	
Carriage outwards	400	2,550
Net profit		9,950

It can be seen that the three versions of K Wade's trial balance have all been concerned with the same overall amount of goods bought and sold by the business, at the same overall prices. Therefore, in each case, the same gross profit of £12,500 is shown. The net profit of £9,950 also remains the same.

Before you proceed further you are advised to attempt Exercises 12.1 and 12.2X.

12.4 The second year of a business

Following on from Exhibit 11.2 in the previous chapter, we assume that B Swift carries on his business for another year. He then extracts a trial balance as on 31 December 2014 as shown as Exhibit 12.4. At that date inventory (stock) was valued at £5,500.

Exhibit 12.4

B Swift
Trial Balance as at 31 December 2014

	Dr £	*Cr* £
Sales		67,000
Purchases	42,600	
Electricity	1,900	
Rent	2,400	
Wages: store assistant	5,200	
General expenses	700	
Carriage outwards	1,100	
Buildings	20,000	
Fixtures and fittings	7,500	
Accounts receivable	12,000	
Accounts payable		9,000
Bank	1,200	
Cash	400	
Loan from J Marsh		10,000
Drawings	9,000	
Capital		21,000
Inventory (at 31 December 2013)	3,000	
	107,000	107,000

Adjustments needed for inventory

So far we have prepared the accounts for new businesses only. When a business starts it has no inventory brought forward. B Swift started his new business on 1 January 2013 so his first year of trading ended on 31 December 2013 when he had a closing inventory of £3,000. Therefore, when preparing his income statement for that year we are only concerned with the closing inventory figure of £3,000. When we prepare the income statement for the second year we can see the difference.

In the income statement for the first year of trading, i.e. the year ended 31 December 2013, only one figure for inventory appears; that is the closing inventory of £3,000. This figure of closing inventory for the year ended 31 December 2013 becomes the opening inventory for the second year of trading and will be entered into the trading account in Swift's second year of trading. Therefore, both opening and closing inventory figures are shown in the trading and profit and loss account section of the income statement for the year ended 31 December 2014.

The inventory figure shown in the trial balance given in Exhibit 12.4 is that brought forward from the previous year on 31 December 2013; it is, therefore, the opening inventory. The closing inventory at 31 December 2014 can only be found by an inventory check; assume that it amounts to £5,500.

The opening and closing inventory figures for Swift for the two years can now be summarised as follows:

Trading Account for period →	**Year to 31 December 2013**	**Year to 31 December 2014**
Opening inventory 1.1.2013	None	
Closing inventory 31.12.2013	£3,000	
Opening inventory 1.1.2014		£3,000
Closing inventory 31.12.2014		£5,500

Double entry for inventory

To enable you to understand the double entry aspect of inventory, both the inventory account and the trading account for B Swift for the year ended 31 December 2014 are shown below:

Inventory Account

2013		£	2013		£
Dec 31	Trading a/c	3,000	Dec 31	Balance c/d	3,000
2014			2014		
Jan 1	Balance b/d	3,000	Dec 31	Trading a/c	
Dec 31	Trading a/c			(Opening inventory)	3,000
	(Closing inventory)	5,500	Dec 31	Balance c/d	5,500
		8,500			8,500

B Swift
Trading and Profit and Loss Account for the year ended 31 December 2014

	£		£
Opening inventory	3,000	Sales	67,000
Purchases	42,600	Closing inventory	5,500
Gross profit c/d	26,900		
	72,500		72,500

The inventory at 31 December 2014 is £5,500 and had not been entered into the accounts previously. The entries above show how this has been recorded using double entry:

Debit: inventory account £5,500
Credit: trading account £5,500.

Calculation of cost of goods sold

Let us now calculate the cost of goods sold for B Swift for the year ended 31 December 2014:

	£
Inventory of goods at start of the year	3,000
Add Purchases	42,600
Total goods available for sale	45,600
Less What remains at the end of the year:	
(i.e. Closing inventory)	5,500
Therefore the cost of goods that have been sold	40,100

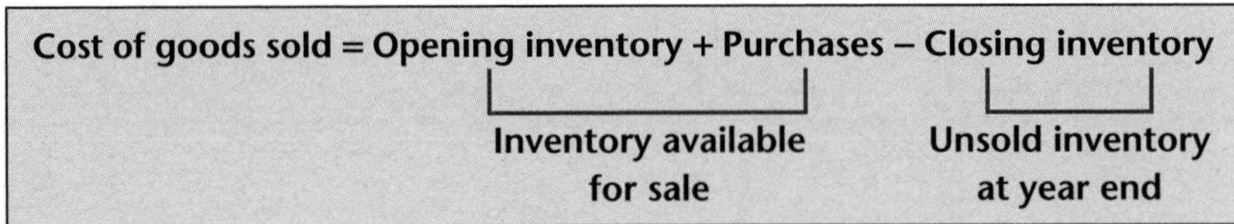

The gross profit can now be found by taking into consideration the effect the closing inventory has on the gross profit. Remember that sales less cost of goods sold equals gross profit therefore:

	£
Sales	67,000
Less Cost of goods sold (see above)	40,100
Gross profit	26,900

Now the income statement and statement of financial position can be drawn up as shown in Exhibits 12.5 and 12.6.

Exhibit 12.5

B Swift Income Statement for the year ended 31 December 2014		
	£	£
Sales		67,000
Less Cost of goods sold		
Opening inventory	3,000	
Add Purchases	42,600	
	45,600	
Less Closing inventory	5,500	
		40,100
Gross profit		26,900
Less Expenses		
Wages	5,200	
Carriage outwards	1,100	
Electricity	1,900	
Rent	2,400	
General expenses	700	
		11,300
Net profit		15,600

Exhibit 12.6

B Swift Statement of Financial Position as at 31 December 2014		
	£	£
Non-current assets		
Buildings		20,000
Fixtures and fittings		7,500
		27,500
Current assets		
Inventory	5,500	
Accounts receivable	12,000	
Cash at bank	1,200	
Cash in hand	400	
	19,100	
Less Current liabilities		
Accounts payable	9,000	
Net current assets		10,100
		37,600
Non-current liabilities		
Loan from J Marsh		10,000
Net assets		27,600
Financed by		
Capital account		
Balance at 1 January 2014		21,000
Add Net profit for the year		15,600
		36,600
Less Drawings		9,000
		27,600

12.5 Financial statements

The term **financial statements** is often given to the accounting statements which a business prepares at the end of its accounting period. These consist of the income statement previously known as the trading and profit and loss account and the statement of financial position previously known as the balance sheet. These financial statements are sometimes referred to as **final accounts**: however, this term can be somewhat confusing since none of the financial statements are really 'accounts' in the book-keeping sense. Many people do, however, still refer to them as the 'final accounts' or just simply 'the accounts' of a business.

12.6 Other expenses in the trading account

The costs of putting goods into a saleable condition should be charged in the trading account section of the income statement. In the case of a trader these are relatively few. An example might be a trader who sells clocks packed in boxes. If he bought the clocks from one source and the boxes from another source, both of these items would be charged in the trading account as purchases. In addition, if a person is paid wages to pack the clocks, then such wages would be charged in the trading account.

For goods imported from abroad it is usual to find that the costs of import duty, marine insurance and freight charges are also treated as part of the cost of goods sold and are, therefore, debited to the trading account.

12.7 Losses incurred by a business

So far, we have looked at the situation in which both a gross profit and a net profit have been made by a business. This will not always be the case in every business. For all kinds of reasons, such as poor trading conditions, bad management, or unexpected increases in expenses, the business may trade at a loss for a given period.

We will look at two cases, A Barnes, who made a gross profit but a **net loss** for the year, and K Jackson, who made both a gross loss and a net loss. The details for the income statements for the year ended 31 December 2012 for Barnes and Jackson are as follows:

	A Barnes	*K Jackson*
	£	£
Opening inventory 1 January 2012	3,500	9,200
Sales	21,000	33,000
Purchases	15,000	29,800
Closing inventory 31 December 2012	2,200	4,800
Other expenses	6,300	3,900

The income statements for each business can now be prepared, see Exhibits 12.7 and 12.8.

Exhibit 12.7

A Barnes
Income Statement for the year ended 31 December 2012

	£	£
Sales		21,000
Less Cost of goods sold		
Opening inventory	3,500	
Add Purchases	15,000	
	18,500	
Less Closing inventory	2,200	16,300
Gross profit		4,700
Less Other expenses		6,300
Net loss		1,600

In the above example of A Barnes a gross profit of £4,700 was made but since expenses of £6,300 were greater than that the final result is a net loss of £1,600.

Exhibit 12.8

K Jackson
Income Statement for the year ended 31 December 2012

	£	£
Sales		33,000
Less Cost of goods sold		
Opening inventory	9,200	
Add Purchases	29,800	
	39,000	
Less Closing inventory	4,800	34,200
Gross loss		1,200
Add Other expenses		3,900
Net loss		5,100

In the above example of K Jackson a gross loss of £1,200 occurred since the cost of goods sold amounted to £34,200 while sales were only £33,000. Added to this gross loss of £1,200 were the expenses of £3,900 for the period and a resultant net loss of £5,100.

Recording losses in the capital account

If a net loss occurs then it will be recorded in the owner's capital account as follows:

Debit: capital account
Credit: profit and loss account.

12.8 Step-by-step guide to preparing financial statements (preliminary level)

Many students have difficulty in the preparation of the financial statements and in remembering the layout. The following step-by-step guide should help you in their preparation:

Preparing the financial statements

1 Before starting the exercise in the trial balance, rule lines connecting each item. This avoids selecting a wrong figure which is easily done under the stress of an examination.
2 Decide which section of the financial statement each item should be entered *before* you start, i.e. trading account, profit and loss account section of the income statement or the statement of financial position. On the left-hand side of the trial balance use the following abbreviations to identify where each item should be entered:
   - T for trading account section
   - P/L for profit and loss account section
   - SF for the statement of financial position.
3 An *almost* infallible rule:
   - Each item displayed in the trial balance must only be entered *once* in the final statements.
   - Any item below a trial balance exercise should be dealt with *twice* (i.e. in the exercises following notice that the closing inventory figure is shown under the totals of the trial balance).

Dealing with adjustments in financial statements

1 **Sales returns** and **purchases returns:**
   (*a*) sales returns - deduct from sales in the trading account section
   (*b*) purchases returns - deduct from purchases in the trading account section.
2 **Carriage inwards** and **carriage outwards:**
   (*a*) carriage inwards - add to purchases in the trading account section
   (*b*) carriage outwards - charge as an expense in the profit and loss account section.

Note: In Appendix B you will find a model layout of the income statement and statement of financial position of a sole trader. Further step-by-step instructions in the preparation of the financial statements are also shown in Chapter 29.

Chapter summary

- The sales returns should always be deducted from the sales and the purchases returns deducted from the purchases; both are shown in the trading account section.
- The name 'carriage' means the cost of transport.
- Carriage inwards is the cost of transporting the goods purchased 'into' the business and, as such, is always *added* to the cost of purchases in the trading account section.
- Carriage outwards is the cost of delivering the goods sold to the customers and is shown as an expense in the profit and loss account section.
- When a new business first starts it has no opening inventory; however, at the end of the first year of trading an inventory check is carried out to ascertain the amount of inventory unsold, the closing inventory.
- The closing inventory of one year becomes the opening inventory of the next year.
- The inventory account is updated to record the closing inventory figure and to carry forward the balance from one period to the next.
- When preparing a trading account for the first year of business only the closing inventory figure is shown since there is no opening inventory.

- In the second year of business both the opening and closing inventory figures are shown in the trading account section.
- The calculation of the figure for *cost of goods sold* is shown which appears under this heading in the trading account section.
- The preparation of the income statement is shown including adjustments for sales returns, purchases returns, carriage inwards, and both the opening and closing inventory in the trading account section. Carriage outwards is shown as an expense in the profit and loss account section.
- A statement of financial position is shown indicating the entry of the closing inventory figure under the 'current asset' section.
- Any expenses incurred with getting the goods into a saleable condition are charged in the trading account.
- How to prepare an income statement if either a gross loss or net loss occurs is also shown.

EXERCISES

Note: Questions with the suffix 'X' shown after the question number do ***not*** *have answers shown at the back of the book. Answers to the other questions are shown in Appendix E.*

12.1 From the following details, prepare the trading account section of the income statement for the year ended 31 December 2012 for T Clarke.

		£
Carriage inwards		670
Sales		38,742
Purchases		26,409
Inventory of goods:	1 January 2012	6,924
	31 December 2012	7,489

12.2X The following details for the year ended 31 March 2012 are available. Prepare the trading account section of the income statement for that year for M Parkin.

		£
Inventory:	31 March 2011	16,492
	31 March 2012	18,504
Purchases		36,905
Carriage inwards		1,122
Sales		54,600

12.3 Prepare the income statement for the year ended 31 December 2013, in respect of T Mann, from the following details:

		£
Sales returns		490
Purchases returns		560
Purchases		31,000
Sales		52,790
Inventory of goods:	1 January 2013	5,690
	31 December 2013	4,230
Carriage inwards		1,700
Salaries and wages		5,010
Rent		1,460
Motor expenses		3,120
General expenses		420
Carriage outwards		790

12.4X An income statement for the year ended 31 December 2012 is to be prepared for K Lake from the following:

		£
Carriage outwards		490
Carriage inwards		210
Sales returns		1,500
Purchases returns		1,580
Salaries and wages		6,250
Rent		1,750
Sundry expenses		360
Sales		99,500
Purchases		64,570
Inventory of goods:	1 January 2012	18,280
	31 December 2012	17,360

12.5 From the following trial balance of Suzanne Curtis, draw up an income statement for the year ended 30 June 2013, and statement of financial position as at that date.

	Dr	*Cr*
	£	£
Inventory 1 July 2012	14,208	
Carriage outwards	1,200	
Carriage inwards	1,860	
Sales returns	1,230	
Purchases returns		1,932
Purchases	71,244	
Sales		111,600
Salaries and wages	23,172	
Rent and rates	1,824	
Insurance	468	
Motor expenses	2,656	
Telephone and internet	2,624	
Electricity	996	
General expenses	1,884	
Buildings	50,000	
Motor vehicles	10,800	
Fixtures and fittings	2,100	
Accounts receivable	23,376	
Accounts payable		20,386
Cash at bank	2,892	
Drawings	7,200	
Capital		85,816
	219,734	219,734

Inventory at 30 June 2013 was £17,700.

12.6X The trial balance shown below was extracted from the books of J Collins on 31 March 2013. Prepare the income statement for the year ended 31 March 2013 and a statement of financial position as at that date using the trial balance and the note regarding inventory.

J Collins
Trial Balance as at 31 March 2013

	Dr £	*Cr* £
Sales		74,400
Purchases	46,224	
Inventory 1 April 2012	15,104	
Carriage outwards	1,304	
Carriage inwards	936	
Salaries and wages	11,788	
Printing and stationery	810	
Telephone	756	
Travel expenses	490	
Rent	1,824	
Rates	1,080	
Sundry expenses	2,808	
Computer equipment	9,600	
Fixtures and fittings	2,400	
Accounts receivable	18,308	
Accounts payable		12,180
Cash at bank	15,504	
Cash in hand	480	
Drawings	8,540	
Capital		51,376
	137,956	137,956

Inventory at 31 March 2013 was £19,992.

12.7X G Bowyer manufactures sportswear, and for the year ended 31 October 2012 his sales were £76,540. He also paid carriage outwards of £4,275 to transport the sportswear to customers.

The materials purchased in the year amounted to £33,325, with an additional amount paid for carriage inwards of £2,715. Bowyer had inventory of £8,255 on 1 November 2011, and of £7,985 on 31 October 2012. He was owed £6,285 by customers, and owed £4,825 to suppliers on 31 October 2012. His bank balance was overdrawn by £3,335, and he had equipment valued at £11,125 and a van valued at £2,225 on that date.

His overheads for the year ended 31 October 2012 were:

	£
Rent and rates	6,000
Motor expenses	3,110
Salaries	7,450
Telephone	495
Insurance	500
General expenses	750

He drew £3,675 in the year to 31 October 2012 and had a balance brought forward on his capital account on 1 November 2011 of £5,485.

You are required to draw up the income statement for the year ended 31 October 2012, and a statement of financial position for G Bowyer at that date.

12.8 The following is the trial balance of J Smailes as at 31 March 2012. Draw up an income statement and statement of financial position for the year ended 31 March 2012.

	Dr	*Cr*
	£	£
Inventory 1 April 2011	18,160	
Sales		92,340
Purchases	69,185	
Carriage inwards	420	
Carriage outwards	1,570	
Purchases returns		640
Wages and salaries	10,240	
Rent and rates	3,015	
Communication expenses	624	
Commissions payable	216	
Insurance	405	
Sundry expenses	318	
Buildings	20,000	
Accounts receivable	14,320	
Accounts payable		8,160
Fixtures	2,850	
Cash at bank	2,970	
Cash in hand	115	
Loan from K Ball		10,000
Drawings	7,620	
Capital		40,888
	152,028	152,028

Inventory at 31 March 2012 was £22,390.

12.9X L Stokes drew up the following trial balance as at 30 September 2013. You are required to prepare an income statement for the year to 30 September 2013 and a statement of financial position.

	Dr	*Cr*
	£	£
Loan from P Owens		5,000
Capital		25,955
Drawings	8,420	
Cash at bank	3,115	
Cash in hand	295	
Accounts receivable	12,300	
Accounts payable		9,370
Inventory 30 September 2012	23,910	
Motor van	4,100	
Office equipment	6,250	
Sales		130,900
Purchases	92,100	
Sales returns	550	
Carriage inwards	215	
Purchases returns		307
Carriage outwards	309	
Motor expenses	1,630	
Rent	2,970	
Telephone charges	405	
Wages and salaries	12,810	
Insurance	492	
Office expenses	1,377	
Sundry expenses	284	
	171,532	171,532

Inventory at 30 September 2013 was £27,475.

CHAPTER 13

Accounting standards, rules and concepts

Learning objectives

After you have studied this chapter you should be able to:

- understand how the regulatory framework of accounting has developed in providing 'rules' for use in the preparation and presentation of financial statements via: 1. Accounting Standards; 2. Company Law; 3. Framework for the Preparation and Presentation of Financial Statements
- appreciate the growth of the Accounting Standards Board (ASB) and the development of accounting standards
- be aware of the formation of the International Accounting Standards Board (IASB) and its function
- understand what is meant by an accounting concept
- understand the main accounting concepts, i.e. business entity, going concern, accruals, materiality, consistency and prudence
- understand the other accounting concepts, i.e. realisation, historical cost, money measurement and dual aspect
- distinguish between 'objectivity' and 'subjectivity'
- understand the importance of confidentiality.

13.1 Introduction

So far in this book we have dealt with recording transactions and in this section we have dealt with the preparation of the financial statements of a sole trader from a trial balance. There are, however, other issues to consider with the preparation of the financial statements which are known as accounting concepts or 'rules' of accounting.

These concepts or rules have evolved over the years for practical as much as theoretical reasons. As a consequence this has made the preparation of the financial statements more standardised enabling the information to be more easily understood and reliable, and to enable clearer comparisons between different businesses.

13.2 The regulatory framework of accounting

The 'rules' of accounting which form the basis on which financial statements are prepared and presented is governed by the regulatory framework of accounting which includes:

1 Accounting Standards
2 Company Law
3 Framework for the Preparation and Presentation of Financial Statements.

The regulatory framework has developed and evolved over a number of years to help provide a basis for the preparation and presentation of financial statements. Such statements need to be reliable to users such as investors, employees, customers, suppliers and the government. They need to be presented in accordance with the standards, and be easily read and understood. This then allows for inter-business comparisons to be made by any interested party since the financial statements will be prepared using the same accounting rules and presentation format.

13.3 Accounting standards

At one time there were quite wide differences in the ways that accountants calculated profits, but in the late 1960s a number of high profile cases in the UK led to a widespread outcry against the lack of uniformity in financial reporting. Therefore, the past 40 years or so have seen many changes and developments in the financial reporting system.

Initially the Accounting Standards Committee (ASC) was formed by the UK accounting bodies in 1971 and this committee was responsible for issuing many Statements of Standard Accounting Practice (SSAPs) which accountants and auditors were expected to comply with. This body was replaced with the Accounting Standards Board (ASB) in 1990 and while this body took over the practices still in use at the time (SSAPs) they developed further standards known as Financial Reporting Standards (FRSs). More recently we have seen the introduction of Statement of Principles for Financial Reporting (SOP) which aims to set out the principles to be followed when preparing the financial statements.

In 1973 the International Accounting Standards Committee (IASC) was formed which later become the International Accounting Standards Board (IASB) in 2000. This board has been responsible for introducing International Accounting Standards (IASs) and International Financial Reporting Standards (IFRSs).

13.4 Company law

The Companies Acts of 1985, 1989 and 2006 state that all limited companies must prepare their financial statements in accordance with applicable accounting standards and comply with European Union Directives. It is, therefore, a legal requirement to comply with the rules.

13.5 Framework for the preparation and presentation of financial statements

This framework, developed by the International Accounting Standards Board (IASB), sets out the objectives used to form the basis on which financial statements are prepared and presented. It aims to provide a logical and consistent form of reference to be used by the IASB in the development of future international standards. The framework is not, however, an accounting standard, instead it is to be used as an aid to the standard setting process which underlies the principles in the preparation and presentation of financial statements.

13.6 The International Accounting Standards Board

Most of UK's larger companies, together with companies in the European Union, now comply with the International Accounting Standards which they were required to adopt in 2005. With the increase of multi-national organisations and the continued growth in international investment there are obvious advantages of adopting international standards such as:

- standardisation of the financial statements which enables companies operating in different countries to adhere to the same accounting standards
- making it easier for inter-business comparisons to be made since companies will be using the same presentation format and accounting standards.

13.7 Accounting concepts

There are a number of accounting concepts which form the basis on which the financial statements of an organisation are prepared and presented. These are outlined in two documents, namely:

- the framework for the preparation and presentation of financial statements
- the International Accounting Standard 1 (IAS 1) – Presentation of Financial Statements.

The main concepts will now be discussed but first we need to define an 'accounting concept'.

Definition of an accounting concept

A concept may be thought of as an idea. Therefore, an **accounting concept** is an idea that underpins the preparation of the financial statements of an organisation. Accounting concepts have developed over time to form the basic rules of accounting.

13.8 The main accounting concepts

The main accounting concepts which are used in preparing the financial statements of a business are shown in Exhibit 13.1.

Exhibit 13.1

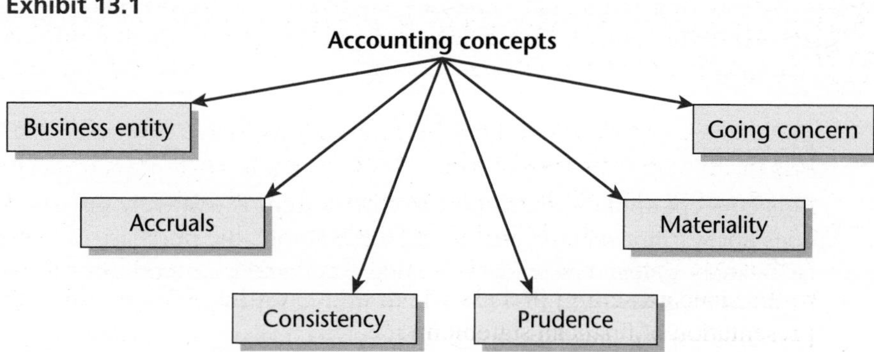

Business entity concept

The **business entity concept** implies that the affairs of a business are to be treated as being quite separate from the personal activities of the owner(s) of the business. In other words, only the activities of the business are recorded and reported in the business's financial statements. Any transactions involving the owner(s) are kept separate and are excluded.

The only time that the personal resources of the owner(s) affect the business's accounting records is when they introduce new capital into the business or take drawings.

Going concern concept

The **going concern concept** implies that the business will continue to operate for the foreseeable future. In other words, it is assumed that the business will continue to trade for a long period of time and there are no plans to cease trading and/or liquidate the business.

Accruals concept (or matching concept)

The **accruals concept** says that net profit is the difference between revenues and expenses rather than the difference between cash received and cash paid.

Revenues – Expenses = Net Profit

Sales are **revenues** when the goods or services are sold and *not* when the money is received, which can be after the end of the accounting period. Purchases are **expenses** when goods are bought, *not* when they are paid for. As we shall see in Chapter 29, items such as rent, insurance and motor expenses are treated as expenses when they are incurred, not when they are paid for. Adjustments are made when preparing financial statements for expenses owing (accruals) and those paid in advance (prepayments). Other adjustments that have to be made include adjusting for the depreciation of non-current assets and for probable bad debts, both of which will be discussed later.

Identifying the expenses used up to obtain the revenues is referred to as *matching* expenses against revenues, which is why this concept is also called the **matching concept**.

By showing the actual expenses *incurred* in a period matched against revenues *earned* in the same period, a correct figure of net profit will be shown in the income statement.

Materiality concept

This concept applies when the value of an item is relatively insignificant and as such does not warrant separate recording, for example, the purchase of a box of paper clips, calculator or small clock for the office. Such small expenditures are regarded as 'not material' and would be recorded in a general expense account, whereas, a non-current asset e.g. machinery would be classed as capital expenditure.

Consistency concept

The **consistency concept** requires that the same treatment be applied when dealing with similar items not only in one period but in all subsequent periods. The concept states that when a business has adopted a method for the accounting treatment of an item it should treat all similar items that follow in the same way when preparing the financial statements. Examples of when the consistency concept is used include:

- methods of depreciation (see Chapter 26)
- inventory valuation (see Chapter 31).

This concept is important since it assists in analysis of financial information and decision making, and it is vital that the organisation uses the same accounting principles each year. If the organisation was constantly changing its methods then this would result in misleading profits being calculated and inaccurate analyses and comparisons, hence the reason why the convention of consistency is used. However, this does not mean that the business must always use a particular method; it may make changes provided it has good reason to do so and each change is declared in the notes to the financial statements.

Prudence concept

When preparing financial statements accountants often have to use their judgement in determining the valuation of a particular asset or perhaps deciding whether an outstanding debt will ever be paid. It is the accountant's duty and responsibility to ensure that the financial statements are prepared as accurately as possible in disclosing the appropriate facts about a business. Therefore, the accountant should ensure that assets are not overvalued and similarly all liabilities should be identified. In other words, the accountant should display a certain amount of caution when forecasting a business's net profit or when valuing assets which are shown in the statement of financial position.

The **prudence concept** means that accountants will take the figure that will understate rather than overstate the profit. They must also ensure that all losses are recorded in the books but equally so ensure that profits are not anticipated by recording them before they have been gained.

The term **conservatism** was widely used to describe this concept until it was generally replaced by 'prudence'.

Other accounting concepts

In addition to the main accounting concepts there are several other concepts which are followed when preparing the financial statements of a business as shown in Exhibit 13.2.

Exhibit 13.2

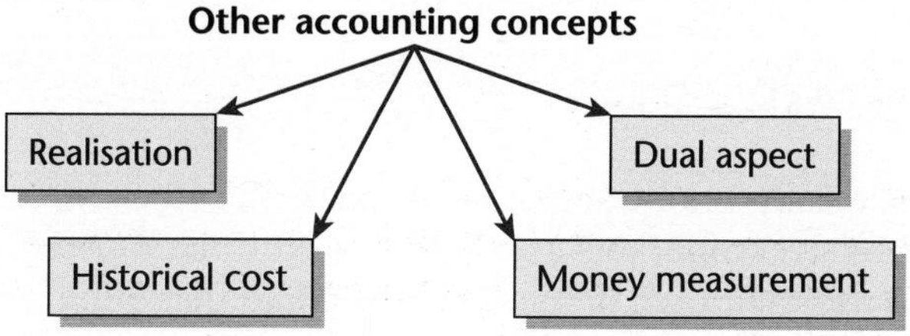

Other accounting concepts

- Realisation
- Historical cost
- Money measurement
- Dual aspect

Realisation concept

This accounting concept considers that profit should only be included in the income statement when it is reasonably certain that it has been earned. Profit is normally said to be earned when:

- goods or services are provided to the buyer, and
- the buyer incurs liability for them.

This concept of profit is known as the **realisation concept**. Note that it is *not*:

- when the order is received, or
- when the customer pays for the goods.

Historical cost concept

The assets of the business are recorded in the accounting records at cost price, i.e. the actual price paid for them, and this is known as the **historical cost concept**. For example, if a building cost £100,000 it will appear in the statement of financial position at that value.

The advantage of using the cost method of valuation is that the assets can be easily verified since there will be a source document (invoice) which can be used to check the amount entered in the books of account.

Money measurement concept

This concept states that only transactions and activities that can be measured in terms of money and whose monetary value can be assessed with reasonable objectivity will be entered into the accounting records.

Dual aspect concept

The concept whereby all transactions affect two aspects and as such affect two double entry accounts, one on the debit side and one on the credit side. The two aspects are always equal to each other. In other words:

Assets = Capital + Liabilities

As mentioned above double entry is the name given to the method of recording the transactions under the **dual aspect concept**.

13.9 Objectivity and subjectivity

It is especially important in accounting that the procedures or methods used are agreed by everyone, this approach is said to be *objective*. If, however, the owner(s) wish to use their own method or procedure that other people may not agree to, then this approach would be *subjective*.

Financial accounting seeks **objectivity** (rather than **subjectivity**) and must have rules which lay down the way in which the activities of the business are recorded. As we have already seen from the above these rules are known as **accounting concepts**.

13.10 Confidentiality

Although confidentiality is not a concept of accounting, employees who work within financial departments of an organisation and have access to its financial information should recognise that this information is confidential. They should not disclose sensitive information to anyone within the organisation except to those authorised to receive it.

Such information should only be disclosed 'outside' the organisation to bodies such as HM Revenue and Customs as this is required by legislation.

The organisation's auditors/accountants will also require access to the financial records to enable the preparation of the business's financial statements.

Chapter summary

- Financial statements are prepared for the use of the owner(s) of the business and others using rules known as accounting 'concepts'. If these 'concepts' are followed then it is easier for comparisons to be made between the financial statements of different businesses.
- Accounting concepts have evolved over the years by the regulatory framework which includes: 1. Accounting Standards; 2. Company Law; 3. Framework for the Preparation and Presentation of Financial Statements.
- More recently the UK and other European Union countries have adopted the International Accounting Standards.

- The main accounting concepts are: business entity, going concern, accruals, materiality, consistency and prudence. In addition there are many other concepts pertinent to organisations when preparing their financial statements.
- Objectivity means using a method that everyone can agree to whereas subjectivity means using a method that other people may not agree to, possibly derived from one's own personal preferences.
- Understanding the importance of confidentiality was also explained.

EXERCISES

*Note: Questions with the suffix 'X' shown after the question number do **not** have answers shown at the back of the book. Answers to the other questions are shown in Appendix E.*

13.1 Which accounting concept is used in each of the following accounting treatments? Explain.

(*a*) The cost of a tape dispenser has been charged to an expense account, although in fact it could still be in use in ten years' time.
(*b*) A sole proprietor has sold his private house, but has not recorded anything about it in the business records.
(*c*) A debt has been written off as a bad debt even though there is still a chance that the debtor eventually may be able to pay it.
(*d*) A machine has been bought for an exceedingly low figure, and it has been entered in the asset account at that figure even though it is worth more.
(*e*) An expert says that the value of the management team to the company is worth well over a million pounds, yet nothing is entered for it in the books.
(*f*) A motor van broke down in December 2012. The repair bill for it was not paid until 2013 yet it has been treated as a 2012 expense.
(*g*) A customer saw a carpet in 2012 and said he might well buy it. He phoned in 2013 and asked for the carpet to be delivered. The item was not treated as a sale in 2012 but instead was treated as a sale in 2013.
(*h*) The final day of the financial year saw the passing of a law that would make trading in our sort of goods illegal, and the business will have to close. The accountant says that our inventory figure cannot be shown at cost in the statement of financial position.
(*i*) We have been told that we cannot show our asset of motor cars at cost in one year and at cost plus the price increase the next year when the manufacturer increases prices of all cars, which also includes any of our unsold cars.
(*j*) We have shown all items of machinery costing less than £100 as machinery operating expenses.

13.2X When preparing the final accounts of your company, name the accounting concepts you should follow to deal with each of the following:

(*a*) Electricity consumed during the accounting period is still unpaid at the year end.
(*b*) The owner of the company has invested her private assets in the company.
(*c*) A customer who owes the company a large amount has been declared bankrupt, and the outstanding amount due to the company is now considered to be irrecoverable.
(*d*) The company has suffered substantial losses in the past few years, and it is extremely uncertain whether it can continue to operate next year.

13.3X Accounting concepts are used in preparing financial statements of a business.

(*a*) Briefly explain any three of the following concepts:
- (i) Going concern
- (ii) Accruals
- (iii) Consistency
- (iv) Prudence.

(*b*) Objectivity is important in analysing and preparing accounting information. Explain the term 'objectivity', giving an example as to how it might be applied.

13.4 Explain briefly what you understand by the 'historical cost concept'. Give an advantage of using the cost method of valuation.

13.5 As an accounts clerk you have been checking the 'aged debtors schedule' and have noticed that an account due from the Priory Paper Co for £187.00 has been outstanding for over six months. No response is gained from enquiries by telephone or letter and a visit is made to Priory's last known address by one of your sales representatives. She discovers that the premises are now occupied by a printing company whose owner tells her that the owner of Priory Paper Co is rumoured to have gone abroad.

Which accounting concept would you follow and what action would you recommend your company to take in dealing with this matter?

13.6 James works in the payroll department of a printing company. While having lunch a serior colleague asks him if he could let him know how much one of the directors earns. James is uncertain how to respond to his colleague's request and asks you, as Payroll Manager, what he should do. Draft an email to James advising him what to do in these circumstances.

PART 3

Books of original entry

This part is concerned with the books and journals into which transactions are first entered, together with chapters on business banking and VAT.

CHAPTER 14

Value added tax (VAT)

Learning outcomes

After you have studied this chapter you should be able to:

- understand how the value added tax system operates in the UK
- understand how VAT is collected and paid to HM Revenue and Customs (HMRC)
- be aware of the differences between the various rates of VAT
- appreciate how VAT affects various business categories
- calculate VAT on goods and services including when a cash discount is allowed
- calculate VAT when this is included in the total price of the goods and services
- prepare sales invoices including charges for VAT
- record VAT transactions in the book-keeping system
- complete a VAT Return form.

14.1 Value added tax (VAT)

VAT is a tax charged on the supply of most goods and services supplied by businesses within the UK and that exceed a certain amount of turnover (sales); such businesses must be registered for VAT. The turnover threshold usually increases each year as part of the Chancellor of the Exchequer's budget. VAT is administered in the UK by HMRC that has a very useful website at www.hmrc.gov.uk where information on all aspects of VAT can be found.

Once a business has been registered for VAT it is issued with a VAT Registration Number which must be quoted on all businesses documentation, for example, invoices, sales receipts, etc. When the business makes a sale of its goods or supplies a service to a customer VAT is added to the purchase price of the goods, this is known as **output VAT** to the supplier and **input VAT** to the customer.

There are exceptions to the goods and services supplied to which VAT is charged and this will be discussed later on in this chapter.

VAT is collected by businesses and paid to HMRC, usually on a quarterly basis. However, some businesses may decide to opt for reporting of VAT on an annual basis. There is also a scheme known as the **flat rate scheme** whereby businesses calculate VAT as a percentage of sales thereby avoiding the necessity to calculate input and output VAT on individual transactions. This scheme was designed to help small businesses and to reduce the work involved in accounting for VAT.

14.2 Payment of VAT

Once a business has been registered for VAT it is required to complete a VAT Return (see Exhibit 14.4 later) each quarter (or each year if it is using the annual basis of return) in which details of the business's purchases and sales and the VAT elements are listed. The VAT due for payment to HMRC is calculated as follows:

- the amount of VAT charged on sales, i.e. output VAT

  less

- the amount of VAT paid on purchases, i.e. input VAT.

In most cases businesses have to pay the difference between output VAT and input VAT to HMRC. However, some businesses have more input VAT than output VAT and in these circumstances the business will receive a refund of VAT from HMRC.

14.3 VAT rates

There are three rates of VAT in operation at the time of writing:

- standard rate, currently 20%
- reduced rate, currently 5%
- zero rate.

14.4 Goods and services applicable to VAT

Standard rate VAT

Most goods and services are subject to VAT at the standard rate of 20%.

Reduced rate VAT

This reduced rate of 5% applies to certain goods and services, for example:

- domestic fuel or power
- energy saving materials and security goods
- children's car seats.

Zero-rated goods and services

Some goods and services are zero-rated which means that VAT on these products is charged at 0%. Some examples are:

- food for human consumption (there are some exceptions such as chocolate biscuits, some confectionery, etc.)
- books and periodicals
- clothing and footwear for young children.

Exempt goods and services

There are also goods and services which are exempt from accounting for VAT. Such businesses neither add VAT onto the selling price of their goods or services nor do they obtain a refund of VAT on the amount they pay on the products they purchase. Examples of **exempt supplies** are:

- financial services
- postal services
- certain types of education.

14.5 Business categories

Zero-rated businesses

In the section above, the concept of **zero-rated supplies** was introduced where the rate of VAT charged was 0%. Since supplies in these businesses are subject to a rate of VAT (albeit 0%), any input VAT incurred, relating to the business, may be reclaimed.

Example 1: A book dealer sells £100,000 worth of books in a year and, during that year, purchases book shelving for £10,000 plus VAT at 20%.

The VAT reclaimable is therefore:

	Net (£)	*VAT (£) @ 20%*
Sales	100,000	Nil
Purchases	10,000	2,000
VAT reclaimable		2,000

A further example that would fall into this category would be a shop selling young children's shoes. The business would apply the 0% rate of VAT to the selling price of the children's shoes and would be able to reclaim any input VAT it paid out on the purchase of goods or services incurred in running the shop.

Exempted businesses

These are businesses that do not have to add VAT to the price of goods and services supplied by them, and that cannot obtain a refund of VAT paid on goods and services purchased by them. The type of businesses falling into this category include:

- Those dealing with financial matters, such as banks and credit card companies.
- Small businesses that are not registered for VAT since their turnover is below the VAT registration threshold, £77,000 (at the time of writing). These small businesses do not have to register for VAT unless they want to, in which case they would need to keep full accounting VAT records and charge VAT on the sale of their goods and services.
- Businesses that are registered for VAT can deregister if their turnover falls below a certain level (£75,000 at the time of writing).

The important thing to note is that input VAT directly attributable to exempt supplies or to non-VAT registered businesses cannot be reclaimed from HMRC.

Example 2: An insurance company sells £100,000 worth of insurance, and purchases furniture for its office for £10,000 plus VAT at 20%.

This business cannot reclaim the £2,000 input VAT on the furniture as it does not have any vatable supplies. The total amount paid for the furniture, £12,000, will be the cost to the business. Contrast this situation with the zero-rated supplier in Example 1 above who was able to reclaim £2,000.

Partly exempt business

Some VAT registered traders will sell some goods that are exempt from VAT and others that are either standard-rated or zero-rated. These businesses may reclaim part of the input VAT paid by them, but not all of it. The rules are complicated, but in essence the input VAT reclaimable will usually be proportionate to the standard- and zero-rated percentage of the business's total annual turnover.

14.6 How the VAT system works

In Exhibit 14.1 it can be seen that VAT is payable to HMRC whenever a sale is made. This progressive method of tax collection ensures a steady flow of funds for the government.

A toymaker manufactures toys from scraps of material and sells them to a wholesaler for £200 plus VAT. The wholesaler sells these to a retailer for £300 plus VAT, who in turn retails the toys to a number of private customers who are not VAT registered.

Exhibit 14.1 Calculation of VAT at 20% payable to HMRC

	Net (£)	VAT (£)	Type of VAT	VAT due to HMRC
Toymaker				
Sale of toys	200.00	40.00	Output	
less cost of materials	–	–		
VAT		40.00		£40.00
Wholesaler				
Sale of toys	300.00	60.00	Output	
less cost of toys	200.00	40.00	Input	
VAT		20.00		£20.00
Retailer				
Sale of toys	400.00	80.00	Output	
less cost of toys	300.00	60.00	Input	
VAT		20.00		£20.00
				£80.00

Exhibit 14.1 shows the total tax of £80 has been paid to HMRC at various stages in the distribution of the toys. It also shows that the retailer has charged its customers a total output VAT of £80. These customers are not VAT registered and have no input VAT to offset against the £80 paid by them so bear the full cost of VAT.

14.7 VAT calculations

Adding VAT to the basic cost of goods and/or services

Assuming that the VAT rate is 20% and the cost of goods is £100, the calculation is as follows:

$$£100 \times \frac{20}{100} = £20.00$$

Therefore total cost including VAT = £100.00 + £20.00 = £120.00.

Calculating VAT when it has already been included in the price

Often, only the gross amount of an item is known. This figure will, in fact, be made up of the net amount plus VAT. To find the amount of VAT that has been added to the net amount, the formula below can be used with any rate of VAT.

$$\text{VAT (£)} = \frac{\text{\% rate of VAT}}{(100 + \text{\% rate of VAT})} \times \text{Gross Amount}$$

If the gross amount was £420 and the rate of VAT was 20% it is only necessary to insert these figures in the formula.

$$\text{VAT (£)} = \frac{20}{(100 + 20\%)} \times 420 = \frac{20}{120} \times 420 = £70$$

The net amount would then be £420 – £70 = £350. Alternatively, the net amount can be calculated thus:

$$\textbf{Net Amount (£)} = \frac{100}{(100 + \%\text{ rate of VAT})} \times \textbf{Gross Amount}$$

$$\text{Net Amount (£)} = \frac{100}{(100+20)} \times 420 = \frac{100}{120} \times 420 = £350$$

Note: When calculating VAT, the VAT is always rounded down to the nearest penny, i.e. VAT of £6.3579 becomes £6.35 and not £6.36.

Preparing a sales invoice

If a business is VAT registered it will need to add VAT onto the value of goods sold to a customer when it is preparing its sales invoice. The following example illustrates the preparation of a sales invoice.

Example: On 16 November 2012, S Shah, who runs a business selling electrical appliances, of Park House, Bankside Road, York YK6 24BD, sold the following goods to Cooper's Ltd, Unit 77, Astley Business Park, York YK6 72PQ. Their order number is N/9721:

10 Deluxe Electric Kettles @ £12.00 each
6 Slow Cookers @ £28.00 each
2 Bedside Lamps @ £45.00 each

All goods are subject to 20% VAT. The sales invoice is numbered 4/457 and the VAT registration number is 873 7902 93 – see Exhibit 14.2.

Exhibit 14.2

INVOICE

S Shah
Park House, Bankside Road
York YK6 24BD
VAT Reg No. 873 7902 93

To: Cooper's Ltd
Unit 77
Astley Business Park
York YK6 72PQ
Order No. N/9721

Invoice No. 4/457

Date: 16 November 2012

	£
10 Deluxe Electric Kettles @ £12.00 each	120.00
6 Slow Cookers @ £28.00 each	168.00
2 Bedside Lamps @ £45.00 each	90.00
	378.00
Add VAT 20%	75.60
	453.60
Terms: Net monthly	

14.8 VAT and cash discounts

Where a cash discount is offered for prompt payment, VAT is calculated on an amount represented by the value of the invoice less such a discount. Even if the cash discount is lost because of late payment, the VAT charged will not change.

Exhibit 14.3 shows an example of such a sales invoice, assuming a cash discount offered of 2.5% and a VAT rate at 20%.

Exhibit 14.3

ATC Ltd
18 High Street
London WC2E 9AN

INVOICE No ZT 48910

VAT Reg No: 313 5924 71
Date/tax point: 11 May 2012
Your order no: TS/778

To: R Noble
Belsize Road
Edgeley
Stockport

	£
500 paper dispensers @ £20 each	10,000.00
Less Trade Discount @ 15%	1,500.00
	8,500.00
Add VAT 20%	1,657.50
Terms – 2.5% cash discount if paid within one month.	10,157.50

Using the invoice in Exhibit 14.3 the VAT is calculated as follows.

Step-by-step guide to calculating VAT where cash discounts are involved

1. Calculate the cost of the goods (500 × £20) = £10,000.
2. Calculate the **trade discount** (15% × £10,000) = £1,500.
3. Deduct the trade discount from the cost of the goods to find the net price of the goods (£10,000 – £1,500 = £8,500).
4. Calculate the **cash discount** on the net price of the goods (2.5% × £8,500 = £212.50).
5. Calculate the VAT at 20% on the net amount less the cash discount (20% × (£8,500 – £212.50) = £1,657.50).
6. Add the VAT to the net price of the goods *prior* to deducting the cash discount to arrive at the invoice total (£8,500 + VAT £1,657.50 = £10,157.50).
7. If the cash discount was claimed the amount payable would be £9,945.00.

Note Trade discount is dealt with in Chapter 16 section 16.8 and cash discount is shown in Chapter 21 section 21.7.

14.9 VAT on items other than sales and purchases

VAT is not just paid on purchases of raw materials and goods for resale. It is also payable on many items of expense and on the purchase of non-current assets.

Businesses that *can* get refunds of VAT paid will not include VAT as part of the cost of the expense or non-current asset. Businesses that *cannot* get refunds of VAT paid will include the VAT cost as part of the expense or non-current asset. For example, two businesses buying similar items would treat the following items as shown:

	Business that can reclaim VAT		*Business that cannot reclaim VAT*	
Buys Machinery	Debit Machinery	£200	Debit Machinery	£240
£200 + VAT £40	Debit VAT Account	£40		
Buys Stationery	Debit Stationery	£160	Debit Stationery	£192
£160 + VAT £32	Debit VAT Account	£32		

14.10 VAT owing

VAT owing by or to the business can be included with accounts receivable or accounts payable, as the case may be. There is no need to show the amount(s) owing as separate items.

14.11 Relief from VAT on bad debts

It is possible to claim relief on any debt that is more than six months old and has been written off in the accounts. Should the debt later be paid, the VAT refunded will then have to be paid back to HMRC.

14.12 Purchase of cars

Normally, the VAT paid on a car bought for a business is not reclaimable.

14.13 VAT records

All VAT records must be retained by a business for a period of six years.

14.14 VAT return forms

At the end of each VAT accounting period, a 'Form VAT 100' has to be completed and sent to HMRC. The following example provides the information for completion of the VAT Account and completion of the VAT Return.

Example 1: Bayley (Supplies) Ltd financial data for the quarter ended 30 June 2012 is as follows:

		Purchases	
	Total	*Net*	*VAT*
2012	£	£	£
30 April	12,000	10,000	2,000
31 May	18,000	15,000	3,000
30 June	21,600	18,000	3,600
	51,600	43,000	8,600

		Sales	
	Total	*Net*	*VAT*
2012	£	£	£
30 April	24,000	20,000	4,000
31 May	36,000	30,000	6,000
30 June	43,200	36,000	7,200
	103,200	86,000	17,200

The company's expenses for the quarter were as follows:

		Expenses	
	Total	*Net*	*VAT*
2012	£	£	£
30 April	480	400	80
31 May	720	600	120
30 June	1,200	1,000	200
	2,400	2,000	400

In addition to the above the company purchased a non-current asset on 1 June 2012 for £12,000 plus VAT of £2,400.

Note: The expenses listed above and the purchase of the non-current asset could be entered in the day book alongside other purchases, however, in this example they have been shown separately to demonstrate the various items that are entered into both the VAT account and VAT return.

The above information is now entered into the company's VAT Account as follows:

VAT Account

2012			*2012*		
April 30	Purchases Day Book	2,000	April 30	Sales Day Book	4,000
"	Expenses	80	May 31	Sales Day Book	6,000
May 31	Purchases Day Book	3,000	June 30	Sales Day Book	7,200
"	Expenses	120			
June 30	Purchases Day Book	3,600			
"	Expenses	200			
"	Non-current Assets	2,400			
"	Balance c/d	5,800			
		17,200			17,200
Aug 7	Bank	5,800	July 1	Balance b/d	5,800

The VAT Return is now completed as shown in Exhibit 14.4. The contents of the columns on form VAT 100 are now explained:

1 This box refers to the amount of VAT charged as output tax on sales invoices.
2 This box would show the VAT due (but not paid) on all goods and related services acquired in this period from other EC Member States. In this case there were no such transactions.
3 Total of boxes 1 and 2: the total output tax due.
4 This box contains the total input tax we are able to reclaim on all purchases and expenses incurred during the period. The quarter's total is £11,400.
5 This is the difference between boxes 3 and 4 since £17,200 VAT has been collected from our customers, but only £11,400 has been incurred on all purchases and expenses. Therefore HMRC is owed £5,800, i.e. £17,200 – £11,400 = £5,800.
6 The total value of sales outputs for the period was £86,000, excluding VAT.
7 The total value of purchases inputs, expenses and non-current asset was £57,000 excluding VAT (i.e. purchases £43,000 + expenses £2,000 + fixed asset £12,000).
8 Sales to EC Member States are entered in this box. In our example the company had not made any sales to EC Members States.*
9 Any acquisitions from EC Member States would be entered here. No purchases from EC Member States had been made in our example.*

*See section 14.15.

Only boxes 1, 3, 4 and 5 actually refer to accounting for VAT. The other boxes are for statistical purposes so that the UK government can assess the performance of the economy and similar matters.

Exhibit 14.4

HM Customs and Excise

Value Added Tax Return

For the period

01.04.12 to 30.06.12

For Official Use

SPECIMEN

Registration Number: 531 8210 44

Period: 06.12

Bayley (Supplies) Ltd
Park Lane
Cougleton
CW12 7EJ

You could be liable to a financial penalty if your completed return and all the VAT payable are not received by the due date.

Due date: 31.07.12

For Official Use

Before you fill in this form please read the notes on the back and the VAT leaflets *"Filling in your VAT return"* and *"Flat rate scheme for small businesses"*, if you use that scheme. Fill in all boxes clearly in ink, and write 'none' where necessary. Don't put a dash or leave any box blank. If there are no pence write "00" in the pence column. **Do not** enter more than one amount in any box.

For official use

	Box	£	p
VAT due in this period on **sales** and other outputs	1	17,200	00
VAT due in this period on **acquisitions** from other **EC Member States**	2	NONE	
Total VAT due (**the sum of boxes 1 and 2**)	3	17,200	00
VAT reclaimed in this period on **purchases** and other inputs (including acquisitions from the EC)	4	11,400	00
Net VAT to be paid to Customs or reclaimed by you (Difference between boxes 3 and 4)	5	5,800	00
Total value of **sales** and all other outputs excluding any VAT. **Include your box 8 figure**	6	86,000	00
Total value of **purchases** and all other inputs excluding any VAT. **Include your box 9 figure**	7	57,000	00
Total value of all **supplies** of goods and related costs, excluding any VAT, to other **EC Member States**	8	NONE	00
Total value of all **acquisitions** of goods and related costs, excluding any VAT, from other **EC Member States**	9	NONE	00

If you are enclosing a payment please tick this box. ✓

DECLARATION: You, or someone on your behalf, must sign below.

I, CHARLES BAYLEY declare that the

(Full name of signatory in BLOCK LETTERS)

information given above is true and complete.

Signature L. Bayley Date 14 July 2012

A false declaration can result in prosecution

F

VAT 100

Note: VAT Forms are normally submitted on-line.

14.15 Sales and purchases to EC Member States

In the above example, Bayley (Supplies) Ltd, it was assumed that the company had not made any sales to or purchased goods from EC Member States. However, in the past few years more and more UK businesses are dealing with European businesses; in these cases it will be necessary to complete boxes 8 and 9. This is now illustrated with the following example:

Example 2: Let us assume that in the example above, Bayley (Supplies) Ltd sold £20,000 of goods and also purchased £10,000 of goods from EC Member States in the quarter ended 30 June 2012. These transactions would need to be included in the VAT return as follows:

- Box 8 – enter the £20,000 of goods sold to EC Member States, this figure is then added to the total in Box 6 (i.e. £86,000 + £20,000 = £106,000).
  Note: Sales to EC Member States do not have VAT charged on them provided the company has obtained the VAT registration number from the overseas business.
- The company's acquisitions of £10,000 is dealt with as shown below:
  1. In Box 9 enter the value of the acquisition, i.e. £10,000.
  2. Calculate the VAT on the acquisition, i.e. 20% of £10,000 = £2,000.
  3. In Box 2 enter the figure of VAT £2,000.
  4. Add Box 1 and 2 together to give £17,200 + £2,000 = £19,200 and enter this figure into Box 3.
  5. In Box 4 add the figure of VAT to the VAT reclaimed figure, i.e. £2,000 + £11,400 = £13,400.
  6. In Box 5 the amount of VAT due to be paid remains the same as in our first example, i.e. £5,800.
  7. In Box 7 add the value of the acquisitions, i.e. £10,000, to the total purchases figure of £57,000 to give a figure of £67,000.

The VAT Return shown in Exhibit 14.4 will now need amending – see Exhibit 14.5.

Exhibit 14.5

HM Customs and Excise

Value Added Tax Return

For the period
01.04.12 to 30.06.12

For Official Use

SPECIMEN

Registration Number	Period
531 8210 44	06.12

Bayley (Supplies) Ltd
Park Lane
Cougleton
CW12 7EJ

You could be liable to a financial penalty if your completed return and all the VAT payable are not received by the due date.

Due date: 31.07.12

For Official Use

Before you fill in this form please read the notes on the back and the VAT leaflets *"Filling in your VAT return"* and *"Flat rate scheme for small businesses"*, if you use that scheme. Fill in all boxes clearly in ink, and write 'none' where necessary. Don't put a dash or leave any box blank. If there are no pence write "00" in the pence column. **Do not** enter more than one amount in any box.

For official use		Box	£	p
	VAT due in this period on **sales** and other outputs	1	17,200	00
	VAT due in this period on **acquisitions** from other EC Member States	2	2,000	00
	Total VAT due (**the sum of boxes 1 and 2**)	3	19,200	00
	VAT reclaimed in this period on **purchases** and other inputs (including acquisitions from the EC)	4	13,400	00
	Net VAT to be paid to Customs or reclaimed by you (Difference between boxes 3 and 4)	5	5,800	00
	Total value of **sales** and all other outputs excluding any VAT. **Include your box 8 figure**	6	106,000	00
	Total value of **purchases** and all other inputs excluding any VAT. **Include your box 9 figure**	7	67,000	00
	Total value of all **supplies** of goods and related costs, excluding any VAT, to other **EC Member States**	8	20,000	00
	Total value of all **acquisitions** of goods and related costs, excluding any VAT, from other **EC Member States**	9	10,000	00

If you are enclosing a payment please tick this box. ✓

DECLARATION: You, or someone on your behalf, must sign below.

I, CHARLES BAYLEY declare that the
(Full name of signatory in BLOCK LETTERS)
information given above is true and complete.

Signature L. Bayley Date 14 July 2012

A false declaration can result in prosecution

F

VAT 100

Note: VAT Forms are normally submitted on-line.

Note: All businesses registered for VAT that make sales to businesses registered for VAT in EC Member States will also be required to complete an 'EC Sales List'. The form lists details of the business's EC supplies and is supplied with the VAT Form 100 from HMRC.

14.16 VAT on goods taken for private use

If a trader takes some goods out of his own business inventory for his own private use, the trader should be charged with any VAT due on these goods.

For instance, suppose that Smith, a furniture dealer, takes a table and chairs out of inventory for permanent use in his own home. The cost to the business has been (cost price + value added tax). Therefore the proprietor's drawing should be charged with both the cost price of goods plus the VAT.

The double entry needed, assuming goods taken of £1,000 + VAT at 20%, would, therefore, be:

	£	£
Dr Drawings	1,200	
Cr Purchases		1,000
Cr VAT		200

There can be complicating circumstances, outside the scope of this book, that might influence the amount of VAT to be charged on such drawings.

Note: In this chapter VAT has been introduced and we have shown how businesses that are VAT registered have to charge VAT on the goods and services they offer to their customers. The VAT charge is shown on the invoice (see section 14.7) and the invoice will then need to be entered into the business's books of account.

In Chapter 15 'Business Documents' which follow, you will see further examples of invoices, credit notes and other documentation relative to the purchase and sale of goods and/or services.

Chapters 16–19 explain and demonstrate how the invoices and credit notes are entered into the books of account using day books, ledgers and accounting for VAT.

Chapter summary

- Value added tax (VAT) is a tax levied on sales by the UK government. It is described as an 'indirect tax' and ultimately the tax is paid by the final consumer of the goods or services.
- VAT is administered in the UK by HM Revenue and Customs (HMRC).
- There are currently three rates of VAT, namely: standard rate, currently 20%; reduced rate, currently 5%; and zero rate.
- The way in which the VAT system operates is explained whereby VAT is collected at various stages in the distribution chain.
- Businesses may be classified as standard-rated, zero-rated, exempt or partially exempt.
- The preparation of a sales invoice subject to VAT is demonstrated.

- If a business allows cash discount for prompt payment the VAT is calculated on the sales value less any cash discount offered. If the cash discount is lost because of late payment the VAT will not change.
- VAT may also be incurred on items of expense and the purchase of non-current assets.
- The book-keeping entries for recording VAT are shown in a VAT Account.
- At the end of a particular period, either quarterly or annually, a VAT return form is submitted to HMRC together with any payment due. Alternatively, there may be a refund due.

EXERCISES

Note: Questions with the suffix 'X' shown after the question number do ***not*** *have answers shown at the back of the book. Answers to the other questions are shown in Appendix E.*

14.1 On 1 May 2012, D Wilson Ltd, 1 Hawk Green Road, Stockport, sold the following goods on credit to G Christie & Son, The Golf Shop, Hole-in-One Lane, Marple, Cheshire:

Order No A/496
3 sets of 'Boy Michael' golf clubs at £240.00 per set.
150 Watson golf balls at £8.00 per 10 balls.
4 Faldo golf bags at £30.00 per bag.
Trade discount is given at the rate of $33^1/_3$%.
All goods are subject to VAT at 20%.

Required:
You are required to calculate the following:

(*a*) the total cost before discount
(*b*) the trade discount
(*c*) the total cost after deducting the trade discount
(*d*) the VAT at the rate of 20%
(*e*) the total cost.

14.2 Triton Ltd sells sports bags to retailers at a price of £6.00 per bag (excluding VAT). To promote sales it is offering a trade discount of $33^1/_3$% for orders of ten bags or more. In today's post it receives the following orders from retailers:

(*a*) Ashlea Sports – 20 bags
(*b*) Redferns Camping – 10 bags
(*c*) Base Camp – 5 bags
(*d*) Samuel's Sports – 30 bags.

For each of the above orders you are required to calculate:

- the total cost before trade discount
- the trade discount
- the total cost after deducting the trade discount
- the VAT at the rate of 20%
- the total cost.

In each case show your workings.

14.3 Recalculate the amount due for each of the customers in question 14.2 above after allowing for a 2.5% cash discount.

14.4X You work for Roberts Suppliers which sells hardware, tools, kitchenware, etc. to both cash and credit customers. Sales invoices are prepared on a weekly basis, each Friday, and are made out from the order details which are shown below:

(*a*) Rudkin Superstores – 6 sets of pans at £78.00 per set
– 10 washing-up bowls (deluxe) at £4.50 each
(*b*) Burgess & Son – 5 electric kettles at £10.00 each
– 10 boxes of wine glasses at £14.00 per box
(*c*) Hargreaves Ltd – 4 cutlery sets at £80 per set
– 6 hammers at £9.40 per hammer

You are required to calculate the following for each of the customers' orders shown above:

- the total cost before trade discount
- the trade discount @ 25%
- the total cost after deducting the trade discount
- the VAT at the rate of 20%
- the total cost.

In each case show your workings.

14.5X Recalculate the amount due for each of the customers in 14.4X above after allowing for a 2.5% cash discount.
In each case show your workings.

14.6 At the quarter ending 30 June 2012 the following details of purchases, sales and VAT (at 20%) were extracted from the books of Ivy & Co.

	Purchases		*Sales*	
2012	*Net*	*20% VAT*	*Net*	*20% VAT*
	£	£	£	£
April	50,000	10,000	52,600	10,520
May	42,000	8,400	48,000	9,600
June	55,000	11,000	60,000	12,000

Required:
(*a*) Write up and balance the VAT account in the books of Ivy & Co for the quarter ended 30 June 2012.
(*b*) Explain the significance of the outstanding balance and how it will be cleared.

14.7X The following information was extracted from the books of Mason Motors Ltd for the quarter ended 31 December 2012.

	Purchases		*Sales*	
2012	*Net*	*20% VAT*	*Net*	*20% VAT*
	£	£	£	£
October	37,600	7,520	75,000	15,000
November	39,400	7,880	62,000	12,400
December	52,000	10,400	68,000	13,600

Required:

(*a*) From the above details write up the VAT account for the quarter ended 31 December 2012.
(*b*) For what period of time must VAT records be kept?
(*c*) What book-keeping entries would be required to record a cash refund of £120 (including VAT at 20%) to a customer?

14.8 You have been asked to prepare the sales invoice amount for photographic equipment recently delivered to your customer, Lawton Photography. The total amount of equipment supplied amounted to £2,320 (excluding VAT). The customer is entitled to the following discounts:

- trade discount 12.5%
- cash discount 2.5% (for payment within 7 days)
- calculate VAT at the rate of 20%.

Required:

Calculate the total amount of the sales invoice showing all your workings.

14.9X (*a*) Photoprint Ltd recently purchased 22 reams of special printing paper for Job No. 67 at a cost of £3.75 per ream each plus VAT at 20%. When the job was complete Photoprint Ltd charged the customer £240.00 inclusive of VAT at 20%. How much VAT is owed to HMRC in respect of Job No. 67?

(*b*) The following amounts include VAT at a rate of 20%.
£48.00
£2.10
£66.60
£3.90
For each item calculate both the net and VAT amounts.

CHAPTER 15

Business documentation

Learning objectives

After you have studied this chapter you should be able to:

- understand the various documentation used in the buying and selling process
- follow the purchasing process from the quotation to the purchase order and subsequently the advice note, delivery note and invoice
- appreciate the documents used when goods or services are not satisfactory, i.e. the returns notes and credit notes
- understand the need for the supplier to send a statement of account to the purchaser at the end of the month
- appreciate the use of a remittance advice which is usually provided by the purchaser of the goods or services.

15.1 Introduction

All businesses and organisations are involved in trading, i.e. the buying and selling of goods and/or services in order to make a profit. The financial transaction of buying and selling involves some very important documents which are used by both the buyer and the seller. The documents have been in general use for many years and are part of an established procedure. Their proper use enables trading to proceed smoothly and in the event of a dispute between a buyer and a seller, the matter can normally be settled quickly. Since both parties use the same documents they will be dealt with in the sequence normally found in the trading activity.

A diagram of the flow of documents is shown in Exhibit 15.1.

Exhibit 15.1 The trading activity

THE FLOW OF DOCUMENTS		
Action by seller (supplier)	**Sequence**	**Action by buyer (purchaser)**
Sends	QUOTATION →	Receives
Receives	← PURCHASE ORDER	Sends
Sends	ADVICE NOTE →	Receives
Sends	DELIVERY NOTE (with goods) →	Receives and raises goods received note
Sends	INVOICE →	Receives
Receives and raises goods received note	← RETURNS NOTE* (if goods are faulty, etc.)	Sends
Sends after approval to give credit	CREDIT NOTE* →	Receives
Sends	STATEMENT OF ACCOUNT →	Receives
Receives	← REMITTANCE ADVICE (payment)	Sends

*Both the returns note and the credit note would only be used if there was some problem with the goods supplied.

15.2 Quotation

At the request of a prospective purchaser a company will issue a **quotation** (an offer to supply goods or services). The quotation will normally be in the form of a formal document detailing what is to be supplied, when, where and the price. It will also state the terms and conditions of sale, under which the company is prepared to supply the goods or services. Some suppliers may have a standard range of products to offer and issue a catalogue as the quotation from which purchasers may order goods.

The quotation is a very important document since it could well be the starting point for a contract between the supplier and the purchaser. On receiving the quotation the purchaser should ensure it meets their full requirements before raising a purchase order.

15.3 Purchase order

When a business or organisation decides to buy goods or engage the services of another company it usually issues a **purchase order**.

This document contains the following information:

- name and address of supplier
- purchase order number
- date of order
- details of the goods or services ordered including part numbers or catalogue references
- quantity required
- delivery date
- authorised signature of a senior member of the company such as the buyer.

It is normally raised by the customer's purchasing office and then sent to the supplier. Once it has been accepted by the supplier a formal contract will exist between the two parties.

An example of a purchase order is shown in Exhibit 15.2 where goods have been ordered from a catalogue.

Exhibit 15.2 Purchase order

PURCHASE ORDER

Champion Sports
Fairway,
Leeds, LS2 8BD

Tel: 0131 874428
Ace Sports
High Street
Manchester
MM1 4TC
Please supply

VAT Reg: 811 6571 56
order number: 4355
date: 6 April 2013

Quantity	*Description*	*Unit price* £	£
20	Rugby Shirts ref 25	12.00	240.00
20	Rugby Shirts ref 14	8.00	160.00
			400.00
		VAT at 20%	80.00
			480.00

Delivery Required: Early May

T. Smith
Purchasing Manager

15.4 Advice note

An **advice note** is sent to the customer before the goods are despatched. This means that the customer will know that the goods are on the way and should they not arrive within a reasonable time then the customer will notify the supplier.

The advice note, delivery note and the invoice contain the same information except that the invoice will have the price details.

15.5 Delivery note

When the company supplying the goods is ready to despatch them to the purchaser they prepare a **delivery note** (sometimes called a despatch note). This contains the following information:

- name and address of purchaser
- date and number of customer's purchase order
- details of goods despatched including their description and part number or catalogue reference
- quantity being supplied
- delivery address and any relevant instructions, i.e. must be delivered between 8 a.m. and 6 p.m.

Price details are not shown on this document. When a supplier uses its own transport or the services of a carrier a copy of the delivery note will be signed by the receiving company and this note will be returned to the supplier. This copy will be safely filed as it may be needed as 'proof of delivery' of the goods should a dispute arise as to their safe receipt.

Note: Both the advice note and delivery note are only usually used where the consignments delivered require a proof of receipt.

15.6 Invoice

An invoice is a document prepared by the seller whenever it sells goods or provides services on credit. The invoice is usually numbered for easy identification and for filing in a suitable storage system. It contains the following information:

- seller's name and address
- seller's VAT registration number
- purchaser's name and address
- purchaser's order number and date
- date of delivery
- description of goods and services supplied including part number and catalogue reference
- quantity
- price per item
- VAT payable
- total amount due
- terms and conditions of sale.

From a book-keeper's point of view the invoice is one of the most important documents since details of the transaction need to be entered in the books of account of both the seller and the buyer. Chapters 16 and 17 deal with the entry of invoices.

Exhibit 15.3 shows an invoice.

Exhibit 15.3 Invoice

INVOICE

Ace Sports
High Street, Manchester, MM1 4TC
Tel: 0161 229 9229
VAT Reg: 338 9366 72

Champion Sports
Fairway
Leeds
LS2 8BD

invoice number: 3189
date: 3 May 2013

Quantity	*Description*	*Unit price* £	£
20	Rugby Shirts ref 25	12.00	240.00
20	Rugby Shirts ref 14	8.00	160.00
			400.00
		VAT at 20%	80.00
			480.00

Terms: 30 days

15.7 Pro-forma invoice

In certain circumstances a **pro-forma invoice** is raised and sent to the purchaser who will then make payment before any goods or services are supplied. A supplier might take this action if a purchaser is unknown to the supplier, has not yet established creditworthiness or is known to the supplier as a late or inconsistent payer.

15.8 Returns note

In certain circumstances a purchaser needs to return goods to the supplier because they are damaged, faulty or perhaps not to the specification ordered. The goods will be returned to the supplier accompanied by a **returns note** or **sales returns** note which gives details of the goods being returned and the reason together with the details of the order number, date, etc. The supplier will then have to decide whether or not it is appropriate to give credit for the returned goods.

15.9 Credit note

Once the supplier has decided to give credit then a **credit note** will be raised for the value of the returned goods including the applicable amount of VAT. The note will then be sent to the customer.

A credit note is usually printed in red to distinguish it from an invoice and while it contains similar information to that found in an invoice some details will differ. For instance, the customer may only have returned a part of a consignment and this will need to be clearly identified on the credit note.

Again credit notes are important documents which need to be entered in the books of account as the amount owed by the buyer will be reduced by the amount of the credit note. Chapter 18 deals with the entry of credit notes.

Exhibit 15.4 illustrates a credit note which, as mentioned above, is usually printed in red.

Exhibit 15.4 Credit note

CREDIT NOTE

Ace Sports
High Street, Manchester, MM1 4TC
Tel: 0161 229 9229
VAT Reg: 338 9366 72

Champion Sports
Fairway
Leeds
LS2 8BD

credit note number: 118
date: 11 June 2013

Quantity	*Description*	*Unit price* £	£
6	Rugby Shirts ref 25	12.00	72.00
			72.00
		VAT at 20%	14.40
			86.40

Reason for credit: Faulty stitching

15.10 Statement of account

At the end of each month businesses send out a document known as a **statement of account**. This statement contains details of all the customer's transactions during the previous month, starting off with the opening balance outstanding from the previous month plus the amounts owing from the current month's invoices. Any amounts that are paid are deducted together with any credit note allowances. This gives the total amount outstanding which is then due for payment at the end of the month.

On receipt of the statement of account the customer should check the details with their own records to ensure that they agree with the statement. Provided the invoices listed on the statement have been approved for payment then arrangements will be made to pay the account. Chapter 18 covers the preparation of statements of account.

Exhibit 15.5 shows a statement of account.

Exhibit 15.5 Statement of account

STATEMENT

Ace Sports
High Street, Manchester, MM1 4TC
Tel: 0161 229 9229
VAT Reg: 338 9366 72

Champion Sports
Fairway
Leeds
LS2 8BD

Statement date: 30 June 2013
Account No: C 52
Page No: 1

Date	*Reference*	*Debit*	*Credit*	*Balance*
03/5/13	Invoice No 3189	480.00		480.00
11/6/13	Credit Note No 118		86.40	393.60
			Total outstanding	393.60

Terms: 30 days from date of invoice

15.11 Remittance advice

When payment is made from one business to another it is important that the recipient of the money has details of the payment so that the money may be correctly allocated. Therefore, the business making the payment usually includes a **remittance advice**. This document is rather like a statement, and may in fact be prepared at the same time, in that it shows details of the business's most recent transactions and final balance outstanding which is represented by the accompanying cheque or advice if the payment is made by BACS (see Chapter 20).

If any invoice has not been paid for any reason it will be left outstanding and can then be queried. A remittance advice is shown in Exhibit 15.6.

Exhibit 15.6 Remittance advice

REMITTANCE ADVICE

Champion Sports,
Fairway
Leeds, LS2 8BD

Tel: 0131 874428

VAT Reg: 811 6571 56
Remittance Advice: 6/151
Date: 5 July 2013

Ace Sports
High Street
Manchester
MM1 4TC

Account Number: C 52

Date	*Invoice or credit note no*	*Invoice*	*Credit note*	*Payment*
03/5/13	Invoice No 3189	480.00		480.00
11/6/13	Credit Note No 118		86.40	(86.40)
			Total payment	393.60

15.12 Goods received note (GRN)

When goods are received the purchaser will raise a **goods received note** (GRN) which details exactly what goods have been received. This note is raised as part of the purchaser's internal procedure and is used to advise various departments of their arrival. These departments will include:

- buying office – so that the progress of orders can be monitored
- materials office – so stock records can be updated
- accounts department – the invoice from the supplier will be checked with the GRN as proof of delivery before payment is authorised.

It is important to both the supplier and the purchaser that details on the purchase order, invoice and GRN are correct so as to avoid possible disputes which could result in delayed payment and the loss of goodwill.

If the supplier receives faulty goods back from the purchaser then they will also raise a GRN to inform all the departments concerned of the return of the goods.

A goods received note is shown as Exhibit 15.7.

Exhibit 15.7 Goods received note

Champion Sports			GRN No ________
Goods Received Note O/No ____________ Supplier Ref ____________		Copies	Accounts Dept —— White Purchasing Dept —— Pink Material control —— Green Inspection —— Blue With Goods —— Yellow
Description	Part No	Quantity	Remarks
Received by (signature) ____________ Carrier ____________			Date ________

15.13 Manufacturer's recommended retail price

Looking at an item displayed in a shop window, you will frequently see something like the following:

Digital LCD TV:	Manufacturer's Recommended Retail Price	£500
	Less discount of 20%	£100
	You pay only	£400

Very often the manufacturer's recommended retail price is a figure above what the manufacturer would expect the public to pay for its product. Probably, in the case shown, the manufacturer would have expected the public to pay around £400 for its product.

The inflated figure used for the 'manufacturer's recommended retail price' is simply a sales gimmick. Most people like to feel they are getting a bargain. The salespeople know that someone would usually prefer to get '20% off' and pay £400, rather than for the price simply be shown as £400 with no mention of a discount.

15.14 Abbreviations

Business documents frequently contain abbreviations and terms of trade the most common of which are as follows:

Carriage paid Another word for carriage is transport costs. Thus carriage paid indicates that the cost of transport has been included in the cost of the goods.

COD This abbreviation stands for 'cash on delivery' and means that the goods must be paid for on delivery.

E&OE On some invoices and other documents you will see the initials 'E&OE' printed at the bottom of the invoice. This abbreviation stands for 'errors and omissions excepted'. Basically, this is a warning that there may possibly be errors or omissions which could mean that the figures shown could be incorrect, and that the recipient should check the figures carefully before taking any action concerning them.

Ex works This means that the price of the goods does not include delivery costs.

Net monthly This phrase frequently appears at the foot of an invoice and means that the full amount of the invoice is due for payment within one month of the date of the invoice.

Chapter summary

- Organisations use many documents within their trading activity (see Exhibit 15.1).
- A 'quotation' is a formal document, containing details of the goods or services required, issued by the seller following a prospective buyer's enquiry.
- Once the buyer has decided to purchase the goods or services it issues a 'purchase order' to the supplier. This document details the goods or services required by the purchaser.
- Upon receipt of the purchase order the supplier issues an 'advice note' informing the buyer of the date of despatch of the goods or services.
- Accompanying the goods will be a delivery note (sometimes called a despatch note). This document contains details of the goods being delivered, but without the price details. The recipient will then sign for the receipt on delivery.
- An 'invoice' is then sent by the supplier to the buyer detailing the goods or services supplied and the amount outstanding. The payment details are also included on the invoice.

- A pro-forma invoice is a type of invoice that is occasionally raised when the seller wishes to secure payment prior to the goods or services being supplied.
- When goods are faulty or unsatisfactory they are often returned to the supplier by the buyer who issues a returns note to accompany the goods. The supplier, upon receipt, will then issue the purchaser with a credit note which will give details of the amount to be deducted from the original invoice.
- Usually, at the end of the month, the purchaser receives a statement of account from the supplier detailing the invoices and credit notes issued during the particular period and the total amount outstanding and due for payment. Any payment made should be accompanied by a remittance advice detailing the invoices included in the payment.
- A goods received note is a document raised by the purchaser when the goods or services are received and shows the exact details of goods received.

EXERCISES

Note: Questions with the suffix 'X' shown after the question number do ***not*** *have answers shown at the back of the book. Answers to the other questions are shown in Appendix E.*

15.1 Describe the functions of the following documents:

(*a*) remittance advice
(*b*) goods received note (GRN)
(*c*) credit note
(*d*) invoice.

15.2X (*a*) What is the purpose of a pro-forma invoice?
(*b*) What does it mean if goods are sold COD?
(*c*) What does the term 'net monthly' on an invoice mean?
(*d*) What does the term 'ex works' mean?
(*e*) What does E&OE on an invoice mean?

15.3 You are asked to complete the following sentences:

(*a*) Clover Designs Ltd sends a .... to a supplier to order goods.
(*b*) An .... is sent to the buyer before the goods are delivered to let it know that the goods will be despatched shortly.
(*c*) An .... is sent by the seller to the buyer of goods or services to advise it of how much is owed for the goods or services supplied.
(*d*) Clover Designs Ltd sends a .... with a payment to a supplier to indicate which invoices are being paid.

15.4X You are employed as an accounts clerk for a printing company. At the end of each month one of your tasks is to prepare statements of account to be sent to customers. Below are details from the account of one of your customers John Ashley Ltd.

Invoices sent during the month:

May 2	Invoice No. 7821	£43.75
May 8	Invoice No. 7955	£35.00
May 17	Credit Note No. 304	£10.20
May 23	Invoice No. 8204	£74.50
May 28	Received cheque	£51.50

The amount outstanding on 1 May amounted to £101.50.

You are required to draft a statement of account showing details of how much John Ashley Ltd has outstanding at the end of May.

CHAPTER 16

Division of the ledger: sales day book and sales ledger including VAT

Learning objectives

After you have studied this chapter you should be able to:

- appreciate how the books of original entry are used alongside the ledgers
- explain the use of the sales, purchases, sales returns and purchase returns day books
- distinguish between a cash sale and a credit sale and the way each are recorded in the books of account
- enter invoices into the sales day book and post transactions to the appropriate accounts in the sales ledger and general ledger
- understand what is meant by trade discount
- understand the importance of internal control
- appreciate the need for credit control over accounts receivable
- understand why 'factoring' is used by businesses.

16.1 Introduction

In Chapter 2 we discussed the accounting cycle within which a business operates during its financial year. This included recording all the trading activities from the source documents in the day books, posting to the various ledgers and the preparation of the financial statements at the end of the accounting period. As a business expands additional accounting record books are required to enable the system of recording transactions to be made easier and more efficient.

A small business can satisfactorily maintain the double entry accounts in one account book called the ledger. Larger businesses, however, require a better system due to the amount of financial data that needs recording. Consequently several books are used to record the many different transactions and these are explained below.

16.2 Books of original entry

A **book of original entry** is where a transaction is first recorded. There are separate books for each different kind of transaction: for example, sales will be entered in one book, purchases in another book, cash in another book, and so on. All transactions that are entered into the book-keeping system originate from a **source document** such as an invoice, credit note, cheque book stub, paying-in slip, and so on.

In the next two chapters we will be looking at invoices and credit notes that are raised when goods or services are sold to customers and perhaps returned if a problem arises with the goods, when a credit would be issued. Chapters 20 and 21 cover the banking system and cash books, which illustrate how cash and cheques are recorded in the accounting records.

Types of books of original entry

Let us look at the books or original entry that we will be using to enter sales and purchase invoices and credit notes:

- **sales day book** – for credit sales (this chapter)
- **purchases day book** – for credit purchases (Chapter 17)
- **sales returns day book** – for sales returns from customers (Chapter 18)
- **purchases returns day book** – for goods returned to the supplier (Chapter 18).

16.3 The ledgers

Once the details of the transactions have been entered into the books of original entry the information is then entered into the ledgers by means of the double entry system. This procedure is often referred to as **posting**. Sales transactions are posted to the sales ledger, purchase transactions to the purchase ledger and other items are posted to the accounts in the general ledger.

The various books used in accounting are shown linked in Exhibit 16.1.

Exhibit 16.1 Diagram of accounting books

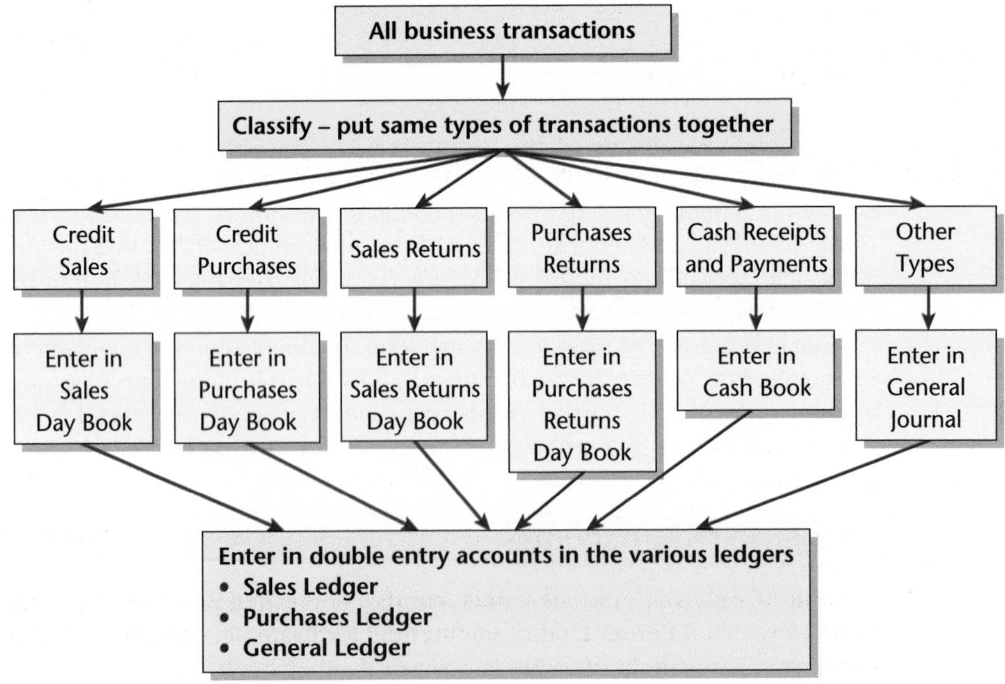

16.4 Cash and credit sales

Cash sales

When goods are purchased by a customer who pays for them immediately by cash, then there is no necessity to enter the sale of these goods into the sales day book or the sales ledger since the customer is not in debt to the business. Keeping details of these customers' names and addresses is, therefore, not needed.

Credit sales

In many businesses most of the sales will be made on credit rather than for cash. In fact, the sales of some businesses or organisations will consist entirely of credit sales.

For each credit sale the supplier will send a document to the buyer showing details and prices of the goods sold. This document is known as a sales invoice to the supplier and a purchase invoice to the buyer. An example of an invoice was shown in Exhibit 15.3. Most businesses have individually designed invoices but inevitably they follow a generally accepted accounting format. All invoices will be numbered and contain the names and addresses of both the supplier and the customer. The invoice in Exhibit 15.3 shows the supplier as Ace Sports and the customer as Champion Sports.

16.5 Sales invoices

Once the goods have been despatched to the buyer a **sales invoice** is made out by the supplier. The top copy of the sales invoice is sent to the buyer, further copies are retained by the supplier for use within the organisation. For example, one copy is usually sent to the accounts department to enable the sale of goods on credit to be recorded in the sales day book and sales ledger, another copy may be passed to the sales department, and so on.

16.6 Entering credit sales into the sales day book

As mentioned above, a copy of the sales invoice is passed to the accounts department where the supplier enters this into the sales day book. This book is merely a list, showing the following:

- date of invoice
- customer's name
- goods (net cost)
- VAT charged
- total amount due.

There is no need to show details of the goods sold in the sales day book. This can be found by looking at copy invoices.

Exhibit 16.2 shows a **sales day book**, which illustrates how the invoices are entered starting with the entry of the invoice shown in Exhibit 15.3. (Assume that the entries are on page 26 of the day book.)

Exhibit 16.2

Sales Day Book					(page 26)
Date	*Details*	*Folio*	*Goods*	*VAT*	*Total*
2013			£	£	£
May 3	Champion Sports	SL12	400.00	80.00	480.00
May 13	BD Sports Ltd	SL39	84.00	16.80	100.80
May 22	Delta Products	SL125	120.00	24.00	144.00
May 29	Zhang Sports	SL249	178.00	35.60	213.60
			782.00	156.40	938.40
			GL44	GL50	*

16.7 Posting credit sales to the sales ledger

Once the invoices have been entered into the sales day book the next step is to post each invoice into the individual customer's account in the sales ledger. At the end of the period, usually each month, the totals in the sales day book are then posted to the 'sales account' and 'VAT account' in the general ledger. The double entry requirements are now shown below:

- **debit** each customer's account in the sales ledger with the ***total*** of each individual invoice (the goods go 'IN' to their account)
- **credit** the sales account with total of the 'net sales' (the sales come 'OUT' from the supplier)
- **credit** the VAT account with the total of the 'VAT' charged (this is a liability and is owed to HMRC).

Note: The 'Total' column in the above sales day book is posted to the 'Sales Control Account' but this will be dealt with in Chapter 25.

An example of posting credit sales

Using the sales day book from Exhibit 16.2 and following the double entry procedures we will now post each of the invoices to the customers' accounts in the sales ledger.

Notice the completion of the folio columns with the sales day book reference in the ledger accounts and the ledger references in the day book.

Sales Ledger

Champion Sports Account *(SL 12)*

	Folio	£	
2013			
May 3 Sales	SB 26	480.00	

BD Sports Account *(SL 39)*

	Folio	£	
2013			
May 13 Sales	SB 26	100.80	

Delta Products Account *(SL 125)*

	Folio	£	
2013			
May 22 Sales	SB 26	144.00	

Zhang Sports Account *(SL 249)*

	Folio	£	
2013			
May 29 Sales	SB 26	213.60	

The postings to the general ledger are shown below:

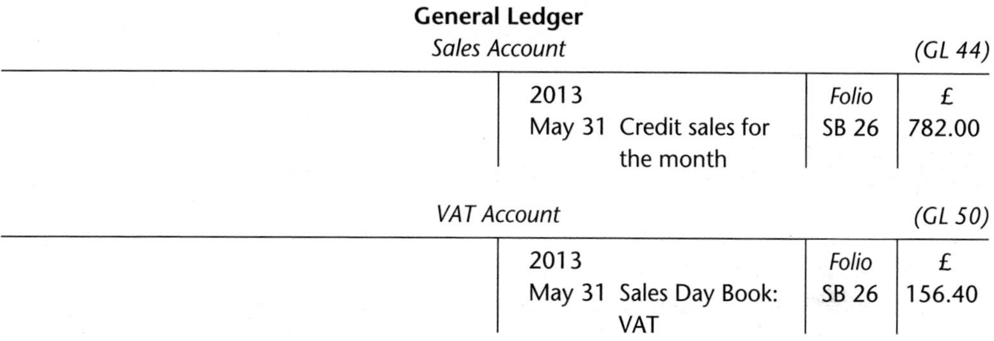

General Ledger

Sales Account *(GL 44)*

			Folio	£
	2013			
	May 31	Credit sales for the month	SB 26	782.00

VAT Account *(GL 50)*

			Folio	£
	2013			
	May 31	Sales Day Book: VAT	SB 26	156.40

The sequence of events is shown in Exhibit 16.3.

Exhibit 16.3 Sales invoices – sequence of entries

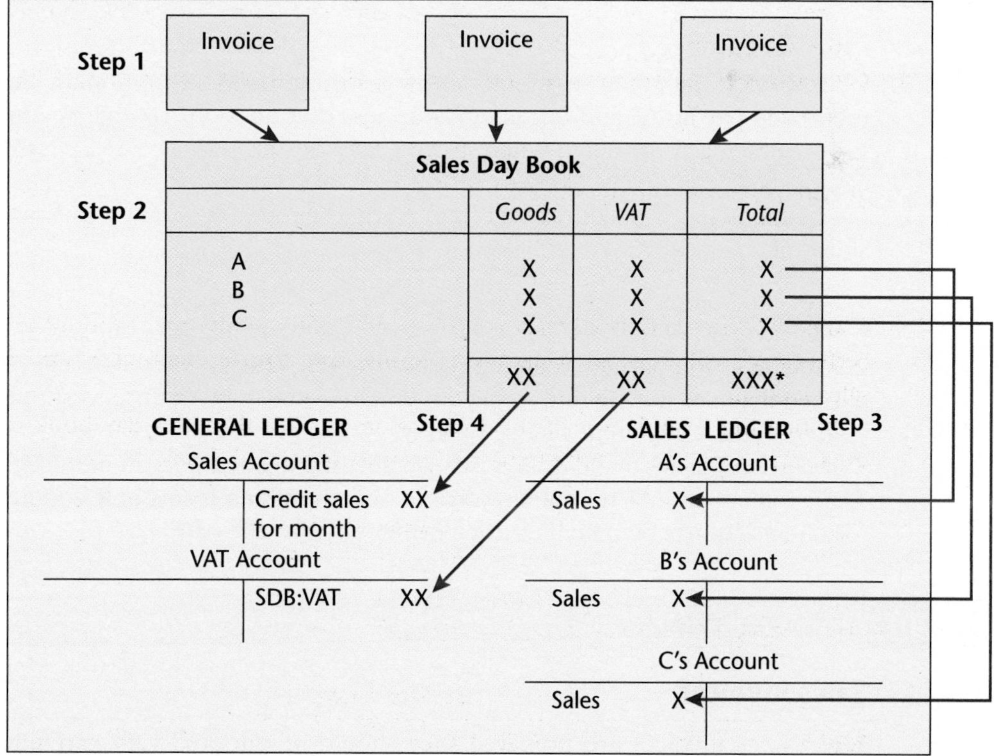

*This total is posted to the sales control account which is dealt with in Chapter 25.

16.8 Trade discounts

Trade discount is an amount deducted by traders from the list price of goods when they are selling to other traders/businesses. While the discount may be allowed to other traders it is not available to the general public. VAT is always calculated on the net amount of the invoice after deduction of the trade discount.

Using Exhibit 15.3 the invoice from Ace Sports to Champion Sports let us assume that the trade discount is 20%. The cost of the rugby shirts was £400.00 plus VAT; if, however, 20% trade discount is allowed the invoice total would be:

	£
Rugby Shirts	400.00
Less Trade discount 20%	80.00
	320.00
Add 20% VAT (20% × £320)	64.00
Invoice total	384.00

It is important to note that trade discount is never shown in the accounts; only the net amount is recorded in the books of account.

Note: *Cash discount* is dealt with in Chapter 21.

16.9 Credit control

Credit control is a crucial function in any organisation that sells goods and/or provides services on credit. It should follow a strict procedure to monitor that accounts receivable pay in full and on time. A business that does not receive payment when it is due may reach the stage when it can no longer pay its accounts payable. In these circumstances, it is very likely to fail.

The following procedures will help the business to maintain a positive cash flow situation:

1 Set a credit limit for each customer which should not be exceeded. The limit should take account of the customer's payment record and its importance to the business.
2 As soon as the payment date has been reached, check to see whether payment has been made or not. Failure to pay on time may mean you refuse to supply any more goods unless payment is made quickly.
3 If payment is not made then it may be decided to sue the customer for the debt.
4 Customers should be made aware in the supplier's terms and conditions of the action that may be taken for non-payment by the due date.

16.10 Internal checks

Sales invoices

When sales invoices are prepared they should be checked very carefully to ensure that the correct quantity of goods supplied is invoiced at the correct price. This also applies when invoicing services. To avoid the possibility of errors being made, or indeed fraud occurring, it is prudent for one member of staff to prepare the invoice, which is then passed to a senior member for checking.

Purchase invoices

Similarly, the purchaser needs to ensure that the goods or services to which the purchase invoice refers have been received and are as the order in terms of price and specification. This is discussed further in Chapter 17, in particular section 17.2.

16.11 Factoring

One of the problems that face many businesses is the time taken by debtors to pay their accounts. Few businesses have so much cash available to them that they do not mind how long the debtor takes to pay. It is a fact that many businesses that become bankrupt do so, not because the business is not making profits, but because the business has run out of cash funds. Once that happens, the confidence factor in business evaporates, and the business then finds that very few people will supply it with goods, and it also cannot pay its employees. Closure of the business then generally happens fairly quickly.

In the case of accounts receivable, the cash problem may be alleviated by using the services of a financial intermediary called a 'factor'. **Factoring** is a financial service designed to improve the cash flow of healthy, growing companies, enabling them to make better use of management time and the money tied up in trade credit to customers. In essence, factors provide their clients with three closely integrated services, covering sales accounting and collection, credit management (which can include protection against bad debts), and the availability of finance against sales invoices.

16.12 Slip system

Some organisations avoid using day books by using the **slip system**. This involves putting information such as lists of invoices in 'slip' form, which can then be entered directly into the ledger accounts. The entry into the appropriate day book is thus eliminated.

For instance, banks use the slip system, whereby a customer makes out a paying-in slip to pay money into his or her account, and the slip is then used to enter the details of the transaction and become the documentary evidence.

Nowadays, with most organisations using computerised accounting systems, invoices tend to be collated into batches prior to entry. The invoices are then entered directly onto the system and the total checked, with the slip, prior to processing the invoices by computer.

The advantages of the slip system are that:

- it is easy to operate
- it is quicker than using day books
- it minimises the risk of error, i.e. batch totals should be verified before processing when using a computerised system of accounting.

The disadvantages are:

- if invoices are lost, this can cause problems
- the risk of fraud is increased
- it is not easy to analyse items, for example, sales of different kinds of goods.

Chapter summary

- As the business expands so does the requirement of additional books to record the accounting transactions.
- Books of original entry are where a transaction is entered first from the source document, i.e. invoice, credit note, etc.
- There are various books of original entry, sales and purchases day books, sales returns and purchases returns day books, the journal, petty cash book and cash book.
- When goods or services are sold for cash it is not necessary to enter the details into the sales day book and sales ledger since the customer is not in debt to the business.
- When goods or services are sold on credit then an invoice will need to be prepared and sent to the buyer. This document is known as a 'sales invoice' to the supplier and a 'purchase invoice' to the buyer. Several copies of the invoice are usually made to enable the accounts staff to record the sale in the books of account, other copies may be required for internal use.
- Sales invoices are a 'source document' and are entered into the sales day book which is a book of original entry. They are then posted to each individual customer's account in the sales ledger. At the end of the period the total net sales are posted to the sales account in the general ledger and the total VAT charged to the VAT account.
- Trade discount is a discount or reduction given to a customer when calculating the price of goods. No entry is made of trade discount in the accounting records.
- Credit control within an organisation is important for the business to maintain a healthy cash flow.
- Other areas that are important include the checking of invoices prior to entry in the books of account and before payment is made.
- Factoring is offered to businesses to help improve their cash flow. This involves 'selling' its accounts receivable to a factoring company who then become responsible for collecting debts as they become due. The factoring company retains a percentage of the amount collected for its services.

EXERCISES

*Note: Questions with the suffix 'X' shown after the question number do **not** have answers shown at the back of the book. Answers to the other questions are shown in Appendix E.*

16.1 For each of the following types of transactions, state the book of original entry, and the ledger and type of account, in which you would enter the transaction:

(*a*) Sales invoice
(*b*) Purchase invoice
(*c*) Sales credit note
(*d*) Sales returns
(*e*) Purchases credit note.

16.2X (*a*) State which document(s) would be entered into the following books of original entry:
(i) Purchases day book
(ii) Sales returns day book
(iii) Sales day book
(iv) Purchases returns day book.

16.3 From the following list of sales invoices you are required to calculate the amount of VAT at 20% for each invoice then enter the invoices in the sales day book using the following columns, 'Goods', 'VAT' and 'Total'.

Post the items to the relevant accounts in the sales ledger and then show the entries in the sales and VAT accounts in the general ledger. Folio references are not required.

2013	*Sales Invoices*	*Net* (£)
Nov 1	T Bates	186.00
Nov 4	D Cope	166.00
Nov 8	F Chan	12.00
Nov 11	T Bates	54.00
Nov 13	B Hope	66.00
Nov 18	D Cope	32.00
Nov 22	M Saka & Sons	20.00
Nov 29	F Chan	320.00

16.4X During July 2013 the following credit sales were made by Select Stationery Supplies:

2013	*Sales Invoices*	*Net* (£)
July 1	Hall Products	520.00
July 5	Ash & Co	62.00
July 8	K Meakin	18.00
July 12	A Ballearic	110.00
July 19	Hall Products	880.00
July 26	G Huang	126.00
July 29	A Ballearic	42.00
July 31	J Stead	98.00

(*a*) For each of the above invoices calculate the amount of VAT to be charged.
(*b*) Draw up a sales day book and enter the above invoices into the day book for the month of July using columns for 'Goods', 'VAT' and 'Total'.
(*c*) Open an account for each customer and post the sales invoices from the sales day book to each account in the sales ledger.
(*d*) Post the net sales to the sales account and the total VAT charged to the VAT account in the general ledger. (Folio references are not required.)

16.5 During April 2013 the following credit sales were made by Dabell's Stationery Supplies Ltd:

Date	*Debtor*	*Net amount*
		£
1 April	Fisher & Co	1,459
3 April	Elder (Office Supplies)	73
5 April	Haigh (Mfr) Ltd	56
11 April	Ardern & Co	1,598
15 April	I Rafiq	540
19 April	Royle's Business Systems	2,456
22 April	Fisher & Co	23
22 April	Ardern & Co	345
25 April	Elder (Office Supplies)	71
26 April	Haigh (Mfr) Ltd	176

Required:

(*a*) From the above list of sales invoices you are required to calculate the amount of VAT at 20% then enter the invoices in the sales day book using columns 'Goods', 'VAT' and 'Total'. The next sales day book page no. is 26.

(*b*) The sales ledger showed the following balances at 1 April 2013.

Customer	*Amount outstanding*
	£
Ardern & Co	472
Elder (Office Supplies)	75
Fisher & Co	231
Haigh (Mfr) Ltd	1,267
I Rafiq	330
Royle's Business Systems	750

Open an account for each of the business customers in the sales ledger and enter the balances outstanding on 1 April 2013.

(*c*) Post the sales invoices for the month of April to the appropriate ledger account in the sales ledger and show the entries in the sales accounts and VAT account in the general ledger. (Folio references are not required.)

(*d*) During April the business received cheques from Fisher & Co for £231, I Rafiq for £330 and £1,000 on account from Haigh (Mfr) Ltd. Post the cheques to the customer's accounts in the sales ledger.

(*e*) Balance each account off at the end of April and draw up a list of outstanding accounts receivable.

16.6X Morton's Garage is situated on the outskirts of Macclesfield and sells petrol and accessories in addition to carrying out repairs and maintenance on vehicles. At 1 January 2013 Morton's sales ledger showed the following balances on their customers' accounts:

	£	
S Brocklehurst	563	Dr
C Crawford	1,078	Dr
L Price & Partners	321	Dr
D Woolham & Co	146	Dr

During January 2013 the garage issued the following invoices in respect of credit sales of petrol, accessories and repairs, which are all subject to VAT at 20%.

2013	*Name*	*Net amount*
		£
2 Jan	D Woolham & Co	230
4 Jan	C Crawford	345
7 Jan	S Brocklehurst	1,980
9 Jan	L Price & Partners	523
14 Jan	D Woolham & Co	56
18 Jan	L Price & Partners	200
21 Jan	C Crawford	340
24 Jan	C Crawford	45
29 Jan	S Brocklehurst	845
31 Jan	L Price & Partners	721

On 31 January 2013 the garage proprietor, Mr Morton, received cheques from the following customers, who settled their account for the previous month:

Customer	*Amount of cheque*
	£
C Crawford	1,078
L Price & Partners	321
D Woolham & Co	146

Required:
Carry out the following tasks (folio references are not required):

(*a*) From the above list of invoices you are required to calculate the amount of VAT at 20%, then enter the invoices in the sales day book using columns, 'Goods', 'VAT' and 'Total' for January 2013.
(*b*) Open an account for each customer and enter the balances as at 1 January 2013. Post the sales from the day book to each account and the amounts received.
(*c*) Balance the customers' accounts at 31 January 2013 and bring down the balances.
(*d*) Post the entries in the sales account and VAT account in the general ledger.

16.7 Why is it important to ensure that sales invoices are thoroughly checked before being sent out to customers?

16.8 What is meant by the term 'factoring'?

CHAPTER 17

Purchases day book and purchases ledger including VAT

Learning objectives

After you have studied this chapter you should be able to:

- appreciate that an invoice is common to both supplier and customer
- enter purchase invoices into the purchases day book
- post the purchases day book to the purchases ledger
- post the purchases day book to the general ledger
- authorise and code invoices for payment.

17.1 Purchase invoices

When a business purchases goods or services from a supplier on credit it is sent a purchase invoice detailing the goods or services supplied and their price. Just as the sales invoices were entered into the sales day book in the previous chapter so purchase invoices (source documents) are entered into a purchases day book as follows:

- date of the invoice
- name of the supplier from whom the goods were purchased
- goods (net cost)
- VAT charged
- total amount due.

An invoice is common to both supplier and customer. The invoice shown in Exhibit 15.3 was prepared and sent by Ace Sports to its customer Champion Sports:

- In the accounting records of Ace Sports it is a **sales invoice**.
- In the accounting records of Champion Sports it is a **purchase invoice**.

Another name for the purchases day book is purchases journal.

Exhibit 17.1 shows a **purchases day book** which has several invoices entered for the month of December 2013.

Exhibit 17.1

Purchases Day Book					(page 38)
Date	*Details*	*Folio*	*Goods*	*VAT*	*Total*
2013			£	£	£
Dec 9	Jarvis & Sons	PL 8	144.00	28.80	172.80
Dec 13	Morton Products	PL 30	280.00	56.00	336.00
Dec 17	K Howard	PL 17	520.00	104.00	624.00
Dec 30	T Joshi	PL 27	72.00	14.40	86.40
			1,016.00	203.20	1,219.20
			GL43	GL67	*

*The 'Total' column in the above purchases day book is posted to the 'Purchases Control Account' but this will be dealt with in Chapter 25.

Posting credit purchases to the purchases ledger

Once the invoices have been entered into the purchases day book the next step is to post each invoice into the individual supplier's account in the purchases ledger. At the end of the period, usually each month, the totals in the purchases day book are then posted to the 'Purchases Account' and 'VAT Account' in the general ledger. The double entry requirements are now shown:

- **credit** each supplier's account in the purchases ledger with the ***total*** of each individual invoice (the goods have come 'OUT' of each supplier)
- **debit** the purchases account with the total of the 'net purchases' (the purchases have come 'IN' to the purchases account)
- **debit** the VAT account with the total of the 'VAT' column (this is the amount of VAT paid by the business on their purchases which can be offset against the liability incurred on sales).

An example of posting credit purchases

Using the purchases day book from Exhibit 17.1 and following the double entry procedures we will now post each of the invoices to the suppliers' accounts in the purchases ledger. Again the folio columns have been completed with the purchases day book page number reference PB38 shown in the purchases ledger while the day book shows the ledger references PL8, PL30, PL17 and PL27.

Purchases Ledger

Jarvis & Sons Account *(PL 8)*

	Folio	£		Folio	£
			2013 Dec 9 Purchases	PB 38	172.80

Morton Products Account *(PL 30)*

	Folio	£		Folio	£
			2013 Dec 13 Purchases	PB 38	336.00

K Howard Account *(PL 17)*

	Folio	£		Folio	£
			2013 Dec 17 Purchases	PB 38	624.00

T Joshi Account *(PL 27)*

	Folio	£		Folio	£
			2013 Dec 30 Purchases	PB 38	86.40

General Ledger

Purchases Account *(GL 43)*

	Folio	£		Folio	£
2013 Dec 31 Credit purchases for the month	PB 38	1,016.00			

VAT Account *(GL 67)*

	Folio	£		Folio	£
2013 Dec 31 Purchases Day Book: VAT	PB 38	203.20			

Exhibit 17.2 Purchase invoices – sequence of events

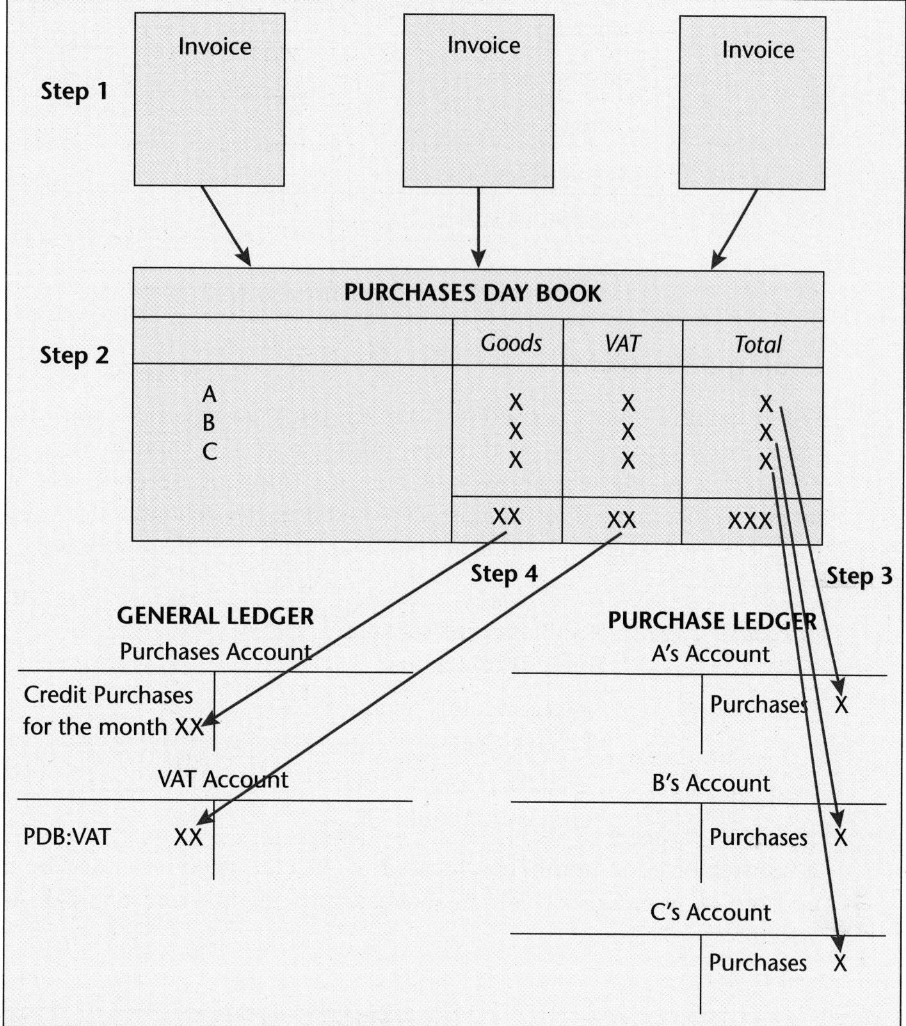

17.2 Authorisation and coding of invoices

Purchase invoices

When purchase invoices are received from various suppliers of goods or services, it is important to check the invoices for accuracy in the calculations and to ensure that the goods invoiced have been received and agree with the relevant purchase order and specifications.

On receipt, each purchase invoice should be numbered, recorded and stamped with an appropriate rubber stamp (see Exhibit 17.3), to enable the invoice to be checked and coded (see below).

Exhibit 17.3

Invoice no	
Purchase order no	
Goods received	
Extensions	
Passed for payment	
Code	

Coding of invoices

When using a computerised accounting package it is necessary to code invoices prior to entering them in the accounting records. Each invoice will need to be checked as mentioned above and then the appropriate code added to enable the invoice to be charged to the correct account in the general ledger. Examples of code numbers used when operating accountancy packages are as follows:

		Account number
Purchase ledger	Needhams Ltd account	0211
	Young Bros account	0245
Sales ledger	Biggs & Bentley account	1078
	J Leigh account	1097
General Ledger	Capital account	4001
	Purchases account	5001

A register of code numbers allocated to specific accounts must be maintained and updated as necessary. This register may be a manual one or held on the computer system.

Chapter summary

- When businesses purchase goods or services from suppliers they are sent a purchase invoice detailing the goods or services and their price. The invoice is used by both buyer and seller: to the buyer it is a purchase invoice and to the seller a sales invoice.
- Only invoices relating to goods bought on credit are entered into the purchases day book which is merely a list showing details of each credit purchase, i.e. the date of purchase, name of supplier, reference number and amount due.
- Each purchase invoice is then posted to the individual customer's account in the purchases ledger (a credit entry).
- At the end of the period, usually a month, the net purchases are posted to the purchases account (debit entry) and the total VAT to the VAT account (debit entry) in the general ledger.
- Many businesses have a system of coding the invoices prior to entry into the books of account. Part of this process involves authorising the invoice for payment.

EXERCISES

*Note 1: Questions with the suffix 'X' shown after the question number do **not** have answers shown at the back of the book. Answers to the other questions are shown in Appendix E.*

Note 2: Folio references are not required in the following exercises.

17.1 As accounts clerk for White Bros one of your tasks is to look after the purchases ledger. During May 2013 the following purchase invoices have been received by the company.

Date	*Supplier*	*Goods*	*VAT*	*Total*
		£	£	£
May 1	Bould & Co	104.00	20.80	124.80
May 7	Harlow & Brown	48.00	9.60	57.60
May 16	T Adams Ltd	234.00	46.80	280.80
May 23	Bould & Co	170.00	34.00	204.00
May 27	JL Products	320.00	64.00	384.00
May 28	Harlow & Brown	62.00	12.40	74.40
May 31	P Yeung Ltd	446.00	89.20	535.20

Required:

(*a*) Draw up a purchases day book, enter the invoices and total up the columns at the end of the month ensuring that the day book balances.

(*b*) Open accounts for each of the suppliers and post the invoices to the suppliers' accounts in the purchases ledger.

(*c*) Post the totals to the purchases account and VAT account in the general ledger.

17.2X Barkers Electrical Co employs an accounts assistant who is responsible for the purchase ledger. During July 2013 the following purchase invoices were received:

Date	*Supplier*	*Goods*	*VAT*	*Total*
		£	£	£
July 3	Peak Electrical	722.00	144.40	866.40
July 8	Leigh Electrics	84.00	16.80	100.80
July 12	Thomas Motors	274.00	54.80	328.80
July 17	Naik & Sons	160.00	32.00	192.00
July 19	Peak Electrical	158.00	31.60	189.60
July 23	WD Services	46.00	9.20	55.20
July 25	Leigh Electrics	210.00	42.00	252.00
July 30	Naik & Sons	178.00	35.60	213.60

Required:

(*a*) Draw up a purchases day book, enter the invoices and total up the columns at the end of the month ensuring that the day book balances.

(*b*) Open accounts for each of the suppliers and post the invoices to the suppliers' accounts in the purchases ledger.

(*c*) Post the totals to the purchases account and VAT account in the general ledger.

17.3 You are employed as accounts assistant for Taylor Ltd. During August 2013 the following purchase invoices, which are all subject to VAT at 20%, are received:

Date	*Supplier*	*Goods*
		£
Aug 1	Barker Ltd	62.00
Aug 6	Fern Bros	48.00
Aug 9	Ash & Co	224.00
Aug 14	Barker Ltd	136.00
Aug 22	Carter Supplies	98.00
Aug 27	Fern Bros	166.00
Aug 29	Singh & Sons	84.00
Aug 30	Ash & Co	366.00

Required:

(*a*) Calculate the amount of VAT (at 20%) and the total invoice amount for each of the invoices listed above.

(*b*) Draw up a purchases day book, enter the invoices and total up the columns at the end of the month ensuring that the day book balances.

(*c*) Open accounts for each of the suppliers and post the invoices to the suppliers' accounts in the purchases ledger.

(*d*) Post the totals to the purchases account and VAT account in the general ledger.

17.4X Why is it important to check invoices prior to payment?

17.5X You are employed as a sales assistant for a small company, Wilshaws Ltd, that sells farm supplies. As the company employs the minimum administrative staff, one of your duties is to look after the purchases ledger. This task involves entering the invoices received from suppliers into the day book and posting to the relevant suppliers' accounts in the purchases ledger.

The following purchase invoices were received in November 2013:

Date	*Supplier*	*Goods*	*VAT*	*Total*
2013		£	£	£
Nov 1	Bould & Co	104.30	20.86	125.16
Nov 4	Hambleton's	140.50	28.10	168.60
Nov 7	Farm Supplies Co	448.10	89.62	537.72
Nov 11	Worthington's Ltd	169.90	33.98	203.88
Nov 12	Sigley Bros	47.00	9.40	56.40
Nov 15	Hambleton's	259.00	51.80	310.80
Nov 20	Harlow's Mfr	84.90	16.98	101.88
Nov 20	Bould & Co	29.10	5.82	34.92
Nov 25	Clark & Robinson	61.60	12.32	73.92
Nov 30	T Adams Ltd	233.80	46.76	280.56

Required:

(*a*) Draw up a purchases day book, enter the invoices shown above and total up at the end of the month ensuring the day book balances.

(*b*) Open accounts for each of the suppliers, using your own folio numbers, and post the invoices to the suppliers' accounts in the purchases ledger.

(*c*) Post the totals to the purchases account and VAT in the general ledger.

CHAPTER 18

Sales returns day book and purchases returns day book

Learning objectives

After you have studied this chapter you should be able to:

- appreciate the need for sales returns and purchases returns to be made when goods or services are unsatisfactory
- enter credit notes in the sales returns day book and post to the appropriate individual customer's account in the sales ledger
- at the end of the period post the total of the sales returns day book into the sales returns account in the general ledger
- enter purchase credit notes in the purchases returns day book and post to the appropriate individual customer's account in the purchases ledger
- at the end of the period post the total of the purchases returns day book to the purchases returns account in the general ledger
- appreciate the need for keeping separate returns accounts
- reconcile ledger accounts with suppliers' statements
- make appropriate book-keeping entries for sales made via credit card.

18.1 Sales returns (returns inwards) and purchases returns (returns outwards)

When goods are bought and sold it is inevitable that occasionally they are unsuitable for various reasons, such as when the goods are:

- faulty or damaged
- not suitable for the particular requirement, for example, wrong type, size, colour
- part of an incomplete consignment
- subject to an overcharge on the invoice.

When this happens the supplier will need to make an allowance to the customer to correct the situation.

Note: there are alternative names which are used for sales and purchases returns. Sales returns are often referred to as **returns inwards** while purchases returns are known as **returns outwards**.

18.2 Sales returns (returns inwards) and credit notes

As mentioned above, if the goods supplied are unsuitable then the supplier will need to rectify the situation. Since the customer will have already been sent an invoice at the time the goods were delivered they will be in debt to the supplier for the value of the goods. Therefore, when the supplier makes an allowance for goods that have been returned, or a reduction in price has been agreed, the supplier will issue a **credit note** to the customer showing the reduction.

An example of a credit note was shown in Chapter 15, Exhibit 15.4.

18.3 Book-keeping entries for sales credit notes

Credit notes are source documents and are listed in a separate day book called the **sales returns day book** also called **returns inwards day book**. In Chapter 16 we entered various invoices into the sales day book, see Exhibit 16.2. Let us assume that two of our customers had a problem with some of the goods invoiced and were each sent a credit note to rectify the situation. The credit notes have been entered into the sales returns day book, as shown in Exhibit 18.1.

Exhibit 18.1

Sales Returns Day Book					*(page 11)*
Date	*Details*	*Folio*	*Goods*	*VAT*	*Total*
2013			£	£	£
June 11	Champion Sports	SL 12	72.00	14.40	86.40
June 24	Zhang Sports	SL 249	56.00	11.20	67.20
			128.00	25.60	153.60
			GL 45	GL 50	*

*The 'Total' column in the above sales returns day book is posted to the 'Sales Control Account' but this will be dealt with in Chapter 25.

Posting credit notes to the sales and general ledger

After entering the credit notes into the sales returns day book, the next step is to post each credit note into the individual customer's accounts. Again at the end of the month the total 'net goods returned' and 'VAT' are posted to the sales returns and VAT accounts in the general ledger. The book-keeping entries are:

- **credit** each customer's accounts in the sales ledger with the ***total*** of each individual credit note
- **debit** the sales returns account with the total of 'net goods returned'
- **debit** the VAT account with the total of the 'VAT' column.

Again, you may find it easier to use 'IN' and 'OUT', i.e. goods returned to us are entered on the 'IN' side of the sales returns account since the goods are coming 'IN' to us, and on the 'OUT' side of the individual customers' accounts as they are sending the goods back to the supplier (OUT).

An example of posting sales credit notes

Using the sales returns day book from Exhibit 18.1 and the sales ledger accounts from the example in Chapter 16 we will now post each of the credit notes to the customers' accounts in the Sales Ledger. The folio references have also been completed.

Sales Ledger

Champion Sports Account *(SL 12)*

2013	*Folio*	£	2013	*Folio*	£
May 3 Sales	SB 26	480.00	June 11 Sales returns	SR11	86.40

Zhang Sports Account *(SL 249)*

2013	*Folio*	£	2013	*Folio*	£
May 29 Sales	SB 26	213.60	June 24 Sales returns	SR11	67.20

The totals from the sales returns day book are now posted to the sales returns and VAT accounts in the general ledger.

General Ledger

Sales Returns Account *(GL 44)*

2013	*Folio*	£		*Folio*	£
June 30 Total SRDB	SR11	128.00			

VAT Account *(GL 50)*

2013	*Folio*	£	2013	*Folio*	£
June 30 Total SRDB	SR11	25.60	May 31 Total SDB	SB 26	156.40

18.4 Purchases returns (returns outwards) and purchases credit notes

When a business buys goods for resale but then has to return some of the goods for any of the reasons already discussed they are known as 'purchases returns' or 'returns outwards'. Once the goods have been returned to the supplier it will issue a credit note which is then sent to the customer.

Book-keeping entries for purchases credit notes

The credit notes are listed in a **purchases returns day book** also called the returns outwards day book. In Chapter 17, Exhibit 17.1, various invoices were entered into the purchases day book. Let us assume that some of the goods received from two of the business's suppliers were not to the specification ordered and had to be returned.

The suppliers then issued credit notes to rectify the situation. The credit notes have been entered below into the Purchases Returns Day Book.

Exhibit 18.2

Purchases Returns Day Book					(page 40)
Date	*Details*	*Folio*	*Goods*	*VAT*	*Total*
2014			£	£	£
Jan 15	Jarvis & Sons	PL 8	32.00	6.40	38.40
Jan 26	K Howard	PL 17	100.00	20.00	120.00
			132.00	26.40	158.40
			GL 45	GL 67	*

*The 'Total' column in the above sales returns day book is posted to the 'Sales Control Account' but this will be dealt with in Chapter 25.

Posting credit notes to the purchases and general ledger

After entering the credit notes into the purchases returns day book the next step is to post each credit note into the individual supplier's accounts. Again at the end of the month the total 'net goods returned' and 'VAT' are posted to the purchase returns and VAT accounts in the general ledger. The book-keeping entries are:

- **debit** each individual suppliers' account in the purchases ledger with the ***total*** of each credit note
- **credit** the purchase returns account with the total of the 'net goods returned'
- **credit** the VAT account with the total of the VAT column.

Using 'IN' and 'OUT', the entries would be as follows: the goods returned by us to the supplier go 'IN' to the suppliers' accounts and come 'OUT' of the purchase returns account.

An example of posting purchase credit notes

Using the purchases returns day book from Exhibit 18.2 and the purchases ledger accounts from the example in Chapter 17 we will now post each of the credit notes to the suppliers' accounts in the purchases ledger. Again the folio columns have been completed.

Purchases Ledger

Jarvis & Sons Account *(PL 8)*

	Folio	£		Folio	£
2014			2013		
Jan 15 Purchase returns	PR 40	38.40	Dec 9 Purchases	PB 38	172.80

K Howard Account *(PL 17)*

	Folio	£		Folio	£
2014			2013		
Jan 26 Purchase returns	PR 40	120.00	Dec 17 Purchases	PB 38	624.00

General Ledger

Purchases Returns Account *(GL 45)*

	Folio	£		Folio	£
			2014		
			Jan 31 Total PRDB	PR 40	132.00

VAT Account *(GL 67)*

	Folio	£		Folio	£
2013			2014		
Dec 31 Total PDB	PB 38	203.20	Jan 31 Total PRDB	PR40	26.40

Exhibit 18.3 Purchasing and selling goods

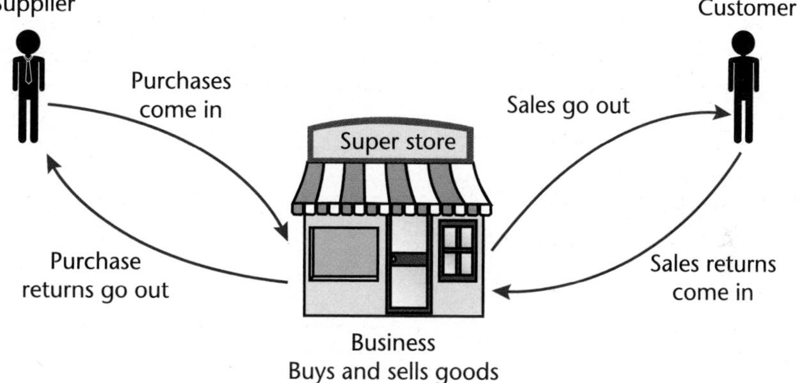

Source: *Edexcel International GCSE Accounting* 1st edn (Robinson, S. 2010) Pearson Education Ltd.

18.5 Double entry and returns

Exhibit 18.4 shows how double entry is made for both sales returns (returns inwards) and purchases returns (returns outwards).

Exhibit 18.4 Posting sales returns and purchases returns

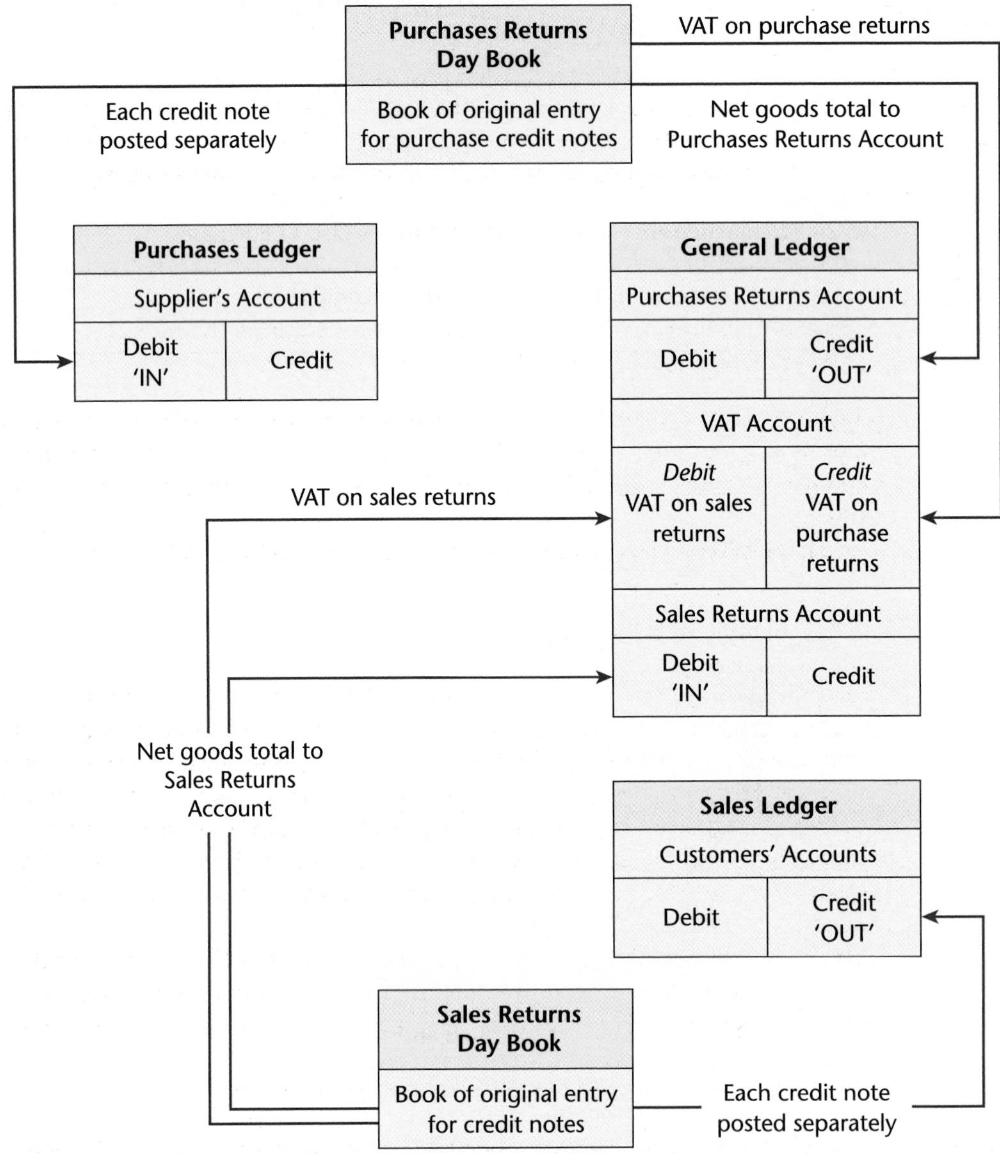

Note that full coverage of the treatment of sales returns and purchases returns in the financial statements have already been shown in section 12.1.

18.6 Reasons for keeping separate returns accounts

It is important for businesses to monitor the amount of goods being returned and the reasons why the goods or services were unsuitable. For this reason separate returns accounts are kept, i.e. sales returns account and purchases returns account. Recording the returns in these accounts would indicate any excessive amounts of sales returns and/or purchases returns which would enable management to investigate the reason.

18.7 Reconciliation of our ledger accounts with suppliers' statements

At the end of each month a **statement of account** should be sent to each customer (accounts receivable) that owes money on the last day of that month. It is really a copy of the customer's account in the seller's books. It should show:

- the amount owing at start of the month
- the amount of each sales invoice sent to the customer during the month
- any credit notes sent to the customer during the month
- cash and cheques received from the customer during the month
- the amount due from the customer at the end of the month.

The customer will use these statements to check that the details shown on the statement agree with their own accounting records. Statements act as a reminder to the customer that money is owed, and will show the date by which payment should be made.

An example of a statement was shown in Chapter 15, Exhibit 15.5.

Reconciliation of suppliers' statements

A supplier's statement of account should be checked against its ledger account in the business's own books and the balance reconciled before making a payment. Sometimes, because of the differences in timing, the balance on a supplier's statement on a certain date can differ from the balance on that supplier's account in the business's purchases ledger. This is similar to a bank statement where the balance may differ from that in the cash book and require the preparation of a **bank reconciliation statement** to reconcile the two balances. This is dealt with in Chapters 21 and 23.

If the balance on the statement of account does differ from the supplier's account in the purchases ledger, then it will be necessary to check the statement against the ledger account and reconcile the difference by preparing a supplier's reconciliation statement.

The reasons for the differences in balances may be due to:

- goods returned by the customer but not recorded by the supplier until after the statement of account has been issued
- a supplier sending goods to a customer, together with an invoice, but neither being received by the customer until a later date: the customer is, therefore, unable to enter the invoice in their books of the account until receipt
- payments in transit
- other errors which may be made by either the supplier or buyer when entering data, i.e. transposing figures, or an error in the calculation of a balance where manual accounts are maintained.

Exhibit 18.5 shows the account of C Young Ltd in the purchases ledger of A. Hall Ltd and the statement of account received from the supplier, C Young Ltd, together with the reconciliation.

Exhibit 18.5

(a) Purchases ledger A Hall Ltd Books

C Young Ltd Account

		£			£
2013			2013		
Jan 10	Bank	1,550	Jan 1	Balance b/d	1,550
Jan 29	Returns (i)	116	Jan 7	Purchases	885
Jan 31	Balance c/d	1,679	Jan 18	Purchases	910
		3,345			3,345
			Feb 1	Balance b/d	1,679

(b) Supplier's statement

C Young Ltd
Market Place, Leeds

STATEMENT

Account Name: A Hall Ltd
Account Number: H93

Date: 31 January 2013

	Debit	*Credit*	*Balance*
2013	£	£	£
Jan 1 Balance			1,550 Dr
Jan 7 Invoice No 3250	885		2,435 Dr
Jan 13 Payment received		1,550	885 Dr
Jan 18 Invoice No 3731	910		1,795 Dr
Jan 31 Invoice No 3894 (ii)	425		2,220 Dr

Comparing the purchases ledger account with the supplier's statement, two differences can be seen:

1 A Hall Ltd returned goods value £116 to C Young Ltd, but it had not received them and recorded them in its books by the end of January.
2 C Young Ltd sent goods to A Hall Ltd, but the latter had not received them and therefore had not entered the £425 in its books by the end of January.

A reconciliation statement can be drawn up by A Hall Ltd as on 31 January 2013.

Reconciliation of Supplier's Statement
C Young Ltd as on 31 January 2013

		£	£
Balance per our purchases ledger			1,679
Add Purchases not received by us	(ii)	425	
Returns not received by supplier	(i)	116	
			541
Balance per supplier's statement			2,220

18.8 Sales and purchases via credit cards

Nowadays, consumers are increasingly using credit cards to purchase goods and services. In effect, the sales are 'cash sales', as far as the purchasers are concerned: they have seen and received goods or obtained services and in their eyes they have paid for them by using their credit card. Such sales are very rarely sales to anyone other than the general public, as compared with sales to professionals in a specific trade.

Once a customer has received the goods or services from the seller, he or she does not need to be entered in the sales ledger as a debtor. All the selling company is then interested in, from a recording point of view, is collecting the money from the credit card company.

The book-keeping entries are as follows:

Sales of items via credit cards:	**Debit:**	Credit card company
	Credit:	Cash sales
Receipt of money from credit card company:	**Debit:**	Bank
	Credit:	Credit card company
Commission charged by credit card company:	**Debit:**	Selling expenses
	Credit:	Credit card company

Credit cards are discussed in more detail in Chapter 20.

Chapter summary

- A credit note is a document issued by a supplier and sent to a purchaser showing details of an allowance made in respect of unsatisfactory goods or services.
- Credit notes are entered into a sales returns day book. The total net goods returned for the month are posted to the debit side of the sales returns account and the total VAT column is posted to the debit side of the VAT account in the general ledger. Each transaction is also posted to the credit side of the individual customers' accounts in the sales ledger.
- A useful hint: goods returned to us are entered on the 'IN' side of the sales returns account and on the 'OUT' side of the individual customers' accounts.
- Purchases credit notes are entered into a purchases returns day book. Each transaction is then posted to the debit side of the individual suppliers' accounts in the purchases ledger. The total net goods returned for the month are posted to the credit side of the purchases returns account and the total of the VAT column is posted to the credit side of the VAT account in the general ledger.
- A useful hint: the goods returned by us to the supplier go 'IN' to the suppliers' accounts and come 'OUT' of the purchases returns account.
- To keep a note of the number of returns being made it is important to have separate accounts for sales returns and purchases returns.
- Statements are issued by suppliers and sent to their customers, requesting payment of amounts due. The customer uses the statement to check the suppliers' records against their own and if correct will make payment against the statement.

- Statements are also used to reconcile the records of the supplier to those of the customer. Differences are identified and if errors or discrepancies have arisen then amendments can be made.
- Credit card sales are treated as cash sales. Commission charged by the credit card company is treated as a selling expense.

EXERCISES

*Note: Questions with the suffix 'X' shown after the question number do **not** have answers shown at the back of the book. Answers to the other questions are shown in Appendix E.*

18.1 From the list shown below calculate the amount of VAT, at 20%, to be added to the cost of the goods on each of the following invoices and credit notes. Enter up the sales day book and the sales returns day book with columns for 'Goods', 'VAT' and 'Total'. Then post to the customers' accounts in the sales ledger and show the transfers to the general ledger. Folio references are not required.

2013
June 3 Credit sales to: J Alcock £180; P Twigg £60
June 7 Credit sales to: Bell Products £140; Travis Ltd £330
June 12 Goods returned to us by: J Alcock £30
June 24 Credit sales to B Seddon £780
June 28 Goods returned to us by Travis Ltd £50
June 28 Credit sales to P Twigg £440

18.2 You are to enter up the purchases day book and the purchases returns day book from the details of the invoices and credit notes listed below. Post the items to the creditors' accounts in the purchases ledger and show the transfers to the relevant accounts in the general ledger at the end of the month. Folio references are not required.

2013
May 1 Credit purchase from J Yau Ltd £120 plus VAT £24
May 6 Credit purchases from the following: S Wager £80 plus VAT £16; Ash Bros £220 plus VAT £44
May 9 Goods returned by us to the following: J Yau Ltd £30 plus VAT £6
May 14 Credit purchase from J Yau Ltd £60 plus VAT £12
May 20 Credit purchases from the following: D Wong £300 plus VAT £60, Rughani & Co £280 plus VAT £56, Ash Bros £80 plus VAT £16
May 27 Goods returned by us to the following: D Wong £40 plus VAT £8
May 31 Credit purchases from: A Davies £50 plus VAT £10, Rughani & Co £170 plus VAT £34

18.3X Framework Ltd is a small company which specialises in framing pictures, photographs, certificates, etc. At the beginning of the financial year 1 January 2013 the following balances appeared in the ledgers:

Sales Ledger		*Purchases Ledger*	
	£		£
J Forbes (Fancy Gifts)	745 Dr	M & P Fitzsimons	800 Cr
J Goodwin & Co	276 Dr	L Horne	450 Cr
L & P Moss	390 Dr	M Ward & Sons	245 Cr

During January 2013 the following transactions took place and invoices/credit notes were issued to the company's customers and/or received from their suppliers:

Jan 2 Purchased goods from L Horne £650, plus VAT £130.
Jan 3 Purchased goods from M Ward & Sons £334, plus VAT £66.80.
Jan 11 Sold goods to J Goodwin & Co £328, plus VAT £65.60.
Jan 12 Received credit note from L Horne £42, plus VAT £8.40, in respect of goods returned as unsuitable.
Jan 22 Purchased goods from M & P Fitzsimons, £756, plus VAT £151.20.
Jan 23 Sold goods to J Forbes (Fancy Gifts) £1,234, plus VAT £246.80.
Jan 28 Sold goods to L & P Moss, £2,500, plus VAT £500.
Jan 28 Received credit note from M & P Fitzsimons £200, plus VAT £40 in respect of faulty goods returned.

On 31 January the company received a cheque from J Forbes (Fancy Gifts) for £745 and a cheque for £200 on account from L & P Moss.

On the same day the company paid cheques to M & P Fitzsimons £500 on account and M Ward & Sons £245.

Required:

(*a*) Open personal accounts for the company's customers (accounts receivable) and suppliers (accounts payable) and enter the outstanding balances as at 1 January 2013.
(*b*) Enter the purchase invoices in the purchases day book, the sales invoices in the sales day book and the credit notes in the purchases returns day book .
(*c*) Post the invoices and credit notes to the customer's and supplier's accounts in the sales and purchases ledgers.
(*d*) Total up the day books and post the relevant totals to the purchases account, sales account, purchases returns account and VAT account in the general ledger.
(*e*) Post the cheques received to the customer's accounts in the sales ledger.
(*f*) Post the cheques paid to the supplier's accounts in the purchases ledger.
(*g*) Balance the accounts in the sales and purchases ledger at the 31 January and bring down the balances on 1 February 2013.
(*h*) Prepare a list of outstanding accounts receivable (debtors) and outstanding accounts payable (creditors) as at 31 January 2013.

18.4X You are employed as an accounts clerk for Elder's Printing Co, 36 High Street, Shrewsbury SH4 8JK. One of your tasks is to prepare statements of account which are sent out to customers at the end of each month. Two of the customers' accounts are shown below.

Sales Ledger

D Hammond Ltd Account

2013		£	2013		£
Jan 1	Balance b/d	1,403	Jan 7	Bank	1,380
Jan 3	Sales	177	Jan 12	Credit note	23
Jan 10	Sales	527			
Jan 25	Sales	200			

Alex Richards Ltd Account

2013		£	2013		£
Jan 1	Balance b/d	346	Jan 7	Bank	292
Jan 7	Sales	27	Jan 7	Discount	8
Jan 9	Sales	521	Jan 12	Credit note	46
Jan 28	Sales	400			
Jan 31	Sales	53			

The addresses of the above customers are as follows:

D Hammond Ltd Bay House Heath Road Shrewsbury SH7 3KL	Alex Richards Ltd Unit 12 Greenways Industrial Estate Chester CE21 9HU

Required:

(*a*) Balance each of the above accounts off, and state the amount owing by each of the customers.

(*b*) Draft a statement of account to be sent to each customer.

18.5X As accounts clerk for Perris Design Company one of your tasks is to reconcile the company's suppliers' accounts statements with the purchases ledger accounts prior to payment. Shown below are two statements which have been received from two of your suppliers; Bennetts Ltd and Kirkhams Products Ltd.

Prepare reconciliation statements reconciling the statements with the ledger accounts.

STATEMENT

BENNETTS LTD
The Green, Brentwood, Essex.

Tel: 0277 371832
Date: 31st July 2013

Customer:
Perris Design Co
Deansgate
Ipswich.

Account No: 47310

Date 2013	*Description/reference*	*Debit* £ p	*Credit* £ p	*Balance* £ p
30 June	Balance b/f			252.41
2 July	003061 Inv.	84.96		
9 July	003123 Inv.	42.50		379.87
16 July	Cash		252.41	127.46
23 July	003972 Inv.	696.32		823.78
30 July	003989 Inv.	121.50		945.28
AMOUNT NOW DUE				

Interest will be charged on overdue accounts

STATEMENT

KIRKHAMS PRODUCTS LTD
Riverside Works, Romford.

Tel: 0708 649685
Date: 31st July 2013

Customer:
Perris Design Co
Deansgate
Ipswich.

Account No: PX/32971

Date	*Description/reference*	*Debit* £ p	*Credit* £ p	*Balance* £ p
July 1	Balance b/f			1,829.00
July 15	Invoice No. 82300	531.75		
July 18	Invoice No. 82663	54.62		
July 22	Invoice No. 84133	459.23		
July 24	Invoice No. 84624	68.42		2,943.02
July 30	Cash		1,432.30	1,510.72

AMOUNT NOW DUE   N.B. Our Inv. No. 82076 for £396.70 is overdue

Interest will be charged on overdue accounts

PURCHASES LEDGER

Bennetts Ltd a/c

2013			2013		
July 10	Bank	252.41	July 1	Balance b/d	252.41
27	Returns	63.50	2	Purchases	84.96
31	Balance c/d	760.28	9	Purchases	42.50
			23	Purchases	696.32
		1,076.19			1,076.19
			Aug 1	Balance b/d	760.28

Kirkhams Products Ltd

2013			2013		
July 30	Bank	1,432.30	July 1	Balance b/d	1,829.00
30	Purchases Returns	54.62	15	Purchases	531.75
31	Balance c/d	1,387.68	18	Purchases	54.62
			22	Purchases	459.23
		2,874.60			2,874.60
			Aug 1	Balance b/d	1,387.68

CHAPTER 19

Analytical day books

Learning objectives

After you have studied this chapter you should be able to:

- enter invoices into analytical sales and purchases day books
- post transactions from analytical sales and purchases day books to the personal accounts in the sales and purchases ledgers
- post totals from the analytical day books to the general ledger
- complete a VAT account from the day books.

19.1 Introduction

In the previous three chapters the sales, purchases and returns day books were shown using three columns, namely 'Goods', 'VAT' and 'Total'. In many businesses operating the day books using three columns to record the purchases and sales on credit is quite sufficient. However, some businesses find it useful to analyse their sales and purchases between different types of goods bought and sold. Furthermore many organisations find it useful to analyse their sales between different departments and their purchases between goods bought for resale and expenses, such as stationery, motor expenses and so on. For example, a coffee shop may sell refreshments and gifts and wish to ascertain the profit on the two different sales areas. In this example, it would be advantageous to analyse both sales and purchases to reflect the goods/services bought or sold in each area. The purchases day book could be ruled as follows:

Purchases Day Book						
Date	*Details*	*Folio*	*Total*	*VAT*	*Gifts*	*Food*
			£	£	£	£

19.2 Entering sales invoices into an analytical sales day book

When a business requires additional information from its records, the books can easily be adapted to meet particular needs.

Let us consider a retail computer shop that sells hardware and software to the public, local businesses and schools. The proprietor, Mr Harlow, wishes to monitor the sales of each of these lines separately. Exhibit 19.1 shows an example of Mr Harlow's **analytical sales day book**.

Exhibit 19.1

Sales Day Book *(page 7)*

Date	*Details*	*Folio*	*Total*	*VAT*	*Software*	*Hardware*
			£	£	£	£
April 1	Mount Hey School	SL 1	720	120		600
3	Ashby Marketing	SL 2	576	96	480	
15	Davenport Manufacturing	SL 3	4,800	800		4,000
20	St James College	SL 4	24,000	4,000		20,000
			30,096	5,016	480	24,600
				GL 3	GL 1	GL 2

19.3 Posting credit sales

Each sale now has to be posted to the individual customer accounts in the sales ledger, as follows:

(i) The total of each sales invoice (i.e. the net price of the goods plus VAT) is posted to each customer's account on the debit side, since the goods are going 'into' their account.

(ii) At the end of the period, the sales day book is added up and the totals posted on the credit, or 'OUT', side of the following accounts:

- sales of software account
- sales of hardware account
- VAT account.

The results are shown below:

Sales Ledger

Mount Hey School Account *SL 1*

	Folio	£	
April 1 Sales	SB 7	720	

Ashby Marketing Co Account *SL 2*

	Folio	£	
April 3 Sales	SB 7	576	

Davenport Manufacturing Co Account *SL 3*

	Folio	£			
April 15 Sales	SB 7	4,800			

St James College Account *SL 4*

	Folio	£			
April 20 Sales	SB 7	24,000			

General Ledger

Sale of Software Account *GL 1*

				Folio	£
			April 30 Credit sales for April	SB 7	480

Sale of Hardware Account *GL 2*

				Folio	£
			April 30 Credit sales for April	SB 7	24,600

VAT Account *GL 3*

				Folio	£
			April 30 VAT on credit sales for April	SB 7	5,016

19.4 Entering purchases invoices into an analytical purchases day book

Another business might wish to monitor its purchases that include goods for resale and business expenses such as electricity, motor expenses, etc. The example shown in Exhibit 19.2 illustrates how a business could analyse its purchases invoices using an **analytical purchases day book**.

Exhibit 19.2

Purchases Day Book *(page 3)*

Date	*Details*	*Folio*	*Total*	*VAT*	*Goods*	*Motor Exp*	*Stationery*
			£	£	£	£	£
Nov 1	Bould & Co	PL 1	4,320	720	3,600		
10	Sigley's (Stat)	PL 2	48	8			40
17	T Adams Ltd	PL 3	960	160	800		
30	Robinson's Garage	PL 4	192	32		160	
			5,520	920	4,400	160	40
				GL 3	GL 1	GL 2	GL 3

19.5 Posting credit purchases

Each purchase now has to be posted to the individual supplier accounts in the purchases ledger, as follows:

(i) The *total* of each purchase invoice (i.e. the net price of the goods, plus VAT) is posted to each supplier's account on the *credit* side, since the goods are coming 'OUT' of their accounts.

(ii) At the end of the period, the purchases day book is added up and the totals are posted on the *debit*, or 'IN', side of the following accounts:

- purchases account
- motor expenses account
- stationery account
- VAT account.

Purchases Ledger

Bould & Co Account — *PL 1*

				Folio	£
			Nov 1 Purchases	PB 3	4,320

Sigley's Stationers Account — *PL 2*

				Folio	£
			Nov 10 Purchases	PB 3	48

T Adams Ltd Account — *PL 3*

				Folio	£
			Nov 17 Purchases	PB 3	960

Robinson's Garage Account — *PL 4*

				Folio	£
			Nov 30 Purchases	PB 3	192

General Ledger

Purchases Account — *GL 1*

	Folio	£			
Nov 30 Credit purchases for November	PB 3	4,400			

Motor Expenses Account — *GL 2*

	Folio	£			
Nov 30 Purchases day book	PB 3	160			

Stationery Account — *GL 3*

	Folio	£			
Nov 30 Purchases day book	PB 3	40			

VAT Account — *GL 4*

	Folio	£			
Nov 30 Purchases day book	PB 3	920			

19.6 Further example of the VAT account

In the above sections and previous three chapters it has been shown that VAT is recorded in a separate column in both the sales and purchases day book. You have also seen that the total of the VAT columns have been transferred into the VAT account at the end of each month. In the same way that VAT is recorded in the sales and purchases day books there are also separate VAT columns in both the sales returns and purchases returns day books as shown in Chapter 18. Taking these into account the VAT account is as follows:

VAT Account

(Input tax)	*(Output tax)*
VAT on purchases	VAT on sales and/or services
VAT on sales returns	VAT on purchases returns
VAT on expenses	VAT on other income
VAT on purchases of non-current assets (except cars)*	VAT on sale of non-current assets*

*The purchase and sale of non-current assets is discussed later on in this book in Chapters 26 and 27.

The following example shows the VAT account including sales, purchases, sales returns and purchases returns.

Example: The following financial information has been extracted from the books of Morridge Products Ltd for the period 1 January to 31 March 2012. Prepare the VAT account for the quarter ended 31 March 2012 and state the amount of VAT to be paid to HMRC.

	Purchases		*Purchases Returns*	
2012	*Net (£)*	*VAT (£)*	*Net (£)*	*VAT (£)*
January	20,000	4,000	1,000	200
February	15,000	3,000	400	80
March	18,000	3,600	–	–
	53,000	10,600	1,400	280

	Sales		*Sales Returns*	
2012	*Net (£)*	*VAT (£)*	*Net (£)*	*VAT (£)*
January	40,000	8,000	1,200	240
February	28,000	5,600	–	–
March	35,000	7,000	800	160
	103,000	20,600	2,000	400

The account is shown below:

VAT Account

2012		2012		
Jan 31 Purchases Day Book	4,000	Jan 31 Sales Day Book	8,000	
Jan 31 Sales Returns Day Book	240	Jan 31 Purchases Returns Day Book	200	
Feb 28 Purchases Day Book	3,000	Feb 28 Sales Day Book	5,600	
Mar 31 Purchases Day Book	3,600	Feb 28 Purchases Returns Day Book	80	
Mar 31 Sales Returns Day Book	160	Mar 31 Sales Day Book	7,000	
Mar 31 Balances c/d	9,880			
	20,880		20,880	
		Apr 1 Balance b/d	9,880	

The amount of VAT due to be paid to HMRC for the quarter ended 31 March 2012 is £9,880. Until this payment is made it is a liability and would appear in the trial balance on the credit side as follows:

Trial balance as at 31 March 2012

	Dr £	*Cr* £
VAT owing to HMRC		9,880

In some cases where the VAT on **inputs** exceeds the output VAT then a refund would be due to the company from HMRC. For example if input VAT for the quarter ended 30 June 2012 amounted to £1,000 and the output VAT was £750 then a refund of £250 would be due to the company. This would appear on the trial balance as a debit entry, see below:

Trial balance as at 30 June 2012

	Dr £	*Cr* £
VAT due from HMRC	250	

19.7 Advantages of analysis books

The advantages of analysis books are that businesses can be provided with exactly the information that they need, at the time when they want it. Different businesses have different needs, and they therefore analyse their books in different ways.

Analysis books enable businesses to do such things as:

- calculate the profit or loss made by each part of a business
- draw up control accounts for the sales and purchases ledgers (see Chapter 25)
- keep a check on the sales of each type of goods
- keep a check on goods sold in different locations, departments or sections
- identify purchasers of each type of good offered for sale.

Chapter summary

- Many organisations use analytical day books for entering sales and purchases invoices, they are books of original entry.
- Analytical day books are especially useful for the recording of VAT since the day book contains several analysis columns allowing the VAT content of an invoice to be recorded. The additional columns enable further analysis to be made, for example, recording sales for different sections of the business or different types of expenditure in the purchases day book.
- Invoices are entered and analysed according to the type of sale or expense at the time the transaction is recorded.
- The total amount of the invoice (i.e. the amount of the goods plus the VAT) is posted to the individual customer's and supplier's account.
- At the end of the month the total of the VAT column and other columns, appropriately analysed, will be posted to the accounts in the general ledger.
- At the end of the period the VAT account is prepared from the sales, purchases, sales returns and purchases returns accounts.
- There are many advantages of using analytical day books.

EXERCISES

*Note: Questions with the suffix 'X' shown after the question number do **not** have answers shown at the back of the book. Answers to the other questions are shown in Appendix E.*

19.1 The Curtain Design Company sells both ready-made and custom-made curtains to local hotels, nursing homes and the public. It operates an analytical sales day book, where it analyses the sales into sales of ready-made curtains and custom-made curtains.

The following invoices were sent during November 2012. All goods are subject to VAT at 20%.

Date	*Customer*	*Ready-made* £	*Custom-made* £
Nov 1	Jarvis Arms Hotel		2,300
Nov 8	Springs Nursing Home	1,000	
Nov 15	J P Morten	220	
Nov 17	Queen's Hotel		1,500
Nov 30	W Blackshaw	90	

You are required to:

(*a*) record the above transactions in an analytical sales day book

(*b*) post the invoices to the personal accounts in the sales ledger

(*c*) post the totals to the appropriate accounts in the general ledger.

(Use your own folio references.)

19.2 The Hall Engineering Company manufactures small engineering components for the motor-car industry. It operates an analytical purchases day book, in which the purchases invoices are recorded.

During May 2012, the following invoices were received. All goods are subject to VAT at 20%.

			£
May 1	Black's Engineering Co	Engineering goods	520
May 3	Ace Printing Co	Printing catalogues	145
May 24	Morgan's Garage	Petrol Account	120
May 26	Martin's Foundry	Engineering parts	700
May 28	Office Supplies	Stationery	126
May 29	Black's Engineering Co	Engineering parts	220

Required:

(*a*) Enter the purchase invoices in an analytical purchases day book using the following analysis columns:

- Engineering parts
- Printing and stationery
- Motor expenses
- VAT.

(*b*) Post the transactions to the personal accounts in the purchases ledger.

(*c*) Post the totals to the appropriate accounts in the general ledger.

(Use your own folio references.)

19.3 The following credit transactions took place in May 2013 and have been entered into the sales day book as shown below. No entries have been made in the ledgers.

Sales Day Book					
Date	*Details*	*Invoice Number*	*Goods*	*VAT*	*Total*
2013			£	£	£
May 2	McGrath Ltd	5013	110.00	22.00	132.00
May 10	Ashley Products	5014	640.00	128.00	768.00
May 21	Denson Bros	5015	70.00	14.00	84.00
May 30	Chang Supplies	5016	360.00	72.00	432.00
			1,180.00	236.00	1,416.00

(*a*) What will be the entries in the sales ledger?

Select your answer from the following list: Chang Supplies, Sales Account, Sales Returns Account, McGrath Ltd, Sales Ledger Control Account, Denson Bros, Cash, VAT, Ashley Products, Purchases Account.

Sales Ledger

Account name	*Amount*	*Debit*	*Credit*
	£	✓	✓

(*b*) Post the totals of the sales day book to the sales account and VAT account in the general ledger. Draw up your own 'T' accounts.

19.4X Adel Garden Centre divides its purchases of stock into two main departments: Outdoor Furniture and Garden Tools. Credit purchases during the month of October 2013 were as set out below, with VAT at 10% to be included on all transactions.

2 October	Oakland Supplies 6 steel spades at £18.75 each 8 garden forks at £10.50 each Less trade discount 20%
14 October	Airedale Products 4 patio furniture sets at £49.60 each Less trade discount 15%
22 October	Oakland Supplies 6 garden tool sets at £34.90 each 4 garden forks at £10.50 each Less trade discount 20% 8 sun loungers at £39.95 each Less trade discount 25%
20 October	Airedale Products 1 patio furniture set invoiced on 14 October was returned because it was damaged. A credit note was issued.
28 October	Oakland Supplies 2 garden tool sets were returned because they were faulty. A credit note was issued.

You are required to do the following:

(*a*) Draw up a purchases day book and purchases returns day book with analysis columns for Total, Outdoor Furniture, Garden Tools and VAT. Enter the date, name of supplier and the amounts of money into the appropriate columns. (Details of invoices are NOT required in the day books.)

(*b*) Total the day books.

(*c*) Write up the purchases ledger accounts from the day books, and balance the accounts at the end of the month.

OCR

CHAPTER 20

Business banking

Learning objectives

After you have studied this chapter you should be able to:

- appreciate the legal relationship with the bank and the customer
- differentiate between current, deposit and loan accounts
- understand the various methods of transferring money by the banking system
- appreciate the services offered by a bank
- understand the clearing system
- be aware of the security measures necessary when using electronic methods of banking
- appreciate the use of the bank statement.

20.1 Introduction

The trading activity, in which all businesses are engaged, involves the transfer of money as goods and/or services are bought and sold. In order to facilitate money transfer all businesses will require a bank account. Banks can offer their business customers three main types of accounts:

1 *Current accounts* are used for regular payments into and out of a bank account. A cheque book will be given by the bank to the holder of the account, who will use it to make payments to people to whom they owe money. Payment may also be made by standing order or direct debit. The holder will be given a paying-in book to enable money to be paid into their current account. An overdraft facility can often be made available by the bank but prior arrangements need to be made. Current accounts do not normally earn interest but more recently some banks have been offering interest on these accounts to attract customers.

2 *Deposit accounts* are for holding money that is not required for making payments in the foreseeable future, i.e. savings. Interest is given by the bank on money kept in such accounts.

3 *Loan accounts* provide funds to an individual or business usually to finance the purchase of a capital item such as a motor vehicle, plant and equipment. Loans are usually for a fixed period, for example, three years, and interest is charged to the customer.

The opening of such accounts will involve a contract between the bank and its customer clearly stating the relationship between the two parties and the terms relating to the operation of the account/s.

The banking system has changed dramatically over the past few years and there are now a number of different ways in which money can be transferred between businesses and their customers.

20.2 Transferring money

This can be received or paid by a business or organisation by various methods, including the following:

- cash
- cheques
- debit cards
- credit cards
- bank giro credit (BGC) transfer
- Bankers' Automated Clearing Service (BACS)
- standing order
- direct debits
- bank draft
- Clearing House Automated Payment System (CHAPS)
- Internet business transactions
- paying-in slips.

20.3 Cash

Receiving cash

Cash is still used extensively in the retail business by customers purchasing goods. Security is a major problem in a number of ways for the business receiving the cash as shown below:

- it must be counted and checked to ensure that it corresponds with any documentation showing the amount to be received
- it must be stored safely and taken to the bank as soon as possible
- counterfeit money can be in circulation and detection equipment could be needed to prevent this type of fraud
- there should be regular internal checks to ensure that the persons handling cash are honest and funds do not go astray.

Most cash sales are made where electronic cash tills are in operation and these issue receipts automatically. The receipts should be kept by customers, not only as proof of payment, but, as evidence of the purchase should the goods have to be returned if faulty or unsuitable.

The electronic operation of the system ensures that the amount of cash received over a particular period is recorded automatically. The amounts received can easily be checked against the till records enabling cash deposits to the bank to be readily made.

A till receipt is shown in Exhibit 20.1.

Exhibit 20.1 Receipt for a cash sale

Name of store ______	**MILO'S SUPERSTORE** **MANCHESTER**	
VAT registration number ______	VAT No. 212 5212 78	
	RECEIPT	
Goods bought ______	Superjet travel game	17.50
	Bulendo magic tricks	11.25
	Junior chess set	9.12
Total price due ______	3 items: TOTAL	37.87
Cash given ______	CASH	40.00
Change to be given ______	CHANGE	2.13
	Please keep receipt for refunds or queries	
Location of cash till ______	Cash till No. 5	
Date/time/reference number of transaction __	14/12/2013 11.58	1216 44/16

Cash that needs to be banked will be detailed on a paying-in slip – this is described in section 20.14.

Paying by cash

When payments are made by a business it is safer and easier to use a non-cash method such as cheques or the BACS system (this is described in section 20.9). Many businesses who employ weekly paid staff still pay wages in cash and this method involves all the security problems which have been discussed previously. However, small value purchases can be made using the petty cash system. This is described in Chapter 22.

20.4 Cheques

Receiving cheques

Most customers who have received goods and/or services pay for them by cheque. These customers will have established a credit account with the business after credit worthiness checks have been carried out.

Cheques received from these well-established credit account customers should be carefully examined for the following:

- that the cheque is drawn payable to the receiver
- that the correct amount is stated both in words and in figures
- that the cheque is dated and is not out of date or postdated
- that the cheque has been properly signed.

If any of these factors are not in order the cheque will have to be returned to the drawer for amendment or for a new cheque to be issued. The UK Domestic Cheque Guarantee Card Scheme closed on 30 June 2011 which means that the cheque guarantee hologram has been removed from **debit cards**. This has ensured that cheque payment by casual customers has virtually ceased and has resulted in a vast increase in the use of debit cards.

Paying by cheque

When a business pays by cheque for goods or services it must be signed by an authorised signatory. The person signing the cheque for the business must have the approval of the company. The bank will also have previously been notified of the name of this person and will have carried out checks to verify this person's identity. They are legally bound to carry out this procedure to prevent fraud and to counter money-laundering activities. Larger businesses will usually insist on at least two authorised signatories to ensure proper payments are made.

It is vital that the business's account has sufficient money in it to cover the amounts paid otherwise the bank will not process the cheque.

The person writing the cheque and using it for payment is known as the **drawer**. The person to whom the cheque is paid is known as the **payee** and the **drawee** is the bank. A completed cheque is shown in Exhibit 20.2.

Exhibit 20.2

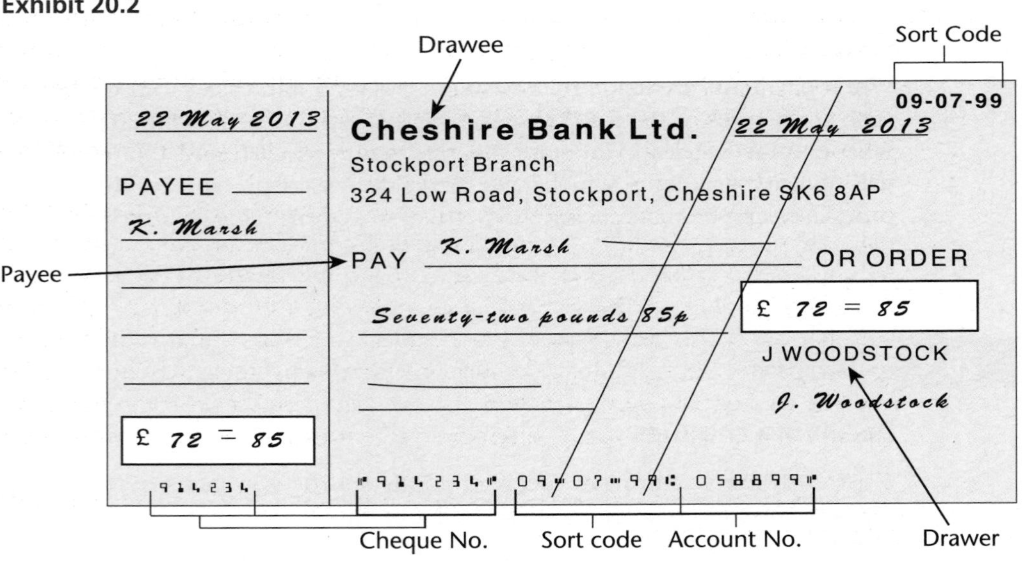

The completed cheque shows that J Woodstock, the drawer, is paying K Marsh, the sum of £72.85 on 22 May 2013. The counterfoil, at the left-hand side of the cheque, is also completed and retained by J Woodstock as a record of the transaction. It will be used to enter the details in the cash book which is covered in a later chapter.

Security of cheques

All cheques used by businesses will be crossed with two diagonal lines pre-printed on the face of the cheque as shown in Exhibit 20.2. This ensures that it must be paid into a bank account, building society account or saving account. The bank will ensure that it is paid into the payee's account if the words 'A/c Payee Only' are written between the diagonal lines.

Cheque clearing

It is important to understand that when a cheque is sent from one business to another it takes time to clear or process it. The business receiving the cheque will pass this to its bank who will in turn seek approval from the drawer's bank to transfer the amount shown on the cheque. The process involves an exchange centre where each bank collects the cheques drawn on accounts held with the centre. Typically the process takes three to five working days. It is important that cheques received by a business are banked on the same day to ensure that the funds are recorded as early as possible.

20.5 Credit cards

Receiving money by credit card

Credit cards are a method for customers to purchase goods without needing to pay by cash or make out a cheque. They can also be used when the customer wishes to make a purchase by telephone, fax or via the internet. Credit cards are issued by organisations such as Visa and Mastercard who operate the system. A recent development has been the 'chip and pin' system which involves the bank issuing a card with a unique four-digit number to each customer.

The business will have an electronic card acceptance point into which the customer places the card. When the system has recognised the card the customer is requested to enter his or her unique number and upon validation the purchase value will be accepted. The business bank account will be credited with the purchase sum automatically. This new system has resulted in a substantial reduction in fraudulent transactions. It has eliminated the need for the business to check the card details and the customer's signature which saves time. However, extreme care should be taken when entering the PIN number so that it cannot be seen by other customers or employees.

When customers are remote from the business they will have to provide the following information:

- card number – 16-digit and on some occasions the last three digits of the security number on the reverse side of the card
- expiry date of the card
- name printed on the card.

Again the purchase sum is transferred automatically to the business and the customer's account with the company is charged.

Paying by credit card

Some organisations provide business credit cards to their staff usually to pay for such things as hotel accommodation, travel expenses, etc. When these are used the charge will be made to the business, not to the person who has used the card. The business will set limits of expenditure on the card and will require copy vouchers and any other form of receipt to be handed in regularly. These will then be compared with the monthly account received from the credit card company.

20.6 Debit cards

Debit cards are issued by a number of banks in conjunction with Visa, Mastercard, etc., and are used in a very similar way to credit cards. Customers operate the same 'chip and pin' system, the crucial difference is that at the time of making payment by debit card, funds are electronically transferred from the purchaser's bank to the supplier's bank account.

Most banks now provide their customers with debit cards having more than one function. In addition to being able to make payments debit cards can be used for making withdrawals from cash machines both in the UK and abroad. This is a popular way for customers to purchase all types of goods and services since it is quick and efficient, cash free and from the point of view of the supplier payment goes directly to their account once the purchase has been validated by the system.

The most important aspect of using debit cards is to ensure that the customer has adequate funds in their account before attempting to use these facilities.

20.7 Electronic funds transfer at point of sale (EFTPOS)

The **EFTPOS** system is used when credit card and debit card transactions are made as described in sections 20.5 and 20.6. In the case of credit cards the supplier usually receives payment within two days whereas the use of debit cards means the purchaser's bank account is debited at the point of sale and the supplier's bank account is credited with the customer's purchase amount.

20.8 Bank giro credit transfer

This is a safe and convenient way of receiving and paying money. Money paid by this method will be received directly into the business's bank account and the sums received will be shown on its bank statement.

Paying by this method requires the business to prepare the payments in the usual way but in addition prepares a list and bank giro credit slips detailing each payee's banking details and the amount due. The list and slips are then sent to the bank with one cheque to cover all the payments. These will be automatically sent to the various bank accounts through a centralised system.

This form of money transfer is still in use but larger organisations have adopted the BACS system.

20.9 BACS (Bankers' Automated Clearing Service)

The service enables the business to receive money due to it and to make payments. BACS is a company owned by the Bank of England, the high street banks and some building societies, which offers a computerised payment transfer system that organisations may use to pay not only wages and salaries but also suppliers, dividends, grants, pensions, etc.

Processing the transfers is a three-day cycle. Information is stored by the BACS system to enable payments to be made on pre-set days, such as salary payments.

It is important to note that a remittance advice should be sent to the supplier when using BACS. Failing this the supplier will not know that the payment has been made until they receive their bank statement. They may also have difficulty in tracing the identity of the business paying the amount.

When the business receives payment from their customers they will also need a remittance advice from the customer for exactly the same reason as explained above and to know which invoices have been covered by the payment.

20.10 Standing order

A person may make a regular payment from their bank account, or receive a regular amount into their account by standing order. This is a straightforward method of making regular fixed payments over which the payer has full control. The steps necessary to make payments by a standing order are as follows:

- **payer** instructs the bank in writing to pay a certain amount, on a particular day to a specific organisation
- bank makes payment via the computer banking system.

The payer can instruct the bank to cease or amend the payment at any time by giving written notification.

20.11 Direct debit

This has become a common method of paying both fixed and variable amounts of money. Many businesses offer discounts on payment since they are so anxious for their customers to use this method. The system of operation is as follows:

- the proposed receiver (**payee**) of the money sends a mandate to the payer
- **payer** completes the mandate and returns it to the payee
- payee sends the mandate to the payer's bank who will arrange to send the money to the payee's bank via the computer banking system.

The amounts that the payer has authorised to be withdrawn from their own account can vary as the payee makes changes. Typical examples of variations are usually increases in insurance premiums, business rates and loan repayments. It is normal for the payee to advise the payer of such increases.

Payees prefer this method of regular payment since they have control over them and should the payer wish to cancel a direct debit they have to do so through the bank/payee. While this method of payment is convenient for both parties, the payer should exercise great care in giving permission for the setting up of direct debits.

The process of setting up a direct debit mandate as described above is quite laborious and time-consuming. However, it is now possible to set up a direct debit by telephone or online using the **Automated Direct Debit Instruction Service (AUDDIS)**. This is a fast way of arranging for a business to make repayments almost immediately for, say, the purchase of computer equipment and to pay by instalments. The safeguards of the Direct Debit Guarantee apply to both a paper-based mandate and paperless mandate.

20.12 Large transfers of money

Bank drafts

When a business wants to make a large purchase from a supplier with whom they have no credit account it could mean it having to use a **bank draft**. A bank draft is raised by the business's bank from funds held by the business and is passed to the supplier for whom it is a secure and guaranteed method of payment.

Clearing House Automated Payments System (CHAPS)

The CHAPS computerised system has been developed to offer same-day sterling fund transfer of large amounts of money. It is particularly useful for the sale and purchase of residential and commercial property. CHAPS also offers low value transactions via its Faster Payments Service.

20.13 Internet business transactions

Most businesses nowadays have websites where the goods or services on offer can be viewed and purchases made online. Since the purchaser and supplier are remote from each other transactions are made using a credit card or a debit card. The use of these cards is covered in sections 20.5 and 20.6.

The online facilities provided by businesses for selling their goods/services are being used increasingly. Consumers can quickly search a number of like suppliers for the keenest prices and best delivery, without leaving home. The supplier will then despatch the goods to them.

Security of online buying is still of concern and businesses must ensure they have systems installed to guard against attempted fraud. Fraudulent transactions can come from a number of sources including:

- computer hackers accessing consumers' and businesses' files
- cloning of credit and debit cards which are then used to access legitimate consumers' bank accounts

- identity fraud where the criminal can apply to a bank for credit/debit cards based on the victim's details.

The encoding of data ('encryption') needs to be constantly reviewed and updated to prevent this type of crime.

20.14 Paying-in slips

A paying-in slip is prepared when the business wants to pay money into its current account. Details of cash and cheques that are to be paid into the bank are entered on the slip. The completed slip, cash and cheques are then taken to the bank. Normally a business deals with one particular branch of its bank but the bank giro credit shown in Exhibit 20.3 can be used to pay money into its account at any branch of any bank.

Exhibit 20.3

(a) Face of paying-in slip

Counterfoil:

Date *22 May 2013*
Cashier's stamp and initials

A/c *J WOODSTOCK*

Cash *23 - 92*
Cheques POs etc *249 - 59*

£ *273 – 51*

Paying-in slip:

Date *22 May 2013*
Cashier's stamp and initials

bank giro credit

Destination Branch Code number *09 - 07 - 99*

Bank *Cheshire Bank*

Branch *Stockport*

Account Name (Block letters) & A/c. No *J. WOODSTOCK 058899*

Paid in by *J Woodstock*

Details for advice to recipient

	pounds	pence
£50 notes	20	
£20 notes	3	
£10 notes		50
£5 notes		30
£2 coins		12
£1 coins		
50p coins		
Other silver		
Bronze coin		
Total cash	23	92
Cheques, POs etc. (see over)	249	59
£	273	51

Counterfoil retained by Woodstock

Paying-in slip and cash and cheques handed in to bank

(b) Reverse side of paying-in slip

Details of Cheques, POs etc

for cheques please specify Drawer's name and	Bank Code Number as shown in top right corner				Counterfoil	
E. KANE & SON	*02-58-76*	184	15		184	15
J. GALE	*05-77-85*	65	44		65	44
In view of the risk of loss in course of clearing, customers are advised to keep an independent record of the drawers of cheques.	Total carried over £	249	59		249	59

Reverse of counterfoil

20.15 Bank statements

All the monies received and paid out of a business's current account are recorded in its cash book. The bank will also have a record of the transactions in its account for the business and will issue a statement of account on a regular basis, usually monthly.

It is important for the business to check the bank statement against the bank column in its own cash book to ensure that there are no errors (see section 21.2). A bank reconciliation statement is usually prepared to reconcile the bank's balance with those in the business's cash book. This topic is covered in Chapter 23.

Chapter summary

- The trading activity is emphasised as meaning the sale of goods and/or services between organisations.
- Fundamental to the trading activity is the receipt and payment of money.
- There are three main bank accounts, namely the current, deposit and loan accounts.
- Transferring money in the business can be carried out in various ways: cash, cheque, credit cards, debit cards, EFTPOS, bank giro credit transfer, BACS, standing order and direct debits.
- Larger sums of money can be transferred via bank draft or by using the clearing house automated payments system (CHAPS).
- Internet business transactions are becoming more and more popular for the online sale and purchase of goods and services. It is important to ensure good security measures are in place to avoid fraudulent transactions taking place.
- Each of the above methods is discussed and reasons given as to why a business might use a particular method(s).
- Paying-in slips are described since they can be used to deposit both cash and cheques into a bank account.
- The use of the bank statement enables the business to check bank transactions against its cash book records.

EXERCISES

Note: Questions with the suffix 'X' shown after the question number do ***not*** *have answers shown at the back of the book. Answers to the other questions are shown in Appendix E.*

20.1 Businesses in the retail sector are highly likely to receive cash from their customers in payment for goods/services. State what steps a business should take in the handling, storage and transfer of cash to a bank.

20.2 State briefly what other non-cash methods are available to businesses in both receiving and paying out money.

20.3 BACS is an organisation formed to handle the transfer of money between businesses. State the full name of BACS and briefly describe how the organisation carries out this function.

20.4 Morridge Products Ltd receives a cheque which has the normal crossing but, in addition, the words 'A/c payee only' have been written between the lines. Explain how a bank would process this cheque.

20.5X Direct debits are a convenient method of making payments. Explain how the system operates and say what the advantages are for the payer and payee.

20.6X The cheque below has been received today.

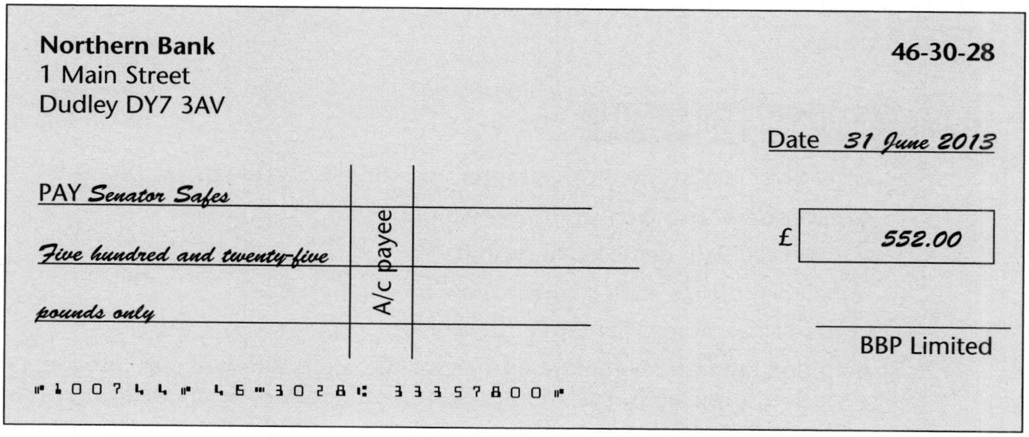

Northern Bank
1 Main Street
Dudley DY7 3AV

46-30-28

Date *31 June 2013*

PAY *Senator Safes*

Five hundred and twenty-five pounds only

A/c payee

£ *552.00*

BBP Limited

⑈100744⑈ 46⑉3028⑆ 33357800⑈

(*a*) Give *three* reasons why the cheque will not be honoured by the bank.
(*b*) What is the branch sort code number on the cheque?
(*c*) What document would you expect to be sent with a cheque in payment of an account?

AAT

20.7 Howard Photographics banks with The Central Bank and has recently sent a cheque to a supplier, Ben Brown Ltd. Give the name of the drawer, the drawee and the payee.

AAT

CHAPTER 21

Cash books

Learning objectives

After you have studied this chapter you should be able to:

- enter data into two- and three-column cash books
- enter 'contra' items in the cash book
- balance off the cash book at the end of a period
- use folio columns for cross-referencing purposes
- understand and complete entries for discounts allowed and discounts received both in the cash book, and at the end of a period, in the discount accounts in the general ledger
- enter data into a cash book with columns for VAT.

21.1 Introduction

The cash book consists of the cash account and the bank account put together in one book. Initially, we showed these two accounts on different pages of the ledger; now it is easier to put the two sets of account columns together. This means that we can record all money received and paid out on a particular date on the same page.

In the cash book, the debit column for cash is put next to the debit column for bank. The credit column for cash is put next to the credit column for bank.

21.2 Drawing up a cash book

In Exhibit 21.1 the cash account and bank account are shown as separate accounts whereas in Exhibit 21.2 the cash and bank accounts are shown together in a cash book. The bank columns contain details of the payments made by cheque and direct transfer from the bank account and the money received and paid into the bank account. The bank will also keep a copy of the customer's account in its own records.

Periodically, or on request, the bank sends a copy of the account in its books to the business. This document is known as a **bank statement**. Upon receipt of the bank statement the business will check the transactions against the bank columns in its own cash book to ensure that there are no errors.

Exhibit 21.1

Cash Account

2013		£	2013		£
Aug 2	T Moore	33	Aug 8	Postage	20
Aug 5	K Charles	25	Aug 12	C Potts	19
Aug 15	F Hughes	37	Aug 28	Stationery	25
Aug 30	H Howe	18	Aug 31	Balance c/d	49
		113			113
Sept 1	Balance b/d	49			

Bank Account

2013		£	2013		£
Aug 1	Capital	1,000	Aug 7	Rates	105
Aug 3	W P Ltd	244	Aug 12	F Small Ltd	95
Aug 16	K Noone	408	Aug 26	K French	268
Aug 30	H Sanders	20	Aug 31	Balance c/d	1,204
		1,672			1,672
Sept 1	Balance b/d	1,204			

Exhibit 21.2

Cash Book

2013		*Cash* £	*Bank* £	2013		*Cash* £	*Bank* £
Aug 1	Capital		1,000	Aug 7	Rates		105
" 2	T Moore	33		" 8	Postage	20	
" 3	W P Ltd		244	" 12	C Potts	19	
" 5	K Charles	25		" 12	F Small Ltd		95
" 15	F Hughes	37		" 26	K French		268
" 16	K Noone		408	" 28	Stationery	25	
" 30	H Sanders		20	" 31	Balance c/d	49	1,204
" 30	H Howe	18					
		113	1,672			113	1,672
Sept 1	Balances b/d	49	1,204				

'Money in' 'Money out'

21.3 Cash paid into the bank

In Exhibit 21.2 the payments into the bank were cheques received by the business, which were banked on receipt. We must now consider cash being paid into the bank.

1 Let us look at the position when a customer pays his account in cash, and later, a part of this cash is paid into the bank. The receipt of the cash is debited to the cash column on the date received, the credit entry being in the customer's personal account. The cash banked has the following effect, needing action as shown:

Effect	Action
(a) Asset of cash is decreased	Credit the asset account, i.e. the cash account that is represented by the cash column in the cash book.
(b) Asset of bank is increased	Debit the asset account, i.e. the bank account that is represented by the bank column in the cash book.

Now let us look at an example:

Example 1: A cash receipt of £100 from M Davies on 1 August 2013, later followed by the banking on 3 August of £80 of this amount, would appear in the cash book as follows:

Cash Book					
	Cash	*Bank*		*Cash*	*Bank*
2013	£	£	2013	£	£
Aug 1 M Davies	100		Aug 3 Bank	80	
Aug 3 Cash		80			

The details column shows entries against each item stating the name of the account in which the completion of double entry has taken place. Against the cash payment of £80 appears the word 'bank', showing the £80 is to be found in the bank column, on the debit side of the cash book.

2 Where the whole of the cash received is banked immediately, the receipt can be treated in exactly the same manner as a cheque received, i.e. it can be entered directly in the bank column.

3 If the business requires cash it may withdraw this from the bank by presenting one of its own cheques to the bank in exchange for cash.

The twofold effect and the action required is:

Effect	Action
(a) Asset of bank is decreased	Credit the asset account, i.e. the bank column in the cash book.
(b) Asset of cash is increased	Debit the asset account, i.e. the cash column in the cash book.

This can be shown in the following example:

Example 2: A withdrawal of £75 cash on 1 June 2013 from the bank would appear in the cash book as:

Cash Book					
	Cash	*Bank*		*Cash*	*Bank*
2013	£	£	2013	£	£
June 1 Bank	75		June 1 Cash		75

Both the debit and credit entries for this item are in the same book. When this happens it is known as a **contra** item.

21.4 The use of folio columns

As already illustrated the 'details column' in an account contains the name of the account in which the other part of the double entry has been entered. Anyone looking through the books should, therefore, be able to find the other half of the double entry in the ledgers. However, when many books are being used, just to mention the name of the other account may not be enough information to find the other account quickly. More information is needed, and this is given by using **folio columns**.

In each account and in each book being used, a folio column is added, always shown on the left of the money columns. In this column, the name of the other book and the number of the page in the other book where the other part of the double entry was made is stated against each and every entry. The double entry must always be completed before the folio columns are filled in.

An entry for receipt of cash from C Kelly whose account was on page 45 of the sales ledger, and the cash recorded on page 37 of the cash book, would have the following folio column entries:

- in the cash book, the folio column entry would be SL 45
- in the sales ledger, the folio column entry would be CB 37.

Note how each of the titles of the books is abbreviated so that it can fit into the space available in the folio column. Each of any contra items (transfers between bank and cash) being shown on the same page of the cash book and would use the letter 'C' (for 'contra') in the folio column. There is no need to also include a page number in this case. The act of using one book as a means of entering transactions into the accounts, in order to complete the double entry, is known as **posting** the items.

21.5 Advantages of folio columns

The advantages of using folio columns are as follows:

- Folio references are essential to help locate where entries have been posted to (see section 21.4).
- Entering references in the folio columns confirms the transaction has been posted. Therefore, any item without a reference can easily be identified and subsequently posted.

21.6 Example of a cash book with folio columns

The following transactions are written up in the form of a cash book. The folio columns are filled in as though double entry had been completed to other accounts.

2013		£
Sept 1	Proprietor puts capital into a bank account for the business	10,940
Sept 2	Received cheque from M Boon	115
Sept 4	Cash sales	1,102
Sept 6	Bought stationery and paid by cash	35
Sept 7	Banked £400 of the cash held by the business	400
Sept 15	Cash sales paid direct into the bank	40
Sept 23	Paid cheque to S Wills	277
Sept 29	Withdrew cash from bank for business use	120
Sept 30	Paid wages in cash	518

Cash Book

	Folio	Cash	Bank		Folio	Cash	Bank
2013		£	£	2013		£	£
Sept 1 Capital	GL 1		10,940	Sept 6 Stationery	GL 65	35	
" 2 M Boon	SL 98		115	" 7 Bank	C	400	
" 4 Sales	GL 87	1,102		" 23 S Wills	PL 23		277
" 7 Cash	C		400	" 29 Cash	C		120
" 15 Sales	GL 87		40	" 30 Wages	GL 39	518	
" 29 Bank	C	120		" 30 Balances	c/d	269	11,098
		1,222	11,495			1,222	11,495
Oct 1 Balances	b/d	269	11,098				

'Money in' 'Money out'

The abbreviations used in the folio column are as follows: GL = General Ledger; SL = Sales Ledger; C = Contra; PL = Purchases Ledger.

21.7 Cash discounts

Businesses prefer it if customers pay their accounts quickly. A business may accept a smaller sum in full settlement if payment is made within a certain period of time. The amount of the reduction of the sum to be paid is known as a **cash discount**. The term 'cash discount' thus refers to the allowance given for quick payment. It is still called a cash discount even if the account is paid by cheque or by direct transfer into the bank account.

The rate of cash discount is usually stated as a percentage. Full details of the percentage allowed, and the period within which payment is to be made, are quoted on all sales documents by the selling company. A typical period during which a discount may be allowed is one month from the date of the original transaction.

Note: The treatment of cash discount when calculating VAT on sales is fully discussed in Chapter 14, section 14.8.

21.8 Discounts allowed and discounts received

A business may have two types of cash discounts in its books. These are:

- **Discounts allowed** – cash discounts allowed by a business to its customers when they pay their accounts quickly.
- **Discounts received** – cash discounts received by a business from its suppliers when it pays their accounts quickly.

We can now see the effect of discounts by looking at two examples.

Example 1: W Clarke owed us £100. He pays on 2 September 2013 by cash within the time limit laid down and the business allows him 5% cash discount. So he will pay £100 – £5 cash discount = £95 in full settlement of his account.

Effect	Action
1 Of cash: Cash is increased by £95. Asset of accounts receivable is decreased by £95.	 Debit: Cash Account, i.e. enter £95 in debit column of cash book. Credit: W Clarke £95.
2 Of discounts: Asset of accounts receivable is decreased by £5. (After the cash was paid there remained a balance of £5. As the account has been paid this asset must now be cancelled.) Expenses of discounts allowed increased by £5.	 Credit: W Clarke £5. Debit: Discounts allowed account £5.

This means that W Clarke's debt of £100 has now been shown as fully settled, and exactly how the settlement took place has also been shown.

Example 2: The business owed S Small £400 and pays him on 3 September 2013 by cheque. Since it pays within the specified 30 days it can claim $2\frac{1}{2}$% cash discount. The business will pay S Small £400 less £10 cash discount = £390 in full settlement of the account.

Effect	Action
1 Of cheque: Asset of bank is reduced by £390. Liability of accounts payable is reduced by £390.	 Credit: Bank, i.e. enter in credit bank column, £390. Debit: S Small's account £390.
2 Of discounts: Liability of accounts payable is reduced by £10. (After the cheque was paid, the balance of £10 remained. As the account has been paid, the liability must now be cancelled.) Revenue of discounts received increased by £10.	 Debit: S Small's account £10. Credit: Discounts received account £10.

The accounts in the business's books for both W Clarke and S Small would be as follows:

Cash Book *(page 32)*

	Folio	*Cash*	*Bank*		*Folio*	*Cash*	*Bank*
2013		£	£	2013		£	£
Sept 2 W Clarke	SL 12	95		Sept 3 S Small	PL 75		390

General Ledger

Discounts Allowed Account *(page 17)*

2013	*Folio*	£		*Folio*	£
Sept 2 W Clarke	SL 12	5			

Discounts Received Account *(page 18)*

	Folio	£	2013	*Folio*	£
			Sept 3 S Small	PL 75	10

Sales Ledger

W Clarke Account *(page 12)*

2013	*Folio*	£	2013	*Folio*	£
Sept 1 Balance	b/d	100	Sept 2 Cash	CB 32	95
			Sept 2 Discount	GL 17	5
		100			100

Purchases Ledger

S Small Account *(page 75)*

2013	*Folio*	£	2013	*Folio*	£
Sept 3 Bank	CB 32	390	Sept 1 Balance	b/d	400
Sept 3 Discounts	GL 18	10			
		400			400

It is accounting custom to enter the word 'Discount' in the personal accounts, not stating whether it is a discount received or a discount allowed.

21.9 Discount columns in the cash book

The discounts allowed account and the discounts received account are in the general ledger, along with all the other revenue and expense accounts. It has already been stated that every effort should be made to avoid too much reference to the general ledger.

In the case of discounts, this is done by adding an extra column on each side of the cash book in which the amounts of discounts are entered. Discounts received are entered in the discounts column on the credit side of the cash book, and discounts allowed in the discounts column on the debit side of the cash book.

The cash book, if completed for the two examples so far dealt with, would appear thus:

Cash Book									(page 32)
	Folio	*Discount*	*Cash*	*Bank*		*Folio*	*Discount*	*Cash*	*Bank*
2013		£	£	£	2013		£	£	£
Sept 2 W Clarke	SL 12	5	95		Sept 3 S Small	PL 75	10		390

There is no alteration to the method of showing discounts in the personal accounts.

To make entries in the discount accounts in the general ledger

Total of discounts column on receipts side of cash book	Enter on debit side of discounts allowed account
Total of discounts column on payments side of cash book	Enter on credit side of discounts received account

21.10 A worked example

The following is an example of a three-column cash book for the whole of a month, showing the ultimate transfer of the totals of the discounts columns to the discount accounts in the general ledger.

2013		£
May 1	Balances brought down from April:	
	Cash Balance	29
	Bank Balance	654
	Accounts receivable:	
	B King	120
	N Campbell	280
	D Shand	40
	Accounts payable:	
	U Barrow	60
	A Allen	440
	R Long	100
May 2	B King pays us by cheque, having deducted $2\frac{1}{2}$% cash discount £3	117
May 8	We pay R Long his account by cheque, deducting 5% cash discount £5	95
May 11	We withdrew £100 cash from the bank for business use	100
May 16	N Campbell pays us his account by cheque, deducting $2\frac{1}{2}$% discount £7	273
May 25	We paid expenses in cash	92
May 28	D Shand pays us in cash after having deducted $2\frac{1}{2}$% cash discount	38
May 29	We pay U Barrow by cheque less 5% cash discount £3	57
May 30	We pay A Allen by cheque less $2\frac{1}{2}$% cash discount £11	429

Cash Book *(page 64)*

	Folio	*Discount*	*Cash*	*Bank*		*Folio*	*Discount*	*Cash*	*Bank*
2013		£	£	£	2013		£	£	£
May 1 Balances	b/d		29	654	May 8 R Long	PL 58	5		95
May 2 B King	SL 13	3		117	May 11 Cash	C			100
May 11 Bank	C		100		May 25 Expenses	GL 77		92	
May 16 N Campbell	SL 84	7		273	May 29 U Barrow	PL 15	3		57
May 28 D Shand	SL 91	2	38		May 30 A Allen	PL 98	11		429
					May 31 Balances	c/d		75	363
		12	167	1,044			19	167	1,044
Jun 1 Balances	b/d		75	363					

Sales Ledger

B King Account *Page 13*

2013	*Folio*	£	2013	*Folio*	£
May 1 Balance	b/d	120	May 2 Bank	CB 64	117
			May 2 Discount	CB 64	3
		120			120

N Campbell Account *Page 84*

2013	*Folio*	£	2013	*Folio*	£
May 1 Balance	b/d	280	May 16 Bank	CB 64	273
			May 16 Discount	CB 64	7
		280			280

D Shand Account *Page 91*

2013	*Folio*	£	2013	*Folio*	£
May 1 Balance	b/d	40	May 28 Cash	CB 64	38
			May 28 Discount	CB 64	2
		40			40

Purchases Ledger

U Barrow Account *Page 15*

2013	*Folio*	£	2013	*Folio*	£
May 29 Bank	CB 64	57	May 1 Balance	b/d	60
May 29 Discount	CB 64	3			
		60			60

R Long Account *Page 58*

2013	*Folio*	£	2013	*Folio*	£
May 8 Bank	CB 64	95	May 1 Balance	b/d	100
May 8 Discount	CB 64	5			
		100			100

A Allen Account *Page 98*

2013	*Folio*	£	2013	*Folio*	£
May 30 Bank	CB 64	429	May 1 Balance	b/d	440
May 30 Discount	CB 64	11			
		440			440

General Ledger

Expenses Account *Page 77*

2013	*Folio*	£		*Folio*	£
May 25 Cash	CB 64	92			

Discounts Received Account *Page 88*

	Folio	£	2013	*Folio*	£
			May 31 Cash book	CB 64	19

Discounts Allowed Account *Page 90*

2013	*Folio*	£		*Folio*	£
May 31 Cash book	CB 64	12			

Is the above method of entering discounts correct? You can easily check. See the following:

Discounts in Ledger Accounts	Debits		Credits	
		£		£
Discounts received	U Barrow	3	Discounts	
	R Long	5	Received	
	A Allen	11	Account	19
		19		
				£
Discounts allowed	Discounts		B King	3
	Allowed		N Campbell	7
	Account	12	D Shand	2
				12

You can see that proper double entry has been carried out. Equal amounts, in total, have been entered on each side of the accounts.

21.11 Bank overdrafts and the cash book

A business may borrow money from a bank by means of a **bank overdraft**. This means that the business is allowed to pay more out of the bank account, by paying out cheques, than the total amount available in the account.

Up to this point the bank balances have all been money at the bank, and so they have all been assets, i.e. debit balances. When the account is overdrawn, the business owes money to the bank and so the account is a liability and the balance a credit one.

Taking the cash book shown, suppose that the amount payable to A Allen was £1,429 instead of £429. Thus the amount in the bank account, £1,044, is exceeded by the amount withdrawn. The cash book would appear as follows:

Cash Book							
	Discount	*Cash*	*Bank*		*Discount*	*Cash*	*Bank*
2013	£	£	£	2013	£	£	£
May 1 Balances b/d		29	654	May 8 R Long	5		95
" 2 B King	3		117	" 11 Cash			100
" 11 Bank		100		" 25 Expenses		92	
" 16 N Campbell	7		273	" 29 U Barrow	3		57
" 28 D Shand	2	38		" 30 A Allen	11		1,429
" 31 Balance c/d			637	" 31 Balance c/d		75	
	12	167	1,681		19	167	1,681
Jun 1 Balance b/d		75		Jun 1 Balance b/d			637

On a balance sheet, a bank overdraft will be shown as an item included under the heading Current Liabilities.

Full coverage of the treatment of discounts allowed and discounts received in the financial statements is shown in Chapter 29.

21.12 Cash books with columns for VAT

Some businesses use a cash book with columns for VAT received on cash sales and VAT paid on expenses. The following example shows a cash book with columns for VAT and Bank which has been written up for the month of June.

Cash Book

	VAT	Bank		VAT	Bank
2013	£	£	2013	£	£
June 1 Balance b/d		4,800.00	June 2 Rates		420.00
June 4 Cash sales	74.00	444.00	June 6 M Lake		1,560.00
June 12 T Hughes		329.40	June 8 Stationery	15.00	90.00
June 18 Cash sales	30.00	180.00	June 18 Rent		500.00
June 23 Belmont Ltd		241.50	June 26 Printing	32.00	192.00
June 30 Cash sales	80.00	480.00	June 30 Balance c/d		3,712.90
	184.00	6,474.90		47.00	6,474.90
July 1 Balance b/d		3,712.90			

At the end of the month the total VAT columns are posted to the VAT account as follows:

VAT Account

2013	Folio	£	2013	Folio	£
June 30 Bank (Cash Book)		47.00	June 30 Bank (Cash Book)		184.00

Chapter summary

- A cash book is made up of a cash account and a bank account put together into one book.
- Entries made on the debit side of the cash book are in respect of monies received via cash, cheque or bank transfer. The money comes 'into' the business and is therefore entered on the debit 'in' side of the cash book.
- Entries made on the credit side of the cash book are in respect of monies paid out via cash, cheque or bank transfer. Money is paid 'out' of the business so entries are made on the 'out' side of the account.
- Folio columns are used in the cash book so that items may easily be traced to other accounts in the ledgers and to provide assurance that the double entries have been completed.
- Cash discounts are given to encourage prompt payment of outstanding accounts. The discount is referred to as cash discount irrespective of whether the account is settled by cash, cheque or bank transfer.
- Discount allowed is the amount of discount allowed by a business to its customers when their accounts are settled promptly and within the time limit.
- Discount received is when the business's suppliers allow them to deduct discount if they pay the account within the stated terms of trade.
- Discounts allowed and received are entered into the appropriate column in the cash book, totalled at the end of the period, and the amount transferred to the discount accounts in the general ledger.
- Should the balance at the bank go into an overdraft position then the balance brought down will appear on the credit side of the cash book.
- A cash book containing columns for VAT is illustrated.

EXERCISES

*Note: Questions with the suffix 'X' shown after the question number do **not** have answers shown at the back of the book. Answers to the other questions are shown in Appendix E.*

21.1 A two-column cash book is to be written up from the following, carrying the balances down to the following month:

2013
Jan 1 Started business with £4,000 in the bank
Jan 2 Paid for fixtures by cheque, £660
Jan 4 Cash sales £225: Paid rent by cash, £140
Jan 6 T Thomas paid us by cheque, £188
Jan 8 Cash sales paid direct into the bank, £308
Jan 10 J King paid us in cash, £300
Jan 12 Paid wages in cash, £275
Jan 14 J Walters lent us £500 paying by cheque
Jan 15 Withdrew £200 from the bank for business use
Jan 20 Bought stationery paying by cash, £60
Jan 22 We paid J French by cheque, £166
Jan 28 Cash drawings £100
Jan 30 J Scott paid us by cheque, £277
Jan 31 Cash sales £66.

21.2 You work for Stott & Co, a medium-sized clothes manufacturer, whose offices and works are situated in Derby. As book-keeper to the firm, one of your main duties is to enter up the cash book on a regular basis.

Required:
From the information given below, enter up the transactions for May 2013, balance off at the end of the month, and bring the balances down.

		£
May 1	Balances b/d	
	Cash in hand	14.72
	Bank (overdrawn)	820.54
May 2	Bought stationery by cash	10.00
May 3	Banked cheques received from:	
	P Wrench	432.36
	R Whitworth	634.34
	J Summers	341.00
May 6	South West Rail Ltd, cheque for travel expenses of company secretary to London	37.50
May 9	Paid the following accounts by cheque:	
	Fabulous Fabrics Ltd	450.80
	Mellors Manufacturing Co	348.32
May 12	Received from cash sale	76.00
May 14	Paid employees PAYE and NI to the HMRC, by cheque	221.30
May 17	Received cheque from Trentam Traders	32.81
May 20	Foreign currency drawn from bank for director's visit to Italy	250.00
	Bank charges re currency	3.20
May 24	Received cash from sale of goods	350.00
May 26	Cash to bank	300.00
May 27	Salaries by cheque	5,720.00
May 31	Received cheques from the following:	
	J Summers	1,231.00
	Bradnop Manufacturing Co	725.00
	Taylors	2,330.50

21.3X As a trainee accounts clerk at Jepsons & Co you have as one of your tasks the job of entering up the business's cash book at the end of each month.

Required:
From the details listed below, enter up the cash book for February 2013, balance off at the end of the month, and bring the balances down.

2013		£
Feb 1	Balances brought down from January:	
	Cash in hand	76.32
	Cash at bank	2,376.50
Feb 2	Paid electricity bill by cheque	156.00
Feb 4	Paid motor expenses by cash	15.00
Feb 6	Received cheques from the following accounts receivable:	
	D Hill	300.00
	A Jackson	275.00
	H Wardle	93.20
Feb 7	Paid for stationery by cash	3.70
Feb 10	Sold goods for cash	57.10
Feb 12	Paid for purchases from Palmer & Sons by cheque	723.50
Feb 14	Received loan by cheque from D Whitman	500.00
Feb 16	Paid Wright Brothers by cheque for repairs to office machinery	86.20
Feb 17	The proprietor, Stan Jepson, took cash for his own use.	50.00
	He asks you to pay his personal telephone bill by cheque to the post office	140.60
Feb 22	J Smith paid his account by cheque	217.00
Feb 23	Petrol bill paid by cash	21.00
Feb 26	Received cheque for sale of goods	53.00
Feb 27	Bought new photocopier from Bronsons of Manchester and paid by cheque	899.00
Feb 28	Paid monthly salaries by cheque	2,400.00

21.4 Enter up a three-column cash book from the following details. Balance off at the end of the month, and show the relevant discount accounts as they would appear in the general ledger.

2013
May 1 Started business with £6,000 in the bank
May 1 Bought fixtures paying by cheque, £950
May 2 Bought goods paying by cheque, £1,240
May 3 Cash sales £407
May 4 Paid rent in cash, £200
May 5 N Morgan paid us his account of £220 by a cheque for £210, we allowed him £10 discount
May 7 Paid S Thompson & Co £80 owing to them by means of a cheque £76, they allowed us £4 discount
May 9 We received a cheque for £380 from S Cooper, discount having been allowed £20
May 12 Paid rates by cheque, £410
May 14 L Curtis pays us a cheque for £115
May 16 Paid M Monroe his account of £120 by cash £114, having deducted £6 cash discount
May 20 P Exeter pays us a cheque for £78, having deducted £2 cash discount
May 31 Cash sales paid direct into the bank, £88.

21.5 From the following details, write up a three-column cash book, balance off at the end of the month, and show the relevant discount accounts as they would appear in the general ledger.

2013
Mar 1 Balances brought forward:
Cash in hand £211
Cash at bank £3,984
Mar 2 We paid each of the following accounts by cheque, in each case we deducted a 5% discount: T Adams £80; C Bibby £260; D Clarke £440
Mar 4 C Potts pays us a cheque for £98
Mar 6 Cash sales paid direct into the bank, £49
Mar 7 Bought stationery £65 and paid by cash
Mar 9 The following persons pay us their accounts by cheque, in each case they deducted a discount of $2\frac{1}{2}$%: R Smiley £160; J Turner £640; R Pimlott £520
Mar 12 Paid motor expenses by cash, £100
Mar 18 Cash sales, £98
Mar 21 Paid for insurance by cheque, £120
Mar 23 Paid expenses by cash, £60
Mar 28 Received a cheque for £500 being a loan from R Godfrey
Mar 31 Paid for stationery by cheque, £27.

21.6X You are to write up a three-column cash book for M Pinero from the details that follow. Then balance off at the end of the month and show the discount accounts in the general ledger.

2013
May 1 Balances brought forward:
Cash in hand £58
Bank overdraft £1,470
May 2 M Pinero pays further capital into the bank, £1,000
May 3 Bought office fixtures by cheque, £780
May 4 Cash sales, £220
May 5 Banked cash, £200
May 6 We paid the following by cheque, in each case deducting $2\frac{1}{2}$% cash discount: B Barnes £80; T Horton £240; T Jacklin £400
May 8 Cash sales, £500
May 12 Paid motor expenses in cash, £77
May 15 Cash withdrawn from the bank, £400
May 16 Cash drawings, £120
May 18 The following firms paid us their accounts by cheque, in each case deducting a 5% discount: L Graham £80; B Crenshaw £140; H Green £220
May 20 Wages paid in cash, £210
May 22 T Weiskopf paid us his account in cash, £204
May 26 Paid insurance by cheque, £150
May 28 We banked all the cash in our possession except for £20 in the cash till
May 31 Bought motor van, paying by cheque, £4,920.

CHAPTER 22

Petty cash and the imprest system

Learning objectives

After you have studied this chapter you should be able to:

- understand why organisations use a petty cash book
- recognise the need for a petty cash voucher
- understand the imprest system
- make entries in a petty cash book
- post the appropriate amounts from the petty cash book to the various accounts in the general ledger at the end of the period.

22.1 Petty cash

All businesses frequently incur low-value (petty) items of expenditure which are paid for in cash by employees. Such expenditure could include train and bus expenses, car mileage expenses, postage, stationery, cleaning materials, hospitality expenses, and so on. The petty cash procedure enables staff members who have purchased items or incurred expenditure to readily seek reimbursement provided a receipt is available to verify the expense.

A junior member of the finance department is normally made responsible for making payments to claimants for the cost of purchases or expenditure incurred and for keeping records of the expenses. The float is a sum of money made available for a period, i.e. a month; it is normally held in a secure box which is additionally held in a safe or lockable desk or cupboard.

To make a claim the staff member must complete a petty cash voucher showing the date and details of the item(s) purchased or expenditure incurred, including VAT if applicable, be signed by the claimant and countersigned by their manager (see Exhibit 22.1). If the claim exceeds the authority of the petty cashier, say £25, then the claim would have to be referred to the senior cashier or accountant.

When the petty cash voucher is entered into the petty cash book it will be numbered for future reference purposes and then filed. An example of a petty cash voucher is shown in Exhibit 22.1.

Exhibit 22.1

Petty Cash Voucher	No. *1* Date *2 May 2013*
Description	*Amount*
Stationery *(including VAT £2.35)*	£ p *14 10*
Signature *Ken Boardman* Authorised *Sandra Ashford*	

Only items of expenditure approved by the business will be reimbursed unless prior agreement has been received for a particular expense claim.

The petty cash book is a book of original entry since items, i.e. petty cash vouchers, are first entered into it.

22.2 The imprest system

The imprest system simply means topping up a previously established petty cash allowance of, say £150, by the amount of expenses incurred in a particular period. If the expenses for a period amounted to, say, £145 then the accountant would give the petty cashier £145 to restore the amount back to £150, often called the **cash float**. The periods involved can be weekly or more usually monthly. Exhibit 22.2 illustrates the above example:

Exhibit 22.2

		£
Period 1	The cashier gives the petty cashier	150
	The petty cashier pays out in the period	145
	Petty cash now in hand	5
	The cashier now gives the petty cashier the amount spent	145
	Petty cash in hand at the end of period	150

The amount of the cash float can be increased if deemed necessary. If it was decided to increase the float to £180 the amount given to the petty cashier would be £145 to reimburse for the expenses incurred + £30 to increase the float = £175. Then with the balance of £5 + £175 = £180, the cash float is increased.

Advantages of the imprest system

- The task of maintaining the imprest system is straightforward and can be carried out by a junior member of the finance department.
- The amount of cash can be checked at any time since the cash in the float plus the total of the vouchers should equal the original amount of the float.
- Using the petty cash book means many small value items are eliminated from being entered in the main cash book and ledgers.

22.3 Worked example of an analytical petty cash book

A small company offering secretarial services to local businesses incurs the following items of expenditure during May 2013. The items shown in Exhibit 22.3 will initially require entering in the petty cash book.

Exhibit 22.3

2013
May 1 The petty cashier received a cash float of £200.00 from the cashier
May 2 Stationery £14.10 including VAT £2.35 (see petty cash voucher no. 1)
May 4 Postage stamps, £22.00
May 6 Tea and coffee for office visitors, £8.00
May 9 Travel expenses, £16.00
May 10 Computer disks, £12.60 including VAT £2.10
May 12 Postage on parcel, £3.60
May 15 Office cleaner, £25.00
May 22 Milk for office, £4.20
May 25 Received £6.00 from Anita Kerr, office manager, for personal photocopying*
May 27 Office cleaner, £25.00
May 27 Cleaning materials, £4.67 plus VAT 93p, total spent £5.60
May 31 Travel expenses, £23.00
May 31 The cashier reimbursed the petty cashier with the amount spent during the month.

Each of the above items will have had a petty cash voucher completed by the person who had incurred the expenditure on behalf of the business. For illustration purposes just one petty voucher is shown, petty cash voucher no. 1, see previous Exhibit 22.1.

*Receipts

Occasionally, a member of staff may wish to purchase stamps from the petty cashier or perhaps have some photocopying done for their own personal use. In these cases the petty cashier will issue a receipt to the staff member for the amount received. For example, see Exhibit 22.4.

Exhibit 22.4

RECEIPT

Received from: *Anita Kerr* **Date:** *25 May 2013*
The sum of: *Six pounds only* **No.** *26*

	£	p
Cheque	–	–
Cash	*6*	*00*
	6	*00*

Re: *Photocopying*

Kim Patel
WITH THANKS

The above items of expenditure and the receipt are entered in the petty cash book as illustrated in Exhibit 22.5.

Exhibit 22.5

Petty Cash Book *(page 31)*

Receipts £ p	Date	Details	Voucher Number	Total £ p	VAT £ p	Postage £ p	Cleaning £ p	Travel Expenses £ p	Stationery £ p	Sundry Expenses £ p
	2013									
200.00	May 1	Cash	CB 19							
	May 2	Stationery	1	14.10	2.35				11.75	
	May 4	Postage stamps	2	22.00		22.00				
	May 6	Tea, coffee	3	8.00						8.00
	May 9	Travel expenses	4	16.00				16.00		
	May 10	Computer disks	5	12.60	2.10				10.50	
	May 12	Postage on parcel	6	3.60		3.60				
	May 15	Office cleaner	7	25.00			25.00			
	May 22	Milk	8	4.20						4.20
*6.00	May 25	Anita Kerr Photo-copying	26							
	May 27	Office cleaner	9	25.00			25.00			
	May 27	Cleaning materials	10	5.60	0.93		4.67			
	May 31	Travel expenses	11	23.00				23.00		
				159.10	5.38	25.60	54.67	39.00	22.25	12.20
	May 31	Balance	c/d	46.90	GL 17	GL 19	GL 29	GL 44	GL 56	GL 60
206.00				206.00						
46.90	June 1	Balance	b/d							
153.10	June 1	Cash	CB 22							

Reimbursement equals the total amount spent in May 2013 (£159.10 – £6.00 Receipt ∴ £153.10 reimbursed)

Total amount spent in May 2013

Entering the petty cash book

On 1 May the petty cashier received £200.00 cash from the main cashier. This is the amount of the float for the period of May.

The cashier would enter this item on the credit side of the cash book, the money comes 'OUT' of the bank. The debit entry is now shown on the 'Receipts' side of the petty cash book, the money comes 'INTO' the petty cash. Note the folio reference 'CB 19' (Cash Book page 19) is also entered to cross-reference the entry.

Each petty cash voucher is then entered in date order as follows:

- Enter the date.
- Enter the details of each payment.
- A voucher number is then given to each petty cash voucher and entered on the voucher itself and in the 'voucher number' column.

- The total amount of the expenditure incurred is then entered in the 'total' column.
- The expenditure is then analysed into an appropriate expense column.
- If VAT has been incurred then the VAT amount is entered in the 'VAT' column and the remaining expense in the appropriate column. For example, the petty cash voucher shown in Exhibit 22.1 is for stationery amounting to £14.10. In the total column £14.10 is entered, £2.35 is then entered in the VAT column and the cost of the stationery £11.75 is then entered in the stationery column.

Any money received from the sale of sundry items to a member of staff, as in the case of Anita Kerr who had some personal photocopying, then the receipt of the cash is entered into the 'receipts' column, in this example £6.00. The date, details and receipt number are also entered in the appropriate columns.

The petty cash book now requires balancing off at the end of the month as follows:

- Add up the 'total' column.
- Add up each of the expense columns. The total of all the expense columns added together should now equal the amount shown in the 'total' column.
  In Exhibit 22.5 this would be:

	£ p
VAT	5.38
Postage	25.60
Cleaning	54.67
Travel expenses	39.00
Stationery	22.25
Sundry expenses	12.20
Total	159.10

- The petty cashier now needs to calculate the amount of money needed to restore the imprest to £200.00 for the beginning of the next period. This is as follows:

	£ p
Amount of float at beginning of May	200.00
Money received during month	
Anita Kerr – Photocopying	6.00
	206.00
Less Amount spent (see above)	159.10
Cash in hand at 31 May 2013	46.90
Amount of float	200.00
Less Cash in hand at 31 May 2013	46.90
Cash required to restore the imprest	153.10

- The balance of cash in hand at 31 May 2013, £46.90, is now entered into the petty cash book and shown as '*balance c/d*', £46.90 (see Exhibit 22.5).
- The '*receipts*' and '*total*' columns are now added up and should equal each other, i.e. £206.00. These totals should be shown on the same line and both double underlined.
- The '*Balance b/d*' on 1 June, £46.90, is now entered in the *receipts* column and underneath that entry the amount received from the cashier to restore the imprest £153.10 is also entered.

The double entry for each of the expense columns is now carried out:

- The total of each expense column is debited to the expense account in the general ledger.
- The folio number of each general ledger account is entered under each of the expense columns in the petty cash book. This enables cross-referencing and also means that the double entry to the ledger account had been completed.

The double entry for all the items in Exhibit 22.5 appears as Exhibit 22.6.

Exhibit 22.6

Cash Book (Bank column only) *Page 19*

				Folio	£
			2013		
			May 1 Petty Cash	PCB 31	200.00
			June 1 Petty Cash	PCB 31	153.10

General Ledger

VAT Account *Page 17*

	Folio	£			
2013					
May 31 Petty Cash	PCB 31	5.38			

Postages Account *Page 19*

	Folio	£			
2013					
May 31 Petty Cash	PCB 31	25.60			

Cleaning Account *Page 29*

	Folio	£			
2013					
May 31 Petty Cash	PCB 31	54.67			

Travel Expenses Account *Page 44*

	Folio	£			
2013					
May 31 Petty Cash	PCB 31	39.00			

Stationery Account *Page 56*

	Folio	£			
2013					
May 31 Petty Cash	PCB 31	22.25			

Sundry Expenses Account *Page 60*

	Folio	£			
2013					
May 31 Petty Cash	PCB 31	12.20			

Paying creditors from petty cash

Occasionally a supplier may be paid their account out of the petty cash. If this arises then the book-keeping entries would be to record the payment in the petty cash book, using a column headed 'ledger accounts', then post the item to the debit side of the supplier's account in the purchases ledger. This transaction is very rare and would only occur where the item to be paid was small, or if a refund was made out of petty cash to a customer who may have overpaid their account.

22.4 Bank cash book

In a business with both a cash book and a petty cash book, the cash book is often known as a **bank cash book**. This means that *all* cash payments are entered in the petty cash book, and the bank cash book will contain *only* bank columns and discount columns. When this arrangement is in operation, any cash sales will be paid directly into the bank.

Chapter summary

- The petty cash book is used to record transactions involving small items of expenditure incurred by a member of staff on behalf of the organisation.
- Claims for reimbursement of monies paid out are usually made on a petty cash voucher. The voucher should be completed with all the relevant details together with receipt (if possible), duly signed and authorised.
- The imprest system is used by many organisations to operate the petty cash system. Here an amount of money called a 'float' is given to the petty cashier at the start of a period. At the end of the period the amount spent by the petty cashier is reimbursed by the cashier to restore the imprest to its original amount.
- The advantages of using a petty cash system is that it enables a junior member of staff to be appointed petty cashier so allowing the cashier or accountant to concentrate on other areas of work.
- Using the petty cash book saves both the cash book and the ledger account from containing many small items of expenditure.
- The imprest system enables the cash to be checked at any time.
- Entries made into the petty cash book include not only petty cash vouchers for expenses incurred on behalf of the business but also receipts of money that may have been received in respect of sundry sales to staff members.
- The petty cash book is totalled, balanced off and the double entry completed with postings to the ledger accounts in the general ledger.
- The name of the cash book is sometimes called a bank cash book when it only contains bank columns. Cash sales having been banked direct and the petty cash book used for small sundry cash items.

EXERCISES

Note: Questions with the suffix 'X' shown after the question number do **not** *have answers shown at the back of the book. Answers to the other questions are shown in Appendix E.*

22.1 You are employed as accounts clerk for Kitchen Designs who operate their petty cash using the imprest system. At the beginning of the month there was £18.52 left in the petty cash box from the previous month and the cashier has just given you £131.48 to restore the imprest to £150.

The following are details of the petty cash vouchers that have been authorised for payment by the cashier for June 2013, together with a receipt for cash received.

2013		£
June 1	Window cleaner	10.00
June 3	Postage stamps	7.60
June 4	Petrol (including VAT of £6.26)	37.60
June 6	Stationery (including VAT of £1.62)	9.75
June 10	Sold stamps to Jean Ford £2.00 (receipt no. 8)	
June 14	Office cleaner	20.00
June 17	Parcel postage	1.35
June 19	Magazine for reception (no VAT)	3.00
June 21	Computer disks (including VAT £1.32)	7.95
June 24	Petrol (including VAT £2.35)	14.10
June 27	Refreshments for clients (no VAT)	4.20
June 28	Office cleaner	20.00

Required:

(*a*) Enter the balance brought down and the cash received to restore the imprest in the petty cash book on 1 June 2013. The petty cash book page number to use is 47.

(*b*) Enter the above transactions into the petty cash book using the following analysis columns, VAT, postage, cleaning, motor expenses, stationery and sundry expenses. The next petty cash voucher number is 32.

(*c*) Total and balance the petty cash book on 30 June and bring down the balance on 1 July. Show the amount of cash received from the cashier to restore the imprest to £150.

22.2X Singh's Estate Agents operates their petty cash system on a fortnightly basis using the imprest system with a float of £100. On 15 October 2013 there was an opening balance of £23.40 in the petty cash box. The following transactions took place during the period commencing 15 October 2013.

2013		£
Oct 15	Received amount from cashier to restore the imprest	
Oct 16	Envelopes and files (including VAT of £1.94)	11.66
Oct 17	Tea, coffee and milk (for clients no VAT)	7.40
Oct 18	Special delivery postage charges	8.60
Oct 21	Office cleaner	20.00
Oct 21	Cleaning materials (including VAT 70p)	4.20
Oct 23	Received £3.50 from M Lloyd for sale of stationery (receipt no. 78)	
Oct 23	Postage stamps	7.00
Oct 25	Travel expenses	16.42
Oct 28	Flowers for reception (including VAT 83p)	4.99
Oct 28	Photocopying paper (including VAT £1.56)	9.40
Oct 31	Received cash to restore imprest	

Required:

(*a*) Enter the balance brought down and the cash received to restore the imprest on 15 October 2013 in the petty cash book page 33.

(*b*) Enter the above transactions into the petty cash book using the following analysis columns, VAT, postage, cleaning, travel expenses, stationery and sundry expenses. The next petty cash voucher number is 80.

(*c*) Total and balance the petty cash book on 31 October and bring down the balance on 1 November. Show the amount of cash received from the cashier to restore the imprest to £100.

22.3 You work for S Dickinson (Estate Agents) as a receptionist, although some of your duties include administration tasks and dealing with the business's petty cash, which is operated using the imprest system. A float of £120 is used by the business for petty cash and this is given to you on 1 March.

Required:

(*a*) From the following petty cash vouchers (Exhibit 22.7), you are required to enter them in the petty cash book using analysis columns as you think appropriate. Balance off at the end of the month and obtain cash to restore the imprest from Ms Dickinson.

(*b*) Post the petty cash expense columns to the accounts in the general ledger and enter the cash obtained to restore the imprest in the cash book.

(*c*) What are the advantages to using the imprest system? Draft a short memo outlining these to Ms Dickinson.

Exhibit 22.7

No 1

Petty Cash Voucher

Date 1/3/2013

For what required	Amount £	p
Postage Stamps	6	50
	6	50

Signature A. Bond
Passed by SMD

No 2

Petty Cash Voucher

Date 4 March 2013

For what required	Amount £	p
Second-class rail fare to Stourbridge	23	—
	23	—

Signature G. Jones
Passed by SMD

Exhibit 22.7 *(continued)*

No 3

Petty Cash Voucher

Date *7th March 2013*

For what required	Amount £	p
Parcel Post to London	4	—
	4	—

Signature *A. Bond*

Passed by *SMD*

No 4

Petty Cash Voucher

Date *9th March 2013*

For what required	Amount £	p
Window cleaning	8	—
	8	—

Signature *C. Cotton*

Passed by *SMD*

No 5

Petty Cash Voucher

Date *12th March 2013*

For what required	Amount £	p
Envelopes	2	59
VAT		51
	3	10

Signature *A. Bond*

Passed by *SMD*

No 6

Petty Cash Voucher

Date *14th March 2013*

For what required	Amount £	p
Tea etc (Hospitality)	6	40
	6	40

Signature *A. Bond*

Passed by *SMD*

No 7

Petty Cash Voucher

Date *16th March 2013*

For what required	Amount £	p
Petrol	10	—
(including VAT @ 20%)		
	10	—

Signature *G. Jones*

Passed by *SMD*

No 8

Petty Cash Voucher

Date *19th March 2013*

For what required	Amount £	p
Computer Discs	10	84
VAT @ 20%	2	16
	13	—

Signature *S. Dickinson*

Passed by *SMD*

Exhibit 22.7 *(continued)*

No 9

Petty Cash Voucher

Date 20 March 2013

For what required	Amount £	p
Dusters & Polish	1	44
VAT @ 20%		29
	1	73

Signature J. Pratt

Passed by SMD

No 10

Petty Cash Voucher

Date 23 March 2013

For what required	Amount £	p
Postage Stamps	2	40
	2	40

Signature A. Bond

Passed by SMD

No 11

Petty Cash Voucher

Date 27th March 2013

For what required	Amount £	p
Payment of creditors:-		
J. Cheetham (A/c No C44)	7	30
	7	30

Signature S. Dickinson

Passed by SMD

No 12

Petty Cash Voucher

Date 29 March 2013

For what required	Amount £	p
Magazines, Newspapers	6	40
etc. (for reception)		
	6	40

Signature A. Bond

Passed by SMD

22.4X You are employed as junior accountant's assistant of Morridge Products Ltd and one of your main tasks is that of petty cashier. The company uses an analytical petty cash book with columns for travelling expenses, postage, stationery, cleaning, sundry expenses and VAT, and they operate the imprest system.

Required:

(*a*) On 1 January 2013 the company's accountant, Mr Brammer, restores the petty cash float to £100 and gives you the petty cash vouchers shown in Exhibit 22.8. You are required to enter them in the petty cash book, balance off the book at the end of January, and obtain reimbursement from Mr Brammer to restore the imprest.

(*b*) Mr Brammer is anxious for you to become involved with all the financial aspects of the business and would like you to complete the book-keeping entries by posting the totals of the 'petty cash analysis columns' to the relevant accounts in the general ledger.

(*c*) Unfortunately, you have to go in hospital for a few days and will probably be absent from work for a couple of weeks. Mr Brammer asks you to write out a set of instructions in note form on the operation of the petty cash book as Jenny Cadwaller, his secretary, will be taking over in your absence. Ensure the instructions are clear, concise and easy to follow.

Exhibit 22.8

Petty Cash Voucher

No 1

Date 1st Jan 2013

For what required	Amount £	p
Travelling Expenses to Crewe	5	36
	5	36

Signature Jim Steadman

Passed by G Brammer

Petty Cash Voucher

No 2

Date 5 Jan 2013

For what required	Amount £	p
Office Cleaning	10	—
	10	—

Signature A. Duffy

Passed by G. Brammer

Petty Cash Voucher

No 3

Date 9 Jan 2013

For what required	Amount £	p
Parcel to Northampton	1	98
	1	98

Signature Tom Finikin

Passed by G Brammer

Petty Cash Voucher

No 4

Date 10 Jan 2013

For what required	Amount £	p
Milk & Coffee for Office	6	50
	6	50

Signature J. Cadwaller

Passed by G. Brammer

Petty Cash Voucher

No 5

Date 12 Jan 2013

For what required	Amount £	p
Air-mail Stationery	7	00
VAT	1	40
	8	40

Signature J. Cadwaller

Passed by G. Brammer

Petty Cash Voucher

No 6

Date 15 Jan 2013

For what required	Amount £	p
Light Bulbs & 3 plugs.	3	57
VAT		71
	4	28

Signature Tom Finikin

Passed by G Brammer

Exhibit 22.8 (*continued*)

Petty Cash Voucher

No 7

Date 21 Jan 2013

For what required	Amount £	p
Office cleaning	20	—
	20	—

Signature A. Duffy

Passed by G Brammer

Petty Cash Voucher

No 8

Date 22 Jan 2013

For what required	Amount £	p
1 Ream Copier Paper	4	21
+ VAT		84
	5	05

Signature J. Cadwaller

Passed by G. Brammer

Petty Cash Voucher

No 9

Date 24 Jan 2013

For what required	Amount £	p
Car Allowance: Manchester – Visiting Customer	15	—
	15	—

Signature J. Steadman

Passed by G. Brammer

Petty Cash Voucher

No 10

Date 24 Jan 2013

For what required	Amount £	p
Financial Times & Economist for Reception	2	10
	2	10

Signature J. Cadwaller

Passed by G Brammer

Petty Cash Voucher

No 11

Date 30 Jan 2013

For what required	Amount £	p
Milk	1	50
	1	50

Signature P. Fisher

Passed by G. Brammer

Petty Cash Voucher

No 12

Date 31 Jan 2013

For what required	Amount £	p
First Class Stamps	4	80
	4	80

Signature J. Cadwaller

Passed by G. Brammer

CHAPTER 23

Bank reconciliation statements

Learning objectives

After you have studied this chapter you should be able to:

- understand the reason for preparing bank reconciliation statements
- reconcile cash book balances with bank statement balances
- understand how bank overdrafts affect the reconciliation process
- make necessary entries in the account for dishonoured cheques.

23.1 Introduction

In Chapter 21 we saw how businesses record monies coming into and out of the business in their cash book. Cash items being entered in the 'cash columns' and cheques and other bank items being entered in the 'bank columns'.

The bank will also be recording the business's bank transactions in the business account at the bank. If all the items entered in the cash book were the same as those entered in the business's account with the bank, then obviously the bank balance per the business's books and the bank balance per the bank's books would equal each other. However, this is not usually the case.

There may be items paid into or out of the business bank account which have not been recorded in the cash book. There may also be items entered in the cash book which have not yet been entered in the bank's records of the business's account. To see if any differences have occurred between the two balances the business will need to obtain a bank statement from the bank and use this to compare its records with those of the bank.

Banks usually issue bank statements to their customers on a regular basis but one can easily be obtained from the bank on request.

An example of a cash book and a bank statement is shown in Exhibit 23.1. The items that are the same in both sets of records are ticked off.

Exhibit 23.1

Cash Book (bank columns only)

2013			£	2013			£
June 1	Balance b/f		80	June 27	I Gordon	✓	35
June 28	D Jones	✓	100	June 29	B Tyrell		40
				June 30	Balance c/d		105
			180				180
July 1	Balance b/d		105				

Bank Statement

2013			Dr £	Cr £	Balance £
June 26	Balance b/f	✓			80 Cr
June 28	Banking	✓		100	180 Cr
June 30	I Gordon	✓	35		145 Cr

By comparing the cash book and the bank statement, it can be seen that the only item that was not in both of these was the cheque payment to B Tyrell for £40 in the cash book. The reason why this was entered in the cash book but does not appear on the bank statement is simply one of timing. The cheque had been posted to B Tyrell on 29 June, but there had not been time for it to be banked by Tyrell and passed through the banking system. Such a cheque is called an **unpresented cheque** because it has not yet been presented at the drawer's bank.

To prove that the balances are not different because of errors, even though they show different figures, a bank reconciliation statement is drawn up. This is shown in Exhibit 23.2.

Exhibit 23.2

Bank Reconciliation Statement as at 30 June 2013

	£
Balance in hand as per cash book	105
Add unpresented cheque: Tyrell	40
Balance in hand as per bank statement	145

It would have been possible for the bank reconciliation statement to have started with the bank statement balance:

Bank Reconciliation Statement as at 30 June 2013

	£
Balance in hand as per bank statement	145
Less unpresented cheque: Tyrell	40
Balance in hand as per cash book	105

Note that in the business's cash book the bank account shows a debit balance brought down because, to the business, the balance is an asset since it is money in the bank. In the bank's books, however, the account will show a credit balance because it is a liability, i.e. money owed by the bank to the business.

23.2 Reasons for differences in balances

We can now look at a more complicated example in Exhibit 23.3. Similar items in both cash book and bank statement are shown ticked.

Exhibit 23.3

Cash Book

		£			£
2013			2013		
Dec 27 Total b/f		2,000	Dec 27 Total b/f		1,600
Dec 29 J Potter	✓	60	Dec 28 J Jacobs	✓	105
Dec 31 M Johnson (B)		220	Dec 30 M Chatwood (A)		15
			Dec 31 Balance c/d		560
		2,280			2,280
2014					
Jan 1 Balance b/d		560			

Bank Statement

2013		Dr £	Cr £	Balance £
Dec 27 Balance b/f				400 Cr
Dec 29 Cheque	✓		60	460 Cr
Dec 30 J Jacobs	✓	105		355 Cr
Dec 30 BGC*: L Shaw (C)			70	425 Cr
Dec 30 Bank charges (D)		20		405 Cr

*BGC = bank giro credit.

The balance brought forward in the bank statement £400 is the same figure as that in the cash book, i.e. totals b/f £2,000 – £1,600 = £400. However, items (A) and (B) are in the cash book only, and (C) and (D) are on the bank statement only. We can now examine these in detail:

(A) This is a cheque recently sent by us to Mr Chatwood. It has not yet passed through the banking system nor been presented to our bank, and it is therefore an unpresented cheque.

(B) This is a cheque banked by us on our visit to the bank when we collected the copy of our bank statement and would not appear on the statement.

(C) A customer, L Shaw, has paid his account by instructing his bank to pay us direct through the banking system, instead of paying by cheque. Such a transaction is usually called a **bank giro credit (BCG)**.

(D) A charge of £20 for operating our account has been taken by the bank.

Having taken into account the above differences the bank reconciliation statement can now be prepared. As mentioned earlier there are two ways in which a bank reconciliation statement can be prepared. You can start with the balance as shown in the cash book (see first example shown below) or, alternatively, you can start with the balance as shown on the bank statement in the second example.

Examining bodies may ask for either method of presentation so ensure you know exactly which method is required before attempting the question.

Bank Reconciliation Statement as at 31 December 2013

	£	£
Balance in hand as per cash book		560
Add Unpresented cheque – M Chatwood	15	
Bank giro credits	70	
		85
		645
Less Bank charges	20	
Bank lodgement not yet entered on bank statement	220	
		240
Balance in hand as per bank statement		405

A bank reconciliation statement starting with the bank statement balance appears thus:

Bank Reconciliation Statement as at 31 December 2013

	£	£
Balance in hand as per bank statement		405
Add Bank charges	20	
Bank lodgement not yet entered on bank statement	220	
		240
		645
Less Unpresented cheque – M Chatwood	15	
Bank giro credits	70	
		85
Balance in hand as per bank statement		560

23.3 Updating the cash book before attempting a reconciliation

The easiest way to prepare a reconciliation statement is first to complete any outstanding entries in the cash book. All items on the bank statement will then be in the cash book. This means that the only differences will be items in the cash book but not on the bank statement. At the same time, any errors found in the cash book by such a check can be corrected.

Although this would be the normal way to proceed before actually drawing up a bank reconciliation statement, it is possible that an examiner will ask you not to do it this way. If, in Exhibit 23.3 the cash book had been written up before the bank reconciliation statement was drawn up, then the cash book and the reconciliation statement would have appeared as follows in Exhibit 23.4.

Exhibit 23.4

Cash Book

2013		£	2013		£
Dec 27	Total b/fwd	2,000	Dec 27	Total b/fwd	1,600
Dec 29	J Potter	60	Dec 28	J Jacobs	105
Dec 31	M Johnson	220	Dec 30	M Chatwood	15
Dec 31	BGC:		Dec 31	Bank charges*	20
	L Shaw*	70	Dec 31	Balance c/d	610
		2,350			2,350
2014					
Jan 1	Balance b/d	610			

*Adding items that appear in the bank statement but not in the cashbook.

Bank Reconciliation Statement as on 31 December 2013

	£
Balance in hand as per cash book	610
Add Unpresented cheque – M Chatwood	15
	625
Less Bank lodgement not yet entered on bank statement	220
Balance in hand as per bank statement	405

23.4 Bank overdrafts

When there is a bank overdraft (shown by a credit balance in the cash book), the adjustments needed for reconciliation work are opposite to those needed for a debit balance.

Exhibit 23.5 shows a cash book, and a bank statement showing an overdraft. Only the cheque for G Cumberbatch (A) £106 and the cheque paid to J Kelly (B) £63 need adjusting. Work through the reconciliation statement in Exhibit 23.5 and then compare the reconciliation statements in Exhibits 23.4 and 23.5.

Exhibit 23.5

Cash Book (bank columns only)

2013		£	2013		£
Dec 5	I Howe	308	Dec 1	Balance b/f	709
Dec 24	L Mason	120	Dec 9	P Davies	140
Dec 29	K King	124	Dec 27	J Kelly (B)	63
Dec 31	G Cumberbatch (A)	106	Dec 29	United Trust	77
Dec 31	Balance c/f	380	Dec 31	Bank charges	49
		1,038			1,038
			2014		
			Jan 1	Balance b/f	380

Bank Statement

2013	Dr £	Cr £	Balance £
Dec 1 Balance b/f			709 O/D
Dec 5 Cheque		308	401 O/D
Dec 14 P Davies	140		541 O/D
Dec 24 Cheque		120	421 O/D
Dec 29 K King: BGC		124	297 O/D
Dec 29 United Trust: Standing order	77		374 O/D
Dec 31 Bank charges	49		423 O/D

Note: On a bank statement an overdraft is often shown with the letters O/D following the amount; or else it is shown as a debit balance, indicated by the letters DR after the amount.

Bank Reconciliation Statement as at 31 December 2013

	£
Overdraft as per cash book	380
Add Bank lodgements not on bank statement	106
	486
Less Unpresented cheque	63
Overdraft per bank statement	423

Now compare the reconciliation statements in Exhibits 23.4 and 23.5. This comparison reveals the following:

	Exhibit 23.4 *Balances*	***Exhibit 23.5*** *Overdrafts*
Balance/Overdraft per cash book	XXXX	XXXX
Adjustments		
Unpresented cheque	PLUS	LESS
Banking not entered	LESS	PLUS
Balance/Overdraft per bank statement	XXXX	XXXX

Adjustments are, therefore, made in the opposite way when there is an overdraft.

23.5 Dishonoured cheques

When a cheque is received from a customer and paid into the bank, it is recorded on the debit side of the cash book. It is also shown on the bank statement as a deposit to the bank. However, at a later date, it may be found that the customer's bank will not pay us the amount due on the cheque. The cheque is therefore worthless. It is known as a **dishonoured cheque**.

There are several possible reasons for this. As an example, let us suppose that K King gave us a cheque for £5,000 on 20 May 2013. We banked it, but on 25 May 2013 our bank returned the cheque to us. Typical reasons are:

- King had put £5,000 in figures on the cheque, but had written it in words as five thousand five hundred pounds. You will have to give the cheque back to King for amendment or reissue.

- King had put the year 2012 on the cheque instead of 2013. Normally, cheques are considered 'stale' six months after the date on the cheque; in other words, the banks will not pay cheques over six months' old.
- King simply did not have sufficient funds in his bank account. Suppose he had previously only got a £2,000 balance and yet he has given us a cheque for £5,000. His bank has not allowed him to have an overdraft. In such a case the cheque would be dishonoured. The bank would write on the cheque 'refer to drawer', and we would have to get in touch with King to see what he was going to do to settle his account.

In all of these cases the bank would show the original banking as being cancelled, by showing the cheque paid out of our bank account. As soon as this happens, they will notify us. We will then also show the cheque being cancelled by a credit in the cash book. We will then debit that amount to this account.

When King originally paid his account, our records would appear as:

K King Account

2013		£	2013		£
May 1	Balance b/d	5,000	May 20	Bank	5,000

Bank Account

2013		£			
May 20	K King	5,000			

After our recording the dishonoured cheque, the records will appear as:

K King Account

2013		£	2013		£
May 1	Balance b/d	5,000	May 20	Bank	5,000
May 25	Bank: cheque dishonoured	5,000			

Bank Account

2013		£	2013		£
May 20	K King	5,000	May 25	K King: cheque dishonoured	5,000

In other words, King is once again shown as owing us £5,000.

23.6 Some other reasons for differences in balances

Another reason why there is a difference between the balance in the business's cash book and the balance on the bank statement is because of standing orders and direct debits, which were discussed in Chapter 20. To recap:

- **Direct debits** – where the business gives permission for an organisation to collect amounts owing direct from its bank account. This method is often used to pay mortgages, insurance premiums, etc.

- **Standing order** – instructions given by a business to a bank to pay specified amounts at given dates.

Both these payments are made by the bank on behalf of the business and until the bank statement is received by the business the entries into the cash book may not have been made.

A more recent method of making payments is by **Bankers' Automated Clearing Service (BACS)** which is a computerised payment transfer system that is a very popular way of paying creditors, wages and salaries. Again details of such payments will appear on the bank statement and will require entry into the business's cash book.

23.7 Terms used in banking

There are many terms used in the banking system with which a student of accountancy needs to be familiar. In Chapter 20 many of these were discussed in detail. As a recap some of these are listed below together with additional terms:

- Bank charges and interest – charges made by the bank for providing the services of a bank account while interest charged is for making funds available to a business when it is overdrawn.
- Bank giro credits (also referred to as credit transfers) – a method used by businesses to pay creditors, wages and salaries.
- Bank lodgement – money deposited by a business into its account at the bank.
- Bank overdraft – an overdraft is a facility provided by the bank where it will continue to make payments from a current account even though there are insufficient funds to cover the payment. This is a short-term loan, on which the bank charges interest on a day-to-day basis.
- Bank reconciliation statement – a calculation comparing the cash book balance with the bank statement balance.
- Bankers' Automated Clearing Service (BACS) – a computerised payment transfer system that is a very popular way of paying creditors, wages and salaries.
- Direct debits – where the business gives permission for an organisation to collect amounts owing direct from its bank account. This method is often used to pay mortgages, insurance premiums, etc.
- Dishonoured cheques – when a bank dishonours a cheque it will not process the cheque because there are insufficient funds in the drawer's (the person making the payment) account.
- Out-of-date cheques – a cheque becomes 'stale' six months after the date on the cheque. Banks will not generally pay cheques over six months old.
- Standing order – instructions given by a business to a bank to pay specified amounts at given dates.
- Unpresented cheques – cheques that have been sent but have not yet gone through the recipient's bank account.

Chapter summary

- The purpose of preparing a bank reconciliation statement is to find the reasons for the differences in the balance as shown in the cash book with that shown on the bank statement.

- By preparing a bank reconciliation statement errors may be identified in either the cash book or the bank statement and be corrected.
- The differences in balances may be caused by quite valid reasons and are usually due to the varying dates that the business and the bank record monies paid into and out of their particular account.
- It is easier to write up the cash book first before preparing a bank reconciliation statement since the only differences will be items in the cash book but not on the bank statement.
- If the account is showing a bank overdraft then preparing a bank reconciliation statement is the opposite to when there is a balance in the account.
- If a business receives a cheque from a customer which ultimately 'bounces', i.e. insufficient funds in the account for the cheque to be paid, then it is known as a 'dishonoured cheque'.
- How to make the appropriate entries in the account to record a dishonoured cheque.
- Typical terms used in banking are summarised.

EXERCISES

Note: Questions with the suffix 'X' shown after the question number do **not** *have answers shown at the back of the book. Answers to the other questions are shown in Appendix E.*

23.1 The following are extracts from the cash book and the bank statement of J Roche. You are required to:

(*a*) write the cash book up to date, and state the new balance as on 31 December 2013.
(*b*) draw up a bank reconciliation statement as on 31 December 2013.

Cash Book

2013	£	2013	£
Dec 1 Balance b/f	1,740	Dec 8 A Dailey	349
Dec 7 T J Masters	88	Dec 15 R Mason	33
Dec 22 J Ellis	73	Dec 28 G Small	115
Dec 31 K Wood	249	Dec 31 Balance c/d	1,831
Dec 31 M Barrett	178		
	2,328		2,328

Bank Statement

2013	*Dr* £	*Cr* £	*Balance* £
Dec 1 Balance b/f			1,740
Dec 7 Cheque		88	1,828
Dec 11 A Dailey	349		1,479
Dec 20 R Mason	33		1,446
Dec 22 Cheque		73	1,519
Dec 31 BGC: J Walters		54	1,573
Dec 31 Bank charges	22		1,551

23.2X The following are extracts from the cash book and bank statement of Preston & Co:

Cash Book

2013		£	2013		£
Dec 1	Balance b/d	8,700	Dec 6	S Little	1,745
Dec 7	T J Blake	440	Dec 14	L Jones	165
Dec 20	P Dyson	365	Dec 21	E Fraser	575
Dec 30	A Veale	945	Dec 31	Balance c/d	9,155
Dec 31	K Woodburn	300			
Dec 31	N May	890			
		11,640			11,640

Bank Statement

2013	*Dr* £	*Cr* £	*Balance* £
Dec 1 Balance b/d			8,700
Dec 9 Cheque		440	9,140
Dec 10 S Little	1,745		7,395
Dec 19 L Jones	165		7,230
Dec 20 Cheque		365	7,595
Dec 26 BGC: P Todd		270	7,865
Dec 31 Bank charges	110		7,755

You are required to:

(*a*) write up the cash book and state the new balance on 31 December 2013.

(*b*) prepare a bank reconciliation statement as on 31 December 2013.

23.3 The bank statement for James Baxter for the month of March 2013 is as follows:

Bank Statement

2013	*Dr* £	*Cr* £	*Balance* £
Mar 1 Balance b/d			2,598 O/D
8 L Young	61		2,659 O/D
16 Cheque		122	2,537 O/D
20 A Duffy	104		2,641 O/D
21 Cheque		167	2,474 O/D
31 BGC: A May		929	1,545 O/D
31 Standing Order: Oak plc	100		1,645 O/D
31 Bank charges	28		1,673 O/D

The cash book for March 2013 is shown below:

Cash Book

2013		£	2013		£
Mar 16	N Morris	122	Mar 1	Balance b/d	2,598
" 21	P Fraser	167	" 6	L Young	61
" 31	Southern Elect. Co	160	" 30	A Duffy	104
" 31	Balance c/d	2,804	" 30	C Clark	490
		3,253			3,253

You are required to:

(*a*) write the cash book up to date

(*b*) draw up a bank reconciliation statement as at 31 March 2013.

23.4X Following is the cash book (bank columns) of E Flynn for December 2013:

Cash Book

2013		£	2013		£
Dec 6	J Hall	155	Dec 1	Balance b/d	3,872
Dec 20	C Walters	189	Dec 10	P Wood	206
Dec 31	P Miller	211	Dec 19	M Roberts	315
Dec 31	Balance c/d	3,922	Dec 29	P Phillips	84
		4,477			4,477

The bank statement for the month is:

2013	*Dr* £	*Cr* £	*Balance* £
Dec 1 Balance			3,872 O/D
Dec 6 Cheque		155	3,717 O/D
Dec 13 P Wood	206		3,923 O/D
Dec 20 Cheque		189	3,734 O/D
Dec 22 M Roberts	315		4,049 O/D
Dec 30 Mercantile: Standing order	200		4,249 O/D
Dec 31 K Saunders: BGC		180	4,069 O/D
Dec 31 Bank charges	65		4,134 O/D

You are required to:

(*a*) write the cash book up to date to take the necessary items into account

(*b*) draw up a bank reconciliation statement as on 31 December 2013.

23.5 On 31 December 2013 the bank columns of K Talbot's cash book showed a balance of £4,500. The bank statement as at 31 December 2013 showed a credit balance of £8,850 on the account. You checked the bank statement with the cash book and found that the following had not been entered in the cash book:

(i) A standing order to RB Insurance for £600 had been paid by the bank.

(ii) Bank interest receivable of £720 had not been entered into the account.

(iii) Bank charges of £90 had been made.

(iv) A credit transfer of £780 from KB Ltd had been paid direct into the account.

(v) Talbot's deposit account balance of £4,200 had been transferred into her bank current account.

(vi) A returned cheque of £210, dishonoured by C Hill, had been entered on the bank statement.

You also found that two cheques, payable to L Young £750 and K Clark £870, had been entered in the cash book but had not been presented for payment. In addition, a cheque for £2,070 had been paid into the bank on 31 December 2013 but had not been credited on the bank statement until 2 January 2014.

Required:

(*a*) Starting with the cash book debit balance of £4,500, write the cash book up to date.

(*b*) Draw up a bank reconciliation statement as on 31 December 2013.

23.6X On 2 May 2013 Real Kitchen Suppliers received the following bank statement for the previous month ending 30 April 2013:

National Bank plc
31 The Street
Marchtown

Account Name: Real Kitchen Suppliers
Account Number: 3419765 — Date: 30 April 2013

STATEMENT OF ACCOUNT

Date	*Detail*	*Payments* £	*Receipts* £	*Balance* £
2013				
01 April	Balance B/f			8,000Cr
16 April	Cheque 10123	1,200		6,800Cr
08 April	Cash Paid In		800	7,600Cr
12 April	Cheque 10124	1,300		6,300Cr
14 April	Cash Paid In		550	6,850Cr
15 April	Direct Debit: Marchtown Council	250		6,600Cr
20 April	Direct Debit: Premier Insurance	80		6,520Cr
21 April	Cash Paid In		650	7,170Cr
22 April	Credit Transfer from M Bell		1,230	8,400Cr
28 April	Bank Charges	120		8,280Cr
30 April	Dishonoured Cheque	280		8,000Cr

(*a*) Explain the meaning of the term 'dishonoured cheque' shown in the bank statement.

(*b*) You are required to update the cash book (below) with the relevant items from the bank statement, and bring down the balance at the end of the month.

Date	*Narration*	£	*Date*	*Narration*	£
Apr 1	Balance b/d	8,000	Apr 2	F Bashir (10123)	1,200
Apr 7	Sales Banked	800	Apr 8	M Tyler (10124)	1,300
Apr 13	Sales Banked	550	Apr 15	H Joshi (10125)	1,250
Apr 20	Sales Banked	650			
Apr 30	Sales Banked	750			

(*c*) Prepare a bank reconciliation statement as at 30 April 2013.

Edexcel International GCSE Accounting 1st edn, Edexcel (Robinson, S. 2010) Pearson Education Ltd.

23.7X Cunningham & Co is an old-established business of accountants in Huddersfield. You have been employed as book-keeper to the company to assist the senior partner, Mr Cunningham, with the accounting records and day-to-day routine duties. The company's policies when dealing with both payments and receipts is extremely strict. All cash and cheques received are to be banked immediately. Any payments over £10 must be made by cheque. Small cash payments are all paid by the petty cash system.

One of your tasks is to enter the company's cash book and reconcile this with the bank statement. This task must be carried out on a weekly basis.

Required:

(*a*) Having obtained the company's cheque book and paying-in book (Exhibits 23.6 and 23.7), enter up the cash book (bank columns only) for the week commencing 3 November 2013. Unfortunately, on that date the company was overdrawn by £2,356.00.

(*b*) Balance up the cash book at the end of the week and bring the balance down.

(*c*) From the bank statement (Exhibit 23.8) you are required to prepare:

(i) The corrected cash book balance as at 10 November 2013.

(ii) A bank reconciliation statement as at 10 November 2013.

Exhibit 23.6 Details of cheque book stubs – Cunningham & Co

Date	Payee	Amount £	Cheque no.
4 Nov 2013	Post Office Stamps	146.50	001763
4 Nov 2013	The Law Society	121.80	001764
4 Nov 2013	Bayleys Office Supplies	94.10	001765
5 Nov 2013	Lower Bents Garage (Petrol A/c – Sept)	450.15	001766
6 Nov 2013	Wages	489.20	001767
11 Nov 2013	Petty Cashier (Restoring Imprest)	46.00	001768

Exhibit 23.7 Details from paying-in book – Cunningham & Co

Date	4 Nov 2013
A/c	Cunningham & Co
Cash	
Cheques	Mrs Stoddard £540.00
£	540.00

Date	5 Nov 2013
A/c	Cunningham & Co
Cash	Bent Garage £221.00
	P Ralphs £53.00
Cheques	Gardeners £1500.00
£	1774.00

Date	6 Nov 2013
A/c	Cunningham & Co
Cash	Mr Prince £130.50
Cheques	Stephens & Smith £523.10
£	653.60

Date	7 Nov 2013
A/c	Cunningham & Co
Cash	
Cheques	Rileys (Printers) & Co £759.00
£	759.00

Date	7 Nov 2013
A/c	Cunningham & Co
Cash	Brindle Bros £165.50
Cheques	Robert Andrews Ltd £325.00
£	490.50

Exhibit 23.8 Bank statement – Cunningham & Co

TUDOR BANK | **CONFIDENTIAL**

High Street
Huddersfield

Account: Cunningham & Co
Chestergate
Huddersfield

Account No: 0012770123

Sheet No: 67
Date: 8 November 2013

2013			*Dr*	*Cr*	*Balance*	
Nov 3	Balance b/d				2,356.00	O/D
4	Cheque	001763	146.50		2,502.50	O/D
4	Deposit			540.00	1,962.50	O/D
5	Deposit			1,774.00	188.50	O/D
6	S/O Noble Insurance		62.00		250.50	O/D
6	Cheque	001767	489.20		739.70	O/D
6	Deposit			653.60	86.10	O/D
7	Deposit			759.00	672.90	
7	Bank charges		22.45		650.45	
7	Cheque	001765	94.10		556.35	

CHAPTER 24

The journal

Learning objectives

After you have studied this chapter you should be able to:

- identify the journal as an original book of entry
- use the journal for entering a range of different transactions
- post items from the journal to the ledgers
- appreciate the advantages of using a journal.

24.1 Introduction

In earlier chapters we have seen that transactions are initially entered into a book of original entry. For example, all items involving receipts and payments are recorded in the cash book while purchase and sales invoices are entered in the respective day books. Occasionally it is necessary to record a much less common transaction like writing off a bad debt or perhaps when a customer is unable to pay an outstanding invoice and offers an asset in full settlement of the debt. It is just as important to record these transactions as it is to record the purchase of goods for resale. Such a transaction is therefore recorded in another book of original entry – the **journal**.

The layout of the journal is shown below:

The Journal

Date		*Folio*	*Dr*	*Cr*
	The name of the account to be debited. The name of the account to be credited. The narrative.			

The journal is like a diary in which details of less common transactions are recorded prior to them being posted to the ledger accounts. For each transaction the following details are recorded:

- the date
- the name of the account to be debited and the amount

- the name of the account to be credited (slightly indented) and the amount
- a description and explanation of the transaction, which is known as the **narrative**
- a reference number for the source document as proof of the transaction
- finally rule off the entry.

Typical uses of the journal

Some of the less common transactions that the journal may be used for include:

- the purchase and sale of non-current assets on credit
- writing off bad debts
- other items – adjustments to any of the entries in the ledgers
- the correction of errors.

24.2 Writing up journal entries

One of the areas that examiners of book-keeping and accounting often highlight as being a problem topic is a student's ability to answer questions involving journal entries. The problem seems to arise because students find it difficult to decide which account needs to be debited and which account credited while trying to complete the journal entry.

The journal entry is really just like a diary which gives specific instructions about transactions that need to be recorded in the ledgers. Therefore, before being able to prepare the journal entry it is necessary to think double entry!

You may find it useful when answering journal questions to take it step-by-step as follows:

1. Assume you are the book-keeper of the business.
2. Think double entry:
   - Which account to debit?
   - Which account to credit?

   Remember: a debit entry is always an asset or an expense; a credit entry is always a liability, capital or income.
3. On your examination paper write up a heading marked 'Workings' then draw up 'T' accounts entering the names of the accounts to be used to record the transaction.
4. Enter the transaction in the 'T' accounts, i.e. ensuring that one account is debited and one account credited. If you have difficulty working out which is the debit and which is the credit entry look at the reminder in point 2 above, for example:

   'A business purchases a motor vehicle for £10,000 on credit from Ace Garages Ltd.'

   the double entry required is:

   - **debit** – motor vehicle account (this is an asset)
   - **credit** – Ace Garages Ltd (this is a liability – the business owes £10,000 to the garage).
5. Record the journal entry as shown above remembering to rule off the entry once you have written the narrative.

Note: It is important to make sure you complete the journal entry after working out your answer in the 'T' accounts. Failure to do so would result in no marks being awarded.

We will now look at some examples, including the folio references.

24.3 Examples of journal entries

1 Purchase and sale of non-current assets

Example 1: On 1 July 2013 a machine was purchased for £5,500 on credit from Toolmakers Ltd (ignore VAT). Purchase Inv. No. 7/159.

This transaction involves the acquisition of a new machine, which is a non-current asset, and the business incurring a liability to Toolmakers Ltd for £5,500. The double entry for this transaction is:

- **debit** – machine account (an asset)
- **credit** – Toolmakers Ltd account (a liability).

We will now show the above entry in 'T' accounts under the heading 'Workings'.

WORKINGS

General Ledger

Machinery Account *(Folio GL 1)*

	Folio	£			
2013					
Jul 1 Toolmakers	PL 55	5,500			

Purchase Ledger

Toolmakers Ltd Account *(Folio PL 55)*

				Folio	£
			2013		
			Jul 1 Machinery	GL 1	5,500

These entries now need recording in the journal. Remember, the journal is simply a kind of diary, not in account form but in ordinary written form. It says which account has to be debited, which account has to be credited, then gives a narrative that simply describes the nature of the transaction.

For the transaction above, the journal entry will appear as follows:

The Journal

Date	*Details*	*Folio*	*Dr*	*Cr*
			£	£
2013				
Jul 1	Machinery	GL 1	5,500	
	Toolmakers	PL 55		5,500
	Purchase of milling machine on credit, purchases invoice no. 7/159			

Example 2: On 12 May 2013 a business purchases a computer for use by one of the managers at a cost of £600 plus VAT at 20% on credit from Newdata Systems Ltd.

This example includes VAT so initially it is necessary to calculate the VAT payable, i.e. 20% of £600 = £120, making the total amount owing to Newdata Systems Ltd £720. Assuming that the business is VAT registered and can claim a refund of the VAT paid (see section 14.9) the double entry required to enter this transaction would be:

- **debit** – computer equipment account with £600 (as asset)
- **debit** – VAT account with £120 (amount to be offset against VAT charged on sales)
- **credit** – Newdata Systems Ltd account with £720 (a liability).

Again, the above double entry is shown in the 'T' accounts under the heading 'Workings', prior to preparing the journal entry.

WORKINGS

General Ledger

Computer Equipment Account *(Folio GL 16)*

	Folio	£		*Folio*	£
2013					
May 12 Newdata Systems Ltd	PL 37	600			

VAT Account *(Folio GL 73)*

	Folio	£		*Folio*	£
2013					
May 12 Newdata Systems Ltd	PL 37	120			

Purchase Ledger

Newdata Systems Ltd Account *(Folio PL 37)*

	Folio	£		*Folio*	£
			2013		
			May 12 Journal	GL 16	720

Note that the cost of purchasing the computer is £600 since the business will be able to reclaim £120 VAT. If, however, the business had not been registered for VAT then the cost would be £720.

The journal entries to record the above transaction are as follows:

The Journal

Date	*Details*	*Folio*	*Dr*	*Cr*
2013			£	£
May 12	Computer equipment	GL 16	600	
May 12	VAT	GL 73	120	
May 12	Newdata Systems Ltd	PL 37		720
	Purchase of computer on credit,			
	Purchase invoice no. 7890			

Example 3: Office furniture that is no longer required is sold for £300 on credit to K King on 2 July 2013. Here again, it is not difficult to work out what entries are needed in the double entry accounts. They are as follows:

WORKINGS

Sales Ledger

K King Account *(Folio SL 79)*

	Folio	£			
2013					
Jul 2 Office furniture	GL 51	300			

The furniture goes 'into' King's Account.

General Ledger

Office Furniture Account *(Folio GL 51)*

				Folio	£
			2013		
			Jul 2 K King	SL 79	300

The furniture comes 'out of' the Office Furniture Account.

These are shown in journal form as follows:

The Journal

Date	*Details*	*Folio*	*Dr*	*Cr*
			£	£
2013				
Jul 2	K King	SL 79	300	
	Office furniture	GL 51		300
	Sale of some office furniture no longer required – see letter ref: CT 568			

2 Writing off bad debts

Example 4: A debt of £78 owing to us by H Mander is written off as a bad debt on 31 August 2013. This means that we will need to credit H Mander's account to cancel the amount out of his account. A bad debt is an expense so we will debit the amount to the bad debts account.

In double entry form this is shown as:

WORKINGS

General Ledger

Bad Debts Account *(Folio GL 16)*

	Folio	£			
2013					
Aug 31 H Mander	SL 99	78			

Sales Ledger

H Mander Account *(Folio SL 99)*

	Folio	£		Folio	£
2013			2013		
Aug 1 Balance	b/d	78	Aug 31 Bad debts	GL 16	78

The journal entry showing the same transaction would be as follows:

The Journal

Date	Details	Folio	Dr	Cr
2013			£	£
Aug 31	Bad debts	GL 16	78	
	H Mander	SL 99		78
	Debt written off as bad. See letter in file 9/8906			

3 Opening entries

Example 5: J Brew, after being in business for some years without keeping proper records, now decides to keep a double entry set of books. On 1 July 2013, he establishes that his assets and liabilities are as follows:

- *Assets*: Motor van £4,840, Fixtures £700, Inventory £390, Accounts receivable – B Young £95, D Blake £45, Bank £5,080, Cash £20.
- *Liabilities*: Accounts payable – M Quinn £129, C Walters £41.

The assets therefore total (£4,840 + £700 + £390 + £95 + £45 + £5,080 + £20) = £11,170; and the liabilities total (£129 + £41) = £170. The capital in the business consists of assets minus liabilities, which in Brew's case is £11,170 – £170 = £11,000.

We start writing up of the books on 1 July 2013 as follows:

1 Open asset accounts, one for each asset. Each opening asset is shown as a debit balance.
2 Open liability accounts, one for each liability. Each opening liability is shown as a credit balance.
3 Open an account for the capital. Show it as a credit balance.

Record the details of the above transactions in the journal.

Exhibit 24.1 shows:

- the journal
- the opening entries in the double entry accounts.

Exhibit 24.1

The Journal *Page 5*

Date	Details	Folio	Dr	Cr
2013			£	£
July 1	Motor van	GL 1	4,840	
	Fixtures	GL 2	700	
	Inventory	GL 3	390	
	Accounts receivable – B Young	SL 1	95	
	D Blake	SL 2	45	
	Bank	CB 1	5,080	
	Cash	CB 1	20	
	Accounts payable – M Quinn	PL 1		129
	C Walters	PL 2		41
	Capital	GL 4		11,000
	Assets and liabilities at the date entered to open the books		11,170	11,170

General Ledger

Motor Van Account *Page 1*

	Folio	£				
2013						
July 1 Balance	J 5	4,840				

Fixtures Account *Page 2*

	Folio	£				
2013						
July 1 Balance	J 5	700				

Inventory Account *Page 3*

	Folio	£				
2013						
July 1 Balance	J 5	390				

Capital Account *Page 4*

					Folio	£
				2013		
				July 1 Balance	J 5	11,000

Sales Ledger

B Young Account *Page 1*

	Folio	£				
2013						
July 1 Balance	J 5	95				

D Blake Account *Page 2*

	Folio	£				
2013						
July 1 Balance	J 5	45				

Purchases Ledger

M Quinn Account *Page 1*

					Folio	£
				2013		
				July 1 Balance	J 5	129

C Walters Account *Page 2*

					Folio	£
				2013		
				July 1 Balance	J 5	41

Cash Book

Page 1

	Folio	Cash	Bank			
		£	£			
2013						
July 1 Balances	J 5	20	5,080			

Once the opening balances have been recorded in the books, the day-to-day transactions are entered in the normal way. Opening entries are needed only *once* in the life of the business.

4 Other items

These can be of many kinds and it is impossible to write out a complete list. Several examples are as follows:

Example 6: K Young, a customer, owes £2,000 on 1 July 2013. He was unable to pay his account in cash, but offers a motor car in full settlement of the debt. The offer is accepted on 5 July 2013.

The personal account is now no longer owed and, therefore, needs to be credited. On the other hand, the business now has an extra asset, a motor car, and therefore the motor car account needs to be debited with £2,000, the value that has been assigned to the motor car.

The double entry records are therefore:

WORKINGS

Sales Ledger

K Young Account *(SL 333)*

	Folio	£		Folio	£
2013			2013		
July 1 Balance	b/d	2,000	July 5 Motor car	GL 171	2,000

General Ledger

Motor Car Account *(GL 171)*

	Folio	£	
2013			
July 5 K Young	SL 333	2,000	

This is shown in the journal as follows:

The Journal

		Folio	Dr	Cr
2013			£	£
July 5	Motor car	GL 171	2,000	
	K Young	SL 333		2,000
	Accepted motor car in full settlement of debt per letter dated 5/7/2013			

Example 7: T Jones is a supplier. On 10 July 2013 his business is taken over by A Lee, to whom the debt of £150 is to be paid.

Here, one supplier is being exchanged for another. The action needed is to cancel the amount owing to T Jones by debiting his account, and to show it owing to A Lee by opening an account for A Lee and crediting it.

The double entry records are therefore thus:

WORKINGS

T Jones Account (SL 92)

	Folio	£		Folio	£
2013			2013		
July 10 A Lee	SL 44	150	July 1 Balance	b/d	150

A Lee Account (SL 44)

				Folio	£
			2013		
			July 10 T Jones	SL 92	150

The journal entries are thus:

The Journal

		Folio	Dr	Cr
			£	£
2013				
July 10	T Jones	SL 92	150	
	A Lee	SL 44		150
	Transfer of indebtedness as per letter ref G/1335			

Example 8: An office photocopier bought on credit from RS Ltd for £1,310 was found to be faulty and returned to the supplier on 12 July 2013. The supplier agreed to make an allowance of the full amount outstanding, £1,310, which the business accepted. Ignore VAT.

The double entry records are therefore thus:

WORKINGS

Purchases Ledger

RS Ltd Account (PL 124)

	Folio	£		Folio	£
2013			2013		
July 12 Office machinery	GL 288	1,310	July 1 Balance	b/d	1,310

General Ledger

Office machinery Account (GL 288)

	Folio	£		Folio	£
2013			2013		
July 1 Balance	b/d	1,310	July 12 RS Ltd	PL 124	1,310

The journal entries are thus:

The Journal

		Folio	Dr	Cr
			£	£
2013				
July 12	RS Ltd	PL 124	1,310	
	Office machinery	GL 288		1,310
	Faulty photocopier returned to supplier.			
	Full allowance given. See letter 10/7/2013			

5 Correction of errors

Journal entries for these will be found in Chapters 32 and 33.

6 Recap on journal entries

Remember that when entering an unusual transaction that needs to go via the journal you need to think double entry, i.e. which account needs to be debited and which account should be credited. In the above examples we have shown the double entry accounts first followed by the journal entry. This is to help the student to overcome the problem in recording journal entries. However, in practical circumstances the journal entry is always done first followed by posting the transaction from the journal to the double entry accounts, see Exhibit 24.2.

Exhibit 24.2

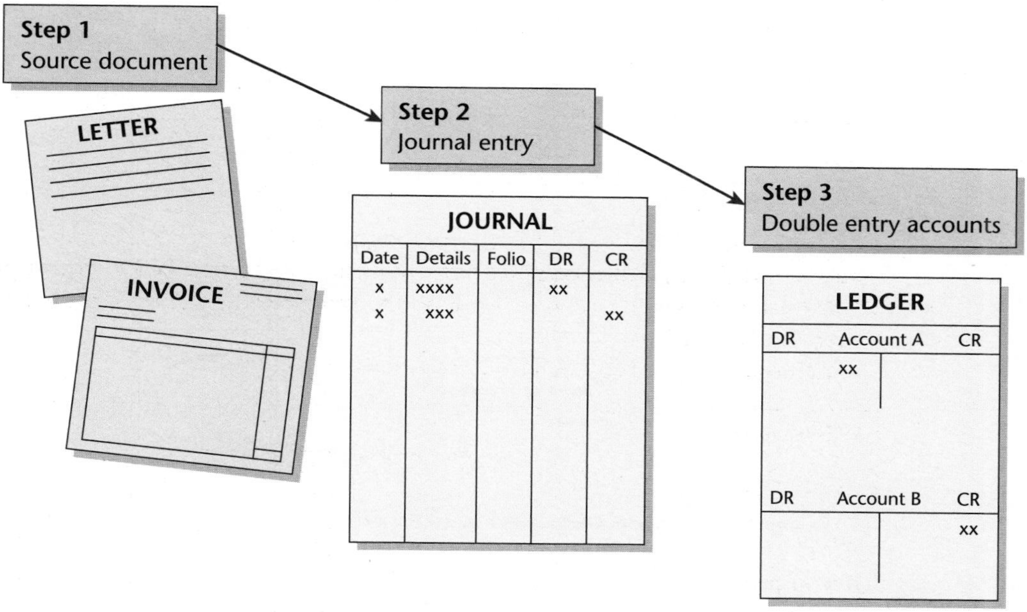

24.4 Advantages of using the journal

Recording transactions in the journal has the following advantages:

- There is less chance of further errors occurring by ensuring that the item is recorded properly and posted in the appropriate double entry accounts.
- Without such a record in the journal fraudulent transactions could occur more easily.
- There is a permanent record of the transaction with reference to the prime source document.
- If a record of the transaction is kept it saves relying on a member of staff to remember all the details. Also, if the member of staff leaves then it becomes almost impossible at a later date to understand why a particular book-keeping entry was made in the accounting books.

Despite these advantages many businesses do not use a journal.

24.5 Examination guidance

Later on in your studies, you may find that some of the journal entries become rather more complicated than those you have seen so far. The best plan for nearly all students would be to follow the step-by-step guide show in section 24.2, i.e. prepare a 'Workings' sheet with 'T' accounts to help you decide which account needs debiting and which account needs crediting. Then prepare the journal entry.

See Exhibit 24.3.

Exhibit 24.3

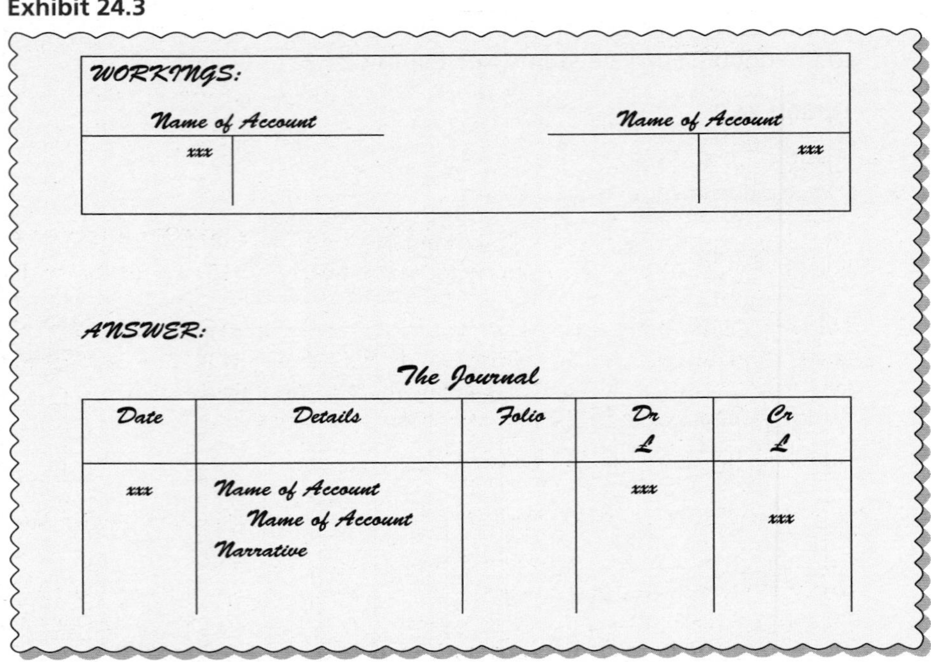

If you are already confident about dealing with these questions and you feel that you can manage them without showing your workings, then you may wish to leave out your workings from your answer.

Chapter summary

- The journal is an original book of entry and is used to record rare or exceptional transactions that do not appear in the other books of original entry.
- Typical uses of the journal include the purchase and sale of non-current assets, writing off bad debts, correction of errors and opening entries.
- When preparing a journal entry the date is entered first followed by the name of the account to be debited and amount, this is followed by entering the name of the account to be credited, slightly indented, and the amount. Finally, a narrative, giving a brief description of the transaction is written.

- Since many students have problems answering examination questions involving journal entries it is recommended that they prepare 'a working section' to show the double entry aspect prior to preparing the journal entry which usually forms the 'Answer' to the question.
- The advantages of using the journal include:
  (*a*) a reduced possibility of an error occurring
  (*b*) a permanent record of the transaction
  (*c*) less risk of fraudulent transactions.

EXERCISES

Note: Questions with the suffix 'X' shown after the question number do ***not*** *have answers shown at the back of the book. Answers to the other questions are shown in Appendix E.*

24.1 Show the journal entries to record the following:

2013
Jan 1 Bought computer on credit from Data Systems for £4,000
Jan 5 Goods taken from the business for own use, £120. The goods were not paid for by the proprietor
Jan 8 A debt of £220 owing to us by J Oddy is written off as a bad debt
Jan 15 Bought a motor vehicle from Smithy Garage paying by cheque, £15,500
Jan 29 J Street owes us £250. She is unable to pay her debt and we agree to take some filing cabinets valued at £250 from her to cancel the debt.

Narratives are not required. (Ignore VAT.)

24.2X Show the journal entries for April 2013 necessary to record the following items:

(*a*) Apr 1 Bought fixtures on credit from J Harper, £1,809
(*b*) Apr 4 We take £500 goods out of the business stock without paying for them
(*c*) Apr 9 £28 worth of the goods taken by us on 4 April are returned back into stock by us. We do not take any money for the return of the goods
(*d*) Apr 12 K Lamb owes us £500. He is unable to pay his debt. We agree to take some office equipment from him at the value and so cancel the debt
(*e*) Apr 18 Some of the fixtures bought from J Harper, £65 worth, are found to be unsuitable and are returned to him for full allowance
(*f*) Apr 24 A debt owing to us by J Brown of £68 is written off as a bad debt
(*g*) Apr 30 Office equipment bought on credit from Super Offices for £2,190.

Narratives are not required. (Ignore VAT.)

24.3 (*a*) J Green's financial position at 1 May 2013 is as follows:

		£
Bank		2,910
Cash		160
Equipment		5,900
Premises		25,000
Accounts payable:	R Smith	890
	T Thomas	610
Accounts receivable:	J Carnegie	540
Loan from:	J Higgins	4,000

You are required to show the opening entries needed to open a double entry set of books for Green as at 1 May 2013. Then open up the necessary accounts in J Green's ledger to record the above, as well as the succeeding transactions.

(*b*) During May 2013, Green's transactions were as follows:

2013
May 2 Bought goods from T Thomas on credit, £2,100
May 5 Paid R Smith on account by cheque, £500
May 12 Repaid J Higgins by cheque, £1,000
May 24 Sold goods to J Carnegie on credit, £2,220
May 31 Total cash sales for the month £8,560, of which £8,000 banked on 31 May
May 31 J Carnegie returned goods to us, £400
May 31 Paid loan interest to Higgins by cheque, £200.

You are required to post all accounts and to extract a trial balance as at 31 May 2013, but only the cash book needs balancing down. Note that the sales, purchases and returns day books are *not* needed. (Ignore VAT.)

24.4X M Maxwell is in business as a trader. During February 2013, the following transactions took place:

February
3 Purchased a motor vehicle from J Saunders costing £5,000 paying 50% of the total cost by cheque with the remainder due in 6 months.
8 Purchased fixtures and fittings on credit from J McNulty. List price £200 less trade discount of 15%.
9 M Maxwell put a further £10,000 into the business, 25% went into cash and the remainder into the business's bank account.
10 A Robinson, a debtor owing £250 was declared bankrupt. M Maxwell received 10% of the amount outstanding by cheque. The remainder to be written off to bad debts.
16 It was found that the £5,000 paid for the motor vehicle purchased on 3 February included Road Fund Licence valued at £150.
22 An account of £50 for petrol for M Maxwell's private car had been posted to the business's Motor Expenses Account.
24 Rent received of £125 had been posted to the Commissions Received Account.
24 Purchased a piece of machinery on credit from C Mattey. The list price was £6,000 but a trade discount of 20% was allowed.
26 The machine, purchased on 24 February, had chipped paintwork. Maxwell kept it but Mattey agreed to a credit of £100.

You are required to enter these transactions (including cash) into the journal, giving suitable brief narratives. (Ignore VAT.)

OCR

CHAPTER 25

Control accounts

Learning objectives

After you have studied this chapter you should be able to:

- understand the need for control accounts
- prepare a sales ledger control account from entries in the day books, cash book and ledger accounts
- prepare a purchases ledger control account from entries in the day books, cash book and ledger accounts
- appreciate the advantages of control accounts
- understand the meaning and use of memorandum accounts.

25.1 Need for control accounts

Where a business is small all the accounting records may be contained in one ledger and at the end of an accounting period the accounts are balanced off and a trial balance prepared to check the accuracy of the book-keeping entries. However, it must be remembered that certain errors may not be revealed by the trial balance (refer to Chapter 8). If a trial balance fails to balance this usually indicates that an error or errors may have been made and needs to be identified.

As the business expands the accounting requirements increase and the work has to be divided into various ledgers and consequently errors are more difficult to find. To help alleviate the problem of identifying errors more easily a type of mini trial balance is used for the sales and purchases ledgers and this is called a **control account**. The two main control accounts are as follows:

- **sales ledger control account** – an account which summarises the customer accounts (accounts receivable) in the sales ledger
- **purchases ledger control account** – an account which summarises all the supplier accounts (accounts payable) in the purchases ledger.

Thus it is only the ledgers where the control accounts do not balance that need detailed checking to locate any errors.

25.2 The principle of control accounts

Control accounts are often referred to as 'total accounts' since they contain the 'totals' of the various transactions that have taken place during the period. Therefore, if the total of the opening balances for each individual ledger account is known, together with information of the total additions and total deductions made into these accounts during a particular period, then the total amount outstanding at the end of that period can be calculated.

The total amount outstanding in the control account can then be checked against a list of the individual balances of the ledger accounts. Provided that no errors have occurred then the two total figures should agree. As mentioned above control accounts act like a mini trial balance and if an error has occurred in the ledger it can be identified more easily if control accounts are maintained since a control account failing to balance would mean the error lies within that particular ledger.

Exhibit 25.1 The principle of control accounts

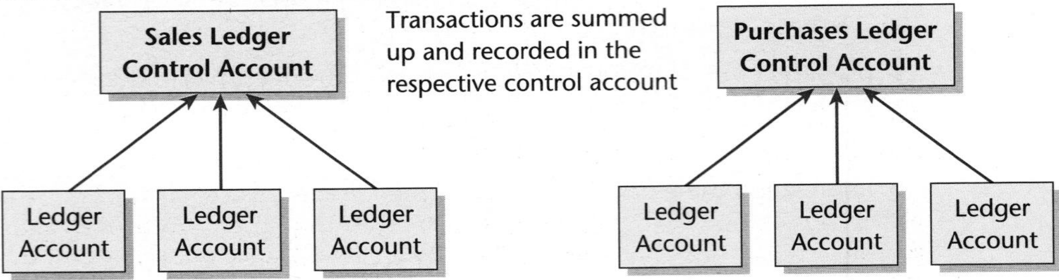

Let us now look at the following sales ledger. Suppose there were only four accounts in the sales ledger for the month of May 2013 as shown below:

Sales Ledger

T Allen Account

			£				£
2013				2013			
May	1	Balance b/d	850	May	7	Bank	820
"	4	Sales	900	"	7	Discounts allowed	30
"	30	Sales	350	"	31	Balance c/d	1,250
			2,100				2,100
Jun	1	Balance b/d	1,250				

P May Account

			£				£
2013				2013			
May	1	Balance b/d	1,500	May	9	Sales returns	200
"	28	Sales	400	"	14	Bank	900
				"	14	Discounts allowed	20
				"	31	Balance c/d	780
			1,900				1,900
Jun	1	Balance b/d	780				

K White Account

2013		£	2013	£
May 1	Balance b/d	750	May 20 Sales returns	110
" 15	Sales	600	" 31 Balance c/d	1,240
		1,350		1,350
Jun 1	Balance b/d	1,240		

C Young Account

2013		£	2013	£
May 1	Balance b/d	450	May 28 Bad debts	450

A **control account**, in this case a ***sales ledger*** **control account**, would consist only of the totals of each of the items in the sales ledger. Let us therefore first list the totals for each type of item.

May 1 Balances b/d:	£850 + £1,500 + £750 + £450 = £3,550
Sales in May:	£900 + £350 + £400 + £600 = £2,250
Cheques received in May:	£820 + £900 = £1,720
Discounts allowed in May:	£30 + £20 = £50
Sales returns in May:	£200 + £110 = £310
Bad debts written off in May:	£450

Now, looking at the totals only, it is possible to draw up a sales ledger control account. Debits are shown as usual on the left-hand side, and credits on the right-hand side. Thus:

Sales Ledger Control Account

2013		£	2013	£
May 1	Balance b/d	3,550	May 31 Bank	1,720
" 31	Sales for the month	2,250	" 31 Discounts allowed	50
			" 31 Sales returns	310
			" 31 Bad debts	450
			" 31 Balances c/d (A)	?
		5,800		5,800
Jun 1	Balances b/d (B)	?		

From your studies so far of double entry, you should be able to see that the Balance c/d (A) is the figure needed to balance the account, i.e. the difference between the two sides, i.e. £5,800 – £2,530 = £3,270.

We can now look at the ledger and see if that is correct. The balances are £1,250 + £780 + £1,240 = £3,270. As this has now proved to be correct, the figure of £3,270 can be shown in the sales ledger control account as the balances carried down (A) and the balances brought down (B).

In the above straightforward example, there were only four ledger accounts. Suppose instead that there were 400 – or 4,000 or 40,000 – ledger accounts. In these cases, the information concerning the totals of each type of item cannot be obtained so easily.

Remember that the main purpose of a control account is to act as a check on the accuracy of the entries in the ledgers. The total of a list of all the balances extracted from the ledger should equal the balance on the control account. If not, a mistake, or even many mistakes, may have been made and will have to be found.

25.3 Information for control accounts

The following tables show where information is obtained from in order to draw up control accounts.

Sales Ledger Control	Source
A Opening accounts receivable	List of customers' balances drawn up at the end of the previous period.
B Credit sales	Total from sales day book.
C Sales returns	Total of sales returns day book.
D Cheques received	Cash book: Bank column on debit (received) side. List extracted or total of a special column for cheques which have been included in the cash book.
E Cash received	Cash book: Cash column on debit (received) side. List extracted or total of a special column which has been included in the cash book.
F Discounts allowed	Total of discounts allowed column in the cash book.
G Closing accounts receivable	List of customers' balances drawn up at the end of the period.

Refer to Exhibit 25.2.

Purchases Ledger Control	Source
A Opening accounts payable	List of suppliers' balances drawn up at the end of the previous period.
B Credit purchases	Total from purchases day book.
C Purchases returns	Total of purchases returns day book.
D Cheques paid	Cash book: Bank column on payments side. List extracted or total of a special column which has been included in the cash book.
E Cash paid	Cash book: Cash column on payments side. List extracted or total of a special column which have been included in the cash book.
F Discounts received	Total of discounts received column in the cash book.
G Closing accounts payable	List of suppliers' balances drawn up at the end of the period.

Refer to Exhibit 25.3.

25.4 Form of control accounts

Control accounts are normally prepared in the same form as an account, with the totals of the debit entries in the ledger on the left-hand side of the control accounts, and the totals of the various credit entries in the ledger on the right-hand side.

Exhibit 25.2 shows how information is used to construct a sales ledger control account for the month of May 2013. The letters A, B, C, etc. from the above tables, relate to the items in the diagram.

Exhibit 25.2 Sales ledger control account – source of data

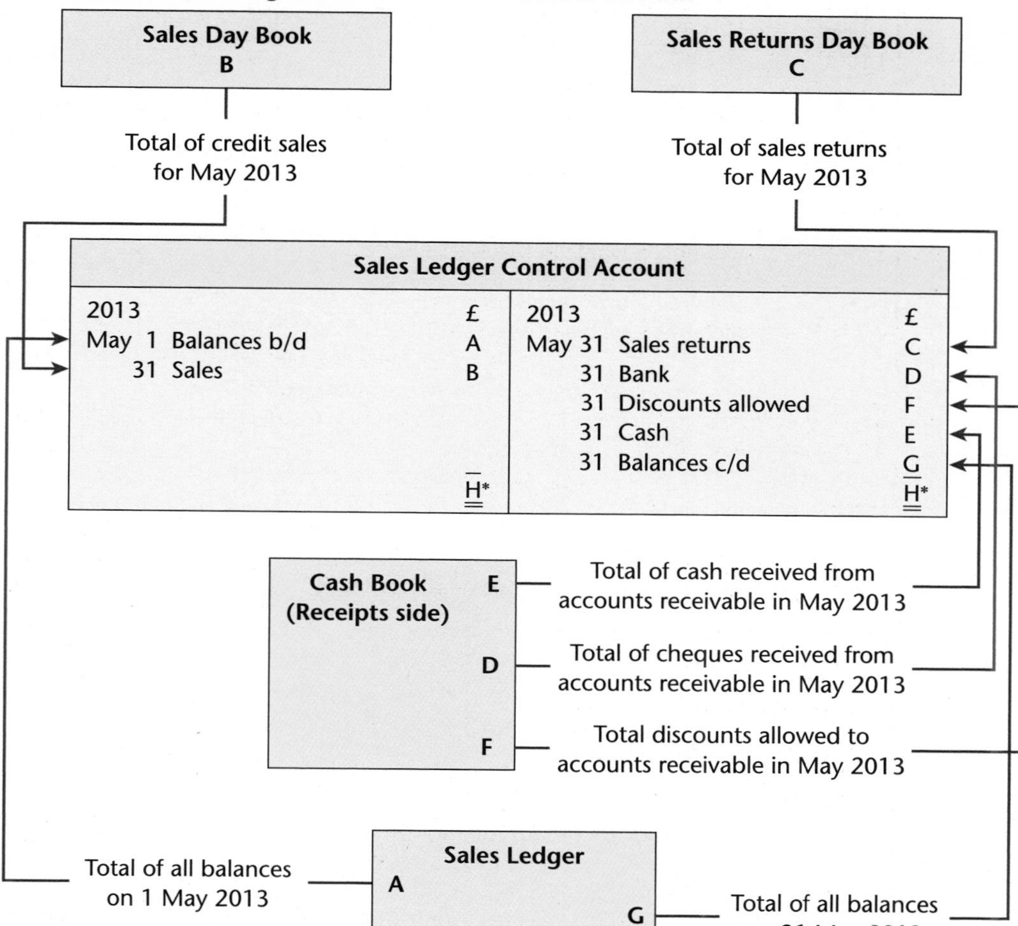

*H: If the two totals labelled H are not equal to each other, then there is an error somewhere in the books.

Exhibit 25.3 now shows the construction of a **purchases ledger control account** for May 2013.

Exhibit 25.3 Purchases ledger control account – source of data

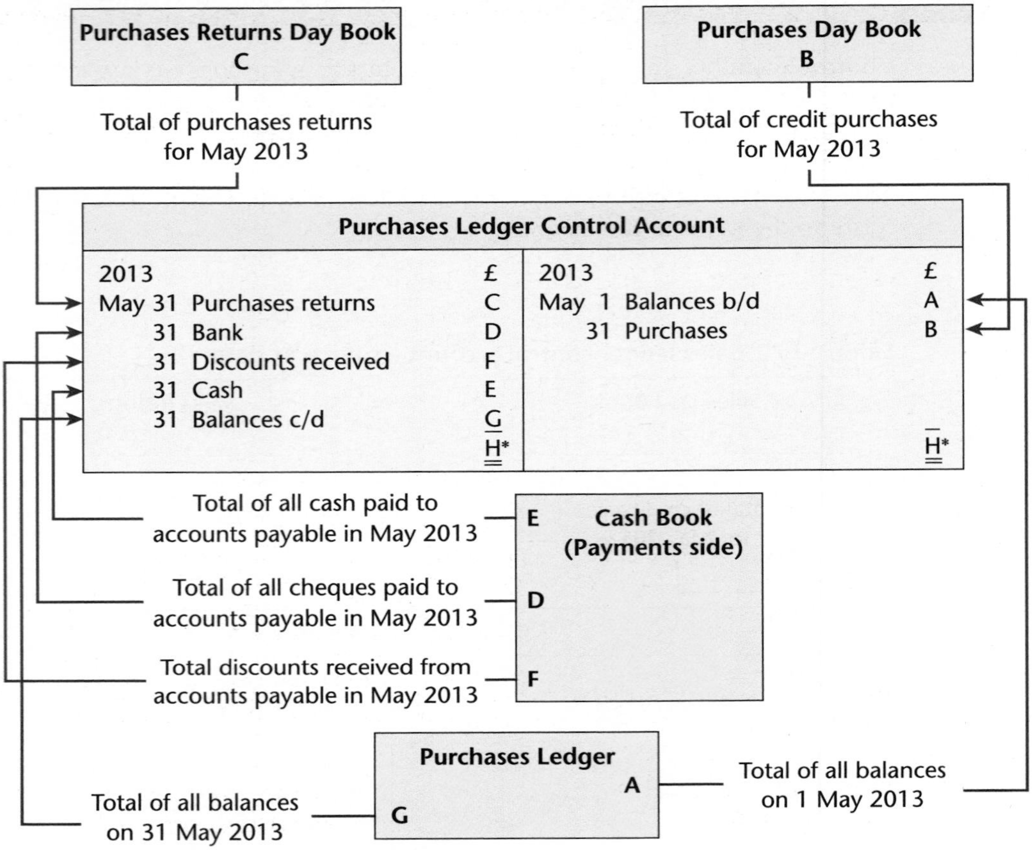

*H: If the two totals labelled H are not equal to each other, then there is an error somewhere in the books.

Exhibit 25.4 shows an example of a sales ledger control account for a sales ledger in which all the entries are arithmetically correct.

Exhibit 25.4

Sales ledger	£
Debit balances on 1 January 2013	1,894
Total credit sales for the month	10,290
Cheques received from customers in the month	7,284
Cash received from customers in the month	1,236
Sales returns from customers during the month	296
Debit balances on 31 January as extracted from the sales ledger	3,368

Sales Ledger Control Account

2013	£	2013	£
Jan 1 Balances b/d	1,894	Jan 31 Bank	7,284
31 Sales	10,290	31 Cash	1,236
		31 Sales returns	296
		31 Balances c/d	3,368
	12,184		12,184

We have proved the ledger to be arithmetically correct because the totals of the control account equal each other. If the totals were not equal, then this would prove that there is an error somewhere.

Exhibit 25.5 shows an example where an error is found to exist in a purchases ledger. The ledger will have to be checked in detail, the error found, and the control account then corrected.

Exhibit 25.5

Purchases ledger	£
Credit balances on 1 January 2013	3,890
Cheques paid to suppliers during the month	3,620
Purchases returns to suppliers in the month	95
Bought from suppliers in the month	4,936
Credit balances on 31 January as extracted from the purchases ledger	5,151

Purchases Ledger Control Account

2013	£	2013	£
Jan 31 Bank	3,620	Jan 1 Balances b/d	3,890
31 Purchases returns	95	31 Purchases	4,936
31 Balances c/d	5,151		
	8,866*		8,826*

*As can be seen from the totals at the bottom of the control account, there is a £40 (£8,866 – £8,826) error in the purchases ledger. We will have to check that ledger in detail to find the error.

Notice that a double line does not appear under the totals figures. The account will not be finalised and ruled off until the error is traced and corrected.

25.5 Other transfers

Transfers to bad debt accounts will have to be recorded in the sales ledger control account because they involve entries in the sales ledgers.

Similarly, a contra account, whereby the same business is both a supplier and a customer and inter-indebtedness is set off, will also need entering in the control accounts. An example of this follows:

(i) The business has sold A Hughes £600 goods on 1 May
(ii) Hughes has supplied the business with £880 goods on 12 May
(iii) The £600 owing by Hughes is set off against £880 owing to him on 30 May
(iv) This leaves £280 owing to Hughes on 31 May

Sales Ledger

A Hughes Account

		£	
May 1 Sales	**(i)**	600	

Purchases Ledger
A Hughes Account

					£
			May 12 Purchases	(ii)	880

The set-off now takes place:

Sales Ledger
A Hughes Account

		£			£
May 1 Sales	(i)	600	May 30 Set-off: Purchases ledger	(iii)	600

Purchases Ledger
A Hughes Account

		£			£
May 30 Set-off: Sales ledger	(iii)	600	May 12 Purchases	(ii)	880
May 31 Balance c/d	(iv)	280			
		880			880
			Jun 1 Balance b/d	(iv)	280

The transfer of the £600 will appear on the credit side of the sales ledger control account and on the debit side of the purchases ledger control account.

Students often find it difficult to work out which side of each control account contra items (set-offs) are shown. Think of it as cash received and cash paid, the entries go on the same sides of the control accounts as these items. Thus a contra item will appear on the credit side of the sales ledger control account (the same side as cash received from accounts receivable) and will appear on the debit side of the purchases ledger control account (the same side as cash paid to accounts payable would appear). Remember this and you won't get it wrong.

25.6 A more complicated example

Exhibit 25.6 shows a worked example of a more complicated control account. You will see that there are sometimes credit balances in the sales ledger as well as debit balances. Suppose, for instance, that we sold £500 goods to W Young, she then paid in full for them, and then afterwards she returned £40 goods to us. This would leave a credit balance of £40 on the account, whereas usually the balances in the sales ledger are debit balances.

There may also be reason to write off a debt as bad where a business finds it impossible to collect the debt. If this happens, the double entry would be as follows:

Debit: bad debts account
Credit: individual account receivable.

Ultimately, the bad debts account would be credited and the profit and loss account would be debited (see Chapter 28). The sales ledger control account would also be credited, as shown in Exhibit 25.6.

Exhibit 25.6

2013		£
Aug 1	Sales ledger – debit balances	3,816
Aug 1	Sales ledger – credit balances	22
Aug 31	Transactions for the month:	
	Cash received	104
	Cheques received	6,239
	Sales	7,090
	Bad debts written off	306
	Discounts allowed	298
	Sales returns	664
	Cash refunded to a customer who had overpaid his account	37
	Dishonoured cheques	29
	Interest charged by us on overdue debt	50
	At the end of the month:	
	Sales ledger – debit balances	3,429
	Sales ledger – credit balances	40

Sales Ledger Control Account

2013		£	2013		£
Aug 1	Balances b/d	3,816	Aug 1	Balances b/d	22
Aug 31	Sales	7,090	Aug 31	Cash	104
	Cash refunded	37		Bank	6,239
	Bank: dishonoured cheques	29		Bad debts	306
	Interest on debt	50		Discounts allowed	298
	Balances c/d	40		Sales returns	664
				Balances c/d	3,429
		11,062			11,062

25.7 Control accounts and double entry

When a business operates control accounts, it has to decide where the control accounts should be kept within the book-keeping system. There are two options:

1 keep the control accounts within the double entry system
2 keep control accounts as memorandum accounts.

These two options are discussed next.

Control accounts within the double entry system

In order to maintain the control accounts within the general ledger, the control account becomes part of the double entry system and the individual accounts receivable and accounts payable accounts become memorandum accounts (see Exhibit 25.7).

Exhibit 25.7 Control account as part of a double entry system

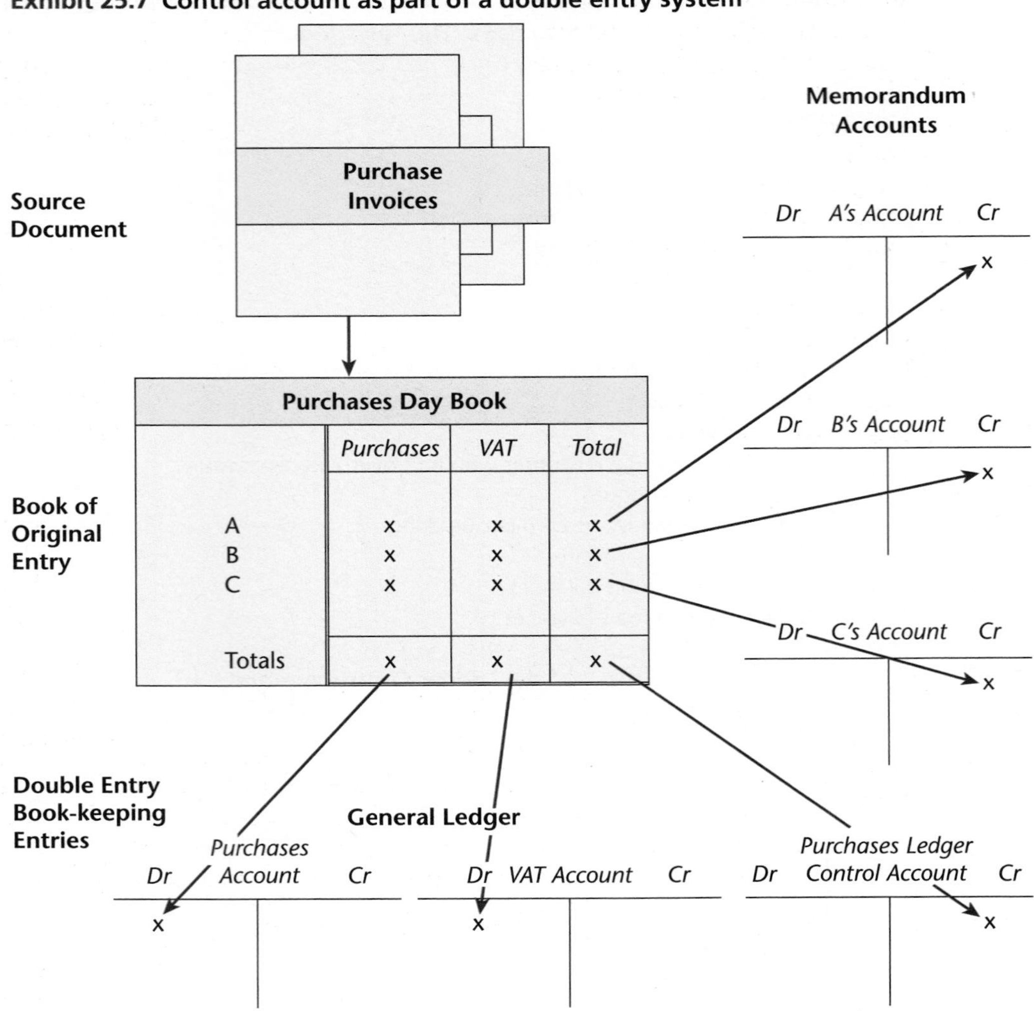

In Exhibit 25.7, the balance of outstanding accounts payable is taken from the control account and included in the trial balance at the end of the month or year end, as required. In this case, the personal accounts of the accounts payable (i.e. A Account, B Account, C Account, etc.) are not part of the double entry and are referred to as **memorandum accounts**. It is, however, important to balance the memorandum accounts periodically with the purchases ledger control accounts so that errors can be located and corrected. The same procedure would apply to the sales.

Control accounts as memorandum accounts

In order to maintain the control accounts in the sales and purchases ledgers, the control accounts become memorandum accounts. Using this method, the accounts receivable and accounts payable personal accounts are included in the double entry system via the sales and purchases ledgers, while the control account becomes the memorandum account. Exhibit 25.8 illustrates this procedure with the purchases ledger. The sales would be similar.

If a transaction involving either an account receivable or an account payable is made via the journal, for example, writing off a bad debt, it is necessary to record the entry in both the individual account receivable or account payable ledger account and also in the respective control account.

Exhibit 25.8 Control account as a memorandum account

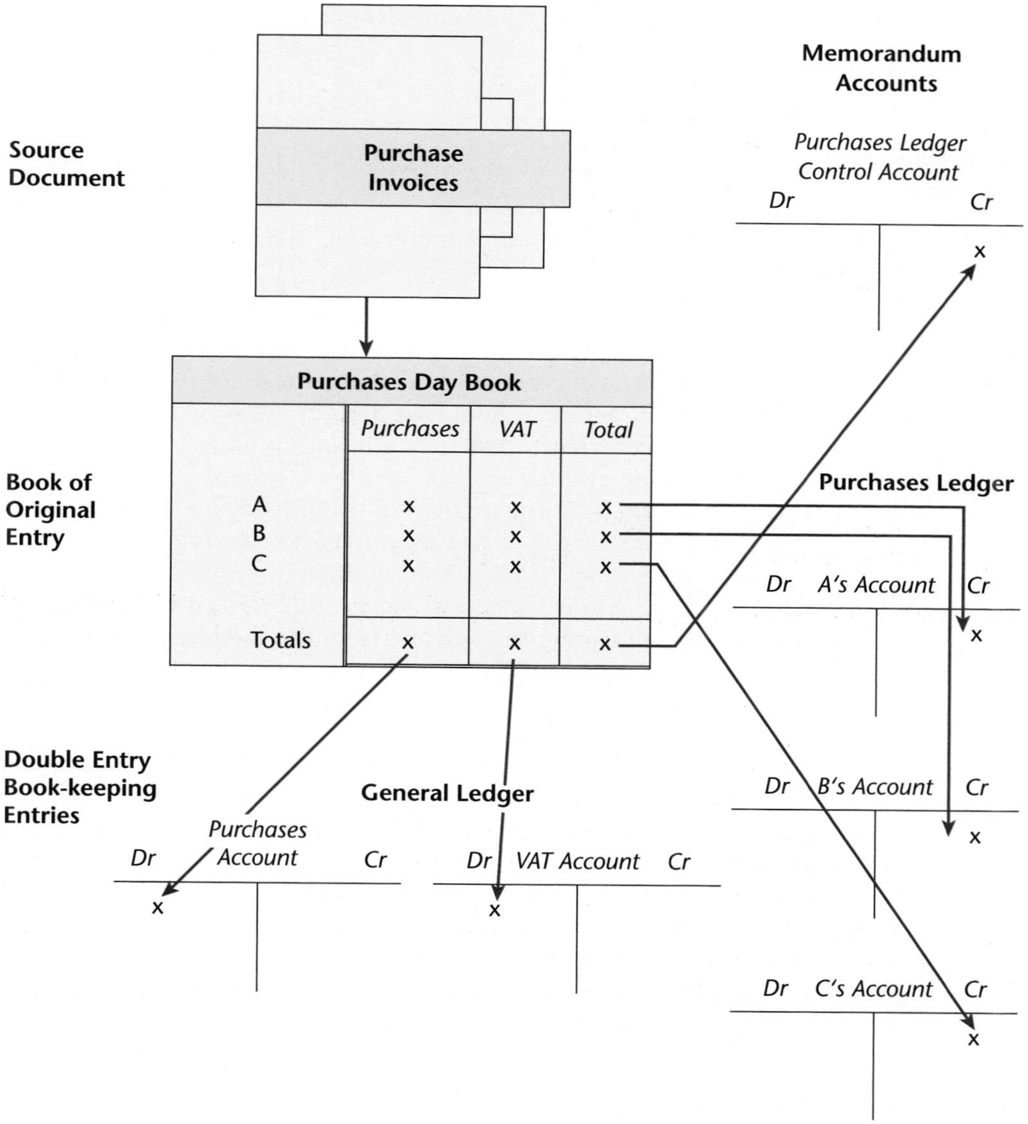

25.8 Control accounts and computerised accounting systems

Control accounts are used by many organisations especially those using manual accounting systems. For organisations using computerised accounting systems the control accounts are an integral part of the accounting package and are prepared automatically. This is because computerised systems ensure that all double entry transactions are completed upon entry thereby ensuring that the ledgers all balance. However, even these businesses with computerised accounting packages often prepare their own manual control accounts to ensure that the ledgers balance and to detect any errors.

25.9 Advantages of control accounts

There are several advantages an organisation can benefit from by using control accounts as shown below:

- *Location of error* – By preparing control accounts any arithmetical errors that may have occurred are identified. Also, if a clerk has inadvertently omitted entering an invoice or payment in the personal accounts these too would be identified since the control account acts as a mini trial balance. However, it must be pointed out that there are other errors that may still be contained in the ledgers such as mispostings or compensating errors.
- *Prevention of fraud* – Normally the control accounts are under the supervision of a senior member of the accounting team or accounts manager. This makes fraud more difficult since any transaction entered into a ledger account must also be included in the control account. Since a different member of staff would be responsible for maintaining the ledgers, from the member supervising the control account, it would be more difficult to carry out fraudulent transactions. Therefore the supervisor or manager provides an internal check on the procedures.
- *Information for management* – For management purposes the balances on the control accounts can always be taken to equal accounts receivable and accounts payable without waiting for an extraction of individual balances. Management control is thereby aided because the speed at which information is obtained is one of the prerequisites of efficient control.

25.10 Other sources of information for control accounts

With a large organisation there may well be more than one sales ledger or purchases ledger. The accounts in the sales ledger may be divided up in ways such as:

- *Alphabetically* – thus we may have three sales ledgers, split: A–F, G–O and P–Z.
- *Geographically* – this could be split: Europe, Far East, Africa, Australasia, North and South America.

For each ledger we must therefore have a separate control account.

Note that many students become confused when making postings to control accounts. You might find it useful to remember that when posting entries to control accounts the entry goes on the same side as it would in the personal account. Another useful hint can also be applied when entering 'contra' or 'set-off' items: here, think of the contra or set-off as *cash* and enter the item where you would normally enter cash on the respective control account (as mentioned previously in section 25.5).

25.11 Multiple-choice questions

Now attempt set No. 2 of the multiple-choice questions in Appendix C. This set contains 35 questions.

Chapter summary

- Control accounts are 'total' accounts which contain the total of the various individual personal account balances which are held in subsidiary ledgers such as the 'sales ledger' or 'purchases ledger' and information gathered from the various accounting books including, sales and purchases day books, sales returns and purchases returns day books and cash book.
- The two main control accounts are:
  1 sales ledger control account
  2 purchases ledger control account.
- Control accounts are usually prepared at the end of each month or period. By comparing the balance on the control account with the total outstanding balances in a subsidiary ledger the arithmetical accuracy can be checked, and errors easily located and corrected.
- Transfers between the sales and purchases ledgers are called 'contra entries' or sometimes 'set-offs'. Remember to enter these on the same side in the control account as you would normally enter cash either received or paid, i.e.:
  1 purchases ledger control account is debited
  2 sales ledger control account is credited.
- The advantages of using control accounts include:
  1 helping to locate errors
  2 preventing fraud
  3 providing up-to-date information to management on the total accounts receivable (debtors) and accounts payable (creditors).
- If the sales ledger control account and the purchases ledger control account are maintained in the general ledger then they are part of the double entry system and the sales ledger and purchases accounts (i.e. the personal accounts) are classed as 'memorandum accounts'.
- If, however, the sales ledger and purchases ledger are part of the double entry system, then the control accounts are classed as 'memorandum accounts'.
- Finally, remember that when making entries into the control accounts the entry goes on exactly the same side as it would do in the personal account.

EXERCISES

*Note: Questions with the suffix 'X' shown after the question number do **not** have answers shown at the back of the book. Answers to the other questions are shown in Appendix E.*

25.1 You are required to prepare a sales ledger control account from the following:

2013		£
May 1	Sales ledger balances	4,560
	Total of entries for May:	
	Sales day book	10,870
	Sales returns day book	460
	Cheques and cash received from customers	9,615
	Discounts allowed	305
May 31	Sales ledger balances	5,050

25.2 You are to prepare a sales ledger control account from the following. Deduce the closing figure for the sales ledger balance as at 31 March 2013.

2013		£
Mar 1	Sales ledger balances	6,708
	Totals for March:	
	Discounts allowed	300
	Cash and cheques received from accounts receivable	8,970
	Sales day book	11,500
	Bad debts written off	115
	Sales returns day book	210
Mar 31	Sales ledger balances	?

25.3X Draw up a purchases ledger control account from the following:

2013		£
June 1	Purchases ledger balances	3,890
	Totals for June:	
	Purchases day book	5,640
	Purchases returns day book	315
	Cash and cheques paid to creditors	5,230
	Discounts received	110
June 30	Purchases ledger balances	?

25.4X The following is a summary of sales activities during the month of November.

	£
Balance of accounts receivable at 1 November 2013	220,617
Goods sold on credit	99,300
Money received from credit customers	109,262
Sales returns from credit customers	2,000
Journal credit to correct an error	550

(*a*) Prepare a sales ledger control account from the above details. Show clearly the balance carried down at 30 November 2013, and brought down at 1 December 2013.

The following closing balances were in the Subsidiary (Sales) Ledger on 30 November.

Robertson Mechanics	£15,016	Dr
Parkes and Company	£52,109	Dr
JJP Limited	£13,200	Dr
Components Limited	£42,982	Dr
OKK Parts	£44,798	Dr
Stevens Limited	£550	Dr
Mechanics Supplies	£40,000	Dr

(*b*) Reconcile the balances shown above with the sales ledger control account balance you have calculated in part (*a*).

	£
Sales ledger control account balance as at 30 November 2013	
Total of Subsidiary (Sales) Ledger accounts as at 30 November 2013	
Difference	

(*c*) What may have caused the difference you calculated in part (*b*) above?

Association of Accounting Technicians

25.5X Draw up a sales ledger control account from the following.

2013		£
Apr 1	Debit balances	4,960
	Credit balances	120
	Totals for April:	
	Sales day book	8,470
	Cash and cheques received from accounts receivable	7,695
	Discounts allowed	245
	Debit balances in the sales ledger set off against credit balances in the purchases ledger	77
Apr 30	Debit balances	?
	Credit balances	46

25.6 At the end of December 2013 the sales ledger of Ravi Singh showed total accounts receivable (debtors) to be £78,540. Ravi believes this figure may be incorrect and obtains the following figures from his books for the period 1 January to 31 December 2013.

	£
Opening balance in the sales ledger at 1 January 2013	65,000
Credit sales	453,900
Returns inwards	6,430
Receipts from accounts receivable (debtors)	432,000
Discount allowed	7,540
Bad debts	650
Purchases ledger balance set off	1,650
Customer's cheque returned by bank	750

(*a*) Prepare the sales ledger control account for the period 1 January–31 December 2013 clearly showing the closing balance.
(*b*) Explain the reason why Ravi believes there may have been errors in his sales ledger.
(*c*) Explain, with reasons, where the closing balance of the sales ledger control account would appear in the final accounts of Ravi Singh.

Edexcel International GCSE Accounting 1st edn
Edexcel (Robinson, S. 2010) Pearson Education Ltd.

25.7X Carl Barber runs a small business selling electrical components to wholesalers. Since he has numerous accounts receivable and accounts payable he keeps sales and purchases ledgers and maintains both sales and purchases control accounts.

The following information is available from Carl's books for the year ended 31 December 2013.

	£
Balances as at 1 January 2013:	
Purchases ledger debit balance	131
Purchases ledger credit balance	7,794
Sales ledger debit balance	10,030
Sales ledger credit balance	71
Totals for the year:	
Cash received in respect of debit balance in purchases ledger	131
Purchases day book	50,099
Purchases returns day book	669
Sales day book	79,660
Discounts allowed	2,910
Discounts received	1,843
Cheques paid to suppliers	46,634
Cheques received from customers	69,015
Sales returns day book	1,578
Bad debts written off	408
Amount due from customer offset against amount due to the same business in our accounts payable ledger (offset via contra)	543

Note: The credit balance of £71 in the Sales Ledger brought forward on 1 January 2013 is to be carried forward as at 31 December 2013.

Required:
(*a*) Prepare Carl's sales ledger control account as at 31 December 2013.
(*b*) Prepare Carl's purchases ledger control account as at 31 December 2013.
(*c*) Why is it important to maintain control accounts? Discuss the advantages.

PART 4

Adjustments for financial statements

This part is concerned with the adjustments that are needed and the use of the extended trial balance in preparing the financial statements.

CHAPTER 26

Depreciation of non-current assets

Learning objectives

After you have studied this chapter you should be able to:

- define depreciation
- explain why depreciation is charged
- calculate depreciation using the straight line method, the diminishing (reducing) balance method and the revaluation method.

26.1 Depreciation of non-current assets

Non-current assets are those assets of material value that are purchased for use in the business, are not for resale and which have a long life. While assets such as buildings, machinery, fixtures and fittings are used in the business for many years they do not last indefinitely: therefore, when they are disposed of the difference between the cost price and the amount received on disposal is called **depreciation**.

Depreciation as an expense

Depreciation is part of the original cost of a non-current asset consumed during its period of use by the business. Since depreciation is an expense, it will have to be charged to the profit and loss account in the same way as expenses such as wages, rent, insurance, etc. and will, therefore, reduce net profit. The amount charged each year for depreciation is based upon an estimate of how much economic use of the non-current asset has been used up in that accounting period.

For example, if a business purchased computer equipment costing £4,000 which was expected to last for four years, then each year a quarter of the overall usefulness would be consumed. The charge for depreciation would be a quarter of the cost of the computer equipment, i.e. £1,000. The net profit for the year would be reduced by £1,000 and the value of the equipment in the statement of financial position would be reduced from £4,000 to £3,000.

26.2 Causes of depreciation

Non-current assets such as machinery, motor vehicles, plant and equipment, etc. tend to fall in value (depreciate) for various reasons such as physical deterioration, economic factors, time and depletion. These are described more fully below:

Physical depreciation

1 *Wear and tear* – non-current assets as described above eventually wear out, some last many years while others wear out more quickly.
2 *Erosion, rust, rot and decay* – land may be eroded or wasted away by the action of wind, rain, sun or other elements. Similarly, the metals in motor vehicles or machinery will rust away. Wood will rot eventually. Decay is a process that is present due to the elements and lack of proper attention.

Economic factors

Economic factors may be said to be the reasons for an asset being put out of use even though it is in good physical condition. The two main factors are usually **obsolescence** and **inadequacy**:

1 *Obsolescence* – this occurs when an asset becomes out of date due to advanced technology or a change in processes. For example, in the car industry much of the assembly work is now done by robots.
2 *Inadequacy* – this arises when an asset is no longer used because of the growth and change in the size of the business due to new regulations. The transport industry is now able to use much larger vehicles than previously resulting in the selling off of smaller vehicles.

Both obsolescence and inadequacy do not necessarily mean that the asset is destroyed: it is merely put out of use by the business, and another business will often buy it.

The time factor

There are some assets that have a legal life fixed in terms of years, for example a **lease**. A business may decide to rent a property for ten years and takes out a lease, and a legal agreement is drawn up between the parties. Each year a proportion of the cost of the lease is depreciated until the lease expires and the value is nil. In such cases the term **amortisation** may be used instead of the term depreciation.

Depletion

Some assets are of a 'wasting nature' such as the extraction of raw materials from mines or quarries or oil from oil wells. Such natural resources are often sold in their raw state to other businesses for processing. To provide for the consumption of an asset of a wasting character is called provision for **depletion**.

26.3 Land and buildings

Prior to the accounting regulation known as SSAP 12 'Accounting for depreciation' which applied after 1977, freehold and long leasehold properties were very rarely subject to a charge for depreciation. It was contended that, as property values tended to rise instead of fall, it was inappropriate to charge depreciation.

However, SSAP 12 requires that depreciation be charged over the property's useful life, with the exception that freehold land will not normally require a provision for depreciation. This is because land does not normally depreciate. Buildings do, however, eventually fall into disrepair or become obsolete and must be subject to a charge for depreciation each year. When a revaluation of property takes place, the depreciation charge must be on the revalued figure.

FRS 15 'Tangible fixed assets' replaced SSAP 12 in 1999 and repeated the requirements of the original standard and also dealt with the problem of the distinction between the cost of freehold land and the cost of the buildings upon it, by insisting that each cost should be separated.

The International Standards that deal with issues relating to non-current assets and have the same requirements as FRS 15 are IAS 16 'Property, plant and equipment', which sets out the accounting treatment for property, plant and equipment (PPE). IAS 23 'Borrowing costs', deals with interest and other costs that an organisation incurs with the borrowing of funds and IAS 36 'Impairment of assets', sets out the accounting procedures in relation to the way the assets are shown on the statement of financial position.

The International Accounting Standards Board has a useful website www.iasb.org.uk where full details of all the standards are shown and to which you may wish to refer later on in your studies.

26.4 Appreciation

At this stage, readers may well begin to ask themselves about the assets that increase (appreciate) in value. The answer to this is that normal accounting procedure would be to ignore any such **appreciation**, as to bring appreciation into account would be to contravene both the historical cost concept and the prudence concept (as discussed in Chapter 13). However, one of the problems when SSAP 12 was introduced was that the UK was in the middle of a property boom when businesses could see the market value of their properties rising. At the same time, they were being instructed by the accounting standard to charge their profit and loss account with depreciation that represented a fall in the value of the property over the period. Not surprisingly, this didn't make sense. Therefore, SSAP 12 allowed non-current assets to be revalued and for depreciation to then be calculated on the basis of the revalued amount. FRS 15 also permits this to be done. IAS 16 also allows non-current assets to be revalued at a fair value for land and buildings or market value for plant and equipment. Depreciation is then calculated on the new value.

26.5 Provision for depreciation as an allocation of cost

Depreciation in total over the life of an asset can be calculated quite simply as cost less amount received when the asset is put out of use by the business. The amount received on disposal is often referred to as the **residual value** or **scrap value**. If an item is bought and sold for a lower amount within the same accounting period, then the difference in value is charged as depreciation in arriving at that period's net profit.

The difficulties start when the asset is used for more than one accounting period; an attempt has to be made to charge each period with the appropriate amount of depreciation.

Although depreciation provisions are now intended to allocate the cost of the non-current asset to each accounting period in which it is in use, it does not follow that there is any true and accurate method of performing even this task. All that can be said is that the cost should be allocated over the life of the asset in such a way as to charge it as equitably as possible to the periods in which the asset is used. The difficulties involved are considerable and include:

- Apart from a few assets, such as a lease, how accurately can a business assess an asset's useful life? Even a lease may be put out of use if the premises leased have become inadequate due to the expansion of the business.
- How is 'use' measured? A car owned by a business for two years may have been driven one year by a very careful driver and another year by a reckless driver. The standard of driving will affect the motor car and also the amount of cash receivable on its disposal. How should such a business apportion the car's depreciation costs?
- There are other expenses beside depreciation, such as repairs and maintenance of the non-current asset. As both of these affect the rate and amount of depreciation, should they not also affect the depreciation provision calculations?
- How can a business possibly know the amount receivable in a number of years' time when the asset is put out of use?

These are only some of the difficulties. Therefore, accounting has developed various methods of calculating depreciation as shown below.

26.6 Methods of calculating depreciation charges

The two main methods in use for calculating depreciation charges are the **straight line method** and the **diminishing (reducing) balance method**. Most accountants think that, although other methods may be needed in certain cases, the straight line method is the one that is generally most suitable. Both methods are now described.

Straight line method

This method involves the cost price of a non-current asset, the estimated years of its use and the expected disposal value. The depreciation charge each year can be calculated thus:

$$\text{Depreciation charge per year} = \frac{\text{Cost price} - \text{Disposal value}}{\text{Number of years of use}}$$

For example, if a car was purchased for £22,000 and the business decided to keep it for four years and then sell it for £2,000, the depreciation to be charged would be:

$$\frac{\text{Cost price} - \text{Disposal value}}{\text{Number of years of use}} = \frac{£22{,}000 - £2{,}000}{4} = £5{,}000 \text{ depreciation per year}$$

The depreciation charge of £5,000 would then be charged for four years.

If, after four years, the car had no disposal value, the charge for depreciation would have been:

$$\frac{\text{Cost price}}{\text{Number of years of use}} = \frac{£22{,}000}{4} = £5{,}500 \text{ depreciation each year for 4 years}$$

This method may sometimes be referred to as the 'fixed instalment method'.

Diminishing (reducing) balance method

Depreciation to be charged involves deciding on a percentage amount to be used each year. This percentage is then deducted from the cost price for the first year and in subsequent years from the reducing balances. This is illustrated in the following example:

Example: If a machine is bought for £10,000 and depreciation is to be charged at 20%, the calculations for the first three years would be as follows:

	£
Cost	10,000
First year: depreciation (20% of £10,000)	2,000
	8,000
Second year: depreciation (20% of £8,000)	1,600
	6,400
Third year: depreciation (20% of £6,400)	1,280
Net book value at the end of the third year	5,120

Note that **net book value** means the cost of the non-current asset with depreciation deducted. It is sometimes simply known as 'book value'.

Using this method means that much larger amounts are charged in the earlier years of use as compared with the latter years of use. It is often said that repairs and upkeep in the early years will not cost as much as when the asset becomes old. This means that:

In the early years		In the later years
A higher charge for depreciation + A lower charge for repairs and upkeep	will tend to be fairly equal to	A lower charge for depreciation + A higher charge for repairs and upkeep

The worked example in section 26.7 gives a comparison of the calculations using the two methods, when the same cost applies to both methods.

26.7 A worked example

A business has just bought a machine for £8,000. It will be kept in use for four years, and then it will be disposed of for an estimated amount of £500. The business's management asks for a comparison of the amounts charged as depreciation using both methods.

For the straight line method the depreciation is calculated as follows:

$$\frac{\text{Cost price} - \text{Disposal value}}{\text{Number of years of use}} = \text{Depreciation per year}$$

$$\frac{£8{,}000 - £500}{4} = \frac{£7{,}500}{4}$$

$$= £1{,}875 \text{ depreciation per year}$$

For the diminishing balance method a percentage figure of 50% will be used.

	Method 1 Straight Line		**Method 2 Reducing Balance**
	£		£
Cost	8,000		8,000
Depreciation: year 1	1,875	(50% of £8,000)	4,000
	6,125		4,000
Depreciation: year 2	1,875	(50% of £4,000)	2,000
	4,250		2,000
Depreciation: year 3	1,875	(50% of £2,000)	1,000
	2,375		1,000
Depreciation: year 4	1,875	(50% of £1,000)	500
Disposal value	500		500

Exhibit 26.1 illustrates the fact that using the diminishing balance method there is a much higher charge for depreciation in the early years, and lower charges in the later years: whereas for the straight line method the charge remains the same each year.

Exhibit 26.1 Comparing depreciation charges for the above worked example

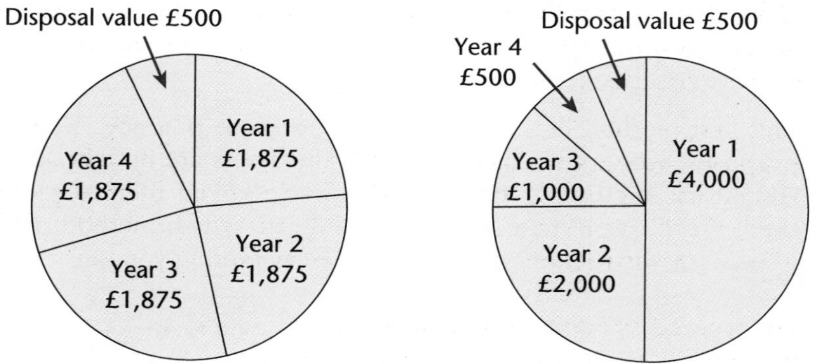

Revaluation method

Another method of depreciation used mainly by self-employed people, such as joiners, electricians, plumbers, etc. is the revaluation method. These small businesses may have a number of low cost tools and equipment such as saws, drills, spanners and so on which are needed to enable them to carry out their jobs. It would be very difficult to use one of the previously discussed methods of depreciation for such low cost tools and equipment: therefore the revaluation method is used.

With this method the tools and equipment, etc. are valued at the beginning of the financial year; any further items purchased during the year for use in the business which are not for resale are added to the initial valuation. After using the tools, etc. during the year they are valued again at the end of the financial year. This figure is then deducted from the initial valuation plus tools, etc. purchased during the year to find the depreciation to be charged to the profit and loss account. The following example shows the depreciation calculation for a joiner:

Example

	£
Value of tools and equipment as start of period	2,500
Add Cost of items purchased during the period	500
	3,000
Less Value at close of the period	2,000
Depreciation for the year	1,000

26.8 Depreciation provisions and assets bought or sold

There are two main methods of calculating depreciation provisions for assets bought or sold during an accounting period.

1. Ignore the dates during the year that the assets were bought or sold and merely calculate a full period's depreciation on the assets in use at the end of the period. Thus, assets sold during the accounting period will have no provision made for depreciation for that last period irrespective of how many months they were in use. Conversely, assets bought during the period will have a full period of depreciation provision charged even though they may not have been owned throughout the whole period.
2. Provide for depreciation made on the basis of one month's ownership equals one month's depreciation. Fractions of months are usually ignored. This is obviously a more precise method than method 1.

The first method is the one normally used in practice. However, for examination purposes, where the dates on which the assets are bought and sold are shown, you should use method 2. If no such dates are given then, obviously, method 1 is the one to use. Often the question will indicate which method to use so it is important to read the instructions carefully before attempting your answer.

Chapter summary

- Depreciation is charged on fixed assets in use during an accounting period.
- Non-current assets are defined as those assets of material value that are intended to be used in the business over a period of time and have not been bought with the intention of resale.
- Depreciation is an expense of the business and as such is charged to the profit and loss account.
- The main causes of depreciation are physical deterioration, economic factors, the time factor and depletion.
- The increase in value over the cost of an asset, usually land and buildings, is called appreciation.
- The straight line method is where an equal amount of depreciation is charged each year.
- The diminishing balance method is where a fixed percentage for depreciation is taken from the cost of the asset in the first year. In the second and later years the same percentage is taken from the diminishing balance (i.e. cost *less* depreciation already charged).
- With the revaluation method the assets are valued at the start of the period; additions are added to this figure from which the value of the assets at the end of the period is deducted. The difference is depreciation, which is charged to the profit and loss account.

EXERCISES

Note: Questions with the suffix 'X' shown after the question number do ***not*** *have answers shown at the back of the book. Answers to the other questions are shown in Appendix E.*

26.1 K Richardson runs a small manufacturing business and purchases a new machine for £40,000. It has an estimated life of five years and a scrap value of £5,000. Richardson is not sure whether to use the straight line or diminishing method of depreciation for the purpose of calculating depreciation on the machine.

You are required to calculate the depreciation on the machine using both methods, showing clearly the balance remaining in the machine account at the end of the five years for each method. Assume that 40% per annum is to be used for the diminishing balance method.

26.2 A printing press cost £37,500 and will be kept for four years when it will be traded in at an estimated value of £15,360. Show the calculations of the figures for depreciation (to the nearest £) for each of the four years using:

(*a*) the straight line method, and
(*b*) the diminishing balance method, using a depreciation rate of 20%.

26.3X A motor vehicle costs £19,200 and will be kept for four years, and then sold for an estimated value of £1,200. Calculate the depreciation for each year using:

(*a*) the diminishing balance method, using a depreciation rate of 50%, and
(*b*) the straight line method.

26.4X A photocopier costs £5,120. It will be kept for five years, and then sold at an estimated figure of £1,215. Show the calculations of the figures for depreciation for each year using:

(*a*) the straight line method, and
(*b*) the diminishing balance method, using a depreciation rate of 25%.

26.5X A tractor cost £72,900 and has an estimated life of five years after which it will be traded in at an estimated value of £9,600. Show your calculations of the amount of depreciation each year using:

(*a*) the diminishing balance method at a rate of 33¹/₃%, and
(*b*) the straight line method.

26.6 A dumper is bought for £6,000. It will last for three years and will then be sold back to the supplier for £3,072. Show the depreciation calculations for each year using:

(*a*) the diminishing balance method with a rate of 20%, and
(*b*) the straight line method.

26.7X From the following information, which shows the depreciation for the first two years of use for two assets, you are required to answer the questions set out below.

	Machinery	*Fixtures*
	£	£
Cost Year 1	8,000	3,600
Year 1 Depreciation	1,600	900
	6,400	2,700
Year 2 Depreciation	1,600	675
	4,800	2,025

(*a*) Which type of depreciation method is used for each asset?
(*b*) What will be the book value of each of the assets after four years of use?
(*c*) If, instead of the method used, the machinery had been depreciated by the alternative method but using the same percentage rate, what would have been the book value after four years? (Calculate your answer to the nearest £.)

26.8X Harry Green is the owner of HG Computers, a business that buys and sells computer equipment whose financial year end is 31 October 2013. As book-keeper to the company you have just prepared the trial balance which you pass to Harry Green. Harry looks at the figures in the trial balance and tells you that he:

- sees that there is an account called 'Computer equipment at cost';
- understands that he has several computers that he uses to run the business;
- hopes to keep these computers for about three years;
- thought that all his computers were treated as stock (inventory).

Task:
Write a memo to Harry Green explaining why computers used by the business would not be classified as stock (inventory).

AAT

CHAPTER 27

Double entry records for depreciation and the disposal of assets

Learning objectives

After you have studied this chapter you should be able to:

- record book-keeping entries relating to depreciation charges
- record book-keeping entries relating to the disposal of a non-current asset.

27.1 Recording depreciation

When a business purchases non-current assets the cost price is recorded in the respective non-current asset account. Any depreciation subsequently charged on that asset is recorded separately in an 'Accumulated provision for depreciation account' where the depreciation charge accumulates each year. The following example illustrates the purchase of machinery and the depreciation charge which is recorded using double entry principles:

Example: A business purchases machinery for use in the business's workshop for £2,000 on 1 January 2013. The company uses the diminishing (reducing) balance method of depreciation using a rate of 20% per annum and their financial year end is 31 December. The accounting records for the first three years are illustrated in Exhibit 27.1.

1 The machinery is purchased on 1 January 2013 and paid for by cheque:
   - **Debit** the machinery account £2,000
   - **Credit** the bank account £2,000 (not shown in our example).

2 At the end of the financial year the asset is depreciated at 20% per annum using the diminishing balance method. First of all we need to calculate the amount of depreciation to be charged each year:

	£
Cost of machinery	2,000
First year: depreciation (20% of £2,000)	400
Reduced balance year 1	1,600
Second year: depreciation (20% of £1,600)	320
Reduced balance year 2	1,280
Third year: depreciation (20% of £1,280)	256
Net book value at end of third year	1,024

Note: Net book value = Cost price − Depreciation = 2,000 − 976 = £1,024

3 To record the depreciation:
- **Debit** the 'profit and loss account' with the amount of depreciation each year.
- **Credit** the 'accumulated provision for depreciation – machinery account' with the amount of the depreciation charged each year.

4 In the statement of financial position the non-current asset and accumulated depreciation would be shown under the non-current asset section as follows:
- The asset, i.e. 'machinery', is always shown at **cost price**, i.e. £2,000.
- The total depreciation to date, i.e. £400 + £320 + £256 = £976, is shown as a deduction from the cost price of the machinery to arrive at the **net book value**, £2,000 – £976 = £1,024.

Exhibit 27.1

Machinery Account

		£			£
2013			2013		
Jan 1	Cash	2,000	Dec 31	Balance c/d	2,000
2014			2014		
Jan 1	Balance b/d	2,000	Dec 31	Balance c/d	2,000
2015			2015		
Jan 1	Balance b/d	2,000	Dec 31	Balance c/d	2,000
2016					
Jan 1	Balance b/d	2,000			

Accumulated Provision for Depreciation – Machinery Account

		£			£
2013			2013		
Dec 31	Balance c/d	400	Dec 31	Profit and loss a/c	400
2014			2014		
Dec 31	Balance c/d	720	Jan 1	Balance b/d	400
			Dec 31	Profit and loss a/c	320
		720			720
2015			2015		
Dec 31	Balance c/d	976	Jan 1	Balance b/d	720
			Dec 31	Profit and loss a/c	256
		976			976
			2016		
			Jan 1	Balance b/d	976

Profit and Loss Account (extracts) for the year ended 31 December

		£	
2013	Acc Provn for Depn: Machinery	400	
2014	Acc Provn for Depn: Machinery	320	
2015	Acc Provn for Depn: Machinery	256	

Income Statement (extracts) for the years ending 31 December

		£
2013	Depreciation	400
2014	Depreciation	320
2015	Depreciation	256

Now, the balance on the machinery account is shown on the statement of financial position at the end of each year, less the balance on the accumulated provision for depreciation account.

Statement of Financial Position (extracts) as at 31 December

	Cost	*Total depreciation*	*Net book value*
2013	£	£	£
Machinery	2,000	400	1,600
2014			
Machinery	2,000	720	1,280
2015			
Machinery	2,000	976	1,024

Another example is now shown in Exhibit 27.2. This is of a business with financial years ending 30 June. A motor car is bought on 1 July 2013 for £8,000. Another car is bought on 1 July 2014 for £11,000. Each car is expected to be in use for five years, and the disposal value of the first car is expected to be £500 and of the second car £1,000. The method of depreciation to be used is the straight line method. The first two years' accounts are shown in the Exhibit.

Depreciation per year – straight line method:

Motor Car No. 1 bought on 1 July 2013 at a cost price of £8,000.

$$\text{Depreciation charge per year} = \frac{\text{Cost price} - \text{Disposal value}}{\text{Number of years of use}}$$

$$= \frac{8{,}000 - 500}{5}$$

$$= \text{£}1{,}500 \text{ depreciation charge per year}$$

Motor Car No. 2 bought on 1 July 2014 at a cost price of £11,000.

$$\text{Depreciation charge per year} = \frac{\text{Cost price} - \text{Disposal value}}{\text{Number of years of use}}$$

$$= \frac{11{,}000 - 1{,}000}{5}$$

$$= \text{£}2{,}000 \text{ depreciation charge per year}$$

Note: The entries in the cash book have not been shown in this example.

Exhibit 27.2

Motor Cars Account

		£			£
2013			2014		
Jul 1	Bank	8,000	Jun 30	Balance c/d	8,000
2014			2015		
Jul 1	Balance b/d	8,000	Jun 30	Balance c/d	19,000
Jul 1	Bank	11,000			
		19,000			19,000
2015					
Jul 1	Balance b/d	19,000			

Accumulated Provision for Depreciation – Motor Cars Account

		£			£
2014			2014		
Jun 30	Balance c/d	1,500	Jun 30	Profit and loss a/c	1,500
			Jul 1	Balance b/d	1,500
2015			2015		
Jun 30	Balance c/d	5,000	Jun 30	Profit and loss a/c	3,500
		5,000			5,000
			Jul 1	Balance b/d	5,000

Profit and Loss Account (extracts) for the year ended 30 June

		£	
2014	Acc Provn for Depn: Motor Cars	1,500	
2015	Acc Provn for Depn: Motor Cars	3,500	

Income Statement (extracts) for the years ending 30 June

		£
2014	Depreciation	1,500
2015	Depreciation	3,500

Statement of Financial Position (extract) as at 30 June 2014

	Cost	*Total depreciation*	*Net book value*
	£	£	£
Motor car	8,000	1,500	6,500

Statement of Finiancial Position (extract) as at 30 June 2015

	Cost	*Total depreciation*	*Net book value*
	£	£	£
Motor cars	19,000	5,000	14,000

27.2 The disposal of a non-current asset

Reason for accounting entries

Once a non-current asset is sold it will need deleting from the accounts. This means that the cost of that asset needs to be taken out of the asset account. In addition, the accumulated depreciation of the asset that has been sold will have to be taken out of the accumulated depreciation provision. Finally, the profit or loss on sale, if any, will have to be calculated.

As we have already seen in the previous chapter depreciation charges have to be estimated. When a non-current asset is purchased initially the business will not know at that time exactly when the asset will be disposed of and for how much. Therefore, when the asset is eventually disposed of, the amount received is usually different from the original estimate.

Accounting entries needed

On the sale of a non-current asset, i.e. machinery, the following entries are needed.

A Transfer the cost price of the asset sold to an assets disposal account (in this case a machinery disposals account):
- **debit** machinery disposals account
- **credit** machinery account.

B Transfer the depreciation already charged to the assets disposal account:
- **debit** accumulated provision for depreciation – machinery account
- **credit** machinery disposals account.

C For the amount received on disposal:
- **debit** cash book
- **credit** machinery disposal account.

D Transfer the difference (i.e. the amount to balance the machinery disposal account) to the profit and loss account.

(a) If the machinery disposals account shows a difference on the debit side of the account, it is a profit on sale:
- **debit** machinery disposals account
- **credit** profit and loss account.

(b) If the machinery disposals account shows a difference on the credit side of the account, it is a loss on sale:
- **debit** profit and loss account
- **credit** machinery disposals account.

These entries can be illustrated by looking at those needed if the machinery already shown in Exhibit 27.1 was sold. The records to 31 December 2015 show that the cost of the machine was £2,000 and a total of £976 has been written off as depreciation, leaving a net book value of (£2,000 – £976) = £1,024. If, therefore, the machine is sold on 2 January 2016 for *more than* £1,024, a profit on sale will be made; if, on the other hand, the machine is sold for *less than* £1,024, then a loss on disposal will be incurred.

Exhibit 27.3 shows the entries needed when the machine has been sold for £1,070 and a small profit on sale has been made. Exhibit 27.4 shows the entries where the machine has been sold for £950, thus incurring a loss on the sale. In both cases the sale is on 2 January 2016 and no depreciation is charged for the two days' ownership in 2016. The letters (A) to (D) in Exhibits 27.3 and 27.4 are references to the sequence of instructions shown above. Note: Cash book entries are not shown.

Exhibit 27.3 Non-current asset sold at a profit

Machinery Account

			£				£
2013				2016			
Jan 1	Cash		2,000	Jan 2	Machinery disposals	(A)	2,000

Accumulated Provision for Depreciation: Machinery Account

			£				£
2016				2016			
Jan 2	Machinery disposals	(B)	976	Jan 1	Balance b/d		976

Machinery Disposals Account

			£				£
2016				2016			
Jan 2	Machinery	(A)	2,000	Jan 2	Cash	(C)	1,070
Dec 31	Profit and loss a/c	(D)	46	2	Accumulated provision for depreciation	(B)	976
			2,046				2,046

Profit and Loss Account

				£
	2016			
	Dec 31	Machinery disposals (profit)	(D)	46

Income Statement (extract) for the year ended 31 December 2016

	£
Gross Profit	xxx
Add Profit on sale of machinery	46

Exhibit 27.4 Non-current asset sold at a loss

Machinery Account

			£				£
2013				2016			
Jan 1	Cash		2,000	Jan 2	Machinery disposals	(A)	2,000

Accumulated Provision for Depreciation: Machinery Account

			£				£
2016				2016			
Jan 2	Machinery disposals	(B)	976	Jan 1	Balance b/d		976

Machinery Disposals Account

			£				£
2016				2016			
Jan 2	Machinery	(A)	2,000	Jan 2	Cash	(C)	950
				2	Accumulated provision for depreciation	(B)	976
				Dec 31	Profit and loss	(D)	74
			2,000				2,000

Profit and Loss Account

2016				
Dec 31	Computer disposals (loss)	(D)	74	

Income Statement (extract) for the year ended 31 December 2016

		£
Gross Profit		xxx
Less Loss on sale of machinery	(D)	74

In this chapter, all unnecessary difficulties have been avoided. For instance, all assets have been bought, or sold, on the first day of a financial year. Exactly what happens when assets are sold or bought part way through the year is dealt with in *Business Accounting 1* by Frank Wood and Alan Sangster.

27.3 Depreciation provisions and the replacement of assets

Making a provision for depreciation does not mean that money is invested somewhere to finance the replacement of the asset when it is put out of use. It is simply a book-keeping entry, and the end result is that lower net profits are shown because the provisions have been charged to the profit and loss account.

It is not surprising to find that people who have not studied accounting misunderstand the situation. They often think that a provision is the same as money kept somewhere with which to replace the asset eventually.

On the other hand, lower net profits may also mean lower drawings by the owner(s) of the business. If this is the case, then there will be more money in the bank with which to replace the asset. However, there is no guarantee that lower profits mean lower drawings.

Note: A step-by-step guide dealing with depreciation in final accounts is shown in section 29.14.

Chapter summary

- Non-current assets are shown at cost price in the appropriate asset account, any depreciation charge is shown separately and accumulating in an 'Accumulated provision for depreciation account'.
- The depreciation charge for the period is then debited to the Profit and Loss Account.
- In the statement of financial position the asset is shown at cost price, less the accumulated depreciation so giving the 'Net book value' of the asset.
- On disposal of a non-current asset the book-keeping entries will involve a new account, i.e. 'asset disposal account'. It is then necessary to transfer the cost price of the asset, the accumulated depreciation and the cash received to this account when the asset is sold. The balancing figure in the asset disposal account may be either a profit or loss on disposal.

- If there is a profit on disposal this will then be added to the gross profit in the profit and loss account.
- If there is a loss on disposal this will be charged as an expense in the profit and loss account.
- Providing for depreciation does not mean that funds are invested elsewhere for financing the replacement of the asset.

EXERCISES

Note: Questions with the suffix 'X' shown after the question number do ***not*** *have answers shown at the back of the book. Answers to the other questions are shown in Appendix E.*

27.1 A White, an exporter, bought a new car for his business on 1 January 2010 for £12,500. He decided to write off depreciation at the rate of 20%, using the diminishing balance method.

Show the following for each of the financial years ended 31 December 2010, 2011 and 2012.

(*a*) motor cars account
(*b*) accumulated provision for depreciation account
(*c*) extracts from the profit and loss accounts
(*d*) extracts from the statement of financial position.

27.2X H Slater, a jewellery manufacturer, purchased a new machine for £18,000 on 1 November 2009. Her business year end is 31 October, but she cannot decide which method of depreciation she should use in respect of the machine – the straight line method or the diminishing balance method.

Required:
In order to assist her in making a decision, draw up the machinery account and the accumulated provision for depreciation account for the three years from 1 November 2009 using:

(*a*) the straight line method
(*b*) the reducing balance method.

Each account must indicate which method is being used, and each account should be balanced at the end of each of the three years. In both cases the rate of depreciation is to be 10%, and calculations should be made to the nearest £.

(*c*) Also show the extracts from the profit and loss accounts and statement of financial position for each of the three years.

27.3 On 1 January 2010, the first day of the financial year, T Young bought computer equipment for £9,500. The equipment is to be depreciated by the straight line method at the rate of 20%, ignoring salvage value. On 1 January 2013 the system was sold for £4,250.

Show the following for the complete period of ownership.

(*a*) The computer equipment account.
(*b*) The accumulated provision for depreciation.
(*c*) The computer equipment disposal account.
(*d*) The extracts from profit and loss accounts for four years.
(*e*) The extracts from three years' statements of financial position 2010, 2011 and 2012.

27.4 Show the relevant disposal account for each of the following cases, including the transfers to the profit and loss account.

(*a*) Motor vehicle: cost £12,000; depreciated £9,700 to date of sale; sold for £1,850.
(*b*) Machinery: cost £27,900; depreciated £19,400 to date of sale; sold for £11,270.
(*c*) Fixtures: cost £8,420; depreciated £7,135 to date of sale; sold for £50.
(*d*) Buildings: cost £200,000; depreciated straight line 5% on cost for 11 years to date of sale; sold for £149,000.

27.5X Wai Lan Chung owns a Chinese restaurant. The business's non-current assets include some kitchen equipment which cost £38,000 when it was purchased on 1 January 2010.

It was decided that kitchen equipment should be depreciated using the straight line method. It was estimated that the equipment has a useful life of five years and a likely scrap value of £2,000. Depreciation is recorded in the accounts on 31 December each year.

On 28 March 2012 some of the kitchen equipment was sold for cash £520. The equipment had cost £4,400 on 1 January 2010; at date of sale the equipment had a net book value of £2,000.

Tasks:

(*a*) Give *one* cause of depreciation.
(*b*) Explain why it is important for businesses to make an annual charge for depreciation of fixed assets.
(*c*) Prepare the disposal account recording the profit or loss on the sale of the kitchen equipment.

Southern Examining Group AQA

Please note that this question is NOT from the live examinations for the current specification.

27.6X (*a*) What is meant by the term depreciation?
(*b*) Which accounting concept is being ignored if a business changes the method of charging depreciation each year?
(*c*) Name *two* methods of charging depreciation provision.
(*d*) The accountant for a business recommends that, because of the size of the organisation, all items of machinery less than £500 should be treated as revenue expenditure. What accounting concept or convention is being applied in this example?
(*e*) A business whose financial year ends on 31 December each year purchased a delivery van by cheque for £20,000 on 1 January 2009. Depreciation is to be charged on delivery vans at 20% p.a. on cost. The delivery van was sold on 30 June 2011 for a cheque of £13,000. Depreciation is not charged in the year of disposal. Show the *relevant entries* in *each* of the following accounts for the years ended 31 December 2009, 2010 and 2011:
   (i) delivery van account
   (ii) provision for depreciation account
   (iii) delivery van disposal account
   (iv) profit and loss account.

NEAB (GCSE)

CHAPTER 28

Bad debts and allowances for doubtful debts

Learning objectives

After you have studied this chapter you should be able to:

- understand how bad debts are written off
- explain why allowances for doubtful debts are made
- make the accounting entries necessary for recording allowances for doubtful debts
- make the accounting entries for increasing or reducing allowances for doubtful debts
- make all the entries in respect of the allowance for doubtful debts in the income statement and statement of financial position
- make accounting entries in respect of bad debts recovered.

28.1 Bad debts

If a business finds that it is impossible to collect a debt, then that debt should be written off as a **bad debt**. This could happen if the debtor is suffering a loss in the business, or may even have gone bankrupt and is thus unable to pay the debt. A bad debt is, therefore, an expense on the business that is owed the money.

An example of debts being written off as bad is shown next.

Example 1: We sold £50 goods to K Leeming on 5 January 2012, but that business became bankrupt. On 16 February 2012 we sold £240 goods to T Young. Young managed to pay £200 on 17 May 2012, but it became obvious that he would never be able to pay the final £40.

When drawing up our final accounts to 31 December 2012, we decided to write these off as bad debts. The accounting entries are shown in the table below.

Accounting entries	Explanation
Debit: Bad debts account Credit: Accounts receivable account	To transfer the amount of unpaid debt to the bad debts account To reduce the liability of the customer who is unable to settle the debt
Debit: Profit and loss account Credit: Bad debts account	To record the amount of bad debts of the period concerned To transfer the amount of bad debts to profit and loss account

The accounts would appear as follows:

K Leeming Account

2012		£	2012		£
Jan 5	Sales	50	Dec 31	Bad debts	50

T Young Account

2012		£	2012		£
Feb 16	Sales	240	May 17	Cash	200
			Dec 31	Bad debts	40
		240			240

Bad Debts Account

2012		£	2012		£
Dec 31	K Leeming	50	Dec 31	Profit and loss a/c	90
Dec 31	T Young	40			
		90			90

Profit and Loss Account

2012		£			
Dec 31	Bad debts	90			

The bad debts written off will appear in the Income Statement as follows:

Income Statement (extract) for the year ending 31 December 2012

	£
Gross profit	xxx
Less Expenses:	
Bad debts	90

28.2 Allowance for doubtful debts

Example 1:

Let us look, as an example, at the accounts of K Clark, who started in business on 1 January 2012 and has just completed his first year of trading on 31 December 2012.

He has sold goods for £50,000 and they cost him £36,000, so his gross profit was (£50,000 – £36,000) = £14,000. However, included in the £50,000 sales was a credit sale to C Yates for £250. C Yates has died, leaving no money, and he had not paid his account. The £250 debt is, therefore, a bad debt and should be charged in the profit and loss account as an expense.

Beside that debt, a credit sale of £550 on 1 December 2012 to L Hall is unlikely to get paid. Although Clark is not certain of this he has been informed that Hall has not paid debts owing to other businesses. As Clark had given three months' credit to Hall, the debt is not repayable until 28 February 2013.

However, he has been requested by his bank to provide his financial statements for the year 2012. Unfortunately, Clark cannot wait until after 28 February 2013 to see whether the debt of £550 owing by Hall will be paid or not.

If it is not paid then it will become a bad debt but in the meantime it is a **doubtful debt**.

What, therefore, can Clark do? When he presents his financial statements to the bank he wants to achieve the following objectives:

(*a*) to charge as an expense in the income statement for the year 2012 an amount representing debts that will never be paid
(*b*) to show in the statement of financial position as correct a figure as possible for the true value of accounts receivable at the date of the statement of financial position.

He can carry out (*a*) above by writing off Yates' debt of £250 and then charging it as an expense in his income statement.

For (*b*) he cannot yet write off Hall's debt of £550 as a bad debt because he is not certain about it being a bad debt. If he does nothing about it, then the accounts receivable shown on the statement of financial position will include a debt that is probably of no value. The accounts receivable on 31 December 2012, after deducting Yates' £250 bad debt, amount to £10,000.

The answer to this is as shown in Exhibit 28.1.

Exhibit 28.1

K Clark
Income Statement for the year ended 31 December 2012

	£	£
Sales		50,000
Less Cost of goods sold:		36,000
Gross profit		14,000
Less Expenses:		
Other expenses	5,000	
Bad debts	250	
Allowance for doubtful debts	550	
		5,800
Net profit		8,200

K Clark
Statement of Financial Position as at 31 December 2012 (extracts)

	£	£
Accounts receivable	10,000	
Less Allowance for doubtful debts	550	
		9,450

In the above exhibit 'bad debts' and 'allowance for doubtful debts' have been shown as expenses in the year in which the sales were made and the accounts receivable figure in the statement of financial position represents their true value. The double entry is explained in section 28.4.

28.3 Allowances for doubtful debts: estimating provisions

The estimates of allowances for doubtful debts can be made thus:

- by looking into each debt, and estimating which ones will be bad debts
- by estimating, on the basis of experience, what percentage of the debts will result in bad debts.

It is well known that the longer a debt is owing, the more likely it will become a bad debt. Some businesses draw up an **ageing schedule for doubtful debts**, showing how long debts have been owing. Older accounts receivable need higher percentage estimates of bad debts than newer accounts receivable. Exhibit 28.2 gives an example of such an ageing schedule.

Exhibit 28.2 Ageing schedule for doubtful debts

Period debt owing	*Amount*	*Estimated percentage doubtful*	*Allowance for doubtful debts*
	£		£
Less than 1 month	5,000	1	50
1 month to 2 months	3,000	3	90
2 months to 3 months	800	4	32
3 months to 1 year	200	5	10
Over 1 year	160	20	32
	9,160		214

In the above example the calculation of the allowance for doubtful debts has been specifically detailed. Many businesses do not go to this level of detail; instead they apply a percentage based upon the experience that has been established within the business over a number of years. For example, they may decide to use 5% of the accounts receivable figure as an allowance for doubtful debts.

28.4 Accounting entries for allowances for doubtful debts

The accounting entries required when first setting up an 'allowance for doubtful debts account' are as follows:

- **Debit**: profit and loss account with the amount of the allowance
- **Credit**: allowance for doubtful debts account.

Let us look at an example that shows the entries needed when first creating the allowance for doubtful debts account.

Example 2: As at 31 December 2012, the accounts receivable figure for a business amounted to £10,000 after writing off £422 of definite bad debts. It is estimated that 2% of debts (i.e. £10,000 × 2% = £200) will eventually prove to be bad debts, and it is decided to make an allowance for these. The accounts would appear as follows:

Profit and Loss Account

		£		
2012				
Dec 31	Bad debts	422		
Dec 31	Allowance for doubtful debts	200		

Allowance for Doubtful Debts Account

		£			£
2012			2012		
Dec 31	Balance c/d	200	Dec 31	Profit and loss a/c	200
			2013		
			Jan 1	Balance b/d	200

In the financial statements the allowance for doubtful debts is shown as follows:

Income Statement (extract) for the year ending 31 December 2012

		£
Gross profit		xxx
Less Expenses:		
Bad debts	422	
Allowance for doubtful debts	200	

Statement of Financial Position (extracts) 31 December 2012

	£	£
Current assets		
Accounts receivable	10,000	
Less Allowance for doubtful debts	200	9,800

28.5 Increasing the allowance

Taking the same example as shown in Example 2 above, let us suppose that at the end of the following year, on 31 December 2013, the doubtful debts allowance needed to be increased. This was because the allowance was kept at 2% but the accounts receivable had risen to £12,000. Not included in the figure of £12,000 accounts receivable is £884 in respect of debts that had already been written off as bad debts during the year. An allowance of £200 had been brought forward from the *previous* year, but we now want a total allowance of £240 (i.e. 2% of £12,000). All that is needed is an allowance for an extra £40.

The double entry will be:

- **Debit**: profit and loss account with the increase in the allowance (i.e. £40)
- **Credit**: allowance for doubtful debts account.

These entries are illustrated below:

Profit and Loss Account

2013		£			
Dec 31	Bad debts	884			
Dec 31	Allowance for doubtful debts (increase)	40			

Allowance for Doubtful Debts Account

2013		£	2013		£
Dec 31	Balance c/d	240	Jan 1	Balance b/d	200
			Dec 31	Profit and loss a/c	40
		240			240
			2014		
			Jan 1	Balance b/d	240

Income Statement (extract) for the year ending 31 December 2013

	£	£
Gross profit		xxx
Less Expenses:		
Bad debts	884	
Allowance for doubtful debts (increase)	40	

Statement of Financial Position as at 31 December 2013 (extracts)

	£	£
Current assets		
Accounts receivable	12,000	
Less Allowance for doubtful debts	240	11,760

28.6 Reducing the allowance

Outstanding accounts receivable can reduce as well as increase and if a business finds that the amount outstanding has decreased it may decide to reduce the allowance for doubtful debts. Reducing an allowance is the opposite of increasing an allowance.

In the allowance for doubtful debts account a credit balance is shown, therefore, to reduce it we would need a debit entry in the allowance account. The credit would be in the profit and loss account. Again, using Example 2 above, let us assume that on 31 December 2014 the accounts receivable figure had fallen to £10,500 but the allowance remained at 2%, i.e. £210 (2% of £10,500). As the allowance had previously been £240, it now needs a reduction of £30. Bad debts of £616 had already been written off during the year and are not included in the accounts receivable figure of £10,500.

The double entry is:

- **Debit**: allowance for doubtful debts account
- **Credit**: profit and loss account,

and the relevant accounts look thus:

Profit and Loss Account

		£			£
2014			2014		
Dec 31	Bad debts	616	Dec 31	Allowance for doubtful debts	30

Allowance for Doubtful Debts Account

		£			£
2014			2014		
Dec 31	Profit and loss a/c	30	Jan 1	Balance b/d	240
Dec 31	Balance c/d	210			
		240			240
			2015		
			Jan 1	Balance b/d	210

Income Statement (extract) for the year ending 31 December 2014

	£	£
Gross profit		xxx
Add Reduction in allowance for doubtful debts		30
		xxx
Less Expenses:		
Bad debts	616	

Statement of Financial Position as at 31 December 2014 (extracts)

	£	£
Current assets		
Accounts receivable	10,500	
Less Allowance for doubtful debts	210	10,290

The main points that you have to remember about allowances for doubtful debts are:

Year 1 – allowance first made:
(*a*) debit profit and loss account with full allowance
(*b*) show in statement of financial position as a deduction from the accounts receivable.

Later years:
(*a*) only the increase, or decrease, in the allowance is shown in the profit and loss account, as follows:
- *to increase*: debit the profit and loss account, and credit the allowance for doubtful debts account.
- *to decrease*: credit the profit and loss account, and debit the allowance for doubtful debts account.

(*b*) the statement of financial position will show the amended figure of the allowance as a deduction from the accounts receivable.

28.7 A worked example

Let us now look at a comprehensive example.

Example 3: A business started on 1 January 2010 and its financial year end is 31 December. A table of accounts receivable, the bad debts written off and the estimated doubtful debts at the rate of 2% of accounts receivable at the end of each year, as well as the double entry accounts and the extracts from the final accounts, follow as Exhibit 28.3.

Exhibit 28.3

Year to 31 December	*Accounts receivable at end of year (after bad debts written off)*	*Bad debts written off during year*	*Debts thought at end of year to be impossible to collect: 2% of accounts receivable*
	£	£	£
2010	6,000	423	120 (2% of £6,000)
2011	7,000	510	140 (2% of £7,000)
2012	7,750	604	155 (2% of £7,750)
2013	6,500	610	130 (2% of £6,500)

Allowance for Doubtful Debts Account

		£			£
2010			2010		
Dec 31	Balance c/d	120	Dec 31	Profit and loss a/c	120
2011			2011		
Dec 31	Balance c/d	140	Jan 1	Balance b/d	120
			Dec 31	Profit and loss a/c	20
		140			140
2012			2012		
Dec 31	Balance c/d	155	Jan 1	Balance b/d	140
			Dec 31	Profit and loss a/c	15
		155			155
2013			2013		
Dec 31	Profit and loss a/c	25	Jan 1	Balance b/d	155
Dec 31	Balance c/d	130			
		155			155
			2014		
			Jan 1	Balance b/d	130

Bad Debts Account

		£			£
2010			2010		
Dec 31	Various accounts receivable	423	Dec 31	Profit and loss a/c	423
2011			2011		
Dec 31	Various accounts receivable	510	Dec 31	Profit and loss a/c	510
2012			2012		
Dec 31	Various accounts receivable	604	Dec 31	Profit and loss a/c	604
2013			2013		
Dec 31	Various accounts receivable	610	Dec 31	Profit and loss a/c	610

Profit and Loss Account

		£			£
2010					
Dec 31	Bad debts	423			
Dec 31	Allowance for doubtful debts	120			
2011					
Dec 31	Bad debts	510			
Dec 31	Allowance for doubtful debts	20			
2012					
Dec 31	Bad debts	604			
Dec 31	Allowance for doubtful debts	15			
2013			2013		
Dec 31	Bad debts	610	Dec 31	Allowance for doubtful debts	25

Income Statements (extracts) for the years ending 31 December

		£	£
Gross profit for 2010, 2011, 2012			xxx
2010	*Less* Expenses:		
	Bad debts	423	
	Allowance for doubtful debts (increase)	120	543
2011	*Less* Expenses:		
	Bad debts	510	
	Allowance for doubtful debts (increase)	20	530
2012	*Less* Expenses:		
	Bad debts	604	
	Allowance for doubtful debts (increase)	15	619
2013	Gross profit for 2013		xxx
	Add Reduction in allowance for doubtful debts		25
			xxx
	Less Bad debts		610
			xxx

Statement of Financial Position (extracts) as at 31 December

		£	£
2010	Accounts receivable	6,000	
	Less Allowance for doubtful debts	120	5,880
2011	Accounts receivable	7,000	
	Less Allowance for doubtful debts	140	6,860
2012	Accounts receivable	7,750	
	Less Allowance for doubtful debts	155	7,595
2013	Accounts receivable	6,500	
	Less Allowance for doubtful debts	130	6,370

28.8 Bad debts recovered

It is not uncommon for a *debt written off* in previous years to be *recovered* in later years. When this occurs, the book-keeping procedures are that you should reinstate the debt by making the following entries:

- **Debit**: the customer's account
- **Credit**: **bad debts recovered** account.

The reason for reinstating the debt in the ledger account of the customer is to have a detailed history of the account as a guide for granting credit in the future. By the time a debt is written off as bad, it will be recorded in the customer ledger account. Thus, when such a debt is recovered, it must also be shown in the customer ledger account.

When cash or a cheque is later received from the customer in settlement of the account or part thereof, other book-keeping entries are necessary:

- **Debit**: cash/bank with the amount received
- **Credit**: customer's account with the amount received.

At the end of the financial year, the credit balance on the bad debts recovered account will be transferred to either the bad debts account or direct to the credit side of the profit and loss account. The net effect of either of these entries is the same, since the bad debts account will be transferred to the profit and loss account at the end of the financial year. In other words, the net profit will be the same no matter which method is used.

Note: A step-by-step guide to dealing with bad debts and allowances for doubtful debts in the financial statements is shown in section 29.14.

Chapter summary

- If a debt is unlikely to be paid then it is known as a bad debt.
- When the debt has been outstanding for a length of time the business usually decides to write it off. The debt is debited to the bad debts account and the customer's account is credited. The bad debt account is later credited and the profit and loss account debited where it is charged as an expense.
- An allowance for doubtful debts is created in case some of the outstanding debts are not paid. The allowance is charged to the profit and loss account and then deducted from the accounts receivable in the statement of financial position, thereby showing a realistic figure of the debts owed and what payment the business expects to receive.
- The allowance for doubtful debts is calculated after any bad debts have been written off and deducted from the outstanding accounts receivable.
- The allowance for doubtful debts can be adjusted if the accounts receivable at the end of the financial year either increase or decrease.
- To increase the allowance debit the profit and loss account and credit the allowance for doubtful debts account with the amount of the increase.
- To reduce the allowance debit the allowance for doubtful debts account and credit the profit and loss account with the amount of the reduction.
- A debt that has previously been written off but is subsequently paid by the customer is known as a bad debt recovered.

EXERCISES

Note: Questions with the suffix 'X' shown after the question number do ***not*** *have answers shown at the back of the book. Answers to the other questions are shown in Appendix E.*

28.1 Data Computer Services commences in business on 1 January 2012, and during its first year of trading the following debts are found to be bad and the business decided to write them off as bad:

2012		
April 30	H Gordon	£1,110
August 31	D Bellamy Ltd	£640
October 31	J Alderton	£120

On 31 December 2010, the schedule of remaining accounts receivable totalling £68,500 is examined, and it is decided to make an allowance for doubtful debts of £2,200.

You are required to show:

(*a*) the bad debts account and the allowance for doubtful debts account
(*b*) the charge to the income statement
(*c*) the relevant extracts from the statement of financial position as at 31 December 2012.

28.2 A business started on 1 January 2010, and its financial year end is 31 December.

Date: 31 Dec	*Total accounts receivable*	*Profit and loss*	*Dr/Cr*	*Final figure for statement of financial position*
2010	7,000			
2011	8,000			
2012	6,000			
2013	7,000			

The table shows the figure of outstanding accounts receivable appearing in a trader's books on 31 December of each year from 2010 to 2013. The allowance for doubtful debts is to be 1% of accounts receivable from 31 December 2010. Complete the table indicating the amount to be debited or credited to the profit and loss accounts for the year ended on each 31 December, and the amount for the final figure of accounts receivable to appear in the statement of financial position on each date.

28.3X A business started on 1 January 2010 and its financial year end is 31 December annually. The table shows the accounts receivable, the bad debts written off and the estimated doubtful debts at the end of year.

Year to 31 December	*Accounts receivable at end of year (after bad debts written off)*	*Bad debts written off during the year*	*Debts thought at end of year to be unlikely to collect*
2010	12,000	298	100
2011	15,000	386	130
2012	14,000	344	115
2013	18,000	477	150

Show the bad debts account and allowance for doubtful debts account, as well as the extracts from the income statements for each year and statement of financial position extracts.

28.4 At the end of April, Steven is advised that one of his customers, A Carter, is unable to pay his outstanding amount of £500. Steven decides to write this off as a bad debt.

(*a*) Prepare the journal entry for this transaction. Steven has experienced problems in the past year in collecting payments from credit customers. He has been advised by his accountant to introduce an allowance for doubtful debts account at the end of the accounting period.
(*b*) State the double entry required to create the allowance for doubtful debts at the end of the accounting period.
(*c*) Using the allowance for doubtful debts as an example, evaluate the importance of the prudence concept to the preparation of the trading and profit and loss account and the statement of financial position.

Edexcel International GCSE Accounting 1st edn, Edexcel (Robinson, S. 2010) Pearson Education Ltd.

28.5X From the details below, write up the accounts shown in the ledger of C Bedford Ltd, a wholesaler, for the year ended 31 December 2013. You should show clearly the amounts transferred to the profit and loss account. Information of relevance is as follows:

- At 1 January 2013, T Strange owed C Bedford Ltd £2,000. On 30 November 2013, C Bedford Ltd is notified that T Strange has been declared bankrupt and Bedford receives a cheque for 25p for each £1 owed. The balance owing by T Strange is written off as a bad debt.
- C Bedford Ltd also maintains an allowance for doubtful debts equivalent to 1% of outstanding debts at the end of the year. On 1 January 2013 the balance on this account is £500. At 31 December 2013 C Bedford is owed £52,000 by customers.

NEAB (GCSE)

28.6X (*a*) On 1 January 2010, there was a balance of £2,500 in the allowance for doubtful debts account and it was decided to maintain the allowance at 5% of accounts receivable at the end of each year. The accounts receivable on 31 December each year were as follows:

	£
2010	60,000
2011	40,000
2012	40,000

You are required to show the accounting entries for the three years ended 31 December 2010, 2011 and 2012 as follows:
(i) the allowance for doubtful debts account
(ii) the income statement
(iii) extracts from the statements of financial position.

(*b*) Explain the difference between bad debts and an allowance for doubtful debts.
(*c*) As more and more businesses are experiencing difficulty collecting debts they find it important to create an allowance for doubtful debts to provide for such a contingency. What is the purpose of creating such an allowance, and which accounting concept covers this area.

CHAPTER 29

Accruals, prepayments and other adjustments for financial statements

Learning objectives

After you have studied this chapter you should be able to:

- distinguish between amounts accrued and prepaid
- adjust expense accounts for amounts owing (accruals) and paid in advance (prepayments)
- adjust revenue accounts for amounts owing
- show accruals, prepayments and revenue accounts receivable in the statement of financial position
- ascertain the amounts of expense and revenue items to be shown in the income statement after making adjustments for accruals and prepayments
- enter up the necessary accounts in respect of goods taken for own use
- prepare financial statements for service sector organisations
- understand what is meant by goodwill and distinguish between the various kinds of capital
- enter discounts allowed and received in the financial statements
- prepare financial statements incorporating the above mentioned adjustments, for a sole trader using the fully worked example and step-by-step guide.

29.1 Introduction

The trading and profit and loss account sections of the income statement that have been prepared in the previous chapters have included sales for a specific period and shown *all* the expenses deducted appertaining to the period, resulting in either a net profit or net loss. So far, it has been assumed that the expenses incurred have belonged exactly to the specific period of the income statement.

While this generally applies to most expenses incurred by a business there are occasions when some items of expenditure are paid in arrears and/or in advance. For example, a business may have some repair work carried out in one year but the invoice for the work may not be received until the following year. In order to show a correct figure of profit for the period the amount of the repair bill should be accrued and charged against the profit for the period. Similarly, if an expense is paid in advance at the end of the period an adjustment needs to be made to ensure that the profit for the period is correct. This is discussed more fully below.

29.2 Adjustments needed for expenses owing or paid in advance

Not all businesses pay their rent exactly on time and, indeed, some businesses prefer to pay for their rent in advance. The following examples will illustrate the adjustments necessary if expenses are either owing, or paid in advance, at the end of a financial period.

Two businesses rent their premises for £1,200 per year.

1 Business A pays £1,000 during the year and owes £200 rent at the end of the year:

   Rent expense used up during the year = £1,200
   Rent actually paid in the year = £1,000.

2 Business B pays £1,300 during the year, including £100 in advance for the following year:

   Rent expense used up during the year = £1,200
   Rent actually paid for in the year = £1,300.

An income statement for the 12 months needs 12 months' rent as an expense, i.e. £1,200. This means that in the above two examples the double entry accounts will have to be adjusted.

In all the examples following in this chapter, the income statements are for the period ended 31 December 2013. All entries in the income statement are in the 'profit and loss section', unless stated otherwise. All mentions of 'profit and loss' refer to the ledger account which is ultimately summarised on the income statement.

29.3 Accrued expenses (i.e. expenses owing)

Assume that rent of £4,000 per year is payable at the end of every three months but that the rent is not always paid on time. Details are given in the table below.

Amount	Rent due	Rent paid
£1,000	31 March 2013	31 March 2013
£1,000	30 June 2013	2 July 2013
£1,000	30 September 2013	4 October 2013
£1,000	31 December 2013	5 January 2014

The rent account appears thus:

Rent Account

2013		£			
Mar 31	Cash	1,000			
Jul 2	Cash	1,000			
Oct 4	Cash	1,000			

The rent for the last quarter was paid on 5 January 2014 and will appear in the books for the year 2014 as part of the double entry.

The expense for 2013 is obviously £4,000 as that is the year's rent, and this is the amount needed to be transferred to the profit and loss account. But if £4,000 was put on the credit side of the rent account (the debit being in the profit and loss account), the account would not balance. We would have £4,000 on the credit side of the account and only £3,000 on the debit side.

To make the account balance, the £1,000 rent owing for 2013 but paid in 2014 must be carried down to 2014 as a credit balance because it is a liability on 31 December 2013. Instead of rent owing, it could be called rent accrued (or just simply an **accrual**). The completed account can now be shown, thus:

Rent Account

2013		£	2013		£
Mar 31	Cash	1,000	Dec 31	Profit and loss	4,000
Jul 2	Cash	1,000			
Oct 4	Cash	1,000			
Dec 31	**Accrued c/d**	**1,000**			
		4,000			4,000
			2014		
			Jan 1	Accrued b/d	**1,000**

The balance c/d has been described as 'accrued c/d', rather than as a balance. This is to explain what the balance is for; it is for an **accrued expense**.

29.4 Prepaid expenses

Insurance for a business is at the rate of £840 a year, starting from 1 January 2013. The business has agreed to pay this at the rate of £210 every three months. However, payments were not made at the correct times. Details were:

Amount	Insurance due	Insurance paid
£210	31 March 2013	£210 28 February 2013
£210 £210	30 June 2013 30 September 2013	£420 31 August 2013
£210	31 December 2013	£420 18 November 2013

The insurance account for the year ended 31 December 2013 will be shown in the books as:

Insurance Account

	£		
2013	£		
Feb 28 Bank	210		
Aug 31 Bank	420		
Nov 18 Bank	420		

The last payment shown of £420 is not just for 2013; it can be split as £210 for the three months to 31 December 2013 and £210 for the three months ended 31 March 2014. For a period of 12 months the cost of insurance is £840 and this is, therefore, the figure needing to be transferred to the profit and loss account.

If this figure of £840 is entered, then the amount needed to balance the account will be £210 and at 31 December 2013 there is a benefit of a further £210 paid for but not used up – an asset that needs carrying forward as such to 2014, i.e. as a debit balance. It is a **prepaid expense** (or **prepayment**). The account can now be completed as follows:

Insurance Account

2013	£	2013	£
Feb 28 Bank	210	Dec 31 Profit and loss	840
Aug 31 Bank	420		
Nov 18 Bank	420	Dec 31 Prepaid c/d	210
	1,050		1,050
2014			
Jan 1 Prepaid b/d	**210**		

Prepayment happens when items other than purchases are bought for use in the business and they are not fully used up in the period. For instance, packing materials and stationery items are normally not entirely used up over the period in which they are bought, there being inventory left at the end of the accounting period. This inventory is, therefore, a form of prepayment and needs carrying down to the following period in which it will be used. This can be seen in the following example:

> Year ended 31 December 2013:
> Packing materials bought in the year £2,200
> Inventory of packing materials in hand as at 31 December 2013 £400.

Looking at the example, it can be seen that in 2013 the packing materials used up will have been (£2,200 – £400) = £1,800. We will have an inventory of £400 packing materials at 31 December 2013, to be carried forward to 2014 as an asset balance (debit balance). Thus:

Packing Materials Account

		£			£
2013			2013		
Dec 31	Bank	2,200	Dec 31	Profit and loss	1,800
			Dec 31	**Inventory c/d**	**400**
		2,200			2,200
2014					
Jan 1	**Inventory b/d**	**400**			

The inventory of packing materials is not added to the inventory of unsold goods in hand in the statement of financial position, but it is added to the other prepayments of expenses in the statement.

29.5 Revenue owing at the end of period

The revenue owing for sales is already shown in the books as debit balances on our customers' accounts, i.e. accounts receivable. There may be other kinds of revenue, all of which have not been received by the end of the period (e.g. rent receivable). An example now follows.

Example: A business's warehouse is larger than is needed. The business rents part of it to another business for £2,000 per annum. Details for the year ended 31 December are as shown in the table below.

Amount	Rent due	Rent received
£500	31 March 2013	4 April 2013
£500	30 June 2013	6 July 2013
£500	30 September 2013	9 October 2013
£500	31 December 2013	7 January 2014

The account for 2013 will appear as follows:

Rent Receivable Account

					£
			2013		
			Apr 4	Bank	500
			Jul 6	Bank	500
			Oct 9	Bank	500

The rent received of £500 on 7 January 2014 will be entered in the books in 2014 (not shown).

Any rent paid by the business would be charged as a debit to the profit and loss account. Any rent received, being the opposite, is transferred to the credit of the profit and loss account, since it is revenue/income.

The amount to be transferred for 2013 is that earned for the 12 months, i.e. £2,000. The rent received account is completed by carrying down the balance owing as a debit balance to 2014. The £500 owing is an asset on 31 December 2013.

The rent receivable account can now be completed:

Rent Receivable Account

2013		£	2013	£
Dec 31	Profit and loss	2,000	Apr 4 Bank	500
			Jul 6 Bank	500
			Oct 9 Bank	500
			Dec 31 Accrued c/d	**500**
		2,000		2,000
2014				
Jan 1	**Accrued b/d**	**500**		

29.6 Expenses and revenue account balances and the statement of financial position

In all the cases dealing with adjustments in the financial statements, there will still be a balance on each account after the preparation of the income statement. All such balances remaining should appear in the statement of financial position. The only question left is where and how they should be shown.

The amounts owing for expenses are usually added together and shown as one figure. These could be called 'expenses payable', 'expenses owing' or 'accrued expenses'. We will refer to them as 'accruals'. The items would appear in the statement of financial position under current liabilities as they are expenses that have to be discharged in the near future.

The items prepaid are also added together and are called 'prepayments', 'prepaid expenses' or 'payments in advance'. They are shown in the statement of financial position under the current assets after accounts receivable. Amounts owing for rents receivable or other revenue owing are usually added to accounts receivable.

The statement of financial position in respect of the accounts so far seen in this chapter would appear thus:

Statement of financial position as at 31 December 2013 (extract)

	£	£	£
Current assets			
Inventory		xxx	
Accounts receivable		500	
Prepayments (210 + 400)		610	
Bank		xxx	
Cash		xxx	
		x,xxx	
Less Current liabilities			
Trade accounts payable	xxx		
Accrued expenses	1,000	xxx	
Net current assets			xxx

29.7 Expenses and revenue accounts covering more than one period

Students are often asked to draw up an expense or revenue account for a full year where there are amounts owing or prepaid at both the beginning and end of a year. We can now see how this is done.

Example 1: The following details are available:

(A) On 31 December 2012, three months' rent of £3,000 is owing.
(B) The rent chargeable per year is £12,000.
(C) The following payments are made in the year 2013: 6 January £3,000; 4 April £3,000; 7 July £3,000; 18 October £3,000.
(D) The final three months' rent for 2013 is still owing.

Now we can look at the completed rent account. The letters (A) to (D) refer to the details above.

Rent Account

			£				£
2013				2013			
Jan 6	Bank	(C)	3,000	**Jan 1**	**Owing b/d**	**(A)**	**3,000**
Apr 4	Bank	(C)	3,000	Dec 31	Profit and loss	(B)	12,000
Jul 7	Bank	(C)	3,000				
Oct 18	Bank	(C)	3,000				
Dec 31	**Accrued c/d**	**(D)**	**3,000**				
			15,000				15,000
				2014			
				Jan 1	**Accrued b/d**		**3,000**

Example 2: The following details are available:

(A) On 31 December 2013, packing materials in hand amount in value to £1,850.
(B) During the year to 31 December 2013, £27,480 is paid for packing materials.
(C) There are no inventory of packing materials on 31 December 2013.
(D) On 31 December 2013, we still owed £2,750 for packing materials already received and used.

The packing materials account will appear thus:

Packing Materials Account

			£			£
2013				2013		
Jan 1	**Inventory b/d**	**(A)**	**1,850**	Dec 31	Profit and loss	32,080
Dec 31	Bank	(B)	27,480			
Dec 31	**Owing c/d**	**(D)**	**2,750**			
			32,080			32,080
				2010		
				Jan 1	**Owing b/d**	**2,750**

The figure of £32,080 is the difference on the account, and is transferred to the profit and loss account. We can prove it is correct through the following:

	£	£
Inventory at start of year		1,850
Add Bought and used:		
Paid for	27,480	
Still owed for	2,750	30,230
Cost of packing materials used in the year		32,080

Example 3: Where different expenses are put together in one account, it can get even more confusing. Let us look at where rent and rates are joined together. Here are the details for the year ended 31 December 2013:

(A) Rent is payable of £6,000 per annum.
(B) Rates of £4,000 per annum are payable by instalments.
(C) At 1 January 2013, rent £1,000 has been prepaid in 2012.
(D) On 1 January 2013 rates are owed of £400.
(E) During 2013, rent of £4,500 is paid.
(F) During 2013, rates of £5,000 were paid.
(G) On 31 December 2013, rent £500 is owing.
(H) On 31 December 2013, rates of £600 have been prepaid.

A combined rent and rates account is to be drawn up for the year 2013 showing the transfer to the profit and loss account, and the balances to be carried down to 2014. Thus:

Rent and Rates Account

			£				£
2013				2013			
Jan 1	**Rent prepaid b/d**	**(C)**	**1,000**	**Jan 1**	**Rates owing b/d**	**(D)**	**400**
Dec 31	Bank: rent	(E)	4,500	Dec 31	Profit & loss a/c	(A)+(B)	10,000
Dec 31	Bank: rates	(F)	5,000				
Dec 31	**Rent owing c/d**	**(G)**	**500**	**Dec 31**	**Rates prepaid c/d**	**(H)**	**600**
			11,000				11,000
2014				2014			
Jan 1	**Rates prepaid b/d**	**(H)**	**600**	**Jan 1**	**Rent owing b/d**	**(G)**	**500**

29.8 Goods for own use

Traders will often take inventory out of their business for their own use, without paying for them. There is nothing wrong about this, but an entry should be made to record the event. This is done as follows:

- **Debit** the drawings account, to show that the proprietor has taken the goods for private use
- **Credit** the purchases account, to reduce cost of goods available for sale.

In the United Kingdom, an adjustment may be needed for value added tax. If goods supplied to a trader's customers have VAT added to their price, then any such goods taken for own use will need such an adjustment. This is because the VAT regulations state that VAT should be added to the cost of goods taken. The double entry for the VAT content would be:

- **Debit** the drawings account
- **Credit** VAT account.

Adjustments may also be needed for other private items. For instance, if a trader's private insurance had been incorrectly charged to the insurance account, then the correction would be:

- **Debit** the drawings account
- **Credit** the insurance account.

29.9 Goodwill

Definition of goodwill

Goodwill is the value of a business over and above the total value of its net assets. For example a business may have the following assets:

	£
Buildings	450,000
Equipment	150,000
Accounts receivable	60,000
Inventory	80,000
	740,000

The owner decides to sell the business as a going concern to Ms Lee for £800,000. Ms Lee has, therefore, paid £60,000 more than the total of all the assets. This extra payment of £60,000 is for what is known as 'goodwill'.

Ms Lee has paid this extra amount because she wanted to take over the business as a going concern. Thus,

Purchased goodwill = Total price *less* the value of identifiable assets.

Goodwill is an intangible asset, that is, an asset that cannot be physically seen or touched. It represents the excess amount that has to be paid to acquire a part or whole of a business as a going concern over and above the value of the net assets owned by the business.

Reasons for payment of goodwill

When a business has been established for some time it has many possible advantages that are important to a prospective purchaser of the business, such as:

- good reputation
- large customer base
- experienced, efficient and reliable employees

- the business is situated in a good location
- good contact with suppliers
- possible good brand names that are known and recognised within the industry.

Few of the above advantages are available to a completely new business. For this reason, many people will decide to buy an existing business and pay an extra amount for goodwill.

29.10 Distinctions between various kinds of capital

The capital account represents the claim of the proprietor against the assets of a business at a point in time. The word 'capital' is, however, often used in a specific sense. The main uses are listed below.

Capital invested

This means the actual amount of money, or monetary value of everything, brought into a business by the proprietor from outside interests. The amount of **capital invested** is not affected by the amounts of profits made by the business or any losses incurred.

Capital employed

The term **capital employed** has many meanings but basically it means the amount of money that is being used (or 'employed') in the business. If, therefore, all the assets were added up in value and the liabilities of the business deducted, the difference is the amount of money employed in the business (i.e. the net assets).

Another way of looking at the calculation of capital employed is to take the balance of the capital account and add this to any long-term loan. The result will be the same as the net assets, i.e. the capital employed.

Working capital (net current assets)

The difference between the current assets and current liabilities is often referred to as **working capital** or 'net current assets'. This amount represents the money that is available to pay the running expenses of the business and, ideally, the current assets should exceed the current liabilities twice over, i.e. in the ratio 2:1. In simple terms it means that, for every £1 owed, the business should be able to raise £2.

29.11 Financial statements in the services sector

All the accounts considered so far have been accounts for businesses that trade in some sort of goods. To enable the business to ascertain the amount of gross profit made on selling the goods, a trading account has been drawn up. There are, however, many organisations that do not deal in goods but instead supply customers with a 'service'. These will include professional businesses such as accountants, solicitors, doctors, estate agents, management consultants and advertising agencies. Also businesses that provide such services as window cleaning, gardening, hairdressing, repairs and maintenance to washing machines, computer repairs, leisure and health clubs and so on. Since they do not deal in 'goods' there is no need for trading accounts to be drawn up; an income statement, together with a statement of financial position, is prepared instead.

The first item in the income statement will be the revenue which might be called 'fees', 'charges', 'accounts rendered', 'takings', etc., depending on the nature of the organisation. Any other item of income will also be added (e.g. rent receivable). Following this, the expenses incurred in running the business will be deducted to arrive at the net profit or loss.

An example of the income statement of a solicitor is illustrated in Exhibit 29.1.

Exhibit 29.1

E B Brown, Solicitor
Income Statement for the year ended 31 December 2013

	£	£
Revenue:		
Fees charged		87,500
Insurance commissions		1,300
		88,800
Less Expenses:		
Wages and salaries	29,470	
Rent and rates	11,290	
Office expenses	3,140	
Motor expenses	2,115	
General expenses	1,975	
Depreciation	2,720	50,710
Net profit		38,090

29.12 Treatment of discounts allowed and discounts received in financial statements

In Chapter 21 we dealt with recording cash discounts in the cash book and ledgers and you will recall that such a discount could be either 'discounts allowed', which represents a reduction given to our customers for prompt payment of their account or 'discounts received' when the reduction is given by a supplier to us when we pay their account within a specified period.

Using the example below of D Marston (Exhibit 29.2) let us assume that the discount allowed amounted to £310 and the discount received totalled £510. These items would appear in the income statement as follows:

Exhibit 29.2

Income Statement of D Marston
for the year ended 31 December 2013

	£	£
Gross profit		30,500
Less Expenses		
Discounts allowed	310	
Other expenses	10,000	10,310
		20,190
Add Income		
Discounts received		510
Net profit		20,700

29.13 Worked example of the financial statements for a sole trader

We have now covered all the adjustments that may be necessary before preparing the financial statements for a business. The adjustments covered are depreciation, from Chapter 27, writing off bad debts and the allowance for doubtful debts from Chapter 28, and in this chapter we have dealt with accruals, prepayments, discounts allowed and received. You may also recall that Chapter 12 dealt with closing inventory and sales returns and purchases returns and carriage inwards and outwards.

Shown in Exhibit 29.3 is a fully worked example that includes all the items mentioned above and in section 29.14 you will find another step-by-step guide that deals with these rather tricky adjustments; remember there is also a step-by-step guide to preparing financial statements, preliminary level, in section 12.8.

Exhibit 29.3

G Lea, a sole trader, extracted the following trial balance from his books for the year ended 31 March 2013.

G Lea
Trial Balance as at 31 March 2013

	Dr	*Cr*
	£	£
Purchases and sales	224,000	419,700
Inventory 1 April 2012	51,600	
Capital 1 April 2012		72,000
Bank overdraft		43,500
Cash	900	
Carriage inwards	4,600	
Discounts	14,400	9,300
Sales returns	8,100	
Purchases returns		5,700
Carriage outwards	21,600	
Rent and insurance	17,400	
Allowance for doubtful debts		6,600
Office equipment	20,000	
Delivery vans	27,000	
Accounts receivable and payable	119,100	61,200
Drawings	28,800	
Bad debts written off	400	
Wages and salaries	89,000	
General office expenses	4,500	
Provision for depreciation		
Office equipment		8,000
Delivery vans		5,400
	631,400	631,400

Notes:

(1) Inventory on 31 March 2013 was valued at £42,900
(2) Wages and salaries accrued £2,100 and office expenses owing £200 at 31 March 2013
(3) Rent prepaid 31 March 2013 was £1,800
(4) Increase the allowance for doubtful debts to £8,100
(5) Provide for depreciation on the office equipment at 20% per annum using the straight line method
(6) Provide for depreciation on the delivery vans at 20% per annum using the diminishing balance method.

You are required to prepare an income statement for the year ended 31 March 2013 together with a statement of financial position as at that date.

G Lea
Income Statement for the year ended 31 March 2013

		£	£	£
Sales				419,700
Less Sales returns				8,100
				411,600
Less Cost of goods sold				
Opening inventory			51,600	
Add Purchases		224,000		
Add Carriage inwards		4,600		
		228,600		
Less Purchases returns		5,700	222,900	
			274,500	
Less Closing inventory			42,900	231,600
Gross Profit				180,000
Add Discounts received	(G)			9,300
				189,300
Less Expenses				
Wages and salaries (89,000 + 2,100)	(C)		91,100	
Discounts allowed	(F)		14,400	
Carriage outwards			21,600	
Rent and insurance (17,400 – 1,800)	(A)		15,600	
Bad debts written off	(N)		400	
General office expenses (4,500 + 200)	(D)		4,700	
Increase in allowance for doubtful debts (8,100 – 6,600)	(L)		1,500	
Depreciation:				
Office equipment	(H)		4,000	
Delivery vans	(J)		4,320	157,620
Net Profit				31,680

G Lea
Statement of Financial Position as at 31 March 2013

Non-current Assets			*Cost*	*Total Depreciation*	*Net Book Value*
		£	£	£	£
Office equipment	(I)		20,000	12,000	8,000
Delivery vans	(K)		27,000	9,720	17,280
			47,000	21,720	25,280
Current Assets					
Inventory			42,900		
Accounts receivable		119,100			
Less Allowance for doubtful debts	(M)	8,100	111,000		
Prepaid expenses	(B)		1,800		
Cash in hand			900	156,600	
Less Current Liabilities					
Accounts payable			61,200		
Bank overdraft			43,500		
Expenses owing (2,100 + 200)	(E)		2,300	107,000	
Net Current Assets					49,600
					74,880
Financed by:					
Capital					72,000
Add Net Profit					31,680
					103,680
Less Drawings					28,800
					74,880

29.14 Step-by-step guide dealing with further adjustments to financial statements

Note: The letters (A) to (N) shown after each adjustment can be cross referenced to the income statement and statement of financial position of G Lea.

1 Prepayments (amounts paid in advance)
In the financial statements

(*a*) If a trial balance is provided in a question then ensure that you *deduct* the amount of the prepayment from the appropriate expense account and put the resultant figure in the income statement. Ensure that only the expenses incurred for that particular period are charged against the profits for that period. Refer to the worked example, note (3) rent prepaid £1,800. This amount should be deducted from the rent in the trial balance, i.e. £17,400 – £1,800 = £15,600, this figure should be entered as an expense in the income statement (A).

(*b*) In the statement of financial position show the amount of the *prepayment* in the current assets section directly under accounts receivable, i.e. prepaid expenses £1,800 (B).

2 Accruals (amount owing)

In the financial statements

(*a*) If a trial balance is provided in a question then *add* the amount of the accrual to the appropriate expense account and put this figure in the income statement. Refer to the worked example, note (2) wages and salaries accrued £2,100 and office expenses owing £200. These figures should be added as follows:

Wages and salaries	£89,000 + £2,100 = £91,100
General office expenses	£4,500 + £200 = £4,700

The amounts to be charged as expenses in the income statement are thus, wages and salaries £91,100 (C) and general office expenses £4,700 (D).

(*b*) In the statement of financial position show the amount of the *accrual* under the heading current liabilities section directly under accounts payable, i.e. expenses owing £2,100 + £200 = £2,300 (E).

3 Discounts allowed and received

Discount allowed

Charge as an expense in the income statement. Refer to the worked example where the discount allowed £14,400 has been charged as an expense (F).

Discount received

Add as income in the income statement directly underneath the gross profit figure. Again, refer to the worked example where there is discount received of £9,300 that has been added as income (G).

4 Depreciation

Straight line method (Refer to the worked example, note 5)

(*a*) Find the cost price of the office equipment	£20,000
(*b*) Using percentage given	20%
calculate 20% of £20,000	= £4,000

then

(*c*) Charge £4,000 as an expense in the income statement (H).

(*d*) In the statement of financial position, deduct *total* depreciation £4,000 from this year plus depreciation deducted in previous years £8,000* = £12,000 from the cost price of the asset to give you the net book value of the asset £20,000 – £12,000 = £8,000. Enter each of these figures in the appropriate columns in the statement of financial position (I). (*See trial balance credit side.)

Diminishing balance method (Refer to the worked example, note 6)

(*a*) Find the cost price of the delivery vans	£27,000
(*b*) Find the total amount of depreciation to date (refer to trial balance credit side)	£5,400
(*c*) Find the difference (£27,000 – £5,400)	£21,600
(*d*) Using percentage given	20%
calculate 20% of £21,600	= £4,320

then

(*e*) Charge £4,320 as an expense in the income statement (J).

(*f*) In the statement of financial position, deduct *total* depreciation £4,320 from this year plus depreciation deducted in previous years £5,400* = £9,720 from the cost price of the asset to give you the net book value of the asset

£27,000 – £9,720 = £17,280. Enter these figures in the appropriate columns in the statement of financial position (K). (*See trial balance credit side.)

5 Allowance for doubtful debts

Creating an allowance

(*a*) If an allowance is to be created for the first time look in the question for details of the amount to be set aside. Let us assume in our worked example that an allowance had been created in 2012 amounting to £6,600.

(*b*) The *allowance for doubtful debts £6,600* would have been charged to the income statement as an expense in 2012.

(*c*) In the statement of financial position, the *allowance for doubtful debts £6,600* would have been deducted from the accounts receivable which are to be found under the heading of current assets.

Increasing the allowance

(*a*) Refer to your question and ascertain the new allowance, in our example the new allowance is £8,100 for this year (see note 4).

(*b*) Find last year's allowance, using our example the figure is £6,600 (this figure can be found in the trial balance, credit side).

(*c*) Charge the difference between the new and old allowance, £8,100 – £6,600 = £1,500 to the income statement (L).

(*d*) In the statement of financial position, deduct the *new allowance £8,100* from the accounts receivable (M).

Reducing the allowance

(*a*) Refer to your question and ascertain the new allowance. Using our worked example we will assume that in 2014 it was decided to reduce the allowance to £5,000.

(*b*) Find the old allowance, again using our example this would be £8,100.

(*c*) Take the difference between the old and the new allowance, £8,100 – £5,000 = £3,100 then add this amount as income in the income statement.

(*d*) Deduct the *new allowance for doubtful debts £5,000* from accounts receivable in the statement of financial position.

6 Bad debts

Simply write them off as an expense in the income statement. In our example you will see that bad debts written off are £400, this is shown as an expense in the income statement (N).

Note: A model layout of the financial statements of a sole trader is shown in Appendix B.

Chapter summary

- It is important to ensure that expenses incurred in a particular period are charged against the profit for that period whether or not they have been paid. In the same way revenue earned in a period should be included as income for that period irrespective of whether the money has been received or is still owed.
- Items owing are called 'accruals', items paid in advance are called 'prepayments'.
- Adjustments need to be made in the expense and revenue accounts to ensure that expenses incurred or revenue due for the period are included in that year's financial statements.

- Expenses owing (accruals) are shown in the statement of financial position under the heading of current liabilities while expenses prepaid (prepayments) are shown under current assets. Amounts owing for rents receivable or other revenue due is usually added to the accounts receivable.
- If the owner of a business takes goods for his or her own use without paying for them then an adjustment is made by crediting the purchases account and debiting the drawings account, plus an adjustment for VAT if appropriate.
- Goodwill is the extra amount paid for an existing business above the value of its other assets.
- There are various forms of 'capital' used in a business; capital invested, capital employed and working capital.
- A fully worked example of the financial statements for a sole trader, including all adjustments, is illustrated using the step-by-step guide.

EXERCISES

*Note: Questions with the suffix 'X' shown after the question number do **not** have answers shown at the back of the book. Answers to the other questions are shown in Appendix E.*

29.1 C Homer's first year of trading ended on 31 December 2013. You are required to write up the ledger accounts in respect of the items shown below. Balance the accounts off at the end of the year and show the balances carried down and amounts transferred to the financial statements for the year 2013.

(*a*) Rent: paid in 2013 amounted to £1,600; owing at 31 December 2013, £400.
(*b*) Insurance: paid in 2013 amounted to £900. Of the amount paid £265 was in respect of insurance for 2014.
(*c*) Motor expenses: paid in 2013, £7,215; owing at 31 December 2013, £166.
(*d*) Rates: paid six months' rates on 1 January 2013, £750; on 1 July 2013 paid nine months' rates for the period 31 March 2014, £1,125.
(*e*) K Whalley rented part of the buildings from C Homer for £400 per month from 1 January 2013. On 15 April 2013 he paid C Homer £2,000 and on 15 December 2013 he paid £4,400. Show these transactions in C Homer's accounts.

29.2 The following accounts are from T Norton's books during his first year of trading to 31 December 2013.

(*a*) General expenses: paid in 2013, £615; still owing at 31 December 2013, £56.
(*b*) Telephone: paid in 2013, £980; owing at 31 December 2013, £117.
(*c*) Norton received commission from the sale of goods. In 2013 he received £3,056 and was owed a further £175 on 31 December 2013.
(*d*) Carriage outwards: paid in 2013, £666; still owing at 31 December 2013, £122.
(*e*) Insurance: paid 1 January 2013 for nine months' insurance, £1,080; paid 1 October 2013 the sum of £1,080 for insurance to 30 June 2014.

Write up the ledger accounts, balance them off at the end of the year and show the balances carried down and amounts transferred to the finiancial statements for the year 2013.

29.3X T Dale's financial year ended on 30 June 2013. Write up the ledger accounts, showing the transfer to the financial statements.

(*a*) Stationery: paid for the year to 30 June 2013, £855; inventory of stationery at 30 June 2012, £290; and at 30 June 2013, £345.

(*b*) General expenses: paid for the year to 30 June 2013, £590; owing at 30 June 2012, £64; owing at 30 June 2013, £90.
(*c*) Rent and rates (combined account): paid in the year to 30 June 2013, £3,890; rent owing at 30 June 2012, £160; rent paid in advance at 30 June 2013, £250; rates owing at 30 June 2012, £205; rates owing at 30 June 2013, £360.
(*d*) Motor expenses: paid in the year to 30 June 2013, £4,750; owing as at 30 June 2012, £180; owing as at 30 June 2013, £375.
(*e*) Dale earned commission from the sales of goods. Received for the year to 30 June 2013, £850; owing at 30 June 2012, £80; owing at 30 June 2013, £145.

29.4 The following balances were part of the trial balance of C Cainen on 31 December 2013:

	Dr	*Cr*
	£	£
Inventory at 1 January 2013	2,050	
Sales		18,590
Purchases	11,170	
Rent	640	
Wages and salaries	2,140	
Insurance	590	
Bad debts	270	
Telephone	300	
General expenses	180	

On 31 December 2013 you ascertain that:

(*a*) the rent for four months of 2014, £160, has been paid in 2013
(*b*) £290 is owing for wages and salaries
(*c*) insurance has been prepaid £190
(*d*) a telephone bill of £110 is owed
(*e*) inventory is valued at £3,910.

Draw up Cainen's income statement for the year ended 31 December 2013.

29.5X The following were part of the trial balance of K Tyler on 31 December 2013:

	Dr	*Cr*
	£	£
Inventory at 1 January 2013	8,620	
Sales		54,190
Purchases	30,560	
Sales returns	200	
Wages and salaries	4,960	
Motor expenses	2,120	
Rent and rates	1,200	
Discounts allowed	290	
Lighting expenses	580	
Computer running expenses	1,210	
General expenses	360	

Given the information that follows, you are to draw up an income statement for the year ended 31 December 2013.

(*a*) inventory on 31 December 2013 is £12,120
(*b*) items prepaid: rates £160; computer running expenses £140
(*c*) items owing: wages £510; lighting expenses £170
(*d*) £700 is to be charged as depreciation of motor vehicles.

29.6 From the following trial balance of J Sears, a store owner, prepare an income statement for the year ended 31 December 2013 and a statement of financial position as at that date, taking into consideration the adjustments shown below:

Trial Balance as at 31 December 2013

	Dr £	*Cr* £
Sales		80,000
Purchases	70,000	
Sales returns	1,000	
Purchases returns		1,240
Inventory at 1 January 2013	20,000	
Allowance for doubtful debts		160
Wages and salaries	7,200	
Telephone	200	
Store fittings	8,000	
Motor van	6,000	
Accounts receivable and payable*	1,960	1,400
Bad debts	40	
Capital		35,800
Bank balance	600	
Drawings	3,600	
	118,600	118,600

Adjustments:

(*a*) closing inventory at 31 December 2013 is £24,000
(*b*) accrued wages £450
(*c*) telephone prepaid £20
(*d*) allowance for doubtful debts to be increased to 10% of accounts receivable
(*e*) depreciation on store fittings £800, and motor van £1,200.

**Note*: Sometimes, in examinations, two items will be shown on the same line. The examiner is testing to see whether the student knows which of the figures relate to the account titles. In Exercises 29.6 and 29.7X the item 'Accounts receivable and payable' is shown on the same line.

29.7X The following trial balance was extracted from the records of L Robinson, a trader, as at 31 December 2013:

	Dr	*Cr*
	£	£
Discounts allowed	410	
Discounts received		506
Carriage inwards	309	
Carriage outwards	218	
Sales returns	1,384	
Purchases returns		810
Sales		120,320
Purchases	84,290	
Inventory at 31 December 2012	30,816	
Motor expenses	4,917	
Repairs to premises	1,383	
Salaries and wages	16,184	
Sundry expenses	807	
Rates and insurance	2,896	
Premises at cost	40,000	
Motor vehicles at cost	11,160	
Provision for depreciation – motors		3,860
Accounts receivable and payable*	31,640	24,320
Cash at bank	4,956	
Cash in hand	48	
Drawings	8,736	
Capital		50,994
Loan from P Hall (repayable 2016)		40,000
Bad debts	1,314	
Allowance for doubtful debts		658
	241,468	241,468

**Note*: See footnote to Exercise 29.6 for an explanation of why two figures are on one line.

The following matters are to be taken into account at 31 December 2013:

(*a*) inventory £36,420
(*b*) expenses owing: sundry expenses £62; motor expenses £33
(*c*) prepayment: rates £166
(*d*) allowance for doubtful debts to be reduced to £580
(*e*) depreciation for motor vehicles to be £2,100 for the year
(*f*) part of the premises were let to a tenant, who owed £250 at 31 December 2013
(*g*) loan interest owing to P Hall £4,000.

Draw up an income statement for the year ended 31 December 2013 and a statement of financial position as at that date.

29.8 Freddy Tuilagi is a baker. His trial balance as at 30 September is as follows:

	Dr	Cr
	£	£
Motor van (at cost)	7,000	
Discount received		230
Bank		50
Opening inventory	850	
General expenses	610	
Provision for depreciation: Equipment		2,000
Drawings	1,400	
Sales		30,490
Cash	30	
Accounts payable		845
Purchases	13,725	
Wages	3,880	
Advertising	420	
Telephone	160	
Equipment (at cost)	17,000	
Capital		11,460
	45,075	45,075

The following additional information is available at 30 September:

(1) Inventory at cost amounted to £960.
(2) Over the year Freddy Tuilagi took purchases for his own use, at cost £320.
(3) The advertising was prepaid by £46.
(4) Depreciation is to be provided for as follows:
   - Equipment 30% diminishing balance method
   - Motor van 15% straight line (on cost) method.
(5) Discounts received of £80 have not yet been entered in the books.

Required:

(*a*) Prepare Freddie Tuigali's income statement for the year ended 30 September.
(*b*) Prepare Freddie Tuigali's statement of financial position as at 30 September.

City & Guilds Pitman qualifications

29.9X Ben Axtell owns a sports shop. His business's financial year ended on 31 March 2013. The trading account for the year ended on that date has been prepared. The following information was gathered from the business's accounting records in order that the other year end financial statements could be prepared.

	£
Gross profit	56,738
Rent of shop premises	9,340
Business rates	4,070
Wages of shop assistants	19,360
Discounts received	133
Accounts payable	4,839
Inventory in trade, 31 March 2013	32,980
Maintenance and servicing charges	740
Cash at bank	3,354
Advertising	1,450
Light and heat	1,740
Capital on 1 April 2012	32,056
Insurance	580
Drawings	17,240
Loan from Kay French	8,000
Loan interest	1,212
Shop furniture, fittings and equipment	
at cost	14,000
provision for depreciation, 1 April 2012	4,300

Additional information:

- Business rates, £320, were outstanding on 31 March 2013.
- Advertising costs, £414, were paid by cheque on 30 March 2013. This transaction was omitted from the accounting records.
- Insurance premiums, £65, were prepaid at 31 March 2013.
- The shop furniture, fittings and equipment should be depreciated by 15% per annum using the straight line method.
- The loan from Kay French is due to be repaid in 2016.

Tasks:

(*a*) Prepare the income statement for the year ended 31 March 2013.

(*b*) Prepare a statement of financial position as at 31 March 2013 which should show clearly the subtotal for working capital.

(*c*) Show how the following accounts should appear in the ledger:
 (i) business rates;
 (ii) insurance.

Note: The accounts should show the figures given in the list above, and any entries arising from the additional information including the transfer of the correct amount to the income statement.

Balance the accounts and bring down the balances.

Southern Examining Group

Please note that this question is NOT from the live examinations for the current specification.

CHAPTER 30

Extended trial balance

Learning objectives

After you have studied this chapter you should be able to:

- enter balances from the general ledger and other records on the extended trial balance
- deal with adjustments, including accruals and prepayments, and enter them correctly on the extended trial balance
- enter the closing inventory valuation on the extended trial balance
- deal with other adjustments such as depreciation and allowances for doubtful debts and enter them on the extended trial balance
- deal with any errors and discrepancies and enter them on the extended trial balance
- extend the extended trial balance entries into appropriate columns of adjustments, income statement and statement of financial position and total them correctly.

30.1 Introduction

As previously mentioned in Chapter 8, a **trial balance** is a list of all balances on the double entry (the ledgers) accounts and the cash book at a particular point in time. The main purpose of the trial balance is to ensure that the books 'balance' and, if any errors are identified, to make the necessary corrections. Another important function of the trial balance is to provide the balances to be used in preparation of the financial statements of the business, the income statement and the statement of financial position.

30.2 The extended trial balance

The extended trial balance is often referred to as a 'worksheet' which provides a useful aid where a large number of adjustments are needed prior to the preparation of the financial statements. The extended trial balance is drawn up on specially preprinted stationery on which suitable columns are printed. Exhibit 30.1 shows an example of an extended trial balance. You may wish to photocopy this format and use it when carrying out some of the student activities at the end of the chapter.

Exhibit 30.1 Format for an extended trial balance

Description	*Ledger Balances*		*Adjustments*		*Income Statement*		*Statement of Financial Position*	
	Dr	*Cr*	*Dr*	*Cr*	*Dr*	*Cr*	*Dr*	*Cr*
	£	£	£	£	£	£	£	£

It should be noted, however, that some examining bodies may require a slightly different format which needs more columns. It is advisable to find out in which format the examining body, whose syllabus you are studying, require the extended trial balance to be shown.

30.3 Preparing the extended trial balance

Once the trial balance has been drawn up and balanced off correctly, the next task is to implement the following adjustments:

- accruals and prepayments
- include the closing inventory valuation
- make provision for depreciation and allowances for doubtful debts
- correct any errors.

30.4 A worked example

In Exhibit 30.2 you will find the trial balance which was extracted from the books of D Simpson, a retailer, at 31 December 2013.

Exhibit 30.2

Trial Balance of D Simpson as at 31 December 2013

	£	£
Purchases	138,872	
Sales		202,460
Carriage inwards	490	
Carriage outwards	1,406	
Sales and purchases returns	424	2,280
Inventory 1 January 2013	9,820	
Wages and salaries	29,950	
Rent	11,000	
Rates and insurance	3,900	
Heating and lighting	1,254	
Motor vehicle	9,000	
Motor expenses	2,500	
Capital 1 January 2013		37,896
Bank overdraft		5,638
Fixtures and fittings	6,400	
Drawings	27,900	
Accounts receivable	23,200	
Accounts payable		17,842
	266,116	266,116

Notes:

(*a*) Rent owing amounted to £1,000 as at 31 December 2013.

(*b*) Rates paid in advance amounted to £500.

(*c*) Closing inventory was valued at £12,042 as at 31 December 2013.

(*d*) Depreciate the motor vehicle at 20% using the straight line method.
[*Note*: Fixtures and fittings are not to be depreciated in this example.]

(*e*) Provide for the creation of an allowance for doubtful debts amounting to 2% of the accounts receivable.

You are required to:

1 Prepare an extended trial balance at 31 December 2013.
2 Prepare an income statement for the year ended 31 December 2013 and a statement of financial position as at that date.

Since many students have difficulty in preparing extended trial balances the above example will be carried out using the 'step-by-step guide' shown below.

Step-by-step guide

Step 1

First of all draw up a trial balance in the usual way (refer to section 8.3). Remember:

Debit Balances are Assets or Expenses
and
Credit Balances are Liabilities, Capital or Income

If there have been no errors then the two sides should agree. Refer to Exhibit 30.3 and note that the balances have now been entered on the **extended trial balance (ETB)** under the heading 'ledger balances'.

Step 2

Deal with the adjustments at the bottom of the trial balance.
Note: Each item must be dealt with twice to comply with the double entry rules.

Adjustments fall into four categories:

1 **Accruals**
2 **Prepayments**
3 **Closing inventory valuation**
4 **Other adjustments:**
   depreciation provision
   allowances for doubtful debts
   correction of errors

When dealing with adjustments think double entry, i.e.

which account should be debited
and
which account should be credited.

When entering the adjustment on the extended trial balance first of all look to see if there is already an 'Account' for the transaction and, if so, use it. If not, then open an account at the foot of the extended trial balance. (This is illustrated in the following examples.)

Step 3

Deal with accruals and prepayments.

1 Accruals (amounts owing)
For example, referring to Exhibit 30.2(a) rent owing amounts to £1,000, which is entered as follows:

Debit Rent Account £1,000
Credit Accruals – Rent £1,000 (as this item is a liability).

This transaction is now shown in Exhibit 30.3 as '(a)' under the 'adjustments' column - see the debit entry of £1,000 next to the 'Rent Account' and the credit entry of £1,000 entered below the totals of the trial balance under the heading 'Accruals - Rent'.

2 Prepayments (amounts paid in advance)
Exhibit 30.2(b) shows a rates prepayment of £500, which is entered as follows:

Debit Prepayments – rates £500
Credit Rates account £500.

This again is shown in Exhibit 30.3(b) under the adjustments column - see the debit entry of £500 entered below the totals of the trial balance under the heading 'Prepayment - rates £500' and the corresponding credit entry shown next to the 'rates account'.

3 Dealing with the closing inventory valuation
At the end of the financial year a business usually undertakes an inventory valuation. Exhibit 30.2(c) shows a closing inventory of £12,042, which is entered as follows:

Debit Inventory account (to be shown in the statement of financial position as an asset)
Credit Inventory account (shown in the income statement as a deduction from the cost of goods sold calculation).

This is shown in Exhibit 30.3(c) under the trial balance totals is the adjustments column.

4 Dealing with other adjustments
Depreciation provision Exhibit 30.2(d) requires provision for depreciation of 20% on motor vehicles using the straight line method. Motor vehicles cost £9,000, therefore, 20% of cost equals £1,800 depreciation to be charged in the income statement. This transaction is entered on the extended trial balance under the adjustments column, see note (d) as follows:

Debit Depreciation of motor vehicle £1,800 (amount to be charged in the income statement)
Credit Depreciation provision of motor vehicle £1,800 (amount to be shown as a deduction from the value of the asset in the statement of financial position).

Allowance for doubtful debts Exhibit 30.2(e) requires the creation of an allowance for doubtful debts amounting to 2% of the accounts receivable figure of £23,200 which amounts to £464. The entry in the extended trial balance will appear in the adjustments column - note (e) as follows:

Debit Creation of allowance for doubtful debts £464 (this amount to be charged in the income statement)
Credit Allowance for doubtful debts £464 (this amount to be shown as deduction from the accounts receivable in the statement of financial position).

Correction of errors To keep the worked example as straightforward as possible, no errors require correcting in Exhibit 30.2. This topic will be covered later in this chapter.

Step 4

The next step is to add up both parts of the adjustments column. Providing the adjustments have been carried out correctly, the two columns should agree – in other words, the adjustments column acts rather like a mini trial balance.

Step 5

It is now necessary to add/subtract the figures *across* the extended trial balance and enter the *total* in either the income statement or statement of financial position column. This step requires a certain amount of skill from the students since they must be fully conversant with the position of each balance figure in the financial statements. A useful hint is to carry out this identification *before* starting the analysis by entering either of the following immediately before the description column (*see* Exhibit 30.3), namely:

IS Income Statement
S Statement of financial position

to indicate which analysis column to use.

It is important to note when carrying out the analysis that if the balance is shown as a debit balance in the ledger balance column then it will appear as a debit balance in either the income statement column or the statement of financial position column. The same thing applies to the credit balances, which will appear in either the income statement column or the statement of financial position column as a credit balance. While carrying out the analysis, any figures appearing in the adjustments column must be taken into consideration; for example, referring to Exhibit 30.3(a), the balance of rent will be analysed as:

Rent £11,000 plus £1,000 (owing) = £12,000

This will be analysed into the income statement column as a debit balance of £12,000.

Note: Refer to Exhibit 30.3 where this task has been carried out.

A further example can also be seen in Exhibit 30.3(b) where the prepayment of rates £500 will be analysed as follows:

Rates and Insurance	£3,900
Less amount paid in advance	500
	£3,400

The amount to be shown in the income statement column will be £3,400 debit balance.

Exhibit 30.3 D Simpson – extended trial balance at 31 December 2013

	Description	Ledger Balances		Adjustments		Income Statement		SofFP*	
		Dr	Cr	Dr	Cr	Dr	Cr	Dr	Cr
		£	£	£	£	£	£	£	£
IS	Purchases	138,872				138,872			
IS	Sales		202,460				202,460		
IS	Carriage inwards	490				490			
IS	Carriage outwards	1,406				1,406			
IS	Sales and purchases returns	424	2,280			424	2,280		
IS	Inventory 1 January 2013	9,820				9,820			
IS	Wages and salaries	29,950				29,950			
IS	Rent	11,000		(a) 1,000		12,000			
IS	Rates and insurance	3,900			(b) 500	3,400			
IS	Heating and lighting	1,254				1,254			
S	Motor vehicle	9,000						9,000	
IS	Motor expenses	2,500				2,500			
S	Capital 1 January 2013		37,896						37,896
S	Bank overdraft		5,638						5,638
S	Fixtures and fittings	6,400						6,400	
S	Drawings	27,900						27,900	
S	Accounts receivable	23,200						23,200	
S	Accounts payable		17,842						17,842
		266,116	266,116						
S	Accrual – Rent				(a) 1,000				1,000
S	Prepayment – Rates			(b) 500				500	
S	Inventory 31 December 2013			(c) 12,042				12,042	
IS	Inventory 31 December 2013				(c) 12,042		12,042		
IS	Depreciation – Motor vehicle			(d) 1,800		1,800			
S	Depreciation – Provision for motor vehicle				(d) 1,800				1,800
IS	Allowance for doubtful debts			(e) 464		464			
S	Allowance for doubtful debts				(e) 464				464
				15,806	15,806				
				(Step 4)					
	Net profit (Step 6)					14,402			14,402
						216,782	216,782		
								79,042	79,042
								(Step 7)	

*SofFP = Statement of Financial Position

Step 6

Add up the income statement columns. The difference between the two figures will represent a profit or loss for the period. In our example of D Simpson the difference between these two columns is £14,402, representing a net profit. This figure will now be entered on the extended trial balance as net profit £14,402, a *debit entry* in the income statement column.

The corresponding *credit entry* will appear as under the statement of financial position columns.

Step 7

The only remaining task to carry out is to add up the statement of financial position column totals and, provided all transactions have been carried out correctly, the totals should agree.

Note: Refer to Exhibit 30.3 where you can see that the extended trial balance balances with a total of £79,042.

The income statement and statement of financial position of D Simpson for the year ended 31 December 2013 is shown in Exhibit 30.4.

Exhibit 30.4

D Simpson
Income Statement for the year ended 31 December 2013

	£	£	£
Sales		202,460	
Less Sales returns		424	202,036
Less Cost of goods sold:			
Opening inventory		9,820	
Purchases		138,872	
Carriage inwards		490	
		149,182	
Less Purchase returns	2,280		
Closing inventory	12,042	14,322	134,860
Gross profit			67,176
Less Expenses:			
Carriage outwards		1,406	
Wages and salaries		29,950	
Rent (11,000 + 1,000)		12,000	
Rates and insurance (3,900 – 500)		3,400	
Heating and lighting		1,254	
Motor expenses		2,500	
Depreciation – Motor vehicle		1,800	
Creation of allowance for doubtful debts		464	52,774
Net profit			14,402

D Simpson
Statement of Financial Position as at 31 December 2013

		Cost	Total Dep'n	Net Book Value
	£	£	£	£
Non-current assets:				
Fixtures and fittings		6,400	–	6,400
Motor vehicles		9,000	1,800	7,200
		15,400	1,800	13,600
Current assets:				
Inventory		12,042		
Accounts receivable	23,200			
Less Allowance for doubtful debts	464	22,736		
Prepayments		500	35,278	
Less Current liabilities:				
Bank overdraft		5,638		
Accounts payable		17,842		
Accruals		1,000	24,480	
Net current assets				10,798
				24,398
Financed by:				
Capital: Balance 1 January 2013				37,896
Add Net profit for the year				14,402
				52,298
Less Drawings				27,900
				24,398

30.5 Other considerations

In the above example of D Simpson the transactions involving depreciation and allowance for doubtful debts was kept as straightforward as possible to avoid complications. However, assuming it is the next accounting period of D Simpson, the following adjustments will now be shown:

1 Depreciate the motor vehicle by 20% using the straight line method (for the second year).
2 Increase the allowance for doubtful debts to £550.
3 Write off a bad debt amounting to £100.

1 Depreciate the motor vehicle by 20% using the straight line method

First of all the amount of depreciation to be charged in the income statement account needs to be calculated. As the method of depreciation to be used is the straight line method, the amount of depreciation will be the same each year, namely, 20% of £9,000 = £1,800. This amount is then entered on the extended trial balance as follows:

D Simpson
Extended Trial Balance (extract) as at 31 December 2014

Description	*Ledger balances*		*Adjustments*		*Income statement*		*Statement of financial position*	
	Dr £	*Cr* £	*Dr* £	*Cr* £	*Dr* £	*Cr* £	*Dr* £	*Cr* £
Motor vehicle	9,000						9,000	
Provision for depreciation motor vehicle*		1,800		1,800				3,600
Depreciation of motor vehicle			1,800		1,800			

The above example shows that the motor vehicle account remains a debit balance of £9,000 which appears in the statement of financial position column as a debit (an asset). The provision for depreciation of motor vehicle* appears under the ledger balances column as £1,800, representing the amount of depreciation charged for the first year. To this figure another £1,800 is added representing the depreciation for this year showing a total of depreciation to date of £3,600. This is shown as a credit balance in the statement of financial position column of the extended trial balance.

When the statement of financial position is prepared it will appear as follows:

D Simpson
Statement of Financial Position (extract) as at 31 December 2014

	Cost	*Total dep'n*	*Net book value*
Non-current assets	£	£	£
Motor vehicle	9,000	3,600	5,400

The remaining debit balance of depreciation of motor vehicle £1,800 will be charged in income statement. This is shown in the extended trial balance under the income statement column as a debit balance (see above in the extended trial balance extract).

2 Increase the allowance for doubtful debts to £550

In the accounts for the year ended 31 December 2013, D Simpson created an allowance for doubtful debts equal to 2% of the accounts receivable which amounted to £464 (this is illustrated in the extract from extended trial balance below).

In the year to 31 December 2014 it was decided to increase the allowance to £550, representing an increase of £86 (£550 *less* £464). To record this increase the following entries need to be made:

- Show the increase of the allowance for doubtful debts of £86 as a debit entry in the adjustments column to be charged in the income statement.
- Increase the existing 'allowance for doubtful debts account' by £86 to £550; this will be shown as a credit entry in the adjustments column of the extended trial balance. This figure is then extended to the statement of financial position column as £550 (credit entry).

This can now be seen in the following extract from the extended trial balance.

D Simpson
Extended Trial Balance (extract) as at 31 December 2014

Description	*Ledger balances*		*Adjustments*		*Income statement*		*Statement of financial position*	
	Dr £	*Cr* £	*Dr* £	*Cr* £	*Dr* £	*Cr* £	*Dr* £	*Cr* £
Allowance for doubtful debts		464		86				550
Increase in allowance for doubtful debts			86		86			

3 Write off a bad debt amounting to £100

After the preparation of the draft accounts one of the business's customers was reported to have been declared bankrupt. The balance on the customer's account was £100 and it was decided to write the debt off as bad.

This would be entered on the extended trial balance as follows:

D Simpson
Extended Trial Balance (extract) as at 31 December 2014

Description	*Ledger balances*		*Adjustments*		*Income statement*		*Statement of financial position*	
	Dr £	*Cr* £	*Dr* £	*Cr* £	*Dr* £	*Cr* £	*Dr* £	*Cr* £
Accounts receivable (say)	26,000			100			25,900	
Bad debts			100		100			

The above entries show that the accounts receivable, which we have assumed are £26,000 for this year ended 2014, have been reduced by £100 and will appear in the statement of financial position as £25,900. The bad debt will also be charged in the income statement. This is shown as a debit entry in both the adjustments column and the income statement column.

30.6 A more complicated example

Exhibit 30.5 shows a worked example of a more complicated extended trial balance.

Exhibit 30.5

J Blake is a sole trader. He extracted the following list of balances from the books of his business on 31 March 2013:

	Dr	*Cr*
	£	£
Sales		80,650
Purchases	45,380	
Sales returns	510	
Purchases returns		930
Discounts allowed	1,120	
Discounts received		390
Inventory at 1 April 2012	12,460	
Motor van, at cost	12,500	
Office equipment	9,600	
Provision for depreciation of motor van 1 April 2012		3,800
Provision for depreciation of office equipment 1 April 2012		2,150
Salaries and wages	17,620	
Motor van running expenses	3,910	
Sundry expenses	1,140	
Rent and rates	3,200	
Bad debts	375	
Allowance for doubtful debts 1 April 2012		320
Accounts receivable	12,870	
Accounts payable		9,100
Bank	8,040	
Cash	60	
Drawings	7,000	
Capital		38,445
	135,785	135,785

This additional information is available at 31 March 2013:

(*a*) Inventory was valued at £20,100.

(*b*) Salaries and wages of £490 are to be accrued.

(*c*) The following have been prepaid: rent and rates £790.

(*d*) An additional £270 is to be written off as bad debts, and the allowance for doubtful debts is to be adjusted to 2% of accounts receivable after writing off bad debts.

(*e*) Goods taken by Blake for his private use during the year amounted at cost to £370. No record of this has yet been made in the books.

(*f*) Depreciation is to be written off as follows: motor van £2,000; office equipment at 15% using the straight line method.

Exhibit 30.6 J Blake – extended trial balance at 31 March 2013

	Description	*Ledger Balances*		*Adjustments*		*Income Statement*		*SofFP**	
		Dr	*Cr*	*Dr*	*Cr*	*Dr*	*Cr*	*Dr*	*Cr*
		£	£	£	£	£	£	£	£
IS	Sales		80,650				80,650		
IS	Purchases	45,380			370	45,010			
IS	Sales returns/Purchase returns	510	930			510	930		
IS	Discounts	1,120	390			1,120	390		
IS	Inventory at 1 April 2012	12,460				12,460			
S	Motor van, at cost	12,500						12,500	
S	Office equipment, at cost	9,600						9,600	
S	Provision for dep'n – Motor van 1.4.2012		3,800		2,000				5,800
S	Provision for dep'n – Office equip. 1.4.2012		2,150		1,440				3,590
IS	Salaries and wages	17,620		490		18,110			
IS	Motor van running expenses	3,910				3,910			
IS	Sundry expenses	1,140				1,140			
IS	Rent and rates	3,200			790	2,410			
IS	Bad debts	375		270		645			
S	Allowance for doubtful debts 1.4.2012		320	68					252
S	Accounts receivable	12,870			270			12,600	
S	Accounts payable		9,100						9,100
S	Bank	8,040						8,040	
S	Cash	60						60	
S	Drawings	7,000		370				7,370	
S	Capital		38,445						38,445
		135,785	135,785						
S	Accrual – Salaries and wages				490				490
S	Prepayment – Rent and rates			790				790	
S	Inventory – 31 March 2013			20,100				20,100	
IS	Inventory – 31 March 2013				20,100		20,100		
IS	Depreciation – Motor van			2,000		2,000			
IS	Depreciation – Office equipment			1,440		1,440			
IS	Reduction in allowance for doubtful debts				68		68		
				25,528	25,528				
S	Net profit (balancing figure)					13,383			13,383
						102,138	102,138		
								71,060	71,060

*SofFP = Statement of Financial Position

You are required to:

1 Prepare an extended trial balance as at 31 March 2013.
2 Prepare an income statement for the year ended 31 March 2013 and a statement of financial position as at that date.

Remember to follow the 'Step-by-step guide' to assist you in following the workings of Exhibit 30.5 and note the order of dealing with the 'adjustments':

- accruals and prepayments
- deal with the closing inventory valuation
- make provision for depreciation and allowance for doubtful debts
- other adjustments
  - writing off the bad debt (refer back to section 30.5(3) and Chaper 28)
  - goods taken for own use (see the worked example, Exhibit 30.6).

The extended trial balance of J Blake is now shown in Exhibit 30.6 and the income statement and statement of financial position is shown in Exhibit 30.7 as follows:

Exhibit 30.7

J Blake
Income Statement for the year ended 31 March 2013

	£	£	£
Sales		80,650	
Less Sales returns		510	80,140
Less Cost of goods sold:			
Opening inventory		12,460	
Add Purchases (45,380 – 370 own use)	45,010		
Less Purchase returns	930	44,080	
		56,540	
Less Closing inventory		20,100	36,440
Gross profit			43,700
Add Income:			
Discount received		390	
Reduction in allowance for doubtful debts			
(320 – 2% of (12,870 – 270))		68	458
			44,158
Less Expenses:			
Discounts allowed		1,120	
Salaries and wages (17,620 + 490)		18,110	
Motor van running expenses		3,910	
Rent and rates (3,200 – 790)		2,410	
Sundry expenses		1,140	
Bad debts (375 + 270)		645	
Depreciation: Motor van		2,000	
Office equipment		1,440	30,775
Net profit			13,383

J Blake
Statement of Financial Position at 31 March 2013

		Cost	*Total dep'n*	*Net book value*
Non-current assets:	£	£	£	£
Office equipment		9,600	3,590	6,010
Motor van		12,500	5,800	6,700
		22,100	9,390	12,710
Current assets:				
Inventory		20,100		
Accounts receivable (12,870 – 270)	12,600			
Less Allowance for doubtful debts	252	12,348		
Prepayments		790		
Cash at bank		8,040		
Cash in hand		60	41,338	
Less Current liabilities				
Accounts payable		9,100		
Accruals		490	9,590	
Net current assets				31,748
				44,458
Financed by:				
Capital				38,445
Add Net profit				13,383
				51,828
Less Drawings (7,000 + 370 goods for own use)				7,370
				44,458

Chapter summary

- The extended trial balance is often referred to as a 'worksheet' since it provides a useful aid where a large number of adjustments are needed prior to the preparation of the financial statements.
- Initially a trial balance is prepared in the usual way with debit balances consisting of assets or expenses and credit balances being liabilities, capital or income.
- At the end of the financial year there are often several adjustments to be made. These consist of accruals and prepayments, closing inventory valuation and making provisions for depreciation and doubtful debts.
- It is important to remember that each adjustment must be recorded *twice* on the extended trial balance, one being a debit entry and the other the credit entry.
- A careful systematic approach must be applied when entering items in the extended trial balance. Each category must be entered one step at a time, i.e. accruals, prepayments, dealing with the closing inventory valuation and then other adjustments.
- It is important to ensure that the 'adjustment columns' add up correctly, rather like a mini-trial balance.

- The next step is to add/subtract the figures across the extended trial balance entering the total in either the income statement or statement of financial position columns. The balancing figure in the income statement columns represents the *profit* or *loss* for the period which is also entered in the statement of financial position columns. All columns are then added up with each section agreeing.
- Finally, the financial statements can be prepared, i.e. the income statement and the statement of financial position.

EXERCISES

Note 1: Questions with the suffix 'X' shown after the question number do **not** *have answers shown at the back of the book. Answers to the other questions are shown in Appendix E.*

Note 2: A blank worksheet for preparing extended trial balance exercises is given in Appendix B.

30.1 Reconstruct the trial balance after making the necessary corrections.

S Dickinson
Trial Balance as at 30 September 2013

	Dr £	*Cr* £
Capital	59,868	
Motor vehicles	22,500	
Computer equipment	18,000	
Accounts receivable	31,059	
Accounts payable		30,690
Purchases	245,259	
Sales		358,317
Wages and salaries		38,476
Motor expenses		3,428
Printing and stationery	3,600	
General expenses	8,235	
Cash at bank	5,850	
Inventory 1 October 2012	23,004	
Rent and rates	31,500	
Heating and lighting		6,624
Interest received	6,417	
Insurance		10,332
Rent received	5,175	
Drawings		12,600
	460,467	460,467

30.2 From the following list of balances taken from the books of G Brammer you are required to draw up a trial balance as at 31 December 2013.

	£
Capital	100,000
Premises	66,250
Motor vehicle	17,000
Office equipment	2,438
Wages	19,637
Purchases	37,455
Sales	56,170
Commission received	1,050
Electricity	925
Telephone	1,125
Motor expenses	1,500
Printing, stationery and advertising	2,050
Accounts payable	8,500
Accounts receivable	12,012
General expenses	2,371
Bank overdraft	3,505
Drawings	6,462

30.3X From the list of balances from the accounts of Fraser & Co, you are required to prepare a trial balance as at 31 December 2012.

Fraser & Co
List of Outstanding Balances as at 31 December 2012

	£
Purchases	334,500
Sales	511,050
Sales returns	10,050
Purchases returns	8,400
Inventory 1 January 2012	33,000
Discount allowed	6,900
Discount received	8,250
Wages and salaries	55,750
Carriage inwards	2,100
Carriage outwards	3,300
Printing and stationery	4,200
Electricity	7,300
Motor expenses	18,250
Telephone	3,100
General expenses	2,900
Accounts receivable	51,000
Accounts payable	32,400
Bad debts written off	1,650
Allowance for doubtful debts at 31 December 2012	675
Cash in hand	1,200
Bank overdraft	35,100
Capital	57,825
Property	75,000
Plant and equipment	96,000
Provision for depreciation at 31 December 2012	
Property	15,000
Plant and equipment	37,500

30.4 The following is a list of balances extracted from the books of J Steadman, a sole trader, as at 31 January 2013.

J Steadman
List of Balances as at 31 January 2013

	£
Capital	58,260
Equipment	11,250
Furniture and fittings	6,000
Motor vehicles	17,370
Sales	96,030
Purchases	59,220
Cash at bank	750
General expenses	1,800
Wages	17,820
Rent, rates and insurance	7,650
Heating and lighting	2,100
Accounts receivable	24,000
Accounts payable	10,800
Inventory 1 February 2012	17,130

The following additional information is available as at 31 January 2013:

(*a*) Wages unpaid amounted to £351.
(*b*) Insurance paid in advance £600.
(*c*) Closing inventory was valued at £14,730.

You are required to take the above adjustments into account and prepare the figures for the financial statements for J Steadman for the year ended 31 January 2013, using the extended trial balance.

Note: Remember to use the blank extended trial balance worksheet in Appendix B.

30.5X The following is a list of balances taken from the ledgers of Rigby & Co as at 31 July 2013, the end of the financial year.

Rigby & Co
List of Balances as at 31 July 2013

	£
Inventory at 1 August 2012	29,150
Purchases	243,800
Sales	509,450
Sales returns	3,805
Purchases returns	2,655
Discounts allowed	6,620
Discounts received	5,750
Wages and salaries	76,500
Lighting and heating	9,250
Telephone, stationery and advertising	13,600
Motor expenses	10,500
General expenses	3,005
Rates and insurance	15,000
Motor vehicles:	
At cost	20,000
Accumulated depreciation	5,000
Fixtures and fittings:	
At cost	22,100
Accumulated depreciation	9,945
Accounts payable	21,900
Accounts receivable	31,700
Drawings	22,325
Cash in hand	995
Cash at bank	10,985
Capital	114,635
Land and buildings	150,000

The following additional information is available as at 31 July 2013:

(*a*) Motor expenses owing £200.
(*b*) Insurance paid in advance £3,500.
(*c*) Closing inventory was valued at £30,700.
(*d*) Depreciate motor vehicles at 25% and fixtures and fittings at 15% per annum using the straight line method.

You are required to take the above adjustments into account and prepare the figures for the financial statements of Rigby & Co for the year ended 31 July 2013, using the extended trial balance.

30.6 Amanda Carver is the proprietor of Automania, a business which supplies car parts to garages to use in servicing and repair work.

At the end of the financial year, on 30 April 2013, the balances were extracted from the general ledger and have been entered onto a trial balance, as shown below:

Automania
Trial Balance as at 30 April 2013

Description	*Ledger balances*	
	Dr	*Cr*
	£	£
Capital		135,000
Drawings	42,150	
Rent	17,300	
Purchases	606,600	
Sales		857,300
Sales returns	2,400	
Purchases returns		1,260
Salaries and wages	136,970	
Motor vehicles (M.V.) at cost	60,800	
Provision for depreciation (M.V.)		16,740
Fixtures and fittings (F&F) at cost	40,380	
Provision for depreciation (F&F)		21,600
Bank		3,170
Cash	2,100	
Lighting and heating	4,700	
VAT		9,200
Inventory at 1 May 2012	116,100	
Bad debts	1,410	
Allowance for doubtful debts		1,050
Sales control account	56,850	
Purchases control account		50,550
Sundry expenses	6,810	
Insurance	1,300	
Accruals		
Prepayments		
Depreciation		
Allowance for doubtful debts – Adjustment		
Closing inventory – Income statement		
Closing inventory – Statement of financial position		
	1,095,870	1,095,870

The following adjustments need to be taken into account as at 30 April 2013:

(*a*) Rent payable by the business is as follows:
- For the period to 31 July 2012 – £1,500 per month
- From 1 August 2012 – £1,600 per month

(*b*) The insurance balance includes £100 paid for the period 1 May 2013 to 31 May 2013.

(*c*) Depreciation is to be calculated as follows:
- Motor vehicles – 20% per annum straight line method
- Fixtures and fittings – 10% per annum diminishing balance method

(*d*) The allowance for doubtful debts is to be adjusted to a figure representing 2% of accounts receivable.

(*e*) Inventory has been valued at cost on 30 April 2013 at £119,360. However, this figure includes old goods, the details of which are as follows:
- Cost price of old goods – £3,660
- Net realisable value of old goods – £2,060

Also included is a badly damaged car door which was to have been sold for £80 but will now have to be scrapped. The cost price of the door was £60.

(*f*) A credit note received from a supplier on 5 April 2013 for goods returned was filed away with no entries having been made. The credit note has now been discovered and is for £200 net plus £35 VAT.

Required:

(i) Make appropriate entries in the adjustments columns of the extended trial balance taking account of the above information. Show all workings.

(ii) Complete the extended trial balance showing clearly the profit or loss made by Automania for the year ended 30 April 2013.

Note: Use a photocopy of the blank extended trial balance form in Appendix B for your answer.

Association of Accounting Technicians (Amended)

30.7X Helen Grant is the owner of Road Runner, a business that buys and sells car tyres.

- The financial year end is 30 April 2013.
- You are employed to assist with the book-keeping.
- The business uses a manual system consisting of a general ledger, a sales ledger and a purchases ledger.
- Double entry takes place in the general ledger. Individual accounts of accounts receivable and accounts payable are kept in memorandum accounts.
- You use a purchases day book and a sales day book. Totals from the day books are transferred into the general ledger.

At the end of the financial year on 30 April 2013, the following balances were taken from the general ledger.

	£
Sales	689,250
Purchases	414,875
Inventory at 1 May 2012	69,376
Salaries and wages	115,654
General expenses	82,440
Shop fittings at cost	48,140
Provision for depreciation, shop fittings	17,890
Computer equipment at cost	12,900
Provision for depreciation, computer equipment	7,460
Sales control account	58,200
Purchases control account	45,320
Bad debts	1,850
Allowance for doubtful debts	2,010
Bank (debit balance)	4,658
Cash	550
VAT (credit balance)	13,500
Discount allowed	8,740
Discount received	3,658
Drawings	22,000
Bank deposit account	20,000
Capital	80,295

The following adjustments need to be made for the year ended 30 April 2013.

(*a*) Inventory was valued at cost on 30 April 2013 at £58,450.
(*b*) Depreciation needs to be provided as follows:
- Shop fittings – 10% per annum straight line method
- Computer equipment – 25% per annum diminishing balance method.

(*c*) General expenses include insurance of £2,400, which was paid for the year ended 31 October 2013.
(*d*) The allowance for doubtful debts should be adjusted to 2.5% of accounts receivable.
(*e*) £2,000 is owed in wages on 30 April 2013.
(*f*) The bank deposit account was opened on 1 November 2012. Interest is paid at a fixed rate of 6% per annum.

Tasks:

1 Using the blank extended trial form in Appendix B enter the balances into the trial balance and total both columns, before taking into account the additional information.
2 Prepare journal entries to record the above adjustments; dates and narratives are not required.
3 Make appropriate entries in the adjustment columns of the extended trial balance taking account of all the journal entries.
4 Complete the extended trial balance showing clearly the profit or loss made by Helen Grant.

Association of Accounting Technicians (Amended)

CHAPTER 31

Inventory valuation

Learning objectives

After you have studied this chapter you should be able to:

- understand that there can be more than one way of valuing inventory
- calculate the value of inventory using three different methods
- understand how the closing inventory valuation affects the profit figures
- appreciate the affect of IAS 2 Valuation of inventories
- adjust inventory valuations in respect of goods on sale or return
- understand the importance of the final inventory valuation figure that appears in the statement of financial position and maintaining appropriate inventory levels.

31.1 Introduction to the valuation of inventory

Inventory is the name given to goods purchased for re-sale; it can also include work in progress and raw materials, which you will learn about later in Chapter 38, Manufacturing accounts.

Most people would assume that there can only be one figure for the valuation of inventory. This is, however, untrue. This chapter will examine how the valuation of inventory can be calculated using different figures.

Assume that a business has just completed its first financial year and is about to value inventory on hand at cost price. The business has only dealt with one type of goods. A record of the transactions is now shown in Exhibit 31.1.

Exhibit 31.1

Bought				Sold			
2013			£	2013			£
January	10	at £30 each	300	May	8	for £50 each	400
April	10	at £34 each	340	November	24	for £60 each	1,440
October	20	at £40 each	800				
	40		1,440		32		1,840

The balance of inventory on hand at 31 December 2013 is 8 units. The total figure of purchases is £1,440 and that of sales is £1,840. The trading account for the first year of trading can now be completed if the closing inventory is brought into the calculations.

But what value do we put on each of the 8 units left in stock at the end of the year? If all of the units bought during the year had cost £30 each, then the closing inventory would be 8 × £30 = £240. However, we have bought goods at different prices. This means that the valuation depends on which goods are taken for this calculation: the units at £30, or those at £34, or yet others at £40.

Many businesses do not know exactly whether they have sold all the oldest units before they sell new units. For instance, a business selling spanners may not know whether the oldest spanners had been sold before the newest spanners.

The inventory valuation will, therefore, be based on an accounting custom, and not on the facts of exactly which units were still in the inventory at the year end. The three main methods of doing this are now shown.

31.2 Inventory valuation methods

The three inventory methods comprise of:

- first in, first out
- last in, first out
- average cost.

First in, first out method

This is usually known as **FIFO**, the first letters of each word. The method says that, as far as the accounts are concerned, the first goods to be received are the first to be issued. Using the figures in Exhibit 31.1, we can now calculate the closing figure of inventory as follows:

2013	Received	Issued	Inventory	£	£
Jan	10 × £30 each		10 × £30		300
April	10 × £34 each		10 × £30 10 × £34	300 340	640
May		8 × £30 each	2 × £30 10 × £34	60 340	400
Oct	20 × £40 each		2 × £30 10 × £34 20 × £40	60 340 800	1,200
Nov		2 × £30 each 10 × £34 each 12 × £40 each	8 × £40		320

The closing inventory at 31 December 2013 is therefore valued at £320 using the FIFO method.

Last in, first out method

This is usually known as **LIFO**. As each issue of goods is made, the goods are said to be from the last batch received before that date. Where there is not enough left of the last batch, then the balance of goods needed is said to come from the previous batch still unsold.

From the information shown in Exhibit 31.1, the calculation under this basis can now be shown.

2013	Received	Issued	Inventory	£	£
Jan	10 × £30 each		10 × £30		300
April	10 × £34 each		10 × £30 10 × £34	300 340	640
May		8 × £34 each	10 × £30 2 × £34	300 68	368
Oct	20 × £40 each		10 × £30 2 × £34 20 × £40	300 68 800	1,168
Nov		20 × £40 each 2 × £34 each 2 × £30 each	8 × £30		240

The closing inventory at 31 December 2013 is therefore valued at £240 using the LIFO method.

Average cost method

Using what is known as the **AVCO** method, with each receipt of goods the average cost for each item of inventory is recalculated. Further issues of goods are then at that figure, until another receipt of goods means that another recalculation is needed.

From the information in Exhibit 31.1, the calculation can be shown thus:

2013	Received	Issued	Average cost per unit of inventory held	Number of units in inventory	Total value of inventory
			£		£
January	10 × £30		30	10	300
April	10 × £34		32*	20	640
May		8 × £32 ←	32	12	384
October	20 × £40		37**	32	1,184
November		24 × £37 ←	37	8	296

Notes: *In April, the average cost is calculated as follows:
inventory 10 × £30 = £300 + inventory received (10 × £34) £340 = total £640.
20 units in inventory, so the average is £640 ÷ 20 = £32.

**In October, the average is calculated as follows:
inventory 12 × £32 = £384 + inventory received (20 × £40) £800 = £1,184.
32 units in inventory, so the average is £1,184 ÷ 32 = £37.

The closing inventory at 31 December 2013 is therefore valued at £296 using the AVCO method.

31.3 Inventory valuation and the calculation of profits

Using the figures from Exhibit 31.1, with inventory valuations shown by the three methods of FIFO, LIFO and AVCO, the trading accounts would appear as set out in the table.

Trading Account for the year ended 31 December 2013

	FIFO		LIFO		AVCO	
	£	£	£	£	£	£
Sales		1,840		1,840		1,840
Less Cost of sales						
Purchases	1,440		1,440		1,440	
Less Closing inventory	320	1,120	240	1,200	296	1,144
Gross Profit		720		640		696

As can be seen from the table above, different methods of inventory valuation will mean that different profits are shown.

31.4 International Accounting Standard 2 – (IAS 2) Valuation of Inventories

This international accounting standard sets out the accounting techniques to be applied when valuing inventories. Since there are many different types of businesses, and conditions within them, there cannot be one system of inventory valuations. Therefore the standard states *'that stock should be valued at the lower of cost or net realisable value'*.

Businesses usually keep records of inventory items either on a manual or computerised system. At the end of the financial period it is usual to carry out a physical inventory check where all the goods held are counted, valued and checked against the records and if necessary adjustments are made to the records. The total value of the inventory is then used when preparing the financial statements, as shown in earlier chapters. The value of the inventory is, therefore, an important element in determining the profits of a business.

IAS 2 applies to the following inventories:

- raw materials*
- work-in-progress*
- finished goods.

*These will be dealt with in Chapter 38.

In all the above valuations it must be remembered that the valuation of the inventory is always *'the lower of cost or net realisable value'*, i.e.:

- **Cost of purchase** comprises the purchase price including, if appropriate, import duties, transport and handling costs and any other directly attributable costs, less trade discounts, rebates and subsidies.
- **Net realisable value** consists of the expected selling price *less* any expenses needed to complete the item or get it in a condition to be sold. This may be below cost because of stock deterioration, obsolescence and similar factors.

The concept of **prudence** is used when inventory is valued. Inventory should not be over-valued, otherwise profits shown will be too high. Therefore, if the net realisable value of inventory is less than the cost of the inventory, prudence dictates that the figure to be used in the financial statements is that of net realisable value.

Example: A machine was purchased at a cost price of £300. Unfortunately, the machine was damaged in the warehouse and the cost of repair and repainting amounted to £50 after which it was estimated it could be sold for £200. The machine would be valued at:

Saleable value £200, less cost of repair and repainting £50
= Net realisable value of £150

31.5 Goods on sale or return

Goods received on sale or return

In this situation goods are received from a supplier on a **sale or return** basis. For example, a supplier may want to promote a range of garden pots and a garden centre agrees to put them on sale for a trial period.

The garden centre does not own or pay for the goods nor includes them in its inventory until they are sold. Any unsold items will be returned to the supplier at the end of the trial period.

Goods sent to customers on sale or return

Should a business send goods on a **sale or return** basis to a customer they will continue to belong to the business until sold. At the business's date of its inventory check any unsold goods held at the customer's premises should be included in the business's inventory valuation.

31.6 The inventory check and the statement of financial position

Students often think that all the counting and valuing of inventory is done on the last day of the accounting period. This might be true in a small business, but it is often impossible in larger businesses. There may be too many items of inventory to do it so quickly.

This means that the inventory check may take place over a period of days. To get the figure of the inventory valuation as on the last day of the accounting period, we will have to make adjustments. Exhibit 31.2 gives an example of such calculations.

Exhibit 31.2

Lee Ltd has a financial year that ends on 31 December 2013. The inventory check is not in fact done until 8 January 2014. When the items in the inventory on that date are priced out, it is found that the inventory value amounts to £28,850. The following information is available about transactions between 31 December 2013 and 8 January 2014.

(*a*) Purchases since 31 December 2013 amounted to £2,370 at cost.
(*b*) Sales returns since 31 December 2013 were £350 at selling price.
(*c*) Sales since 31 December 2013 amounted to £3,800 at selling price.
(*d*) The selling price is always cost price + 25%.

Lee Ltd
Computation of stock as on 31 December 2013

			£
Inventory (at cost) as at 8 January 2014			28,850
Add Items which were in stock on 31 December 2013 (at cost)			
		£	
Sales		3,800	
Less Profit content (20% of selling price)*		760	3,040
			31,890
Less Items which were not in the inventory on 31 December 2013 (at cost)			
	£	£	
Sales returns	350		
Less Profit content (20% of selling price)*	70	280	
Purchases (at cost)		2,370	2,650
Inventory in hand as on 31 December 2013			29,240

*Note: Inventory is at cost (or net realisable value) and not at selling price. As this calculation has a sales figure in it, which includes profit, we must deduct the profit part to get to the cost price. This is true also for sales returns.

The professional accounting bodies encourage auditors to be present at the inventory check if at all possible.

31.7 Inventory levels

One of the most common faults found in the running of a business is that too high a level of inventory is maintained. A considerable number of businesses that have problems with a shortage of finance will find that they can help matters by having a sensible look at the amounts of inventory they hold. It would be a very rare business indeed which, had it not investigated the matter previously, could not reduce its inventory level. The cash saved could be used more profitably and could also improve cash flow.

Chapter summary

- There are three methods of valuing inventory namely: first in, first out (FIFO), last in, first out (LIFO) and the average cost method (AVCO).
- Each of the above methods gives a different closing inventory valuation that subsequently affects the profit figure. The lower the closing inventory figure the lower the profit while the higher the closing inventory figure the higher the profit.
- Net realisable value is the sales value of goods less expenses before sale – as per IAS 2 Valuation of inventories.
- When a business supplies goods to a customer on sale or return they belong to the supplier until such time as the customer decides they wish to purchase them and an order is placed.
- It may be necessary to make adjustments to the final inventory figure which appears in the statement of finanical position depending upon when the physical inventory check has taken place.
- It is important that businesses do not maintain a high level of inventory since this means funds are tied up and could cause a cash flow problem.

EXERCISES

Note: Questions with the suffix 'X' shown after the question number do ***not*** *have answers shown at the back of the book. Answers to the other questions are shown in Appendix E.*

31.1 (*a*) From the following figures, calculate the closing inventory that would be shown using (i) FIFO, (ii) LIFO, (iii) AVCO methods.

2013	*Bought*	*2013*	*Sold*
January	24 at £10 each	June	30 at £16 each
April	16 at £12.50 each	November	34 at £18 each
October	30 at £13 each		

(*b*) Draw up trading accounts for 2013 using each of the three methods for inventory valuation.

31.2X (*a*) From the following figures, calculate the closing inventory that would be shown using (i) FIFO, (ii) LIFO, (iii) AVCO methods.

2013	*Bought*	*2013*	*Sold*
January	30 at £12 each	July	24 at £15.50 each
May	30 at £14 each	November	16 at £18 each

(*b*) Draw up trading accounts for 2013 using each of the three methods for inventory valuation.

31.3 DC Ltd, whose financial year end was 31 December 2013, does not take an inventory check until 8 January 2014, when it is shown to be £50,850 at cost. It is then established that:

(*a*) a calculation of 1,000 items at £1.60 was shown as £160
(*b*) during the period from the year end to 8 January 2014, no purchases were made but sales of £500 were made. The profit margin is 20%
(*c*) some goods costing £560 had a net realisable value of £425
(*d*) one inventory sheet has been added up to be £2,499. The total should have been £4,299.

Calculate the correct value of the inventory on 31 December 2013.

31.4X You are valuing inventory at your business as it was at 31 December 2013. The actual date on which the inventory was checked was 7 January 2014. The inventory valuation shows a total of £85,980 at cost as on that date. You are to adjust this figure to ascertain the value of the inventory as at 31 December 2013. The rate of gross profit is 25% on selling price.

On further scrutiny you find:

(*a*) goods received after 1 January and for which invoices bear the date of January amount to £3,987
(*b*) one of the inventory sheets has been added up to give a total of £4,897 instead of £4,798
(*c*) goods selling at £480 have been sent to a customer on 'sale or return' during December – these had not been sold by the customer but they had been omitted from the inventory figures
(*d*) an item of 360 units priced at £1.60 each has been extended on the inventory sheets as £420
(*e*) goods amounting to £98 have been returned to suppliers during the first week of January.

31.5X (*a*) If the closing inventory of a business had been mistakenly overvalued by £5,000 and the error has gone unnoticed, what would be the effect of the error on:
(i) this year's profit?
(ii) next year's profit?

(*b*) A company that sells videos and electrical goods values its closing inventory at £72,050 (cost price) at 30 June 2013. However, it has found that this figure includes the following:
(i) Five flat screen televisions that had cost £300 each have now been replaced by an improved model. In order to sell these obsolete models, it is thought that they will have to be sold at £250 each.
(ii) A hi-fi system that cost £500 has been damaged and it is estimated that repairs will cost £100 before it can be sold.

Calculate the value of the closing inventory after taking into the account the above adjustments.

31.6 On 30 November 2013, the last day of its financial year, The Pine Warehouse made a cash sale of some pine tables and chairs. These had originally cost £1,000 and were sold for £1,500. Although the sale was immediately recorded in the accounts of the business and the cash had been paid at the time of the sale, the customer asked for delivery to take place on 22 December 2013. The tables and chairs were therefore still in the inventory at the financial year end. The proprietor of the business, Pat Hall, has suggested that the tables and chairs should be included in the valuation of the closing inventory at the selling price of £1,500. Pat Hall comments to you: 'This seems to be in accordance with the prudence concept since profits can be recognised once they are realised.'

You are required to write a memo to Pat Hall stating whether or not you agree with the proposed accounting treatment for the tables and chairs. Clearly explain the reasons for your answer.

AAT

31.7X (*a*) You are required to value the closing inventory, after taking into account the necessary adjustments, in the following separate situations:
(i) Closing inventory was valued at cost at £43,795. However, this figure includes two items, cost price £175 each, which have been damaged in storage. It has been estimated that if a total of £35 was spent on repairing them, they could be sold for £140 each.
(ii) The value of the closing inventory had been valued at cost on 31 October 2013 at £107,300. However, this includes some discontinued kitchen cabinets the details of which are as follows:

Cost	£2,300
Normal selling price	£3,500
Net realisable value	£1,800

(*b*) Inventory has always been valued by Electronics World Ltd on a FIFO basis and this includes the closing inventory figure of £198,650 as at 31 May 2013. It has been suggested that the closing inventory figure should now be recalculated on a LIFO basis.

(i) Assuming that the prices of electronic goods have been gradually rising throughout the year, would the change suggested increase profit for the year ended 31 May 2013, decrease profit or would profit remain the same?

(ii) Which accounting concept states that the company should not normally change its basis for valuing inventory unless it has very good reasons for doing so?

AAT

CHAPTER 32

Errors not affecting trial balance agreement

Learning objectives

After you have studied this chapter you should be able to:

- appreciate that accounting transactions are entered twice; once on the debit side and once on the credit side on an account
- understand that there are two types of error, those that affect the agreement of the trial balance and those that do not
- appreciate that errors are usually identified after a period of time has elapsed
- distinguish between the different kinds of errors
- correct errors using the journal.

32.1 Introduction

In Part 1 of this book the system of double entry book-keeping was introduced whereby each transaction recorded in the books of account required two entries:

1 one entry must be on the debit side of an account, and
2 one entry must be on the credit side of an account.

At the end of an accounting period each account is balanced up and a trial balance drawn up to check the arithmetical accuracy of the book-keeping entries. Provided that every item has been entered correctly, the two sides of the trial balance should equal each other, i.e.

Total debit balances = Total credit balances

However, it is inevitable that errors will occur when data is entered into the books of account. There are two main classifications of errors:

1 those that affect the balancing of the trial balance
2 those that do not affect the balancing of the trial balance.

32.2 Errors affecting trial balance agreement

These errors result in the total of the debit columns in the trial balance *not* being the same as the total of the credit column. Suppose we correctly entered cash received of £103 from H Lee, our customer, in the cash book as shown below:

Cash Book (debit side only)

	Cash	Bank	
2013	£	£	
May 1 H Lee	103		

However, when posting this item to H Lee's account we entered the amount received on the credit side as £13, see below:

Sales Ledger
H Lee Account

		2013	£
		May 1 Cash	13

When the trial balance is drawn up the totals will be different by (£103 – £13) = £90. This effect will arise in every case where a debit entry does not equal a credit entry for a transaction. Correction of these types of errors is covered in Chapter 33. In this present chapter errors that do not affect the trial balance agreement will be discussed.

32.3 Errors not affecting trial balance agreement

Although the trial balance totals agree, complete accuracy cannot be guaranteed. Certain errors can still be made which do not affect the balancing of the trial balance, i.e. the trial balance would still appear to balance even though certain errors have occurred. The errors that lead to this situation are listed below:

- **Errors of commission** – where a correct amount is entered, but in the wrong person's account, for example, a sale of goods to J. Black is entered in error, in J. Blake's account.
- **Errors of principle** – where an item is entered in the wrong type of account, for example, a non-current asset such as a motor car or computer equipment is entered in an expense account.
- **Error of original entry** – where an item is entered using an incorrect amount, for example, an invoice received showing goods purchased to the value of £925 is entered in both the purchases account and the supplier's account as £92.50.
- **Error of omission** – where a transaction is completely omitted from the books for example if a purchase invoice is accidentally thrown away and therefore never entered in the books of account.

- **Compensating errors** – where two errors of equal amounts but on opposite sides of the accounts cancel out each other.
- **Complete reversal of entries** – where the correct amounts are entered in the correct accounts but each item is shown on the wrong side of each account.

In sections 32.5 to 32.10, to follow, each of the above errors are illustrated together with the journal entries required to correct the error.

32.4 Correction of errors

Most errors are discovered after a period of time has elapsed. Once identified they need to be corrected properly via the journal and not by crossing out items or tearing a page out of a ledger or even using correcting fluid. If the latter was permitted then there is more risk of fraudulent transactions taking place.

Corrections are recorded in the journal which, as already mentioned in Chapter 24, is a book of original entry. By entering them in the journal a permanent record is made for future reference.

Since many students have difficulty with journal entries you may remember from Chapter 24 that it is often useful to think 'double entry' before entering the details in the journal. In other words, when dealing with 'correction of errors' think where the transaction has been entered in the double entry accounts and then where the entry should have been made; this then gives you the basis for preparing the journal entry. Work through the following sections with this in mind; you may wish to refer to the step-by-step guide in Chapter 24, section 24.2.

32.5 Errors of commission

An **error of commission** arises when a correct amount is entered in the books, but in the wrong person's account.

Example 1: D Long paid us £50 by cheque on 18 May 2013. The transaction is correctly entered in the cash book but was entered by mistake in the account of D Longman. This means that there has been both a debit and credit entry for £50, therefore, the trial balance will still balance. The entry appeared in the personal account of D Longman as shown below, but remember this entry is wrong!

WORKINGS

D Longman Account

		2013	£
		May 18 Bank	50

The error was found on 31 May 2013 and will now have to be corrected and requires two entries:

Accounting entries	Explanation
Debit D Longman's account	To cancel out the error on the credit side of that account
Credit D Long's account	To enter the amount in the correct account

The accounts will now appear as follows:

D Longman Account

2013	£	2013	£
May 31 D Long: Error corrected	50	May 18 Bank	50

D Long Account

2013	£	2013	£
May 1 Balance b/d	50	May 31 Cash entered in error in D Longman's account	50

The journal

The ways by which errors have been corrected should all be entered in the journal. The correction has already been shown in double entry 'workings' above. In fact, the journal entries should be made before completing the double entry accounts for the transaction. For teaching purposes only in this chapter, the journal entries are shown last.

The journal entry will be:

The Journal

	Dr	*Cr*
2013	£	£
May 31 D Longman	50	
D Long		50
Cheque received . . . entered in wrong personal account, now corrected.		

32.6 Errors of principle

An **error of principle** is where a transaction is entered in the wrong type of account. For instance, the purchase of a non-current asset, e.g. shop fittings, motor van, etc. should be debited to the non-current asset account. If in error it is debited to an expense account, then it has been entered in the wrong type of account.

Example 2: The purchase of a motor car for £5,500 by cheque on 14 May 2013 has been debited in error to a motor expenses account. In the cash book it is shown correctly. This means that there has been both a debit of £5,500 and a credit of £5,500, hence the trial balance will balance despite the error.

It will have been entered in error in the expense account Motor Expenses, as:

WORKINGS

Motor Expenses Account

	£		
2013			
May 14 Bank	5,500		

Remember, this entry is wrong!

The error is detected on 31 May 2013 and is corrected by making the following two entries:

Accounting entry	**Explanation**
Debit Motor Car account	To put the amount in the correct account
Credit Motor Expenses account	To cancel the error previously made in the Motor Expenses account

The accounts when corrected are as follows:

Motor Expenses Account

	£		£
2013		2013	
May 14 Bank	5,500	May 31 Motor car error corrected	5,500

Motor Car Account

	£		
2013			
May 31 Bank: entered originally in Motor expenses	5,500		

The journal

The journal entries to correct the error will be shown as:

The Journal

	Dr	*Cr*
	£	£
2013		
May 31 Motor car	5,500	
Motor expenses		5,500
Correction of error whereby purchase of motor car was debited to motor expenses account.		

32.7 Errors of original entry

An **error of original entry** occurs where an original amount is entered incorrectly in the accounting records.

Example 3: Sales of £150 to T Higgins on 13 May 2013 have been entered as both a debit and a credit of £130. The accounts would appear as follows:

WORKINGS

T Higgins Account

2013	£		
May 13 Sales	130		

Sales Account

		2013	£
		May 31 Sales day book (part of total)	130

Remember the entries in the above accounts are wrong! The amount has been entered as £130 instead of £150.

The error is found on 31 May 2013 and the entries to correct the mistake are now shown:

T Higgins Account

2013	£		
May 13 Sales	130		
May 31 Sales: error	20		

Sales Account

		2013	£
		May 31 Sales day book	130
		May 31 T Higgins: error corrected	20

The journal

In the journal the difference of £20, between the correct amount, £150, and the amount entered in error, £130, is shown in the journal entry.

The Journal

	Dr	*Cr*
2013	£	£
May 31 T Higgins	20	
Sales		20
Correction of error. Sales of £150 had been incorrectly entered as £130.		

32.8 Errors of omission

Errors of omission are where transactions are not entered into the books at all.

Example 4: The purchase of goods from T Hope for £250 on 13 May 2013 had been completely omitted from the books. The error was found on 31 May 2013. The entries to correct it will be as follows:

WORKINGS

Purchases Account

	£		
2009			
May 31 T Hope: error corrected	250		

T Hope Account

			£
		2013	
		May 31 Purchases: error corrected	250

Since this entry was completely omitted it only needs to be entered in the accounting records as shown above.

The journal

The journal entries to record this omission are now shown:

The Journal

	Dr	*Cr*
	£	£
2013		
May 31 Purchases	250	
T Hope		250
Correction of error. Purchase omitted from books.		

32.9 Compensating errors

These errors are where they cancel each other out.

Example 5: Let us take a case where incorrect totals had purchases of £7,900 and sales of £9,900. The purchases day book adds up to be £100 too much. In the same period, the sales day book also adds up to be £100 too much.

If these were the only errors in our books, the trial balance totals would equal each other. Both totals would be wrong – they would both be £100 too much – but they would be equal. In this case, the accounts would have appeared as follows:

WORKINGS

Purchases Account

2013	£		
May 31 Purchases	7,900		
Wrong entry!			

Sales Account

		2013	£
		May 31 Sales	9,900
		Wrong entry!	

When corrected, the accounts will appear as:

Purchases Account

2013	£	2013	£
May 31 Purchases	7,900	May 31 The Journal: error corrected	100

Sales Account

2013	£	2013	£
May 31 The Journal: error corrected	100	May 31 Sales	9,900

The journal

Journal entries to correct these two errors will be thus:

The Journal

	Dr	Cr
2013	£	£
May 31 Sales	100	
Purchases		100
Correction of compensating errors. Totals of both purchases and sales day books incorrectly added up to £100 too much.		

32.10 Complete reversal of entries

This error is where the correct amounts are entered in the correct accounts, but each item is shown on the wrong side of each account.

Example 6: We pay a cheque for £200 on 28 May 2013 to D Charles. We enter it as follows in accounts with the letter (A). There has, therefore, been both a debit and a credit of £200.

WORKINGS

Cash Book (A)

	Cash	Bank		Cash	Bank
	£	£		£	£
2013					
May 28 D Charles		200			
			Entry should be on the credit side		

D Charles (A)

			£
		2013	
		May 28 Bank	200
Entry should be on the debit side			

This is incorrect. It should have been debit D Charles Account £200, credit Bank £200. Both items have been entered in the correct accounts, but each is on the wrong side of its account.

The way to correct this is more difficult to understand than with other errors. Let us look at how the items would have appeared if we had done it correctly in the first place. We will show the letter (B) behind the account names.

WORKINGS

Cash Book (B)

	Cash	Bank		Cash	Bank
	£	£		£	£
			2013		
			May 28 D Charles		200

D Charles (B)

	£	
2013		
May 28 Bank	200	
		These entries are correct

We found the error on 31 May and it was corrected as follows:

1 First we have to cancel the error. This would mean entering these amounts:

Dr:	D Charles	£200	
Cr:	Bank		£200

2 Then we have to enter up the transaction:

Dr:	D Charles	£200	
Cr:	Bank		£200

Altogether then, the entries to correct the error are twice the amounts first entered.

When corrected, the accounts appear as follows, marked (C).

WORKINGS

Cash Book (C)

	Cash	Bank		Cash	Bank
	£	£		£	£
2013			2013		
May 8 D Charles		200	May 31 D Charles: error corrected		400
Original wrong entry!			*Entry to correct error*		

D Charles Account (C)

	£		£
2013		2013	
May 28 Bank: error corrected	400	May 28 Bank	200
Entry to correct error		*Original wrong entry!*	

You can see that accounts (C) give the same final answer as accounts (B).

			£	£
(B)	*Dr:*	D Charles	200	
	Cr:	Bank		200
(C)	*Dr:*	D Charles (£400 – £200)	200	
	Cr:	Bank (£400 – £200)		200

The journal

Journal entries. These would be shown as follows:

The Journal

	Dr	*Cr*
	£	£
2013		
May 31 D Charles	400	
Bank		400
Payment of £200 on 28 May 2013 to D Charles incorrectly credited to his account, and debited to bank. Error now corrected.		

32.11 Casting

You will often notice the use of the expression **casting**, which means adding up. **Overcasting** means incorrectly adding up a column of figures to give an answer that is *greater* than it should be. **Undercasting** means incorrectly adding up a column of figures to give an answer that is *less* than it should be.

Chapter summary

- Periodically businesses balance their accounts and prepare a trial balance to check the arithmetical accuracy of the book-keeping entries. However, agreement in the trial balance does not necessarily mean that no errors have occurred.
- There are two types of errors: those that affect the balancing of the trial balance and those that do not.
- Errors that can occur and yet the trial balance still agree are errors of commission, principle, original entry, omission, compensating and complete reversal of entries.
- Once identified the errors are corrected by using the journal. However, it is sometimes easier for students to carry out the double entry first followed by the journal entry. In normal circumstances you would prepare the journal entry first followed by postings to the appropriate ledger accounts.
- The term 'casting' refers to figures that are added up. Overcasting means adding figures up to an amount greater than they should be, whereas, undercasting means adding a column of figures up to less than it should be.

EXERCISES

*Note: Questions with the suffix 'X' shown after the question number do **not** have answers shown at the back of the book. Answers to the other questions are shown in Appendix E.*

32.1 Show the journal entries necessary to correct the following errors:

(*a*) A sale of goods £678 to J Harkness had been entered in J Harker's account.
(*b*) The purchase of a machine on credit from L Pearson for £4,390 had been completely omitted from our books.
(*c*) The purchase of a motor vehicle for £10,800 had been entered in error in the motor expenses account.
(*d*) A sale of £221 to E Fletcher had been entered in the books – both debit and credit – as £212.
(*e*) Commission received £257 had been entered in error in the sales account.

32.2X Show the journal entries needed to correct the following errors:

(*a*) Purchases £699 on credit from K Webb had been entered in H Weld's account.
(*b*) A cheque of £189 paid for advertisements had been entered in the cash column of the cash book instead of in the bank column.
(*c*) Sale of goods £443 on credit to B Maxim had been entered in error in B Gunn's account.
(*d*) Purchase of goods on credit from K Innes £89 entered in two places in error as £99.
(*e*) Cash paid to H Mersey £89 has been entered on the debit side of the cash book and the credit side of H Mersey's account.

32.3 Tom Ainsworth runs a successful stationery business. After preparation of his month end accounts the following errors were revealed:

(*a*) The sale of unwanted fixtures and fittings for £1,000 had been credited to the sales account.
(*b*) Expenditure incurred repairing the motor van £420 had been debited to motor van account.
(*c*) A payment of £800 received from C. Clark had been posted in error to the credit of C. Clarkson's account.
(*d*) Drawings of £500 taken by Mr Ainsworth had been debited to the salaries account.
(*e*) A payment of £240 for office cleaning had been debited to office equipment account in error.

Required:
Write up the journal entries, including narratives, to correct the above errors.

32.4X (*a*) You are employed as accounts clerk for a small photographic company. While tidying your desk at the end of the day you discover two purchase invoices that have not been entered into the books of account as follows:

	Supplier	*Invoice Date*	*Net*	*VAT*	*Total*
			£	£	£
(i)	Logan Logistics	4 June 2013	96.00	19.20	115.20
(ii)	Abbott Supplies	6 June 2013	30.20	6.04	36.24

You are required to prepare journal entries with suitable narratives for each of the two invoices shown above.

(*b*) Your accountant, Ms Smart, asks you to deal with the following issues that have occurred during the last month.

(i) Stationery amounting to £96.00 has been wrongly charged to office equipment.

(ii) A cheque for £134.00 received from J Broad had been correctly entered in the cash book but by mistake credited to the account of J Brooks.

(iii) A standing order payment for insurance of £210.00 has been entered on the debit side of the bank account and the credit side of the insurance account.

(iv) Express Photos who owe the company £117.40 have been declared bankrupt. Please write the debt off as a bad debt.

You are required to prepare journal entries, with suitable narratives, to record the necessary amendments. Date your entries 30 June.

32.5X Joe Jogia has recently opened a retail business trading in ladies' and children's clothing. His accountant has suggested that his book-keeper prepare a trial balance at the end of each quarter to ensure there are no errors in the books of account. Joe is not sure what a trial balance is or what purpose it serves.

(*a*) Define a trial balance.
(*b*) Describe two advantages of using a trial balance.
(*c*) Explain the limitations of a trial balance.
(*d*) Illustrate one example where the limitations of a trial balance may occur.

32.6 The following errors have been found in the accounting records of Shaw Supplies at the year end 31 March 2012:

(*a*) A receipt of £400 from Paul Palmer, a customer, had been entered in the cash book correctly but was posted to the account of Brian Palmer in error.

(*b*) The purchase of a new computer costing £3,000 had been posted in error to the stationery account.

(*c*) A purchase invoice from Belfields and Machin Ltd amounting to £683 had accidentally been thrown away and not entered in the accounting records. The error was only discovered when Belfields rang asking for payment of the outstanding invoice.

(*d*) A sales invoice for goods sold on credit to Kirkham & Co for £760 had been entered in both the sales account and the personal account of Kirkham & Co as £670.

Required:
Prepare journal entries to correct the errors shown above with suitable narratives. (Ignore VAT.)

32.7X D Singh, a retail trader, has a lot still to learn about accounting but has managed to draw up the following trial balance from his business records.

	£	£
Inventory 1 April 2012		21,400
Inventory 31 March 2013	15,600	
Discounts allowed		620
Discounts received	900	
Purchases	188,000	
Purchase returns	2,800	
Sales		264,200
Sales returns	2,200	
Buildings at cost	140,000	
Provision for depreciation of buildings	7,000	
Motor vehicles at cost	30,000	
Provision for depreciation of motor vehicles	9,000	
Capital: D Singh		169,200
Bank	14,200	
Accounts receivable		22,600
Allowance for doubtful debts	1,920	
Accounts payable	15,200	
General expenses	33,200	
Drawings	18,000	
	478,020	478,020

Required:

(*a*) Prepare a corrected trial balance as at 31 March 2013.

(*b*) After the preparation of the corrected trial balance, but before drawing up the financial statements, the following items were discovered:

(i) No entry had been made in the books regarding a credit note for £148 received from FH Ltd in respect of faulty goods returned by Mr Singh.

(ii) No entry has been made in the books in respect of £333 goods taken for own use.

(iii) A receipt from a customer, T Hall, of £168 has been credited in error to T Hallworth's account.

(iv) Free samples sent to a customer, L Shah, have been charged to him as though they were sales for £88.

(v) A discount allowed to K Young of £64 was found to be incorrect. It should have been £94.

Show the journal entries needed for items (i) to (v) above.

CHAPTER 33

Suspense accounts and errors

Learning objectives

After you have studied this chapter you should be able to:

- understand the reason for using a suspense account
- create a suspense account in order to balance the trial balance
- correct errors using a suspense account
- recalculate profits after errors have been corrected
- appreciate the limitations of trial balances.

33.1 Introduction

In the previous chapter errors that did not affect the balancing of the trial balance were discussed. However, many errors may occur that do affect the balancing of the trial balance, for example:

- incorrect additions in any account
- making an entry on only one side of the accounts – for example, a debit but no credit, or a credit but no debit
- entering a different amount on the debit side from the amount on the credit side.

33.2 Suspense accounts

If a trial balance does not balance it is important that errors are located and corrected as soon as possible. When they cannot be found, then the trial balance totals should be made to agree with each other by inserting the amount of the difference between the two sides in a **suspense account**. This occurs in Exhibit 33.1 where there is a difference of £40.

Exhibit 33.1

Trial Balance as at 31 December 2013

	Dr	Cr
	£	£
Totals after all the accounts have been listed	100,000	99,960
Suspense account		40
	100,000	100,000

To make the two totals the same, a figure of £40 for the suspense account has been shown on the credit side. A suspense account is opened and the £40 difference is also shown there on the credit side.

Suspense Account

		£
	2013	
	Dec 31 Difference per trial balance	40

33.3 Suspense account and the statement of financial position

If the errors are not found before the financial statements are prepared, the suspense account balance will be included in the statement of financial position. Where the balance is a credit balance, it should be included under current liabilities on the statement of financial position. When the balance is a debit balance, it should be shown under current assets on the statement of financial position. Large errors should always be found before the financial statements are drawn up.

33.4 Correction of errors

When errors are found, they must be corrected using double entry. Each correction must initially be entered in the journal giving a description of the particular error and then posted in the relevant accounts.

However, as mentioned in the previous chapters on the journal, you may find it easier to carry out the entries in the double entry accounts first and then prepare the journal entry, as shown below:

One error only

We will look at two examples:

Example 1: Assume that the error of £40 as shown in Exhibit 33.1 is found in the following year on 31 March 2014, the error being that the sales account was undercast by £40. The action taken to correct this is:

- Debit the suspense account to close it: £40.
- Credit the sales account to show item where it should have been: £40.

The accounts now appear as Exhibit 33.2.

Exhibit 33.2

Suspense Account

2014	£	2013	£
		Dec 31 Difference per	
Mar 31 Sales	40	trial balance	40

Sales Account

		2014	£
		Mar 31 Suspense	40

This can be shown in journal form as follows:

The Journal

	Dr	Cr
2014	£	£
Mar 31 Suspense	40	
Sales		40
Correction of undercasting of sales by £40 in last year's accounts.		

Example 2: The trial balance on 31 December 2013 shows a difference of £168. It was a shortage on the debit side. A suspense account is opened and the difference of £168 is entered on the debit side.

On 31 May 2014 the error is found. We had made a payment of £168 to D Miguel to close his account. It was correctly entered in the cash book, but it was not entered in Miguel's account.

To correct the error, the account of D Miguel is debited with £168, as it should have been in 2013, and the suspense account is credited with £168 so that the account can be closed. The accounts and journal entry now appear as in Exhibit 33.3.

Exhibit 33.3

D Miguel Account

2014	£	2014	£
May 31 Bank	168	Jan 1 Balance b/d	168

Suspense Account

2013	£	2014	£
Dec 31 Difference			
per trial balance	168	May 31 D Miguel	168

The Journal	Dr	Cr
	£	£
2014		
May 31 D Miguel	168	
Suspense		168
Correction of non-entry of payment last year in D Miguel's account.		

More than one error

We can now look at an example where the suspense account difference has been caused by more than one error.

Example 3: A trial balance at 31 December 2013 shows a difference of £77, being a shortage on the debit side. A suspense account is opened, and the difference of £77 is entered on the debit side of the account.

On 28 February 2014 all the errors from the previous year were found:

(*a*) A cheque of £150 paid to L Kent had been correctly entered in the cash book, but had not been entered in Kent's account.
(*b*) The purchases account has been undercast by £20.
(*c*) A cheque of £93 received from K Sand has been correctly entered in the cash book but has not been entered in Sand's account.

These three errors have resulted in a net error of £77, shown by a debit of £77 on the debit side of the suspense account.

These are corrected by:

- making correcting entries in the accounts for (*a*), (*b*) and (*c*)
- recording the double entry for these items in the suspense account.

L Kent Account

	£		
2014			
Feb 28 Suspense (*a*)	150		

Purchases Account

	£		
2014			
Feb 28 Suspense (*b*)	20		

K Sand Account

			£
		2014	
		Feb 28 Suspense (*c*)	93

Suspense Account

	£		£
2014		2014	
Jan 1 Balance b/d	77	Feb 28 L Kent (*a*)	150
Feb 28 K Sand (*c*)	93	Feb 28 Purchases (*b*)	20
	170		170

The Journal	Dr	Cr
2014	£	£
Feb 28 L Kent	150	
Suspense		150
Cheque paid omitted from Kent's account		
Feb 28 Purchases	20	
Suspense		20
Undercasting of purchases by £20 in last year's accounts		
Feb 28 Suspense	93	
K Sand		93
Cheque received omitted from Sand's account		

Only those errors that make the trial balance totals different from each other have to be corrected via the suspense account.

33.5 The effect of errors on profits

Some of the errors will have meant that the calculation of original profits will be wrong. Other errors will have no effect upon profits. We will use Exhibit 33.4 to illustrate the different kinds of errors. Exhibit 33.4 shows a set of financial statement in which errors have been made.

Exhibit 33.4

S Brough
Income Statement for the year ended 31 December 2013

		£	£
Sales	(A)		165,000
Less Cost of goods sold			
Opening inventory		10,000	
Purchases	(B)	122,000	
		132,000	
Less Closing inventory		14,000	
			118,000
Gross profit			47,000
Less Expenses			
Rent	(C)	7,000	
Insurance	(D)	1,400	
Lighting		1,600	
Depreciation		5,000	
			15,000
Net profit			32,000

S Brough
Statement of Financial Position as at 31 December 2013

		£	£	£
Non-current assets		*Cost*	*Depreciation*	
Equipment		44,000	16,000	28,000
Current assets				
Inventory		14,000		
Accounts receivable	(E)	13,000		
Cash at bank		6,800		
Suspense	(G)	200	34,000	
Current liabilities				
Accounts payable	(F)	12,000	12,000	
Net current assets				22,000
Net assets				50,000
Financed by				
Capital Account				
Balance as at 1 January 2013				36,000
Add Net profit for the year				32,000
				68,000
Less Drawings				(18,000)
				50,000

Errors that *do not* affect profit calculations

If an error affects items only in the statement of financial position, then the original calculated profit will not need altering. The example below shows this:

Example 4: Assume that in Exhibit 33.4 the £200 debit balance on the suspense account shown in the statement of financial position was due to the following error:

On 1 November 2013, we paid £200 to a supplier T Monk and it was correctly entered in the cash book, but it was not entered anywhere else. The error was found on 1 June 2014.

We can see that when this error is corrected, only two items in the financial statements will have to be altered. These are (F) accounts payable, which will have to be reduced by £200, and (G) suspense account, which will now be cancelled and not shown in the statement of financial position. Once the errors have been corrected by the journal entries, see below, the statement will be correct. This means that in the income statement the profit for 2013 will not be affected.

The double entry records needed are as follows:

T Monk Account

2014	£	2014	£
June 1 Suspense (Correction)	200	Jan 1 Balance b/d	200

Suspense Account

2014	£	2014	£
Jan 1 Balance b/d (Difference in last year's trial balance)	200	June 1 T Monk	200

The journal entries to correct it will be thus:

The Journal	Dr	Cr
2014	£	£
June 1 T Monk	200	
Suspense		200
Payment to T Monk on 1 November 2013 not entered in his account. Correction now made.		

Errors that *do* affect profit calculations

If the error is in one of the numbers labelled (A), (B), (C) or (D) shown in the income statement in Exhibit 33.4, then the original profit will need altering. Example 5 shows this:

Example 5: Assume that in Exhibit 33.4 the £200 debit balance was because the rent account (C) was added up incorrectly: it should be shown as £7,200 instead of £7,000. The error was found on 1 June 2014. The journal entries to correct it are:

The Journal	Dr	Cr
2014	£	£
June 1 Rent	200	
Suspense		200
Correction of rent undercast last year.		

Rent last year should have been increased by £200. This would have reduced net profit by £200. A statement of corrected profit for the year is now shown.

S Brough
Statement of Corrected Net Profit for the year ended 31 December 2013

	£
Net profit per the accounts	32,000
Less Rent understated	200
Corrected net profit for the year	31,800

Where there have been several errors

Example 6: Let us assume that in Exhibit 33.4 there had been four errors found in the ledger accounts of S Brough on 31 March 2014, their correction can now be seen. Assume that the net difference had also been £200, with the four errors as:

		£
(A)	Sales overcast by	210
(B)*	A credit purchase from C Hall of £59 was entered in the books, debit and credit entries, as	95
(D)	Insurance undercast by	40
(E)	Cash received from a customer, L Young entered in the cash book only	50

Note*: Error (B) is known as an **error of transposition, the figures have been transposed.

Error (A) affected the profits: both gross and net profit were shown £210 too much because of this error. It also affected the suspense account (G).

Error (B) showed purchases too high by (£95 – £59) = £36. This means that gross and net profits were shown £36 too little. The other item affected is (F) Accounts payable, which is shown as being £36 too much. This error does not affect (G) suspense account.

Error (D) needs insurance increasing by £40. This will reduce the net profit by £40. It also affects the suspense account (G).

Error (E) does not affect the profits at all. It affects only items in the statement of financial position, namely (E) accounts receivable and (G) suspense.

The entries in the ledger accounts are as follows:

General Ledger **Sales Account**

		£			£
2014					
Mar 31 Suspense (Correction)	(A)	210			

General Ledger **Purchases Account**

		£			£
			2014		
			Mar 31 C Hall (Correction)	(B)	36

Purchases Ledger **C Hall Account**

		£			£
2014					
Mar 31 Purchases (Correction)	(B)	36			

General Ledger **Insurance Account**

		£			£
2014					
Mar 31 Suspense (Correction)	(D)	40			

Sales Ledger **L Young Account**

		£			£
			2014		
			Mar 31 Suspense (Correction)	(E)	50

The entries in the suspense account and the journal entries will be as follows:

General Ledger **Suspense Account**

		£			£
2014			2014		
Jan 1 Balance b/d		200	Mar 31 Sales	(A)	210
Mar 31 L Young	(E)	50	" 31 Insurance	(D)	40
		250			250

The Journal		Dr	Cr
2014		£	£
(A) Mar 31	Sales	210	
	Suspense		210
	Sales overcast of £70 in 2013.		
(B) Mar 31	C Hall	36	
	Purchases*		36
	Credit purchase of £59 entered both as debit and credit as £95 in 2013.		
(D) Mar 31	Insurance	40	
	Suspense		40
	Insurance expense undercast by £40 in 2013.		
(E) Mar 31	Suspense	50	
	L Young		50
	Cash received omitted from L Young's account in 2013.		

Note: *In (B), the correction of the understatement of purchases does not pass through the suspense account.

Now we can calculate the corrected net profit for the year 2013. Only items (A), (B) and (D) affect figures in the income statement. These are the only adjustments to be made to profit.

S Brough
Statement of Corrected Net Profit for the year ended 31 December 2013

		£	£
Net profit per the accounts			32,000
Add Purchases overstated	(B)		36
			32,036
Less Sales overcast	(A)	210	
Insurance undercast	(D)	40	250
Corrected net profit for the year			31,786

33.6 Limitations of trial balances

In this and the previous chapter, you have seen various kinds of errors. Those in Chapter 32 were not revealed by trial balance totals being unequal. This shows a serious limitation in depending completely on the trial balance as an absolute check on the accuracy of the entries in the books of account. To refresh your memory, the kinds of *errors not disclosed by a trial balance* are:

- errors of commission
- errors of principle
- errors of original entry
- errors of omission

- compensating errors
- complete reversal of entries.

Even when the balances in a trial balance agree, there can be very large errors of various kinds, which may mean that profits have been wrongly calculated and that the statement of financial position is incorrect. This current chapter has demonstrated these kinds of errors, where they have resulted in a difference being put into a suspense account until the error(s) have been found.

A very small amount in a suspense account could hide very large errors. For instance, a £50 credit in a suspense account could eventually be found to be either of the following:

- Sales overcast £10,000, accounts receivable total overcast £10,050. If the errors are not found, then both the gross and net profits will be overstated by £10,000 and the figure of accounts receivable in the statement of financial position overstated by £10,050.
- Rent expense undercast by £2,000, total of accounts payable undercast by £1,950. In this case the net profit will be shown at £2,000 more than it should be, while accounts payable in the statement of financial position will be understated by £1,950.

This shows that there is always a possibility of serious errors occurring without it being obvious at first sight.

Every attempt should be made to find errors. Opening a suspense account should be done only if all other efforts have failed.

33.7 Suspense accounts: examinations and business

Examinations

Unless it is part of a question, *do not* make your statement of financial position totals agree by using a suspense account. The same applies to trial balances. Examiners are very likely to penalise you for including a suspense account when it should not be required.

Business

When preparing financial statements for a business every effort should be made to ensure that the trial balance and statement of financial position balance. However, if all else fails it may be necessary to open a suspense account and hopefully the error(s) may subsequently be located and posted to the suspense account, as shown in this chapter, and the balance eliminated.

Chapter summary

- If the totals in the trial balance do not agree it may be necessary to open a suspense account and enter the difference into the account until the error(s) can be located.
- In the unlikely event that the error(s) are not found when the statement of financial position is prepared it may be necessary to include the suspense account. If the

suspense account shows a credit balance then it should be entered under the current liabilities whereas a debit balance would be shown under current assets.

- Any errors found should be corrected using a journal and subsequently posted to the appropriate double entry accounts. If the error affects the suspense account then the posting should be made to that account.
- Some errors may affect the gross profit and net profit calculations and adjustments have to be made to these profit figures.
- Other errors that do not affect the profit calculations may affect a figure in the statement of financial position. If this is the case then the figure in the statement of financial position will require amending.
- While the balancing of the trial balance is seen to ensure that the book-keeping entries have been carried out correctly the trial balance does have limitations in that certain errors occur which are not revealed by the trial balance agreement.

EXERCISES

*Note: Questions with the suffix 'X' shown after the question number do **not** have answers shown at the back of the book. Answers to the other questions are shown in Appendix E.*

33.1 On 31 March 2013 the following items are to be corrected via the journal. Show the corrections. Narratives are not required.

(*a*) T Thomas, a customer, had paid us a cheque for £900 to settle his debt. The cheque has now been returned to us marked 'Dishonoured'.
(*b*) We had allowed C Charles, a customer, a cash discount of £35. Because of a dispute with her, we have now disallowed the cash discount.
(*c*) Office equipment bought for £6,000 has been debited to motor vehicles account.
(*d*) The copy sales invoice of sales to J Graham £715 was lost, and therefore was completely omitted from our books.
(*e*) Cash drawings of £210 have been correctly entered in the cash book, but have been credited to the wages account.

33.2 Jaspa West wishes to record the following in his books of account:

1 A cash receipt of £55 for rent has been recorded as a debit entry in the rent received account. The cash book entry had been correctly made. This matter should be corrected.
2 A debt of £150 owing by Mary Beagle will not be received and is to be written off as a bad debt.
3 The sales account has been overcast by £350. Therefore, this needs to be corrected.
4 A motor vehicle, costing £3,500, has been purchased on credit from C Williams.
5 An allowance for doubtful debts of £225 is to be created.

Required:
(*a*) Write up the journal entries to record the above transactions.
(*b*) Give two examples of book-keeping errors which would not be revealed by the trial balance.

City & Guilds Pitman qualifications

33.3X John Laundau has just extracted a trial balance at 30 August, the end of his financial year. The debit side was greater than the credit side by £520 and a suspense account was opened for that amount. The auditors subsequently found the following errors:

1 £200 cash received from the sale of an old computer has been credited to the rent received account.
2 A payment of £100 for water entered in the cash book had not been entered in the water account.

3 The sales account had been undercast by £260.
4 A private purchase of a £1,000 computer had been included in the computer account.
5 Sale of goods to Lynne Beagle had been correctly entered in the sales account as £2,150 but had been entered in the personal account as £2,510.
6 No allowance against doubtful debts had been created. This should have been 3% of the end of year total debtors of £7,000.

Required:

(*a*) Make appropriate journal entries, with narrative, to rectify the errors.
(*b*) Show how the suspense account would be cleared by the appropriate entries.

City & Guilds Pitman qualifications

33.4 H Logan extracted a trial balance as at 31 December 2013. He was unable to balance it, but as he urgently needed his accounts for tax purposes, he opened a suspense account and entered £705 debit balance in it.

The following year he found the errors now listed:

(*a*) The sales returns day book had been undercast by £100.
(*b*) Drawings of £80 had been debited to wages account.
(*c*) Carriage inwards £75 had been debited to carriage outwards.
(*d*) A payment of bank charges £270 had not been posted to the expense account.
(*e*) A sale of goods £385 to K Abbott on 30 December 2013 had not been entered at all.
(*f*) Discounts allowed of £218 had been credited to the discounts allowed account.
(*g*) A rent rebate of £200 had been entered in the cash book but not posted elsewhere.
(*h*) The purchases day book had carried forward a figure of £24,798 when it should have been £24,897.

Required:

1 Show the journal entries needed to correct the errors. Narratives are not required.
2 Show the suspense account balanced off.
3 If the original incorrect gross profit was shown as £129,487 and the original net profit was shown as £77,220 calculate the corrected figures for gross and net profits after the above items have been corrected.

33.5 The following trial balance was extracted by K Woodburn from her books as at 30 June 2012. She is unable to get the totals to agree.

Trial Balance as at 30 June 2012

	Dr £	*Cr* £
Sales		87,050
Purchases	62,400	
Discounts allowed and received	305	410
Salaries and wages	3,168	
General expenses	595	
Fixtures	10,000	
Inventory 1 July 2011	12,490	
Accounts receivable and accounts payable	8,120	5,045
Bank	6,790	
Drawings	4,520	
Capital		17,017
Suspense	1,134	
	109,522	109,522

The following errors are found:

(i) Sales day book overcast by £350.
(ii) Discounts allowed undercast by £100.
(iii) Fixtures, bought for £850, have been entered in the cash book but not in the fixtures account.
(iv) Credit purchases of £166 was entered in the purchases day book only, but not in the supplier's account.
(v) Cheque payment to a supplier of £490 had been debited to the drawings account in error.

You are required to:
(*a*) draw up the suspense account to record the corrections
(*b*) redraft the trial balance after all corrections have been made.

33.6X T Sawyer extracted the following trial balance from his books. He could not get the totals to agree with each other.

Trial Balance as at 31 December 2013

	Dr	*Cr*
	£	£
Capital		25,621
Drawings	13,690	
Sales		94,630
Purchases	60,375	
Sales and purchases returns	1,210	1,109
Wages and salaries	14,371	
Sundry expenses	598	
Inventory 1 January 2013	8,792	
Accounts receivable and payable	11,370	4,290
Loan from J Chandler		5,000
Equipment	16,000	
Bank	5,790	
Suspense		1,546
	132,196	132,196

The following errors are discovered:

(i) Purchases day book was overcast by £258.
(ii) A repayment of loan £2,000 was debited in error to the wages account.
(iii) A cheque payment for equipment £1,500 has been entered in the equipment account but not in the cash book.
(iv) Purchases returns £168 have been entered in the purchases returns day book but not in the supplier's account.
(v) Sundry expenses £44 have been entered in the cash book but not in the sundry expenses account.

You are required to:
(*a*) draw up the suspense account, showing corrections
(*b*) redraft the trial balance after all corrections have been made.

33.7 The trial balance of Philip Hogan as at 31 December 2013 does not balance. The difference of £5,400 has been credited to a suspense account. The following errors were subsequently discovered:

(*a*) The sales day book is undercast by £3,000.
(*b*) Purchases received from Dawson & Co, amounting to £1,147, had been received on 31 December 2013, and included in the closing inventory at that date. Unfortunately, the invoice had not been entered in the purchases day book.
(*c*) Motor repairs of £585 have been charged to the motor vehicles account.
(*d*) Credit sales of £675 made to J Greenway have been debited to the account of J Green.
(*e*) A payment of £425 in respect of electricity has been debited to the electricity account as £575.
(*f*) A cheque for £2,250 received from Teape Ltd, a customer, has been correctly entered in the cash book but no entry has been made in Teape's account.

Required:
(i) Show the journal entries, including narratives, to correct the above errors
(ii) Write up the suspense account after correction of the above errors.

33.8X A trial balance does not balance and a suspense account has been opened with a credit balance of £510. The following errors are then discovered.

(i) Cash purchases of £450 were recorded in both the cash book and ledger as £540.
(ii) The total of the motor expenses account was undercast by £70.
(iii) Cash received from a customer £150 is entered in the cash book only.
(iv) The sales account was undercast by £350.
(v) The insurance account was overcast by £80.

Required:
(*a*) Show the journal entries to correct the errors.
(*b*) Write up the suspense account showing correction of the errors.
(*c*) The net profit figure originally calculated for the year ended 31 December 2013 was £12,250. Calculate the corrected net profit figure.

NEAB (AQA) (GCSE)

PART 5

Financial statements of other organisations

This part is concerned with the accounting procedures that have to be followed with different forms of organisations. It also includes a chapter outlining the basic ratios that are used for analysis and interpretation of accounts.

CHAPTER 34

Single entry and incomplete records

Learning objectives

After you have studied this chapter you should be able to:

- appreciate why it is not always appropriate to use double entry for recording transactions
- understand the difference between mark-up and margin
- use accounting ratios to calculate missing figures in financial statements
- appreciate that many businesses use single entry for recording transactions
- ascertain the profit figure from incomplete records
- ascertain sales and purchases from incomplete records
- prepare financial statements from incomplete records.

34.1 Introduction

There are many types of businesses that are run by a person on their own such as the shopkeeper, market stall holder, window cleaner, and so on. In such cases it may be impractical for them to record their finances by the use of a full double entry system of book-keeping. In fact many of them would be unable to write up double entry records, it is more likely that they would enter details of a transaction once only thereby using a **single entry** system. Also many would fail to record every transaction resulting in **incomplete accounting records**.

Since accounting is carried out to assist management in the successful running of a business it is important to remember that the task should not be too onerous for the owner of the business. Many small businesses, like small retail shops, have all the information they require just by keeping a cash book and a record of their accounts receivable and accounts payable, which in most cases is not recorded using double entry.

Where businesses use a single entry system of recording their financial transactions and indeed where not every transaction is recorded, resulting in incomplete accounting records, then the accountant may have to use ratios to help ascertain missing information.

The ratios, mark-up and margin, can be used to calculate missing figures from incomplete records and to show the relationship between profit and cost price and profit and selling price respectively.

34.2 Mark-up and margin

The purchase cost, gross profit and selling price of goods or services may be shown as:

Cost price + Gross profit = Selling price

The gross profit when shown as a fraction or percentage of the **cost price** is known as the **mark-up**. The gross profit when shown as a fraction or percentage of the **selling price** is known as the **margin**.

The mark-up and margins can now be calculated using this example:

$$\text{Cost price} + \text{Gross profit} = \text{Selling price}$$
$$£4 \quad + \quad £1 \quad = \quad £5$$

Mark-up $= \dfrac{\text{Gross profit}}{\text{Cost price}}$ as a fraction, or if required as a percentage, multiply by 100:

$$£\frac{1}{4} = \frac{1}{4}, \text{ or } \frac{1}{4} \times 100 = 25\%$$

Margin $= \dfrac{\text{Gross profit}}{\text{Selling price}}$ as a fraction, or if required as a percentage, multiply by 100:

$$£\frac{1}{5} = \frac{1}{5}, \text{ or } \frac{1}{5} \times 100 = 20\%$$

Author's hint

Students often confuse the relationship between the selling price and profit (margin) and cost price and profit (mark-up). This can easily be remembered using the mnemonic 'MRS MUC', as shown in Exhibit 34.1.

Exhibit 34.1

34.3 Calculating missing figures

We can now use the ratios given in section 34.2 to complete trading accounts where some of the figures are missing. For ease of illustrating this fact, all examples in this chapter:

- assume that all the goods in a business have the same rate of mark-up
- ignore wastages and theft of goods.

Example 1: The following figures apply for the year 2013:

	£
Inventory 1.1.2013	400
Inventory 31.12.2013	600
Purchases	5,200

A uniform rate of mark-up of 20% is applied.

Required: Find the gross profit and the sales figure.

First of all you need to prepare the trading account section of the income statement. Write out the trading account entering in all the figures that you know. In our example you will see that we have entered in the inventory and purchases figures. If a figure is not known, i.e. in our case the figure for sales, then initially put in a ? mark preferably in pencil. This is illustrated below:

The Trading Account section of the Income Statement for the year ended 31 December 2013

	£	£
Sales		?
Less Cost of goods sold		
Inventory 1.1.2013	400	
Add Purchases	5,200	
	5,600	
Less Inventory 31.12.2013	600	
		5,000
Gross profit		?

Then work out your answer as follows:

Answer:

It is known that:	Cost of goods sold + Gross profit = Sales
and you know that you can use mark-up to find profit, because	Cost of goods sold + % mark-up = Sales
	£5,000 + 20% = Sales
So sales =	£5,000 + £1,000 = £6,000

The trading account can now be completed as shown below:

The Trading Account section of the Income Statement for the year ended 31 December 2013

	£	£
Sales		6,000
Less Cost of goods sold		
Inventory 1.1.2013	400	
Add Purchases	5,200	
	5,600	
Less Inventory 31.12.2013	600	5,000
Gross profit		1,000

Example 2: Another business has the following figures for 2012:

	£
Inventory 1.1.2012	500
Inventory 31.12.2012	800
Sales	6,400

A uniform rate of margin of 25% is in use.

Required: Find the gross profit and the figure of purchases.

The Trading Account section of the Income Statement
for the year ended 31 December 2012

	£	£
Sales		6,400
Less Cost of goods sold		
Inventory 1.1.2012	500	
Add Purchases	?	
	?	
Less Inventory 31.12.2012	800	?
Gross profit		?

Answer:

	Cost of goods sold + Gross profit	= Sales
Rearranging items:	Sales – Gross profit	= Cost of goods sold
	Sales – 25% Margin	= Cost of goods sold
	£6,400 – £1,600 (25% of £6,400)	= £4,800

Now the following figures are known:

		£	£
Cost of goods sold:			
Inventory 1.1.2012		500	
Add Purchases	(A)	?	
	(B)	?	
Less Inventory 31.12.2012		800	
			4,800

The two missing figures are found by normal arithmetical deduction:

(B) *less* £800	= £4,800
Therefore (B)	= £5,600

So that:

£500 opening inventory + (A)	= £5,600
Therefore (A)	= £5,100

The completed trading account section of the income statement can now be shown:

The Trading Account section of the Income Statement for the year ended 31 December 2012

	£	£
Sales		6,400
Less Cost of goods sold		
Inventory 1.1.2012	500	
Add Purchases	5,100	
	5,600	
Less Inventory 31.12.2012	800	4,800
Gross profit		1,600

This technique is found very useful by retail stores when estimating the amount to be bought if a certain sales target is to be achieved. Alternatively, inventory levels or sales figures can be estimated if information is given on purchases and the opening inventory figures.

34.4 The relationship between mark-up and margin

As both of these figures refer to the same profit but are expressed as a fraction or a percentage of different figures, there is a relationship between them. If one is known as a fraction, the other can soon be found.

If the mark-up is known, in order to find the margin you need to take the same numerator to be the numerator of the margin. Then, for the denominator of the margin, take the total of the mark-up's denominator *plus* the numerator. An example can now be shown:

Mark-up	Margin
$\frac{1}{4}$	$\frac{1}{4+1} = \frac{1}{5}$
$\frac{2}{11}$	$\frac{2}{11+2} = \frac{2}{13}$

If the margin is known, to find the mark-up take the same numerator to be the numerator of the mark-up. Then, for the denominator of the mark-up, take the figure of the margin's denominator *less* the numerator:

Margin	Mark-up
$\frac{1}{6}$	$\frac{1}{6-1} = \frac{1}{5}$
$\frac{3}{13}$	$\frac{3}{13-3} = \frac{3}{10}$

34.5 Preparing financial statement from incomplete records

When a business has not kept full accounting records it is still necessary to prepare financial statements at the end of the business's financial year. The method used to prepare the accounts in these circumstances is to compare the capital at the *beginning* and *end* of the accounting period.

The only way that capital can be increased is by the owner putting in additional funds or by making profits. Consider a business where capital at the end of 2011 is £20,000. During 2012 there had been no drawings or extra cash brought in by the owner. At the end of 2012 the capital was £30,000. The profits of the business for the year can be found as follows:

	This year's capital		Last year's capital	
Net profit =	£30,000	−	£20,000	= £10,000

If on the other hand the drawings had been £7,000, the profits must have been £17,000, calculated thus:

Last year's capital	+	Profits	−	Drawings	=	This year's capital
£20,000	+	?	−	£7,000	=	£30,000

We can see that £17,000 profits was the figure needed to complete the formula, filling in the missing figure by normal arithmetical deduction:

$$£20{,}000 + £17{,}000 - £7{,}000 = £30{,}000$$

Exhibit 34.2 shows the calculation of profit where insufficient information is available to draft an income statement. The only information available is about the assets and liabilities.

Exhibit 34.2

H Taylor has not kept proper book-keeping records, but he has kept notes in diary form of the transactions of his business. He is able to give you details of his assets and liabilities as at 31 December 2012 and at 31 December 2013 as follows:

			£
At 31 December 2012	*Assets:*	Motor van	10,000
		Fixtures	7,000
		Inventory	8,500
		Accounts receivable	9,500
		Bank	11,100
		Cash	100
	Liabilities:	Accounts payable	8,000
		Loan from J Ogden	6,000
At 31 December 2013	*Assets:*	Motor van (after depreciation)	8,000
		Fixtures (after depreciation)	6,300
		Inventory	9,900
		Accounts receivable	11,240
		Bank	11,700
		Cash	200
	Liabilities:	Accounts payable	8,700
		Loan from J Ogden	4,000
	Drawings were £9,000		

First of all a **statement of affairs** is drawn up as at 31 December 2012 which is just a statement of financial position. The capital is the difference between the assets and liabilities.

H Taylor
Statement of Affairs as at 31 December 2012

	£	£
Non-current assets		
Motor van		10,000
Fixtures		7,000
		17,000
Current assets		
Inventory	8,500	
Accounts receivable	9,500	
Bank	11,100	
Cash	100	
	29,200	
Less Current liabilities		
Accounts payable	8,000	
Net current assets		21,200
		38,200
Less Long-term liability		
Loan from J Ogden		6,000
		32,200
Financed by		
Capital (difference)		32,200

A second statement of affairs is now drafted up as at the end of 2013. The formula of opening capital + profit – drawings = closing capital is then used to deduce the figure of profit.

H Taylor
Statement of Affairs as at 31 December 2013

	£		£
Non-current assets			
Motor van			8,000
Fixtures			6,300
			14,300
Current assets			
Inventory	9,900		
Accounts receivable	11,240		
Bank	11,700		
Cash	200		
	33,040		
Less Current liabilities			
Accounts payable	8,700		
Net current assets			24,340
			38,640
Less Long-term liability			
Loan from J Ogden			4,000
			*34,640
Financed by			
Capital balance at 1.1.2013			32,200
Add Net profit		(C)	?
		(B)	?
Less Drawings			9,000
		(A)	?

Deduction of net profit:

Opening capital + net profit – drawings = closing capital. Find the missing figures (A), (B) and (C) by deduction:

(A) the figure needed is £34,640, which is the total shown at the top half of the statement marked *.
(B) is therefore £34,640 + £9,000 = £43,640;
(C) is therefore £43,640 – £32,200 = £11,440.

To check:

		£
Capital		32,200
Add Net profit	(C)	11,440
	(B)	43,640
Less Drawings		9,000
	(A)	34,640

Obviously, this method of calculating profit is very unsatisfactory as it is much more informative when an income statement can be drawn up. Therefore, whenever possible, the 'comparison of capital' method of ascertaining profit should be avoided and financial statements drawn up from the available records.

34.6 Step-by-step guide to incomplete records

In preparing financial statements from a single entry set of records a formal approach should be followed as shown below.

Note: You may find it useful to use this guide when studying the example shown below in the accounts of M Cole.

Step 1

Prepare a statement of affairs on the closing day of the *last* accounting period to ascertain the initial *opening capital*. Remember to include the cash and bank balances. (In our example the opening capital is £43,000.)

Step 2

Either draw up and balance a cash and bank summary or, if a cash and bank summary is shown, it may only be necessary to balance off the account. Remember to include the *final cash and bank balances in the statement of financial position*. (In our example the balances at 31 December 2013 are cash £100 and bank £30,500.)

Step 3

Calculate the figures for purchases and sales to be shown in the trading account section of the income statement. Remember that there are *two ways* that this may be achieved: either as a calculation or by using double entry 'T' accounts. (In our example the purchases are £74,500 and the sales £102,200.)

Step 4

Calculate the figures for expenses. If there are no accruals or prepayments either at the beginning or end of the accounting period, the expenses paid will equal the expenses used up during the period. If, however, there *are* accruals and prepayments, then it will be necessary to make adjustments, again, this may be carried out as a calculation or by using 'T' accounts. (In our example there is an 'accrual for rent', therefore it is necessary to calculate the rent for the year using either of the aforementioned methods, and the figure for the year is £3,000.) Remember that 'accounting for prepaid expenses' has been shown in section 29.4.

Step 5 Depreciation

Check to see if you need to take account of any depreciation before preparing the financial statements. The amount of depreciation may be given or, alternatively, you may have to compare the value of each asset at the beginning of the period with that at the end of the period – the difference being **depreciation**. (In our example under (*f*) below we are told the value of the asset of 'fixtures' is £8,000 and they are to be depreciated at 10% per annum. Thus 10% of £8,000 = £800 depreciation which has been charged to the profit and loss account section of the income statement and shown as a deduction from the fixtures in the statement of financial position.)

Remember to check to see if there are any additions to assets and, if so, ensure that you include them in the statement of financial position and depreciate them as indicated above.

Finally, prepare the financial statements:

- the income statement, and
- statement of financial position.

The above guide is now used in the following example to demonstrate the various stages. M Cole requires his financial statement to be drawn up for the year ended 31 December 2013 but has not kept full accounting records. He has, however, been able to provide the following information.

(*a*) The sales are mostly on a credit basis. No record of sales has been made, but £100,000 has been received, £95,000 by cheque and £5,000 by cash, from persons to whom goods have been sold.
(*b*) Amount paid by cheque to suppliers during the year = £72,000.
(*c*) Expenses paid during the year: by cheque, rent £2,000, general expenses £1,800; by cash, rent £500.
(*d*) M Cole took £100 cash per week (for 52 weeks) as drawings.
(*e*) Other information is available:

	At 31.12.2012	At 31.12.2013
	£	£
Accounts receivable	11,000	13,200
Accounts payable	4,000	6,500
Rent owing	–	500
Bank balance	11,300	30,500
Cash balance	800	100
Inventory	15,900	17,000

(*f*) The only non-current asset consists of fixtures that were valued at 31 December 2012 at £8,000. These are to be depreciated at 10% per annum.

A step-by-step guide, shown below, is now used to demonstrate the various stages.

Step-by-step guide

Step 1

First, draw up a statement of affairs, taking into account all the opening figures, on the closing day of the last accounting period. This is shown below:

M Cole
Statement of Affairs as at 31 December 2012

	£	£
Non-current Assets		
Fixtures		8,000
Current Assets		
Inventory	15,900	
Accounts receivable	11,000	
Bank	11,300	
Cash	800	
	39,000	
Less Current Liabilities		
Accounts payable	4,000	
Net current assets		35,000
		43,000
Financed by		
Capital (difference)		43,000
		43,000

Step 2

Next, a cash and bank summary, showing the totals of each separate item plus opening and closing balances, is drawn up. Thus:

	Cash	*Bank*		*Cash*	*Bank*
	£	£		£	£
Balances 31.12.2012	800	11,300	Suppliers		72,000
Receipts from			Rent	500	2,000
accounts receivable	5,000	95,000	General Expenses		1,800
			Drawings	5,200	
			Balances 31.12.2013	100	30,500
	5,800	106,300		5,800	106,300

Step 3

Calculate the figures for purchases and sales to be shown in the trading account section. Remember that the figures needed are the same as those which would have been found if double entry records had been kept.

Purchases

In double entry, purchases means the goods that have been bought in the period, irrespective of whether or not they have been paid for during the period. The figure of payments to suppliers must therefore be adjusted to find the figure for purchases. In our example we have:

	£
Paid during the year	72,000
Less Payments made, but which were for goods which were purchased in a previous year (accounts payable 31.12.2012)	4,000
	68,000
Add Purchases made in this year, but for which payment has not yet been made (accounts payable 31.12.2013)	6,500
Goods bought in this year, i.e. purchases	74,500

The same answer could have been obtained if the information had been shown in the form of a total accounts payable account, the figure for purchases being the amount required to make the account totals agree:

Total Accounts Payable Account

	£		£
Cash paid to suppliers	72,000	Balances b/f	4,000
Balances c/d	6,500	Purchases (missing figure)	74,500
	78,500		78,500

Sales

Where all the sales in a business are for cash then obviously this will be the figure for sales. However, if goods or services are sold on credit as well as for cash then the figures will need adjusting to find the 'sales' for the accounting period. This can be found in one of two ways, i.e.:

	£
Amount received during the year:	
Cash	5,000
Bank	95,000
	100,000
Less Receipts for goods sold in the previous year (accounts receivable 31.12.12)	11,000
	89,000
Add Sales made this year but payment not yet received (accounts receivable 31.12.13)	13,200
Goods sold during this year, i.e. sales	102,200

This too could have been obtained if the information had been shown in a total accounts receivable account, the figure for sales* being the amount required to make the totals agree.

Total Accounts Receivable Account

	£		£
Balances b/f	11,000	Receipts: Cash	5,000
		Cheque	95,000
Sales (missing figure)*	102,200	Balances c/d	13,200
	113,200		113,200

Step 4 Expenses

Where there are no accruals or prepayments either at the beginning or end of the accounting period, then expenses paid will equal the expenses used up during the period. These figures will be charged to the income statement.

In contrast, where such prepayments or accruals exist, then an expense account should be drawn up for that particular item. When all known items have been entered, the missing figure will be the expenses to be charged for the accounting period.

In our example, only the rent account needs to be drawn up:

Rent Account

	£		£
Cheques	2,000	Rent (missing figure)	3,000
Cash	500		
Accrued c/d	500		
	3,000		3,000

Alternatively, the rent for the year can be found using the following calculation:

Accrual – Rent

		£
Paid:	Bank	2,000
	Cash	500
		2,500
Add: Owing 31.12.2013		500
Rent for the year		3,000

Step 5

Check to see if any depreciation needs to be charged to the income statement. In our example, Section 34.6 (*f*), it states that the fixtures are valued at £8,000 and should be depreciated at 10% per annum. Therefore, depreciation charge for the year is 10% of £8,000 = £800; this amount should be charged to the income statement. In the statement of financial position remember to deduct the depreciation from the fixtures, i.e. £8,000 – £800 = £7,200 to give you the net book value of the asset.

Now prepare the financial statements using all the information given in the details and the figures you have calculated.

M Cole
Income Statement for the year ended 31 December 2013

	£	£
Sales (Step 3)		102,200
Less Cost of goods sold		
Inventory at 1.1.2013	15,900	
Add Purchases (Step 3)	74,500	
	90,400	
Less Inventory at 31.12.2013	17,000	73,400
Gross profit		28,800
Less Expenses		
Rent (Step 4)	3,000	
General expenses	1,800	
Depreciation: Fixtures	800	5,600
Net profit		23,200

Statement of Financial Position at 31 December 2013

	£	£	£
Non-current Assets			
Fixtures at 1.1.2013		8,000	
Less Depreciation (Step 5)		800	7,200
Current Assets			
Inventory		17,000	
Accounts receivable		13,200	
Bank (Step 2)		30,500	
Cash (Step 2)		100	
		60,800	
Less Current Liabilities			
Accounts payable	6,500		
Rent owing	500	7,000	
Net current assets			53,800
			61,000
Financed by			
Capital (Step 1)			
Balance 1.1.2013 (per opening statement of affairs)			43,000
Add Net profit			23,200
			66,200
Less Drawings			5,200
			61,000

34.7 Incomplete records and missing figures

In practice, part of the information relating to cash receipts or payments is often missing. If the missing information is in respect of one type of payment, then it is normal to assume that the missing figure is the amount required to make both totals agree in the cash column of the cash and bank summary. This does not happen with bank items since another copy of the bank statement can always be obtained from the bank.

Exhibit 34.3 shows an example when the drawings figure is unknown.

Exhibit 34.3

The following information on cash and bank receipts and payments is available:

	Cash	*Bank*
	£	£
Cash paid into the bank during the year	30,000	
Receipts from accounts receivable	41,250	60,800
Paid to suppliers	2,320	64,930
Drawings during the year	?	–
Expenses paid	250	15,900
Balances at 1.1.2013	4,135	2,200
Balances at 31.12.2013	115	12,170

	Cash	*Bank*		*Cash*	*Bank*
	£	£		£	£
Balances 1.1.2013	4,135	2,200	Bankings C	30,000	
Received from accounts receivable	41,250	60,800	Suppliers	2,320	64,930
			Expenses	250	15,900
Bankings C		30,000	Drawings	?	
			Balances 31.12.2013	115	12,170
	45,385	93,000		45,385	93,000

The amount needed to make the two sides of the cash columns agree is £12,700. Therefore, this is taken as the figure of drawings.

Exhibit 34.4 is an example of where the cash received from accounts receivable in unknown.

Exhibit 34.4

Information of cash and bank transactions is available as follows:

	Cash	*Bank*
	£	£
Receipts from accounts receivable	**?**	**96,080**
Cash withdrawn from the bank for business use (this is the amount which is used besides cash receipts from accounts receivable to pay drawings and expenses)		10,920
Paid to suppliers		70,800
Expenses paid	3,640	15,230
Drawings	20,180	315
Balances at 1.1.2013	40	1,560
Balances at 31.12.2013	70	375

	Cash	*Bank*		*Cash*	*Bank*
	£	£		£	£
Balances 1.1.2013	40	1,560	Suppliers		70,800
Received from accounts receivable	?	96,080	Expenses	3,640	15,230
Withdrawn from Bank C	10,920		Withdrawn from Bank C		10,920
			Drawings	20,180	315
			Balances 31.12.2013	70	375
	23,890	97,640		23,890	97,640

Receipts from accounts receivable is, therefore, the amount needed to make each side of the cash column agree, namely £12,930, i.e. £23,890 – (10,920 + 40).

It must be emphasised that balancing figures are acceptable only when all the other figures have been verified. Should, for instance, a cash expense be omitted when cash received from accounts receivable is being calculated, then this would result in an understatement not only of expenses but also ultimately of sales.

34.8 Where there are two missing pieces of information

If both cash drawings and cash receipts from accounts receivable were not known, it would not be possible to deduce both of these figures. The only course available would be to estimate whichever figure was more capable of being accurately assessed, use this as a known figure, and deduce the other figure. However, this is a most unsatisfactory position as both of the figures are no more than pure estimates, the accuracy of one relying entirely upon the accuracy of the other.

34.9 Cash transactions for sales and purchases

Where there are cash sales as well as sales on credit terms, then the cash sales must be added to sales on credit to give the total sales for the year. This total figure of sales will be the one shown in the trading account part of the income statement.

Similarly, purchases for cash will need adding to credit purchases to give the figure of total purchases for the trading account part of the income statement.

Chapter summary

- Both margin and mark-up are based upon the formula, Cost price + Gross profit = Sales. When gross profit is shown as a percentage of the cost price this gives the mark-up. If the gross profit is shown as a percentage of the selling price this gives the margin. Remember *MRS MUC*!
- Mark-up and margin can be used to ascertain missing figures in incomplete records.

- In many small businesses it may not be practical to use a full double entry accounting system; instead single entry is used.
- Where no proper accounts are kept, possibly the only way to ascertain the amount of profit is to compare the capital account at the beginning and end of an accounting period. Provided no additional funds have been invested in the business or drawings taken out then the difference must be either profit or loss.
- A statement of affairs is often prepared to ascertain the capital of the proprietor. This statement shows the value of the assets and liabilities at a specific date and by using the accounting equation the capital can be found.
- Using the step-by-step method the financial statements can be prepared from records not kept by the double entry system of book-keeping (see section 34.6).
- Where there are missing figures it is possible to deduce the figure by careful analysis of data available and process of elimination.
- The disadvantage of single entry is that insufficient financial information is available to the owner(s) of the business.

EXERCISES

*Note: Questions with the suffix 'X' shown after the question number do **not** have answers shown at the back of the book. Answers to the other questions are shown in Appendix E.*

34.1 (*a*) If an item costs £20 and is sold for £25, what are the mark-up and margin, expressed as percentages?
(*b*) If the mark-up on a unit is 33⅓%, what is the margin?
(*c*) If the margin is 16⅔%, what is the mark-up?

34.2X (*a*) If an item costs £60 and is sold for £90, what are the mark-up and margin, expressed as percentages?
(*b*) If the margin on a unit is 50%, what is the mark-up?
(*c*) If the mark-up is 50%, what is the margin?

34.3 T Ashby is a trader who marks up the selling price of his goods to 25% above cost. His books give the following information at 31 July 2013:

	£
Inventory as at 1 August 2012	19,744
Inventory as at 31 July 2013	25,240
Sales for the year	120,000

You are required to create the trading account section of the income statement for Ashby showing:
(*a*) the cost of goods sold
(*b*) the value of purchases during the year
(*c*) the profit that Ashby made.

34.4 T Rigby produced from his trial balance as at 31 August 2013 the following information:

	£
Inventory as at 1 September 2012	20,000
Purchases for the year	180,000

Rigby has a 'mark-up' of 50% on 'cost of sales'.
His average inventory during the year was valued at £40,000.

You are required to:

(*a*) calculate the closing inventory for Rigby as at 31 August 2013

(*b*) prepare the trading account section of the income statement for the year ended 31 August 2013

(*c*) ascertain the total amount of expenses that Rigby *must not exceed* if he is to maintain a net profit on sales of 10%.

34.5 The following figures have been extracted from the records of K Rogers, who does not keep a full record of his transactions on the double entry system:

			£
1 November	2012	Accounts receivable	2,760
1 November	2012	Accounts payable	1,080
1 November	2012	Inventory	2,010
31 October	2013	Accounts receivable	3,090
31 October	2013	Accounts payable	1,320
31 October	2013	Inventory	2,160

All goods were sold on credit and all purchases were made on credit. During the year ended 31 October 2013, cash received from accounts receivable amounted to £14,610, whereas cash paid to accounts payable amounted to £9,390.

Required:

(*a*) Calculate the amount of sales and purchases for the year ended 31 October 2013.

(*b*) Draw up the trading account section of the income statement for the year ended 31 October 2013.

34.6X The following figures for a business are available:

			£
1 June	2012	Inventory	11,590
1 June	2012	Accounts payable	3,410
1 June	2012	Accounts receivable	5,670
31 May	2013	Inventory	13,425
31 May	2013	Accounts payable	4,126
31 May	2013	Accounts receivable	6,108
Year to 31 May 2013:			
Received from accounts receivable			45,112
Paid to accounts payable			29,375

All goods were bought or sold on credit.

Required:

Draw up the trading account section of the income statement for the year 31 May 2013, deducing any figures that might be needed.

34.7 On 1 July 2012, D Lewinski commenced business with £60,000 in his bank account. After trading for a full year, he ascertained that his position on 30 June 2013 was as follows:

	£		£
Plant	36,000	Fixtures	3,600
Accounts payable	7,200	Bank balance	6,000
Accounts receivable	9,300	Inventory	13,500
Cash in hand	1,350	Drawings	16,000

You are required to:

(*a*) calculate D Lewinski's capital at 30 June 2013

(*b*) prepare D Lewinski's statement of financial position at 30 June 2013 (assuming a profit of £18,550).

34.8 J Marcano is a dealer who has not kept proper books of account. At 31 August 2012 her state of affairs was as follows.

	£
Cash	115
Bank balance	2,209
Fixtures	3,500
Inventory	16,740
Accounts receivable	11,890
Accounts payable	9,952
Motor van (at valuation)	3,500

During the year to 31 August 2013, her drawings amounted to £7,560. Winnings from the national lottery of £12,800 were put into the business. Extra fixtures were bought for £2,000. At 31 August 2013 Marcano's assets and liabilities were: cash £84; bank overdraft, £165; inventory, £24,891; accounts payable for goods £6,002; accounts payable for expenses £236; fixtures to be depreciated by £300; motor van to be valued at £2,800; accounts receivable, £15,821; prepaid expenses, £72.

You are required to draw up a statement showing the profit or loss made by Marcano for the year ended 31 August 2013.

34.9X A Hanson is a sole trader who, although keeping very good records, does not operate a full double entry system. The following figures have been taken from his records:

	31 March 2012	*31 March 2013*
	£	£
Cash at bank	14,600	17,400
Office furniture	6,000	5,000
Inventory	23,200	26,200
Cash in hand	600	800

Accounts receivable on 31 March 2012 amounted to £29,800 and sales for the year ended 31 March 2013 to £115,200. During the year ended 31 March 2013, cash received in respect of accounts receivable amounted to £108,200.

Accounts payable on 31 March 2012 amounted to £18,800 and purchases for the year ended 31 March 2013 to £81,200. During the year ended 31 March 2013, cash paid to accounts payable amounted to £77,800.

During the year to 31 March 2013 no bad debts were incurred. Also during the same period, there was neither discounts allowed nor discounts received.

Required:

(*a*) Calculate accounts receivable and accounts payable as at 31 March 2013.

(*b*) Calculate Hanson's capital as at 31 March 2012 and 31 March 2013.

(*c*) Calculate his net profit for the year ended 31 March 2013, allowing for the fact that during the year Hanson's drawings amounted to £25,400.

(Show all your workings)

34.10 Leigh Osawa had not kept full accounting records. On 31 March 2013 he attempted to prepare his financial statements for his business but was unable to calculate the figure for total sales, rent and business rates for the year ended on that date.

The following information is available:

	Balance 1 April 2012	*Balance 31 March 2013*
	£	£
Accounts receivable	23,460	28,270
Rent due	1,040	730
Business rates prepaid	390	440

The bank statements for the year ended 31 March 2013 reveal:

	£
Receipts from accounts receivable	226,820
Payment for	
Rent	12,290
Business rates	4,680

It should be noted that accounts receivable were allowed discounts of £280 during the year under review.

Set out detailed calculations of the amounts to be included in the financial statements for the year ended 31 March 2013 for:

(*a*) sales
(*b*) rent
(*c*) business rates.

Southern Examining Group AQA

Please note that this question is NOT from the live examinations for the current specification.

34.11X Ruth Eridge has not kept proper accounting records for her business which opened on 1 April 2012. On that date she opened a business bank account with £30,000 of her private funds.

A summary of her bank account for the year ended 31 March 2013 is shown below:

	£		£
Capital introduced	30,000	Drawings	14,500
Cash sales	64,200	Purchase of non-current assets	25,000
		Payments to suppliers of inventory	27,800
		Business expenses	18,100
		Balance at bank 31 March 2013	8,800
	94,200		94,200

On 31 March 2013:

- unsold inventory was valued at £7,700
- there were business expenses of £200 prepaid
- non-current assets were to be depreciated by £4,000
- accounts payable owing amounted to £3,200.

Tasks:

(*a*) Prepare the business's income statement for the year ended 31 March 2013.
(*b*) Ruth Eridge would like to expand her business but will need £25,000 to finance the expansion. Advise Ruth of *two* ways in which she could finance the expansion of the business. In each case explain the financial implications of your suggestion.

Southern Examining Group AQA

Please note that this question is NOT from the live examinations for the current specification.

CHAPTER 35

Accounting for non-profit-making organisations

Learning objectives

After you have studied this chapter you should be able to:

- appreciate that non-profit-making organisations such as clubs, charities, associations and societies prepare different financial statements from profit-making organisations
- prepare a receipts and payments account
- prepare income and expenditure accounts and statements of financial position for non-profit-making organisations
- calculate profits and losses from special activities and incorporate them into the financial statements
- appreciate that various forms of income may need special treatment
- be aware of treasurer's responsibilities.

35.1 Non-profit-making organisations

The organisations we have covered so far have all been profit-making businesses. However, there are other organisations whose objective is not to make a profit but instead provide facilities for their members to pursue a hobby, sporting activity or provide voluntary services. These clubs and associations do not have to produce income statements. Instead the financial statements prepared by them are either 'receipts and payments accounts' or 'income and expenditure accounts'.

35.2 Receipts and payments account

Receipts and payments accounts are usually prepared by the treasurer of the club or association. This account is a summary of the cash book for the period and if the organisation has no assets (other than cash) and no liabilities, a summary of the cash book tells the members all they need to know about the financial activities during a period. Exhibit 35.1 is an example of a receipts and payments account.

Exhibit 35.1

The Homers Running Club
Receipts and Payments Account for the year ended 31 December 2013

Receipts	£	*Payments*	£
Bank balance 1.1.2013	2,360	Groundsman's wages	10,000
Subscriptions received for 2013	11,640	Sports ground expenses	1,760
Rent received	1,000	Committee expenses	280
		Printing and stationery	110
		Bank balance 31.12.2013	2,850
	15,000		15,000

35.3 Income and expenditure accounts

When assets are owned, and/or there are liabilities, the receipts and payments account is not sufficient. Other than the cash received and paid out, it shows only the cash balances; the other assets and liabilities are not shown at all.

What is required is:

- a statement of financial position, and
- a statement showing whether the association's capital has increased.

The second of these two requirements is provided via an **income and expenditure account** that follows the same rules as an income statement, the only differences being the terms used.

A comparison of terms used now follows:

Profit-making organisation	**Non-profit-making organisation**
1 Income statement	1 Income and expenditure account
2 Net profit	2 Surplus of income over expenditure
3 Net loss	3 Excess of expenditure over income

35.4 Profit or loss for a special purpose

Sometimes there are reasons why a **non-profit-making organisation** would want to prepare an income statement. This is where something is done to make a profit. The profit is not to be kept, but used to pay for the main purpose of the organisation.

For instance, a football club may have discos or dances that people pay to attend. Any profit from these events helps to pay football expenses. For these discos and dances either a trading account or an income statement would be drawn up. Any profit (or loss) would be transferred to the income and expenditure account.

35.5 Accumulated fund

A sole trader or a partnership would have capital accounts. A non-profit-making organisation would instead have an **accumulated fund**. It is in effect the same as a capital account, for it is the difference between assets and liabilities.

For a sole trader or partnership:

Capital = Assets – Liabilities

In a non-profit-making organisation:

Accumulated Fund = Assets – Liabilities

35.6 Drawing up income and expenditure accounts

We can now look at the preparation of an income and expenditure account and a statement of financial position of a club. This is drawn up on the basis of a trial balance.

Long Lane Football Club
Trial Balance as at 31 December 2013

	Dr	*Cr*
	£	£
Sports equipment	8,500	
Club premises	29,600	
Subscriptions received		6,490
Staff wages	4,750	
Furniture and fittings	5,260	
Rates and insurance	1,910	
General expenses	605	
Accumulated fund 1 January 2013		42,016
Donations received		360
Telephone and postage	448	
Bank	2,040	
Bar purchases	9,572	
Accounts payable for bar supplies		1,040
Bar sales		14,825
Bar inventory 1 January 2013	2,046	
	64,731	64,731

The following information is also available:

(i) Bar inventory at 31 December 2013 amounts in value to £2,362.
(ii) Provide for depreciation: sports equipment £1,700; furniture and fittings £1,315.

Initially a 'Bar Trading Account' is prepared to ascertain the profit/loss made by the club on bar sales. This is shown below:

Long Lane Football Club
Bar Trading Account for the year ended 31 December 2013

	£	£
Sales		14,825
Less Cost of goods sold		
Opening inventory	2,046	
Purchases	9,572	
	11,618	
Closing inventory	2,362	
		9,256
Gross profit		5,569

The result of the club bar operation has been calculated separately as shown above and the gross profit of £5,569 will be incorporated into the club's income and expenditure account for calculation of the overall result, as shown below:

Income and Expenditure Account
for the year ended 31 December 2013

	£	£
Income		
Gross profit from bar		5,569
Subscriptions		6,490
Donations received		360
		12,419
Less Expenditure		
Staff wages	4,750	
Rates and insurance	1,910	
Telephone and postage	448	
General expenses	605	
Depreciation: Furniture	1,315	
Sports equipment	1,700	
		10,728
Surplus of income over expenditure		1,691

Statement of Financial Position as at 31 December 2013

	£	£	£
Non-current assets	*Cost*	*Depreciation*	*Net book value*
Club premises	29,600	–	29,600
Furniture and fittings	5,260	1,315	3,945
Sports equipment	8,500	1,700	6,800
	43,360	3,015	40,345
Current assets			
Inventroy of bar stocks		2,362	
Cash at bank		2,040	
		4,402	

	£	£	£
Current liabilities			
Accounts payable for bar supplies		1,040	
Net current assets			3,362
Net assets			43,707
Accumulated fund			
Balance at 1 January 2013			42,016
Add Surplus of income over expenditure			1,691
			43,707

35.7 Subscriptions

No subscriptions owing

Where there are no **subscriptions** owing, or paid in advance, at the beginning and the end of a financial year, then the amount shown on the credit side of the subscriptions account can be transferred to the credit side of the income and expenditure account, as follows:

Subscriptions

2013		£	2013		£
Dec 31	Income & expenditure a/c	3,598	Dec 31	Bank (total received)	3,598

Income and Expenditure Account
for the year ended 31 December 2013 (extract)

	£
Income:	
Subscriptions	3,598

Subscriptions owing

On the other hand, there may be subscriptions owing at both the start and the end of the financial year. In a case where £325 was owing at the start of the year, a total of £5,668 was received during the year, and £554 was owing at the end of the year, then this would appear as follows:

Subscriptions

2013		£	2013		£
Jan 1	Owing b/d	325	Dec 31	Bank (total received)	5,668
Dec 31	Income & expenditure a/c (difference)	5,897	Dec 31	Balance c/d	554
		6,222			6,222

Income and Expenditure Account
for the year ended 31 December 2013 (extract)

	£
Income:	
Subscriptions	5,897

In the statement of financial position, the subscription owing at the end of December 2013 would be shown under the heading of 'Current assets' as accounts receivable for subscriptions, as shown below:

Statement of Financial Position as at 31 December 2013 (extract)

	£
Current assets	
Inventory	x,xxx
Accounts receivable for subscriptions	xxx

Subscriptions owing and paid in advance

In the third case, at the start of the year there are both subscriptions owing from the previous year and also subscriptions paid in advance. In addition, there are also subscriptions paid in the current year for the next year (in advance) and subscriptions unpaid (owing) at the end of the current year. The example below concerns an amateur theatre organisation.

The organisation charges its members an annual subscription of £20 per member. It accrues for subscriptions owing at the end of each year and also adjusts for subscriptions received in advance. The following applies:

(A) On 1 January 2002, 18 members owed £360 for the year 2001.
(B) In December 2001, 4 members paid £80 for the year 2002.
(C) During the year 2002, the organisation received cash subscriptions of £7,420.

For 2001	£360
For 2002	£6,920
For 2003	£140
	£7,420

(D) At the close of 31 December 2002, 11 members had not paid their 2002 subscriptions.

Note: Dates have been deliberately set as 2001, etc., for easier understanding of this topic.

These facts are translated into the accounts as set out below:

Subscriptions

2002			£	2002			£
Jan 1	Owing b/d	(A)	360	Jan 1	Prepaid b/d	(B)	80
Dec 31	Income and expenditure a/c		*7,220	Dec 31	Bank	(C)	7,420
Dec 31	Prepaid c/d	(C)	140	Dec 31	Owing c/d	(D)	220
			7,720				7,720
2003				2003			
Jan 1	Owing b/d	(D)	220	Jan 1	Prepaid b/d	(C)	140

*The difference between the two sides of the account.

**Income and Expenditure Account
for the year ended 31 December 2002 (extract)**

	£
Income:	
Subscriptions	7,220

In this last case in the statement of financial position as at 31 December 2002, the amounts owing for subscriptions (D), £220, will be shown under current assets as accounts receivable for subscriptions. The subscriptions (C) paid in advance for 2003 will appear as an item under current liabilities as subscriptions received in advance, £140, as shown below:

Statement of Financial Position as at 31 December 2002 (extract)

Current Assets	
Inventory	xxx
Accounts receivable for subscriptions	xxx
Current Liabilities	
Subscriptions received in advance	140

Note: Treasurers of clubs and societies are very much aware that if subscriptions are outstanding for a long time it is unlikely that they will ever be paid, the member may have lost interest or moved on to another organisation. Consequently, many clubs and indeed charities do not include unpaid subscriptions as an asset in the statement of financial position.

35.8 Donations

Any **donations** received are shown as income in the year that they are received.

35.9 Entrance fees

New members often have to pay an entrance fee in the year that they join, in addition to the membership fee for that year. Entrance fees are normally included as income in the year that they are received.

35.10 Life membership

In some clubs and societies members can pay a one-off amount for **life membership**. In this case, all of the money received from life membership should not be credited to the income and expenditure account of the year in which it is received.

In a club where members joined at age 20 and would probably be members for 40 years, then one-fortieth ($2\frac{1}{2}$%) of the life membership fee should be credited in the income and expenditure account each year. The balance not transferred to the income and expenditure account would appear in the statement of financial position as a long-term liability. This is because it is the liability of the club to allow the members to use the club for the rest of their lives without paying any more for membership.

On the other hand, a club especially for people over the age of 60 would transfer a much bigger share of the life membership fee paid to the income and expenditure account. This is because the number of years of future use of the club will be far less because people are already old when they join. It may be, in those circumstances, that 10% of the life membership fee per year would be transferred to the credit of the income and expenditure account.

35.11 Treasurers' responsibilities

Treasurers of clubs or societies have a responsibility for maintaining proper accounting records in the same way as an accountant has when looking after the financial affairs of a business. It is important to ensure that any monies paid out by the treasurer have been properly authorised, especially when purchasing an item of capital expenditure (such as new sound equipment for a dramatic society). In such cases, the authorisation for purchase will more than likely have been approved at a committee meeting and noted in the minutes of the meeting. For smaller items of expenditure such as postages, telephone calls, etc., the club's or society's rules will provide the treasurer with the authority to make payments against receipted bills.

It is also important for the treasurer to keep all invoices, receipted accounts and any other documents as evidence against payments. Treasurers should also provide receipts for any monies received. All documents should be filed and available at the year end for the club's auditor to carry out an audit and for preparation of the club's year-end financial statements.

Chapter summary

- The main objective of non-profit-making organisations is to provide members with facilities to pursue a leisure activity and not to trade and make profits.
- The financial statements prepared for non-profit-making organisations may either be a 'receipts and payments account' or 'income and expenditure account'.
- A 'receipts and payments account' is very much like a cash book summary.
- An 'income and expenditure account' is very similar to an income statement except that the terminology used is different. A profit/surplus in the Income and Expenditure Account is expressed as 'surplus of income over expenditure'. A loss would be referred to as 'excess of expenditure over income'.
- The 'accumulated fund' is basically the same as a capital account.
- Although clubs and societies are non-profit-making sometimes activities are held to generate profits for the benefit of the organisation and its members.
- The treatment of members' subscriptions may involve subscriptions owing and/or paid in advance.
- Donations should be treated as income in the year in which they are received.
- Entrance fees are usually treated as income in the year in which the member joins the organisation.
- Life membership subscriptions should be spread over the anticipated length of membership which is usually decided by the club's committee or may be set out in the rules and regulations.
- Club treasurers carry an important role and, as such, are responsible for maintaining the organisation's accounting records and looking after their financial affairs.

EXERCISES

*Note: Questions with the suffix 'X' shown after the question number do **not** have answers shown at the back of the book. Answers to the other questions are shown in Appendix E.*

35.1 You are given the following details of the Horton Hockey Club for its year to 30 June 2013:

	£
Payments:	
Teams' travel expenses	1,598
Groundsman's wages	3,891
Postage and stationery	392
Rent of pitches and clubhouse	4,800
General expenses	419
Cost of prizes for raffles	624
Receipts:	
Subscriptions	8,570
Donations	1,500
Receipts from raffles	3,816

Cash and bank balances:	£
1 July 2012	2,715
30 June 2013	4,877

You also find out that members owe £160 subscriptions on 30 June 2013. On that date, the club owed £400 for rent and £75 for wages.

You are required to draw up:

(*a*) a receipts and payments account for the year ended 30 June 2013.

(*b*) an income and expenditure account for the year ended 30 June 2013.

35.2X These are the financial details of the Superball Football Club for the year to 31 May 2013:

	£
Payments:	
Hire of transport	3,710
Ground maintenance costs	1,156
Groundsman's wages	5,214
Committee expenses	906
Costs of disco	1,112
Rent of ground	2,450
General expenses	814
Receipts:	
Members' subscriptions	8,124
Prize money for winning cup	1,000
Receipts from disco	3,149
Collections at matches	5,090

Cash and bank balances:	£
1 June 2012	905
31 May 2013	2,906

Members' subscriptions owing on 31 May 2012 amount to £160 and on 31 May 2013 to £94. On 31 May 2013 the rent had been prepaid £200, and owing were transport hire £90 and committee expenses £170.

You are required to draw up:

(*a*) a receipts and payments account for the year ended 31 May 2013.

(*b*) an income and expenditure account for the year ended 31 May 2013.

35.3 The following receipts and payments account for the year ending 31 May 2013 was prepared by the treasurer of the Bradnop Bowling Club.

Receipts	£	*Payments*	£
Balance at bank 1 June 2012	1,716	Purchases of new equipment	996
Subscriptions	810	Bar inventory purchased	2,382
Net proceeds of jumble sale	546	Hire of rooms	384
Net proceeds of dance	732	Wages of part-time staff	1,188
Sale of equipment	480	Balance at bank 31 May 2013	2,112
Bar takings	2,778		
	7,062		7,062

Notes:

(i) On 1 June 2012, the club's equipment was valued at £2,040. Included in this total, valued at £552, was the equipment sold during the year for £480.

(ii) Bar inventory was valued as follows: 31 May 2012, £528; 31 May 2013, £606. There were no accounts payable for bar supplies on either of these dates.

(iii) Allow £180 for depreciation of equipment during the year ending 31 May 2013. This is additional to the loss on equipment sold during the year.

(iv) No subscriptions were outstanding at 31 May 2012, but on 31 May 2013 subscriptions due but unpaid amounted to £84.

Required (with calculations shown):

(*a*) Calculate the accumulated fund of the club as at 1 June 2012.

(*b*) Prepare a bar trading account for the year ending 31 May 2013.

(*c*) Draw up the income and expenditure account of the club for the year ending 31 May 2013.

35.4X The following trial balance was extracted from the books of the Upper Harbour Sports Club at the close of business on 31 March 2013:

	Dr	*Cr*
	£	£
Club premises	13,500	
Sports equipment	5,100	
Bar purchases and sales	9,540	15,270
Bar inventory 1 April 2012	2,190	
Balance at bank	2,790	
Subscriptions received		8,640
Accumulated fund 1 April 2012		22,290
Salary of secretary	3,600	
Wages of staff	5,280	
Postage and telephone	870	
Office furniture	1,200	
Rates and insurance	1,230	
Cash in hand	60	
Sundry expenses	840	
	46,200	46,200

Notes:

(i) All bar purchases and sales are on a cash basis. Bar inventory at 31 March 2013 was £2,460.

(ii) No subscriptions have been paid in advance but subscriptions in arrears at 31 March 2013 amounted to £90.

(iii) Rates pre-paid at 31 March 2013: £60.

(iv) Provision for depreciation as follows: sports equipment £600; office furniture £120.

Required:
Prepare the bar trading account and the income and expenditure account of the club for the year ended 31 March 2013, together with a statement of financial position as on that date. For this purpose, the wages of staff £5,280 should be shown in the income and expenditure account and not the bar trading account.

35.5 Amit Mall is the treasurer of the local tennis club. He needs to prepare some financial statements and has asked you to help.

The following information is available for the year ended 30 November 2013.

- The bank summary shows:

	£		£
Opening balance	850	Bar purchases	6,400
Subscriptions	33,000	Wages	25,500
Bar sales	8,700	General expenses	4,850
Bank loan	5,400	Purchase of land	12,000
Closing balance	800		
	48,750		48,750

- The year end balances are:

	30 November 2012	*30 November 2013*
	£	£
Bar inventory	680	890
Accounts payable for bar purchases	1,000	540
Subscriptions in arrear	1,000	4,000
Accrual for general expenses	150	250

- 20% of wages relate to the bar, 80% to other activities
- 30% of expenses relate to the bar, 70% to other activities
- the loan was taken out on 1 January 2012 at a rate of interest of 8% per annum
- the subscription is £100 per member per year.

Tasks:
1 Calculate the purchases made for the bar for the year ended 30 November 2013.
2 Calculate the net profit or loss made from the bar for the year ended 30 November 2013.
3 Calculate the total number of members who should have paid a subscription to the tennis club for the year ended 30 November 2013.
4 Calculate the surplus or deficit made by the tennis club for the year ended 30 November 2013.
5 List the assets and liabilities held by the tennis club on 30 November 2013.
6 The tennis club does not provide for depreciation of land. Briefly explain why.

Association of Accounting Technicians

35.6 The treasurer of a local amateur dramatic society is trying to ascertain the amount of subscriptions to transfer to the society's income and expenditure account for the year ended 31 December 2002 and asks for your help.

The following information is made available to you:

	2001	*2002*
	£	£
Subscriptions in arrears	235	185
Subscriptions in advance	220	140

In addition, you are told that the amount received from members during the year 2002 amounted to £2,600, all of which was banked immediately.

Note: Dates have deliberately set as 2001, etc., to make it easier for students answering this question.

You are required to draw up the society's subscriptions account for the year ended 31 December 2002, showing clearly the amount of subscriptions to be transferred to the income and expenditure account.

35.7X Pat Hall is the treasurer of a local tennis club that has 420 members. The subscription details for the club are as follows:

Subscriptions for year to 31 December 2010 – £220 per member
Subscriptions for year to 31 December 2011 – £240 per member
Subscriptions for year to 31 December 2012 – £250 per member

On 31 December 2010, six members had prepaid their subscriptions for 2011. By 31 December 2011, eight members will have prepaid their subscriptions for 2012. All other members have paid, and will continue to pay their subscriptions during the relevant year.

You are required (showing all your workings) to:

(*a*) calculate the subscriptions figure to be entered in the income and expenditure account for the year ended 31 December 2011

(*b*) calculate the total amount of money received for subscriptions during the year ended 31 December 2011.

Association of Accounting Technicians

35.8X Harry Green is the treasurer of his golf club.

- During the year ended 30 November 2012, the club received £110,000 in cash and cheques from members for annual subscriptions.
- The annual subscription is £50 per member.
- On 30 November 2011, four members were in arrears and two had paid in advance.
- On 30 November 2012, three members were in arrears and five had paid in advance.

Tasks:

(*a*) Prepare the subscription account, clearly showing the amount of subscriptions to be entered in the income and expenditure account for the year ended 30 November 2012.

(*b*) How many members does the golf club have?

Association of Accounting Technicians

35.9X The following items represented the assets and liabilities of the Torrevieja Club at 1 January 2013:

	£
Rent paid in advance	400
Cash at bank	800
Subscriptions in advance	1,200
Equipment	40,000
Lawn mower	600
Subscriptions in arrears	200
Insurance in arrears	100
Heating in advance	200

The Receipts and Payments Account for the year to 31 December 2013 reveals the following:

	£		£
Subscriptions	26,000	Purchase of lawn mower	1,100
Dinner and dance ticket sales	4,650	Soft drink purchases	3,600
Sale of existing lawn mower	700	Insurance	1,050
Soft drink sales	7,200	Rent	4,420
		Heating	1,450
		Dinner dance expenses	3,200

The following additional information is also available:

(i) The club depreciates its lawn mowers by 15% on those in existence at 31 December 2013.

(ii) Subscriptions in arrears at 31 December 2013 amounted to £750, while those in advance amounted to £590.

(iii) Unsold soft drinks at 31 December 2013 amounted to £1,400.

(iv) Dinner dance expenses in arrears at 31 December amounted to £160.

(v) Insurance paid in advance at 31 December 2013 amounted to £180.

You are required to:

(*a*) calculate the club's accumulated fund at 1 January 2013

(*b*) prepare the club's income and expenditure account for the year ended 31 December 2013

(*c*) prepare the club's statement of financial position as at 31 December 2013.

City & Guilds Pitman qualifications

CHAPTER 36

Partnership accounts

Learning objectives

After you have studied this chapter you should be able to:

- understand exactly what a partnership is and the rules relating to the number of partners
- distinguish between limited and unlimited partners
- describe the main features of a partnership agreement
- understand the position if no partnership agreement exists
- draw up the capital and current accounts for the partnership
- prepare the financial statements of a partnership.

36.1 The need for partnerships

So far, we have considered mainly businesses owned by only one person. Businesses that set up to make a profit can often have more than one owner and there are various reasons for multiple ownership. There are two types of multiple ownership: **partnerships** and limited companies. This chapter deals only with partnerships. Limited companies will be the subject of later chapters.

Advantages of partnerships

Partnerships are easier to set up than limited companies and have much lower set-up costs. The advantages of partnerships include:

- More capital can be raised, i.e. with additional partners.
- Additional partners bring in a variety of skills and expertise that benefit the partnership.
- The experience or ability required to manage the business cannot always be provided by one person working alone.
- The responsibility of management could be shared by additional partners.
- A partnership of family members can bring a stronger desire to succeed within a dependable environment.

- Partnerships are ideal organisations for professional practices such as medicine, law and accounting.
- Profits from partnership are taxed as the personal income of the partnership.

Disadvantages of partnerships

The disadvantages include:

- The partners have unlimited liability (except a **limited partner**, see section 36.3) and may be responsible for the debts of other partners.
- A partnership is dissolved on the death of a partner.
- It is difficult to liquidate or transfer partnerships.
- A partnership may have difficulty in raising sufficient capital for large-scale operations. Increased unlimited liability could also be a deterrent to expanding the business.
- There may be disagreements between the partners.

36.2 Nature of a partnership

A partnership has the following characteristics:

1. It is formed to make profits.
2. It must obey the law as given in the Partnership Act 1890. If there is a limited partner, as described in section 36.3, the Limited Partnerships Act of 1907 must also be complied with.
3. Normally, there can be a minimum of two and a maximum of 20 partners. Exceptions are banks, where there cannot be more than ten partners; also, there is no maximum limit for partnerships of accountants, solicitors, stock exchange members or other professional bodies receiving the approval of the relevant government body for this purpose.
4. Each partner (except for limited partners, described below) must pay his or her share of any debts that the partnership is unable to pay; they are personally liable. If necessary, partners could be forced to sell their private possessions to pay their share of any debts. This can be said to be 'unlimited' liability.

36.3 Limited partners

A partnership may be unlimited as previously discussed or limited. In a **limited partnership** there must be at least one partner who is not limited. All limited partnerships must be registered with the Registrar of Companies. Limited partners are not liable for the debts as in section 36.2 (4) above. The following characteristics are found in limited partnerships:

1. Their liability for the debts of the partnership is limited to the capital they have invested in the partnership. They can lose that capital, but they cannot be asked for any more money to pay the debts unless they break the regulations relating to the involvement in the partnership (2 and 3 below).

2 The partners are not allowed to take out or receive back any part of their contribution to the partnership during its lifetime.
3 They are not allowed to take part in the management of the partnership business.
4 All the partners cannot be limited partners as mentioned above; there must be at least one partner with unlimited liability.

36.4 Partnership deed or agreement

Partnership deeds or agreements in writing are not necessary for partnerships, however, it is advisable to have a written **partnership deed** or **agreement** drawn up by a solicitor or accountant to prevent problems between partners occurring. The written agreement can contain as much, or as little, as the partners want since there are no requirements in law as to what it must contain. The usual accounting contents are as follows:

1 The capital to be contributed by each partner.
2 The ratio in which profits (or losses) are to be shared.
3 The rate of interest, if any, to be paid on capital before the profits are shared.
4 The rate of interest, if any, to be charged on partners' drawings.
5 Salaries to be paid to partners.
6 Performance-related payments to partners.
7 Arrangement for the admission of a new partner.
8 Procedures to be carried out when a partner retires or dies.

Points 1 to 6 in the list above are now examined. Points 7 and 8 are outside the scope of this book but are covered in *Business Accounting 1* by Frank Wood and Alan Sangster.

1 Capital contributions

Partners need not contribute equal amounts of capital. What matters is how much capital each partner *agrees* to contribute.

2 Profit (or loss) sharing ratios

Although partners can in fact agree to share profits/losses in any ratio that they desire, it is often thought by students that profits should be shared in the same ratio as that in which capital is contributed. For example, suppose the capitals were Allen £20,000 and Beet £10,000; many people would share the profits in the ratio of two-thirds to one-third, even though the work to be done by each partner is similar. A look at the division of the first few years' profits on such a basis would be:

Years	*1*	*2*	*3*	*4*	*5*	*Total*
	£	£	£	£	£	£
Net profits	18,000	24,000	30,000	30,000	36,000	
Shared:						
Allen $^2/_3$	12,000	16,000	20,000	20,000	24,000	92,000
Beet $^1/_3$	6,000	8,000	10,000	10,000	12,000	46,000

It can be seen from the above table that Allen would receive £92,000, or £46,000 more than Beet. To treat each partner fairly, the difference between the two shares of profit when the duties of the partners are the same should be adequate to compensate Allen for putting extra capital into the business. Some might feel that £46,000 extra profits is far more than adequate for this purpose.

Consider, too, the position of capital-ratio sharing of profits when one partner has put in £99,000 and the other £1,000 as capital. In this case, one partner would get 99/100ths of the profits, while the other would get only 1/100th!

To overcome the difficulty of compensating for the investment of extra capital, the concept of interest on capital was devised.

3 Interest on capital

If the work to be done by each partner is of equal value but the capital contributed is unequal, it is reasonable to grant **interest on the partners' capital**. This interest is treated as a deduction prior to the calculation of profits and its distribution according to the profit-sharing ratio. The rate of interest is a matter of agreement between the partners, but it should equal the return that they would have received if they had invested the capital elsewhere.

Taking Allen and Beet's business again, but sharing the profits equally after charging 5% per annum interest on capital, the division of profits would become:

Years	*1*	*2*	*3*	*4*	*5*	*Total*
	£	£	£	£	£	£
Net profits	18,000	24,000	30,000	30,000	36,000	
Interest on capital						
Allen	1,000	1,000	1,000	1,000	1,000	
Beet	500	500	500	500	500	
Remainder shared:						
Allen 1/2	8,250	11,250	14,250	14,250	17,250	65,250
Beet 1/2	8,250	11,250	14,250	14,250	17,250	65,250

Summary	*Allen*	*Beet*
	£	£
Interest on capital	5,000	2,500
Balance of profits	65,250	65,250
	70,250	67,750

Here Allen has received £2,500 more than Beet which the partners consider appropriate for his having invested a larger amount over five years.

4 Interest on drawings

It is clearly in the best interests of the business that cash is withdrawn from the business by the partners in accordance with the two basic principles of: (*a*) as little as possible, and (*b*) as late as possible. The more cash that is left in the business, the more expansion can be financed, the greater the economies of having ample cash to take advantage of bargains and of not missing cash discounts.

To deter the partners from taking out cash unnecessarily, the concept can be used of charging the partners **interest on each withdrawal**, calculated from the date of withdrawal to the end of the financial year. The amount charged to them helps to swell the profits divisible between the partners. The rate of interest should be sufficient to achieve this without being too harsh.

Suppose that Allen and Beet have decided to charge interest on drawings at 5% per annum, and that their year end is 31 December. The following drawings are made:

Allen

Drawings		*Interest*		£
1 January	£1,000	5% of £1,000 for 1 year	=	50
1 March	£2,400	5% of £2,400 for 10 months	=	100
1 May	£1,200	5% of £1,200 for 8 months	=	40
1 July	£2,400	5% of £2,400 for 6 months	=	60
1 October	£ 800	5% of £800 for 3 months	=	10
		Interest charged to Allen	=	260

Beet

Drawings		*Interest*		£
1 January	£ 600	5% of £600 for 1 year	=	30
1 August	£4,800	5% of £4,800 for 5 months	=	100
1 December	£2,400	5% of £2,400 for 1 month	=	10
		Interest charged to Beet	=	140

The interest charged to each partner would vary depending on when and how much money was taken out as drawings.

5 Salaries to partners

One partner may have more responsibility or tasks than others. As a reward for this and rather than change the profit and loss sharing ratio, that partner may have a **partnership salary**, which is deducted before sharing the balance of profits.

6 Performance-related payments to partners

Partners may agree that commission or performance-related bonuses should be payable to some or all the partners in a way that is linked to their individual performance. As with salaries, these would be deducted before sharing the balance of profits.

36.5 An example of the distribution of profits

Taylor and Clarke have been in partnership for one year, sharing profits and losses in the ratio of Taylor three-fifths and Clarke two-fifths. They are entitled to 5% per annum interest on capital, Taylor having put in £20,000 and Clarke £60,000. Clarke is to have a salary of £20,000. They charge interest on drawings, Taylor being charged

£500 and Clarke £1,000. The net profit, before any distributions to the partners, amounts to £50,000 for the year ended 31 December 2013.

The results are shown in Exhibit 36.1.

Exhibit 36.1

	£	£	£
Net profit			50,000
Add Charged for interest on drawings:			
Taylor		500	
Clarke		1,000	
			1,500
			51,500
Less Salary: Clarke		20,000	
Interest on capital (@ 5%)			
Taylor	1,000		
Clarke	3,000		
		4,000	
			24,000
			27,500
Balance of profits shared:			
Taylor (three-fifths)		16,500	
Clarke (two-fifths)		11,000	27,500
			27,500

The £50,000 net profits have therefore been shared as follows:

	Taylor	*Clarke*
	£	£
Balance of profits	16,500	11,000
Interest on capital	1,000	3,000
Salary	–	20,000
	17,500	34,000
Less Interest on drawings	500	1,000
	17,000	33,000
	£50,000	

36.6 The financial statements

If the sales, inventory and expenses of a partnership were exactly the same as that of a sole trader, then the income statement would be identical with that prepared for the sole trader. However, a partnership would have an extra section shown at the end of the income statement. This section is called the **profit and loss appropriation account**, and it is in this account that the distribution of profits is shown. The heading to the income statement does not include the words 'appropriation account'. It is purely an accounting custom not to include it in the heading.

The profit and loss appropriation account of Taylor and Clarke from the details given would appear as shown in Exhibit 36.2.

Exhibit 36.2

Taylor and Clarke
Income Statement for the year ended 31 December 2013

(Trading Account – same as for sole trader)
(Profit and Loss Account – same as for sole trader)
Profit and loss appropriation account

	£	£	£
Net profit			50,000
Interest on drawings:			
Taylor		500	
Clarke		1,000	1,500
			51,500
Less:			
Interest on capital:			
Taylor	1,000		
Clarke	3,000	4,000	
Salary		20,000	24,000
			27,500
Balance of profits shared:			
Taylor (three-fifths)		16,500	
Clarke (two-fifths)		11,000	27,500
			27,500

36.7 Fixed and fluctuating capital accounts

There is a choice available in partnership accounts. Partnerships can operate either fixed capital accounts plus current accounts, or fluctuating capital accounts. Each option is described below, with a final comment on which is generally preferable.

Fixed capital accounts plus current accounts

With **fixed capital accounts**, the capital account for each partner remains year by year at the figure of capital put into the business by the partners. The profits, interest on capital, and the salaries to which the partner may be entitled are then credited to a separate current account for the partner, and the drawings and the interest on drawings are debited to it. The balance of the current account at the end of each financial year will then represent the amount of undrawn (or withdrawn) profits. A credit balance will be undrawn profits, while a debit balance will be drawings in excess of the profits to which the partner is entitled.

Using the financial information from sections 36.5 and 36.6 for Taylor and Clarke their capital and current accounts, assuming drawings of £12,000 for Taylor and £20,000 for Clarke, would appear as follows:

Taylor
Capital Account

			£
		2013	
		Jan 1 Bank	20,000

Clarke
Capital Account

			£
		2013	
		Jan 1 Bank	60,000

Taylor
Current Account

	£		£
2013		2013	
Dec 31 Cash: Drawings	12,000	Dec 31 Profit and loss appropriation account:	
Dec 31 Profit and loss appropriation account:		Interest on capital	1,000
Interest on drawings	500	Share of profits	16,500
Dec 31 Balance c/d	5,000		
	17,500		17,500
		2014	
		Jan 1 Balance b/d	5,000

Clarke
Current Account

	£		£
2013		2013	
Dec 31 Cash: Drawings	20,000	Dec 31 Profit and loss appropriation account:	
Dec 31 Profit and loss appropriation account:		Interest on capital	3,000
Interest on drawings	1,000	Share of profits	11,000
Dec 31 Balance c/d	13,000	Salary	20,000
	34,000		34,000
		2014	
		Jan 1 Balance b/d	13,000

Notice that the salary of Clarke was not paid to him but was merely credited to his account. If in fact it was paid in addition to his drawings, the £20,000 cash paid would have been debited to the current account, changing the £13,000 credit balance into a £7,000 debit balance.

Examiners often ask for the capital accounts and current accounts to be shown in columnar form. For the previous accounts of Taylor and Clarke, these would appear as follows:

Capital Accounts

	Taylor	*Clarke*		*Taylor*	*Clarke*
	£	£	2013	£	£
			Jan 1 Bank	20,000	60,000

Current Accounts

	Taylor	Clarke		Taylor	Clarke
2013	£	£	2013	£	£
Dec 31 Cash: Drawings	12,000	20,000	Dec 31 Interest on capital	1,000	3,000
Dec 31 Interest on drawings	500	1,000	Dec 31 Share of profits	16,500	11,000
Dec 31 Balances c/d	5,000	13,000	Dec 31 Salary	–	20,000
	17,500	34,000		17,500	34,000
			2014		
			Jan 1 Balances b/d	5,000	13,000

Fluctuating capital accounts

In this arrangement of **fluctuating capital accounts** the distribution of profits would be credited to the capital account, and the drawings and interest on drawings is debited. Therefore, the balance on the capital account will change each year, i.e. it will fluctuate.

If fluctuating capital accounts had been kept for Taylor and Clarke, they would have appeared:

Taylor
Capital Account

2013	£	2013	£
Dec 31 Cash: Drawings	12,000	Jan 1 Bank	20,000
Dec 31 Profit and loss appropriation account:		Dec 31 Profit and loss appropriation account:	
Interest on drawings	500	Interest on capital	1,000
Dec 31 Balance c/d	25,000	Share of profits	16,500
	37,500		37,500
		2014	
		Jan 1 Balance b/d	25,000

Clarke
Capital Account

2013	£	2013	£
Dec 31 Cash: Drawings	20,000	Jan 1 Bank	60,000
Dec 31 Profit and loss appropriation account:		Dec 31 Profit and loss appropriation account:	
Interest on drawings	1,000	Interest on capital	3,000
Dec 31 Balance c/d	73,000	Salary	20,000
		Share of profits	11,000
	94,000		94,000
		2014	
		Jan 1 Balance b/d	73,000

Fixed capital accounts preferred

The keeping of fixed capital accounts plus current accounts is considered preferable to operating fluctuating capital accounts. When partners are taking out greater amounts than the share of the profits that they are entitled to, it is shown up by a debit balance on the current account and so acts as a warning.

36.8 Where no partnership agreement exists

Where no formal partnership agreement exists – either expressed or implied – Section 24 of the Partnership Act 1890 governs the situation. The accounting content of this section states:

- Profits and losses are to be shared equally.
- There is to be no interest allowed on capital.
- No interest is to be charged on drawings.
- Salaries are not allowed.
- If a partner puts a sum of money into a business in excess of the capital he or she has agreed to subscribe, that partner is entitled to interest at the rate of 5% per annum on such an advance.

Section 24 applies where there is no agreement. There may be an agreement not by a partnership deed but in a letter, or it may be implied by conduct – for instance, when a partner signs a statement of financial position that shows profits shared in some ratio other than equally. Where a dispute arises as to whether agreement exists or not, and this cannot be resolved by the partners, only the courts will be competent to decide.

36.9 The statement of financial position

In a partnership, the capital section of the statement of financial position will appear as follows. Note that figures in brackets, e.g. '(20,000)', is an accounting convention indicating a negative amount.

Statement of Financial Position as at 31 December 2013

	£	£	£
Capital accounts	Taylor	Clarke	Total
Balance	20,000	60,000	80,000
Current accounts			
Interest on capital	1,000	3,000	
Share of profits	16,500	11,000	
Salary	–	20,000	
	17,500	34,000	
Less Drawings	(12,000)	(20,000)	
Interest on drawings	(500)	(1,000)	
	5,000	13,000	18,000

If one of the current accounts had finished in debit – for instance, if the current account of Taylor had finished up as £5,000 debit – the figure of £5,000 would appear in brackets and the balances would appear net in the totals column:

	Taylor	*Clarke*	
	£	£	£
Closing balance	(5,000)	13,000	8,000

If the net figure, for example, the £8,000 just shown, turned out to be a debit figure, then this would be deducted from the total of the fixed capital accounts.

36.10 A fully worked exercise

We can now look at a fully worked exercise covering nearly all the main points shown in this chapter.

Kidd and Mellor are in partnership. They share profits in the ratio: Kidd three-fifths to Mellor two-fifths. The following trial balance was extracted as at 31 March 2013:

Trial balance as at 31 March 2013

	Dr	*Cr*
	£	£
Equipment at cost	26,000	
Motor vehicles at cost	36,800	
Provision for depreciation at 31.3.2012:		
Equipment		7,800
Motor vehicles		14,720
Inventory at 31 March 2012	99,880	
Accounts receivable and accounts payable	83,840	65,100
Cash at bank	2,460	
Cash in hand	560	
Sales		361,480
Purchases	256,520	
Salaries	45,668	
Office expenses	1,480	
Motor expenses	2,252	
Heating and lighting	2,000	
Current accounts at 31.3.2012:		
Kidd		5,516
Mellor		4,844
Capital accounts:		
Kidd		86,000
Mellor		50,000
Drawings:		
Kidd	16,000	
Mellor	22,000	
	595,460	595,460

The financial statements for the year ended 31 March 2013 for the partnership are to be drawn up. The following notes are applicable at 31 March 2013:

(i) Inventory at 31 March 2013 was valued at £109,360.
(ii) Office expenses owing £440.
(iii) Provision for depreciation: motor vehicles 20% of cost, equipment 10% of cost.
(iv) Charge interest on capital at 6%.
(v) Charge interest on drawings: Kidd £628, Mellor £892.
(vi) Charge £15,000 for salary for Mellor.

The financial statements are now shown in Exhibit 36.3.

Exhibit 36.3

Kidd and Mellor
Income Statement for the year ended 31 March 2013

	£	£	£
Sales			361,480
Less Cost of sales:			
Opening inventory		99,880	
Add Purchases		256,520	
		356,400	
Less Closing inventory		109,360	247,040
Gross profit			114,440
Less Expenses:			
Salaries*		45,668	
Heating and lighting		2,000	
Office expenses (1,480 + 440)		1,920	
Motor expenses		2,252	
Depreciation: Motor vehicles	7,360		
Equipment	2,600	9,960	61,800
Net profit			52,640
Add Interest on drawings: Kidd		628	
Mellor		892	1,520
			54,160
Less Interest on capital: Kidd		5,160	
Mellor		3,000	8,160
			46,000
Less Salary: Mellor			15,000
			31,000
Balance of profits shared: Kidd (3/5ths)		18,600	
Mellor (2/5ths)		12,400	31,000
			31,000

*Does not include partner's salary.

Kidd and Mellor
Statement of Financial Position as at 31 March 2013

	Cost	*Depreciation*	*NBV*
Non-current assets	£	£	£
Equipment	26,000	10,400	15,600
Motor vehicles	36,800	22,080	14,720
	62,800	32,480	30,320
Current assets			
Inventory	109,360		
Accounts receivable	83,840		
Bank	2,460		
Cash	560	196,220	
Less Current liabilities			
Accounts payable	65,100		
Expenses owing	440	65,540	
Net Current assets			130,680
			161,000
Capital accounts	*Kidd*	*Mellor*	*Total*
Balance	86,000	50,000	136,000
Current accounts			
Balances as at 1.4.2012	5,516	4,844	
Add Interest on capital	5,160	3,000	
Add Salary	–	15,000	
Add Share of profits	18,600	12,400	
	29,276	35,244	
Less Drawings	(16,000)	(22,000)	
Less Interest on drawings	(628)	(892)	
Balances as at 31.3.2013	12,648	12,352	25,000
			161,000

Chapter summary

- Partnerships are formed with two or more partners carrying on in business with a view to making a profit.
- There are two types of partnership, an unlimited and a limited partnership.
- Where there is a limited partnership there must be at least one unlimited partner within the partnership. Limited partnerships should be registered with the Registrar of Companies and comply with the Limited Partnership Act 1907.
- Limited partners cannot withdraw any of the capital they invested in the partnership nor may they take part in the management of the partnership.
- It is advisable for all partnerships to draw up a partnership deed or agreement detailing the accounting requirements of the partnership (section 36.4).
- If there is no partnership agreement then the provisions of the Partnership Act 1890 will apply (section 36.8).
- The partners may use either fixed or fluctuating capital accounts.

- The financial statements of a partnership are: an income statement that has an additional section called the 'appropriation account' and the statement of financial position which show the capital and current accounts of all the partners.

EXERCISES

Note: Questions with the suffix 'X' shown after the question number do ***not*** *have answers shown at the back of the book. Answers to the other questions are shown in Appendix E.*

36.1 Stead and Jackson are partners in a retail business in which they share profits and losses equally. The balance on the partners' capital and current accounts at the year end 31 December 2013 were as follows:

	Capital Account	*Current Account*
	£	£
Stead	24,000	2,300 Cr
Jackson	16,000	3,500 Cr

During the year, Stead had drawings amounting to £15,000 and Jackson £19,000. Jackson was to receive a partnership salary of £5,000 for extra duties undertaken. The net profit of the partnership, before taking any of the above into account, was £45,000.

You are required to:

(*a*) draw up the appropriation account for the partnership for the year ended 31 December 2013.

(*b*) show the partners' capital and current accounts.

36.2X Wain, Brown and Cairns own a garage, and the partners share profits and losses in the ratio of Wain 50%, Brown 30% and Cairns 20%. Their financial year end is 31 March 2013 and the following details were extracted from their books on that date:

	Wain	*Brown*	*Cairns*
	£	£	£
Capital account balances	30,000	50,000	70,000
Current account balances	2,400 Cr	3,100 Cr	5,700 Cr
Partnership salaries	10,000	8,000	–
Drawings	12,000	15,050	14,980

The net profit for the year ended 31 March 2013 amounted to £60,000 before taking any of the above into account.

You are required to:

(*a*) prepare an appropriation account for the year ended 31 March 2013.

(*b*) draw up the partners' capital and current accounts in columnar form for the year ended 31 March 2013.

36.3X The following balances were extracted from the books of Bradford and Taylor as at 31 December 2013:

	£
Capital accounts	
Bradford	40,000
Taylor	30,000
Current accounts	
Bradford	3,450 Cr
Taylor	2,680 Dr
Drawings	
Bradford	8,000
Taylor	12,000
Net profit for the year	44,775

The following information is also available from their partnership agreement:

(i) The partners are entitled to receive 5% interest on capital.
(ii) Taylor is to receive a partnership salary of £6,000.
(iii) Interest is to be charged on drawings as follows: Bradford £200; Taylor £125.
(iv) Bradford and Taylor are to share profits and losses in the ratio 3:2.

Required:

(*a*) Show the profit and loss appropriation account for the year ended 31 December 2013.
(*b*) Show the partners' capital and current accounts for the year ended 31 December 2013.
(*c*) Show how the profits and losses would be distributed and how much each partner would receive if there was no partnership agreement.

36.4 Simpson and Young are in partnership, sharing profits and losses in the ratio 3:2. At the close of business on 30 June 2013 the following trial balance was extracted from their books:

		Dr	*Cr*
		£	£
Buildings		28,000	
Motor van (cost £16,000)		11,000	
Office equipment (cost £8,400)		5,600	
Inventory 1 July 2012		18,000	
Purchases		184,980	
Sales			254,520
Wages and salaries		32,700	
Rent, rates and insurance		3,550	
Electricity		980	
Stationery and printing		420	
Motor expenses		3,480	
General office expenses		1,700	
Accounts receivable and accounts payable		28,000	15,200
Capital accounts:	Simpson		50,000
	Young		20,000
Drawings:	Simpson	10,000	
	Young	5,000	
Current accounts:	Simpson		640
	Young		300
Cash at bank		7,250	
		340,660	340,660

Notes:

(i) Interest is to be allowed on capital accounts at the rate of 10% per annum, and no interest is to be charged on drawings.

(ii) Rates prepaid at 30 June 2013 amount to £250.

(iii) Wages due at 30 June 2013 are £500.

(iv) Provision for depreciation is as follows: motor van at 20% per annum on cost; office equipment at 10% using the reducing balance method.

(v) Inventory 30 June 2013 was valued at £19,000.

Required:

Prepare an income statement and profit and loss appropriation account for the year ended 30 June 2013, and a statement of financial position as at that date.

36.5X Kirkham and Keeling are in partnership, sharing profits and losses in the ratio of 3:2. Their partnership agreement also provides for interest on capital to be given to the partners at 10% per annum, but no interest may be charged on drawings. The following trial balance was drawn up at the end of the financial year:

Trial Balance of Kirkham and Keeling as at 30 June 2013

		£	£
Premises		59,200	
Motor vehicles (cost £30,000)		24,000	
Computer equipment (cost £12,000 at 1.7.2011)		8,000	
Cash at bank		12,500	
Accounts receivable		56,000	
Accounts payable			30,400
Sales			509,040
Purchases		369,960	
Inventory 1 July 2012		36,000	
Salaries		65,400	
Electricity		1,960	
Telephone		840	
Motor expenses		3,960	
Printing, stationery and advertising		3,000	
Rates and insurance		7,100	
General expenses		3,400	
Capital accounts:	Kirkham		100,000
	Keeling		40,000
Current accounts:	Kirkham		1,280
	Keeling		600
Drawings:	Kirkham	20,000	
	Keeling	10,000	
		681,320	681,320

Notes:

(i) The closing inventory has been valued at £38,000.

(ii) Insurance paid in advance at 30 June 2013 amounted to £1,000.

(iii) Motor expenses owing at 30 June 2013 amounted to £400.

(iv) You are to provide for depreciation on the motor vehicles at 20% on cost. The computer equipment is expected to last three years from the date of purchase.

You are required to prepare the income statement and profit and loss appropriation account for the year ended 30 June 2013 and a statement of financial position as at that date.

36.6 Bhayani and Donnell are in partnership, sharing profits and losses in the ratio 2:1. The following trial balance was extracted after the preparation of their trading account for the year ended 31 December:

		Dr	*Cr*
		£	£
Provision for depreciation: Vehicles			3,000
Provision for depreciation: Fittings			2,000
Bank balance			950
Drawings:	Bhayani	2,000	
	Donnell	600	
Vehicles (at cost)		35,000	
Fittings (at cost)		12,000	
Premises (at cost)		20,000	
Rent received			500
Accounts receivable and accounts payable		25,700	15,600
Current accounts: Bhayani		600	
	Donnell	nil	nil
Allowance for doubtful debts			950
Gross profit			32,000
Heating and lighting		1,400	
Wages and salaries		4,100	
Cash		600	
Capital accounts: Bhayani			35,000
	Donnell		12,000
		102,000	102,000

At 31 December the following information needs to be taken into consideration:

(i) The allowance for doubtful debts is to be maintained at 3% of accounts receivable.
(ii) Rent received of £100 has been paid in advance.
(iii) A heating invoice of £100 has yet to be paid.
(iv) £200 of wages have been prepaid.
(v) Depreciation needs to be provided for on the following basis:
- vehicles at 10% straight line method
- fittings at 15% reducing (diminishing) balance method.

(vi) The partnership agreement provides for the following:
- interest on drawings is charged at 6% per annum
- interest on capital is allowed at 8% per annum
- Donnell is to receive a salary of £3,263.

You are required to:
(*a*) prepare the partnership income statement for the year ended 31 December
(*b*) prepare the partnership appropriation account for the year ended 31 December
(*c*) prepare each partner's current account at 31 December
(*d*) prepare the partnership statement of financial position as at 31 December.

City & Guilds Pitman qualifications

36.7X Jane Hanford and Kevin Pearson are partners in a travel agency. They share profits and losses equally. On 31 March 2013 the business's financial statements were prepared. The following balances remained in the accounts.

	£
Cash at bank	3,460
Expenses due	240
Expenses prepaid	160
Furniture and equipment at net book value	45,000
Net profit for the year ended 31 March 2013	31,280
Accounts receivable	6,300
Accounts payable	7,500
Capital accounts	
Jane Hanford	25,000
Kevin Pearson	20,000
Drawings for the year	
Jane Hanford	17,000
Kevin Pearson	13,000
Current account balances at 1 April 2012	
Jane Hanford	2,100
Kevin Pearson	1,200

From this information the partners' current accounts were prepared.

Current Accounts

	Jane Hanford £	Kevin Pearson £		Jane Hanford £	Kevin Pearson £
Drawings	17,000	13,000	Opening Balances	2,100	1,200
Balances c/f	740	3,840	Net Profit	15,640	15,640
	17,740	16,840		17,740	16,840

(*a*) Prepare the business's statement of financial position as at 31 March 2013.

(*b*) Jane and Kevin want to expand the business but they disagree how this should be financed. Jane thinks that they ought to get a loan from the bank. Kevin thinks they ought to take on a new partner who could provide additional finance. What method of finance do you think they should choose? Give reasons for your choice.

AQA

CHAPTER 37

Limited company accounts

Learning objectives

After you have studied this chapter you should be able to:

- appreciate the reasons for forming a limited company
- understand the features of a limited company
- distinguish between a public limited company, private limited company and a company limited by guarantee
- appreciate the legal status of a limited company
- distinguish between the different types of share capital
- distinguish between ordinary and preference shares and debentures
- understand and prepare the financial statements of limited companies
- appreciate the concept of reserves and distinguish between revenue and capital reserves.

37.1 Features of a limited company

In the previous chapter we considered partnerships which were owned and run by more than one person. Another type of business organisation is a **limited company**. If a business wishes to expand it will inevitably require additional capital; forming a limited company makes it possible to raise the required funds and also provides additional features that are attractive to the owner(s) as follows:

- **Limited liability** – the capital of a limited company is divided into **shares**. Shares can be of any nominal amount, for example, 10p, 25p, £1, £5, £10 per share. To become a member of a limited company, or a **shareholder**, a person must buy one or more of the shares.

  A shareholder can only lose the price paid for the shares invested in the company or the balance due on shares; their personal assets are safe.
- **Separate legal entity** – one of the most important features of a limited company is its status in law as a separate legal entity. This means that the company is treated separately from the shareholders who own the company. Thus, a company may sue someone in its own name and likewise be sued in the company name.

- Raising capital – one of the main reasons for forming a limited company is to raise large amounts of capital to finance the business. The way in which companies raise capital is by issuing shares to prospective investors. In smaller private companies shares are issued to family and business colleagues who then become shareholders (i.e. members) of the company. Large public limited companies issue their shares to the general public, hence the name 'public' limited companies.

37.2 The Companies Acts

Limited companies are governed by the various Companies Acts 1985, 1989 and more recently the Companies Act 2006. There are two main classes of company: the **public limited company** (abbreviated to PLC) and the **private limited company** (abbreviated to Ltd). There are also companies limited by guarantee.

Public limited company (PLC)

Under the Companies Act 2006 a public company must fulfil the following requirements:

- have issued share capital of at least £50,000
- have at least two shareholders
- have at least two directors
- have a qualified company secretary
- be registered (incorporated) at Companies House.

A public limited company can raise funds by selling shares on the stock exchange to the general public, hence, they are called 'public limited companies'. However, this does not mean that such companies have to raise funds in this way, they may chose not to do so for whatever reason.

Private limited company (Ltd)

In the UK private limited companies far outnumber public limited companies and are defined in the Companies Act 2006 as 'any company that is not a public company'. Many small businesses form a private limited company to take advantage of limited liability (see section 37.1). The features of a private limited company are:

- no minimum requirement for issued share capital.
- at least one member (shareholder) and one director who may be the sole shareholder.
- be registered (incorporated) at Companies House.
- no need to have a company secretary – but if it has one it must notify Companies House.
- no need to hold an **Annual General Meeting (AGM)** unless it really wishes to.

Company limited by guarantee

These companies do not have a share capital, instead they rely on the guarantee of the members to contribute to the assets in the event of insolvency. Such companies include charities and educational organisations.

37.3 Company documents

The two documents governing the formation of limited companies are:

1 Memorandum of Association – this document confirms the following:
   - that the subscribers would like to form a company under the Act, and
   - that all subscribers wish to become members of the company and have at least one share each.

2 Articles of Association – this document details the internal regulations of running a company and regulates the affairs of the company to the outside world. It contains the following:
   - the constitution of the company
   - the rules for running the company
   - details of the director's powers and responsibilities.

37.4 Share capital

The **share capital** is the capital of a company which is divided into shares which are then bought and owned by the shareholders. There are two main types of share capital namely, **authorised share capital** and **issued share capital**, it is important to distinguish between the two:

1 **Authorised share capital** – the total of the share capital that the company would be allowed to issue also called the 'nominal capital'.
   Note: In the Companies Act 2006 a company will no longer be required to have authorised share capital and only the issued/allotted share capital will be included in the financial statements. However, since many of the examining bodies may still be using existing syllabuses when setting examination papers it was felt necessary to include the definition of authorised share capital.

2 **Issued share capital** – the amount of share capital actually issued and allotted to shareholders.

If all of the authorised share capital has been issued then items (1) and (2) above are the same. The authorised share capital is included in the statement of financial position as *a note to the accounts* for information only, whereas the issued capital is included in the *Equity* section. If all the share capital has not been issued then the amount of the authorised share capital will be greater than the issued capital. The difference between the two being the *unissued capital* (see below).

There are also other meanings relating to share capital:

- **Called-up capital** – where only part of the amounts payable on each share has been asked for, the total amount requested on all the shares is known as the 'called-up capital'.
- **Uncalled capital** – the amount that is to be received in future, but which has not yet been requested.
- **Calls in arrear** – the amount for which payment has been requested (i.e. called for), but has not yet been paid by shareholders.
- **Paid-up capital** – the total of the amount of share capital that has been paid for by shareholders.

Exhibit 37.1 illustrates these different meanings.

Exhibit 37.1 Better Enterprises Ltd

Better Enterprises Ltd was formed with the legal right to be able to issue 100,000 shares of £1 each. The company has actually issued 75,000 shares. None of the shares has yet been fully paid-up; so far the company has made calls of 80p (£0.80) per share. All of the calls have been paid by shareholders, except for £200 owing from one particular shareholder. On this basis, therefore:

(*a*) *Authorised (or nominal) share capital is £100,000.
(*b*) Issued share capital is £75,000.
(*c*) Called-up capital is (75,000 × £0.80) = £60,000.
(*d*) Calls in arrear amounted to £200.
(*e*) Paid-up capital is £60,000 less (*d*) £200 = £59,800.

*See note above re authorised share capital.

37.5 Shares and dividends

Two main types of shares are issued by companies:

1 **Ordinary shares** – these are by far the most popular way that companies use to raise capital. Ordinary shareholders will receive a variable share of the profits in the form of a **dividend** based on the number of shares that each shareholder owns. If a company makes a loss no dividend would likely to be paid.

As owners of an ordinary share, shareholders can attend the **annual general meeting** and other company meetings and vote on agenda items. As stated earlier if a company fails, shareholders could lose all their investment since other creditors have first call on any assets left in the company.

2 **Preference shares** – shareholders buy these shares knowing that they will get an agreed percentage rate of dividend. They will be paid this agreed amount before dividends are paid to ordinary shareholders. Preference shareholders can attend company meetings but have no voting rights.

A successful company is very likely to pay a dividend based on its net profit. It is, however, unlikely that all this profit will be available for distribution since the company may decide to retain a proportion in the form of **revenue reserves**.

Exhibit 37.2 shows how dividends are distributed between ordinary and preference shareholders.

Exhibit 37.2

Dee Dee Transport has issued 30,000 5% preference shares of £1 each and 300,000 ordinary shares of £1 each, which have all been taken up. The profit available for dividends over the past four years has been:

Year 1 – £12,000
Year 2 – £19,500
Year 3 – £24,000
Year 4 – £34,500

The profit would have been distributed as follows:

Year	1	2	3	4
	£	£	£	£
Profits available for dividends	12,000	19,500	24,000	34,500
Preference shares	1,500	1,500	1,500	1,500
Balance for Ordinary shares	(3.5%) 10,500	(6%) 18,000	(7.5%) 22,500	(11%) 33,000

In the above example, the preference share dividend remains constant at 5% whereas the ordinary share dividend depends upon the success or otherwise of the company's performance. In the above case the company has achieved a yearly growth in profits.

37.6 Loans and debentures

Companies often require extra funds, other than the money supplied by the shareholders, and, therefore, borrow monies from a bank or other sources in the form of a loan or debenture:

- **Loans** – are usually monies borrowed on a medium- or long-term basis from a bank or other sources such as other companies; in the case of small companies this may be from the directors in the form of a 'directors' loan'.

  Such loans are often secured on the company assets, such as property, should the lender be unable to repay the loan.
- **Debentures** – these too are long-term loans taken out by limited companies and are monies borrowed from a bank or other investors for which a 'debenture certificate' is issued. The features of a debenture are as follows:
  - a fixed rate of interest – known as **debenture interest** – is paid by the company to the investor annually
  - the interest must be paid irrespective of whether the company makes a profit
  - debentures are often secured on the non-current assets of the business, thereby making them a safer investment for the investor
  - if the company gets into financial difficulties the debenture holders are one of the first claimants to be paid.

37.7 The financial statements of a limited company

The financial statements of a limited company consist of the following:

- **income statement**
- **statement of changes in equity**
- **statement of financial position**
- **statement of cash flows.**

Income statement

The **income statements** of both private and public companies are prepared in exactly the same way as they would be for sole traders and partnerships. While there is no difference to the trading account section of the income statement the profit and loss account section does contain *two* additional types of expense:

1 **Directors' remuneration** – **directors** are appointed by the shareholders and are employees of the company. As such they are entitled to receive what is termed directors' remuneration, in other words payment in return for services rendered to the company. Such remuneration is charged to the profit and loss account section of the income statement.

2 **Debenture interest** – as mentioned above this is interest that has to be paid each year to the debenture holder for lending the company money. The interest is usually at a fixed rate and has to be paid even if the company makes a loss.

The above new items now appear in the income statement, as shown in the layout below:

Name of Company . . . Limited
Income statement for the year ended . . .

	£	£
Sales		xxx
Less Cost of goods sold		
Opening inventory	xxx	
Add: Purchases	xxx	
	xxx	
Less Closing inventory	xxx	
Cost of sales		xxx
Gross profit		**xxx**
Less Expenses:		
Directors' remuneration	**xx**	
Debenture interest	**xx**	
Other overhead expenses	xx	
		xxx
Net profit		**xxx**

Statement of changes in equity

In Chapter 36 it was shown when preparing partnership income statements that after the net profit had been found another section was added to the statement in the form of a 'Profit and Loss Appropriation Account'. This account showed the distribution of the profits, etc. between the partners. When preparing limited company accounts, rather than produce an appropriation account a 'Statement of Changes in Equity' is produced that shows the following:

- the **profit** for the year
- plus any retained profit bought forward from the previous period
- less any transfers of the profits to reserve accounts
- less the distribution of the equity, i.e. any dividends paid

- the remaining retained profit which is then included in the statement of financial position and carried forward to the next period.

Note: Later on in your studies you will see that the statement of changes in equity includes further items such as the contribution of equity (i.e. any share issues) and also an analysis of the various categories of equity. These are outside the scope of this book.

Exhibit 37.3 shows the changes in equity of Delta Ltd, a new business, for the first three years of trading.

Exhibit 37.3

Delta Ltd has a share capital of 400,000 ordinary shares of £1 each and 200,000 5% preference shares of £1 each.

- The net profits for the first three year of business ending on 31 December are as follows:
  2011 = £107,808; 2012 = £122,184; 2013 = £142,500
- Transfers to reserves are made as follows:
  2011 = Nil; 2012 = General reserve £40,000; 2013 = Non-current asset replacement reserve £50,000
- Dividends were paid for each year on the preference shares at 5% and on the ordinary shares at:
  2011 = 6%; 2012 = 8%; 2013 = 10%

The statements of changes in equity for Delta Ltd for the three years would be as follows:

Delta Ltd
Statement of changes in equity (extracts)
(1) For the year ended 31 December 2011

	£	£
Profit for the year		107,808
Less Appropriations:		
Dividends:		
Preference dividend 5% (5% × £200,000)	10,000	
Ordinary dividend 6% (6% × £400,000)	24,000	34,000
Retained profits carried forward		73,808

(2) For the year ended 31 December 2012

	£	£
Profit for the year		122,184
Add Retained profits brought forward		73,808
		195,992
Less Appropriations:		
Transfer to general reserve	40,000	
Dividends:		
Preference dividend 5% (5% × £200,000)	10,000	
Ordinary dividend 8% (8% × £400,000)	32,000	82,000
Retained profits carried forward		113,992

(3) For the year ended 31 December 2013

	£	£
Profit for the year		142,500
Add Retained profits brought forward		113,992
		256,492
Less Appropriations:		
Transfer to non-current assets replacement reserve	50,000	
Dividends:		
Preference dividend 5% (5% × £200,000)	10,000	
Ordinary dividend 10% (10% × £400,000)	40,000	100,000
Retained profits carried forward		156,492

Statement of financial position

This statement lists the assets, liabilities and equity (capital) of the company at the end of the financial period.

Many years ago companies could draw up their financial statements in any way they wished provided they disclosed all the relevant information. However, the Companies Act of 1981 stopped this practice and laid down precise details of how the statements should be presented. In the more recent Companies Act 2006 this has not changed although the current legal requirements are noted in the Companies Act 1985. Since the UK is now conforming to International Standards it must be noted that they are not specific about the layout, so UK companies continue to use the Companies Acts layout.

Exhibit 37.4 shows a statement of financial position for a limited company which contains more detailed information while the statement in Exhibit 37.5 has less detail. Both are prepared for internal use and explanations are given below the examples.

Note: Published statements of financial position of limited company accounts are outside the scope of this book and students are advised to refer to *Business Accounting 1* and *2* where the topic is discussed fully.

Exhibit 37.4 Statement of financial position showing more detailed information

Statement of Financial Position as at 31 December 2013

		Cost	*Depreciation to date (b)*	*Net book value*
		£	£	£
Non-current assets	(a)			
Goodwill		100,000	20,000	80,000
Buildings		100,000	28,000	72,000
Machinery		60,000	16,000	44,000
Motor vehicles		26,000	6,000	20,000
		286,000	70,000	216,000
Current assets				
Inventory			40,000	
Accounts receivable			36,000	
Bank			28,000	
				104,000
Total assets				320,000
Less Current liabilities				
Accounts payable		48,000		
			48,000	
Less Non-current liabilities				
Debenture loan			64,000	
Total liabilities				112,000
Net assets				208,000
Equity				
Share capital				
Issued 160,000 ordinary shares of £1, fully paid	(c)			160,000
Revenue reserves	(d)			
General reserve			40,000	
Retained profits			8,000	
				48,000
Total equity	(e)			208,000

The letters (a) to (e) in the statement of financial position above are explained in the notes below.

Study notes:

(a) Non-current assets are assets of a more permanent nature and are purchased for use within the business. They are not for resale and are usually shown at cost price.

(b) The total depreciation charged from the date of purchase to the date of the statement of financial position.

(c) The amount of share capital of a company that has been issued to shareholders.

(d) Reserves consist of the transfer of apportioned profits to accounts (i.e. general reserve) for use in the future and unused profits remaining in the 'retained profits'. See section 37.8.

(e) The total of the share capital and reserves is known as the 'total equity' or 'shareholders' funds'.

Exhibit 37.5 Statement of financial position with less detail

Statement of Financial Position as at 31 December 2013

		£	£	£
Non-current assets				
Intangible assets	(A)			
Goodwill				80,000
Tangible assets	(B)			
Buildings			72,000	
Machinery			44,000	
Motor vehicles			20,000	
				136,000
				216,000
Current assets				
Inventory			40,000	
Accounts receivable			36,000	
Bank			28,000	
				104,000
Total assets				320,000
Less Current liabilities	(C)			
Accounts payable		48,000		
			48,000	
Less Non-current liabilities	(D)			
Debenture loan			64,000	
Total liabilities				112,000
				208,000
Equity				
Called-up share capital	(E)			160,000
Revenue reserves				
General reserve				40,000
Retained profits				8,000
Total equity				208,000

The letters (a) to (e) in the statement of financial position above are explained in the notes below.

Study notes:

(A) **Intangible assets** are those not having a 'physical' existence; for instance, you can see and touch tangible assets under (B), i.e. buildings, machinery, etc., but you cannot see and touch goodwill or intellectual property rights, etc.

(B) Tangible non-current assets are shown under a separate heading. Notice that figures are shown net of depreciation. In a note accompanying the accounts, the cost and depreciation on these assets would be given.

(C) Only items payable within one year go under this heading.

(D) These particular debentures are repayable several years hence. If they had been payable within one year, they would have been shown under (C).

(E) An analysis of share capital will be given in supplementary notes to the statement of financial position.

Statement of cash flows

This is a financial document that shows how the profit of the company is linked to the cash flow.

This topic is outside the scope of this book but details can be found in *Business Accounting 2* by Frank Wood and Alan Sangster.

37.8 Reserves in the statement of financial position

In the above statements of financial position (Exhibits 37.4 and 37.5) there is a section, '*Equity*' incorporating *share capital* and *revenue reserves.* **Revenue reserves** are profits of the company which are transferred to a **reserve account** for use in future years. There are two types of reserves in a company:

1. **Revenue reserves** are reserves that are transferred from the trading activities of the company, i.e. the net profit, and set aside for future use by the company. They often appear under the heading of *general reserve*. Another revenue reserve is retained profit, i.e. the balance of profit remaining after distribution of dividends and transfers to reserve accounts. This figure is shown at the bottom of the *statement of changes in equity* as *retained profit carried forward* and is subsequently included in the statement of financial position where it is shown as *retained profits*.
2. **Capital reserves**, unlike revenue reserves, cannot be used for payment of dividends. The two most common capital reserves are the *share premium account* and the *revaluation reserve account*.

   The **share premium** account arises when shares are issued at a premium, i.e. above their par or nominal value. For example, a company may wish to expand its business and require additional funds. The nominal value of its ordinary shares is £1 but the valuation of each share is calculated to be £3. The extra funds acquired in this case, £2 per share, will be put into the share premium account while the remainder will be part of the ordinary share capital.

   The revaluation reserve account arises when an asset of the company is revalued, for example, premises and buildings may have been purchased when the company was first established many years ago and since then have increased in value. The asset is thus revalued and the new valuation figure is shown in the non-current assets section in the statement of financial position. The difference between the original value, i.e. the cost price and the revaluation figure, is shown in the statement under the heading 'Reserves' and is described as 'revaluation reserve account'.

Note: It is thought by many that reserves represent money available whenever the company needs extra funding but this is not the case. Both revenue and capital reserves are not cash funds; they are reserves which are represented by the net assets owned by the company. The assets belong to the company which is owned by the shareholders.

37.9 Investments

Where a company buys shares in another company as an investment, the investment is shown as an asset in the statement of financial position. It is shown as a separate item in the accounts between the non-current assets and the current assets. The market value of such investments is shown in the statement of financial position as a note, or in brackets, for example:

Statement of Financial Position (Extracts)

	£
Investments at cost (market value £100,000)	75,000

In the above case, the market value is above cost. If the market value falls below cost, then the difference is written off in the income statement, so that the statement of financial position will then show the investment at the written-down figure.

37.10 Loan capital

The term **loan capital** includes money owing on debentures, and loans from banks and other sources not repayable in the next 12 months.

37.11 Equity/shareholders' funds

This is the amount of share capital and reserves owned by the shareholders. In Exhibit 37.6, Ashford Ltd, the equity in the statement of financial position will be shown as follows:

	£
Called-up capital	150,000
General reserve	10,000
Retained profits	63,521
	223,521

37.12 The treatment of dividends in the financial statements

In section 37.5 we discussed the types of shares available to shareholders for investment and how the dividend was calculated on both ordinary and preference shares. Dividends are distributions of the profits to shareholders in return for their investment and are usually paid out twice a year. During the year the company may pay out an ***interim dividend*** and at the end of the year a ***final dividend*** is declared depending on the profits for the year. This final dividend has then to be approved by the shareholders at the Annual General Meeting (AGM) of the company and is usually paid out at the beginning of the next financial year.

Note that the treatment of dividends in the financial statements differs depending upon whether the dividend is *paid* or whether it is *proposed*:

- **Dividends paid** – the amount of dividend *paid* (e.g. the interim dividend) is calculated and then entered in the 'Statement of changes in equity' as an appropriation of the profits.
- **Dividends proposed but not paid** – again the amount of dividend is calculated, payment of which has to be approved by the shareholders at the company's AGM as mentioned above. Since the amount cannot be paid until approved by the shareholders it is not entered in the financial statements, but appears as a note to the accounts.

37.13 A fully worked example of the financial statements

Two examples of a limited company's financial statements are now shown as Exhibits 37.6 and 37.7. In the first exhibit new items applicable to limited company accounts are shown while Exhibit 37.7 contains a more complicated example including preference shares and debentures.

Exhibit 37.6

The following trial balance is extracted from the books of an imaginary company called Ashford Ltd as at 31 December 2013 and is presented showing more detail. Note that the new items specific to limited companies have been highlighted in bold.

Ashford Ltd
Trial Balance as at 31 December 2013

	Dr £	*Cr* £
Ordinary share capital		**150,000**
Premises at cost	97,500	
Equipment at cost	82,500	
Provision for depreciation on equipment		23,700
Purchases	302,547	
Sales		475,215
Wages and salaries	61,310	
Directors' remuneration	**20,000**	
General expenses	48,252	
Rates and insurance	6,450	
Electricity	2,324	
Bad debts	1,122	
Allowance for doubtful debts		1,291
Accounts receivable	32,676	
Accounts payable		26,240
Inventory as at 1 January 2013	38,534	
Bank	27,151	
Retained profits as at 31.12.12		**51,420**
Interim ordinary dividend paid	**7,500**	
	727,866	727,866

The following adjustments are needed:

(i) The issued share capital is divided into 150,000 shares of £1 each and a final dividend of 5% has been declared on these shares for 2013.
(ii) Inventory at 31 December 2013 is valued at £43,713.
(iii) Wages and salaries due at 31 December 2013 amount to £872.
(iv) Rates and insurance paid in advance at 31 December 2013 amount to £450.
(v) The allowance for doubtful debts is to be increased to £1,407.
(vi) A depreciation charge is to be made on equipment at the rate of 10% per annum on cost.
(vii) A transfer of £10,000 to a general reserve account is required.

Ashford Ltd
Income Statement
for the year ended 31 December 2013

		£	£
Sales			475,215
Less Cost of goods sold:			
Opening inventory		38,534	
Add Purchases		302,547	
		341,081	
Less Closing inventory		43,713	297,368
Gross profit			177,847
Less Expenses:			
Salaries and wages (61,310 + 872)		62,182	
Directors' remuneration	**(A)**	**20,000**	
General expenses		48,252	
Rates and insurance (6,450 – 450)		6,000	
Electricity		2,324	
Bad debts		1,122	
Increase in allowance for doubtful debts (1,407 – 1,291)		116	
Depreciation: Equipment		8,250	148,246
Net profit			29,601

Statement of changes in equity
for the year ended 31 December 2013

			£
Profit for the year			29,601
***Add* Retained profits brought forward**			**51,420**
			81,021
Less Appropriations:			
Transfer to general reserve		**10,000**	
Ordinary share dividends (interim) paid	**(B)**	**7,500**	**17,500**
Retained profits carried forward			**63,521**

Ashford Ltd
Statement of Financial Position as at 31 December 2013

		Cost	Depreciation to date	Net book value
Non-current assets		£	£	£
Premises		97,500	–	97,500
Equipment		82,500	31,950	50,550
		180,000	31,950	148,050
Current assets				
Inventory			43,713	
Accounts receivable (32,676 + 450 – 1,407)			31,719	
Bank			27,151	102,583
Total assets				250,633
Less current liabilities				
Accounts payable (26,240 + 872)		27,112		
			27,112	
				27,112
Net assets				223,521
Equity	**(C)**			
Called-up share capital				**150,000**
Revenue reserves	**(D)**			
General reserve			**10,000**	
Retained profits			**63,521**	**73,521**
				223,521

Note to the accounts:
The proposed final dividend of 5% on the ordinary shares, £7,500, for the year ended 31 December 2013 is subject to approval by shareholders at the Annual General Meeting and has not been included in the above financial statements as a liability. **(E)**

Study notes:
(A) Directors' remuneration is shown as an expense in the income statement.
(B) This is the interim dividend paid on the ordinary shares
(C) The total of the share capital and reserves is known as the 'total equity' or 'shareholders funds'.
(D) 'Reserves' consist either of those undistributed profits remaining in the retained profits, or those profits transferred to a reserve account appropriately titled (e.g. general reserve or non-current assets replacement reserve) – refer to section 37.8.
(E) This is the proposed final dividend of 5% on the ordinary shares (5% × 150,000 = £7,500) and since it has to be approved by the shareholders at their AGM, prior to payment, it is not included in the financial statements.

Exhibit 37.7

This worked example is presented for internal use, shows less detail and includes preference shares, debentures and the share premium account. The following trial balance was extracted from the books of an imaginary company called Dobson Ltd as at 31 December 2013:

Dobson Ltd
Trial Balance as at 31 December 2013

	Dr £	*Cr* £
8% Preference share capital		35,000
Ordinary share capital		125,000
10% Debentures (repayable 2018)		20,000
Share premium		21,000
Retained profits 31.12.2012		13,874
Interim ordinary dividend paid	6,250	
Equipment at cost	122,500	
Motor vehicles at cost	99,750	
Provision for depreciation: Equipment		29,400
Provision for depreciation: Motor vehicles		36,225
Inventory 1.1.2013	136,132	
Sales		418,250
Purchases	232,225	
Sales returns	4,025	
General expenses	1,240	
Salaries and wages	46,260	
Directors' remuneration	18,750	
Rent, rates and insurance	18,095	
Motor expenses	4,361	
Debenture interest	1,000	
Bank	6,501	
Cash	630	
Accounts receivable	94,115	
Accounts payable		93,085
	791,834	791,834

The following adjustments are needed:

(i) Inventory at 31.12.2013 was £122,000.
(ii) Accrue rent £2,000.
(iii) Accrue debenture interest £1,000.
(iv) Depreciate the equipment at 10% on cost and motor vehicles at 20% on cost.
(v) Transfer to general reserve £5,000.
(vi) It is proposed to pay the 8% preference dividend and a final dividend of 6% on the ordinary shares.
(vii) Authorised share capital is £35,000 in preference shares and £200,000 in £1 ordinary shares.

Dobson Ltd
Income Statement for the year ended 31 December 2013

		£	£
Sales			418,250
Less Sales returns			4,025
			414,225
Less Cost of goods sold:			
Opening inventory		136,132	
Add Purchases		232,225	
		368,357	
Less Closing inventory		122,000	246,357
Gross profit			167,868
Less Expenses:			
Salaries and wages		46,260	
Rent, rates and insurance (18,095 + 2,000)		20,095	
Motor expenses		4,361	
General expenses		1,240	
Directors' remuneration	(A)	18,750	
Debenture interest (1,000 + 1,000)	(B)	2,000	
Depreciation:			
Equipment (10% × 122,500)		12,250	
Motor vehicles (20% × 99,750)		19,950	124,906
Net profit			42,962

Statement of changes in equity

		£
Profit for the year		42,962
Add Retained profits brought forward		13,874
		56,836
Less Appropriations		
Transfer to general reserve	5,000	
Ordinary share dividend (interim) paid	6,250	11,250
Retained profits carried forward		45,586

Study notes:
(A) Directors' remuneration is shown as an expense in the income statement.
(B) Debenture interest is an expense to be shown in the income statement.

Dobson Ltd
Statement of Financial Position as at 31 December 2013

		£	£	£
Non-current assets				
Tangible assets	(A)			
Equipment*			80,850	
Motor vehicles*			43,575	124,425
Current assets				
Inventory			122,000	
Accounts receivable			94,115	
Bank			6,501	
Cash			630	223,246
Total assets				347,671
Less Current liabilities				
Accounts payable (93,085 + 2,000)		95,085		
Debenture interest due		1,000		
			96,085	
Less Non-current liabilities				
10% Debentures			20,000	
Total liabilities				116,085
				231,586
Equity				
Share capital				
Issued 160,000 Ordinary shares of £1 fully paid			125,000	
Issued 35,000 – 8% Preference shares of £1 each fully paid			35,000	160,000
Capital reserve				
Share premium	(B)			21,000
Revenue reserves	(C)			
General reserve			5,000	
Retained profit			45,586	
				50,586
				231,586

Note: The proposed final dividends are as follows:
(i) 8% on the Preference shares (8% × 35,000 = £2,800)
(ii) 6% on the Ordinary shares (6% × 125,000 = £7,500).

For the year ended 31 December 2013 these are subject to approval by the shareholders at the AGM and have not been included in the above financial statements.

Notes:
(A) Notes to be given in an appendix as to cost, acquisitions and sales in the year and depreciation.
(B) The share premium account is a capital reserve – refer to section 37.8.
(C) 'Reserves' consist either of those undistributed profits remaining in the retained profit, or those transferred to a reserve account appropriately titled (e.g. general reserve and non-current assets replacement reserve) – refer to section 37.8.

**Workings*:
Equipment cost £122,500 less depreciation to date £41,650 (£29,400 + £12,250) gives a net book value of £80,850. Motor vehicles cost £99,750 less depreciation to date £56,175 (£36,225 + £19,950) gives a net book value of £43,575.

Chapter summary

- Limited companies are owned by shareholders who appoint directors to manage the company on their behalf.
- There are many features which make forming a limited company attractive to investors including limited liability whereby a shareholder may lose the amount invested in the company but their personal assets are safe.
- A limited company is a separate legal entity to the shareholders and as such it can sue and be sued in its own name.
- A public company is one that can issue its shares publicly but has an issued share capital of at least £50,000. The company must also have at least two shareholders (there is no maximum), two directors and a company secretary.
- In a private limited company there must be a least one member (shareholder) and one director who may be the sole shareholder. There is no minimum requirement for issued share capital and the company can only issue its shares privately.
- A company limited by guarantee does not have a share capital instead relies on the guarantee of the members to contribute to the assets in the event of insolvency. Such companies include charities and educational organisations.
- Company documents include the Memorandum of Association, which details the subscribers of a company, and the Articles of Association showing the company's internal regulations.
- Authorised share capital is the maximum amount of share capital or number of shares the company would be allowed to issue. Note that in the Companies Act 2006, from October 2009, there will no longer be a requirement to have an authorised share capital.
- Issued share capital is the amount of share capital actually issued to shareholders, i.e. the called-up capital.
- There are two main types of shares: (1) preference shares – here the shareholders get an agreed percentage rate of dividend before the ordinary shareholders receive anything; (2) ordinary shares – the shareholders are entitled to a dividend after the preference shareholders have been paid their dividends. The amount they receive fluctuates depending on the profits available.
- A debenture is a loan to the company upon which a fixed rate of interest is paid annually. The interest must be paid even if the company makes a loss. Debentures are often secured on the assets of the business.
- The financial statements for a limited company consist of an income statement, statement of changes in equity, statement of financial position and statement of cash flows. (Note that the last is outside the scope of this book but is dealt with in *Business Accounting 1* by Frank Wood and Alan Sangster.)
- Both debenture interest and directors' remuneration are charged to the income statement.
- Any retained profits are carried forward to the next accounting period and must also be shown in the statement of financial position.
- Reserve accounts contain appropriated profits that have been transferred for use in future years such as a general reserve or non-current asset reserve account. They are classed as revenue reserves and may be distributed to shareholders as dividend.
- Share premium is another class of reserve that arises when shares are issued above the face or nominal value. The extra amount received above the nominal value is credited to the share premium account. This account is classed as a capital reserve, which means it cannot be distributed to shareholders as dividend.

EXERCISES

*Note: Questions with the suffix 'X' shown after the question number do **not** have answers shown at the back of the book. Answers to the other questions are shown in Appendix E.*

37.1 Lear Ltd has a share capital of 300,000 ordinary shares of £1 each and 100,000 6% preference shares of £1 each. The following information is also available:

- The net profit for the first two years of business ending on 31 December 2013 are: 2012 – £164,500; 2013 – £182,330.
- Transfers to reserves made during the two years are: 2012 – Nil; 2013 – General reserve £60,000.
- Dividends:
  - The preference dividend was paid each year.
  - Ordinary dividend: 2012 – interim dividend paid 4%; Final dividend proposed 4% (paid in 2013); 2013 – interim dividend paid 5%; proposed final dividend of 6%.

You are required to draw up a statement of change in equity for the two years ending 31 December 2012 and 2013.

37.2 Draw up a statement of financial position for Croft Ltd from the following as at 31 December 2012 for internal use.

	£
Buildings at cost	315,000
Machinery at cost	168,000
Fixtures at cost	84,000
Inventory	106,000
Bank	44,000
Accounts receivable	63,000
Depreciation to date:	
Buildings	47,250
Machinery	50,400
Fixtures	33,600
Issued share capital: Fully paid	250,000
Debentures: 10%	20,000
Accounts payable	80,000
General reserve	200,000
Retained profit (balancing figure, for you to ascertain)	?

37.3X CA Company Ltd, who manufacture agricultural implements, made a net profit of £210,000 for the year to 31 December 2013. Retained profits at 31 December 2012 amounted to £17,000. At the directors' meeting, the following appropriations were agreed:

	£
To be transferred to general reserve	30,000
To be transferred to foreign exchange reserve	16,000

It had also been agreed that a dividend of 10% be proposed on the ordinary share capital. This amounted to 500,000 shares of £2 each. Preference share dividends of 10% have been paid during the year on 250,000 preference shares of £1 each.

You are required to draw up the company's statement of changes in equity for the year ended 31 December 2013.

37.4 The trial balance extracted from the books of Chang Ltd at 31 December 2013 was as follows:

	£	£
Issued share capital (100,000 shares of £1 each)		100,000
Retained profits		34,280
Freehold premises at cost	65,000	
Machinery at cost	55,000	
Provision for depreciation on machinery account as at 31 December 2012		15,800
Purchases	201,698	
Sales		316,810
General expenses	32,168	
Wages and salaries	54,207	
Rent	4,300	
Lighting expenses	1,549	
Bad debts	748	
Allowance for doubtful debts as at 31 December 2012		861
Accounts receivable	21,784	
Accounts payable		17,493
Inventory as at 31 December 2012	25,689	
Bank balance	18,101	
Interim dividend paid on the ordinary shares	5,000	
	485,244	485,244

You are given the following additional information:

(i) Inventory as at 31 December 2013 was £29,142.
(ii) Wages and salaries due at 31 December 2013 amounted to £581.
(iii) Rent paid in advance at 31 December 2013 amounted to £300.
(iv) A final dividend of 5% is proposed for the year ended 31 December 2013.
(v) The allowance for doubtful debts is to be increased to £938.
(vi) A depreciation charge is to be made on machinery at the rate of 10% per annum at cost.

Required:
Draw up an income statement, a statement of changes in equity for the year ended 31 December 2013 and a statement of financial position as at 31 December 2013.

37.5X On 30 September 2012, Reynolds Ltd had an authorised capital of £250,000, divided into 200,000 ordinary shares of £1 each and 50,000 7% preference shares of £1 each. All the preference shares were issued and fully paid, while 150,000 of the ordinary shares were issued and fully paid. The company also had a balance on the general reserve account of £45,000 and retained profits brought forward of £30,000.

During the year ended 30 September 2013, the company made a net profit of £70,000, out of which a transfer of £8,000 was made to the general reserve account. The directors had paid an interim dividend of 6p per share on the ordinary share capital and the preference dividend. They proposed to pay a final dividend of 14p per share on the ordinary share capital.

From the information given above you are required to prepare for Reynolds Ltd:

(*a*) A statement of changes in equity for the year ended 30 September 2013.
(*b*) The capital and reserves section of the statement of financial position as at 30 September 2013.

37.6 Newton Ltd has an authorised share capital of £300,000, divided into 200,000 ordinary shares of £1 each and 100,000 8% preference shares of £1 each, both fully paid. The following balances remained in the accounts of the company after the preparation of the income statement for the year ended 31 December 2012:

	Dr	*Cr*
	£	£
Premises at cost	360,800	
Bank balance		42,534
Preference dividend paid	8,000	
3% interim dividend paid on the ordinary shares	6,000	
Heating and lighting prepaid	5,067	
Provision for depreciation on machinery		38,720
Machinery at cost	96,800	
Preference share capital: fully paid		100,000
Ordinary share capital: fully paid		200,000
Retained profit brought forward: 1 January 2012		122,667
Accounts receivable	106,700	
Accounts payable		68,846
Inventory	75,000	
Wages and salaries accrued		5,600
Net profit (for the year ended 31 December 2012)		80,000
	658,367	658,367

You are given the following additional information:

1 Transfer £20,000 to the general reserve.
2 The directors have proposed a final dividend of 4% on the ordinary shares.

You are required to:

(*a*) prepare the statement of changes in equity for the year ended 31 December 2012
(*b*) prepare the statement of financial position as at 31 December 2012.

37.7X Harper plc has an authorised capital of 500,000 £1 ordinary shares and 250,000 £1 (6%) preference shares. The following balances remained in the books after the income statement has been prepared for the year ended 31 December 2013:

	Dr	*Cr*
	£	£
300,000 £1 ordinary shares (fully paid)		300,000
100,000 £1 (6%) preference shares		100,000
Retained profit brought forward 1 January 2013		33,000
Premises at cost	300,000	
Motor vehicles at cost	120,000	
Fixtures and fittings at cost	65,000	
Provision for depreciation on motor vehicles		72,000
Provision for depreciation on fixtures and fittings		26,000
Accounts receivable	50,800	
Accounts payable		66,000
Bank	84,000	
Preference dividend paid	6,000	
Expenses prepaid and accrued	8,000	4,000
Inventory 31 December 2013	87,200	
General reserve		40,000
Net trading profit for the year ended 31 December 2013		80,000
	721,000	721,000

The directors of Harper plc have decided to transfer £20,000 to the general reserve and to recommend a dividend of 10% on ordinary shares.

From the information given, you are required to prepare for Harper plc:

(*a*) a statement of changes in equity for the year ended 31 December 2013
(*b*) a statement of financial position as at 31 December 2013.

37.8X M & J Ltd's financial year ended on 31 March 2013. On this date the following balances remained in the company's books after the preparation of the income statement.

	Dr	*Cr*
	£000	*£000*
3,000,000 £1 ordinary shares (fully paid)		3,000
Premises (cost)	4,000	
Plant and machinery	1,000	
Provision for depreciation on plant and machinery		400
Interim dividend paid on ordinary shares	150	
Trade accounts receivable	312	
Allowance for doubtful debts		18
Debentures (10%)		400
Wages and salaries accrued		20
Expenses prepaid	15	
Share premium		600
Retained profit brought forward, 1 April 2012		273
Trade accounts payable		287
General reserve, 1 April 2012		350
Bank overdraft		161
Inventory	432	
Net profit for the year ended 31 March 2013		400
	5,909	5,909

You are given the following information:

(i) A final dividend of 7.5% is proposed on the ordinary shares for the year ended 31 March 2013.
(ii) The directors have decided to transfer £100,000 to the general reserve account.

You are required to:
(*a*) prepare a statement of changes in equity for the year ended 31 March 2013
(*b*) prepare a statement of financial position as at 31 March 2013.

CHAPTER 38

Manufacturing accounts

Learning objectives

After you have studied this chapter you should be able to:

- understand that a company producing goods records the cost in the manufacturing account
- understand that regular review of production costs can aid management
- calculate the prime cost and production cost of goods manufactured
- define direct costs and indirect costs
- prepare a manufacturing account
- calculate the production cost per unit.

38.1 Manufacturing accounts

So far the book has dealt with businesses solely involved in trading. However, companies with manufacturing activities need to prepare a **manufacturing account** to ascertain the cost of producing goods. This account, which is normally for internal management purposes, will show the production cost and this figure will be transferred to the trading account section of the income statement.

Cost records are essential if an accurate assessment of the production cost is to be achieved. Regular reviews of the production cost by management are vital on, say, a monthly basis. Action can then be taken if, for example, increases in material costs have occurred or production targets are not being met.

38.2 Direct and indirect costs

Direct costs are those that can be directly identified with specific products or jobs. For example, referring to Exhibit 38.1, the direct costs identified are:

- Direct materials – raw materials required for the manufacture of a product.
- Direct labour – wages of the machine operator who makes the product.

- Direct expenses – expenses that can be identified to each unit of production, for example, the hire of a special machine, or the payment of a royalty for the use of a patent or copyright.

The total of all the **direct costs** is known as the **prime cost** (see Exhibit 38.1).

Indirect costs are those that occur in the factory or other places where production is being carried out but cannot be easily traced to the items being manufactured. Examples include:

- rent of premises and business rates
- insurance of premises
- depreciation of equipment
- factory heating and lighting
- wages of supervisors.

Indirect costs are also referred to as indirect manufacturing costs, production overheads or **factory overhead costs** (see Exhibit 38.1).

Exhibit 38.1 Total cost calculation

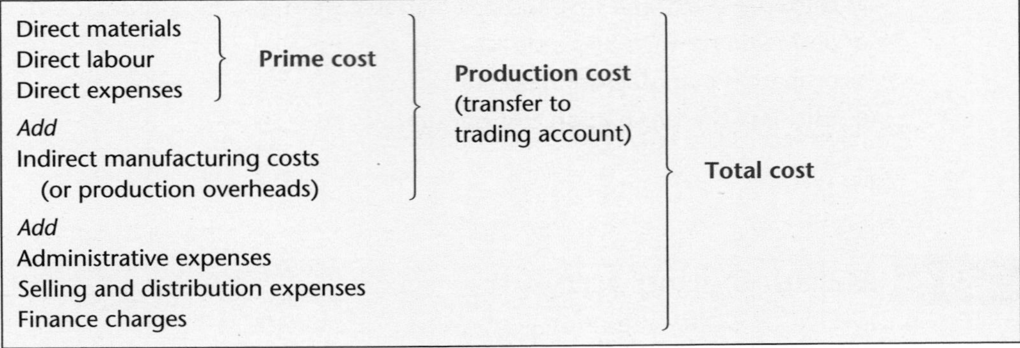

The prime cost and production cost appear in the manufacturing account. The production cost is transferred to the trading account. Administrative expenses, selling and distribution expenses and finance expenses appear in the profit and loss account. This information is then used in the preparation of the income statement (see chapter 10).

38.3 Other expenses

Administration expenses consist of such items as managers' salaries, legal and accountancy charges, the depreciation of office equipment, and secretarial salaries.

Selling and distribution expenses are items such as sales staff salaries and commission, carriage outwards, depreciation of delivery vehicles, advertising and display expenses.

Finance charges are those expenses incurred in providing finance facilities such as interest charged on a loan, bank charges and discounts allowed.

38.4 Format of the financial statements

As previously mentioned, if a company manufactures its own products then it would draw up a manufacturing account prior to preparing the income statement. The financial statements would then consist of the following:

- manufacturing account
- income statement
- statement of financial position.

Manufacturing account section

This is charged with the production cost of goods completed during the accounting period. It consists of:

- *Direct material* – this is found as follows:
  (i) opening inventory of raw materials
  (ii) *add* the cost of purchases of raw materials plus carriage inwards charges
  (iii) *less* closing inventory of raw materials
  (iv) this gives *the cost of raw material consumed.*
  To this figure *add* the following:
- *Direct labour*
- *Direct expenses*
- This now gives the figure of *prime cost.*

Now add:

- *Indirect manufacturing costs* such as wages of supervisor, factory rent, depreciation of equipment, etc.
- *Add* opening work in progress and *deduct* closing work in progress
- This now gives *production cost of goods completed.*

When completed the manufacturing account shows the total production costs relating to the goods manufactured and available for sale during the accounting period. This figure is then transferred to the trading account section of the income statement.

Note: Many students are so used to deducting expenses such as wages, rent, depreciation, etc. in the profit and loss account section of the income statement that they can easily fall into the trap of *deducting* these instead of *adding* them in the manufacturing account. Remember we are building up the cost of manufacture so all costs are *added.*

Trading account section of the income statement

This account includes:

- production cost brought down from the manufacturing account section
- opening and closing inventory of finished goods
- sales.

When completed, this account will disclose the gross profit. This figure will then be carried down to the profit and loss account section of the income statement.

The manufacturing account and the trading account section can be shown in the form of a diagram.

Manufacturing Account

	£
Production costs for the period:	
Direct materials	xxx
Direct labour	xxx
Direct expenses	xxx
Prime cost	xxx
Indirect manufacturing costs (or production overheads)	xxx
***Production cost of goods completed c/d to trading account**	xxx

Trading Account section of the Income Statement

		£	£
Sales			xxx
Less Production cost of goods sold:			
Opening inventory of finished goods	(A)	xxx	
Add ***Production costs of goods completed b/d**		xxx	
Less Closing inventory of finished goods	(B)	xxx	xxx
Gross profit			xxx

(A) is production costs of goods unsold in previous period.
(B) is production costs of goods unsold at end of the period.

Profit and loss account section of the Income Statement

This section includes:

- gross profit brought down from the trading account section
- all administration expenses
- all selling and distribution expenses
- all finance charges.

Since some of the charges usually found in the profit and loss account section will have already been included in the manufacturing account only the remainder need charging to the profit and loss account section.

When complete the profit and loss account section will show the net profit.

Statement of financial position

The statement of financial position of a manufacturing company is virtually the same as statements prepared for other organisations with one exception. In the *current assets* section the closing inventory must include the following:

- inventory of raw materials
- inventory of work-in-progress
- inventory of finished goods.

38.5 A worked example of a manufacturing account

Exhibit 38.2 shows the necessary details for a manufacturing account. It has been assumed that there were no partly completed units (known as **work in progress**) either at the beginning or end of the period.

Exhibit 38.2

Details of production cost for the year ended 31 December 2013:

	£
1 January 2013, inventory of raw materials	3,000
31 December 2013, inventory of raw materials	4,200
Raw materials purchased	48,000
Manufacturing (direct) wages	126,000
Royalties	900
Indirect wages	54,000
Rent of factory – excluding administration and selling and distribution blocks	2,640
Depreciation of plant and machinery in factory	2,400
General indirect expenses	1,860

Manufacturing Account for the year ended 31 December 2013

	£	£
Inventory of raw materials 1.1.2013		3,000
Add Purchases		48,000
		51,000
Less Inventory of raw materials 31.12.2013		4,200
Cost of raw materials consumed		46,800
Manufacturing wages		126,000
Royalties		900
Prime cost		173,700
Indirect Manufacturing Costs		
Rent	2,640	
Indirect wages	54,000	
General expenses	1,860	
Depreciation of plant and machinery	2,400	60,900
Production cost of goods completed c/d		234,600

Sometimes, if a company has produced less than its customers have demanded, the company may well have bought an outside supply of finished goods. In this case, the trading account will have both a figure for purchases and for the production cost of goods completed.

38.6 Work in progress

The production cost to be carried down to the trading account section of the income statement will be the production cost of goods completed during the period. If items have not been completed, they cannot be sold. Therefore, they should not appear in the trading account section.

For instance, if we have the following information, we can calculate the transfer to the trading account section:

	£
Total production costs expended during the year	60,000
Production costs last year on goods not completed last year, but completed in this year (work in progress)	3,600
Production costs this year on goods which were not completed by the year end (work in progress)	5,280

The calculation is:	£
Total production costs expended this year	60,000
Add Costs from last year, in respect of goods completed in this year (work in progress)	3,600
	63,600
Less Costs in this year, for goods to be completed next year (work in progress)	5,280
Production costs expended on goods completed this year	58,320

38.7 A worked example for a manufacturing account

Consider the case whose details are given in Exhibit 38.3.

Exhibit 38.3

	£
1 January 2013, inventory of raw materials	7,200
31 December 2013, inventory of raw materials	9,450
1 January 2013, work in progress	3,150
31 December 2013, work in progress	3,780
Year to 31 December 2013	
Wages: Direct	35,640
Indirect	22,950
Purchase of raw materials	78,300
Fuel and power	8,910
Direct expenses	1,260
Lubricants	2,700
Carriage inwards on raw materials	1,800
Rent of factory	6,400
Depreciation of factory plant and machinery	3,780
Internal transport expenses	11,620
Insurance of factory buildings and plant	11,350
General factory expenses	2,970

Manufacturing Account for the year ended 31 December 2013

	£	£
Inventory of raw materials 1.1.2013		7,200
Add Purchases		78,300
Carriage inwards		1,800
		87,300
Less Inventory of raw materials 31.12.2013		9,450
Cost of raw materials consumed		77,850
Direct wages		35,640
Direct expenses		1,260
Prime cost		114,750
Add Indirect Manufacturing Cost		
Fuel and power	8,910	
Indirect wages	22,950	
Lubricants	2,700	
Rent	6,400	
Depreciation of plant	3,780	
Internal transport expenses	11,620	
Insurance	11,350	
General factory expenses	2,970	70,680
		185,430
Add Work in progress 1.1.2013		3,150
		188,580
Less Work in progress 31.12.2013		3,780
Production cost of goods completed c/d		184,800

The trading account section is concerned with finished goods. If in Exhibit 38.3 there had been £31,500 of finished goods at 1 January 2013 and £39,600 at 31 December 2013, and the sales of finished goods amounted to £275,000, then the trading account section would appear thus:

Trading Account section for the year 31 December 2013

	£	£
Sales		275,000
Less Cost of goods sold		
Inventory of finished goods 1.1.2013	31,500	
Add Production cost of goods completed b/d	184,800	
	216,300	
Less Inventory of finished goods 31.12.2013	39,600	176,700
Gross profit c/d		98,300

The profit and loss account is then constructed in the normal way.

Unit cost of production

Once the total cost of production is calculated the production cost per unit can easily be ascertained. In the above example, 2,100 units were produced at the cost of £184,800 (see the manufacturing account). The cost per unit is as follows:

$$\text{Cost per unit} = \frac{\text{Cost of production}}{\text{No. of units produced}} = \frac{\pounds184{,}800}{2{,}100 \text{ units}} = \pounds88 \text{ per unit}$$

38.8 Apportionment of expenses

Quite often, expenses will have to be divided between:

- Indirect manufacturing costs: to be charged in the manufacturing account section
- Administration expenses:
- Selling and distribution expenses:
- Financial charges:

(Administration expenses, selling and distribution expenses and financial charges: to be charged in the profit and loss account section of the income statement)

An instance of this could be the rent expense. If the rent is paid separately for each part of the organisation, then it is easy to charge the rent to each sort of expense. However, only one figure of rent might be paid, without any indication as to how much is for the factory part, how much is for the selling and distribution part and that for the administration buildings.

How the rent expense will be apportioned in the latter case will depend on circumstances, but will use the most equitable way of doing it. A range of methods may be used, including ones based upon:

- floor area
- property valuations of each part of the buildings and land.

38.9 Full set of financial statements: worked example

A complete worked example is now given. Note that in the profit and loss account section the expenses have been separated to show whether they are administration expenses, selling and distribution expenses, or financial charges.

The trial balance in Exhibit 38.4 has been extracted from the books of J Jarvis, Toy Manufacturer, as on 31 December 2013.

Exhibit 38.4

J Jarvis
Trial Balance as at 31 December 2013

	Dr	*Cr*
	£	£
Inventory of raw materials 1.1.2013	2,100	
Inventory of finished goods 1.1.2013	3,890	
Work in progress 1.1.2013	1,350	
Wages (direct £18,000; factory indirect £14,500)	32,500	
Royalties	700	
Carriage inwards (on raw materials)	350	
Purchases of raw materials	37,000	
Productive machinery (cost £28,000)	23,000	
Computer equipment (cost £2,000)	1,200	
General factory expenses	3,100	
Lighting	750	
Factory power	1,370	
Administrative salaries	4,400	
Salesmen's salaries	3,000	
Commission on sales	1,150	
Rent	1,200	
Insurance	420	
General administration expenses	1,340	
Bank charges	230	
Discounts allowed	480	
Carriage outwards	590	
Sales		100,000
Accounts receivable and accounts payable	14,230	12,500
Bank	5,680	
Cash	150	
Drawings	2,000	
Capital as at 1.1.2013		29,680
	142,180	142,180

Notes at 31.12.2013:

(i) Inventory of raw materials £2,400; inventory of finished goods £4,000; work in progress £1,500.

(ii) Lighting, rent and insurance are to be apportioned: factory five-sixths, administration one-sixth.

(iii) Depreciation on productive machinery and computer equipment is at 10% per annum on cost.

J Jarvis
Manufacturing Account and Income Statement
for the year ended 31 December 2013

	£	£	£
Inventory of raw materials 1.1.2013			2,100
Add Purchases			37,000
Carriage inwards			350
			39,450
Less Inventory of raw materials 31.12.2013			2,400
Cost of raw materials consumed			37,050
Direct labour			18,000
Royalties			700
Prime cost			55,750
Indirect Manufacturing Cost			
General factory expenses		3,100	
Lighting 5/6ths		625	
Power		1,370	
Rent 5/6ths		1,000	
Insurance 5/6ths		350	
Depreciation of plant		2,800	
Indirect labour		14,500	23,745
			79,495
Add Work in progress 1.1.2013			1,350
			80,845
Less Work in progress 31.12.2013			1,500
Production cost of goods completed c/d			79,345
Sales			100,000
Less Cost of goods sold			
Inventory of finished goods 1.1.2013		3,890	
Add Production cost of goods completed		79,345	
		83,235	
Less Inventory of finished goods 31.12.2013		4,000	79,235
Gross profit			20,765
Administration Expenses			
Administrative salaries	4,400		
Rent 1/6th	200		
Insurance 1/6th	70		
General expenses	1,340		
Lighting 1/6th	125		
Depreciation of computer equipment	200	6,335	
Selling and Distribution Expenses			
Sales representatives' salaries	3,000		
Commission on sales	1,150		
Carriage outwards	590	4,740	
Financial Charges			
Bank charges	230		
Discounts allowed	480	710	11,785
Net profit			8,980

J Jarvis
Statement of Financial Position as at 31 December 2013

	Cost	*Total Depreciation*	*Net Book Value*
	£	£	£
Non-current Assets			
Productive machinery	28,000	7,800	20,200
Computer equipment	2,000	1,000	1,000
	30,000	8,800	21,200
Current Assets			
Inventory:			
Raw materials	2,400		
Finished goods	4,000		
Work in progress	1,500		
Accounts receivable	14,230		
Bank	5,680		
Cash	150	27,960	
Less Current Liabilities			
Accounts payable	12,500	12,500	
Net current assets			15,460
			36,660
Financed by			
Capital			
Balance as at 1.1.2013			29,680
Add Net profit			8,980
			38,660
Less Drawings			2,000
			36,660

Unit cost of production

Once the total cost of production is calculated the production cost per unit can easily be ascertained. In the above example let us assume that 2,267 units were produced at the cost of £79,345 (see the Manufacturing Account). The cost per unit is as follows:

$$\frac{\text{Cost of production}}{\text{No. of units produced}} = \text{Cost per unit}$$

$$= \frac{\pounds 79{,}345}{2{,}267 \text{ units}} = \pounds 35.00 \text{ per unit}$$

38.10 Other terms used in manufacturing accounts

Fixed costs are costs that, in the short term, remain the same irrespective of the level of business activity. Examples of a fixed cost would be rent, business rates, insurance, etc., and such costs would have to be paid if the company produced 100 units or 1,000 units.

Variable costs vary depending on the level of production. For example, raw materials used in manufacture would vary depending upon the level of goods produced; the more goods produced the greater the cost of raw materials. If fewer goods were produced the costs of raw materials would be reduced.

Note: Students often find the preparation of manufacturing accounts difficult to grasp and may find it useful to remember the following areas in which they could easily make a mistake:

1 Remember to add any item appearing under the heading of 'Indirect Manufacturing Costs', i.e. rent, wages, depreciation, power and lighting, etc.
2 In the trading account section of the income statement 'Cost of Goods Sold' section ensure you use the **production cost** of goods completed, i.e. £79,345, and *not* the **purchases** figure.
3 In the statement of financial position, under current assets, be sure to include all *three closing inventories* if applicable to your question, i.e.
   (i) inventory of raw materials
   (ii) inventory of work in progress
   (iii) inventory of finished goods.

Chapter summary

- When a company manufactures its own products, rather than purchasing them, the cost of production can be found by preparing a manufacturing account.
- Direct costs are those costs that can be traced to the specific item being manufactured.
- Indirect costs, also known as 'indirect manufacturing costs', are those costs relating to the manufacture of an item that cannot be easily traced, for example, a supervisor's wages.
- The cost of producing an item is made up of direct materials, direct labour and direct expenses to arrive at the prime cost. To this figure is added any indirect manufacturing costs, plus the opening inventory of work in progress less closing inventory of work in progress to find the production cost of goods completed.
- Where a business manufactures its own goods the financial statements consist of: a manufacturing account, which gives the production cost of goods completed; the income statement, which shows the gross and net profits respectively; and the statement of financial position.
- It is important to adjust the manufacturing account for any work in progress at the start and end of the accounting period.
- Fixed costs remain the same whatever the level of productive activity whereas variable costs, such as raw materials, varies according to the number of units produced.
- The areas likely to cause errors when preparing financial statements for manufacturing organisations are:
  1 Manufacturing account – under the heading 'Indirect expenses' remember to *add* the expenses, i.e. rent, power and lighting, depreciation, etc.
  2 Trading account section – when calculating the 'Cost of goods sold' ensure you use the 'Production cost of goods manufactured' not purchases!
  3 Statement of financial position – include all *three* closing inventories under the heading of 'Current assets', i.e. raw materials, work in progress and finished goods.

EXERCISES

*Note: Questions with the suffix 'X' shown after the question number do **not** have answers shown at the back of the book. Answers to the other questions are shown in Appendix E.*

38.1 From the following information, prepare the manufacturing and trading account section of the income statement of E Smith for the year ended 31 March 2013.

	£
Inventory at 1 April 2012:	
Finished goods	6,724
Raw materials	2,400
Work in progress	955
Carriage on purchases (raw materials)	321
Sales	69,830
Purchases of raw materials	21,340
Manufacturing wages	13,280
Factory power	6,220
Other manufacturing expenses	1,430
Factory rent and rates	2,300
Inventory at 31 March 2013	
Raw materials	2,620
Work in progress	870
Finished goods	7,230

38.2X From the following details, you are to draw up a manufacturing account and income statement of P Lucas for the year ended 30 September 2013.

	30.9.2012	*30.9.2013*
	£	£
Inventory of raw materials, at cost	8,460	10,970
Work in progress	3,070	2,460
Finished goods inventory	12,380	14,570
For the year:		£
Raw materials purchased		38,720
Manufacturing wages		20,970
Factory expenses		12,650
Depreciation:		
Plant and machinery		7,560
Delivery vans		3,040
Office equipment		807
Factory power		6,120
Advertising		5,080
Office and administration expenses		25,910
Sales representatives' salaries and expenses		26,420
Delivery van expenses		5,890
Sales		174,610
Carriage inwards		2,720

38.3 The Oldport Manufacturing Co's financial year ended on 30 April 2013. The following list includes some of the balances in the business's book at that date.

	£
Inventory 1 May 2012	
Finished goods	27,900
Raw materials	31,550
Wages	
Direct manufacturing	67,525
Indirect manufacturing	24,390
Office	38,440
Purchases of raw materials	98,560
Factory rent and rates	22,400
Inventory 30 April 2013	
Finished goods	31,280
Raw materials	34,585

Tasks:

(*a*) Set out a detailed calculation of the company's prime cost. Select appropriate items from the information provided.

(*b*) Explain what is meant by the term 'variable costs'. Illustrate your answer with *one* example of a variable cost.

Southern Examining Group AQA

Please note that this question is NOT from the live examinations for the current specification.

38.4 Ace Crafts Ltd makes ornaments, which it sells in wooden cases. The following information is made available to you in respect of the year ended 31 December 2013:

	1 Jan 2013	*31 Dec 2013*
	£	£
Raw materials	36,000	46,400
Wooden cases	18,000	15,360
Work-in-progress	10,000	15,200
The activities for the year ended 31 December 2013 were:		
Raw materials purchased	70,400	
Purchases of wooden cases	18,000	
Carriage outwards	1,680	
Carriage inwards on raw materials	1,120	
Wages	170,000	
Salary of factory manager	33,200	
Factory power	14,560	
Factory rates	2,280	
Lighting	1,800	
Administration expenses	19,200	
Salesmen's salaries	47,600	

The company completely finished the manufacture of 6,250 ornaments. All ornaments were sold immediately on completion for £80 each. In addition:

- Factory plant was valued at £100,000 on 1 January 2013. It depreciates by 20% for 2013.
- 80% of the wages are for productive workers, and 20% for factory overheads.
- 50% of the lighting is for the factory.

Required:

(*a*) Draw up a manufacturing account to disclose:

- (i) cost of raw materials used
- (ii) cost of wooden cases used
- (iii) prime cost
- (iv) factory overheads
- (v) cost of production.

(*b*) Draft the income statement for the year ended 31 December 2013.

(*c*) Ascertain the production cost of each boxed ornament.

(*d*) Calculate the gross profit on each boxed ornament sold.

38.5X The following balances have been extracted from the books of Tan Guat Hoon as at 31 August 2013.

	£
Inventory at 1 September 2012	
Raw materials	16,300
Work in progress	21,200
Finished goods	43,100
Allowance for doubtful debts at 1 September 2012	1,460
Purchases of raw materials	71,200
Returns of raw materials	700
Sales	187,300
Discounts allowed	640
Discounts received	700
Production wages	21,300
Office salaries	11,300
Production equipment (cost £60,000)	29,400
Office equipment (at cost)	5,400
Carriage on raw materials	930
Rent and rates	8,000
Heat and light	1,100
Insurance	500

The following information is also relevant at 31 August 2013:

(i) Closing inventory is:

- Raw materials £15,800
- Work in progress £20,100
- Finished goods £36,400.

(ii) The following amounts remain outstanding:

- Rent and rates £500
- Heat and light £220
- Production wages £2,600.

(iii) £100 insurance has been prepaid.

(iv) Three-quarters of insurance relates to the factory and the remainder to the office.

(v) Two-thirds of heat and light relates to the factory and the remainder to the office.

(vi) 80% of rent and rates relates to the factory and the remainder to the office.

(vii) The allowance for doubtful debts is to be reduced to £1,010.

(viii) Depreciation is to be provided:

- on production equipment at 30% diminishing balance basis
- on office equipment at 40% on cost.

You are required to:

(*a*) prepare a Manufacturing Account for the year ended 31 August 2013

(*b*) prepare an income statement for the year ended 31 August 2013.

City & Guilds Pitman qualifications

38.6X Joey Peterson is a manufacturer of musical instruments. The following balances were extracted from the business records at the end of the financial year, 30 June 2012.

	£
Inventory at 1 July 2011	
Raw materials	81,600
Work in progress	125,300
Finished goods	115,440
Inventory at 30 June 2012	
Raw materials	94,500
Work in progress	154,300
Finished goods	85,440
Insurance	66,900
General expenses	43,200
Factory rent and rates	96,000
Selling and distribution expenses	29,700
Direct factory power	40,000
Purchase of raw materials	314,000
Direct factory wages	450,000
Indirect factory wages	98,600
Administration staff salaries	136,800
Sales of finished goods	2,000,000

The following additional information is available at 30 June 2012 and is to be taken into account:

- direct factory wages £8,900 are accrued
- insurance £6,900 is prepaid
- factory plant and machinery is to be depreciated by £50,000
- expenditure on insurance and general expenses is to be allocated on the following basis: factory one-third: administration two-thirds.

(*a*) Prepare a manufacturing account for the year ended 30 June 2012 showing clearly:
- cost of raw materials consumed
- prime cost
- cost of production.

(*b*) Prepare the trading account section of the income statement for the year ended 30 June 2012 showing clearly:
- cost of goods sold
- gross profit.

Edexcel International GCSE Accounting 1st edn, Edexcel (Robinson, S. 2010) Pearson Education Ltd.

CHAPTER 39

Analysis and interpretation of financial statements

Learning objectives

After you have studied this chapter you should be able to:

- appreciate the importance of analysing financial statements for the benefit of interested parties
- distinguish between profitability and liquidity
- calculate and analyse ratios
- understand the term 'capital employed'
- calculate and understand the importance of working capital.

39.1 Interpretation of accounts

The whole purpose of recording and classifying financial information about a business, and communicating this to the owners and managers in the form of the financial statements, is to assess the performance of the business. The information contained in the financial statements can be used to evaluate various aspects of the company by the use of accounting ratios.

For the ratios to be a reliable guide to performance, two criteria need to be applied:

1 The financial statements used for calculating the current ratios must be *up to date.*
2 Each ratio must be *compared* with the same ratio from the previous year's accounts or with those from a competitor's accounts.

The concept of comparison is crucial, since this identifies trends in the business and allows action to be taken.

The analysis of a business using accounting ratios is widely practised by both internal and external parties and the main ones are listed in Exhibit 39.1.

Exhibit 39.1

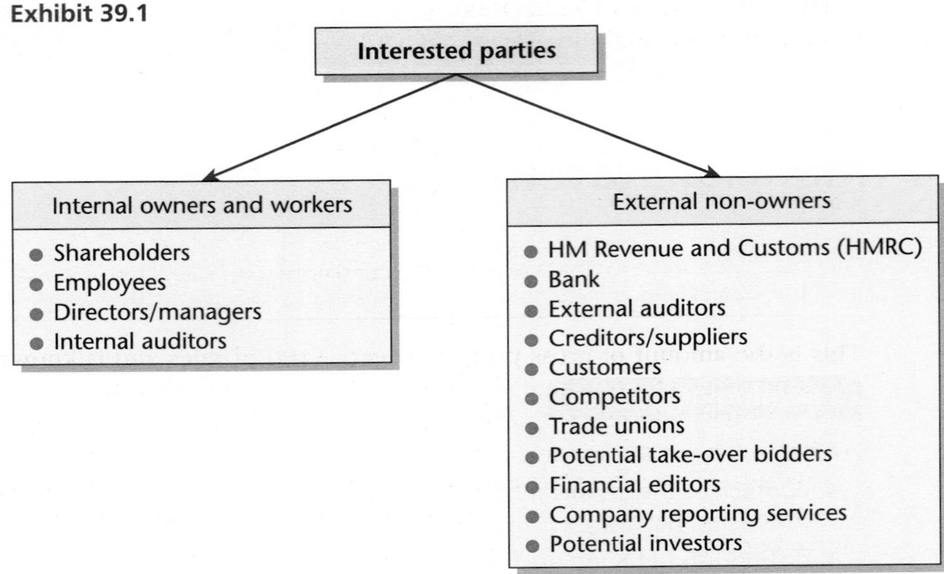

39.2 Profitability and liquidity

There are two basic but essential factors in the operation of a business, the first is to maintain, and if possible, increase profit. The ability to make profit is known as **profitability**.

The second essential factor is for the business to have sufficient funds at all times so that it can pay its debts as they become due. The level of funds available to pay suppliers is known as **liquidity**.

The importance of both these factors cannot be too highly stressed. A business which operates with a good profits record and sound liquidity will become well regarded by both customers and suppliers.

If a business is consistently unable to generate profits it will fail. Even when a business makes a profit but has weak liquidity it would demonstrate a failure to control its cash flow. Late or slow payments to suppliers could lead to them not wishing to deal with the company. Once a business gains a poor financial reputation it could affect its trading performance which would further weaken it and cause it to fail.

39.3 Profitability ratios

The **profitability ratios** measure the success or otherwise of a business's trading activities in respect of profit during an accounting period. The main ratios used to examine profitability are:

- **gross profit margin/sales**
- **gross profit mark-up/cost of sales**
- **net profit margin/sales**

- **expenses (or overheads)/sales**
- **return on capital employed (ROCE)**
- **inventory turnover ratio.**

1 Gross profit as percentage of sales

The basic formula is:

$$\frac{\text{Gross profit}}{\text{Sales}} \times 100 = \text{Gross profit as percentage of sales (Gross profit margin)}$$

This is the amount of gross profit for every £100 of sales and is known as the gross profit margin (refer to Chapter 34 for margin and mark-up). If the answer turns out to be 15% this would mean that for every £100 of sales £15 gross profit is made before any expenses are paid.

This ratio is used as a test of the profitability of the sales. Even if sales are increased it may not mean that the gross profit will increase. The trading accounts in Exhibit 39.2 illustrate this.

Exhibit 39.2

D. Clive
Trading Account sections of the Income Statements for the years ended 31 December 2012 and 2013

	2012		*2013*	
	£	£	£	£
Sales		70,000		80,000
Less Cost of goods sold				
Opening inventory	5,000		9,000	
Add Purchases	60,000		72,000	
	65,000		81,000	
Less Closing inventory	9,000	56,000	11,000	70,000
Gross profit		14,000		10,000

In the year 2012 the gross profit as a percentage of sales was:

$$\frac{14{,}000}{70{,}000} \times 100 = 20\%$$

In the year 2013 it became:

$$\frac{10{,}000}{80{,}000} \times 100 = 12^1/_2\%$$

Sales had increased, but as the gross profit percentage had fallen by a relatively greater amount, the gross profit had fallen. There can be many reasons for such a fall in the gross profit percentage.

- Perhaps the goods being sold have cost more, but the selling price of the goods has not risen to the same extent.
- Perhaps, in order to increase sales, reductions have been made in the selling price of goods.

- There could be a difference in how much has been sold of each sort of goods, called the sales mix, between this year and last, with different kinds of goods carrying different rates of gross profit per £100 of sales.
- There may have been a greater wastage or theft of goods.

These are only some of the possible reasons for the decrease. The point of calculating the ratio is to find out why and how such a change has taken place.

2 Gross profit to cost of sales

The basic formula is:

$$\frac{\text{Gross profit}}{\text{Cost of sales}} \times 100 = \text{Gross profit as a percentage of cost of sales (Gross profit mark-up)}$$

This ratio shows the percentage of profit to the cost of sales, in other words the amount the trader has marked up its products. For example, if a trader buys a product for £1 and decides to mark it up by 20% (20% of £1 = 20p) then the selling price becomes £1.20.

Using the figures in Exhibit 39.2, the gross profit as a percentage of cost of sales would be as follows:

In the year 2012 the gross profit as a percentage of cost of sales:

$$\frac{14{,}000}{56{,}000} \times 100 = 25\%$$

In the year 2013 it became:

$$\frac{10{,}000}{70{,}000} \times 100 = 14.29\%$$

3 Net profit margin to sales

Here the formula is:

$$\frac{\text{Net profit}}{\text{Sales}} \times 100 = \text{Net profit as percentage of sales}$$

This calculation will show how much net profit has been made for every £100 of sales. It brings the expenses (or overheads) into the calculation, as opposed to the gross profit percentage, which ignores expenses. Changes in the ratio will be due either to:

- the gross profit ratio changing, and/or
- the expenses per £100 of sales changing.

When changes are due to expenses, they will be examined to see if anything can be done in future to minimise the expenses and ensure that a reasonable net profit is made.

4 Expenses to sales ratio

This ratio is calculated as follows:

$$\text{Expenses/sales ratio} = \frac{\text{Expenses}}{\text{Sales}}$$

Normally, this is referred to as a percentage and is calculated as follows:

$$\text{Expenses as a percentage of sales} = \frac{\text{Expenses}}{\text{Sales}} \times 100 = x\%$$

It is useful to compare the expenses/sales percentage with the previous results. If an increase was evident this would indicate an increase in the expenses of the business and would require further investigation by management. If the result remained stable or in fact had reduced this would indicate that expenses incurred in running the business had been carefully monitored.

5 Return on capital employed ratio (ROCE)

This ratio is calculated as follows:

$$\text{ROCE ratio} = \frac{\text{Net profit}}{\text{Capital employed}}$$

Normally, this is referred to as a percentage and is calculated as follows:

$$\text{Return of capital employed} = \frac{\text{Net profit}}{\text{Capital employed}} \times 100 = x\%$$

It shows (as a percentage) the net profit made for each £100 of capital employed. The higher the ratio, the more profitable the business. This is the most important ratio of all.

There has never been an agreed definition of the term 'capital employed'. Very often it has been taken to mean the average capital. For this, the opening capital for the period is added to the closing capital and then the total is divided by two. In an examination, use the method stated by the examiner. If you are given only the closing capital, use the closing capital figure.

In the following example, two businesses of sole traders (A) and (B) have made the same profits, but the capital employed in each case is different. From the statements of financial position that follow, the return on capital employed is calculated using the average of the capital account as capital employed.

Statements of Financial Position	(A)	(B)
	£	£
Non-current Assets + Current Assets – Current Liabilities	100,000	160,000
Capital Accounts:		
Opening balance	80,000	140,000
Add Net profits	36,000	36,000
	116,000	176,000
Less Drawings	16,000	16,000
	100,000	160,000

Return on capital employed is calculated thus for the two businesses:

$$(A)\quad \frac{£36{,}000}{(£80{,}000 + £100{,}000) \div 2} \times 100\% = 40\%$$

$$(B)\quad \frac{£36{,}000}{(£140{,}000 + £160{,}000) \div 2} \times 100\% = 24\%$$

The ratio illustrates that what is important is not simply how much profit has been made but how well the capital has been employed. Business (A) has made far better use of its capital, achieving a return of £40 net profit for every £100 invested, whereas (B) has received a net profit of only £24 per £100.

In this case, only the accounts of sole traders have been dealt with, so that a straightforward example could be used. In section 39.6 other meanings of 'capital employed' will be considered, when dealing with:

- sole traders who have received loans to help finance their businesses
- partnerships
- limited companies.

6 Inventory turnover ratio

Every business should operate both to keep its inventory to as low a figure as possible without losing profitability, and to sell its goods as quickly as possible. The inventory turnover ratio measures how well the business is managing to do these things. Any increase in inventory or slowdown in sales will show a lower ratio.

The ratio is calculated as follows:

$$\frac{\text{Cost of goods sold}}{\text{Average inventory}} = \text{Inventory turnover ratio}$$

If only the opening and closing inventory figures are known the average inventory is found by adding these two figures and dividing them by two (i.e. averaging them). The higher this ratio, the more profitable the business. For example, if £5 gross profit was made on a particular product and the inventory turnover is 6 times a year then the business would make a gross profit of £5 × 6 = £30. If, however, the inventory turnover ratio increased to 9, then gross profit would be £5 × 9 = £45.

39.4 Liquidity ratios

A business that has satisfactory liquidity (see section 39.2) will have sufficient funds, normally referred to as 'working capital', to pay suppliers at the required time. The ability to pay suppliers on time is vital to ensure that good business relationships are maintained.

The ratios used to examine liquidity, i.e. the **liquidity ratios**, are:

1 Current ratio (working capital ratio)
2 Acid test ratio (quick ratio)

3 Accounts receivable : sales ratio (customers' collection period)
4 Accounts payable : purchases ratio (suppliers' payment period).

Each of the liquidity ratios stated can be compared period by period to see whether that particular aspect of liquidity is getting better or worse. In the case of the current ratio, it was often thought in the past that the ideal ratio should be around 2:1 and that, ideally, the acid test ratio should be in the region of 1:1 to 1.5:1. However, in recent years it has become recognised that such a fixed figure cannot possibly apply to every business, as the types and circumstances of businesses vary so widely.

1 Current ratio (or working capital ratio)

The current ratio measures current assets against current liabilities. It will compare assets that will be turned into cash within the next 12 months with any liabilities that will have to be paid within the same period. The current ratio is as follows:

$$\text{Current ratio} = \frac{\text{Current assets}}{\text{Current liabilities}}$$

If, therefore, the current assets are £125,000 and the current liabilities are £50,000, the current ratio will be:

$$\frac{£125{,}000}{£50{,}000} = 2.5{:}1\text{, or 2.5 times}$$

If the ratio increases by a large amount, the business may have more current assets than it needs. If the ratio falls by a large amount, then perhaps too little is being kept as current assets.

2 Acid test ratio (or quick ratio)

To determine a further aspect of liquidity, the **acid test ratio** takes into account only those current assets that are cash or can be changed very quickly into cash. This will normally mean Cash + Bank + Accounts receivable. You can see that this means exactly the same as current assets less inventory. The acid test ratio may, therefore, be stated as:

$$\text{Acid test ratio} = \frac{\text{Current assets less inventory}}{\text{Current liabilities}}$$

For instance, if the total of current assets is £40,000 and inventory is £10,000, and the total of current liabilities is £20,000, then the ratio will be:

$$\frac{£40{,}000 - £10{,}000}{£20{,}000} = 1.5{:}1\text{, or 1.5 times}$$

This ratio shows whether there are enough liquid assets to be able to pay current liabilities quickly. It is dangerous if this ratio is allowed to fall to a very low figure. If suppliers and others cannot be paid on time, supplies to the business may be reduced or even stopped completely. Eventually, the business may not have enough inventory to be able to sell properly. In that case, it may have to cease business.

3 Accounts receivable to sales ratio (customers' collection period)

This ratio assesses how long it takes customers to pay what they owe. The calculation is made as follows:

$$\frac{\text{Accounts receivable}}{\text{Sales for the year}} \times 12 = \begin{array}{l}\text{Number of months that customers}\\ \text{(on average) take to pay up}\end{array}$$

For example:

	(C)	(D)
Sales for the year	£240,000	£180,000
Accounts receivable as per statement of financial position	£60,000	£30,000

In business (C), debtors (customers) take three months on average to pay their accounts, calculated from:

$$\frac{\pounds 60{,}000}{\pounds 240{,}000} \times 12 = 3 \text{ months}$$

In business (D), debtors (customers) take two months on average to pay their accounts, given from:

$$\frac{\pounds 30{,}000}{\pounds 180{,}000} \times 12 = 2 \text{ months}$$

If the ratio is required to be shown in days instead of months, the formula should be multiplied by 365 instead of 12. The higher the ratio, the worse a business is at getting its accounts receivable to pay on time. The lower the ratio, the better it is at managing its accounts receivable.

Businesses should make certain that debtors (customers) pay their accounts on time. There are two main reasons for this. First, the longer a debt is owed, the more likely it will become a bad debt. Second, any payment of money can be used in the business as soon as it is received, and so this increases profitability; it can help reduce expenses. For example, it would reduce a bank overdraft and therefore reduce the bank overdraft interest.

4 Accounts payable to purchases ratio (suppliers' payment period)

This ratio shows how long it takes a business (on average) to pay its suppliers. The calculation is made as follows:

$$\frac{\text{Accounts payable}}{\text{Purchases for the year}} \times 12 = \begin{array}{l}\text{Number of months it takes}\\ \text{(on average) to pay up suppliers}\end{array}$$

For example:

	(E)	(F)
Purchases for the year	£120,000	£90,000
Accounts payable as per statement of financial position	£40,000	£22,500

Business (E) therefore takes four months' credit on average from its suppliers, i.e.

$$\frac{£40,000}{£120,000} \times 12 = 4 \text{ months}$$

Business (F) takes on average three months to pay its suppliers, i.e.

$$\frac{£22,500}{£90,000} \times 12 = 3 \text{ months}$$

Taking longer to pay suppliers could be a good thing or a bad thing, depending upon circumstances. If so long is taken to pay that possible discounts are lost, or that suppliers refuse to supply again, then it would be undesirable. On the other hand, paying before it is necessary simply takes money out of the business early without gaining any benefit.

39.5 Other ratios

There are many more ratios that may be used in analysing financial information, too many to mention in this book. There may be the need, say, to ascertain the amount of sales per employee or production ratios in a manufacturing company. However, another ratio that is useful to business organisations is the **non-current assets to sales ratio**.

Non-current assets to sales ratio

This ratio measures the level of efficiency of the non-current assets in generating sales. It is calculated as follows:

$$\frac{\textbf{Sales}}{\textbf{Non-current assets}} = \textbf{Non-current asset to sales ratio}$$

The greater the ratio the higher the level of efficiency, whereas a lower ratio indicates that the company is not operating as effectively. This may be caused by a decrease in sales or an increase in the non-current assets.

39.6 Definition of capital employed in various circumstances

In section 39.3 (5), it was pointed out that there is not one single agreed definition of the term 'capital employed'. In answering an exam question in this area, you must follow the examiner's instructions, if any are given; otherwise, state what basis you have used.

Sole proprietorships

'Capital employed' could mean any of the following:

- closing balance on capital account at the end of a financial period
- average of opening and closing balances on the capital account for the accounting period
- capital balances plus any long-term loans.

Partnerships

'Capital employed' could mean any of the following:

- closing balance on the fluctuating capital accounts at the end of a financial period
- average of opening and closing balances on the fluctuating capital accounts for an accounting period
- total of fixed capital accounts plus total of partners' current accounts at the end of a financial period
- average of opening and closing balances on the partners' capital and current accounts for an accounting period
- any of the above, plus long-term loans to the partnership.

Limited companies

Given the following details, different figures for capital employed may be used.

	£
(*a*) Ordinary share capital	100,000
(*b*) Preference share capital	40,000
(c) Total of different types of reserves including the retained profit shown in the income statement	35,000
(*d*) Debentures	60,000

- To calculate return on ordinary shareholders' funds, it would be (*a*) £100,000 + (c) £35,000 = £135,000.
- To calculate return on total shareholders' fund, it would be (*a*) £100,000 + (*b*) £40,000 + (c) £35,000 = £175,000.
- To calculate return on total capital employed, i.e. including borrowed funds, it would be (*a*) £100,000 + (*b*) £40,000 + (c) £35,000 + (*d*) £60,000 = £235,000.

Any question involving return of capital employed for limited companies should be read very carefully indeed. Use the method suggested by the examiner. If no indication is given, use that of (*a*) + (c) above, but you must state what method you have used.

39.7 Definition of working capital

Working capital is the amount by which current assets exceed current liabilities. It is also known as 'net current assets' (see Chapter 11).

It is vital for businesses to have sufficient working capital to enable them to have funds available to pay everyday running expenses. Working capital tends to circulate through a business, as shown in the diagram in Exhibit 39.3. As it flows, profits are made as inventory is sold to customers; the quicker it is sold, the quicker the business makes profits.

Exhibit 39.3

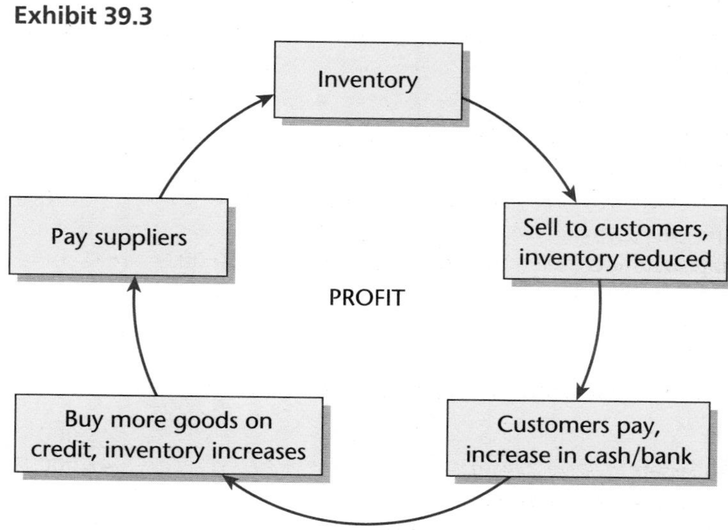

39.8 A fully worked example of calculating ratios

A fully worked example of calculating ratios and interpreting accounts is shown in Exhibit 39.4. Check all the calculations yourself and see whether your conclusions about the changes in the ratios agree with the author's.

Exhibit 39.4

The following are the financial statements for two similar types of retail stores:

Income Statements

	J		K	
	£	£	£	£
Sales		80,000		120,000
Less Cost of goods sold:				
Opening inventory	25,000		22,500	
Add Purchases	50,000		91,000	
	75,000		113,500	
Less Closing inventory	15,000	60,000	17,500	96,000
Gross profit		20,000		24,000
Less Depreciation	1,000		3,000	
Other expenses	9,000	10,000	6,000	9,000
Net profit		10,000		15,000

Statement of Financial Position

	J		K	
Non-current Assets	£	£	£	£
Equipment at cost	10,000		20,000	
Less Depreciation to date	8,000	2,000	6,000	14,000
Current Assets				
Inventory	15,000		17,500	
Accounts receivable	25,000		20,000	
Bank	5,000		2,500	
		45,000		40,000
Total assets		47,000		54,000
Less Current Liabilities				
Accounts payable		5,000		10,000
Net assets		42,000		44,000
Equity:				
Capital				
Balance at start of year		38,000		36,000
Add Net profit		10,000		15,000
		48,000		51,000
Less Drawings		6,000		7,000
		42,000		44,000

We will now calculate the following ratios (with all calculations shown correct to one decimal place):

(*a*) Gross profit as a percentage of sales
(*b*) Net profit as a percentage of sales
(*c*) Expenses as a percentage of sales
(*d*) Inventory turnover ratio
(*e*) Rate of return of net profit on capital employed (use the average of the capital account for this purpose)
(*f*) Current ratio
(*g*) Acid test ratio (quick ratio)
(*h*) Accounts receivable : Sales ratio
(*i*) Accounts payable : Purchases ratio

	J	K
(*a*) Gross profit as a % of sales	$\frac{£20,000}{£80,000} \times 100\% = 25\%$	$\frac{£24,000}{£120,000} \times 100\% = 20\%$
(*b*) Net profit as a % of sales	$\frac{£10,000}{£80,000} \times 100\% = 12.5\%$	$\frac{£15,000}{£120,000} \times 100\% = 12.5\%$
(*c*) Expenses as a % of sales	$\frac{£10,000}{£80,000} \times 100\% = 12.5\%$	$\frac{£9,000}{£120,000} \times 100\% = 7.5\%$
(*d*) Inventory turnover	$\frac{£60,000}{(£25,000 + £15,000) \div 2} = 3 \text{ times}$	$\frac{£96,000}{(£22,500 + £17,500) \div 2} = 4.8 \text{ times}$
(*e*) Rate of return on capital employed	$\frac{£10,000}{(£38,000 + £42,000) \div 2} \times 100\% = 25\%$	$\frac{£15,000}{(£36,000 + £44,000) \div 2} \times 100\% = 37.5\%$
(*f*) Current ratio	$\frac{£45,000}{£5,000} = 9:1$	$\frac{£40,000}{£10,000} = 4:1$
(*g*) Acid test ratio	$\frac{£45,000 - £15,000}{£5,000} = 6:1$	$\frac{£40,000 - £17,500}{£10,000} = 2.25:1$
(*h*) Accounts receivable : Sales ratio	$\frac{£25,000}{£80,000} \times 12 = 3.75 \text{ months}$	$\frac{£20,000}{£120,000} \times 12 = 2 \text{ months}$
(*i*) Accounts payable : Purchases ratio	$\frac{£5,000}{£50,000} \times 12 = 1.2 \text{ months}$	$\frac{£10,000}{£91,000} \times 12 = 1.3 \text{ months}$

Having calculated the ratios, we will now briefly analyse our findings.

Note: It is not suffficient to say that the ratios differ, but also try to give reasous why they differ relevant to the particular business.

Business K is more profitable, both in terms of actual net profits (£15,000 compared with £10,000), but also in terms of capital employed. K has managed to achieve a return of £37.50 for every £100 invested, i.e. 37.5%. J has managed a lower return of 25%.

The conclusions are only possible reasons because you must know more about the business before you can give a definite answer.

- Possibly K managed to sell far more merchandise because of lower prices, i.e. it took only 20% margin as compared with J's 25% margin.
- Maybe K made more efficient use of mechanised means in the business. Note that it has more equipment, and perhaps as a consequence it kept other expenses down to £6,000 as compared with J's £9,000.
- K did not have as much inventory lying idle. K turned his inventory over 4.8 times in the year, as compared with 3 times for J.
- J's current ratio of 9:1 was far greater than normally needed. K kept it down to 4:1. J therefore had too much money lying idle.
- The acid test ratio for J was higher than necessary and followed a similar trend to that shown by the current ratio.
- One reason for the better current and acid test ratios for K was that debts were collected on a two months' average.
- J also paid his suppliers more quickly than K – but only slightly faster.

When all these factors are considered, it is clear that business K is being run much more efficiently and, consequently, more profitably.

39.9 Summary of the formulae

For easy reference the various ratios, percentages and formulae used in this chapter are summarised in Exhibit 39.5.

Exhibit 39.5

Gross profit margin as a percentage of sales $= \dfrac{\text{Gross profit}}{\text{Sales}} \times 100 = x\%$

Gross profit mark-up as a percentage of sales $= \dfrac{\text{Gross profit}}{\text{Cost of sales}} \times 100 = x\%$

Net profit margin as a percentage of sales $= \dfrac{\text{Net profit}}{\text{Sales}} \times 100 = x\%$

Expenses as a percentage of sales $= \dfrac{\text{Expenses}}{\text{Sales}} \times 100 = x\%$

Return on capital employed (ROCE) $= \dfrac{\text{Net profit}}{\text{Capital employed}} \times 100 = x\%$

Inventory turnover $= \dfrac{\text{Cost of goods sold}}{\text{Average inventory}} = x \text{ times a year}$

where average inventory $= \dfrac{\text{Opening inventory} + \text{Closing inventory}}{2}$

Current ratio (working capital ratio) $= \dfrac{\text{Current assets}}{\text{Current liabilities}} = x{:}1$

Acid test ratio (quick ratio) $= \dfrac{\text{Current assets} - \text{Inventory}}{\text{Current liabilities}} = x{:}1$

Accounts receivable : Sales ratio (customers' collection period) = Number of months customers (on average) take to pay

$= \dfrac{\text{Accounts receivable}}{\text{Sales for the year}} \times 12 = x \text{ months}$

(If days instead of months are required, the formula should be multiplied by 365 instead of 12.)

Accounts payable : Purchases ratio (suppliers' payment period) = Number of months it takes (on average) to pay suppliers

$= \dfrac{\text{Accounts payable}}{\text{Purchases for the year}} \times 12 = x \text{ months}$

(If days instead of months are required, the formula should be multiplied by 365 instead of 12.)

Non-current asset : Sales ratio $= \dfrac{\text{Sales}}{\text{Non-current assets}} = x{:}1$

39.10 Multiple-choice questions

Now attempt Set No 3 of the multiple-choice questions in Appendix C, which contains 27 questions.

Chapter summary

- Financial statements are analysed and interpreted for internal and external parties. It is important to remember that a ratio on its own is of no use at all. It must be compared with previous years' results or the results of a competitor to be meaningful.
- Profitability and liquidity are equally important factors when running a business.
- The use of the profitability ratios ensure owners of a business keep a careful check on figures such as cost of goods, sales, expenses, gross and net profits.
- Liquidity ratios measure the ability of a business to pay its debts as they fall due and ensure smooth cash flow.
- Working capital is found by deducting current liabilities from the current assets. It is vital for businesses to have sufficient working capital to ensure they can pay their debts as they fall due.
- There are various methods of calculating capital employed depending upon the type of business, i.e. sole trader, partnership or limited company.

Note: In Appendix B you will find a worksheet that you can photocopy and use to answer questions on ratio analysis.

EXERCISES

*Note: Questions with the suffix 'X' shown after the question number do **not** have answers shown at the back of the book. Answers to the other questions are shown in Appendix E.*

39.1 The following accounts are of two companies that each sell sports goods:

Income Statements

	M Ltd		*N Ltd*	
	£	£	£	£
Sales		360,000		250,000
Less Cost of goods sold:				
Opening inventory	120,000		60,000	
Add Purchases	268,000		191,500	
	388,000		251,500	
Less Closing inventory	100,000	288,000	64,000	187,500
Gross profit		72,000		62,500
Less Expenses:				
Wages	8,000		11,300	
Directors' remuneration	12,000		13,000	
Other expenses	8,800	28,800	3,200	27,500
Net profit		43,200		35,000
Add Retained profits brought forward		16,800		2,000
		60,000		37,000
Less Appropriations:				
General reserve	8,000		2,000	
Dividends	40,000	48,000	30,000	32,000
Retained profits carried forward		12,000		5,000

Statements of Financial Position

	M Ltd		*N Ltd*	
	£	£	£	£
Non-current Assets:				
Fixtures at cost	200,000		180,000	
Less Depreciation to date	50,000	150,000	70,000	110,000
Motor vans at cost	80,000		120,000	
Less Depreciation to date	30,000	50,000	40,000	80,000
		200,000		190,000
Current Assets:				
Inventory	100,000		64,000	
Accounts receivable	60,000		62,500	
Bank	40,000		3,500	
		200,000		130,000
Total Assets		400,000		320,000
Less Current Liabilities				
Accounts payable		50,000		65,000
Net assets		350,000		255,000
Equity:				
Issued share capital		300,000		200,000
General reserve		38,000		50,000
Retained profits		12,000		5,000
		350,000		255,000

Required:

(*a*) Calculate the following ratios to one decimal place:

(i) current ratio
(ii) acid test ratio
(iii) inventory turnover
(iv) Accounts receivable : sales ratio
(v) Accounts payable : purchases ratio
(vi) gross profit as a percentage of sales
(vii) net profit as a percentage of sales
(viii) rate of return on shareholders' funds.

(*b*) Compare the results of the two companies, giving possible reasons for the different results.

39.2X The owners of Hailstone company and Taylor company are having a friendly argument over the relative performance of their two similar businesses. The following information is available:

	Hailstone company	*Taylor company*
	£	£
Cash	4,000	100
Sales	200,000	200,000
Operating expenses	8,000	80,000
Closing inventory	8,000	30,000
Accounts receivable	3,000	33,000
Bank overdraft	nil	5,000
Opening inventory	10,000	40,000
Capital employed	320,000	320,000
Accounts payable	7,500	50,000
Purchases	140,000	60,000

Required:

(*a*) For each company, calculate to one decimal place:
- (i) gross profit margin
- (ii) inventory turnover (use cost of goods sold divided by average inventory)
- (iii) net profit margin
- (iv) return on capital employed
- (v) accounts receivable collection period
- (vi) current ratio.

(*b*) Comment on the performance of each of the companies, using the ratios you have calculated.

City & Guilds Pitman qualifications

39.3X The following figures are extracted from the final accounts of a company for the year ended 31 December 2013:

	£
Opening inventory	5,000
Purchases	32,000
Closing inventory	7,000
Sales	60,000
Accounts receivable	7,500

For the year ended 31 December 2013, calculate:

(*a*) cost of goods sold
(*b*) average inventory
(*c*) inventory turnover rate
(*d*) accounts receivable collection period.

For the year ended 31 December 2012, the following had been calculated.

- Inventory turnover (rate) = 6 times p.a.
- Accounts receivable collection period = 31 days (1 month)

(*e*) With that additional information in mind, state which you think was the better year out of 2012 and 2013. Give *two* reasons to support your answer.

NEAB (GCSE)

39.4 Cruise Furnishings and Holmes Suppliers are two rival businesses. The following information has been extracted from their recent sets of accounts:

	Cruise Furnishings £000	*Holmes Supplies £000*
Results for year ended 31 August 2013		
Turnover	1,800	2,400
Cost of sales	1,200	1,800
Average inventory	120	150
Gross profit	600	600
Net profit	150	160

	Cruise Furnishings *£000*	*Holmes Supplies* *£000*
Balances at 31 August 2013		
Non-current assets	2,136	2,910
Current assets	210	180
Inventory (included in current assets)	111	120
Current liabilities	66	60
Non-current liabilities	30	2,070
Owner's capital	2,250	960

(*a*) Calculate the following for both businesses to two decimal places:
  (i) the gross profit margin
  (ii) the net profit margin
  (iii) the current ratio.

(*b*) Calculate the inventory turnover rate for Cruise Furnishings.

The owner of Holmes Supplies believes the performance of her business is superior to that of her rival, Cruise Furnishings.

(*c*) Using figures and including both profitability and liquidity, evaluate the owner's belief.

Edexcel International GCSE Accounting 1st edn, Edexcel (Robinson, S. 2010) Pearson Education Ltd.

39.5X The following figures were extracted from the books of Haydesh Kordi at the end of the previous two years' trading.

	Year ended 29 February 2012 £	*Year ended 28 February 2013* £
Sales	35,000	52,000
Opening inventory	2,900	4,000
Purchases	14,500	19,500
Closing inventory	4,000	7,000
Gross profit	21,600	35,500
Business expenses	5,600	9,500
Net profit	16,000	26,000

(*a*) Stating clearly the formula used, calculate the net profit margin for *each* of the two years. (Round to *two* decimal places.)

(*b*) Stating clearly the formula used, calculate the mark up for *each* of the two years. (Round to *two* decimal places.)

(*c*) Stating clearly the formula used, calculate the inventory turnover ratio for *each* of the two years.

(*d*) Using the figures calculated in the above sections, evaluate the profitability of the business over the last two years.

Edexcel International GCSE Accounting 1st edn, Edexcel (Robinson, S. 2010) Pearson Education Ltd.

PART 6

Associated accounting topics

This part is concerned with the use of computerised accounting systems. Also covered is a chapter on how ethics affects you personally in the workplace.

CHAPTER 40

Computers and accounting systems

Learning objectives

After you have studied this chapter you should be able to:

- appreciate the uses of computer technology in recording financial information
- appreciate the different types of financial accounting packages available for all types of organisations
- understand the functions and benefits of computer accounting software
- appreciate the benefits of having online facilities within a computer system to provide for internet usage
- realise the importance of backing up data when using a computerised accounting package
- understand the importance of security when using an accounting package and the benefits of using a password
- describe the advantages and disadvantages of using a computerised accounting system.

40.1 Introduction

Today there is widespread use of computers to operate accounting systems. Sophisticated technology is now available at a reasonable cost. Large to medium-sized concerns have used specially written packages for a number of years but smaller enterprises were initially discouraged from setting up their own systems by the cost of such packages. However, small businesses can now afford to use a computerised system using off-the-shelf packages such as Sage or QuickBooks. These packages carry out the same double entry functions of data processing and recording financial information as manual systems and also offer other features such as management information.

The rapid development of the internet means that accounting information and transactions can be carried out online. Consequently businesses that do not have computer facilities could easily get left behind and miss out on the opportunities that internet access provides.

40.2 Functions of computerised accounting packages

A **computerised accounting package** offers all the functions that a manual system provides but in addition it provides useful reports and management information. Since the system is integrated, basic data is entered, processed and automatically posted to supplier and customer accounts and the general (nominal) ledger updated. At the same time inventory records are updated and, in some instances, automatic re-ordering systems are in place. The main functions of a computerised accounting package are listed below.

Sales

Preparation and printing of sales invoices, credit notes and month end statements. Data from the above documents is entered, processed and recorded:

- in the customer accounts in the sales ledger
- by automatic update of the inventory records.

Purchases

Data from the purchase invoice and credit notes is entered, processed and recorded:

- in the supplier accounts in the purchase ledger
- by automatic update of the inventory records
- via a print out of remittance advices.

Bank account

- Recording data such as customer receipts, supplier payments, other payments and receipts.
- Many banks offer online banking facilities which have the added advantage of the organisation's bank account being completely up to date.
- All receipts and payments are linked to the personal accounts of the accounts receivable and accounts payable and the system provides for such transactions to automatically update these accounts.

General (nominal) ledger

Automatic updating of the general (nominal) ledger.

Wages/salaries

Organisations have the option of using a combined computerised accounting and wages/salary package; alternatively, they may use a separate 'payroll package'. Such packages perform all the necessary payroll functions.

Inventory control

As mentioned above under sales and purchases these functions are linked to the inventory records. This means that inventory records are automatically updated after each sales invoice and purchases invoice is entered into the system so providing an accurate figure of inventory held at any particular point in time.

At the end of the financial year when an organisation undertakes an inventory check the use of a computerised system enables up-to-date inventory lists to be made available. These lists are used in the physical inventory check and enable variances to be identified and amended.

The functions are summarised in Exhibit 40.1.

Exhibit 40.1 Integrated computerised accounting system

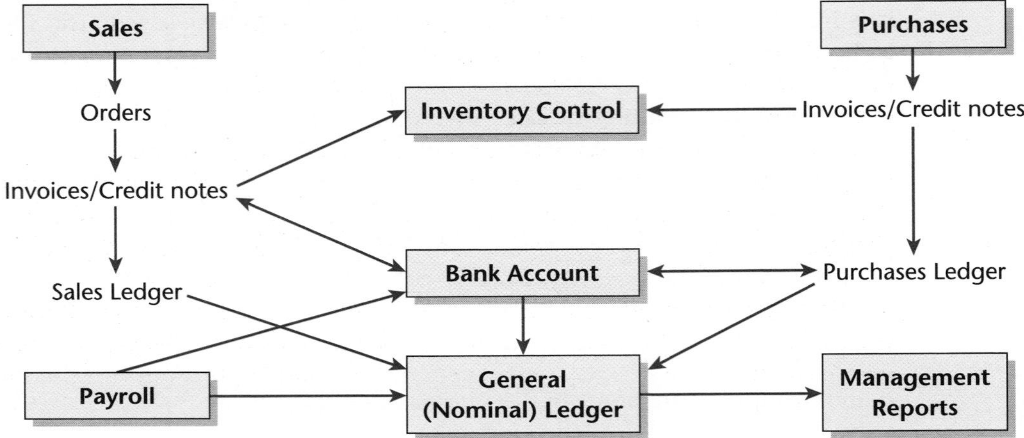

Exhibit 40.1 can be compared to Exhibit 2.1. The source documents and their entry in the books of prime entry are clearly shown.

Management reports

One of the main features of a computerised accounting system is the facility to provide the owners of the business and/or management with useful financial data and reports. At the end of each month or specific accounting period certain 'month end/year end' functions are carried out to provide the following information:

- day books for customers and suppliers
- general (nominal) ledger and bank account transactions
- activity reports on all ledger transactions
- an audit trail
- analysis reports for aged 'accounts receivable' and 'accounts payable'
- financial statements including the trial balance, income statements and statements of financial position
- ratio analysis.

Other useful functions

Spreadsheets The use of spreadsheets is another facility that a computer has to offer. Spreadsheets can be used to provide financial budgets or cash-flow budgets, a non-current asset register, calculation of loan interest payments plus many other uses.

Internet access As mentioned above internet access can provide such things as online banking, payment of suppliers and other payments such as wages/salaries. An organisation having its own website can advertise its products and services and offer online ordering systems. In addition the internet is a useful source of information and data that an organisation may from time to time need to access.

40.3 Data back-up

It is important that data held on the computer is regularly saved. The regularity has to be determined by the business relative to the type of operation and could mean every few minutes, after a specified computer task or after a longer time scale, say, every hour.

It is also vital to back up data held on the system. Back-up can be achieved by copying data onto a floppy disc, a CD or by transferring it to another computer, either on the premises or at a remote location. A recent development for storing information is USB pen drives, or memory sticks, which are small but robust solid state devices and are easily carried in a pocket or briefcase.

Some large organisations may deem it essential to keep their CDs, floppy discs, etc. containing stored information off-site in a secure location. This is particularly the case where the loss of such data could have catastrophic implications for the business.

40.4 Security

All organisations regard their financial information as sensitive and as such it should remain confidential except where legislation demands certain information be made available to external bodies.

Staff working on computerised accounting systems will be allocated passwords which will restrict access to their area of work. Passwords should be changed regularly to help prevent the possibility of non-authorised persons accessing the system.

When a system uses internet connections there is the constant threat of fraudulent access and corruption. Most computer systems have packages to resist viruses and attack by hacking. These have to be constantly reviewed and updated.

40.5 Computerised accounting systems

The following advantages and disadvantages of using accounting packages are detailed below.

Advantages

- Data is inputted and processed very rapidly, far faster than in a manual system.
- Greater accuracy since data is only input once and transactions carried out automatically whereas with a manual system data may have to be entered twice or more.

- Documents such as invoices, credit notes, statements, remittance advices can be produced automatically.
- Constant updating of the accounting records gives the accurate state of customers' accounts enabling remedial action to be taken as necessary.
- Management information can quickly be made available in report form, i.e. aged accounts receivable and accounts payable analysis reports.
- A system connected to the internet can make financial transactions electronically.
- More efficient use of resources, for example, less accounting staff.

Disadvantages

- The cost of installation can be considerable together with the ongoing costs of maintenance and updating.
- The introduction of the system will affect most other areas of the business leading to considerable disruption. Staff may also be resentful of any new system.
- Staff will need to be trained to use the system and training costs have to be considered.
- System downtime can be very disruptive.
- Data back-up is essential at regular intervals.
- Fraudulent access can seriously affect the business operation and its profitability.
- Security measures are vital, for example, passwords for staff and protection against viruses and hacking.
- Health risks associated with the operation of computer keyboards and screens, which include eyestrain, back problems due to poor posture, and muscular fatigue in the arm and wrist from keyboard use. Regular rest intervals away from work stations are essential.

Chapter summary

- Computers are widely used in organisations for operating accounting systems.
- Most computerised accounting packages are integrated systems linking together the sales ledger, purchase ledger, general (nominal) ledger and the bank account.
- The computerised accounting package also produces various documents such as invoices, credit notes, statements and remittance advices.
- Other features include providing financial information for the owners of the business and/or management and the use of the internet for online facilities and spreadsheets for such things as preparing budgets, etc.
- It is essential that users of computerised accounting packages regularly back up data using one of the various methods available.
- Security within any system is paramount for any organisation and every effort must be made to ensure that data is safe and secure.
- Organisations must consider the benefits of operating a computer accounting package such as the speed at which data is entered, accuracy, cost effectiveness and the information output, such as management reports.
- The disadvantages include the cost of installing equipment, buying software and providing training together with security concerns. There may also be some resentment from staff and lack of motivation.

EXERCISES

*Note: Questions with the suffix 'X' shown after the question number do **not** have answers shown at the back of the book. Answers to the other questions are shown in Appendix E.*

40.1 A flag manufacturer's business has recently received a large increase in orders from overseas to meet the requirements of major sporting events. This demand for flags has had a considerable effect on the present manual accounting system. The Finance Director has decided that he would like to introduce a fully integrated computer accounting system. He intends to put his case forward at the next Directors' Meeting and asks you to prepare some notes on his behalf.

Required:
Prepare notes for the Finance Director to present at the meeting including the main advantages to be gained by making the change. You must also anticipate the arguments that may be used by a board member objecting to the proposed change.

40.2 The security of data is a very important consideration when using a computerised accounting package. Explain the measures that a medium-sized company could initiate to provide protection for the company against the security of its financial data and records.

40.3X You work in the accounts department of an advertising agency where a new member of staff has recently joined the accounts team. You have been asked to help her settle in the department and provide training on the computerised accounting system. One of the areas that you feel is very important is security and backing up data.

Required:
Draft a memo to the trainee outlining the importance of security of financial data and the agency's procedures for backing up data.

40.4X (*a*) Outline the benefits that are available to a small business when it has internet facilities.
(*b*) If the firm decided to obtain the services of a web designer to develop a website what benefits would this provide to the business?
(*c*) If the website was developed what do you think are the disadvantages to offering such a service?

40.5X A local garage, which carries out servicing and repairs mainly to cars and small commercial vehicles, is run by the owner with two other employees. The book-keeping and accounting is carried out on a part-time basis by an employee who works one day per week. She uses a manual accounting system to deal with customer invoices and payments, paying suppliers for goods received, banking monies received, petty cash and paying wages.

The owner is considering a computerised accounting system but is unsure as to the benefits to be gained from a large initial investment.

Required:
Put forward the benefits that might be gained but also consider the adverse aspects of such an investment.

CHAPTER 41

Ethics: getting it right as a professional

Learning objectives

After you have studied this chapter you should be able to:

- appreciate how ethics affects you personally at home, with friends and in the workplace
- reflect on the factors on which your ethical behaviour is based
- be aware that codes of ethical behaviour have been introduced by most accountancy bodies
- appreciate that conflict may occur in dealing with an ethical dilemma or problem and the steps to take to resolve this.

41.1 This chapter is for you personally

You may wonder why ethics appears in a book whose aim is to develop your accountancy skills. Since you have reached the final chapter in the book it is assumed that you intend to make a career in finance and accounting.

You will already have been influenced by ethics but may not have been fully aware of how it has affected you. Your upbringing at home, your progress through school and college will have shaped and developed your behaviour. This revolves round the 'right thing to do' and the 'wrong thing to do'. The object of this chapter is to introduce you to the topic and encourage you to reflect on your own values and beliefs and how they affect your personal behaviour.

Accountancy is a profession and being a member of such a profession means more than 'just a job of work'. Being technically competent and nothing else is not sufficient. The way you act and make decisions in the workplace is crucial to the role of being a professional.

41.2 What are you taking to the party?

This question is asking what you have gained from your upbringing and life experiences in developing your personal behaviour. You might describe this as your own 'code of conduct' which will probably have been influenced by family/cultural/religious/educational aspects.

It is expected that you will have gained:

- values – what you have decided will guide you through life
- attitudes – developed through experience and can change through new positive/negative experiences
- beliefs – a conviction that something is true
- awareness – *self:* a developing understanding of a certain subject or situation; *others:* an ability of how to interact with family, friends and colleagues
- discipline – in terms of personal behaviour the ability to maintain self-control.

At this point consider the first three aspects discussed above and then add your own perceptions. Try to think of at least three elements for each aspect below.

An example is done for you.

Values *Honesty* --

Attitudes --

Beliefs --

41.3 Ethics

On a personal level **ethics** may be sufficiently described as the morals governing human behaviour. Professional ethics, however, are more clearly defined and are generally referred to as 'a code of behaviour considered correct for a particular group, association or profession'.

41.4 What you need to be successful in your workplace

The level and range of ethical requirements for each employee in the workplace will change relative to their duties and status. For example, an employee with no contact with clients or customers will have different requirements to employees such as sales staff.

Mechanical

Any aspiring professional should:

- Be skilled up to a technical level appropriate to their job requirements.
- Behave responsibly in carrying out their duties.
- Be prepared to undertake training to enhance their skills in terms of job, technological, environmental and legal requirements. Most professional bodies require members to undertake Continual Professional Development (CPD) to ensure that they are up-to-date and competent in all areas of their work.
- Know the need to keep confidential the work of the business except in permitted circumstances, for example, compliance with legal requirements.

Inter-personal

Any aspiring professional should:

- Work honestly and diligently with colleagues.
- Behave responsibly and fairly in a straightforward and honest manner to all people whether they be colleagues, clients, customers, contractors, etc.
- Conduct oneself courteously at all times.
- Not undermine colleagues to gain a personal advantage.

41.5 Ethical codes

Over the past few years the issue of ethical behaviour in the finance industry has been highly topical. In the USA, during this time, there have been some high-profile corporate failures, which led to the ethical culture and behaviour within these companies being questioned.

As a result the International Federation of Accountants (IFAC), through its ethics committee, issued its Code of Ethics for Professional Accountants, the latest issue being in June 2005. The aim of the code is 'to strengthen the worldwide accountancy profession' and is mandatory for those accountancy bodies that are members of IFAC. Therefore most accountancy bodies in the UK have now adopted the IFAC code with some additions and extra guidance.

As a student or full member of an accountancy institution you will be required to comply with that institution's code. To ensure that members are familiar with the requirements of the codes, seminars and training programmes have been initiated by the professional bodies as part of their CPD programmes. You should also be aware that many institutions have incorporated such codes into the assessment process for student members.

Larger accountancy businesses have their own ethical codes. As an employee you would be expected to comply with that code from the commencement of your employment. It is likely to be covered in your training at the induction stage or by participating in internal sessions.

41.6 Conflict

Until IFAC produced its first Code of Ethics in 2001, most codes of ethics in the accountancy profession consisted of sets of detailed rules that had to be followed to the letter. That was the problem in most of the famous corporate failures; it was the letter rather than the spirit that was being observed. Most regulators were producing ever-increasingly lengthy and unwieldy lists of rules to combat ever-increasing breaches of the regulations. It was then that IFAC decided to produce a code, which was a framework of principles:

A professional accountant is expected to comply with the following fundamental principles:

(a) Integrity – A professional accountant should be straightforward and honest in all professional and business relationships.

(b) *Objectivity – A professional accountant should not allow bias, conflict of interest or undue influence to override professional or business judgements.*

(c) *Professional Competence and Due Care – A professional accountant has a continuing duty to maintain professional knowledge and skill at the level required to ensure that a client or employer receives competent professional service based on current developments in practice, legislation and techniques. A professional accountant should act diligently and in accordance with applicable technical and professional standards when providing professional services.*

(d) *Confidentiality – A professional accountant should respect the confidentiality of information acquired as a result of professional and business relationships and should not disclose any such information to third parties without proper and specific authority unless there is a legal or professional right or duty to disclose. Confidential information acquired as a result of professional and business relationships should not be used for the personal advantage of the professional accountant or third parties.*

(e) *Professional behaviour – A professional accountant should comply with relevant laws and regulations and should avoid any action that discredits the profession.*

Professional accountants, including students, have to abide by these fundamental principles. Although there are detailed examples for guidance, the principles override any illustrations. Therefore, when making professional judgements the professional accountant has to consider these principles sufficiently for any such decisions to be able to withstand professional scrutiny if necessary at a later date.

Problems can arise when we take account of the influences on us when deciding what course of action to follow, whether professional or personal. The influences can include:

- Personal – the need to behave within one's own integrity.
- Company – working in the best interests of your employer.
- Professional body – upholding the aims and standards of your institution or association.
- Public interest – *'a distinguishing mark of a profession is acceptance of its responsibility to the public. Therefore, a professional accountant's responsibility is not exclusively to satisfy the needs of an individual client or employer'* (IFAC Code of Ethics, Introduction). In the first edition (2001) of its Code, it was stated: *'The accountancy profession's public consist of clients, credit grantors, governments, employers, employees, investors, the business and financial community and others who rely on the objectivity and integrity of professional accountants. . . .'*

You can see that all these considerations can lead to uncertainty in arriving at the correct decision. However, remember that management are responsible for implementing and maintaining ethical standards. An ethical dilemma or problem is not the sole responsibility of the person affected but should be dealt with as stated in the Code. This may be as a team in a particular department, as a company-wide issue or at a professional or regulatory disciplinary hearing.

41.7 Your next step

Assuming you are involved in accountancy you need to evaluate your present situation relative to your work, academic studies and your status, even as a student member of an accountancy body. As a junior member in the workplace, professional ethics may have little effect due to your level of work. If you are in the initial stages of your accountancy studies you will need to be familiar with the assessment requirements of your particular accountancy body.

It is worth remembering that professional ethics have an impact on companies, institutions, associations, etc. irrespective of the activity being carried out. You will need to be involved whatever your role.

Chapter summary

- This chapter introduces the concept of your personal behaviour, which can be referred to as your own code of conduct.
- Ethical behaviour is now an important aspect of working as a professional accountant and is referred to under both inter-personal and mechanical aspects.
- Codes of behaviour have been introduced in the UK by most of the professional firms, institutions, associations, etc. Within an organisation, it is management's role to implement and maintain the relevant ethical code. Nevertheless every professional accountant has his or her own responsibilities and has to be accountable for his or her actions.
- Ethical dilemmas and problems are not the sole responsibility of the person affected but should be resolved based on teamwork appropriate to the scale of the problem.

Appendices

The Appendices provide ancillary information to aid understanding of the main narrative of the book. Test questions are also included.

APPENDIX A

Glossary of accounting terms

The chapter number where the term first appears is shown at the end of each definition.

Account	The place in a ledger where all the transactions relating to a particular asset, liability or capital, expenses or revenue item are recorded. Accounts are part of the double entry book-keeping system. They are sometimes referred to as 'T accounts' or ledger accounts. **(4)**
Accounts payable (or creditor)	A person to whom money is owed for goods or services. **(2)**
Accounts payable : purchases ratio	A ratio assessing how long it takes a business to pay its suppliers (creditors). **(39)**
Accounts receivable (or debtor)	A person who owes money to the business for goods or services supplied. **(2)**
Accounts receivable : sales ratio	A ratio assessing how long it takes customers (debtors) to pay a business. **(39)**
Accounting	A skill or practice of maintaining accounts and preparing reports to aid the financial control and management of a business. **(1)**
Accounting concepts	The rules which lay down the way in which the activities of a business are recorded. **(13)**
Accounting equation	If a business starts trading it will require resources, expressed as: resources supplied by the owner = resources in the business or capital = assets – liabilities. **(3)**
Accounting system (cycle)	The period in which a business operates its financial year. It involves recording all trading activities from source documents to the preparation of the financial statements. **(2)**
Accrual	An accrued expense. An amount owing. **(29)**
Accruals concept	Where net profit is the difference between revenues and expenses. **(13)**
Accrued expense	An expense that has been incurred and the benefit received but that has not been paid for at the end of the accounting period. Also referred to as an accrual. **(29)**
Accumulated fund	A form of capital account for a non-profit-making organisation. **(35)**
Acid test ratio	A ratio comparing current assets less inventory with current liabilities. Also known as the 'quick ratio'. **(39)**

Administration expenses Expenses such as managers' salaries, legal fees, the depreciation of office equipment and secretarial salaries which are shown under this heading in the financial statements. (**38**)

Advice note A note sent to a customer by the supplier prior to goods being despatched, advising of the goods to be despatched and the estimated date of delivery. (**15**)

Ageing schedule for doubtful debts A list of amounts owing by customers (debtors) and how long the debt has been outstanding. (**28**)

Allowance for doubtful debts An account showing the expected amounts of debts that are unlikely to be paid at the date of the financial statements. (**28**)

Amortisation A term used instead of depreciation when assets are used up simply because of the time factor. (**26**)

Analytical day books Book of original entry in which sales and/or purchases invoices are entered. The book has various analysis columns, which are totalled at the end of the month and posted to the general ledger and control accounts. (**19**)

Annual General Meeting (AGM) A meeting held every year to which all shareholders in a company are invited to attend. At the meeting, the latest set of financial statements are considered, together with the appointment or removal of directors and/or auditors. (**37**)

Appreciation The increase in value over the cost of an asset, usually land and buildings. (**26**)

Assets Resources owned by the business. (**3**)

Authorised share capital The total amount of share capital or number of shares which a company can have in issue at any given time. (**37**)

Automated Direct Debit Instruction Service (AUDDIS) A fast method for businesses to make repayments. (**20**)

AVCO A method by which the goods used are priced out at average cost. (**31**)

Bad debt A debt owing to a business which is unlikely to be paid. (**28**)

Bad debt recovered A debt, previously written off, that is subsequently paid by the customer. (**28**)

Balancing the account Finding and entering the difference between the two sides of an account. (**7**)

Bank cash book The cash book for other than petty cash. (**22**)

Bank draft This is raised by the bank from funds held by a business and is passed to the supplier for whom it is a secure and guaranteed method of payment. (**20**)

Bank giro credit (BGC) Method used by businesses to pay suppliers, wages and/or salaries. A bank giro credit list and slips containing information about each person or organisation to be paid and the amounts payable are sent to the bank, together with one cheque to cover all the payments. The bank then automatically transfers the funds from the business's account to the account of each of the respective people or organisations. (**23**)

Bank overdraft This occurs when a business has paid more out of their bank account than they have paid into it. Therefore, the business is being financed by the bank in the short term. **(21)**

Bank reconciliation statement A calculation comparing the cash book balance with the bank statement balance. **(18)**

Bank statement Copy of our current account given to us by our bank. **(20)**

Bankers' Automated Clearing Service (BACS) Computerised payment transfer system that is a very popular way of paying suppliers, wages and salaries. **(2)**

Book-keeping The recording of accounting data. **(1)**

Books of original entry Books where the first entry of a transaction is made. **(16)**

Budgets The usual term for financial plans. **(1)**

Business entity concept Concerning only transactions that affect the business, and ignoring the owner's private transactions. **(13)**

Called-up capital Where only part of the amounts payable on each issued share have been asked for, the total amount requested on all the issued shares is known as the 'called-up capital'. **(37)**

Calls in arrear The amount for which payment has been requested (i.e. called for), but has not yet been paid by shareholders. **(37)**

Capital The total of resources supplied to a business by its owner. **(3)**

Capital employed This term has many meanings, but basically it means the amount of money that is being used up (or 'employed') in the business. It is the balance of the capital account plus any long-term loans or, alternatively, the total net assets of the business. **(29)**

Capital expenditure When a business spends money to buy or add value to any non-current asset. **(9)**

Capital invested The amount of money, or money's worth, brought into a business by its proprietor from outside. **(29)**

Capital reserve Reserves which cannot be used for the payment of dividends. The two most common types of capital reserve are the Share Premium Account and Revaluation Reserve Account. (Capital reserves are outside the scope of this book.) **(37)**

Carriage inwards Cost of transport of goods into a business. **(12)**

Carriage outwards Cost of transport of goods to the customers of a business. **(12)**

Carriage paid The cost of transport that has been included in the cost of the goods. **(15)**

Cash book Book of original entry for cash and bank receipts and payments. **(2)**

Cash discount An allowance given for quick payment of an account owing. **(14)**

Cash float The sum held as petty cash. **(22)**

Casting Adding up figures. **(32)**

Cheque A cash free method of transferring money using a form of standard format. It is used to instruct one's own bank to transfer money from one's own account to another person or business. **(20)**

Cheque counterfoil	On which to record details of the cheque issued. **(2)**
Clearing House Automated Payments System (CHAPS)	A computerised system that has developed to facilitate the same day transfer of largeamounts of money. **(20)**
COD	Literally 'Cash on delivery'. **(15)**
Coding of invoices	A process used, particularly in computerised accounting, to code the invoice to the supplier or purchaser, and also to the relevant account in the general ledger. **(17)**
Company limited by guarantee	These do not have share capital but rely on members' guarantees in the event of insolvency. **(37)**
Compensating error	Where two errors of equal amounts but on opposite sides of the accounts, cancel out each other. **(32)**
Complete reversal of entries	Where the correct amounts are entered in the correct accounts but each item is shown on the wrong side of each account. **(32)**
Computerised accounting package	A software accounting package which involves the inputting of packages financial data. The data is recorded in both the individual account and ledgers in one transaction. The package also provides additional financial management reports and information. **(40)**
Conservatism	An older term for 'prudence'. **(13)**
Consistency concept	To keep the same method, except in special cases. **(13)**
Contra	A contra is where both the debit and credit entries are shown in the cash book. **(21)**
Control account	An account which checks the arithmetical accuracy of a ledger. **(25)**
Cost control	The process of recording and monitoring costs incurred by a business to ensure the continued financial viability. **(1)**
Cost of goods sold	This is calculated as follows: Opening inventory plus purchases during the period less the value of the inventory at the end of the period (closing stock). **(10)**
Cost of purchase	The purchase price less trade discounts, etc. **(31)**
Cost price	The basic price before any mark ups, etc. **(27)**
Credit	The right-hand side of the accounts in double entry. **(4)**
Credit card	Issued by organisations such as Visa, Mastercard and involve electronic transfer of money to the seller by the credit card company who will bill the buyer for repayment. **(20)**
Credit control	The measures and procedures a business undertakes to ensure that its customers pay their accounts when they fall due. This includes evaluating the credit worthiness of customers before allowing them credit. **(16)**
Credit note	A document sent to a customer showing allowance given by supplier in respect of unsatisfactory goods. **(2)**
Credit transfer	An amount paid by someone direct into our bank account. **(20)**
Current assets	Assets consisting of cash, goods for resale, or items having a shorter life. **(3)**

Current liabilities Liabilities to be paid for in the near future. **(3)**

Current ratio A ratio comparing current assets with current liabilities. Also known as the 'working capital' ratio. **(39)**

Debenture Loan to a company, often secured on the non-current assets of the business. **(37)**

Debenture interest An agreed percentage of interest paid to a debenture holder for lending a company money. **(37)**

Debit The left-hand side of the accounts in double entry. **(4)**

Debit card A card issued by the bank which allows the account holder to purchase goods/services and pay for them using the debit card. The account holder's account is then charged with the purchase. **(20)**

Debit note A document sent to a supplier showing allowance given for unsatisfactory goods. **(2)**

Delivery note A note which accompanies goods being despatched, enabling the customer to check what goods have been received. The carrier often retains a copy and asks the customer to sign this to verify that the customer has received the goods. **(15)**

Depletion The wasting away of an asset as it is used up. **(26)**

Depreciation The part of the cost of the non-current asset consumed during its period of use by a business. **(26)**

Diminishing balance method See 'reducing balance method. **(26)**

Direct costs Costs which can be traced to the item being manufactured. **(38)**

Direct debit Payment made out of payer's bank, direct to payee's bank, on *payee's* instructions. **(20)**

Directors Officials appointed by shareholders to manage the company for them. **(37)**

Directors' remuneration Directors are legally employees of the company and any pay they receive is called directors' remuneration. **(37)**

Discounts allowed A reduction given to customers who pay their accounts within the time allowed. **(21)**

Discounts received A reduction given to us by a supplier when we pay their account before the time allowed has elapsed. **(21)**

Dishonoured cheque A cheque that the bank refuses to honour (pay). **(23)**

Dividends The amount given to shareholders as their share of the profits of the company. **(37)**

Dividends proposed but not paid The dividend proposed has to be approved by the shareholders and cannot appear in the financial statements but appears as a note to the accounts. **(37)**

Donation A monetary gift donated to the club or society, monies received should be shown as income in the year that they are received. **(35)**

Double entry See Double entry book-keeping. **(4)**

Double entry book-keeping A system where each transaction is entered twice, once on the debit side and once on the credit side. **(2)**

Doubtful debt A debt which may not be paid in the time requested. (**28**)

Drawee The bank on which a cheque is drawn. (**20**)

Drawer The person making out a cheque and using it for payment. (**20**)

Drawings Cash or goods taken out of a business by the owner for private use. (**6**)

Dual aspect concept Dealing with both aspects of a transaction. (**13**)

E&OE Appears on some invoices and other documents. Abbreviation stands for 'errors and omissions excepted'. Basically it is a warning that errors or omissions may exist on documents. (**15**)

EFTPOS Electronic Funds Transfer at Point of Sale. A system used by most large retail businesses which involves the use of electronic cash registers. This automatically transfers payments from the purchaser's account to the seller's bank account. (**20**)

Equity Another name for the capital of the owner. Also described as 'net worth'. (**3**)

Error of commission Where a correct amount is entered, but in the wrong person's account. (**32**)

Errors, complete reversal of entries See 'complete reversal of entries'. (**32**)

Error of omission Where a transaction is completely omitted from the books. (**32**)

Error of original entry Where an item is entered, but both debit and credit entries are of the same incorrect amount. (**32**)

Error of principle Where an item is entered in the wrong type of account, for example, a non-current asset entered in an expense account. (**32**)

Error of transposition Where figures are transposed incorrectly. (**33**)

Ethics The moral principles governing human conduct generally referred to as 'a code of behaviour considered correct for a particular group, association, profession'. (**41**)

Ex works An indication that the price of certain goods does not include delivery costs. (**15**)

Exempted businesses Businesses that do not have to add VAT to the price of goods and services supplied by them, and that cannot obtain a refund of VAT paid on goods and services purchased by them. (**14**)

Exempt supplies Supplies which are outside the scope of VAT and, therefore, VAT cannot be charged. (**14**)

Expenses Costs of operating the business. (**6**)

Expenses : sales ratio A ratio which indicates whether costs are rising against sales or whether sales are falling against expenses. (**39**)

Extended trial balance (ETB) A trial balance with additional columns added to enable adjustments to be made prior to the preparation of the financial statements. The extended trial balance is often referred to as a 'worksheet'. (**30**)

Factoring A system used by a business to improve its cash flow. This involves 'selling' its accounts receivable (debtors) to a factoring company, which is then responsible for collecting debts as they become due and which keeps a percentage of the money collected, usually around 10%. **(16)**

Factory overhead costs Refer to: Indirect manufacturing costs. **(38)**

FIFO A method by which the first goods to be received are said to be the first to be sold. **(31)**

Final accounts At the end of the accounting period or year a business usually prepares its financial statements, which includes the income statement and statement of financial position, these are often referred to as 'final accounts'. **(12)**

Finance charges Expenses incurred in providing finance facilities such as interest charged on a loan, bank charges and discounts allowed, all which appear under this heading in the financial statements. **(38)**

Financial statements Formal documents produced by an organisation to show the financial status of the business at a particular time. These include the income statement and statement of financial position. **(1)**

Fixed capital accounts Capital accounts which consist only of the original capital invested in a partnership. **(36)**

Fixed costs Costs that remain the same (in the short term) irrespective of levels of production or business activity. **(38)**

Flat rate scheme A special VAT scheme for small businesses. **(14)**

Fluctuating capital accounts Capital accounts whose balances change from one period to the next. **(36)**

Folio columns Columns used for entering reference numbers. **(21)**

General ledger All accounts other than those for customers and suppliers. **(2)**

Going concern concept Where a business is assumed to continue for a long time. **(13)**

Goodwill The extra amount paid for an existing business above the value of its other assets. **(29)**

Goods received note A note that details exactly what goods have been received. **(15)**

Gross loss When the 'cost of goods sold' exceeds 'sales', then the business has incurred a gross loss. **(10)**

Gross profit Found by deducting cost of goods sold from sales. **(9)**

Gross profit as a percentage of sales (Gross profit margin) A ratio which states gross profit as a percentage of sales; can indicate how effectively a business has controlled their cost of goods. **(39)**

Gross profit to cost of sales (Gross profit mark-up) The percentage of gross profit to the cost of sales. **(39)**

Historical cost concept The normal means of valuing the assets of a business based on their cost price. **(13)**

Impersonal accounts All accounts other than accounts receivable (debtors') and accounts payable (creditors') accounts. **(2)**

Imprest system A system used for controlling expenditure of small cash items which are recorded in the petty cash book. A cash 'float' of a fixed amount is provided initially to the person responsible for operating the petty cash system. Any cash paid out during a particular period, i.e. a week, is reimbursed to the petty cashier so restoring the 'float' to its original sum. **(22)**

Inadequacy When an asset is no longer used because of changes within an organisation due to growth, competition or product range changes. **(26)**

Income and expenditure account An account for a non-profit-making organisation to find the surplus or loss made during a period. **(35)**

Income statement The financial statement in which both the gross and net profits are calculated. **(1)**

Incomplete records Where only some transactions are recorded in the books of account, the missing information has to be obtained by other means. **(34)**

Indirect (manufacturing) costs Costs which occur in a factory or other production facility but cannot be easily traced to the items being manufactured. **(38)**

Input VAT The VAT charged to a business on its purchases and expenses (inputs). **(14)**

Inputs The value of goods and services purchased by a business. **(14)**

Intangible asset An asset that cannot be physically seen or touched such as goodwill. **(37)**

Interest on capital An amount, at an agreed rate of interest, that is credited to a partner based on the amount of capital contributed by him or her. **(36)**

Interest on drawings/withdrawal An amount, at an agreed rate of interest, that is based on the drawings taken out and is debited to the partners. **(36)**

Inventory Goods purchased by a business for resale. **(3)**

Inventory turnover ratio A ratio comparing the cost of goods sold to average inventory. It shows the number of times inventory is sold in an accounting period. Also known as 'stockturn'. **(39)**

Invoice A document prepared by the seller and sent to the purchaser whenever a business buys goods or services on credit. It gives details of the supplier and the customer, the goods purchased and their price. **(2)**

Issued share capital The amount of the authorised share capital of a company that has been issued to shareholders. **(37)**

Journal A book of account used to record rare or exceptional transactions that should not appear in the other books of original entry in use. **(2)**

Lease An agreement to rent property for a period of time. **(26)**

Liabilities Total of money owed for assets supplied to the business. **(3)**

Life membership Where members pay one amount for membership to last them their lifetime. **(35)**

LIFO A method by which the goods sold are said to have come from the last batch of goods to be received. (**31**)

Limited company An organisation owned by its shareholders, whose liability is limited to their share capital. (**37**)

Limited liability The liability of shareholders, in a company, is limited to any amount they have agreed to invest. (**37**)

Limited partner A partner whose liability is limited to the capital invested in the partnership. (**36**)

Limited partnership A form of partnership in which limited partners' liabilities are limited to their investment and in which general partners with unlimited liability operate the business. (**36**)

Liquidity The ability of a business to pay its debts as they fall due and to meet unexpected expenses within a reasonable settlement period. (**39**)

Liquidity ratios Ratios that attempt to indicate the ability of a business to meet its debts as they become due and include current ratio and acid test ratio. (**39**)

Loan Money borrowed by a company from a bank or other sources. (**37**)

Loan capital Money owing by a company for debentures and for loans from banks and other sources that are not repayable in the near future. (**37**)

Loan interest The extra amount levied by the lender of funds to recompense them for making the loan. (**9**)

Loss Result of selling goods for less than they have cost the business. (**6**)

Manufacturing account An account in which production cost is calculated. (**38**)

Margin Profit shown as a percentage or fraction of the selling price. (**34**)

Mark-up Profit shown as a percentage or fraction of the cost price. (**34**)

Matching concept Another term for the accrual concept. (**13**)

Materiality concept To record something in a special way only if the amount is not a small one. (**13**)

Memorandum account An account which is not part of the double-entry system. These may be the personal accounts of accounts receivable (debtors) or accounts payable (creditors) where the control account is part of the double entry and the personal accounts are classified as 'memorandum accounts'. Alternatively, the sales and purchases ledgers may be part of the double entry and the control accounts classified as 'memorandum accounts'. (**25**)

Money measurement concept Accounting is only concerned with the money measurement of things and where most people will agree to the monetary value of a transaction. (**13**)

Narrative A description and explanation of the transaction recorded in the journal. (**24**)

Net book value The cost of a non-current asset with depreciation deducted, also known as 'book value'. (**26**)

Net current assets The value of current assets less that of current liabilities. Also known as 'working capital'. **(11)**

Net loss This occurs when total expenses exceed the gross profit. **(12)**

Net monthly Appears at the foot of an invoice and means the full amount of the invoice is due for payment within one month of the invoice date. **(15)**

Net profit Gross profit less expenses. **(9)**

Net profit as a percentage of sales A ratio that states net profit as a percentage of sales and brings expenses into the calculation. **(39)**

Net realisable value The value of goods calculated as the selling price less expenses before sale. **(31)**

Net worth See 'equity'. **(3)**

Nominal accounts Accounts in which expenses, revenue and capital are recorded. **(2)**

Nominal ledger Ledger for impersonal accounts (also called general ledger). **(2)**

Non-current assets Assets bought which have a long life and are to be used in the business. **(3)**

Non-current assets to sales ratio A measurement of the efficiency of the non-current assets in generating sales. **(39)**

Non-current liabilities Liabilities not having to be paid for in the near future. **(11)**

Non-profit-making organisations Clubs, associations and societies operated to provide a service or activity for members since their main purpose is not trading or profit making. **(35)**

Non-trading organisations These include clubs, associations and other non-profit-making organisations that are normally run for the benefit of their members to engage in a particular activity. **(1)**

Objectivity Using a method that everyone can agree to. **(13)**

Obsolescence Becoming out of date. **(26)**

Opening entry An entry needed to open a new set of books of account. **(24)**

Ordinary shares Shares entitled to dividends after the preference shareholders have been paid their dividends. **(37)**

Output VAT The VAT charged by a business on its supplies (outputs). **(14)**

Outputs The value of goods and services sold to a business. **(14)**

Overcasting Incorrectly adding up a column of figures to give an answer which exceeds the correct total. **(32)**

Paid-up capital The total of the amount of share capital that has been paid for by shareholders. **(37)**

Partly exempt businesses These will sell some goods that are exempt from VAT and some goods that are either standard-rated or zero-rated. They may reclaim part of the input VAT paid by them. **(14)**

Partnership A group of a minimum of two people and a maximum of 20, who together are carrying on a particular business with a view to making profit. **(1)**

Partnership agreement The contractual relationship, either written or verbal, between partners, which usually covers details such as how profits or losses should be shared and the relevant responsibilities of the partners. **(36)**

Partnership deed See 'partnership agreement'.

Partnership salaries Agreed amounts payable to partners in respect of duties undertaken by them. **(36)**

Payee The person to whom a cheque is paid. **(20)**

Payer The person who pays a cheque. **(20)**

Paying-in slip Form used for paying money into a bank account. **(2)**

Personal accounts Accounts for both accounts payable (creditors) and accounts receivable (debtors). **(2)**

Petty cash book A cash book used for making small (petty) payments. Payments are usually analysed and the totals of each column later posted to the various accounts in the general ledger. The source document used for entry into the petty cash book is a petty cash voucher. **(2)**

Petty cash voucher The form used by anyone requesting payment for a small item of expenditure incurred on behalf of the business. The form gives details of the expense and should be signed and duly authorised. **(2)**

Posting The act of using one book as a means of entering the transactions to another account. **(2)**

Preference shares Shares that are entitled to an agreed rate of dividend before the ordinary shareholders receive anything. **(37)**

Prepaid expense An expense – usually a service – that has been paid for in one accounting period, the benefit of which will not be received until a subsequent period. It is a payment for an expense that has been paid for in advance. **(29)**

Prepayment Also referred to as 'prepaid expense'. **(29)** (See above)

Prime cost Direct materials plus labour plus direct expenses. **(38)**

Prime documents Another term for source documents. **(2)**

Private ledger Ledger for capital and drawings accounts. **(2)**

Private limited company A legal entity which must have at least one shareholder and one director who may be the sole shareholder. The liability of the shareholders is limited to the amount of their investment. The public cannot subscribe for its shares. **(1)**

Production cost Prime cost plus indirect manufacturing costs. **(38)**

Profit The result when goods are sold for more than they cost. (If they are sold for less than they cost, then a *loss* is incurred.) **(1)**

Profit and loss account An account in which net profit is calculated which is included the income statement. **(10)**

Profit and loss appropriation account An addition to the profit and loss account of partnerships which shows how the profit earned is divided. The profits are divided in accordance with the Partnership Deed or Agreement. However, if no such deed or agreement exists the Partnership Act of 1890 governs the situation. **(36)**

Profitability	The effective operation of a business to make ongoing profits to ensure its long-term viability. **(39)**
Profitability ratios	Ratios that attempt to indicate the trend in a business's ability to make profit. These include gross profit and net profit to sales and return on capital employed. **(39)**
Pro-forma invoice	A type of invoice that is occasionally raised when the seller wishes to secure payment prior to the goods or services being supplied. **(15)**
Provision for depreciation account	An account where depreciation is accumulated and shown as a deduction from the cost price of the asset to give the net book value figure in the statement of financial position. **(27)**
Prudence concept	To ensure that profit is not shown as being too high, or assets shown at too high a value. **(13)**
Public limited company	A legal entity with many shareholders since the public can subscribe for its shares. Shareholder liability is limited to the amount of their investment. The issued capital must be at least £50,000. **(1)**
Purchase invoice	A document received by purchaser showing details of goods bought and their prices. **(17)**
Purchase order	This is a document prepared by the purchaser and it contains details of the goods or services required by the purchaser. **(15)**
Purchases	Goods bought by the business for the purpose of selling them again. **(5)**
Purchases day book	Book of original entry for credit purchases. **(2)**
Purchases journal	Another name for the purchases day book. **(2)**
Purchases ledger	A ledger for suppliers' personal accounts. **(2)**
Purchases ledger control account	An account containing the total of the various individual personal account ledger account balances. By comparing the balance on the control account with the outstanding balances in a subsidiary ledger the arithmetical accuracy can be checked and errors rectified. **(25)**
Purchases returns	Goods returned by the business to its suppliers. See also 'returns outwards'. **(5)**
Purchases returns day book	Book of original entry for goods returned to suppliers. **(2)**
Quick ratio	Same as the acid test ratio. **(39)**
Quotation	A formal document prepared by a supplier which is an offer to supply goods or services. **(15)**
Real accounts	Accounts in which property of all kinds is recorded. **(2)**
Realisation concept	The point at which profit is treated as being earned. **(13)**
Receipt	A form acknowledging receipt of money for goods or services rendered. **(2)**
Receipts and payments account	A summary of the cash book of a non-profit-making organisation. **(35)**

Reducing balance method	Depreciation calculation which is at a lesser amount every following period. Also known as the 'diminishing balance method'. **(26)**
Remittance advice	A document which accompanies payments by cheque or via BACS and gives details of the payment. **(15)**
Reserve accounts	The transfer of apportioned profits to accounts for use in future years. **(37)**
Residual value	The amount received on disposal of an asset, also referred to as 'scrap value'. **(26)**
Retained profits	Profits earned in a year but not paid out in dividends. **(37)**
Return on capital employed (ROCE)	A ratio that shows the net profit made for each £100 of capital employed. **(39)**
Returns inwards	Goods returned to the business by its customers. **(18)**
Returns inwards day book	Book of original entry for goods returned by customers. **(2)**
Returns note	Document identifying sales returns. **(15)**
Returns outwards	Goods returned by the business to its suppliers. **(18)**
Returns outwards day book	Book of original entry for goods returned to suppliers. **(2)**
Revenue expenditure	Expenses needed for the day-to-day running of the business. **(9)**
Revenue reserve	Reserves of a company which are available for distribution as a dividend. **(37)**
Revenues	Monetary value of goods and services supplied to the customers. **(6)**
Sale or return	Goods that do not belong to the person holding them. **(31)**
Sales	Goods sold by the business. **(5)**
Sales day book	Book of original entry for credit sales. **(2)**
Sales invoice	A document showing the details of goods sold and the prices of those goods. **(16)**
Sales journal	Another name for sales day book. **(2)**
Sales ledger	A ledger for customers' personal accounts. **(2)**
Sales ledger control account	See 'purchases ledger control account'. **(25)**
Sales returns	Goods returned to the business by its customers. **(5)**
Sales returns day book	Book of original entry for goods returned by customers. **(2)**
Scrap value	See 'residual value'.
Selling and distribution expenses	Expenses such as staff salaries and commission, carriage outwards, depreciation of delivery vehicles, advertising and display expenses, all of which are shown under this heading in the financial statements. **(38)**
Selling price	The price a good/service is sold at. **(34)**
Separate legal entity	A feature of a limited company. **(37)**
Shareholder	An owner of shares in a company. **(37)**
Shares	The division of the capital of a limited company into parts. **(37)**
Share capital	The capital of a company divided into shares owned by its shareholders. **(37)**

Shareholders' funds The amount of share capital and reserves 'owned' by the shareholders. **(37)**

Share premium The excess in price of an issued share over its nominal value. **(37)**

Single entry Where transactions are only recorded once in the books of account. **(34)**

Slip system This involves putting information, such as lists of invoices, in slip form which can then be entered directly into the ledger accounts, eliminating the need to enter them in the day books. Also used by banks whereby a customer makes out a paying-in slip to pay money into their account, the slip is used to enter details of the transaction. The slip is used as documentary evidence. **(16)**

Sole trader A business owned by one person only. **(1)**

Source documents Where original information is found (e.g. sales and purchases invoices and credit notes). **(2)**

Spreadsheets A computer program which consists of rows and columns. The program carries out calculations and is a useful facility when preparing financial budgets such as cash flow forecasts. **(40)**

Standard-rated businesses These will have to add VAT to the value of the sales invoice, but they can also claim back VAT paid on purchases. **(14)**

Standing order Payment made out of payer's bank, direct to payee's bank, on the *payer's* instructions. **(20)**

Statement of account This is normally sent to customers at the end of each month and it states the amount owing to the supplier at the end of that particular month. **(15)**

Statement of affairs A statement from which the capital of the owner is deduced by estimating assets and liabilities. Then Capital = Assets *less* Liabilities. **(34)**

Statement of financial position A statement showing the assets, capital and liabilities of a business. **(1)**

Straight line method Depreciation calculation which remains at an equal amount each year. **(26)**

Subjectivity Using a method which other people may not agree to. **(13)**

Subscriptions Amounts paid by members of a club or society, usually on an annual basis, to enable them to participate in the activities of the organisation. **(35)**

Suspense account This account is used to enter the difference in the trial balance totals when it fails to balance, awaiting further investigation. **(33)**

T accounts Accounts presented in the shape of a 'T'. **(4)**

Trade discount A reduction given to a customer when calculating the selling prices of goods. **(14)**

Trading account Account in which gross profit is calculated and is part of the income statement. **(10)**

Transaction Events which change two items in the statement of financial position. **(4)**

Trial balance A list of all the balances in the books at a particular point in time. The balances are shown in debit and credit columns. These columns should balance provided no errors have occurred. **(2)**

Uncalled capital The amount that is to be received in future, but which has not yet been requested. **(37)**

Undercasting Incorrectly adding up a column of figures to give an answer which is less than the correct total. **(32)**

Unpresented cheque A cheque which has been sent but has not yet gone through the receiver's bank account. **(23)**

Value Added Tax (VAT) A tax charged on the supply of most goods and services. The tax is borne by the final consumer of the goods or services, not by the business selling them to the consumer. VAT is administered by HMRC. **(14)**

Variable costs Costs that vary depending on levels of production or business activity. **(38)**

Work in progress Items not completed at the end of a period. **(38)**

Working capital The amount by which the current assets exceed the current liabilities. Also known as 'net current assets'. **(11)**

Working capital ratio Same as the current ratio. **(39)**

Zero-rated businesses Businesses that do not have to add VAT to goods and services supplied to others by them, but they can receive a refund of VAT paid on goods and services purchased by them. **(14)**

Zero-rated supplies Goods or services where VAT is charged at the rate of 0%. **(14)**

APPENDIX B

Model layouts for financial statements and worksheets

Many students have difficulty remembering the layout of the financial statements of various businesses. In this appendix you will find suggested model layouts of the financial statements, which include the income statement and statement of financial position for the following organisations:

- sole trader
- partnership – including the appropriation account
- limited company
- a manufacturing account.

Also included are suggested working sheets for answering questions on petty cash, ratio analysis and the extended trial balance. You may find it useful to photocopy the above documents and put them in your file for reference and to use when answering questions on these topics.

In this appendix you will find the following suggested model layouts of financial statements and worksheets; these are shown with column lines for ease of working:

- **Financial statements:**
  1 Sole trader
  2 Partnership
  3 Limited company
     Income statement
     Statement of financial position
  4 Manufacturing account

- **Worksheets:**
  5 Petty cash book
  6 Worksheet for accounting ratios
  7 Worksheet for extended trial balance.

1 Sole trader financial statements

Income Statement – Sole trader

Income Statement . . . for the year ended . . .			
		£	£
Sales			xxx
Less Sales returns			xx
			xxx (a)
Less Cost of goods sold			
Opening inventory		x	
Add Purchases		x	
Add Carriage inwards		x	
		xx	
Less Purchases returns		x	
		xx	
Less Closing inventory		x	xxx (b)
Gross profit	(a) – (b)		xxx (c)
Less Expenses			
Bad debts (written off)		x	
Wages and salaries		x	
Rates		x	
Insurance		x	
Rent		x	
General expenses		x	
Postages		x	
Stationery		x	
Carriage outwards		x	
Discounts allowed		x	
Heating		x	
Electricity		x	
Depreciation		x	
Increase in allowance for doubtful debts		x	xxx (d)
	(c) – (d)		xxx (e)
Add income*			
Discounts + interest received		x	
Reductions in allowance for doubtful debts		x	xx (f)
Net profit	(e) + (f)		£xxx (g)

(Side labels: Trading Account section — Sales to Gross profit; Profit and Loss Account section — Less Expenses to Net profit)

**Note*: Alternatively, the income can be added to gross profit before deducting expenses.

Statement of Financial Position – Sole trader

Statement of Financial Position of . . . as at . . .			
	Cost (a)	*Total depreciation (b)*	*Net book value (a) – (b)*
Non-current assets	£	£	£
Premises	x	x	x
Motor vehicle	x	x	x
Office furniture	x	x	x
Office equipment	x	x	x
Machinery	x	x	x
	xx	xx	x (c)
Current assets			
Inventory (closing)	x		
Accounts receivable (*Less* Allowance for doubtful debts)	x		
Prepayments	x		
Cash at bank	x		
Cash in hand	x	xx (d)	
Less Current liabilities			
Accounts payable	x		
Expenses owing	x		
Bank overdraft	x	xx (e)	
Net current assets (d) – (e)			xx (f)
(c) + (f)			xxx (g)
Less Non-current liabilities			
Long-term loan			x (h)
Net assets (g) – (h)			£x,xxx (i)
Financed by			
Capital			xxx
Add Profit			x
			xxx
Less Drawings			x
			£x,xxx (i)

2 Partnership financial statements

Alan and Graham
Income Statement for the year ended . . .

Trading Account section – Same as sole trader
Profit and Loss Account section – Same as sole trader
*Profit and Loss Appropriation Account**

	£	£	£
Net Profit			xxx (a)
Add Interest charged on drawings			
Alan		x	
Graham		x	xx (b)
(a) + (b)			xxx (c)
Less Interest on capital			
Alan	x		
Graham	x	xx	
Salary			
Graham	x	x	xx (d)
(c) – (d)			xxx (e)
Share of Profits:			
Alan		xx	
Graham		xx	
			xxx (e)

*Note: The appropriation account is usually shown under the general heading of 'Income Statement'.

Alan and Graham
Statement of Financial Position as at . . .

Asset section of the statement of financial position – Same as sole trader
Extract showing Financed by section only

Financed by:	£	£	£
Capital Accounts	*Alan*	*Graham*	*Total*
Balance	xx	xx	xxx (a)
Current Accounts			
Balance b/d	xx	xx	
Add Share of profit	x	x	
Salary – Graham	–	x	
Interest on capital	x	x	
	xx	xx	
Less Drawings	(x)	(x)	
Interest on drawings	(x)	(x)	
	xx	xx	
			xxx (b)
	(a) + (b) =		£x,xxx (c)

3 Limited company financial statements

Name of Company . . . Limited
Income Statement for the year ended . . .

		£	£
Sales			xxx
Less Sales returns			x
			xxx (a)
Less Cost of goods sold			
Opening inventory		xxx	
Add Purchases		xxx	
Add Carriage inwards		xxx	
		xxx	
Less Purchases returns		xxx	
		xxx	
Less Closing inventory		xx	xxx (b)
Gross Profit	(a) – (b)		xxx (c)
Less Expenses:			
Salaries and wages		xx	
Directors' remuneration		xx	
General expenses		xx	
Rates and insurance		xx	
Motor expenses		xx	
Debenture interest		xx	
Bad debts written off		xx	
Depreciation – Motors		xx	
– Equipment		xx	xxx (d)
Net Profit	(c) – (d)		xxx (e)

Statement of change in equity for the year ended . . .

		£	£
Retained profit for the year	(e)		xxx
Add Retained profit brought forward	(f)		xxx
	(e) + (f)		xxx (g)
Less Appropriations:			
Transfers to general reserve		xx	
Interim dividends paid:			
Preference shares		xx	
Ordinary shares		xx	
Final dividends paid:			
Preference shares		xx	
Ordinary shares		xx	xxx (h)
Retained profits carried forward	(g) – (h)		£xxx (i)

Note: Statement of financial position showing less detailed information.

Name of Company . . . Limited
Statement of Financial Position as at . . .

		£	£	£	
Non-current assets					
Intangible assets					
Goodwill				xx	(a)
Tangible assets (A)					
Premises			xxx		
Equipment			xxx		
Motors			xxx	xxx	(b)
	(a) + (b)			xxx	(c)
Current assets					
Inventory			xx		
Accounts receivable			xx		
Bank			xx		
Cash			xx		
				xxx	(d)
Total assets	(c) + (d)			xxxx	(e)
Less Current liabilities					
Accounts payable		xx			
Bank overdraft		xx			
Debenture interest due		xx			
	(f)		xxx		
Less Non-current liabilities					
Debentures	(g)		xxx		
Total liabilities	(f) + (g)			xxx	(h)
	(e) – (h)			x,xxx	(i)
Equity					
Share Capital					
Called-up share capital				x,xxx	(j)
Capital reserve					
Share premium				xxx	(k)
Revenue reserves					
General reserve			xxx		
Retained profits			xxx		
				xxx	(l)
	(j) + (k) + (l)			x,xxx	(m)

Notes: Based on UK legislation
(A) Notes to be given in appendix as to cost, acquisitions and sales in the year and depreciation.

Note: Statement of financial position showing more detailed information.

Name of Company . . . Limited
Statement of Financial Position as at . . .

		Cost	*Depreciation to date*	*Net book value*
Non-current assets		£	£	£
Intangible assets				
Goodwill		xxx	–	xxx
Tangible assets				
Premises		xxx	xx	xxx
Equipment		xxx	xx	xxx
Motors		xxx	xx	xxx
		xxx	xxx	xxx (a)
Current assets				
Inventory			xx	
Accounts receivable			xx	
Bank			xx	
Cash			xx	
				xxx (b)
Total assets	(a) + (b)			xxxx (c)
Less Current liabilities				
Accounts payable		xx		
Bank overdraft		xx		
Debenture interest due		xx		
	(d)		xxx	
Less Non-current liabilities				
Debentures	(e)		xxx	
Total liabilities	(d) + (e)			xxx (f)
	(c) – (f)			x,xxx (g)
Equity				
Share Capital				
Called-up share capital				x,xxx (h)
Capital reserve				
Share premium				xxx (i)
Revenue reserves				
General reserve			xxx	
Retained profits			xxx	
				xxx (j)
	(h) + (i) + (j)			x,xxx (k)

4 Manufacturing Account

Name of firm
Manufacturing Account for the year ended . . .

		£	£
Inventory of raw materials (opening)			xxx
Add Purchases			xxx
Add Carriage inwards			xxx
			xxx (a)
Less Inventory of raw materials (closing)			xxx (b)
Cost of raw materials consumed	(a) – (b)		xxx (c)
Direct labour			xxx (d)
Direct expenses			
Royalties			xx (e)
Prime cost	(c) + (d) + (e)		xxx (f)
Add Indirect manufacturing cost			
General factory overheads		xx	
Lighting		xx	
Power		xx	
Rent		xx	
Insurance		xx	
Indirect labour		xx	
Depreciation of plant		xx	xxx (g)
	(f) + (g)		xxx (h)
Add Work in progress (opening)			xx (i)
	(h) + (i)		xxx (j)
Less Work in progress (closing)			xx (k)
Production cost of goods completed c/d	(j) – (k)		xxx

Note: The 'Production cost of goods completed' will be entered in the trading account section of the income statement: refer to Chapter 38. The rest of the income statement is the same as for sole traders and partnerships.

Statement of Financial Position Extract as at . . .

	£	£	£
Current assets			
Inventory – raw materials	xx		
– work in progress	xx		
– finished goods	xx		

Note: All three closing inventories of raw materials, work in progress and finished goods are included in the statement of financial position.

5 Petty Cash Book

Receipts £	*Date*	*Details*	*Voucher Number*	*Total* £	*VAT* £	£	£	£	£	£

6 Accounting ratios – Calculation sheet

Profitability Ratios – Section 39.3			
Ratio	**Formula**	**Year 1**	**Year 2**
1 Gross profit margin as a % of sales	$\frac{\text{GP}}{\text{Sales}} \times 100 = \text{x}\%$		
2 Gross profit mark-up as a % of sales	$\frac{\text{GP}}{\text{Cost of Sales}} \times 100 = \text{x}\%$		
3 Net profit margin as a % of sales	$\frac{\text{NP}}{\text{Sales}} \times 100 = \text{x}\%$		
4 Expenses as a % of sales	$\frac{\text{Expenses}}{\text{Sales}} \times 100 = \text{x}\%$		
5 Return on capital employed (ROCE)	$\frac{\text{NP}}{\text{Capital Employed}} \times 100 = \text{x}\%$		
6 Inventory turnover, e.g. 5 times	$\frac{\text{Cost of Goods Sold}}{\text{Average Inventory}} = \text{x Times a year}$		
Liquidity Ratios – Section 39.4			
1 Current (or working capital ratio)	$\frac{\text{Current Assets}}{\text{Current Liabilities}} = \text{x:1}$		
2 Acid test (or quick ratio)	$\frac{\text{Current Assets – Inventory}}{\text{Current Liabilities}} = \text{x:1}$		
3 Accounts receivable to sales ratio (for months) (debtors' collection period)	$\frac{\text{Accounts receivable}}{\text{Sales for year}} \times 12 = \text{x Months}$		
or Accounts receivable to sales ratio (for days) **4** Accounts payable to purchases (for months) (creditors' payment period)	$\frac{\text{Accounts receivable}}{\text{Sales for year}} \times 365 = \text{x Days}$ $\frac{\text{Accounts payable}}{\text{Purchases for year}} \times 12 = \text{x Months}$		
or Accounts payable to purchases (for days)	$\frac{\text{Accounts payable}}{\text{Purchases for year}} \times 365 = \text{x Days}$		
Asset Utilisation – Section 39.5			
Non-current assets to sales ratio	$\frac{\text{Sales}}{\text{Non-current Assets}} = \text{x:1}$		

7 Format for an extended worksheet

Description	Ledger Balances		Adjustments		Income Statement		Statement of Financial Position	
	Dr	Cr	Dr	Cr	Dr	Cr	Dr	Cr
	£	£	£	£	£	£	£	£

APPENDIX C

Multiple-choice questions

Each multiple-choice question has four suggested answers, either letter (A), (B), (C) or (D). You should read each question and then decide which choice is best, either (A) or (B) or (C) or (D). Write down your answers on a separate piece of paper. You will then be able to repeat the set of questions later without the distraction of previously written attempts.

When you have completed a set of questions, check your answers against those given in Appendix D.

Set No 1: Questions MC1–MC20

MC1 Which of the following statements is *in*correct?

(A) Assets – Liabilities = Capital
(B) Capital – Liabilities = Assets
(C) Assets = Capital + Liabilities
(D) Assets – Capital = Liabilities.

MC2 Which of the following is not an asset?

(A) Accounts receivable
(B) Motor Vehicle
(C) Accounts payable
(D) Inventory.

MC3 Which of the following is a liability?

(A) Cash balance
(B) Loan from J Owens
(C) Accounts receivable
(D) Buildings.

MC4 Which of the following is *in*correct?

	Assets	*Liabilities*	*Capital*
	£	£	£
(A)	9,460	2,680	6,780
(B)	7,390	1,140	6,250
(C)	6,120	2,490	4,630
(D)	8,970	3,580	5,390

MC5 Which of the following statements is *in*correct?

	Effect upon Assets	Effect upon Liabilities
(A) Paid supplier by cheque	– Bank	+ Suppliers
(B) Bought goods on credit	+ Stock	+ Suppliers
(C) Received cash from customer	+ Cash – Customer	
(D) Sold goods for cash	+ Cash – Inventory	

MC6 Which of the following are correct?

	Accounts	To record	Entry in the account
(i)	Assets	a decrease	Debit
		an increase	Credit
(ii)	Capital	a decrease	Debit
		an increase	Credit
(iii)	Liabilities	a decrease	Debit
		an increase	Credit

(A) (i) and (ii)
(B) (i) and (iii)
(C) (ii) and (iii)
(D) None of them.

MC7 Which of the following are correct?

		Account to be debited	Account to be credited
(i)	Bought motor van by cheque	Motor van	Bank
(ii)	Paid a supplier, T Allen, by cheque	Cash	T Allen
(iii)	Loan repaid to C Kirk by cheque	Loan from Kirk	Bank
(iv)	Sold goods for cash	Sales	Cash

(A) (i) and (ii) only
(B) (ii) and (iii) only
(C) (iii) and (iv) only
(D) (i) and (iii) only.

MC8 Which of the following are *in*correct?

		Account to be debited	Account to be credited
(i)	Sold goods on credit to P Moore	P Moore	Sales
(ii)	Bought fixtures on credit from Furnishers Ltd	Fixtures	Furnishers Ltd
(iii)	Introduce more capital in cash	Capital	Cash
(iv)	A customer, L Sellars, pays by cheque	Cash	L Sellars

(A) (iii) and (iv) only
(B) (ii) and (iii) only
(C) (i) and (iv) only
(D) (i) and (iii) only.

MC9 Which of the following should not be called 'sales'?
(A) Goods sold, to be paid for in one month's time
(B) Goods sold, cash being received immediately
(C) Item previously included in purchases, now sold on credit
(D) Sale of a motor lorry no longer required.

MC10 Which of the following should not be called 'purchases'?
(A) Items bought for the prime purpose of resale
(B) Goods bought on credit
(C) Office stationery purchased
(D) Goods bought for cash.

MC11 Which of the following are *in*correct?

		Account to be debited	*Account to be credited*
(i)	B Ash returns goods to us	Sales returns	B Ash
(ii)	Goods bought on credit from L Thomas	L Thomas	Purchases
(iii)	Motor van bought on credit from X L Garages	Purchases	X L Garages
(iv)	Goods sold for cash	Cash	Sales

(A) (i) and (ii) only
(B) (i) and (iii) only
(C) (ii) and (iii) only
(D) (iii) and (iv) only.

MC12 Of the following, which are correct?

		Account to be debited	*Account to be credited*
(i)	Surplus office furniture sold for cash	Cash	Sales
(ii)	We returned goods to F Ward	F Ward	Sales returns
(iii)	Goods bought for cash	Purchases	Cash
(iv)	Goods sold on credit to F Clarke	F Clarke	Sales

(A) (i) and (ii) only
(B) (iii) and (iv) only
(C) (ii) and (iii) only
(D) (ii) only.

MC13 What is the amount of capital, given the following information? Buildings £30,000, Inventory £5,600, Bank £750, Accounts payable £2,200, Loan from K Noone £7,000:
(A) £29,150
(B) £36,350
(C) £41,150
(D) None of the above.

MC14 Which of these statements is *in*correct?
(A) Profit is another word for capital
(B) A loss decreases capital
(C) Profit increases capital
(D) Drawings decreases capital.

MC15 Which of the following are *in*correct?

		Account to be debited	*Account to be credited*
(i)	Paid insurance by cheque	Insurance	Bank
(ii)	Paid telephone bill by cash	Telephone	Cash
(iii)	Received refund of part of motor expenses by cheque	Cash	Motor Expenses
(iv)	Took cash out of business for personal use	Drawings	Capital

(A) (i) and (iii) only
(B) (ii) and (iv) only
(C) (iii) and (iv) only
(D) (iv) only.

MC16 Of the following, which are correct?

		Account to be debited	*Account to be credited*
(i)	Paid rent by cheque	Rent	Cash
(ii)	Received commission in cash	Commissions	Cash
(iii)	Introduced extra capital in cash	Cash	Capital
(iv)	Sold surplus stationery for cash	Cash	Stationery

(A) None of them
(B) (i) and (iv) only
(C) (ii) and (iii) only
(D) (iii) and (iv) only.

MC17 What is the balance on the following account on 30 June 2013?

N Garth

2013		£	2013		£
June 18	Bank	400	June 1	Purchases	870
June 22	Returns	44	June 15	Purchases	245
			June 29	Purchases	178

(A) A debit balance of £849
(B) A credit balance of £829
(C) A credit balance of £849
(D) There is a nil balance on the account.

MC18 What was the balance on the account of N Garth, in MC17, on 20 June?
(A) A credit balance of £671
(B) A debit balance of £715
(C) A credit balance of £715
(D) A debit balance of £671.

MC19 Of the following, which *best* describes a trial balance?
(A) Is the final account in the books
(B) Shows all the asset balances
(C) Is a list of balances on the books
(D) Discloses the financial position of a business.

MC20 When should the trial balance totals differ?
(A) Only when it is drawn up by the accountant
(B) When drawn up before the profit and loss account section of the income statement is prepared
(C) If drawn up half-way through the financial year
(D) Never.

Set No 2: Questions MC21–MC55

MC21 Gross profit is:
(A) Excess of cost of goods sold over sales
(B) Purchases + Sales
(C) Net profit less expenses
(D) Excess of sales over cost of goods sold.

MC22 Net profit is calculated in the:
(A) Trial balance
(B) Trading account section of the income statement
(C) Profit and loss account section of the income statement
(D) Statement of financial position.

MC23 The credit entry for net profit is shown in the:
(A) Capital account
(B) Profit and loss account
(C) Statement of financial position
(D) Trading account.

MC24 The value of closing inventory is found by:
(A) Adding opening inventory to purchases
(B) Deducting purchases from sales
(C) Looking in the inventory account
(D) Doing a stock-taking.

MC25 Which of the following are *not* part of the double entry system?
(i) Trading account
(ii) Statement of financial position
(iii) Trial balance
(iv) Profit and loss account.

(A) (i) and (ii)
(B) (i) and (iii)
(C) (ii) and (iii)
(D) (ii) and (iv).

MC26 Which is the *best* definition of a statement of financial position?
(A) A list of balances after calculating net profit
(B) A statement of all liabilities
(C) A trial balance at a different date
(D) A list of balances before calculating net profit.

MC27 The descending order in which current assets should be shown in the statement of financial position are:

(A) Accounts receivable, Bank, Inventory, Cash
(B) Inventory, Accounts receivable, Bank, Cash
(C) Inventory, Accounts receivable, Cash, Bank
(D) Cash, Bank, Accounts receivable, Inventory.

MC28 Carriage inwards is charged to the trading account because:

(A) It should not go in the statement of financial position
(B) It is not part of motor expenses
(C) Sales returns also goes in the trading account
(D) It is basically part of the cost of buying goods.

MC29 Given figures showing Sales £28,500, Opening inventory £4,690, Closing inventory £7,240, Carriage inwards £570 and Purchases £21,360, the cost of goods sold figure is:

(A) £19,830
(B) £19,380
(C) £18,810
(D) Another figure.

MC30 If someone owns a grocery store, which of the following are *not* capital expenditure?

(i) Rent
(ii) Motor van
(iii) Fixtures
(iv) Fire insurance.

(A) (ii) and (iii)
(B) (i) and (ii)
(C) (i) and (iii)
(D) (i) and (iv).

MC31 The purchases day book is *best* described as:

(A) A list of purchases bought on credit
(B) Containing suppliers' accounts
(C) A list of purchases bought for cash
(D) Part of the double entry system.

MC32 Customers' personal accounts are found in:

(A) The private ledger
(B) General ledger
(C) Purchases ledger
(D) Sales ledger.

MC33 Which of the following are *not* personal accounts?

(i) Accounts receivable
(ii) Drawings
(iii) Rent
(iv) Accounts payable.

(A) (iii) only
(B) (i) and (ii) only
(C) (i) and (iv) only
(D) (ii) and (iii) only.

MC34 A debit balance of £500 in the cash columns of the cash book would mean:
(A) The book-keeper has made a mistake
(B) We have £500 cash in hand
(C) We have spent £500 cash more than we have received
(D) Someone has stolen £500 cash.

MC35 A sum of £200 withdrawn from the bank and placed in the cash till is entered:
(A) Debit bank column £200: Credit bank column £200
(B) Debit cash column £200: Credit bank column £200
(C) Debit bank column £200: Credit cash column £200
(D) Debit cash column £400: Credit cash column £400.

MC36 A contra item is where:
(A) Cash is banked before it has been paid out
(B) Where double entry is completed within the cash book
(C) Where the proprietor has repaid his capital in cash
(D) Where sales have been paid by cash.

MC37 An invoice shows a total of £3,200 less a $2\frac{1}{2}$% cash discount. If this was paid in time, the amount of the cheque paid would be for:
(A) £2,960
(B) £3,040
(C) £3,120
(D) £2,800.

MC38 The total of the discounts received column in the cash book is posted to:
(A) The credit of the discounts received account
(B) The credit of the discounts allowed account
(C) The debit of the discounts allowed account
(D) The debit of the discounts received account.

MC39 A bank overdraft is *best* described as:
(A) A business wasting its money
(B) Having more receipts than payments
(C) A business having bought too many goods
(D) A business having paid more out of its bank account than it has put in it.

MC40 A cash discount is *best* described as a reduction in the sum to be paid:
(A) If goods are bought on credit and not for cash
(B) If either cheque or cash payment is made within an agreed period
(C) If cash is paid instead of cheques
(D) If trade discount is also deducted.

MC41 If a sales invoice shows 12 items of £250 each, less trade discount of 20% and cash discount of 5%, then the amount to be paid, if the payment is made within the credit period, will be for:

(A) £2,440
(B) £2,360
(C) £2,280
(D) £2,500.

MC42 The total of the sales day book is entered on:

(A) The debit side of the sales day book
(B) The credit side of the sales account in the general ledger
(C) The debit side of the sales account in the general ledger
(D) The debit side of the sales day book.

MC43 A trade discount is *best* described as:

(A) A discount given if the invoice is paid
(B) A discount given for cash payment
(C) A discount given to suppliers
(D) A discount given to traders.

MC44 The sales day book does *not* contain:

(A) Credit sales made without deduction of trade discount
(B) Credit sales made to overseas customers
(C) Cash sales
(D) Credit sales which eventually turn out to be bad debts.

MC45 The purchases day book consists of:

(A) Cash purchases
(B) Suppliers' ledger accounts
(C) A list of purchases invoices
(D) Payments for goods.

MC46 The total of the purchases day book is transferred to the:

(A) Debit side of the purchases account
(B) Credit side of the purchases day book
(C) Debit side of the purchases day book
(D) Debit side of the purchases ledger.

MC47 The balances in the purchases ledger are usually:

(A) Credit balances
(B) Contras
(C) Nominal account balances
(D) Debit balances.

MC48 Debit notes are entered in the:

(A) Purchases returns day book
(B) Sales returns day book
(C) Purchases account
(D) Purchases returns account.

MC49 A statement of account:
(A) Is used instead of an invoice
(B) Means that customers need not keep accounts
(C) Saves sending out invoices
(D) Acts as a reminder to the purchaser of the amount owed.

MC50 Originally we bought 80 items at £60 each, less trade discount of 25%. We now return 5 items, so we will issue a debit note amounting to:
(A) £270
(B) £240
(C) £225
(D) £220.

MC51 A cheque given to you by a customer and banked by you, but for which he has proved not to have enough funds to meet it, is known as:
(A) A dishonoured cheque
(B) A debit transfer
(C) A standing order
(D) A bank error.

MC52 Which of the following are not true? A bank reconciliation statement is:
(i) Drawn up by the bank monthly
(ii) Not part of the double entry system
(iii) Part of the double entry system
(iv) Drawn up by our cashier.

(A) (i) and (ii)
(B) (i) and (iii)
(C) (ii) and (iv)
(D) (iii) and (iv).

MC53 The journal is:
(A) Part of the double entry system
(B) A form of sales day book
(C) A form of diary
(D) A supplement to the statement of financial position.

MC54 Given a desired cash float of £700, if £541 is spent in the period and the opening cash float has been £700, how much will be reimbursed at the end of the period?
(A) £541
(B) £700
(C) £159
(D) None of the above.

MC55 A petty cash book:
(A) Is used only in limited companies
(B) Is used when there is a bank overdraft
(C) Is used for small cheque payments
(D) Will keep down the number of entries in the general ledger.

Set No 3: Questions MC56–MC82

MC56 The straight line method of depreciation consists of:
(A) Unequal amounts of depreciation each year
(B) Increasing amounts of depreciation each year
(C) Reducing amounts of depreciation each year
(D) Equal amounts of depreciation each year.

MC57 Depreciation is:
(A) The cost of a current asset wearing away
(B) The cost of a replacement for a non-current asset
(C) The salvage value of a non-current asset plus its original cost
(D) The part of the cost of the non-current asset consumed during its period of use by the business.

MC58 A business bought a machine for £50,000. It is expected to be used for 6 years, then sold for £5,000. What is the annual amount of depreciation if the straight line method is used?
(A) £7,000
(B) £8,000
(C) £7,500
(D) £6,750.

MC59 When a separate provision for depreciation account is in use, then book-keeping entries for the year's depreciation are:
(A) Debit profit and loss: Credit the statement of financial position
(B) Debit profit and loss: Credit asset account
(C) Debit asset account: Credit provision for depreciation account
(D) Debit profit and loss: Credit provision for depreciation account.

MC60 In a trial balance, the balance on the provision for depreciation account is:
(A) Shown as a credit item
(B) Not shown, as it is part of depreciation
(C) Shown as a debit item
(D) Sometimes shown as a credit, sometimes as a debit.

MC61 If a provision for depreciation account is not in use, then the entries for the year's depreciation would be:
(A) Debit asset account, credit profit and loss account
(B) Credit asset account, debit provision for depreciation account
(C) Credit profit and loss account, debit provision for depreciation account
(D) None of the above.

MC62 An allowance for doubtful debts is created:
(A) When debtors become bankrupt
(B) When debtors cease to be in business
(C) To provide for possible bad debts
(D) To write off bad debts.

MC63 When the financial statements are prepared, the bad debts account is closed by a transfer to the:
(A) Statement of financial position
(B) Profit and loss account
(C) Trading account
(D) Allowance for doubtful debts account.

MC64 These questions relate to the following assets and liabilities:

	£		£
Inventory	1,000	Machinery	750
Cash at bank	750	Accounts receivable	750
Cash in hand	50	Fixtures	250
Accounts payable	500	Motor vehicle	750
Capital	3,800		

(i) The statement of financial position totals are (use the vertical presentation):
(A) £4,800. (B) £3,800. (C) £4,000. (D) £4,500.
(ii) Current liabilities are:
(A) £1,750. (B) £500. (C) £3,800. (D) £2,550.
(iii) Working capital is:
(A) £3,050. (B) £2,050. (C) £500. (D) £800.

Pitman Qualifications

MC65 If we take goods for own use, we should:
(A) Debit drawings account: Credit purchases account
(B) Debit purchases account: Credit drawings account
(C) Debit drawings account: Credit inventory account
(D) Debit sales account: Credit inventory account.

MC66 A debit balance brought down on a packing materials account means:
(A) We owe for packing materials
(B) We have no stock of packing materials
(C) We have lost money on packing materials
(D) We have a stock of packing materials unused.

MC67 A credit balance brought down on a rent account means:
(A) We owe that rent at that date
(B) We have paid that rent in advance at that date
(C) We have paid too much rent
(D) We have paid too little in rent.

MC68 Working capital is a term meaning:
(A) The amount of capital invested by the proprietor
(B) The excess of the current assets over the current liabilities
(C) The capital less drawings
(D) The total of the non-current assets + current assets.

MC69 In the trading account section of the income statement, the sales returns should be:
(A) Added to cost of goods sold
(B) Deducted from purchases
(C) Deducted from sales
(D) Added to sales.

MC70 If £750 was added to rent instead of being added to a non-current asset:
(A) Gross profit would not be affected
(B) Gross profit would be affected
(C) Both gross and net profits would be affected
(D) Just the statement of financial position items would be affected.

MC71 Of the following, which should *not* be entered in the journal?
(i) Cash payments for wages
(ii) Bad debts written off
(iii) Credit purchases of goods
(iv) Sale of non-current assets.

(A) (i) and (ii)
(B) (i) and (iii)
(C) (ii) and (iii)
(D) (iii) and (iv).

MC72 Which of the following do *not* affect trial balance agreement?
(i) Purchases £585 from C Owens completely omitted from the books
(ii) Sales £99 to R Morgan entered in his account as £90
(iii) Rent account added up to be £100 too much
(iv) Error on sales invoice of £14 being entered in the books.

(A) (i) and (iv)
(B) (i) and (ii)
(C) (i) and (iii)
(D) (iii) and (iv).

MC73 Which of the following *are* errors of principle?
(i) Rent entered in buildings account
(ii) Purchases £150 completely omitted from books
(iii) Sale of machinery £500 entered in sales account
(iv) Cheque payment to R Kago entered only in cash book.

(A) (ii) and (iii)
(B) (iii) and (iv)
(C) (i) and (ii)
(D) (i) and (iii).

MC74 When trial balance totals do not agree, the difference is entered in:
(A) The balance account
(B) A suspense account
(C) An errors account
(D) The profit and loss account.

MC75 Which of these errors would be disclosed by the trial balance?

(A) Error on a purchase invoice
(B) Purchases from T Morgan entered in C Morgan's account
(C) Carriage outwards debited to sales account
(D) Overcast of total on sales account.

MC76 All these questions refer to the following income statement.

Income Statement			
		£	£
Sales			24,770
Less Sales returns			270
			24,500
Less Cost of goods sold:			
Opening inventory		700	
Add Purchases	18,615		
Less Purchases returns	280		
	18,335		
Add Carriage Inwards	320	18,655	
		19,355	
Less Closing inventory		980	18,375
Gross Profit			6,125
Less Expenses:			
Wages		1,420	
Rent (360 + 90)		450	
General expenses		220	
Carriage outwards		360	?
Net Profit			?

(i) The missing net profit figure should be:
(A) £1,675. (B) £21,675. (C) £3,675. (D) £4,675.

(ii) Total expenses were:
(A) £210. (B) £2,450. (C) £810. (D) £2,575.

(iii) The cost of goods sold totalled:
(A) £18,375. (B) £19,500. (C) £24,500. (D) £24,770.

(iv) The expense item of Rent totalled:
(A) £360. (B) £270. (C) £90. (D) £450.

(v) The turnover is:
(A) £24,770. (B) £24,500. (C) £19,355. (D) £18,375.

(vi) The net cost of purchases is:
(A) £18,615. (B) £18,335. (C) £18,655. (D) £18,375.

(vii) Purchases returned totalled:
(A) £360. (B) £320. (C) £280. (D) £270.

(viii) Gross profit as a percentage on net sales is:
(A) 20%. (B) 30%. (C) 25%. (D) $33^1/_3$%.

(ix) Net profit as a percentage on net sales is:
(A) 10%. (B) 20%. (C) 25%. (D) 15%.

(x) The value of unsold goods was:
(A) £980. (B) £24,500. (C) £6,125. (D) £19,355.

Pitman Qualifications

MC77 Answer the following questions using the following trial balance and the information given below:

Trial Balance as at 31 December

	£	£
Capital		5,600
Furniture and fittings	5,880	
Inventory 1 January	700	
Drawings	1,200	
Bank overdraft		1,260
Salaries	3,560	
General expenses	190	
Purchases/sales	4,020	9,840
Discount all'd/rec'd	150	130
Rent and rates	820	
Sales and purchase returns	90	80
Accounts receivable and payable	1,500	1,070
Allowance for doubtful debts		130
	£18,110	£18,110

Notes:

(*a*) Salaries owing at 31 December – £140
(*b*) Rent and rates paid in advance – £220
(*c*) Depreciate furniture and fittings by 10% p.a.
(*d*) Closing inventory is valued at – £800
(*e*) Increase the allowance for doubtful debts to bring it up to 10% of accounts receivable balances.

(i) What will be the yearly depreciation charge?
(A) £5,292. (B) £6,468. (C) £588. (D) £5,886.

(ii) What will be the salaries figure shown on the profit and loss account?
(A) £140. (B) £3,700. (C) £3,420. (D) £3,560.

(iii) The rent and rates figure shown on the profit and loss account will be:
(A) £600. (B) £820. (C) £220. (D) £1,040.

(iv) The new allowance for doubtful debts will be:
(A) £1,650. (B) £1,450. (C) £150. (D) £110.

(v) What will be the gross profit on the trading account?
(A) £5,910. (B) £5,830. (C) £4,630. (D) £4,430.

(vi) The net profit on the profit and loss account will be:
(A) £1,420. (B) £792. (C) £1,400. (D) £812.

(vii) The book value of furniture and fittings on the statement of financial position will be:
(A) £5,292. (B) £6,000. (C) £6,368. (D) £5,880.

(viii) What will be the turnover for the year?
(A) £9,840. (B) £3,840. (C) £9,750. (D) £4,640.

(ix) Using the adjusted sales figure, the inventory turnover for the year will be:
(A) 10. (B) 11. (C) 12. (D) None of these.

(x) What will be the capital figure at end of year?
(A) £4,100. (B) £5,600. (C) £5,192. (D) £6,392.

Pitman Qualifications

MC78 Given last year's capital as £57,500, this year's capital as £64,300, and drawings as £11,800, then profit must have been:
(A) £18,600
(B) £18,100
(C) £16,600
(D) £19,600.

MC79 Given last year's capital as £74,500, closing capital as £46,200, and drawings of £13,400, then:
(A) Profit for the year was £14,900
(B) Loss for the year was £14,900
(C) Loss for the year was £15,900
(D) Profit for the year was £16,800.

MC80 Given this year's closing capital as £29,360, the year's net profit as £8,460 and drawings as £5,320, what was the capital at the beginning of the year?
(A) £29,360
(B) £26,220
(C) £34,680
(D) None of the above.

MC81 In a commercial business, an 'accumulated fund' would be known as:
(A) Non-current assets
(B) Total assets
(C) Net current assets
(D) Capital.

MC82 A receipts and payments account does not show:
(A) Cheques paid out during the year
(B) The accumulated fund
(C) Receipts from sales of assets
(D) Bank balances.

APPENDIX D

Answers to multiple-choice questions in Appendix C

Set 1

1	B	2	C	3	B	4	C	5	A
6	C	7	D	8	A	9	D	10	C
11	C	12	B	13	D	14	A	15	C
16	D	17	C	18	C	19	C	20	D

Set 2

21	D	22	C	23	A	24	D	25	C
26	A	27	B	28	D	29	B	30	D
31	A	32	D	33	D	34	B	35	B
36	B	37	C	38	A	39	D	40	B
41	C	42	B	43	D	44	C	45	C
46	A	47	A	48	A	49	D	50	C
51	A	52	B	53	C	54	A	55	D

Set 3

56	D	57	D	58	C	59	D	60	A
61	D	62	C	63	B	64	(i) B (ii) B (iii) B	65	A
66	D	67	A	68	B	69	C	70	A
71	B	72	A	73	D	74	B	75	D
76	(i) C (ii) B (iii) A (iv) D (v) B (vi) B (vii) C (viii) C (ix) D (x) A								
77	(i) C (ii) B (iii) A (iv) C (v) A (vi) B (vii) A (viii) C (ix) D (x) D								
78	A	79	B	80	B	81	D	82	B

APPENDIX E

Answers to exercises

*Set out in this Appendix are the answers to the Exercises at the end of each chapter, **excluding** those with suffix 'X' in the Exercise number.*

Chapter 1 Introduction to accounting principles

1.1 Good financial control is important to ensure the continued profitability and success of the business. Also to control costs and cash flow.

1.2 Refer to text, section 1.3.

1.3 Refer to text, section 1.2.

Chapter 2 The accounting system

2.1 Refer to text Section 2.3.

2.2 Refer to text Section 2.3.

2.4 Refer to text Section 2.6.

Chapter 3 The accounting equation and statement of financial position

3.1
(*a*) £26,373
(*b*) £62,486
(*c*) £77,100
(*d*) £986,763
(*e*) £10,265
(*f*) £404,903

3.3
(*a*) Asset
(*b*) Asset
(*c*) Liability
(*d*) Asset
(*e*) Liability
(*f*) Asset

3.5 Wrong:

Assets	-	Accounts payable, Loan from C Shaw
Liabilities	-	Accounts receivable, inventory

3.7

		£
Assets		
Shop premises		50,000
Motor vehicle		10,000
Inventory		5,000
Cash at bank		7,000
Cash in hand		100
		72,100
Less Liabilities		
Loan from Uncle	30,000	
Owing to suppliers	2,100	32,100
CAPITAL INTRODUCED		40,000

3.9 *Statement of Financial Position of T Lymer as at 31 December 2012*

	£	£	£
Non-current assets:			
Office furniture			8,640
Delivery van			12,000
			20,640
Current assets:			
Inventory	4,220		
Accounts receivable	10,892		
Cash at Bank	11,722	26,834	
Less Current liabilities:			
Accounts payable	12,651	12,651	
Net current assets			14,183
			£34,823
Financed by:			
Capital			34,823
			£34,823

3.11

	Assets £	Capital £	Liabilities £
(a)	+ 400		+ 400
(b)	+ 500		+ 500
(c)	− 50		− 50
(d)	− 330		− 330
(e)	+ 5,000	+ 5,000	
(f)	+ 880		
	− 880		
(g)	+ 45		
	− 45		
(h)	+ 77		
	− 77		

Chapter 4 The double entry system for assets, liabilities and capital

4.1

	Account to be debited	Account to be credited
(a)	Motor van	Cash
(b)	Office machinery	J Grant & Son
(c)	Cash	Capital
(d)	Bank	J Beach
(e)	A Barrett	Cash

4.3

Bank

(1) Capital	25,000	(2) Office Furniture	1,500
		(5) Motor Van	6,000
		(16) Planers Ltd	7,500
		(31) Machinery	2,800

Capital

		(1) Bank	25,000

Office Furniture

(2) Bank	1,500	(9) J. Walker & Sons	600

Machinery

(3) Planers Ltd	7,500		
(31) Bank	2,800		

Planers Ltd

(16) Bank	7,500	(3) Machinery	7,500

Motor Van

(5) Bank	6,000		

J. Walker & Sons

(9) Office Furniture	600	(23) Cash	600

Cash

(23) J. Walker & Sons	600		

4.5

A Burton

Capital Account

		(1) Bank	15,000

Bank Account

(1) Capital	15,000	(3) Motor vehicles	6,500
		(9) Furniture	1,150
		(17) Cash	200
		(25) Computex Ltd	1,000
		(27) Motor vehicles	2,450
		(31) Computex Ltd	1,400

Motor Vehicles Account

(3) Bank	6,500		
(27) Bank	2,450		

Furniture Account

(9) Bank	1,150		
(19) Cash	42		
(29) Cash	100		

Computer Equipment Account

(12) Computex Ltd	2,400		

Computex Ltd Account

(25) Bank	1,000	(12) Computer equipment	2,400
(31) Bank	1,400		

Cash Account

(17) Bank	200	(19) Furniture	42
		(29) Furniture	100

Chapter 5 The double entry system for inventory

5.1

	Account to be debited	Account to be credited
(a)	Purchases	P Hart
(b)	Cash	Sales
(c)	Motor vehicles	Morgan Motors
(d)	Purchases	Cohens Ltd
(e)	P Hart	Purchases returns
(f)	H Perkins	Sales
(g)	Bank	Sales
(h)	Cash	Office furniture
(i)	Sales returns	H Perkins
(j)	Purchases	P Griffith

5.3

Paul Garner

Capital

		(1) Cash	4,000

Purchases

(2) Flynn Bros	1,230		
(4) Cash	345		
(20) Flynn Bros	450		

Sales

		(7) Cash	120
		(16) D Knott	600
		(23) Bateson's Ltd	570

Computer Equipment

(14) Bank	1,000		

Bateson's Ltd

(23) Sales	570	(30) Sales returns	109

Sales Returns

(30) Bateson's Ltd	109		

Cash

(1) Capital	4,000	(4) Purchases	345
(7) Sales	120	(10) Bank	3,500

Flynn Bros

(25) Purchases returns	75	(2) Purchases	1,230
(27) Bank	1,605	(20) Purchases	450

Bank

(10) Cash	3,500	(14) Computer Equip	1,000
		(27) Flynn Bros	1,605

D Knott

(16) Sales	600		

Purchases Returns

		(25) Flynn Bros	75

5.4

Grace Andrews

Capital

		(1) Bank	10,000
		(1) Cash	100

Cash

(1) Capital	100	(10) Office furniture	65
(30) Sales	280		

Shop Fittings

(3) Duffy & Son	1,900		

Barrett's Fashions

(15) Purchases returns	180	(5) Purchases	2,378
		(28) Purchases	1,434

Office Furniture

(10) Cash	65		

Purchases Returns

		(15) Barrett's Fashions	180

Bank

(1) Capital	10,000	(9) Computer	1,020
(12) Sales	800	(22) Duffy & Son	1,900
(25) Sales	600	(30) Motor vehicles	4,750

Duffy & Son

(22) Bank	1,900	(3) Shop fittings	1,900

Purchases

(5) Barrett's Fashions	2,378		
(28) Barrett's Fashions	1,434		

Computer

(9) Bank	1,020		

Sales

		(12) Bank	800
		(25) Bank	600
		(30) Cash	280

Motor Vehicles

(30) Bank	4,750		

Chapter 6 The double entry system for expenses and revenues

6.1

	Account to be debited	*Account to be credited*
(*a*)	Rent	Cash
(*b*)	Purchases	Cash
(*c*)	Bank	Rates
(*d*)	General exps	Bank
(*e*)	Cash	Commissions rec'd
(*f*)	T Jones	Purchases returns
(*g*)	Cash	Sales
(*h*)	Office fixtures	Bank
(*i*)	Wages	Cash
(*j*)	Drawings	Cash

6.3

Bank

Jan 1 Capital	20,000	Jan 3 Rent	1,000
Jan 25 Sales	800	Jan 4 Motor van	5,000
		Jan 19 Insurance	220
		Jan 31 Electricity	78

Capital

		Jan 1 Bank	20,000

Rent

Jan 3 Bank	1,000		

Motor Van

Jan 4 Bank	5,000		

Cash

Jan 5 Sales	1,005	Jan 10 Motor expenses	75
		Jan 12 Wages	120
		Jan 31 Wages	135

Motor Expenses

Jan 10 Cash	75		

Wages

Jan 12 Cash	120		
Jan 31 Cash	135		

Insurance

Jan 19 Bank	220		

Electricity

Jan 31 Bank	78		

Purchases

Jan 4 M Parkin	580		
Jan 4 J Kane	2,400		
Jan 17 M Parkin	670		

Sales

		Jan 5 Cash	1,005
		Jan 25 Bank	800

M Parkin

		Jan 4 Purchases	580
		Jan 17 Purchases	670

J Kane

		Jan 4 Purchases	2,400

6.5

Bank

Jul 1 Capital	8,000	Jul 2 Rent	375
		Jul 3 Shop Fittings	800
		Jul 6 Insurance	130
		Jul 13 Printing & Stationery	120
		Jul 30 High Lane Motors	5,000

Capital

		Jul 1 Bank	8,000

Rent

Jul 2 Bank	375		

Shop Fittings

Jul 3 Bank	800		

Insurance

Jul 6 Bank	130		

6.5 *(cont'd)*

Motor Van

Jul 7 High Lane Motors	5,000		

Cash

Jul 11 Sales	1,500	Jul 15 Wages	200
Jul 21 Sales	780	Jul 25 Motor expenses	89
		Jul 31 Wages	300
		Jul 31 Stationery	45

Printing and Stationery

Jul 13 Bank	120		
Jul 31 Cash	45		

Wages

Jul 15 Cash	200		
Jul 31 Cash	300		

Motor Expenses

Jul 25 Cash	89		

Purchases

Jul 5 A Jackson	450		
Jul 5 D Hill	675		
Jul 5 E Frudd	1,490		
Jul 18 A Jackson	890		

Sales

		Jul 11 Cash	1,500
		Jul 21 Cash	780

A Jackson

		Jul 5 Purchases	450
		Jul 18 Purchases	890

D Hill

		Jul 5 Purchases	675

E Frudd

		Jul 5 Purchases	1,490

High Lane Motors

Jul 30 Bank	5,000	Jul 7 Motor van	5,000

Chapter 7 Balancing off accounts

7.1

D Binns

(1) Sales	1,035	(9) Sales returns	60
		(25) Cash	450
		(31) Balance c/d	525
	1,035		1,035
(1) Balance b/d	525		

M Lowe

(3) Sales	99	(31) Balance c/d	99
(1) Balance b/d	99		

C Cade

(1) Sales	450	(12) Bank	450

H Teate

(1) Sales	630	(9) Sales returns	30
		(16) Bank	600
	630		630

J Watts

(3) Sales	627		
(31) Sales	135	(31) Balance c/d	762
	762		762
(1) Balance b/d	762		

7.2

G Birks

(11) Purchases returns	87	(2) Purchases	687
(27) Cash	300	(17) Purchases	120
(31) Balance c/d	420		
	807		807
		(1) Balance b/d	420

B Dixon

(21) Bank	1,320	(5) Purchases	1,320

A Weale

(31) Purchases returns	42	(2) Purchases	180
(31) Balance c/d	138		
	180		180
		(1) Balance b/d	138

T Potts

(11) Purchases returns	33	(2) Purchases	1,012
(31) Balance c/d	979		
	1,012		1,012
		(1) Balance b/d	979

K Lee

(31) Balance c/d	150	(5) Purchases	150
		(1) Balance b/d	150

7.3

D Binns

	Dr £	Cr £	Balance £	
(1) Sales	1,035		1,035	Dr
(9) Sales returns		60	975	Dr
(25) Cash		450	525	Dr

C Cade

	Dr £	Cr £	Balance £	
(1) Sales	450		450	Dr
(12) Bank		450	0	

H Teate

	Dr £	Cr £	Balance £	
(1) Sales	630		630	Dr
(9) Sales returns		30	600	Dr
(16) Bank		600	0	

J Watts

	Dr £	Cr £	Balance £	
(3) Sales	627		627	Dr
(31) Sales	135		762	Dr

M Lowe

	Dr £	Cr £	Balance £	
(3) Sales	99		99	Dr

7.5

T Tickle

(1) Sales	690	(14) Sales returns	46
(31) Balance c/d	30	(25) Bank	674
	720		720

D Stott

(19) Purchases returns	19	(3) Purchases	116
(23) Bank	97		
	116		116

J Rhodes

(31) Balance c/d	98	(3) Purchases	98

J Ahmed

(29) Cash	367	(11) Purchases	367

S Ames

(1) Sales	330	(14) Sales returns	45
(9) Sales	645	(30) Bank	500
		(31) Balance c/d	430
	975		975

D Owen

(19) Purchases returns	36	(3) Purchases	347
(31) Balance c/d	446	(11) Purchases	135
	482		482

T Johnson

(9) Sales	376	(31) Bank	376

Accounts receivable S Ames

Accounts payable T Tickle
D Owen
J Rhodes

Chapter 8 The trial balance

8.1

Capital

		May 1 Bank	2,500

Bank

May 1 Capital	2,500	May 12 K Gibson	76
May 9 C Bailey	250	May 12 D Ellis	370
May 10 H Spencer	150	May 31 C Mendez	87
		May 31 Balance c/d	2,367
	2,900		2,900
Jun 1 Balance b/d	2,367		

8.1 *(cont'd)*

Cash

May 6 Sales	500	May 8 Rent	120
		May 15 Stationery	60
		May 19 Rent	120
		May 31 Balance c/d	200
	500		500
Jun 1 Balance b/d	200		

Rent

May 8 Cash	120	May 31 Balance c/d	240
" 19 Cash	120		
	240		240
Jun 1 Balance b/d	240		

Stationery

May 15 Cash	60		

Purchases

May 2 D Ellis	540	May 31 Balance c/d	1,082
May 2 C Mendez	87		
May 2 K Gibson	76		
May 18 D Ellis	145		
May 18 C Mendez	234		
	1,082		1,082
Jun 1 Balance b/d	1,082		

Sales

May 31 Balance c/d	1,496	May 4 C Bailey	430
		May 4 B Hughes	62
		May 4 H Spencer	176
		May 6 Cash	500
		May 25 C Bailey	90
		May 25 B Hughes	110
		May 25 H Spencer	128
	1,496		1,496
		Jun 1 Balance b/d	1,496

H Spencer

May 4 Sales	176	May 10 Bank	150
May 25 Sales	128	May 31 Balance c/d	154
	304		304
Jun 1 Balance b/d	154		

D Ellis

May 12 Bank	370	May 2 Purchases	540
May 31 Balance c/d	315	May 18 Purchases	145
	685		685
		Jun 1 Balance b/d	315

C Mendez

May 31 Bank	87	May 2 Purchases	87
May 31 Balance c/d	234	May 18 C Mendez	234
	234		234
		Jun 1 Balance b/d	234

K Gibson

May 12 Bank	76	May 2 Purchases	76

C Bailey

May 4 Sales	430	May 9 Bank	250
May 25 Sales	90	May 31 Balance c/d	270
	520		520
Jun 1 Balance b/d	270		

B Hughes

May 4 Sales	62	May 31 Balance c/d	172
May 25 Sales	110		
	172		172
Jun 1 Balance b/d	172		

Trial Balance as at 31 May 2012

	Dr £	*Cr* £
Capital		2,500
Bank	2,367	
Cash	200	
Rent	240	
Stationery	60	
Purchases	1,082	
Sales		1,496
H Spencer	154	
D Ellis		315
C Mendez		234
C Bailey	270	
B Hughes	172	
	4,545	4,545

8.2

Bank

Mar 1 Capital	8,000	Mar 17 M Hyatt	84
Mar 24 J Carlton	95	Mar 21 Betta Ltd	500
		Mar 31 Motor van	4,000
		Mar 31 Balance c/d	3,511
	8,095		8,095
Apr 1 Balance b/d	3,511		

Cash

Mar 5 Sales	870	Mar 6 Wages	140
Mar 30 J King (Loan)	600	Mar 9 Purchases	46
		Mar 12 Wages	140
		Mar 31 Balance c/d	1,144
	1,470		1,470
Apr 1 Balance b/d	1,144		

Capital

		Mar 1 Bank	8,000

Motor Van

Mar 31 Bank	4,000		

Purchases Returns

Mar 31 Balance c/d	44	Mar 18 T Braham	20
		Mar 27 K Henriques	24
	44		44
		Apr 1 Balance b/d	44

Wages

Mar 6 Cash	140	Mar 31 Balance c/d	280
Mar 12 Cash	140		
	280		280
Apr 1 Balance b/d	280		

Purchases

Mar 2 K Henriques	76	Mar 31 Balance c/d	864
Mar 2 M Hyatt	27		
Mar 2 T Braham	560		
Mar 9 Cash	46		
Mar 10 M Hyatt	57		
Mar 10 T Braham	98		
	864		864
Apr 1 Balance b/d	864		

Sales

Mar 31 Balance c/d	1,074	Mar 5 Cash	870
		Mar 7 H Elliott	35
		Mar 7 L Lane	42
		Mar 7 J Carlton	72
		Mar 13 L Lane	32
		Mar 13 J Carlton	23
	1,074		1,074
		Apr 1 Balance b/d	1,074

Shop Fixtures

Mar 15 Betta Ltd	500		

J King (Loan)

		Mar 30 Cash	600

H Elliott

Mar 7 Sales	35		

L Lane

Mar 7 Sales	42	Mar 31 Balance c/d	74
Mar 13 Sales	32		
	74		74
Apr 1 Balance b/d	74		

J Carlton

Mar 7 Sales	72	Mar 24 Bank	95
Mar 13 Sales	23		
	95		95

8.2 *(cont'd)*

K Henriques

Mar 27 Purchases returns	24	Mar 2 Purchases	76
Mar 31 Balance c/d	52		
	76		76
		Apr 1 Balance b/d	52

M Hyatt

Mar 17 Bank	84	Mar 2 Purchases	27
		Mar 10 Purchases	57
	84		84

T Braham

Mar 18 Purchases returns	20	Mar 2 Purchases	560
Mar 31 Balance c/d	638	Mar 10 Purchases	98
	658		658
		Apr 1 Balance b/d	638

Betta Ltd

Mar 21 Bank	500	Mar 15 Shop Fixtures	500

Trial Balance as at 31 March 2012

	Dr £	Cr £
Bank	3,511	
Cash	1,144	
Capital		8,000
Motor van	4,000	
Purchases returns		44
Wages	280	
Purchases	864	
Sales		1,074
Shop fixtures	500	
J King (Loan)		600
H Elliott	35	
L Lane	74	
K Henriques		52
J Braham		638
	10,408	10,408

8.5 **Trial Balance of P Brown as at 31 May 2013**

	Dr £	Cr £
Capital		20,000
Drawings	7,000	
General expenses	500	
Sales		38,500
Purchases	29,000	
Accounts receivable	6,800	
Accounts payable		9,000
Bank	15,100	
Cash	200	
Plant and equipment	5,000	
Heating and lighting	1,500	
Rent	2,400	
	67,500	67,500

8.6 **Trial Balance of S Higton as at 30 June 2013**

	Dr £	Cr £
Capital		19,956
Sales		119,439
Stationery	1,200	
General expenses	2,745	
Motor expenses	4,476	
Cash at bank	1,950	
Inventory 1 July 2012	7,668	
Wages and salaries	9,492	
Rent and rates	10,500	
Office equipment	6,000	
Purchases	81,753	
Heating and lighting	2,208	
Rent received		2,139
Accounts receivable	10,353	
Drawings	4,200	
Accounts payable		10,230
Motor vehicle	7,500	
Interest received		1,725
Insurance	3,444	
	153,489	153,489

Chapter 9 Capital and revenue expenditures

9.1

Newton Data Systems

	Type of expenditure	*Reason*
(*a*)	Revenue	Use up in the short term
(*b*)	Capital	Adds to value of computer equipment
(*c*)	Revenue	Used up in the short term
(*d*)	Revenue	Used up in the short term
(*e*)	Capital	Adds to the value of the computer
(*f*)	Question is not clear	
	(1) If spent on improving building Construction = Capital	Add to value of non-current assets
	(2) If spent on extra wages for Security guards = Revenue	Used up in the short term

9.2

Cairns Engineering Co

		Capital	*Revenue*
		£	£
(*a*)	New stationery and brochures	-	411
(*b*)	New pickup truck	18,000	-
(*c*)	New lathe	5,200	-
(*d*)	Delivery costs - lathe	200	-
(*e*)	Electricity - wiring	1,800	
	- electricity costs		2,100
(*f*)	Wages - Re: improvements	20,000	
	- Other		45,000
		45,200	47,511

Brief description of capital and revenue expenditure - see text.

9.4

T Taylor
Revised Profits Year to 31 December 2013

	£
Gross profit before corrections	95,620
Add (a) Purchases overstated	311
	95,931
Less (c) Sale of building	10,000
Revised gross profit	85,931
Net profit before corrections	28,910
Less Gross profit overstated (10,000 – 311)	9,689
	19,221
Add (d) Loan interest overstated	500
Revised net profit	19,721

Error (b) does not affect gross profit or net profit calculations.

Chapter 10 Income statements: an introduction

10.1

L Simpson
Income Statement
for the year ended 31 December 2012

	£	£
Sales		38,220
Less Cost of goods sold:		
Purchases	24,190	
Less Closing inventory	4,310	19,880
Gross profit		18,340
Less Expenses:		
Rent	4,170	
Wages and salaries	5,390	
Postage and stationery	840	
Electricity expenses	710	
General expenses	370	11,480
Net profit		6,860

10.3

G Singh
Income Statement
for the year ended 31 December 2013

	£	£
Sales		73,848
Less Cost of goods sold:		
Purchases	58,516	
Less Closing inventory	10,192	48,324
Gross profit		25,524
Less Expenses:		
Wages	8,600	
Motor expenses	2,080	
Rates	2,680	
Insurance	444	
General expenses	420	14,224
Net profit		11,300

10.5

Mrs P Stewart
Trial Balance as at 31 March 2013

	Dr £	*Cr* £
Sales		24,765
Purchases	13,545	
Staff wages	2,100	
Drawings	5,500	
Rent and rates	1,580	
Electricity	565	
Motor expenses	845	
Insurance	345	
General expenses	245	
Cash in hand	135	
Cash at bank	2,675	
Accounts payable		3,285
Vehicle	5,875	
Fixtures and fittings	1,495	
Capital		6,855
	34,905	34,905

Closing inventory £2,345

Mrs P Stewart
Income Statement
for the year ended 31 March 2013

	£	£
Sales		24,765
Less Cost of goods sold		
Purchases	13,545	
Less Closing inventory	2,345	
		11,200
Gross profit		13,565
Less Expenses		
Staff wages	2,100	
Rent and rates	1,580	
Electricity	565	
Motor expenses	845	
Insurance	345	
General expenses	245	
		5,680
Net profit		7,885

Chapter 11 Statements of financial position

11.1

G Singh
Statements of Financial Position as at 31 December 2013

	£	£	£
Non-current Assets			
Premises			20,000
Motor vehicle			12,000
			32,000
Current Assets			
Inventory	10,192		
Accounts receivable	7,800		
Cash at bank	6,616		
Cash in hand	160	24,768	
Less Current Liabilities			
Accounts payable	6,418	6,418	
Net current assets			18,350
			50,350
Financed by			
Cash introduced			48,000
Add Net profit for the year			11,300
			59,300
Less Drawings			8,950
			50,350

11.3

Mrs P Stewart
Statement of Financial Position as at 31 March 2013

	£	£	£
Non-current Assets			
Fixtures and fittings			1,495
Motor car			5,875
			7,370
Current Assets			
Inventory	2,345		
Accounts receivable	-		
Bank	2,675		
Cash	135	5,155	
Less Current Liabilities			
Accounts payable	3,285	3,285	
Net current assets			1,870
Total net assets			9,240
Financed by			
Capital			6,855
Add Net profit			7,885
			14,740
Less Drawings			5,500
			9,240

11.4

Miss V Holland
Statement of Financial Position as at 30 June 2013

	£	£	£
Non-current Assets			
Equipment			2,885
Van			3,400
			6,285
Current Assets			
Inventory	1,465		
Accounts receivable	2,375		
Cash in hand	150		
		3,990	
Current Liabilities			
Accounts payable	4,565		
Bank overdraft	1,785		
		6,350	
Net current liabilities			(2,360)
			3,925
Non-current Liabilities			
Loan from mother			2,000
Net assets			1,925
Financed by			
Capital account			
Cash introduced			2,000
Net profit			2,525
			4,525
Drawings			2,600
			1,925

Chapter 12 Income statements and statements of financial position: further considerations

12.1

T Clarke
Trading Account section of the Income Statement
for the year ended 31 December 2012

	£	£
Sales		38,742
Less cost of goods sold		
Opening inventory	6,924	
Add Purchases	26,409	
Add Carriage inwards	670	
	34,003	
Less Closing inventory	7,489	26,514
Gross profit		12,228

12.3

T Mann
Income Statement
for the year ended 31 December 2013

	£	£	£
Sales			52,790
Less Sales returns			490
			52,300
Less Cost of goods sold			
Opening inventory		5,690	
Add Purchases	31,000		
Carriage inwards	1,700		
	32,700		
Less Purchases returns	560	32,140	
		37,830	
Less Closing inventory		4,230	33,600
Gross profit			18,700
Less Expenses:			
Rent		1,460	
Salaries and wages		5,010	
Motor expenses		3,120	
Carriage outwards		790	
General expenses		420	10,800
Net profit			7,900

12.5

Suzanne Curtis
Income Statement
for the year ended 30 June 2013

	£	£
Sales		111,600
Less Sales returns		1,230
		110,370
Less Cost of sales		
Opening inventory	14,208	
Add Purchases	71,244	
Add Carriage inwards	1,860	
	87,312	
Less Purchases returns	1,932	
	85,380	
Less Closing inventory	17,700	67,680
Gross profit		42,690
Less Expenses:		
Salaries and wages	23,172	
Rent and rates	1,824	
Insurance	468	
Motor expenses	2,656	
Telephone internet charges	2,624	
Carriage outwards	1,200	
Electricity	996	
General expenses	1,884	34,824
Net profit		7,866

12.5 *(cont'd)*

Suzanne Curtis
Statement of Financial Position as at 30 June 2013

	£	£	£
Non-current Assets			
Buildings			50,000
Fixtures and fittings			2,100
Motor vehicles			10,800
			62,900
Current Assets			
Inventory	17,700		
Accounts receivable	23,376		
Cash at bank	2,892	43,968	
Less Current Liabilities			
Accounts payable	20,386	20,386	
Net current assets			23,582
			86,482
Financed by:			
Capital – Balance at 1.7.2012			85,816
Add Net profit			7,866
			93,682
Less Drawings			7,200
			86,482

12.8

J Smailes
Income Statement for the year ended 31 March 2012

	£	£	£
Sales			92,340
Less Cost of sales			
Opening inventory		18,160	
Add Purchases	69,185		
Add Carriage inwards	420		
	69,605		
Less Purchases returns	640	68,965	
		87,125	
Less Closing inventory		22,390	64,735
Gross profit			27,605
Less Expenses			
Wages and salaries		10,240	
Carriage outwards		1,570	
Rent and rates		3,015	
Communication expenses		624	
Commissions payable		216	
Insurance		405	
Sundry expenses		318	16,388
Net profit			11,217

J Smailes
Statement of Financial Position as at 31 March 2012

	£	£	£
Non-current Assets			
Buildings			20,000
Fixtures			2,850
			22,850
Current Assets			
Inventory	22,390		
Accounts receivable	14,320		
Bank	2,970		
Cash	115	39,795	
Less Current Liabilities			
Accounts payable	8,160	8,160	
Net current assets			31,635
			54,485
Less Non-current liabilities			
Loan			10,000
			44,485
Capital			
Balance at 1.4.2011			40,888
Add Net profit			11,217
			52,105
Less Drawings			7,620
			44,485

Chapter 13 Accounting standards, rules and concepts

13.1 (*a*) Materiality
(*b*) Business entity
(*c*) Prudence
(*d*) Historical cost
(*e*) Money measurement
(*f*) Accruals
(*g*) Realisation
(*h*) Going concern
(*i*) Consistency
(*j*) Materiality.

13.4 The *historical cost concept* is an accounting concept whereby the assets of a business are recorded in the accounts at cost price.

Advantages of using the cost method of valuation are that the assets can easily be verified since there will be an invoice available for checking the purchase price; and, also, no valuations need be carried out on assets whose value may be subjective. Refer to text, section 13.8.

13.5 The accounting concept the accounts clerk should follow in these circumstances would be that of prudence. Since it appears that the Priory Paper Co has disappeared it is unlikely that the debt of £187.00 will be recovered. In the circumstances the business will have no option but to write the debt off.

13.6

MEMO

To James
From Payroll Manager — Today's date

Further to our conversation I would advise you not to divulge any confidential information to one of your colleagues. As you are no doubt aware any information that you observe in your position within the Payroll Department is confidential and should not be discussed with anyone other than myself as Payroll Manager.

Your colleague should be advised accordingly.

Chapter 14 Value added tax (VAT)

14.1 D Wilson Ltd

Total	*Discount*	*Net Total*	*VAT*	*Invoice Total*
£	£	£	£	£
960.00	320.00	640.00	128.00	768.00

14.2 Triton Ltd

	Total	*Discount*	*Net Total*	*VAT*	*Invoice Total*
	£	£	£	£	£
(*a*)	120.00	40.00	80.00	16.00	96.00
(*b*)	60.00	20.00	40.00	8.00	48.00
(*c*)	30.00	-	30.00	6.00	36.00
(*d*)	180.00	60.00	120.00	24.00	144.00

14.3 Triton Ltd

	Total	*Cash Discount Deducted*	*Total after Cash Discount*	*VAT*	*Invoice Total*
	£	£	£	£	£
(*a*)	80.00	2.00	78.00	15.60	95.60
(*b*)	40.00	1.00	39.00	7.80	47.80
(*c*)	30.00	0.75	29.25	5.85	35.85
(*d*)	120.00	3.00	117.00	23.40	143.40

14.6 (*a*) Ivy & Co

VAT Account

2012			2012		
April 30	Purchases Day Book	10,000	April 30	Sales Day Book	10,520
May 31	Purchases Day Book	8,400	May 31	Sales Day Book	9,600
June 30	Purchases Day Book	11,000	June 30	Sales Day Book	12,000
June 30	Balances c/d	2,720			
		32,120			32,120
			July 1	Balance b/d	2,720

(*b*) The outstanding balance of £2,720 is the amount of VAT due to HMRC for the quarter ending 30 June 2012.

When Ivy & Co pays this amount to HMRC this will clear the amount in the VAT account.

14.8 Lawton Photography

	Calculation	*Amount of invoice*
	£	£
Total amount of equipment delivered	2,320.00	
Less Trade discount of $12\frac{1}{2}$%, £2,320 × $\frac{12.50}{100}$	290.00	
	2,030.00	2,030.00
Less Cash discount of $2\frac{1}{2}$%, £2,030 × $\frac{2.50}{100}$	50.75	
	1,979.25	
Add VAT @ 20%, £1,979.25 × $\frac{20}{100}$	395.85	395.85
		2,425.85

Note: VAT is calculated when $2\frac{1}{2}$% discount has been deducted but the invoice amount ignores this discount since the customer may not pay within the 7 days. If the customer fails to pay within 7 days no adjustment to the VAT needs to be made. See text section 14.8.

Chapter 15 Business documentation

15.1 (*a*) Remittance advice – see section 15.11.
(*b*) Goods received note (GRN) – see section 15.12.
(*c*) Credit note – see section 15.9.
(*d*) Invoice – see section 15.6.

15.3 (*a*) Purchase order.
(*b*) Advice note.
(*c*) Invoice.
(*d*) Remittance advice.

Chapter 16 Division of the ledger: sales day book and sales ledger including VAT

16.1 (*a*) Sales day book/sales ledger/personal account
(*b*) Purchases day book/purchases ledger/personal account
(*c*) Sales returns day book/sales ledger/personal account
(*d*) Sales returns day book/sales ledger/personal account
(*e*) Purchases returns day book/purchases ledger/personal account

16.3

Sales Day Book

Date	*Details*	*Folio*	*Goods*	*VAT*	*Total*
2013			£	£	£
Nov 1	T Bates		186.00	37.20	223.20
Nov 4	D Cope		166.00	33.20	199.20
Nov 8	F Chan		12.00	2.40	14.40
Nov 11	T Bates		54.00	10.80	64.80
Nov 13	B Hope		66.00	13.20	79.20
Nov 18	D Cope		32.00	6.40	38.40
Nov 22	M Saka & Sons		20.00	4.00	24.00
Nov 29	F Chan		320.00	64.00	384.00
			856.00	171.20	1,027.20

Sales Ledger

T Bates Account

(1) Sales	223.20		
(11) Sales	64.80		

F Chan Account

(8) Sales	14.40		
(29) Sales	384.00		

D Cope Account

(4) Sales	199.20		
(18) Sales	38.40		

B Hope Account

(13) Sales	79.20		

M Saka & Sons Account

(22) Sales	24.00		

General Ledger

Sales Account

		(30) Credit sales for the month	856.00

VAT Account

		(30) Sales Day Book: VAT	171.20

16.5 Dabell's Stationery Supplies Ltd.

Sales Day Book					*page 26*
Date	*Details*	*Folio*	*Goods*	*VAT*	*Total*
2013			£	£	£
April 1	Fisher & Co		1,459.00	291.80	1,750.80
April 3	Elder (Office Supplies)		73.00	14.60	87.60
April 5	Haigh (Mfr) Ltd		56.00	11.20	67.20
April 11	Ardern & Co		1,598.00	319.60	1,917.60
April 15	I Rafiq		540.00	108.00	648.00
April 19	Royles Business Sys.		2,456.00	491.20	2,947.20
April 22	Fisher & Co		23.00	4.60	27.60
April 22	Ardern & Co		345.00	69.00	414.00
April 25	Elder (Office Supplies)		71.00	14.20	85.20
April 26	Haigh (Mfr) Ltd		176.00	35.20	211.20
			6,797.00	1,359.40	8,156.40

Sales Ledger

Ardern & Co Account

(1) Balance b/d	472.00	30 Balance c/d	2,803.60
(11) Sales	1,917.60		
(22) Sales	414.00		
	2,803.60		2,803.60
(1) Balance b/d	2,803.60		

Elder (Office Supplies) Account

(1) Balance b/d	75.00	(30) Balance c/d	247.80
(3) Sales	87.60		
(25) Sales	85.20		
	247.80		247.80
(1) Balance b/d	247.80		

Fisher & Co Account

(1) Balance b/d	231.00		(30) Bank	231.00
(1) Sales	1,750.80		(30) Balance c/d	1,778.40
(22) Sales	27.60			
	2,009.40			2,009.40
(1) Balance b/d	1,778.40			

Haigh (Mfr) Ltd Account

(1) Balance b/d	1,267.00		(30) Bank	1,000.00
(5) Sales	67.20		(30) Balance c/d	545.40
(26) Sales	211.20			
	1,545.40			1,545.40
(1) Balance b/d	545.40			

I Rafiq Account

(1) Balance b/d	330.00		(30) Bank	330.00
(15) Sales	648.00		(30) Balance c/d	648.00
	978.00			978.00
(1) Balance b/d	648.00			

Royles Business Systems Account

(1) Balance b/d	750.00		(30) Balance c/d	3,697.20
(19) Sales	2,947.20			
	3,697.20			3,697.20
(1) Balance b/d	3,697.20			

General Ledger

Sales Account

			(30) Credit sales for the month	6,797.00

VAT Account

			(30) Sales Day Book: VAT	1,359.40

List of outstanding accounts receivable as at 30 April 2013

	Amount (£)
Ardern & Co	2,803.60
Elder (Office Supplies)	247.80
Fisher & Co	1,778.40
Haigh (Mfr) Ltd	545.40
I Rafiq	648.00
Royle's Business Systems	3,697.20
	9,720.40

16.7 See text, section 16.10.

16.8 See text, section 16.11.

Chapter 17 Purchases day book and purchases ledger including VAT

17.1 White Bros.

Purchases Day Book

Date	Details	Folio	Goods £	VAT £	Total £
May 1	Bould & Co		104.00	20.80	124.80
May 7	Harlow & Brown		48.00	9.60	57.60
May 16	T Adams Ltd		234.00	46.80	280.80
May 23	Bould & Co		170.00	34.00	204.00
May 27	JL Products		320.00	64.00	384.00
May 28	Harlow & Brown		62.00	12.40	74.40
May 31	P Yeung Ltd		446.00	89.20	535.20
			1,384.00	276.80	1,660.80

Purchases Ledger

T Adams Ltd Account

		(16) Purchases	280.80

Bould & Co Account

		(1) Purchases	124.80
		(23) Purchases	204.00

Harlow & Brown Account

		(7) Purchases	57.60
		(28) Purchases	74.40

J L Products Account

		(27) Purchases	384.00

P Yeung Ltd Account

		(31) Purchases	535.20

General Ledger
Purchases Account

(31) Credit purchases for the month	1,384.00		

VAT Account

(31) Purchases Day Book: VAT	276.80		

17.3 Taylor Ltd

Purchases Day Book

Date	Details	Folio	Goods £	VAT £	Total £
Aug 1	Barker Ltd		62.00	12.40	74.40
Aug 6	Fern Bros		48.00	9.60	57.60
Aug 9	Ash & Co		224.00	44.80	268.80
Aug 14	Barker Ltd		136.00	27.20	163.20
Aug 22	Carter Supplies		98.00	19.60	117.60
Aug 27	Fern Bros.		166.00	33.20	199.20
Aug 29	Singh & Sons		84.00	16.80	100.80
Aug 30	Ash & Co		366.00	73.20	439.20
			1,184.00	236.80	1,420.80

Purchase Ledger
Ash & Co Account

		(9) Purchases	268.80
		(30) Purchases	439.20

Barker Ltd Account

		(1) Purchases	74.40
		(14) Purchases	163.20

Carter Supplies Account

		(22) Purchases	117.60

Fern Bros. Account

		(6) Purchases	57.60
		(27) Purchases	199.20

Singh & Sons Account

		(29) Purchases	100.80

General Ledger
Purchases Account

(31) Credit purchases for the month	1,184.00		

VAT Account

(31) Purchases Day Book: VAT	236.80		

Chapter 18 Sales returns day book and purchases returns day book

18.1

Sales Day Book

Date	Details	Folio	Goods £	VAT £	Total £
June 3	J Alcock		180.00	36.00	216.00
June 3	P Twigg		60.00	12.00	72.00
June 7	Bell Products Ltd		140.00	28.00	168.00
June 7	Travis Ltd		330.00	66.00	396.00
June 24	B Seddon		780.00	156.00	936.00
June 28	P Twigg		440.00	88.00	528.00
			1,930.00	386.00	2,316.00

Sales Returns Day Book

Date	Details	Folio	Goods £	VAT £	Total £
June 12	J Alcock		30.00	6.00	36.00
June 28	Travis Ltd		50.00	10.00	60.00
			80.00	16.00	96.00

Sales Ledger
J Alcock Account

(3) Sales	216.00	(12) Sales returns	36.00

Bell Products Account

(7) Sales	168.00		

B Seddon Account

(24) Sales	936.00		

Travis Ltd Account

(3)	Sales	396.00	(28)	Sales returns	60.00

P Twigg Account

(3)	Sales	72.00			
(28)	Sales	528.00			

General Ledger

Sales Account

			(30)	Credit sales for the month	1,930.00

Sales Returns Account

(30)	Total sales returns day book	80.00			

VAT Account

(30)	Total sales returns day book: VAT	16.00	(30)	Sales day book: VAT	386.00

18.2

Purchases Day Book

Date	*Details*	*Folio*	*Goods* £	*VAT* £	*Total* £
May 1	J. Yau Ltd		120.00	24.00	144.00
May 6	S. Wager		80.00	16.00	96.00
May 6	Ash Bros.		220.00	44.00	264.00
May 14	J. Yau Ltd		60.00	12.00	72.00
May 20	D. Wong		300.00	60.00	360.00
May 20	Rughani & Co		280.00	56.00	336.00
May 20	Ash Bros		80.00	16.00	96.00
May 31	A. Davies		50.00	10.00	60.00
May 31	Rughani & Co.		170.00	34.00	204.00
			1,360.00	272.00	1,632.00

Purchases Returns Day Book

Date	*Details*	*Folio*	*Goods* £	*VAT* £	*Total* £
May 9	J Yau Ltd		30.00	6.00	36.00
May 27	D. Wong		40.00	8.00	48.00
			70.00	14.00	84.00

Purchases Ledger

Ash Account

			(6)	Purchases	264.00
			(20)	Purchases	96.00

A Davies Account

			(31)	Purchases	60.00

Rughani & Co Account

			(20)	Purchases	336.00
			(31)	Purchases	204.00

S Wager

			(6)	Purchases	96.00

D Wong Account

(27)	Purchase Returns	48.00	(20)	Purchases	360.00

J Yau Ltd Account

(9)	Purchase Returns	36.00	(1)	Purchases	144.00
			(14)	Purchases	72.00

General Ledger

Purchases Account

(31)	Total Purchases Day Book	1,360.00			

Purchases Returns Account

			(31)	Total Purchases Returns Day Book	70.00

VAT Account

(31)	Total Purchases Day Book	272.00	(31)	Total Purchases Returns Day Book	14.00

19.1

(a)

Sales Day Book *page 11*

Date	*Details*	*Folio*	*Total*	*VAT*	*Ready-made*	*Custom-made*
2012			£	£	£	£
Nov 1	Jarvis Arms Hotel	SL 1	2,760.00	460.00		2,300.00
Nov 8	Springs Nursing Home	SL 2	1,200.00	200.00	1,000.00	
Nov 15	J P Morten	SL 3	264.00	44.00	220.00	
Nov 17	Queen's Hotel	SL 4	1,800.00	300.00		1,500.00
Nov 30	W Blackshaw	SL 5	108.00	18.00	90.00	
			6,132.00	1,022.00	1,310.00	3,800.00
				GL 3	GL 1	GL 2

(b)

Sales Ledger

Jarvis Arms Hotel Account SL 1

Nov 1 Sales	SDB II	2,760.00					

Spring's Nursing Home Account SL 2

Nov 8 Sales	SDB II	1,200.00					

J P Morten Account SL 3

Nov 15 Sales	SDB II	264.00					

Queen's Hotel Account SL 4

Nov 17 Sales	SDB II	1,800.00					

W Blackshaw Account SL 5

Nov 30 Sales	SDB II	108.00					

(c)

General Ledger

Sales – Ready-Made Account GL 1

			Nov 30 Day book	SDB II	1,310.00

Sales – Custom-Made Account GL 2

			Nov 30 Day book	SDB II	3,800.00

Value Added Tax Account GL 3

			Nov 30 VAT on sales	SDB II	1,022.00

19.2

(a)

Hall Engineering Co
Purchases Day Book *page 5*

Date	*Details*	*Folio*	*Total*	*VAT*	*Engineering parts*	*Printing and stationery*	*Motor expenses*
2012			£	£	£	£	£
May 1	Black's Engineering Co	PL 1	624.00	104.00	520.00		
May 3	Ace Printing Co	PL 2	174.00	29.00		145.00	
May 24	Morgan's Garage	PL 3	144.00	24.00			120.00
May 26	Martin's Foundry	PL 4	840.00	140.00	700.00		
May 28	Office Supplies	PL 5	151.20	25.20		126.00	
May 29	Black's Engineering Co	PL 1	264.00	44.00	220.00		
			2,197.20	366.20	1,440.00	271.00	120.00
				GL 4	GL 1	GL 2	GL 3

(b)

Purchases Ledger

Black's Engineering PL 1

			May 1 Purchases	PDB5	624.00
			May 29 Purchases	PDB5	264.00

Ace Printing Co PL 2

			May 3 Purchases	PDB5	174.00

Morgan's Garage PL 3

			May 24 Purchases	PDB5	144.00

Martin's Foundry PL 4

			May 26 Purchases	PDB5	840.00

Office Supplies PL 5

			May 28 Purchases	PDB5	151.20

(c)

General Ledger

Purchases – Engineering Parts GL 1

May 31 Day book	PDB5	1,440.00			

Printing and Stationery GL 2

May 31 Day book	PDB5	271.00			

Motor Expenses GL 3

May 31 Day book	PDB5	120.00			

VAT GL 4

May 31 VAT on Purchases	PDB5	366.20			

19.3 (*a*)

Sales Ledger

Account name	*Amount* £	*Debit*	*Credit*
McGrath Ltd	132.00	✓	
Ashley Products	768.00	✓	
Denson Bros	84.00	✓	
Chang Supplies	432.00	✓	

(*b*)

General Ledger

Sales Account

		(31) Total SDB	1,180.00

VAT Account

		(31) Total SDB	236.00

Chapter 20 Business banking

20.1, **20.2**, **20.3** and **20.4**
The answer to each question can be found in the chapter text.

20.7 (*a*) Howard Photographics
(*b*) Central Bank
(*c*) Ben Brown Limited.

Chapter 21 Cash books

21.1

Cash Book

	Cash	*Bank*		*Cash*	*Bank*
(1) Capital		4,000	(2) Fixtures		660
(4) Sales	225		(4) Rent	140	
(6) T Thomas		188	(12) Wages	275	
(8) Sales		308	(15) Cash		200
(10) J King	300		(20) Stationery	60	
(14) J Walters (Loan)		500	(22) J French		166
(15) Bank	200		(28) Drawings	100	
(30) J Scott		277	(31) Balances c/d	216	4,247
(31) Sales	66				
	791	5,273		791	5,273
(1) Balances b/d	216	4,247			

21.2

Cash Book

	Cash	*Bank*		*Cash*	*Bank*
(1) Balance b/d	14.72		(1) Balance b/d		820.54
(3) P Wrench		432.36	(2) Stationery	10.00	
(3) R Whitworth		634.34	(6) SW Rail		37.50
(3) J Summers		341.00	(9) Fabulous Fabrics Ltd		450.80
(12) Sales	76.00		(11) Mellors Mfg. Co		348.32
(17) Trentham Traders		32.81	(14) HMRC		221.30
(24) Sales	350.00		(20) Foreign Currency		250.00
(26) Cash C		300.00	(20) Bank Charges		3.20
(31) J Summers		1,231.00	(26) Bank C	300.00	
(31) Bradnop Mfg. Co		725.00	(27) Salaries		5,720.00
(31) Taylors		2,330.50	(31) Balance c/d	130.72	
(31) Balance c/d		1,824.65			
	440.72	7,851.66		440.72	7,851.66
(1) Balance b/d	130.72		(1) Balance b/d		1,824.65

21.4

Cash Book

	Disct	*Cash*	*Bank*		*Disct*	*Cash*	*Bank*
(1) Capital			6,000	(1) Fixtures			950
(3) Sales		407		(2) Purchases			1,240
(5) N Morgan	10		210	(4) Rent		200	
(9) S Cooper	20		380	(7) S Thompson & Co	4		76
(14) L Curtis			115	(12) Rates			410
(20) P Exeter	2		78	(16) M Monroe	6	114	
(31) Sales			88	(31) Balances c/d		93	4,195
	32	407	6,871		10	407	6,871

General Ledger

Discounts Allowed

(31) Cash Book	32		

Discounts Received

		(31) Cash Book	10

21.5

Cash Book

	Disct	Cash	Bank		Disct	Cash	Bank
(1) Balances b/d		211	3,984	(2) T Adams	4		76
(4) C Potts			98	(2) C Bibby	13		247
(6) Sales			49	(2) D Clarke	22		418
(9) R Smiley	4		156	(7) Stationery		65	
(9) J Turner	16		624	(12) Motor expenses		100	
(9) R Pimlott	13		507	(21) Insurance			120
(18) Sales		98		(23) Expenses		60	
(28) R Godfrey (Loan)			500	(31) Stationery			27
				(31) Balances c/d		84	5,030
	33	309	5,918		39	309	5,918

General Ledger

Discounts Allowed

(31) Cash Book	33		

Discounts Received

		(31) Cash Book	39

Chapter 22 Petty cash and the imprest system

22.1

Petty Cash Book *page 47*

Receipts £ p	Date	Details	Voucher Number	Total £ p	VAT £ p	Postage £ p	Cleaning £ p	Motor Expenses £ p	Stationery £ p	Sundry Expenses £ p
2013										
18.52	June 1	Balance b/d								
131.48	June 1	Cash								
	June 1	Window cleaner	32	10.00			10.00			
	June 3	Postage stamps	33	7.60		7.60				
	June 4	Petrol	34	37.60	6.26			31.34		
	June 6	Stationery	35	9.75	1.62				8.13	
2.00	June 10	Jean Ford stamps	8							
	June 14	Office cleaner	36	20.00			20.00			
	June 17	Parcel postage	37	1.35		1.35				
	June 19	Magazine	38	3.00						3.00
	June 21	Computer disks	39	7.95	1.32				6.63	
	June 24	Petrol	40	14.10	2.35			11.75		
	June 27	Refreshments	41	4.20						4.20
	June 28	Office cleaner	42	20.00			20.00			
				135.55	11.55	8.95	50.00	43.09	14.76	7.20
	June 30	Balance c/d		16.45						
152.00				152.00						
16.45	July 1	Balance b/d								
133.55	July 1	Cash								

		£
Amount required to restore imprest =	Float required	150.00
	Less Cash in hand	16.45
	Amount required	133.55

22.3

(a)

Petty Cash Book – S Dickinson (Estate Agents)

Receipts £	*Date* 2013	*Details*	*Voucher no*	*Total payment* £	*VAT* £	*Travelling* £	*Postage* £	*Stationery* £	*Office expenses* £	*Ledger postings* £
120.00	Mar 1	Cash	CB 1							
	1	Postage Stamps	1	6.50			6.50			
	4	Rail Fare	2	23.00		23.00				
	7	Parcel	3	4.00			4.00			
	9	Window Cleaning	4	8.00					8.00	
	12	Envelopes	5	3.10	0.51			2.59		
	14	Office Tea, etc.	6	6.40					6.40	
	16	Petrol	7	10.00	1.66	8.34				
	19	Disks – Computer	8	13.00	2.16			10.84		
	20	Dusters and Polish	9	1.73	0.29				1.44	
	23	Postage Stamps	10	2.40			2.40			
	27	Ledger a/c J Cheetham	11	7.30						7.30
	29	Magazine	12	6.40					6.40	
				91.83	4.62	31.34	12.90	13.43	22.24	7.30
		Balance c/d		28.17						
120.00				120.00						
28.17	Apr 1	Balance b/d			GL 5	GL 1	GL 2	GL 3	GL 4	C 44
91.83	Apr 1	Cash	CB 1							

(b)

General Ledger

Travelling Expenses Account GL 1

(31) Petty Cash	PCB 1	31.34	

Postage Account GL 2

(31) Petty Cash	PCB 1	12.90	

Stationery Account GL 3

(31) Petty Cash	PCB 1	13.43	

Office Expenses Account GL 4

(31) Petty Cash	PCB 1	22.24	

VAT Account GL 5

(31) Petty Cash	PCB 1	4.62	

Cash Book (Bank Column Only) CB 1

			(31) Petty Cash	PCB 1	91.83

Purchase Ledger

J Cheetham Account C 44

(31) Petty Cash	PCB 1	7.30	(1) Balance b/d	7.30

(c)

MEMORANDUM

To Ms S Dickinson | Ref
From Student's Name | Date 31 March 2013
Subject Petty Cash Imprest System

Advantages of Imprest System:

1. *Control*: The petty cash can be checked easily at any time because cash in hand plus vouchers paid out for the period should always equal the amount of the 'float'.
2. *Responsibility*: It is an ideal opportunity to appoint junior staff and give them some responsibility and test their honesty.
3. *Efficiency*: It relieves the accountant by dealing with numerous small cash payments and reduces the posting to the general ledger.

Chapter 23 Bank reconciliation statements

Note: Both in theory and in practice you can start with the cash book balance working to the bank statement balance, or you can reverse this method. Many teachers and lecturers have their preferences, but this is a personal matter only. Examiners sometimes ask for them using one way, sometimes the other. Students should therefore be able to tackle them both ways.

23.1 (*a*) **Cash Book**

2013 (Totals so far)	2,328	2013 (Totals so far)	497
Dec 31 J. Walters	54	Dec 31 Bank charges	22
		Dec 31 Balance c/d	1,863
	2,382		2,382

(*b*) **Bank Reconciliation Statement as at 31 December 2013**

Balance per cash book	1,863
Add Unpresented cheque	115
	1,978
Less Bankings not yet on bank statement (249 + 178)	427
Balance per bank statement	1,551

OR

Bank Reconciliation Statement as at 31 December 2013

Balance per bank statement	1,551
Add Bankings not yet on bank statement (249 + 178)	427
	1,978
Less Unpresented cheque	115
Balance per cash book	1,863

23.3 (*a*) **Cash Book – James Baxter**

	£		£
2013		2013	
Mar 31 BGC		Mar 31 Balance b/d	2,804
- A May	929	Mar 31 Standing order	
Mar 31 Balance c/d	2,003	- Oak plc	100
		Mar 31 Bank charges	28
	2,932		2,932

(*b*) **James Baxter**
Bank Reconciliation Statement as at 31 March 2013

	£
Bank overdraft per cash book	2,003
Add Banking not entered on bank statement	160
	2,163
Less Unpresented cheque	490
Bank overdraft per bank statement	1,673

OR

James Baxter
Bank Reconciliation Statement as at 31 March 2013

	£
Balance per bank statement	1,673 O/D
Less Banking not entered on bank statement	160
	1,513 O/D
Add Unpresented cheque	490
Balance per cash book	2,003 O/D

23.5 (*a*) **Cash Book – K Talbot**

	£		£
Balance b/d	4,500	RB Insurance	600
Bank interest received	720	Bank charges	90
KB Ltd	780	Dishonoured cheque: C Hill	210
Bank deposit account	4,200	Balance c/d	9,300
	10,200		10,200

(*b*) **K Talbot**
Bank Reconciliation Statement as at 31 December 2013

	£
Balance per cash book	9,300
Add Unpresented cheques (750 + 870)	1,620
	10,920
Less Banking not recorded	2,070
Balance per bank statement	8,850

OR

K Talbot
Bank Reconciliation Statement as at 31 December 2013

	£
Balance per bank statement	8,850
Add Cash not yet credited	2,070
	10,920
Less Unpresented cheques (750 + 870)	1,620
Balance per cash book	9,300

Chapter 24 The journal

24.1

The Journal

Date	Details	Dr	Cr
2013		£	£
Jan 1	Computer	4,000	
	Data Systems Ltd		4,000
Jan 5	Drawings	120	
	Purchases		120
Jan 8	Bad debts	220	
	J Oddy		220
Jan 15	Motor vehicle	15,500	
	Bank		15,500
Jan 29	Office furniture and fittings	250	
	J Street		250

24.3 (*a*) **The Journal as at 1 May 2013**

Bank	2,910	
Cash	160	
Equipment	5,900	
Premises	25,000	
Account receivable: J Carnegie	540	
Account payable: R Smith		890
T Thomas		610
Loan: J Higgins		4,000
Capital		29,010
	34,510	34,510

(*b*) **Cash Book**

	Cash	Bank		Cash	Bank
(1) Balances b/d	160	2,910	(5) R Smith		500
(31) Sales	8,560		(12) J Higgins		1,000
(31) Cash C		8,000	(31) Bank C	8,000	
			(31) Loan interest		200
			(31) Balance c/d	720	9,210
	8,720	10,910		8,720	10,910

Equipment

(1) Balance b/d	5,900			

Premises

(1) Balance b/d	25,000		

R Smith

(5) Bank	500	(1) Balance b/d	890

J Carnegie

(1) Balance b/d	540	(31) Sales returns	400
(24) Sales	2,220		

T Thomas

		(1) Balance b/d	610
		(2) Purchases	2,100

J Higgins (Loan)

(12) Bank	1,000	(1) Balance b/d	4,000

Loan Interest

(31) Bank	200		

Capital

		(1) Capital	29,010

Sales Returns

(31) J Carnegie	400		

Sales

		(24) J Carnegie	2,220
		(31) Cash	8,560

Purchases

(2) T Thomas	2,100		

24.3 *(cont'd)*

J Green
Trial Balance as at 31 May 2013

	Dr £	*Cr* £
Cash	720	
Bank	9,210	
Equipment	5,900	
Premises	25,000	
R Smith		390
J Carnegie	2,360	
T Thomas		2,710
J Higgins		3,000
Loan interest	200	
Capital		29,010
Sales		10,780
Purchases	2,100	
Sales returns	400	
	45,890	45,890

Chapter 25 Control accounts

25.1

Sales Ledger Control Account

(1)	Balance b/d	4,560	(31) Sales returns	460
(31)	Sales day book	10,870	(31) Cheques and cash	9,615
			(31) Discounts allowed	305
			(31) Balances c/d	5,050
		15,430		15,430

25.2

Sales Ledger Control Account

(1)	Balances b/d	6,708	(31) Discounts	300
(31)	Sales day book	11,500	(31) Cash and cheques	8,970
			(31) Bad debts	115
			(31) Sales returns	210
			(31) Balances c/d	8,613
		18,208		18,208

25.6 *(a)*

Sales Ledger Control Account

2013			2013		
Jan 1	Balance b/d	65,000	Dec 31	RIDB	6,430
Dec 31	SDB	453,900	Dec 31	Bank	432,000
Dec 31	Returned cheque	750	Dec 31	Discount All	7,540
			Dec 31	Bad debts	650
			Dec 31	Purchases ledger set offs	1,650
			Dec 31	Balance c/d	71,380
		519,650			519,650

(b) Ravi believes there may be errors in his sales ledger because the sales ledger shows £78,540 total accounts receivable (debtors) at the end of December 2013. Having constructed the control account the total accounts receivable (debtors) outstanding amounts to £71,380. Therefore there is a discrepancy of £78,540 – £71,380 – £7,160 which will require investigation.

(c) The closing balance of the sales ledger control account would appear under current assets in the statement of financial position.

IGCSE

Chapter 26 Depreciation of non-current assets

26.1

K Richardson

Straight Line		*Diminishing (Reducing) Balance*	
Cost	40,000	Cost	40,000
Year 1 Depreciation	7,000	Year 1 Depreciation 40% of 40,000	16,000
	33,000		24,000
Year 2 Depreciation	7,000	Year 2 Depreciation 40% of 24,000	9,600
	26,000		14,400
Year 3 Depreciation	7,000	Year 3 Depreciation 40% of 14,400	5,760
	19,000		8,640
Year 4 Depreciation	7,000	Year 4 Depreciation 40% of 8,640	3,456
	12,000		5,184
Year 5 Depreciation	7,000	Year 5 Depreciation 40% of 5,184	2,074
	5,000		3,110

40,000 – 5,000 = 35,000 ÷ 5 = 7,000

26.2

(a) Straight Line		(b) Diminishing (Reducing) Balance	
Cost	37,500	Cost	37,500
Year 1 Depreciation	5,535	Year 1 Depreciation 20% of 37,500	7,500
	31,965		30,000
Year 2 Depreciation	5,535	Year 2 Depreciation 20% of 30,000	6,000
	26,430		24,000
Year 3 Depreciation	5,535	Year 3 Depreciation 20% of 24,000	4,800
	20,895		19,200
Year 4 Depreciation	5,535	Year 4 Depreciation 20% of 19,200	3,840
	15,360		15,360

37,500 − 15,360 = 22,140 ÷ 4 = 5,535

26.6

(a) Diminishing (Reducing) Balance		(b) Straight Line	
Dumper cost	6,000	Dumper cost	6,000
Year 1 Depreciation 20%	1,200	Year 1 Depreciation	976*
	4,800		5,024
Year 2 Depreciation 20% of 4,800	960	Year 2 Depreciation	976
	3,840		4,048
Year 3 Depreciation 20% of 3,840	768	Year 3 Depreciation	976
	3,072		3,072

*Calculation: $\frac{6{,}000 - 3{,}072}{3} = \frac{2{,}928}{3} = 976$

Chapter 27 Double entry records for depreciation and the disposal of assets

27.1 (a)

Motor Cars

2010				
Jan 1 Bank	12,500			

(b)

Accumulated Provision for Depreciation: Motor Cars

		2010	
		Dec 31 Profit and loss	2,500
2011		2011	
Dec 31 Balance c/d	4,500	Dec 31 Profit and loss	2,000
	4,500		4,500
2012		2012	
Dec 31 Balance c/d	6,100	Jan 1 Balance b/d	4,500
		Dec 31 Profit and loss	1,600
	6,100		6,100

(c)

Profit and Loss Account (extracts) – A White

(2010) Acc. provn for depn: Motors	2,500	
(2011) Acc. provn for depn: Motors	2,000	
(2012) Acc. provn for depn: Motors	1,600	

(d)

Statement of Financial Position (extracts) – A White

	2010	*2011*	*2012*
Motor car at cost	12,500	12,500	12,500
Less Acc. Depreciation	2,500	4,500	6,100
Net book value	10,000	8,000	6,400

27.3 (a)

Computer

2010		2013	
Jan 1 Balance b/d	9,500	Jan 1 Computer disposals	9,500

27.3 *(cont'd)*

(b) *Accumulated Provision for Depreciation: Computer*

2010		2010	
Dec 31 Balance c/d	1,900	Dec 31 Profit and loss	1,900
2011		2011	
Dec 31 Balance c/d	3,800	Jan 1 Balance b/d	1,900
		Dec 31 Profit and loss	1,900
	3,800		3,800
2012		2012	
Dec 31 Balance c/d	5,700	Jan 1 Balance b/d	3,800
		Dec 31 Profit and loss	1,900
	5,700		5,700
2013		2013	
Jan 1 Computer disposals	5,700	Jan 1 Balance b/d	5,700

(c) *Computer Disposals*

2013		2013	
Jan 1 Computer	9,500	Jan 1 Acc. provn. for depn.	5,700
Dec 31 Profit and loss	450	" 1 Bank	4,250
	9,950		9,950

(d) *Profit and Loss Account (extracts)*

(2010) Acc. provn. for depn.: Computer	1,900		
(2011) Acc. provn. for depn.: Computer	1,900		
(2012) Acc. provn. for depn.: Computer	1,900		
		(2013) Profit on sale of computer	450

(e) *Statement of Financial Position (extracts)*

	2010	*2011*	*2012*
Computer at cost	9,500	9,500	9,500
Less Depreciation to date	1,900	3,800	5,700
Net book value	7,600	5,700	3,800

27.4 *(a)* *Motor Van Disposals*

Motor van	12,000	Acc. provn. for depn.	9,700
		Bank	1,850
		Profit and loss: loss on sale	450
	12,000		12,000

(b) *Machinery Disposals*

Machinery	27,900	Acc. provn. for depn.	19,400
Profit and loss: profit on sale	2,770	Bank	11,270
	30,670		30,670

(c) *Fixtures Disposals*

Fixtures	8,420	Acc. provn. for depn.	7,135
		Bank	50
		Profit and loss: loss on sale	1,235
	8,420		8,420

(d) *Buildings Disposals*

Buildings	200,000	Acc. provn. for depn.	110,000
Profit and loss: profit on sale	59,000	Bank	149,000
	259,000		259,000

Chapter 28 Bad debts and allowances for doubtful debts

28.1

Data Computer Services

(a) *Bad Debts Account*

	£		£
2012		2012	
Apr 30 H Gordon	1,110	Dec 31 Profit and loss	1,870
Aug 31 D Bellamy	640		
Oct 31 J Alderton	120		
	1,870		1,870

Allowance for Doubtful Debts Account

			£
		2012	
		Dec 31 Profit and loss	2,200

(b) *Income Statement for the year ended 31 December 2012 (extracts)*

Gross profit		xxx
Less Expenses:		
Bad debts written off	1,870	
Allowance for doubtful debts	2,200	4,070

(c) *Statement of Financial Position as at 31 December 2012 (extract)*

Accounts receivable	68,500	
Less Allowance for doubtful debts	2,200	66,300

28.2

Date 31 Dec	Total accounts receivable	Profit and loss	Dr/Cr	Final figure for statement of financial position
2010	7,000	70	Dr	6,930 (net)
2011	8,000	10	Dr	7,920 (net)
2012	6,000	20	Cr	5,940 (net)
2013	7,000	10	Dr	6,930 (net)

28.4 (*a*)

The Journal

Date	*Debit* £	*Credit* £
Apr 30 Bad debts	500	
A Carter		500
Being bad debt written off		

(*b*) Double entry for the creation of an allowance for doubtful debts
Debit: profit and loss account
Credit: allowance for doubtful debts account

(*c*) The prudence concept requires that the financial statements provide a 'true and fair' view of the business at the date of the statement of financial position. In addition profits should also reveal a correct and true figure. Therefore any anticipated losses need to be accounted for in the profit and loss account. Providing for an allowance for doubtful debts' anticipates any potential loss should a debtor fail to pay. By deducting the allowance from the debtors in the statement of financial position a more accurate figure of debtors is given.

Chapter 29 Accruals, prepayments and other adjustments for financial statements

29.1

C Homer

(*a*) *Rent Account*

2013			2013		
Dec 31	Bank	1,600	Dec 31	Profit and loss	2,000
Dec 31	Owing c/d	400			
		2,000			2,000
			2014		
			Jan 1	Owing b/d	400

(*b*) *Insurance Account*

2013			2013		
Dec 31	Bank	900	Dec 31	Profit and loss	635
			Dec 31	Prepaid c/d	265
		900			900
2014					
Jan 1	Prepaid b/d	265			

(*c*) *Motor Expenses Account*

2013			2013		
Dec 31	Bank	7,215	Dec 31	Profit and loss	7,381
Dec 31	Owing c/d	166			
		7,381			7,381
			2014		
			Jan 1	Owing b/d	166

(*d*) *Rates Account*

2013			2013		
Jan 1	Bank	750	Dec 31	Profit and loss	1,500
Jul 1	Bank	1,125	Dec 31	Prepaid c/d	375
		1,875			1,875
2014					
Jan 1	Prepaid b/d	375			

(*e*) *Rents Receivable Account*

2013			2013		
Dec 31	Profit and loss	4,800	Apr 15	Bank	2,000
Dec 31	In advance c/d	1,600	Dec 15	Bank	4,400
		6,400			6,400
			2014		
			Jan 1	In advance b/d	1,600

29.2

T Norton

(*a*) *General Expenses Account*

2013			2013		
Dec 31	Bank	615	Dec 31	Profit and loss	671
Dec 31	Owing c/d	56			
		671			671
			2014		
			Jan 1	Owing b/d	56

(*b*) *Telephone Account*

2013			2013		
Dec 31	Bank	980	Dec 31	Profit and loss	1,097
Dec 31	Owing c/d	117			
		1,097			1,097
			2014		
			Jan 1	Owing b/d	117

29.2 *(cont'd)*

(c) *Commission Received Account*

2013			2013		
Dec 31	Profit and loss	3,231	Dec 31	Bank	3,056
			Dec 31	Owing c/d	175
		3,231			3,231
2014					
Jan 1	Owing b/d	175			

(d) *Carriage Outwards Account*

2013			2013		
Dec 31	Bank	666	Dec 31	Profit and loss	788
Dec 31	Owing c/d	122			
		788			788
			2014		
			Jan 1	Owing b/d	122

(e) *Insurance Account*

2013			2013		
Jan 1	Bank	1,080	Dec 31	Profit and loss	1,440
Oct 1	Bank	1,080	Dec 31	Prepaid c/d	720
		2,160			2,160
2014					
Jan 1	Prepaid b/d	720			

29.4

C Cainen
Income Statement
for the year ended 31 December 2013

Sales		18,590
Less Cost of goods sold:		
Opening inventory	2,050	
Add Purchases	11,170	
	13,220	
Less Closing inventory	3,910	
		9,310
Gross profit		9,280
Less Expenses:		
Rent (640 – 160)	480	
Wages and salaries (2,140 + 290)	2,430	
Insurance (590 – 190)	400	
Bad debts	270	
Telephone (300 + 110)	410	
General expenses	180	4,170
Net profit		5,110

29.6

J Sears
Income Statement
for the year ended 31 December 2013

Sales		80,000
Less Sales returns		1,000
		79,000
Less Cost of goods sold:		
Opening inventory	20,000	
Add Purchases	70,000	
	90,000	
Less Purchase returns	1,240	
	88,760	
Less Closing inventory	24,000	64,760
Gross profit		14,240
Less Expenses:		
Wages and salaries (7,200 + 450)	7,650	
Telephone (200 – 20)	180	
Bad debts	40	
Allowance for doubtful debts (1,960 × 10% – 160)	36	
Depreciation:		
Store fittings	800	
Motor van	1,200	9,906
Net profit		4,334

J Sears
Statement of Financial Position as at 31 December 2013

	Cost	*Depreciation*	*Net Book Value*
Non-current Assets			
Store fittings	8,000	800	7,200
Motor van	6,000	1,200	4,800
	14,000	2,000	12,000
Current Assets			
Inventory		24,000	
Accounts receivable	1,960		
Less Allowance for doubtful debts	196	1,764	
Prepaid expenses		20	
Bank		600	
		26,384	
Less Current Liabilities			
Accounts payable	1,400		
Expenses owing	450	1,850	
Net current assets			24,534
			36,534
Financed by:			
Capital			
Balance 1.1.2013			35,800
Add Net profit			4,334
			40,134
Less Drawings			3,600
			36,534

29.8

Freddy Tuilagi
Income Statement
for the year ended 30 September

Sales		30,490
Less Cost of goods sold:		
Opening inventory	850	
Add Purchases (13,725 – 320)	13,405	
	14,255	
Less Closing inventory	960	13,295
Gross profit		17,195
Add Discounts received (230 + 80)		310
		17,505
Less Expenses:		
General expenses	610	
Wages	3,880	
Advertising (420 – 46)	374	
Telephone	160	
Depreciation - Equipment	4,500	
- Motor van	1,050	10,574
		6,931

Freddy Tuilagi
Statement of Financial Position as at 30 September

	Cost £	*Depreciation* £	*Net Book Value* £
Non-current Assets			
Equipment	17,000	6,500	10,500
Motor van	7,000	1,050	5,950
	24,000	7,550	16,450
Current Assets			
Inventory	960		
Prepayments	46		
Cash in hand	30	1,036	
Less Current Liabilities			
Bank overdraft	50		
Accounts payable (845 – 80)	765	815	
Net current assets			221
			16,671
Financed by:			
Capital			11,460
Add Net profit			6,931
			18,391
Less Drawings (1400 + 320)			1,720
			16,671

Chapter 30 Extended trial balance

30.1

S Dickinson
Trial Balance as at 30 September 2013

	Dr £	*Cr* £
Capital		59,868
Motor vehicles	22,500	
Computer equipment	18,000	
Accounts receivable	31,059	
Accounts payable		30,690
Purchases	245,259	
Sales		358,317
Wages and salaries	38,476	
Motor expenses	3,428	
Printing and stationery	3,600	
General expenses	8,235	
Cash at bank	5,850	
Inventory 1 October 2012	23,004	
Rent and rates	31,500	
Heating and lighting	6,624	
Interest received		6,417
Insurance	10,332	
Rent received		5,175
Drawings	12,600	
	460,467	460,467

30.2

G Brammer
Trial Balance as at 31 December 2013

	Dr £	*Cr* £
Capital		100,000
Premises	66,250	
Motor vehicle	17,000	
Office equipment	2,438	
Wages	19,637	
Purchases	37,455	
Sales		56,170
Commission received		1,050
Electricity	925	
Telephone	1,125	
Motor expenses	1,500	
Printing, stationery and advertising	2,050	
Accounts payable		8,500
Accounts receivable	12,012	
General expenses	2,371	
Bank overdraft		3,505
Drawings	6,462	
	169,225	169,225

30.4

J Steadman – Extended trial balance as at 31 January 2013

	Description	Ledger Balances		Adjustments		Income Statement		Statement of Financial Position	
		Dr	Cr	Dr	Cr	Dr	Cr	Dr	Cr
		£	£	£	£	£	£	£	£
S	Capital		58,260						58,260
S	Equipment	11,250						11,250	
S	Furniture and fittings	6,000						6,000	
S	Motor vehicles	17,370						17,370	
IS	Sales		96,030				96,030		
IS	Purchases	59,220				59,220			
S	Cash at bank	750						750	
IS	General expenses	1,800				1,800			
IS	Wages	17,820		(a) 351		18,171			
IS	Rent, rates and insurance	7,650			(b) 600	7,050			
IS	Heating and lighting	2,100				2,100			
S	Accounts receivable	24,000						24,000	
S	Accounts payable		10,800						10,800
IS	Inventory 1 February 2012	17,130				17,130			
		165,090	165,090						
S	Accrual - Wages				(a) 351				351
S	Prepayment - Insurance			(b) 600				600	
S	Inventory - 31 January 2013			(c) 14,730				14,730	
IS	Inventory - 31 January 2013				(c) 14,730		14,730		
				15,681	15,681				
	Net profit					5,289			5,289
						110,760	110,760	74,700	74,700

30.6 (ii)

Automania – Extended trial balance as at 30 April 2013

	Description	Ledger Balances		Adjustments		Income Statement		Statement of Financial Position	
		Dr	*Cr*	*Dr*	*Cr*	*Dr*	*Cr*	*Dr*	*Cr*
		£	£	£	£	£	£	£	£
S	Capital		135,000						135,000
S	Drawings	42,150						42,150	
IS	Rent	17,300		1,600		18,900			
IS	Purchases	606,600				606,600			
IS	Sales		857,300				857,300		
IS	Sales returns	2,400				2,400			
IS	Purchases returns		1,260		200		1,460		
IS	Salaries and wages	136,970				136,970			
S	Motor vehicles (MV) at cost	60,800						60,800	
S	Provision for depreciation (MV)		16,740		12,160				28,900
S	Fixtures and fittings (F & F) at cost	40,380						40,380	
S	Provision for depreciation (F & F)		21,600		1,878				23,478
S	Bank		3,170						3,170
S	Cash	2,100						2,100	
IS	Lighting and heating	4,700				4,700			
S	VAT		9,200		35				9,235
IS	Inventory 1 May 2012	116,100				116,100			
IS	Bad debts	1,410				1,410			
IS/S	Allowance for doubtful debts		1,050		87				1,137
S	Accounts receivable control account	56,850						56,850	
S	Accounts payable control account		50,550	*235					50,315
IS	Sundry expenses	6,810				6,810			
IS	Insurance	1,300			100	1,200			
		1,095,870	1,095,870						
S	Accruals				1,600				1,600
S	Prepayments			100				100	
IS	Depreciation – Motor vehicles			12,160		12,160			
IS	Depreciation – Fixtures & fittings			1,878		1,878			
IS	Allowance for doubtful debts – Adjustment			87		87			
IS	Closing Inventory – 30.4.13				117,700		117,700		
S	Closing Inventory – 30.4.13			117,700				117,700	
				133,760	133,760				
	Net profit					67,245			67,245
						976,460	976,460	320,080	320,080

*Note: Made up of £200 purchases returns plus VAT £35 = £235

30.6 *(cont'd)*

(i) Workings

			£
(a) Rent:	1.5.2012 to 31.7.2013 = 3 months × 1,500 =		4,500
	1.8.2012 to 30.8.2013 = 9 months × 1,600 =		14,400
			18,900
	Rent paid during year		17,300
	Rent owing at 30.4.2013		1,600
(b) Insurance paid in advance - 100			
(c) Depreciation:			
	Motor vehicles = 20% SLM = 20% of £60,800 =		12,160
	Fixtures and fittings = 10% RBM = F & F cost		40,380
	Less Depreciation to date		21,600
	Net book value		18,780
	Therefore 10% of £18,780 =		1,878
(d) Increase in allowance for doubtful debts to 2% of accounts receivable			
	= 2% of £56,850 (new provision) =		1,137
	Less Old provision =		1,050
	Therefore increase =		87
(e) Inventory valuation 30.4.2013			119,360
	Less Reduction in value of old goods 3,660 – 2,060 =	1,600	
	Less Badly damaged car door =	60	1,660
	New inventory valuation 30.4.2013		117,700
(f) Debit - Accounts payable control		235	
	Credit - Purchases returns		200
	Credit - VAT		35

Chapter 31 Inventory valuation

31.1 *(a)* (i) FIFO 6 × £13 = £78 inventory valuation at 31 December 2013.
(ii) LIFO

2013	*Received*	*Issued*	*Stock*	£	£
Jan	24 × £10		24 × £10		240
April	16 × £12.50		24 × £10 16 × £12.50	240 200	440
June		14 × £10 16 × £12.50	10 × £10		100
Oct	30 × £13		10 × £10 30 × £13	100 390	490
Nov		4 × £10 30 × £13	6 × £10		60

Closing inventory would be valued at £60 on a LIFO basis.

(iii) AVCO

2013	*Received*	*Issued*	*Average cost per unit*	*No. of units in stock*	*Total value of stock*
Jan	24 × £10		£10.00	24	£240
April	16 × £12.50		£11.00	40	£440
June		30	£11.00	10	£110
Oct	30 × £13		£12.50	40	£500
Nov		34	£12.50	6	£75

Closing inventory would be valued at £75 on an average cost basis.

(b) **Trading Accounts for the year ended 31 December 2013**

	FIFO		*LIFO*		*AVCO*	
Sales		1,092		1,092		1,092
Less Cost of goods sold						
Purchases	830		830		830	
Less Closing inventory	78	752	60	770	75	755
Gross Profit		340		322		337

31.3

DC Ltd
Stock Valuation as at 31 December 2013

	£	£
Value at 8 January 2014		50,850
Add (*a*) Error in calculation (1,600 – 160)	1,440	
(*b*) Sales at cost (500 – 100)	400	
(*d*) Casting error (4,299 – 2,499)	1,800	3,640
		54,490
Less (*c*) Reduce to NRV (560 – 425)		135
Corrected value of inventory at 31 December 2013		54,355

31.6 The Pine Warehouse

The tables and chairs sold to the customer on 30 November 2013 should not be included in the closing inventory figure at the end of the financial year since they are no longer the property of The Pine Warehouse; they belong to the customer who has already paid for them and is the legal owner. Inventory should be valued at the lower of 'cost' or 'net realisable value' and certainly not at selling price. In any case, the profit of £500 has already been entered in the books for the year to 30 November 2013, as it was included in cash sales.

Chapter 32 Errors not affecting trial balance agreement

(To economise on space, all narratives for journal entries in these answers are omitted.)

32.1

The Journal

		Dr £	*Cr* £
(*a*)	J Harkness	678	
	J Harker		678
(*b*)	Machinery	4,390	
	L Pearson		4,390
(*c*)	Motor van	10,800	
	Motor expenses		10,800
(*d*)	E Fletcher	9	
	Sales		9
(*e*)	Sales	257	
	Commissions received		257

32.3 Tom Ainsworth

The Journal

		Dr £	*Cr* £
(*a*)	Sales	1,000	
	Fixtures and fittings		1,000
(*b*)	Motor repairs	420	
	Motor van		420
(*c*)	C Clarkson	800	
	C Clark		800
(*d*)	Drawings	500	
	Salaries		500
(*e*)	Office cleaning	240	
	Office equipment		240

32.6 Shaw Supplies

The Journal

		Dr £	*Cr* £
(*a*)	Brian Palmer	400	
	Paul Palmer		400
(*b*)	Computer Equipment	3,000	
	Stationery		3,000
(*c*)	Purchases	683	
	Belfields and Machin Ltd		683
(*d*)	Kirkham & Co	90	
	Sales		90

Chapter 33 Suspense accounts and errors

33.1

The Journal

	Dr £	*Cr* £
(*a*) T. Thomas Bank	900	 900
(*b*) C. Charles Discounts allowed	35	 35
(*c*) Office equipment Motor vehicles	6,000	 6,000
(*d*) J. Graham Sales	715	 715
(*e*) Wages Drawings Suspense	210 210	 420

33.2 (*a*)

Jaspa West

	Dr	*Cr*
(1) Suspense Rent Received *Correction of error rent received £55 debited in error to Rent Received*	110	 110
(2) Bad Debts Mary Beagle *Debt owed by Mary Beagle written off as bad*	150	 150
(3) Sales Suspense *Sales overcast by £350*	350	 350
(4) Motor Vehicle C Williams *Purchase of motor vehicle on credit*	3,500	 3,500
(5) Profit and Loss Allowance for doubtful debts *Creation of allowance for doubtful debts*	225	 225

(*b*) Two examples of errors which would not be revealed by the trial balance would be: Two from, errors of omission, commission, principle, original entry, compensating and complete reversal of entries.

33.4 1.

The Journal

	Dr	*Cr*
(*a*) Sales returns Suspense	100	 100
(*b*) Drawings Wages	80	 80
(*c*) Carriage inwards Carriage outwards	75	 75
(*d*) Bank charges Suspense	270	 270
(*e*) Sales ledger control (K Abbott) Sales	385	 385
(*f*) Discounts allowed (2 × 218) Suspense	436	 436
(*g*) Suspense Rent	200	 200
(*h*) Purchases (24,897 – 24,798) Suspense	99	 99

2.

Suspense Account

	£		£
Balance b/f	705	(*a*) Sales returns	100
(*g*) Rent	200	(*d*) Bank charges	270
		(*f*) Discounts received	436
		(*h*) Purchases	99
	905		905

3.

Original incorrect gross profit			129,487
Add (*e*)	Sales omitted		385
			129,872
Less (*a*)	Sales returns omitted	100	
(*c*)	Carriage inwards understated	75	
(*b*)	Purchases understated	99	274
			129,598
Original net profit			77,220
Add	Increase in gross profit, i.e. it also increases net profit (129,598 – 129,487)		111
			77,331
Add (*b*)	Wages overstated	80	
(*c*)	Carriage outwards overstated	75	
(*g*)	Rent rebate omitted	200	355
			77,686
Less (*d*)	Bank charges omitted	270	
(*f*)	Discounts allowed understated	436	706
Corrected figure of net profit			76,980

33.5 (*a*)

Suspense

Balance as per T.B.	1,134	(i) Sales over-cast	350
(iv) Creditor	166	(ii) Discounts under-cast	100
		(iii) Fixtures omitted	850
	1,300		1,300

(*b*)

K Woodburn
Trial Balance as at 30 June 2012

	Dr	*Cr*
Sales (87,050 – 350)		86,700
Purchases	62,400	
Discounts allowed and received	405	410
Salaries and wages	3,168	
General expenses	595	
Fixtures (10,000 + 850)	10,850	
Inventory 1 July 2011	12,490	
Accounts receivable and Accounts payable	8,120	4,721
Bank	6,790	
Drawings (4,520 – 490)	4,030	
Capital		17,017
	108,848	108,848

Note: Discounts allowed 305 + (ii) 100 = 405
Accounts payable 5,045 + (iv) 166 – (v) 490 = 4,721

33.7

The Journal

	Dr	*Cr*
(*a*) Suspense Sales *Correction of error sales day book undercast by £3,000*	3,000	3,000
(*b*) Purchases Dawson & Co *Goods purchased on credit from Dawson & Co*	1,147	1,147
(*c*) Motor repairs Motor vehicles *Motor repairs posted in error to motor vehicles account*	585	585
(*d*) J Greenway J Green *Goods sold on credit to J Greenway posted in error to J Green's account*	675	675
(*e*) Suspense Electricity *Payment of electricity account incorrectly debited £150 too much*	150	150
(*f*) Suspense Teape Ltd *Payment of £2,250 received from Teape Ltd not credited to their account*	2,250	2,250

Philip Hogan
Suspense Account

	£		£
Sales (*a*)	3,000	Balance b/d	5,400
Electricity (*e*)	150		
Teape Ltd (*f*)	2,250		
	5,400		5,400

Note that items (b), (c) and (d) do not pass through the suspense account, as they do not affect the balancing of the books.

Chapter 34 Single entry and incomplete records

34.1 (*a*) (i) Mark-up = 25%
(ii) Margin = 20%
(*b*) Margin = 25%
(*c*) Mark-up = 20%

34.3 First, draw up the trading account section of the income statement and insert the figures given in the question. The gross profit can now be calculated. Since mark-up is 25%, then margin is 20%. Consequently, gross profit is 20% of £120,000 = £24,000.

Cost of goods sold = Sales – Gross Profit = £120,000 – £24,000 = £96,000. Purchases can now be found arithmetically.

T Ashby
Trading Account section of the Income Statement for the year ended 31 July 2013

	£	£
Sales		120,000
Less Cost of goods sold (a)		
Opening inventory	19,744	
Add Purchases (*b*)	101,496	
	121,240	
Less Closing inventory	25,240	96,000
Gross profit (*c*)		24,000

34.4 (*a*) Average inventory value = £40,000

Therefore $\frac{£20{,}000 + (a)}{2} = £40{,}000$ and (*a*) is found to be £60,000.

Cost of goods sold is then calculated as £140,000. Mark-up is 50%, so sales = £140,000 + (£140,000 × 50%) = £210,000.

(*b*)
T Rigby
Trading Account section of the Income Statement for the year ended 31 August 2013

		£	£
Sales			210,000
Less Cost of sales:			
Opening inventory		20,000	
Add Purchases		180,000	
		200,000	
Less Closing inventory	(*a*)	60,000	140,000
Gross profit			70,000

(*c*) If net profit on sales is not to be less than 10% of sales (= £21,000), this means that Rigby can afford up to £49,000 in expenses, i.e. Gross profit £70,000 – £49,000 expenses = £21,000 net profit.

34.5 (*a*)

Total Accounts Receivable

Balances b/d	2,760	Cash	14,610
Sales (difference)	**14,940**	Balances c/d	3,090
	17,700		17,700

Total Accounts Payable

Cash	9,390	Balances b/d	1,080
Balances c/d	1,320	**Purchases (difference)**	**9,630**
	10,710		10,710

(*b*)
K Rogers
Trading Account section of the Income Statement for the year ended 31 October 2013

	£	£
Sales		14,940
Less Cost of Goods Sold		
Opening Inventory	2,010	
Add Purchases	9,630	
	11,640	
Less Closing Inventory	2,160	9,480
Gross Profit		5,460

34.7 (*a*) Capital at 30 June 2013 = £62,550.

(*b*)
D Lewinski
Statement of Financial Position as at 30 June 2013

	£	£
Non-current assets		
Plant		36,000
Fixtures		3,600
		39,600
Current assets		
Inventory	13,500	
Accounts receivable	9,300	
Bank	6,000	
Cash	1,350	
	30,150	
Less Current liabilities		
Accounts payable	7,200	
Net current assets		22,950
		62,550
Financed by:		
Capital		
Cash introduced		60,000
Add Net profit		18,550
		78,550
Less Drawings		16,000
		62,550

34.8

J Marcano
Statement of Affairs as at 31 August 2012

	£	£
Non-current assets		
Fixtures		3,500
Motor van		3,500
		7,000
Current assets		
Inventory	16,740	
Accounts receivable	11,890	
Bank	2,209	
Cash	115	
	30,954	
Less Current liabilities		
Accounts payable	9,952	21,002
		28,002

Statement of Affairs as at 31 August 2013

	£	£	£
Non-current assets			
Fixtures		5,500	
Less Depreciation		300	5,200
Motor van		3,500	
Less Depreciation		700	2,800
			8,000
Current assets			
Inventory		24,891	
Accounts receivable		15,821	
Prepaid expenses		72	
Cash		84	
		40,868	
Less Current liabilities			
Accounts payable	6,002		
Expenses owing	236		
Bank overdraft	165	6,403	
Net current assets			34,465
			42,465
Capital			
Balance as at 31.8.2012			28,002
Add Cash introduced			12,800
Add Net profit		(C)	9,223
		(B)	50,025
Less Drawings			7,560
		(A)	42,465

(A) Found as the figure to make statement of financial position totals agree 42,465.
(B) Less 7,560 = (A) 42,465, therefore (B) is 50,025.
(C) Missing figure to total 50,025 = 9,223.

34.10

Leigh Osawa

(*a*) *Sales*

Total Accounts Receivable Account

2012		2013	
Apr 1 Balance b/f	23,460	Mar 31 Receipts	226,820
2013			
Mar 31 Sales (missing figure)	231,910	Mar 31 Discounts	280
		Mar 31 Balance c/d	28,270
	255,370		255,370
Apr 1 Balance b/d	28,270		

(*b*) *Rent*

Rent Account

2013		2012	
Mar 31 Bank: rent	12,290	Apr 1 Balance (rent owing) b/d	1,040
Mar 31 Balance (rent owing) c/d	730	2013	
		Mar 31 Profit & Loss	11,980
	13,020		13,020
		Apr 1 Balance (rent owing) b/d	730

(*c*) *Business Rates*

Business Rates Account

2012		2013	
Apr 1 Balance (prepaid) b/d	390	Mar 31 Profit & Loss	4,630
2013			
Mar 31 Bank: business rates	4,680	Mar 31 Balance (prepaid) c/d	440
	5,070		5,070
Apr 1 Balance (prepaid) b/d	440		

Chapter 35 Accounting for non-profit-making organisations

35.1 *(a)*

Horton Hockey Club
Receipts and Payments Account
for the year ended 30 June 2013

Receipts		*Payments*	
Bank balance b/f	2,715	Teams' travel expenses	1,598
Subscriptions	8,570	Groundsman's wages	3,891
Donations	1,500	Postage and stationery	392
Receipts from raffles	3,816	Rent of pitches and club house	4,800
		General expenses	419
		Prizes for raffles	624
		Bank balance c/f	4,877
	16,601		16,601

(b)

Horton Hockey Club
Income and Expenditure Account
for the year ended 30 June 2013

Income:		
Subscriptions (8,570 + 160)		8,730
Donations		1,500
Profit on raffles (3,816 – 624)		3,192
		13,422
Less Expenditure:		
Teams' travel expenses	1,598	
Groundsman's wages (3,891 + 75)	3,966	
Postage and stationery	392	
Rent of pitches and club house (4,800 + 400)	5,200	
General expenses	419	11,575
Surplus of income over expenditure		1,847

35.3 *(a)* Accumulated fund as at 1 June 2012:

Bar inventory	528
Equipment	2,040
Bank	1,716
	4,284

(b)

Bradnop Bowling Club
Bar Trading Account year ended 31 May 2013

	£	£
Sales		2,778
Less Cost of supplies		
Opening inventory	528	
Add purchases of supplies	2,382	
	2,910	
Less Closing inventory	606	2,304
Profit from bar sales		474

Subscriptions Account

May 31 Income and expenditure account	894	May 31 Bank (rec'd)	810
		May 31 Balance c/d	84
	894		894
June 1 Balance (owing)	84		

(c)

Bradnop Bowling Club
Income and Expenditure Account for the year ended 31 May 2013

	£	£
Income		
Profit from bar		474
Subscriptions		894
Net proceeds from jumble sale		546
Net proceeds from dance		732
		2,646
Less Expenses		
Wages	1,188	
Hire of rooms	384	
Loss on sale of equipment	72	
Depreciation	180	1,824
Surplus of income over expenditure		822

35.5 1 Bar Purchases

	£
Payments via Bank	6,400
Less Opening Accounts payable	1,000
	5,400
Add Closing Accounts payable	540
Bar Purchases	5,940

2

Bar
Trading and Profit and Loss Account
for the year ended 30 November 2013

Sales		8,700
Less Cost of bar sales		
Opening inventory	680	
Add Bar purchases (see Task 1)	5,940	
	6,620	
Less Closing inventory	890	5,730
Gross Profit		2,970
Less Expenses		
Wages (20% × 25,500)	5,100	
General expenses ((4,850 + 250 − 150) × 30%)	1,485	6,585
Net Loss		3,615

3

Subscription Account

Balance (owing) b/d	1,000	Bank	33,000
Income and Expenditure Account (difference)	36,000	Balance (owing) c/d	4,000
	37,000		37,000

Total number of members = $\frac{36,000}{100}$ = 360 Members

4

Income and Expenditure Account
for the year ended 30 November 2013

		£
Income		
Subscriptions (See Task 3)		36,000
Expenditure		
Loss on bar (See Task 2)	3,615	
Wages (80% × 25,500)	20,400	
General expenses ((4,850 + 250 − 150) × 70%)	3,465	
Interest on bank loan (8% × 5,400 × 11/12)	396	27,876
Surplus of income over expenditure		8,124

5

	£
Assets	
Land	12,000
Inventory	890
Subscriptions owing	4,000
	16,890
Liabilities	
Bank	800
Accounts payable	540
Accrual (General expenses)	250
Loan	5,400
Interest	396
	7,386

6 Land is usually classified as a non-wasting non-current asset. It does not tend to go down in value and therefore is not normally depreciated.

35.6

Amateur Dramatic Society
Subscriptions Account

In arrears b/d	235	In advance b/d	220
In advance c/d	140	Bank	2,600
Income and expenditure	**2,630**	In arrears c/d	185
	3,005		3,005
In arrears b/d	185	In advance b/d	140

Chapter 36 Partnership accounts

36.1 *(a)*

Stead and Jackson
Appropriation Account
for the year ended 31 December 2013

			£
Net profit			45,000
Less Salary: Jackson			5,000
			40,000
Balance of profits shared:			
Stead	½	20,000	
Jackson	½	20,000	40,000

(b)

Capital Accounts

	Stead	Jackson		Stead	Jackson
			2013		
			Dec 31 Balance b/d	24,000	16,000

Current Accounts

	Stead	Jackson		Stead	Jackson
2013			2013		
Dec 31 Drawings	15,000	19,000	Dec 31 Balance b/d	2,300	3,500
Dec 31 Balances c/d	7,300	9,500	Dec 31 Salary		5,000
			Dec 31 Share of profits	20,000	20,000
	22,300	28,500		22,300	28,500
			2014		
			Jan 1 Balance b/d	7,300	9,500

36.4

Simpson and Young
Income Statement and Profit and Loss Appropriation Account for the year ended 30 June 2013

	£	£
Sales		254,520
Less Cost of sales:		
Opening inventory	18,000	
Add Purchases	184,980	
	202,980	
Less Closing inventory	19,000	183,980
Gross profit		70,540
Less Expenses:		
Wages and salaries (32,700 + 500)	33,200	
Rent, rates and insurance (3,550 – 250)	3,300	
Electricity	980	
Stationery and printing	420	
Motor expenses	3,480	
General office expenses	1,700	
Depreciation: Motor van (20% of 16,000)	3,200	
Office equipment (10% of 5,600)	560	46,840
Net profit		23,700
Less Interest on capital:		
Simpson (10% of 50,000)	5,000	
Young (10% of 20,000)	2,000	7,000
		16,700
Share of profits:		
Simpson 3/5ths	10,020	
Young 2/5ths	6,680	16,700

Simpson and Young
Statement of Financial Position as at 30 June 2013

	Cost	*Accumulated Depreciation*		*Net Book Value*
	£	£		£
Non-current assets				
Buildings	28,000	-		28,000
Office equipment	8,400	3,360	(W1)	5,040
Motor van	16,000	8,200	(W2)	7,800
	52,400	11,560		40,840
Current assets				
Inventory	19,000			
Accounts receivable	28,000			
Prepayments	250			
Cash at bank	7,250	54,500		
Less Current liabilities				
Accounts payable	15,200			
Accruals	500	15,700		
Net current assets				38,800
				79,640
Financed by:				
Capital accounts	*Simpson*	*Young*		*Total*
Balance b/f	50,000	20,000		70,000
Current accounts				
Balance b/f	640	300		
Add Share of profit	10,020	6,680		
Add Interest on capital	5,000	2,000		
	15,660	8,980		
Less Drawings	10,000	5,000		
	5,660	3,980		9,640
				79,640

(W1) Provision for depreciation on office equipment:
8,400 – 5,600 + 560 = 3,360

(W2) Provision for depreciation on motor van:
16,000 – 11,000 + 3,200 = 8,200

36.6 *(a)*

Bhayani and Donnell
Income Statement for the year ended 31 December

	£	£
Gross profit		32,000
Add Reduction in allowance for doubtful debts		179
Add Rent received (500 – 100)		400
		32,579
Less Expenses:		
Heating and lighting (1,400 + 100)	1,500	
Wages and salaries (4,100 – 200)	3,900	
Depreciation: Vehicles (10% of 35,000)	3,500	
Fittings 15% of (12,000 – 2,000)	1,500	10,400
Net profit		22,179

(b)

Bhayani and Donnell
Appropriation Account for the year ended 31 December

Net profit b/fwd			22,179
Add Interest charged on drawings:			
Bhayani	(6% of 2,000)	120	
Donnell	(6% of 600)	36	156
			22,335
Less Salary: Donnell		3,263	
Interest on capital:			
Bhayani	(8% of 35,000)	2,800	
Donnell	(8% of 12,000)	960	7,023
			15,312
Balance of profits shared:			
Bhayani	2/3	10,208	
Donnell	1/3	5,104	15,312

(c)

Bhayani – Current Account

Jan 1 Balance b/d	600	Dec 31 Profit and loss		
Dec 31 Drawings	2,000	appropriation account:		
Dec 31 Profit and loss		Interest on capital	2,800	
appropriation account:		Share of profit	10,208	
Interest on drawings	120			
Dec 31 Balance c/d	10,288			
	13,008		13,008	
		Jan 1 Balance b/d	10,288	

Donnell – Current Account

Dec 31 Drawings	600	Dec 31 Profit and loss	
Dec 31 Profit and loss		appropriation account:	
appropriation account:		Interest on capital	960
Interest on drawings	36	Share of profit	5,104
Dec 31 Balance c/d	8,691	Salary	3,263
	9,327		9,327
		Jan 1 Balance b/d	8,691

(d)

Bhayani and Donnell
Statement of Financial Position as at 31 December

		Cost	*Total Depreciation*	*Net Book Value*
	£	£	£	£
Non-current assets				
Premises		20,000	-	20,000
Fittings		12,000	3,500	8,500
Vehicles		35,000	6,500	28,500
		67,000	10,000	57,000
Current assets				
Accounts receivable	25,700			
Less Allowance for doubtful debts	771	24,929		
Prepayments (wages)		200		
Cash		600		
			25,729	
Less Current liabilities				
Accounts payable		15,600		
Bank overdraft		950		
Accruals (heating)		100		
Rent received in advance		100	16,750	
Net current assets				8,979
				65,979
Financed by:				
Capital accounts		*Bhayani*	*Donnell*	
Balance		35,000	12,000	47,000
Current accounts				
Balance 1 January		(600)	nil	
Add Interest on capital		2,800	960	
Salary			3,263	
Share of profits		10,208	5,104	
		12,408	9,327	
Less Drawings		(2,000)	(600)	
Interest on drawings		(120)	(36)	
		10,288	8,691	18,979
				65,979

37.1

Lear Ltd
Statement of changes in equity (extracts)
(1) For the year ended 31 December 2012

	£	£
Profit for the year		164,500
Less Appropriations:		
Dividends:		
Preference dividend (6% × £100,000)	6,000	
Ordinary dividend interim 4% (4% × £300,000)	12,000	18,000
Retained profits carried forward		146,500

(2) For the year ended 31 December 2013

	£	£
Profit for the year		182,330
Add Retained profits brought forward		146,500
		328,830
Less Appropriations:		
Transfer to general reserve	60,000	
Dividends:		
Preference dividend (6% × £100,000)	6,000	
Ordinary dividend – final 2012 (4% × £300,000)	12,000	
Ordinary dividend – interim (5% × £300,000)	15,000	93,000
Retained profits carried forward		235,830

Note: The proposed final dividend of 6% on the ordinary shares (6% × £300,000 = £18,000), if approved by the shareholders at the Annual General Meeting, will be paid in 2014.

37.2

Croft Ltd
Statement of Financial Position as at 31 December 2012

	Cost	*Depreciation to date*	*Net book value*
Non-current assets	£	£	£
Buildings	315,000	47,250	267,750
Machinery	168,000	50,400	117,600
Fixtures	84,000	33,600	50,400
	567,000	131,250	435,750
Current assets			
Inventory		106,000	
Accounts receivable		63,000	
Bank		44,000	213,000
Total assets			648,750
Less Current Liabilities			
Accounts payable	80,000		
		80,000	
Less Non-current liabilities			
10% Debentures		20,000	
Total liabilities			100,000
			548,750
Equity			
Share capital			
Issued 250,000 ordinary shares of £1 each			250,000
Revenue reserves			
General reserve		200,000	
Retained profits		(C) ?	(B) ?
			(A) ?

Workings:

(A) is the figure needed to make the statement of financial position total agree, i.e. 548,750.

(B) is the figure needed to add up to 548,750; therefore B = 548,750 – 250,000 = 298,750.

(C) + 200,000 = B. (C) must be the missing figure 98,750.

37.4

Chang Ltd
Income Statement for the year ended 31 December 2013

	£	£
Sales		316,810
Less Cost of goods sold:		
Opening inventory	25,689	
Add Purchases	201,698	
	227,387	
Less Closing inventory	29,142	198,245
Gross profit		118,565
Less Expenses:		
Wages and salaries (54,207 + 581)	54,788	
Rent (4,300 – 300)	4,000	
Lighting expenses	1,549	
Bad debts	748	
Allowance for doubtful debts (938 – 861)	77	
General expenses	32,168	
Depreciation: Machinery (55,000 × 10%)	5,500	98,830
Net profit		19,735

Statement of changes in equity
for the year ended 31 December 2013

Profit for the year	19,735
Add Retained profits brought forward	34,280
	54,015
Less Interim dividend paid on the ordinary shares	5,000
Retained profits carried forward	49,015

Chang Ltd
Statement of financial position as at 31 December 2013

	Cost	*Depreciation to date*	*Net book value*
	£	£	£
Non-current assets			
Premises	65,000	-	65,000
Machinery	55,000	21,300	33,700
	120,000	21,300	98,700
Current assets			
Inventory		29,142	
Accounts receivable	21,784		
Less Allowance for doubtful debts	938	20,846	
Prepayments		300	
Bank		18,101	68,389
Total assets			167,089
Less current liabilities			
Accounts payable	17,493		
Expenses owing	581		
		18,074	
Total liabilities			18,074
			149,015
Equity			
Share capital			
Called-up share capital			100,000
Revenue reserves			
Retained profits			49,015
			149,015

Note: The proposed final dividend of 5% on the ordinary shares, £100,000, for the year ended 31 December 2013 is subject to approval by shareholders at the Annual General Meeting and has not been included in the above financial statements as a liability.

37.6

Newton Ltd
Statement of Changes in Equity
for the year ended 31 December 2012

	£	£
Profit for the year		80,000
Add Retained profit brought forward		122,667
		202,667
Less Appropriations		
General reserve	20,000	
Dividends:		
Preference dividend (8% × 100,000)	8,000	
Ordinary dividend (3% × 200,000)	6,000	34,000
Retained profits carried forward		168,667

Newton Ltd
Statement of Financial Position as at 31 December 2012

	Cost	*Depreciation to date*	*Net book value*
	£	£	£
Non-current assets			
Premises	360,800	-	360,800
Machinery	96,800	38,720	58,080
	457,600	38,720	418,880
Current assets			
Inventory		75,000	
Accounts receivable	106,700		
Prepayments	5,067	111,767	186,767
Total assets			605,647
Less Current liabilities			
Accounts payable	68,846		
Accruals	5,600	74,446	
Bank overdraft		42,534	
Total liabilities			116,980
			488,667
Equity			
Share capital			
Issued 100,000 – 8% Preference Shares			100,000
Issued 200,000 Ordinary Shares of £1 each			200,000
Revenue Reserves			
General reserve		20,000	
Retained profit		168,667	188,667
			488,667

Note: The proposed final dividend of 4% on the ordinary shares of £200,000, for the year ended 31 December 2012, is subject to approval by shareholders at the Annual General Meeting and has not been included in the above financial statements as a liability.

Chapter 38 Manufacturing accounts

38.1

E Smith
Manufacturing and Trading Account
for the year ended 31 March 2013

	£	£
Inventory of raw material 1.4.2012		2,400
Add Purchases		21,340
Carriage inwards		321
		24,061
Less Inventory of raw materials 31.3.2013		2,620
Cost of raw materials consumed		21,441
Manufacturing wages		13,280
Prime cost		34,721
Add Factory overhead expenses:		
Rent and rates	2,300	
Power	6,220	
Other expenses	1,430	9,950
		44,671
Add Work in progress 1.4.2012		955
		45,626
Less Work in progress 31.3.2013		870
Production cost of goods completed c/d		44,756
Sales		69,830
Less Cost of goods sold		
Inventory finished goods 1.4.2012	6,724	
Add Production cost of goods completed b/d	44,756	
	51,480	
Less Inventory finished goods 31.3.2013	7,230	44,250
Gross profit		25,580

38.3

The Oldport Manufacturing Co

(*a*) Calculation of prime cost

	£
Inventory raw materials 1 May 2012	31,550
Add Purchases raw materials	98,560
	130,110
Less Inventory raw materials 30 April 2013	34,585
	95,525
Direct Labour – Wages manufacturing	67,525
Prime cost	163,050

(*b*) Variable costs are those costs that change according to the number of units produced.

Examples one from: direct material or direct labour, that may be used, for example, in the manufacture of a wheelbarrow.

38.4 *(a)*

Ace Crafts Ltd
Manufacturing Account for the year ended 31 December 2013

		£	£
Inventory of raw materials 1.1.2013			36,000
Add Purchases		70,400	
Add Carriage inwards		1,120	71,520
			107,520
Less Inventory of raw materials 31.12.2013			46,400
Cost of raw materials used	(i)		61,120
Inventory of cases 1.1.2013		18,000	
Add Purchases		18,000	
		36,000	
Less Inventory of cases 31.12.2013		15,360	
Cost of wooden cases used	(ii)		20,640
Wages (170,000 × $^4/_5$)			136,000
Prime cost	(iii)		217,760
Add Factory overhead expenses:	(iv)		
Indirect wages (170,000 × $^1/_5$)		34,000	
Manager's salary		33,200	
Power		14,560	
Rates		2,280	
Lighting (1,800 × $^1/_2$)		900	
Depreciation		20,000	104,940
			322,700
Add Work-in-progress 1.1.2013			10,000
			332,700
Less Work-in-progress 31.12.2013			15,200
Production cost of goods completed c/d	(v)		317,500

(b)

Ace Crafts Ltd
Income Statement
for the year ended 31 December 2013

	£	£
Sales (80 × 6,250)		500,000
Less Production cost of goods sold b/d		317,500
Gross profit		182,500
Less Expenses:		
Administration expenses	19,200	
Salesmen's salaries	47,600	
Lighting (1,800 × $^1/_2$)	900	
Carriage outwards	1,680	69,380
Net profit		113,120

(c) Production cost = £317,500 ÷ 6,250 = £50.80 per unit.
(d) Gross profit = £182,500 ÷ 6,250 = £29.20 per unit.

Chapter 39 Analysis and interpretation of financial statements

39.1 *(a)*

	M Ltd	*N Ltd*
(i) *Current ratio*	$\frac{£200{,}000}{£50{,}000} = 4:1$	$\frac{£130{,}000}{£65{,}000} = 2:1$
(ii) *Acid test ratio*	$\frac{£200{,}000 - £100{,}000}{£50{,}000} = 2:1$	$\frac{£130{,}000 - £64{,}000}{£65{,}000} = 1:1$
(iii) *Inventory turnover*	$\frac{£288{,}000}{£120{,}000 + £100{,}000 \div 2} = 2.6$ times	$\frac{£187{,}500}{£60{,}000 + £64{,}000 \div 2} = 3.0$ times
(iv) *Accounts receivable : Sales ratio*	$\frac{£60{,}000}{£360{,}000} \times 12$ months = 2 months	$\frac{£62{,}500}{£250{,}000} \times 12$ months = 3 months
(v) *Accounts payable : Purchases ratio*	$\frac{£50{,}000}{£268{,}000} \times 12$ months = 2.2 months	$\frac{£65{,}000}{£191{,}500} \times 12$ months = 4 months
(vi) *Gross profit %*	$\frac{£72{,}000}{£360{,}000} \times 100\% = 20\%$	$\frac{£62{,}500}{£250{,}000} \times 100\% = 25\%$
(vii) *Net profit %*	$\frac{£43{,}200}{£360{,}000} \times 100\% = 12\%$	$\frac{£35{,}000}{£250{,}000} \times 100\% = 14\%$
(viii) *Rate of return on shareholders' funds*	$\frac{£43{,}200}{£350{,}000} \times 100\% = 12.3\%$	$\frac{£35{,}000}{£255{,}000} \times 100\% = 13.7\%$

(b) Briefly N Ltd gives a better return to shareholders because of (viii) above.

Reasons include:

- M Ltd's current ratio is higher. This indicates that M Ltd is in a better liquidity position.
- N Ltd's inventory turnover is higher than that of M Ltd. This shows that N Ltd manages its sales performance more effectively.
- The gross profit percentage of N Ltd is 5% higher than that of M Ltd. This is due to better purchasing and selling prices. Net profit margins differ by a smaller margin of 2%, suggesting, that M Ltd has tighter control of its overhead expenses when compared with its sales volume (8% compared with 11%).

39.4 *(a)*

	Cruise Furnishings	*Holmes Supplies*
(i) Gross profit margin	$\frac{600}{1,800} \times 100 = 33\frac{1}{3}\%$	$\frac{600}{2,400} \times 100 = 25\%$
(ii) Net profit margin	$\frac{150}{1,800} \times 100 = 8.33\%$	$\frac{160}{2,400} \times 100 = 6.67\%$
(iii) Current ratio	$\frac{210}{66} = 3.18 : 1$	$\frac{180}{60} = 3 : 1$

(b) Inventory turnover rate for Cruise Furnishings

$$\frac{1200}{120} = 10 \text{ times a year}$$

(c)

Profitability

Both businesses are making good net profits, Cruise £150,000 and Holmes £160,000. However, both the gross profit percentage and net profit percentage for Cruise is better than Holmes, with the net profit percentage being 8.33% for Cruise against Holmes 6.67%. This could be due to Cruise selling goods at a higher price and their cost of sales being lower.

Liquidity

The current ratio for both Cruise and Holmes are very similiar with Cruise being slightly higher at 3.18 : 1 against Holmes 3 : 1. If we calculate the acid test, i.e. we remove inventory from the calculation,

Cruise

$$\frac{210 - 111}{66} = 1.5 : 1$$

Holmes

$$\frac{180 - 120}{60} = 1 : 1$$

then Cruise is in a stronger position since it could raise £1.50 for every £1 owed compared to Holmes who could raise £1 for every £1 of debt.

Conclusion

While Holmes has a greater turnover than Cruise the company is not as profitable. In terms of liquidity again Cruise is in a stronger position which may in part be due to Holmes non-current liabilities of £2,070,000.

Chapter 40 Computers and accounting systems

40.1

To: Director of Finance
From: Administrative Assistant
Date: June 2013
Re: Proposed Integrated Computerised Accounting System

Points in favour of the new system:

- Faster data input and automatic processing.
- Greater accuracy especially via automatic posting.
- Documentation such as invoices, credit notes, statements, remittance advices produced automatically.
- Up-to-date information on customers' accounts, etc. is readily available.
- Provides management information.
- The system may be linked to the internet to allow for transactions such as ordering goods to be carried out electronically.
- Provides access to the organisation's bank account via the internet.
- More efficient and makes better use of resources.

Arguments against the new system:

- The cost of the installation plus ongoing costs of maintenance and updating software.
- Training costs of staff.
- Staff resentment of new system.
- System downtime may be disruptive.
- Fraudulent access can seriously affect business operation and profitability.
- Security measures that are necessary.
- Health and safety issues associated with using computers.

40.2 Measures a medium-sized company may adopt to safeguard the security of its financial data and records would include:

- All company's financial information should be regarded as confidential except where legislation states otherwise. Staff should be made aware of this requirement in the company's code of conduct.
- Staff should be allocated passwords to monitor accessibility to specific areas of work.
- Passwords need to be changed frequently.
- Installation of anti-virus computer packages to prevent the threat of fraud.
- Ensure data is saved and backed up regularly.
- Store back-up data in an off-site location if deemed necessary.

Index